REPORT

OF THE

SELECT COMMITTEE TO INVESTIGATE

THE

ALLEGED CREDIT MOBILIER BRIBERY,

MADE TO THE

HOUSE OF REPRESENTATIVES,

FEBRUARY 18, 1873.

WASHINGTON:
GOVERNMENT PRINTING OFFICE.
1873.

42D CONGRESS, } HOUSE OF REPRESENTATIVES. { REPORT
3d Session. } { No. 77.

CREDIT MOBILIER INVESTIGATION.

FEBRUARY 18, 1873.—Ordered to be printed with the evidence, and the further consideration postponed until Tuesday next, after the reading of the Journal.

Mr. POLAND, from the select committee to investigate the alleged Credit Mobilier bribery, made the following

REPORT:

The special committee appointed under the following resolutions of the House, to wit:

Whereas accusations have been made in the public press, founded on alleged letters of Oakes Ames, a Representative from Massachusetts, and upon the alleged affidavits of Henry S. McComb, a citizen of Wilmington, in the State of Delaware, to the effect that members of this House were bribed by Oakes Ames to perform certain legislative acts for the benefit of the Union Pacific Railroad Company, by presents of stock in the Credit Mobilier of America, or by presents of a valuable character derived therefrom: Therefore,

Resolved, That a special committee of five members be appointed by the Speaker pro tempore, *whose duty it shall be to investigate whether any member of this House was bribed by Oakes Ames, or any other person or corporation, in any matter touching his legislative duty.*

Resolved further, That the committee have the right to employ a stenographer, and that they be empowered to send for persons and papers;

beg leave to make the following report:

In order to a clear understanding of the facts hereinafter stated as to contracts and dealings in reference to stock of the Credit Mobilier of America, between Mr. Oakes Ames and others, and members of Congress, it is necessary to make a preliminary statement of the connection of that company with the Union Pacific Railroad Company, and their relations to each other.

The Company called the "Credit Mobilier of America" was incorporated by the legislature of Pennsylvania, and in 1864 control of its charter and franchises had been obtained by certain persons interested in the Union Pacific Railroad Company, for the purpose of using it as a construction company to build the Union Pacific road. In September, 1864, a contract was entered into between the Union Pacific Company and H. M. Hoxie, for the building by said Hoxie of one hundred miles of said road from Omaha west.

This contract was at once assigned by Hoxie to the Credit Mobilier Company, as it was expected to be when made. Under this contract and extensions of it some two or three hundred miles of road were built by the Credit Mobilier Company, but no considerable profits appear to have been realized therefrom. The enterprise of building a railroad to the Pacific was of such vast magnitude, and was beset by so many hazards and risks, that the capitalists of the country were generally averse to investing in it, and, notwithstanding the liberal aid granted by the Government, it seemed likely to fail of completion.

In 1865 or 1866, Mr. Oakes Ames, then and now a member of the House from the State of Massachusetts, and his brother Oliver Ames, became interested in the Union Pacific Company and also in the Credit Mobilier Company as the agents for the construction of the road. The Messrs. Ames were men of very large capital, and of known character and integrity in business. By their example and credit, and the personal efforts of Mr. Oakes Ames, many men of capital were induced to embark in the enterprise, and to take stock in the Union Pacific Company and also in the Credit Mobilier Company. Among them were the firm of S. Hooper & Co., of Boston, the leading member of which, Mr. Samuel Hooper, was then and is now a member of the House; Mr. John B. Alley, then a member of the House from Massachusetts, and Mr. Grimes, then a Senator from the State of Iowa. Notwithstanding the vigorous efforts of Mr. Ames and others interested with him, great difficulty was experienced in securing the required capital.

In the spring of 1867 the Credit Mobilier Company voted to add 50 per cent. to their capital stock, which was then two and a half millions of dollars; and to cause it to be readily taken each subscriber to it was entitled to receive as a bonus an equal amount of first-mortgage bonds of the Union Pacific Company. The old stockholders were entitled to take this increase, but even the favorable terms offered did not induce all the old stockholders to take it, and the stock of the Credit Mobilier Company was never considered worth its par value until after the execution of the Oakes Ames contract hereinafter mentioned.

On the 16th day of August, 1867, a contract was executed between the Union Pacific Railroad Company and Oakes Ames, by which Mr. Ames contracted to build six hundred and sixty-seven miles of the Union Pacific road at prices ranging from $42,000 to $96,000 per mile, amounting in the aggregate to $47,000,000. Before the contract was entered into it was understood that Mr. Ames was to transfer it to seven trustees, who were to execute it, and the profits of the contract were to be divided among the stockholders in the Credit Mobilier Company, who should comply with certain conditions set out in the instrument transferring the contract to the trustees. The Ames contract and the transfer to trustees are incorporated in the evidence submitted, and therefore further recital of their terms is not deemed necessary.

Substantially, all the stockholders of the Credit Mobilier complied with the conditions named in the transfer, and thus became entitled to share in any profits said trustees might make in executing the contract.

All the large stockholders in the Union Pacific were also stockholders in the Credit Mobilier, and the Ames contract and its transfer to trustees were ratified by the Union Pacific, and received the assent of the great body of stockholders, but not of all.

After the Ames contract had been executed, it was expected by those interested that by reason of the enormous prices agreed to be paid for the work very large profits would be derived from building the road, and very soon the stock of the Credit Mobilier was understood by those holding it to be worth much more than its par value. The stock was not in the market and had no fixed market-value, but the holders of it, in December, 1867, considered it worth at least double the par value, and in January and February, 1868, three or four times the par value, but it does not appear that these facts were generally or publicly known, or that the holders of the stock desired they should be.

The foregoing statement the committee think gives enough of the historic details, and condition and value of the stock, to make the following detailed facts intelligible:

Mr. Oakes Ames was then a member of the House of Representatives, and came to Washington at the commencement of the session, about the beginning of December, 1867. During that month Mr. Ames entered into contracts with a considerable number of members of Congress, both Senators and Representatives, to let them have shares of stock in the Credit Mobilier Company at par, with interest thereon from the first day of the previous July. It does not appear that in any instance he asked any of these persons to pay a higher price than the par value and interest, nor that Mr. Ames used any special effort or urgency to get these persons to take it. In all these negotiations Mr. Ames did not enter into any details as to the value of the stock or the amount of dividend that might be expected upon it, but stated generally that it would be good stock, and in several instances said he would guarantee that they should get at least 10 per cent. on their money.

Some of these gentlemen, in their conversations with Mr. Ames, raised the question whether becoming holders of this stock would bring them into any embarrassment as members of Congress in their legislative action. Mr. Ames quieted such suggestions by saying it could not-for the Union Pacific had received from Congress all the grants and legislation it wanted, and they should ask for nothing more. In some instances those members who contracted for stock paid to Mr. Ames the money for the price of the stock, par and interest; in others, where they had not the money, Mr. Ames agreed to carry the stock for them until they could get the money or it should be met by the dividends.

Mr. Ames was at this time a large stockholder in the Credit Mobilier, but he did not intend any of these transactions to be sales of his own stock, but intended to fulfill all these contracts from stock belonging to the company.

At this time there were about six hundred and fifty shares of the stock of the company, which had for some reason been placed in the name of Mr. T. C. Durant, one of the leading and active men of the concern.

Mr. Ames claimed that a portion of this stock should be assigned to him to enable him to fulfill engagements he had made for stock. Mr. Durant claimed that he had made similar engagements that he should be allowed stock to fulfill. Mr. McComb, who was present at the time, claimed that he had also made engagements for stock which he should have stock given him to carry out. This claim of McComb was refused, but after the stock was assigned to Mr. Ames, McComb insisted that Ames should distribute some of the stock to his (McComb's) friends, and named Senators Bayard and Fowler, and Representatives Allison and Wilson, of Iowa.

It was finally arranged that three hundred and forty three shares of the stock of the company should be transferred to Mr. Ames to ena ble him to perform his engagements, and that number of shares were set over on the books of the company to Oakes Ames, trustee, to distinguish it from the stock held by him before. Mr. Ames at the time paid to the company the par of the stock and interest from the July previous, and this stock still stands on the books in the name of Oakes Ames, trustee, except thirteen shares which have been transferred to parties in no way connected with Congress. The committee do not find that Mr. Ames had any negotiation whatever with any of these members of Congress on the subject of this stock prior to the commencement of the session of December, 1867, except Mr. Scofield, of Pennsylvania, and it was not claimed that any obligation existed from Mr. Ames to him as the result of it.

In relation to the purpose and motives of Mr. Ames in contracting to let members of Congress have Credit Mobilier stock at par, which he and all other owners of it considered worth at least double that sum, the committee, upon the evidence taken by them and submitted to the House, cannot entertain doubt. When he said he did not suppose the Union Pacific Company would ask or need further legislation, he stated what he believed to be true. But he feared the interests of the road might suffer by adverse legislation, and what he desired to accomplish was to enlist strength and friends in Congress who would resist any encroachment upon or interference with the rights and privileges already secured, and to that end wished to create in them an interest identical with his own. This purpose is clearly avowed in his letters to McComb, copied in the evidence. He says he intends to place the stock "where it will do most good to us." And again, "we want more friends in this Congress." In his letter to McComb, and also in his statement prepared by counsel, he gives the philosophy of his action, to wit, "That he has found there is no difficulty in getting men to look after their own property." The committee are also satisfied that Mr. Ames entertained a fear that, when the true relations between the Credit Mobilier Company and the Union Pacific became generally known, and the means by which the great profits expected to be made were fully understood, there was danger that congressional investigation and action would be invoked.

The members of Congress with whom he dealt were generally those who had been friendly and favorable to a Pacific Railroad, and Mr. Ames did not fear or expect to find them favorable to movements hostile to it; but he desired to stimulate their activity and watchfulness in opposition to any unfavorable action by giving them a personal interest in the success of the enterprise, especially so far as it affected the interest of the Credit Mobilier Company. On the 9th day of December, 1867, Mr. C. C. Washburn, of Wisconsin, introduced in the House a bill to regulate by law the rates of transportation over the Pacific Railroad.

Mr. Ames, as well as others interested in the Union Pacific road, was opposed to this, and desired to defeat it. Other measures apparently hostile to that company were subsequently introduced into the House by Mr. Washburn of Wisconsin, and Mr. Washburne of Illinois. The committee believe that Mr. Ames, in his distributions of stock, had specially in mind the hostile efforts of the Messrs. Washburn, and desired to gain strength to secure their defeat. The reference in one of his letters to "Washburn's move" makes this quite apparent.

The foregoing is deemed by the committee a sufficient statement of facts as to Mr. Ames, taken in connection with what will be subsequently stated of his transactions with particular persons. Mr. Ames made some contracts for stock in the Credit Mobilier with members of the Senate. In public discussions of this subject the names of members of both Houses have been so connected, and all these transactions were so nearly simultaneous, that the committee deemed it their duty to obtain all evidence in their power, as to all persons then members of either House, and to report the same to the House. Having done this, and the House having directed that evidence transmitted to the Senate, the committee consider their own power and duty, as well as that of the House, fully performed, so far as members of the Senate are concerned. Some of Mr. Ames's contracts to sell stock were with gentlemen who were then members of the House, but are not members of the present Congress.

The committee have sought for and taken all the evidence within their reach as to those gentlemen, and reported the same to the House. As the House has ceased to have jurisdiction over them as members, the committee have not deemed it their duty to make any special finding of facts as to each, leaving the house and the country to their own conclusions upon the testimony.

In regard to each of the members of the present House, the committee deem it their duty to state specially the facts they find proved by the evidence, which, in some instances, is painfully conflicting.

MR. JAMES G. BLAINE, OF MAINE.

Among those who have in the public press been charged with improper participation in Credit Mobilier stock is the present Speaker, Mr. Blaine, who moved the resolution for this investigation. The committee have, therefore, taken evidence in regard to him. They find from it that Mr. Ames had conversation with Mr. Blaine in regard to taking ten shares of the stock, and recommended it as a good investment. Upon consideration Mr. Blaine concluded not to take the stock, and never did take it, and never paid or received anything on account of it; and Mr. Blaine never had any interest, direct or indirect, in Credit Mobilier stock or stock of the Union Pacific Railroad company.

MR. HENRY L. DAWES, OF MASSACHUSETTS.

Mr. Dawes had, prior to December, 1867, made some small investments in railroad bonds through Mr. Ames. In December, 1867, Mr. Dawes applied to Mr. Ames to purchase a thousand-dollar bond of the Cedar Rapids road, in Iowa. Mr. Ames informed him that he had sold them all, but that he would let him have for his thousand dollars ten shares of Credit Mobilier stock, which he thought was better than the railroad bond. In answer to inquiries by Mr. Dawes Mr. Ames said the Credit Mobilier Company had the contract to build the Union Pacific road, and thought they would make money out of it, and that it would be a good thing; that he would guarantee that he should get 10 per cent. on his money, and that if at any time Mr. Dawes did not want the stock he would pay back his money with 10 per cent. interest. Mr. Dawes made some further inquiry in relation to the stock of Mr. John B. Alley, who said he thought it was good stock, but not as good as Mr. Ames thought, but that Mr. Ames's guarantee would make it a perfectly safe investment.

Mr. Dawes thereupon concluded to purchase the ten shares, and on the 11th of January he paid Mr. Ames $800, and in a few days thereafter the balance of the price of this stock, at par and interest from July previous. In June, 1868, Mr. Ames received a dividend of 60 per cent. in money on this stock, and of it paid to Mr. Dawes $400, and applied the balance of $200 upon accounts between them. This $400 was all that was paid over to Mr. Dawes as a dividend upon this stock. At some time prior to December, 1868, Mr. Dawes was informed that a suit had been commenced in the courts of Pennsylvania by former owners of the charter of the Credit Mobilier, claiming that those then claiming and using it had no right to do so. Mr. Dawes thereupon informed Mr. Ames that as there was a litigation about the matter he did not desire to keep the stock. On the 9th of December, 1868, Mr. Ames and Mr. Dawes had a settlement of their matters in which Mr. Dawes was allowed for the money he paid for the stock with 10 per cent. interest upon it, and accounted to Mr. Ames for the $400 he had received as a dividend. Mr. Dawes received no other benefit under the contract than to get 10 per cent. upon his money, and after the settlement had no further interest in the stock.

MR. GLENNI W. SCOFIELD, OF PENNSYLVANIA.

In 1866 Mr. Scofield purchased some Cedar Rapids bonds of Mr. Ames, and in that year they had conversations about Mr. Scofield taking stock in the Credit Mobilier Company, but no contract was consummated. In December, 1867, Mr. Scofield applied to Mr. Ames to purchase more Cedar Rapids bonds, when Mr. Ames suggested he should purchase some Credit Mobilier stock, and explained generally that it was a contracting company to build the Union Pacific road; that it was a Pennsylvania corporation, and he would like to have some Pennsylvanians in it; that he would sell it to him at par and interest, and that he would guarantee he should get 8 per cent. if Mr. Scofield would give him half the dividends above that. Mr. Scofield said he thought he would take $1,000 of the stock; but before anything further was done Mr. Scofield was called home by sickness in his family. On his return, the latter part of January, 1868, he spoke to Mr. Ames about the stock, when Mr. Ames said he thought it was all sold, but he would take his money and give him a receipt, and get the stock for him if he could. Mr. Scofield thereupon paid Mr. Ames $1,041, and took his receipt therefor.

Not long after Mr. Ames informed Mr. Scofield he could have the stock, but could not give him a certificate for it until he could get a larger certificate dividend. Mr. Scofield received the bond dividend of 80 per cent., which was payable January 3, 1868, taking a bond for $1,000 and paying Mr. Ames the difference. Mr. Ames received the 60 per cent. cash dividend on the stock in June, 1868, and paid over to Mr. Scofield $600, the amount of it.

Before the close of that session of Congress, which was toward the end of July, Mr. Scofield became, for some reason, disinclined to take the stock, and a settlement was made between them, by which Mr. Ames was to retain the Credit Mobilier stock and Mr. Scofield took a thousand dollars Union Pacific bond and ten shares of Union Pacific stock.

The precise basis of the settlement does not appear, neither Mr. Ames nor Mr. Scofield having any full data in reference to it; Mr. Scofield thinks that he only received back his money and interest upon it, while Mr. Ames states that he thinks Mr. Scofield had ten shares of Union Pacific stock in addition. The committee do not deem it specially important to settle this difference of recollection. Since that settlement Mr. Scofield has had no interest in the Credit Mobilier stock and derived no benefit therefrom.

MR. JOHN A. BINGHAM, OF OHIO.

In December, 1867, Mr. Ames advised Mr. Bingham to invest in the stock of the Credit Mobilier, assuring him that it would return him his money with profitable dividends. Mr. Bingham agreed to take twenty shares, and about the 1st of February, 1868, paid to Mr. Ames the par value of the stock, for which Mr. Ames executed to him some receipt or agreement. Mr. Ames received all the dividends on the stock, whether in Union Pacific bonds, or stock, or money; some were delivered to Mr. Bingham and some retained by Mr. Ames. The matter was not finally adjusted between them until February, 1872, when it was settled, Mr. Ames retaining the twenty shares of Credit Mobilier stock, and accounting to Mr. Bingham for such dividends upon it as Mr. Bingham had not already received. Mr. Bingham was treated as the real owner of the stock from the time of the agreement to take it, in December, 1867, to the settlement in February, 1872, and had the benefit of all the dividends upon it. Neither Mr. Ames nor Mr. Bingham had such records of their dealing as to be able to give the precise amount of those dividends.

MR. WILLIAM D. KELLEY, OF PENNSYLVANIA.

The committee find from the evidence that in the early part of the second session of the Fortieth Congress, and probably in December, 1867, Mr. Ames agreed with Mr. Kelley to sell him ten shares of Credit Mobilier stock at par and interest from July 1, 1867. Mr. Kelley was not then prepared to pay for the stock, and Mr. Ames agreed to carry the stock for him until he could pay for it. On the third day of January, 1868, there was a dividend of 80 per cent. on Credit Mobilier stock in Union Pacific bonds. Mr. Ames received the bonds, as the stock stood in his name, and sold them for 97 per cent. of their face. In June, 1868, there was a cash dividend of 60 per cent., which Mr. Ames also received. The proceeds of the bonds sold, and the cash dividends received by Mr. Ames, amounted to $1,376. The par value of the stock and interest thereon from the previous July amounted to $1,047; so that, after paying for the stock, there was a balance of dividends due Mr. Kelley of $329. On the 23d day of June, 1868, Mr. Ames gave Mr. Kelley a check for that sum on the Sergeant-at-Arms of the House of Representatives, and Mr. Kelley received the money thereon.

The committee find that Mr. Kelley then understood that the money he thus received was a balance of dividends due him after paying for the stock.

All the subsequent dividends upon the stock were either in Union Pacific stock or bonds, and they were all received by Mr. Ames. In September, 1868, Mr. Kelley received from Mr. Ames $750 in money, which was understood between them to be an advance to be paid out of dividends. There has never been any adjustment of the matter between them, and there is now an entire variance in the testimony of the two men as to what the transaction between them was; but the committee are unanimous in finding the facts above stated. The evidence reported to the House gives some subsequent conversations and negotiations between Mr. Kelley and Mr. Ames on this subject. The committee do not deem it material to refer to it in their report.

MR. JAMES A. GARFIELD, OF OHIO.

The facts in regard to Mr. Garfield, as found by the committee, are identical with the case of Mr. Kelley to the point of reception of the check for $329. He agreed with Mr. Ames to take ten shares of Credit Mobilier stock, but did not pay for the same. Mr. Ames received the 80 per cent. dividend in bonds and sold them for 97 per cent., and also received the 60 per cent. cash dividend, which together paid the price of the stock and interest, and left a balance of $329. This sum was paid over to Mr. Garfield by a check on the Sergeant-at-Arms, and Mr. Garfield then understood this sum was the balance of dividends after paying for the stock. Mr. Ames received all the subsequent dividends, and the committee do not find that, since the payment of the $329, there has been any communication between Mr. Ames and Mr. Garfield on the subject until this investigation began. Some correspondence between Mr. Garfield and Mr. Ames, and some conversations between them during this investigation, will be found in the reported testimony.

The committee do not find that Mr. Ames, in his negotiations with the persons above named, entered into any detail of the relations between the Credit Mobilier Company and the Union Pacific Company, or gave them any specific information as to the amount of dividends they would be likely to receive further than has been already stated. They all knew from him, or otherwise, that the Credit Mobilier was a contracting company to build the Union Pacific road, but it does not appear that any of them knew that the profits and dividends were to be in stock and bonds of that company.

The Credit Mobilier Company was a State corporation, not subject to congressional legislation, and the fact that its profits were expected to be derived from building the Union Pacific road did not, apparently, create such an interest in that company as to disqualify the holder of Credit Mobilier stock from participating in any legislation affecting the railroad company. In his negotiations with these members of Congress, Mr. Ames made no suggestion that he desired to secure their favorable influence in Congress in favor of the railroad company, and whenever the question was raised as to whether the ownership of this stock would in any way interfere with or embarrass them in their action as members of Congress, he assured them it would not.

The committee, therefore, do not find, as to the members of the present House above named, that they were aware of the object of Mr. Ames, or that they had any other purpose in taking this stock than to make a profitable investment. It is apparent that those who advanced their money to pay for their stock present more the appearance of ordinary investors than those who did not, but the committee do not feel at liberty to find any corrupt purpose or knowledge founded upon the fact of non-payment alone.

It ought also to be observed that those gentlemen who surrendered their stock to Mr. Ames before there was any public excitement upon the subject, do not profess to have done so upon any idea of impropriety in holding it, but for reasons affecting the value and security of the investment. But the committee believe that they must have felt that there was something so out of the ordinary course of business in the extraordinary dividends they were receiving as to render the investment itself suspicious, and that this was one of the motives of their action.

The committee have not been able to find that any of these members of Congress have been affected in their official action in consequence of their interest in Credit Mobilier stock.

It has been suggested that the fact that none of this stock was transferred to those with whom Mr. Ames contracted was a circumstance from which a sense of impropriety, if not corruption, was to be inferred. The committee believe this is capable of explanation without such inference. The profits of building the road, under the Ames contract, were only to be divided among such holders of Credit Mobilier stock as should come in and become parties to certain conditions set out in the contract of transfer to the trustees, so that a transfer from Mr. Ames to new holders would cut off the right to dividends from the trustees, unless they also became parties to the agreement; and this the committee believe to be the true reason why no transfers were made.

The committee are also of opinion that there was a satisfactory reason for delay on Mr. Ames's part to close settlements with some of these gentlemen for stock and bonds he had received as dividends upon the stock contracted to them. In the fall of 1868 Mr. McComb commenced a suit against the Credit Mobilier Company and Mr. Ames and others, claiming to be entitled to two hundred and fifty shares of the Credit Mobilier stock upon a subscription for stock to that amount. That suit is still pending. If McComb prevailed in that suit, Mr. Ames might be compelled to surrender so much of the stock assigned to him as trustee, and he was not therefore anxious to have the stock go out of his hands until that suit was terminated. It ought also to be stated that no one of the present members of the House above named appears to have had any knowledge of the dealings of Mr. Ames with other members.

The committee do not find that either of the above-named gentlemen, in contracting with Mr. Ames, had any corrupt motive or purpose himself, or was aware that Mr. Ames had any, nor did either of them suppose he was guilty of any impropriety or even indelicacy in becoming a purchaser of this stock. Had it appeared that these gentlemen were aware of the enormous dividends upon this stock, and how they were to be earned, we could not thus acquit them. And here as well as anywhere, the committee may allude to that subject. Congress had chartered the Union Pacific road, given to it a liberal grant of lands, and promised a liberal loan of Government bonds, to be delivered as fast as sections of the road were completed. As these alone might not be sufficient to complete the road, Congress authorized the company to issue their own bonds for the deficit, and secured them by a mortgage upon the road, which should be a lien prior to that of the Government. Congress never intended that the owners of the road should execute a mortgage on the road prior to that of the Government, to raise money to put into their own pockets, but only to build the road.

The men who controlled the Union Pacific seem to have adopted as the basis of their action the right to incumber the road by a mortgage prior to that of the Government to the full extent, whether the money was needed for the construction of the road or not.

It was clear enough they could not do this directly and in terms, and therefore they resorted to the device of contracting with themselves to build the road, and fix a price high enough to require the issue of bonds to the full extent, and then divide the bonds or the proceeds of them under the name of profits on the contract. All those acting in the matter seem to have been fully aware of this, and that this was to be the effect of the transaction. The sudden rise of value of Credit Mobilier stock was the result of the adoption of this scheme. Any undue and unreasonable profits thus made by themselves were as much a fraud upon the Government as if they had sold their bonds and divided the money without going through the form of denominating them profits on building the road.

Now, had these facts been known to these gentlemen, and had they understood they were to share in the proceeds of the scheme, they would have deserved the severest censure.

Had they known only that the profits were to be paid in stock and bonds of the Union Pacific Company, and so make them interested in it, we cannot agree to the doctrine, which has been urged before us and elsewhere, that it was perfectly legitimate for members of Congress to invest in a corporation deriving all its rights from and subject at all times to the action of Congress.

In such case the rules of the House, as well as the rules of decency, would require such member to abstain from voting on any question affecting his interest. But, after accepting the position of a member of Congress, we do not think he has the right to disqualify himself from acting upon subjects likely to come before Congress without some higher and more urgent motive than merely to make a profitable investment.

But it is not so much to be feared that in such case an interested member would vote as that he would exercise his influence by personal appeal to his fellow-members, and by other modes, which often is far more potent than a single silent vote.

We do not think any member ought to feel so confident of his own strength as to allow himself to be brought into this temptation. We think Mr. Ames judged shrewdly in saying that a man is much more likely to be watchful of his own interests than those of other people. But there is a broader view still which we think ought to be taken. This country is fast becoming filled with gigantic corporations, wielding and controlling immense aggregations of money, and thereby commanding great influence and power. It is notorious in many State legislatures that these influences are often controlling, so that in effect they become the ruling power of the State. Within a few years Congress has, to some extent, been brought within similar influences, and the knowledge of the public on that subject has brought great discredit upon the body, far more, we believe, than there were facts to justify.

But such is the tendency of the time, and the belief is far too general that all men can be ruled with money, and that the use of such means to carry public measures is legitimate and proper. No member of Congress ought to place himself in circumstances of suspicion, so that any discredit of the body shall arise on his account. It is of the highest importance that the national legislature should be free of all taint of corruption, and it is of almost equal necessity that the people should feel confident that it is so.

In a free government like ours, we cannot expect the people will long respect the laws, if they lose respect for the law-makers.

For these reasons we think it behooves every man in Congress or in any public position to hold himself aloof, as far as possible, from all such influences, that he may not only be enabled to look at every public question with an eye only to the public good, but that his conduct and motives be not suspected or questioned. The only criticism the committee feel compelled to make on the action of these members in taking this stock is that they were not sufficiently careful in ascertaining what they were getting, and that in their judgment the assurance of a good investment was all the assurance they needed. We commend to them, and to all men, the letter of the venerable Senator Bayard, in response to an offer of some of this stock, found on page 74 of the testimony.

The committee find nothing in the conduct or motives of either of these members, in taking this stock, that calls for any recommendation by the committee of the House.

MR. JAMES BROOKS, OF NEW YORK.

The case of Mr. Brooks stands upon a different state of facts from any of those already given. The committee find from the evidence as follows: Mr. Brooks had been a warm advocate of a Pacific Railroad, both in Congress and in the public press. After persons interested in the Union Pacific road had obtained control of the Credit Mobilier charter and organized under it for the purpose of making it a construction company to build the road, Dr. Durant, who was then the leading man in the enterprise, made great efforts to get the stock of the Credit Mobilier taken. Mr. Brooks was a friend of Dr. Durant, and he made some efforts to aid Dr. Durant in getting subscriptions for the stock, introduced the matter to some capitalists of New York, but his efforts were not crowned with success.

During this period Mr. Brooks had talked with Dr. Durant about taking some of the stock for himself, and had spoken of taking fifteen or twenty thousand dollars of it, but no definite contract was made between them, and Mr. Brooks was under no legal obligation to take the stock, or Durant to give it to him. In October, 1867, Mr. Brooks was appointed by the President one of the Government directors of the Union Pacific road. In December, 1867, after the stock of the Credit Mobilier was understood, by those familiar with the affairs between the Union Pacific and the Credit Mobilier, to be worth very much more than par, Mr. Brooks applied to Dr. Durant, and claimed that he should have two hundred shares of Credit Mobilier stock. It does not appear that Mr. Brooks claimed he had any legal contract for stock that he could enforce, or that Durant considered himself in any way legally bound to let him have any, but still, on account of what had been said, and the efforts of Mr. Brooks to aid him, he considered himself under obligation to satisfy Mr. Brooks in the matter.

The stock had been so far taken up, and was then in such demand, that Durant could not well comply with Brooks's demand for two hundred shares. After considerable negotiation, it was finally adjusted between them by Durant's agreeing to let Brooks have one hundred shares of Credit Mobilier stock, and giving him with it $5,000 of Union Pacific bonds, and $20,000 of Union Pacific stock. Dr. Durant testifies that he then considered Credit Mobilier stock worth double the par value, and that the bonds and stock he was to give Mr. Brooks worth about $9,000, so that he saved about $1,000 by not giving Brooks the additional hundred shares he claimed. After the negotiation had been concluded between Mr. Brooks and Dr. Durant, Mr. Brooks said that as he was a Government director of the Union Pacific road, and as the law provided such directors should not be stockholders in that company, he would not hold this stock, and directed Dr. Durant to transfer it to Charles H. Neilson, his son-in-law. The whole negotiation with Durant was conducted by Mr. Brooks himself, and Neilson had nothing to do with the transaction, except to receive the transfer. The $10,000 to pay for the one hundred shares was paid by Mr. Brooks, and he received the $5,000 of Pacific bonds which came with the stock.

The certificate of transfer of the hundred shares from Durant to Neilson is dated December 26, 1867. On the 3d of January, 1868, there was a dividend of 80 per cent. in Union Pacific bonds paid on the Credit Mobilier stock. The bonds were received by Neilson, but passed over at once to Mr. Brooks. It is claimed, both by Mr. Brooks and Neilson, that the $10,000 paid by Mr. Brooks for the stock was a loan of that sum by him to Neilson, and that the bonds he received from Durant, and those received for the dividend, were delivered and held by him as collateral security for the loan.

No note or obligation was given for the money by Neilson, nor, so far as we can learn from either Brooks or Neilson, was any account or memorandum of the transaction kept by either of them. At the time of the arrangement or settlement above spoken of between Brooks and Durant, there was nothing said about Mr. Brooks being entitled to have 50 per cent. more stock by virtue of his ownership of the hundred shares. Neither Brooks nor Durant thought of any such thing.

Some time after the transfer of the shares to Neilson, Mr. Brooks called on Sidney Dillon, then the president of the Credit Mobilier, and claimed he or Neilson was entitled to fifty additional shares of the stock, by virtue of the purchase of the one hundred shares of Durant.

This was claimed by Mr. Brooks as his right by virtue of the 50 per cent. increase of the stock hereinbefore described. Mr. Dillon said he did not know how that was, but he would consult the leading stockholders, and be governed by them. Mr. Dillon, in order to justify himself in the transaction, got up a paper authorizing the issue of fifty shares of the stock to Mr. Brooks, and procured it to be signed by most of the principal shareholders. After this had been done, an entry of fifty shares was made on the stock-ledger to some person other than Neilson. The name in two places on the book has been erased, and the name of Neilson inserted. The committee are satisfied that the stock was first entered on the books in Mr. Brooks's name.

Mr. Neilson soon after called for the certificate for the fifty shares, and on the 29th of February, 1868, the certificate was issued to him, and the entry on the stock-book was changed to Neilson.

Neilson procured Mr. Dillon to advance the money to pay for the stock, and at the same time delivered to Dillon $4,000 Union Pacific bonds, and fifty shares of Union Pacific stock as collateral security. These bonds and stock were a portion of dividends received at the time, as he was allowed to receive the same percentage of dividends on these fifty shares that had previously been paid on the hundred. This matter has never been adjusted between Neilson and Dillon. Brooks and Neilson both testify they never paid Dillon. Dillon thinks he has received his pay, as he has not now the collaterals in his possession. If he has been paid it is probable that it was from the collaterals in some form. The subject has never been named between Dillon and Neilson since Dillon advanced the money, and no one connected with the transaction seems able to give any further light upon it. The whole business by which these fifty shares were procured was done by Mr. Brooks. Neilson knew nothing of any right to have them, and only went for the certificate when told to do so by Mr. Brooks.

The committee find that no such right to fifty shares additional stock passed by the transfer of the hundred. And from Mr. Brooks's familiarity with the affairs of the company, the committee believe he must have known his claim to them was unfounded. The question naturally arises, How was he able to procure them? The stock at this time by the stockholders was considered worth three or four times its par value. Neilson sustained no relations to any of these people that commanded any favor, and if he could have used any influence he did not attempt it; if he had this right he was unaware of it till told by Mr. Brooks, and left the whole matter in his hands. It is clear that the shares were procured by the sole efforts of Mr. Brooks, and, as the stockholders who consented to it supposed, for the benefit of Mr. Brooks. What power had Mr. Brooks to enforce an unfounded claim, to have for $5,000, stock worth $15,000 or $20,000? Mr. McComb swears that he heard conversation between Mr. Brooks and Mr. John B. Alley, a large stockholder, and one of the executive committee, in which Mr. Brooks urged that he should have the additional fifty shares, because he was or would procure himself to be made a Government director, and also that, being a member of Congress, he "would take care of the democratic side of the House."

Mr. Brooks and Mr. Alley both deny having had any such conversation, or that Mr. Brooks ever made such a statement to Mr. Alley. If, therefore, this matter rested wholly upon the testimony of Mr. McComb, the committee would not feel justified in finding that Mr. Brooks procured the stock by such use of his official position; but all the circumstances seem to point exactly in that direction, and we can find no other satisfactory solution of the question above propounded. Whatever claim Mr. Brooks had to stock, either legal or moral, had been adjusted and satisfied by Dr. Durant. Whether he was getting this stock for himself or to give to his son-in-law, we believe, from the circumstances attending the whole transaction, that he obtained it knowing that it was yielded to its official position and influence, and with the intent to secure his favor and influence in such positions. Mr. Brooks claims that he has had no interest in this stock whatever; that the benefit and advantage of his right to have it he gave to Mr. Neilson, his son-in-law, and that he has had all the dividends upon it. The committee are unable to find this to be the case, for in their judgment all the facts and circumstances show Mr. Brooks to be the real and substantial owner, and that Neilson's ownership is merely nominal and colorable.

In June, 1868, there was a cash dividend of $9,000 upon this one hundred and fifty shares of stock. Neilson received it, of course, as the stock was in his name; but on the same day it was paid over to Mr. Brooks, as Neilson says, to pay so much of the $10,000 advanced by Mr. Brooks to pay for the stock. This, then, repaid all but $1,000 of the loan; but Mr. Brooks continued to hold $16,000 of Union Pacific bonds, which Neilson says he gave him as collateral security, and to draw the interest upon all but $5,000. The interest upon the others, Neilson says, he was permitted to draw and retain, but at one time in his testimony he spoke of the amount he was allowed as being Christmas and New Year's presents. Neilson says that during the last summer he borrowed $14,0..0 of Mr. Brooks, and he now owes Mr. Brooks nearly as much as the collaterals; but, according to his testimony, Mr. Brooks for four years held $16,000 in bonds as security for $1,000, and received the interest on $11,000 of the collaterals. No accounts appear to have been kept between Mr. Brooks and Neilson, and doubtless what sums he has received from Mr. Brooks, out of the dividends, were intended as presents rather than as deliveries of money belonging to him.

Mr. Brooks's efforts procured the stock; his money paid for it; all the cash dividends he has received; and he holds all the bonds, except those Dillon received, which seem to have been applied toward paying for the fifty shares. Without further comment on the evidence, the committee find that the one hundred and fifty shares of stock appearing on the books of the Credit Mobilier in the name of Neilson were really the stock of Mr. Brooks, and subject to his control, and that it was so understood by both the parties. Mr. Brooks had taken such an interest in the Credit Mobilier Company, and was so connected with Dr. Durant, that he must be regarded as having full knowledge of the relations between that company and the railroad company, and of the contracts between them. He must have known the cause of the sudden increase in value of the Credit Mobilier stock, and how the large expected profits were to be made. We have already expressed our views of the propriety of a member of Congress becoming the owner of stock, possessing this knowledge.

But Mr. Brooks was not only a member of Congress, but he was a Government director of the Union Pacific Company. As such it was his duty to guard and watch over the interests of the Government in the road and to see that they were protected and preserved. To insure such faithfulness on the part of Government directors, Congress wisely provided that they should not be stockholders in the road. Mr. Brooks readily saw that, though becoming a stockholder in the Credit Mobilier was not forbidden by the letter of the law, yet it was a violation of its spirit and essence, and therefore had the stock placed in the name of his son in-law. The transfer of the Oakes Ames contract to the trustees and the building of the road under that contract, from which the enormous dividends were derived, were all during Mr. Brooks's official life as a Government director, must have been within his knowledge, and yet passed without the slightest opposition from him. The committee believed this could not have been done without an entire disregard of his official obligation and duty, and that while appointed to guard the public interests in the road he joined himself with the promoters of a scheme whereby the Government was to be defrauded, and shared in the spoil.

In the conclusions of fact upon the evidence, the committee are entirely agreed.

In considering what action we ought to recommend to the House upon these facts, the committee encounter a question which has been much debated: Has this House power and jurisdiction to inquire concerning offenses committed by its members prior to their election, and to punish them by censure or expulsion? The committee are unanimous upon the right of jurisdiction of this House over the cases of Mr. Ames and Mr. Brooks, upon the facts founded in regard to them. Upon the question of jurisdiction the committee present the following views:

The Constitution, in the fifth section of the first article, defines the power of either House as follows:

"Each House may determine the rules of its proceedings, punish its members for disorderly behavior, and with the concurrence of two-thirds expel a member."

It will be observed that there is no qualification of the power, but there is an important qualification of the manner of its exercise—it must be done "with the concurrence of two-thirds."

The close analogy between this power and the power of impeachment is deserving of consideration.

The great purpose of the power of impeachment is to remove an unfit and unworthy incumbent from office, and though a judgment of impeachment may to some extent operate as punishment, that is not its principal object. Members of Congress are not subject to be impeached, but may be expelled, and the principal purpose of expulsion is not as punishment, but to remove a member whose character and conduct show that he is an unfit man to participate in the deliberations and decisions of the body, and whose presence in it tends to bring the body into contempt and disgrace.

In both cases it is a power of purgation and purification to be exercised for the public safety, and, in the case of expulsion, for the protection and character of the House. The Constitution defines the causes of impeachment, to wit, "treason, bribery, or other high crimes and misdemeanors." The office of the power of expulsion is so much the same as that of the power to impeach that we think it may be safely assumed that whatever would be a good cause of impeachment would also be a good cause of expulsion.

It has never been contended that the power to impeach for any of the causes enumerated was intended to be restricted to those which might occur after appointment to a civil office, so that a civil officer who had secretly committed such offense before his appointment should not be subject upon detection and exposure to be convicted and removed from office. Every consideration of justice and sound policy would seem to require that the public interests be secured, and those chosen to be their guardians be free from the pollution of high crimes, no matter at what time that pollution had attached.

If this be so in regard to other civil officers, under institutions which rest upon the intelligence and virtue of the people, can it well be claimed that the law-making Representative may be vile and criminal with impunity, provided the evidences of his corruption are found to antedate his election?

In the report made to the Senate by John Quincy Adams in December, 1807, upon the case of John Smith, of Ohio, the following language is used: "The power of expelling a member for misconduct results, on the principles of common sense, from the interests of the nation that the high trust of legislation shall be invested in pure hands. When the trust is elective, it is not to be presumed that the constituent body will commit the deposit to the keeping of worthless characters. But when a man whom his fellow-citizens have honored with their confidence on a pledge of a spotless reputation, has degraded himself by the commission of infamous crimes, which become suddenly and unexpectedly revealed to the world, defective indeed would be that institution which should be impotent to discard from its bosom the contagion of such a member; which should have no remedy of amputation to apply until the poison had reached the heart."

The case of Smith was that of a Senator, who, after his election, but not during a session of the Senate, had been involved in the treasonable conspiracy of Aaron Burr. Yet the reasoning is general, and was to antagonize some positions which had been taken in the case of Marshall, a Senator from Kentucky; the Senate in that case having, among other reasons, declined to take jurisdiction of the charge for the reason that the alleged offense had been committed prior to the Senator's election, and was matter cognizable by the criminal courts of Kentucky. None of the commentators upon the Constitution or upon parliamentary law assign any such limitation as to the time of the commission of the offense, or the nature of it, which shall control and limit the power of expulsion. On the contrary, they all assert that the power in its very nature is a discretionary one, to be exercised of course with grave circumspection at all times and only for good cause. Story, Kent, and Sergeant, all seem to accept and rely upon the exposition of Mr. Adams in the Smith case as sound. May, in his Parliamentary Practice, page 59, enumerates the causes for expulsion from Parliament, but he nowhere intimates that the offense must have been committed subsequent to the election.

When it is remembered that the framers of our Constitution were familiar with the parliamentary law of England, and must have had in mind the then recent contest over Wilkes's case, it is impossible to conclude that they meant to limit the discretion of the Houses as to the causes of expulsion. It is a received principle of construction that the Constitution is to be interpreted according to the known rules of law at the time of its adoption, and therefore, when we find them dealing with a recognized subject of legislative authority, and while studiously qualifying and restricting the manner of its exercise, assigning no limitations to the subject-matter itself, they must be assumed to have intended to leave that to be determined according to established principles, as a high prerogative power to be exercised according to the sound discretion of the body. It was not to be apprehended that two-thirds of the Representatives of the people would ever exercise this power in any capricious or arbitrary manner, or trifle with or trample upon constitutional rights. At the same time it could not be foreseen what necessities for self-preservation or self-purification might arise in the legislative body. Therefore it was that they did not, and would not, undertake to limit or define the boundaries of those necessities.

The doctrine that the jurisdiction of the House over its members is exclusively confined to matters arising subsequent to their election, and that the body is bound to retain the vilest criminal as a member if his criminal secret was kept until his election was secured, has been supposed by many to have been established and declared in the famous case of John Wilkes before alluded to. A short statement of that case will show how fallacious is that supposition. Wilkes had been elected a member of Parliament for Middlesex, and in 1764 was expelled for having published a libel on the ministry. He was again elected and again expelled for a similar offense on the 3d of February, 1769. Being again elected on the 17th of February, 1769, the commons passed the following resolution: "That John Wilkes, esq., having been in this session of Parliament expelled this house, was and is incapable of being elected a member to serve in this present Parliament." Wilkes was again elected, but the House of Commons declared the seat vacant and ordered a new election. At this election Wilkes was again elected by 1,143 votes, against 296 for his competitor, Luttrell.

On the 15th of April, 1769, the house decided that by the previous action Wilkes had become ineligible, and that the votes given for him were void and could not be counted, and gave the seat to Luttrell. Subsequently, in 1783, the House of Commons declared the resolution of February 17, 1769, which had asserted the incapacity of an expelled member to be re-elected to the same Parliament, to be subversive of the rights of the electors, and expunged it from the journal. It will be seen from this concise statement of Wilkes's case that the question was not raised as to the power of the house to expel a member for offenses committed prior to his election; the point decided, and afterward most properly expunged, was that expulsion *per se* rendered the expelled member legally ineligible, and that votes cast for him could not be counted. Wilkes's offense was of purely a political character, not involving moral turpitude; he had attacked the ministry in the press, and the proceedings against him in Parliament were then claimed to be a partisan political persecution, subversive of the rights of the people and of the liberty of the press. These proceedings in Wilkes's case took place during the appearance of the famous Junius letters, and several of them are devoted to the discussion of them. The doctrine that expulsion creates ineligibility was attacked and exposed by him with great force. But he concedes that if the cause of expulsion be one that renders a man unfit and unworthy to be a member, he may be expelled for that cause as often as he shall be elected.

The case of Matteson, in the House of Representatives, has also often been quoted as a precedent for this limitation of jurisdiction. In the proceedings and debates of the House upon that case it will be seen that this was one among many grounds taken in the debate; but as the whole subject was ended by being laid on the table, it is quite impossible to say what was decided by the House. It appeared, however, in that case that the charge against Matteson had become public, and his letter upon which the whole charge rested had been published and circulated through his district during the canvass preceding his election. This fact, we judge, had a most important influence in determining the action of the House in his case.

The committee have no occasion in this report to discuss the question as to the power or duty of the House in a case where a constituency, with a full knowledge of the objectionable character of a man, have selected him to be their Representative. It is hardly a case to be supposed that any constituency, with a full knowledge that a man had been guilty of an offense involving moral turpitude, would elect him.

The majority of the committee are not prepared to concede such a man could be forced upon the House, and would not consider the expulsion of such a man any violation of the rights of the electors, for while the electors have rights that should be respected, the House as a body has rights also that should be protected and preserved. But that in such case the judgment of the constituency would be entitled to the greatest consideration, and that this should form an important element in its determination, is readily admitted.

It is universally conceded, as we believe, that the House has ample jurisdiction to punish or expel a member for an offense committed during his term as a member, though committed during a vacation of Congress and in no way connected with his duties as a member. Upon what principle is it that such a jurisdiction can be maintained? It must be upon one or both of the following: that the offense shows him to be an unworthy and improper man to be a member, or that his conduct brings odium and reproach upon the body. But suppose the offense has been committed prior to his election, but comes to light afterward, is the effect upon his own character, or the reproach and disgrace upon the body, if they allow him to remain a member, any the less? We can see no difference in principle in the two cases, and to attempt any would be to create a purely technical and arbitrary distinction, having no just foundation. In our judgment, the time is not at all material, except it be coupled with the further fact that he was re-elected with a knowledge on the part of his constituents of what he had been guilty, and in such event we have given our views of the effect.

It seems to us absurd to say that an election has given a man political absolution for an offense which was unknown to his constituents. If it be urged again, as it has sometimes been, that this view of the power of the House, and the true ground of its proper exercise, may be laid hold of and used improperly, it may be answered that no rule, however narrow and limited, that may be adopted can prevent it. If two-thirds of the House shall see fit to expel a man because they do not like his political or religious principles, or without any reason at all, they have the power, and there is no remedy except by appeal to the people. Such exercise of the power would be wrongful, and violative of the principles of the Constitution, but we see no encouragement of such wrong in the views we hold.

It is the duty of each House to exercise its rightful functions upon appropriate occasions, and to trust that those who come after them will be no less faithful to duty, and no less jealous for the rights of free popular representation than themselves. It will be quite time enough to square other cases with right reason and principle when they arise. Perhaps the best way to prevent them will be to maintain strictly public integrity and public honor in all cases as they present themselves. Nor do we imagine that the people of the United States will charge their servants with invading their privileges when they confine themselves to the preservation of a standard of official integrity which the common instincts of humanity recognize as essential to all social order and good government.

The foregoing are the views which we deem proper to submit upon the general question of the jurisdiction of the House over its members. But apart from these general views, the committee are of opinion that the facts found in the present case amply justify the taking jurisdiction over them, for the following reasons:

The subject-matter upon which the action of members was intended to be influenced was of a continuous character, and was as likely to be a subject of congressional action in future Congresses as in the Fortieth. The influences brought to bear on members were as likely to be operative upon them in the future as in the present, and were so intended. Mr. Ames and Mr. Brooks have both continued members of the House to the present time, and so have most of the members upon whom these influences were sought to be exerted. The committee are, therefore, of opinion that the acts of these men may properly be treated as offenses against the present House, and so within its jurisdiction upon the most limited rule.

Two members of the committee, Messrs. Niblack and McCrary, prefer to express no opinion on the general jurisdictional questions discussed in the report, and rest their judgment wholly on the ground last stated.

In relation to Mr. Ames, he sold to several members of Congress stock of the Credit Mobilier Company, at par, when it was worth double that amount or more, with the purpose and intent thereby to influence their votes and decisions upon matters to come before Congress.

The facts found in the report as to Mr. Brooks show that he used the influence of his official positions as member of Congress and Government director in the Union Pacific Railroad Company, to get fifty shares of the stock of the Credit Mobilier Company, at par, when it was worth three or four times that sum, knowing that it was given to him with intent to influence his votes and decisions in Congress, and his action as a Government director.

The sixth section of the act of February 26, 1853, 10 Stat. United States, 171, is in the following words:

"If any person or persons shall, directly or indirectly, promise, offer, or give, or cause or procure to be promised, offered, or given, any money, goods, right in action, bribe, present, or reward, or any promise, contract, undertaking, obligation, or security for the payment or delivery of any money, goods, right in action, bribe, present, or reward, or any other valuable thing whatever, to any member of the Senate or House of Representatives of the United States, after his election as such member, and either before or after he shall have qualified and taken his seat, or to any officer of the United States, or person holding any place of trust or profit, or discharging any official function under or in connection with any Department of the Government of the United States, or under the Senate or House of Representatives of the United States, after the passage of this act, with intent to influence his vote or decision on any question, matter, cause, or proceeding which may then be pending, or may by law, or under the Constitution of the United States, be brought before him in his official capacity, or in his place of trust or profit, and shall thereof be convicted, such person or persons so offering, promising, or giving, or causing or procuring to be promised, offered, or given, any such money, goods, right in action, bribe, present, or reward, or any promise, contract, undertaking, obligation, or security for the payment or delivery of any money, goods, right in action, bribe, present, or reward, or other valuable thing whatever, and the member, officer, or person who shall in anywise accept or receive the same, or any part thereof, shall be liable to indictment as for a high crime and misdemeanor in any of the courts of the United States having jurisdiction for the trial of crimes and misdemeanors; and shall, upon conviction thereof, be fined not exceeding three times the amount so offered, promised, or given, and imprisoned in the penitentiary not exceeding three years; and the person so convicted of so accepting or receiving the same, or any part thereof, if an officer or person holding any such place of trust or profit as aforesaid, shall forfeit his office or place; and any person so convicted under this section shall forever be disqualified to hold any office of honor, trust, or profit under the United States."

In the judgment of the committee, the facts reported in regard to Mr. Ames and Mr. Brooks would have justified their conviction under the above-recited statute and subjected them to the penalties therein provided.

The committee need not enlarge upon the dangerous character of these offenses. The sense of Congress is shown by the severe penalty denounced by the statute itself. The offenses were not violations of private rights, but were against the very life of a constitutional Government by poisoning the fountain of legislation.

The duty devolved upon the committee has been of a most painful and delicate character. They have performed it to the best of their ability. They have proceeded with the greatest care and deliberation, for while they desired to do their full duty to the House and the country, they were most anxious not to do injustice to any man. In forming their conclusions they have intended to be entirely cool and dispassionate, not to allow themselves to be swerved by any popular fervor on the one hand, or any feeling of personal favor and sympathy on the other.

The committee submit to the House and recommend the adoption of the following resolutions:

1. Whereas Mr. Oakes Ames, a Representative in this House from the State of Massachusetts, has been guilty of selling to members of Congress shares of stock in the Credit Mobilier of America, for prices much below the true value of such stock, with intent thereby to influence the votes and decisions of such members in matters to be brought before Congress for action: Therefore,

Resolved, That Mr. Oakes Ames be, and he is hereby, expelled from his seat as a member of this House.

2. Whereas Mr. James Brooks, a Representative in this House from the State of New York, did procure the Credit Mobilier Company to issue and deliver to Charles H. Neilson, for the use and benefit of said Brooks, fifty shares of the stock of said company, at a price much below its real value, well knowing that the same was so issued and delivered with intent to influence the votes and decisions of said Brooks, as a member of the House, in matters to be brought before Congress for action, and also to influence the action of said Brooks as a Government director in the Union Pacific Railroad Company: Therefore,

Resolved, That Mr. James Brooks be, and he is hereby, expelled from his seat as a member of this House.

CREDIT MOBILIER.

WASHINGTON, D. C., *Thursday, December* 12, 1872.

The committee met at 10 a. m. The following members of the committee were present:

Mr. LUKE P. POLAND, (chairman,) of Vermont.

Mr. N. P. BANKS, of Massachusetts.

Mr. GEO. W. MCCRARY, of Iowa.

Mr. WM. E. NIBLACK, of Indiana.

Mr. WM. M. MERRICK, of Maryland.

Mr. Oakes Ames and R. C. McMurtrie, his counsel; Henry S. McComb, with Jeremiah S. Black and Samuel G. Thompson, counsel, were also present.

JAMES G. BLAINE, Speaker of the United States House of Representatives, was sworn, and testified as follows:

With the leave of the committee I will submit my testimony in writing, for the sake of accuracy, and when I have finished, I shall, of course, answer any questions which the committee may desire to ask by way of examination or cross-examination.

And I wish to state, without reservation or qualification, that I never owned a share of stock in the Credit Mobilier in my life, either by gift, purchase, or in any way whatever. Nor did I ever receive, either directly or indirectly, a single cent derived in any manner or shape from the Credit Mobilier or from the Union Pacific Railroad Company. No person holds, or ever did hold, for me, any stock in either corporation as agent or trustee, or in any capacity whatever. I wish my testimony to be taken as exhaustive and as intended to exclude every form or phase of ownership in the Credit Mobilier or the Union Pacific Railroad Company, both past and present.

I desire further to state that some time in the spring of 1868, the precise date I will not affirm, Mr. Oakes Ames asked me one day if I would like to purchase some stock in the Credit Mobilier. He said it would prove a good investment, and he could sell me ten shares of the stock at a rate somewhat above par—I think some ten hundred and sixty dollars for the ten shares. We had some conversation in regard to the matter, and Mr. Ames told me very frankly that in regard to these shares there was a law-suit either pending or threatened, though he said his right to sell the shares was perfect and undoubted. I concluded that I did not desire to purchase the stock, and therefore declined Mr. Ames's offer.

I beg to say, however, in justice to Mr. Ames, but more especially in justice to myself, that it never once occurred to me that he was attempting to bribe me, or in any way influence my vote or action as a Representative. I understood him to say that he was the owner of more of the stock than he wished to carry, and was offering some of it to friends at cost and interest to him, a slight advance above par value. The amount offered to me was very small, and made little impression on my mind; indeed, was well nigh forgotten until recalled by the incidents which led to this investigation.

Mr. Ames never offered me any of the stock at any other time than as I have just narrated, nor was any of the stock ever offered to me at any time by "any other person or corporation."

By the CHAIRMAN:

Question. Have you any knowledge in relation to any dealing between Mr. Ames and any other member of the House of the character referred to?—Answer. None whatever, and I never heard of any until this publication. Mr. Ames is present, and I desire to ask him whether the statement I have just made is correct.

Mr. AMES. Yes, sir; your statement corresponds substantially with my recollection of the facts.

By Mr. MERRICK:

Q. Have you any knowledge of any other member of Congress owning stock in the Credit Mobilier?—A. None whatever; nor the remotest, other than from the general newspaper reports. I have, of course, seen these; and aside from them I have no knowledge of the subject in any shape or manner, except as pertains to myself, as just given in my testimony.

WASHINGTON, D. C., *Friday, December* 13, 1872.

The committee met at 10 a. m., all the members present, except Mr. Banks.

Mr. Ames and Mr. McComb, with their counsel, were also present.

HENRY S. MCCOMB sworn and examined.

By the CHAIRMAN:

Question. State to the committee what knowledge or information you have in regard to shares of Credit Mobilier stock disposed of by Mr. Ames to members of Congress.—Answer. If the committee please, I would prefer to have them ask me questions, and let me give direct answers. I have with me my sworn testimony in the suit in Pennsylvania, which has been instituted on this subject, which, if the committee desire to refer to, will give them all the information I have.

Q. I see that you state in this testimony in your examination-in-chief that three hundred and forty-three shares of the Credit Mobilier stock were put in the control of Oakes Ames, and were given to members of Congress. The question was then asked, "Where did you gain your information enabling you to make that precise answer?" And the answer given here is, "From Oakes Ames."

The WITNESS. Yes, sir; and I repeat that answer.

Q. Are you a stockholder in this Credit Mobilier Company of America?—A. I am.

Q. Were you connected with it otherwise than as a stockholder, and are you familiar with its history and proceedings?—A. I have been connected as a stockholder only, not as a director or manager. I was familiar with its proceedings until the present officers took position, since which time everything has been kept secret, and I have never been able to see the books or ascertain what has been going on. When I speak of the present officers I refer to Sidney Dillon, president, and John B. Alley, of the executive committee. I have never been able to get anything out of them as to the management of the company in any way or manner. The books are always withheld from my personal examination.

Q. Was Oakes Ames a member of that company?—A. He was a stockholder.

Q. Was he an officer?—A. He was never an officer, but was an intimate friend of all the officers and all concerned.

Q. There is a litigation pending now in the courts of Pennsylvania, as the committee understand, in reference to your right to certain shares in this company?—A. Yes, sir; a suit commenced four years ago.

Q. You claim to be entitled to three hundred and seventy-five shares?—A. Yes, sir; to two hundred and fifty of the original shares, with the accretions or increase, which would make three hundred and seventy-five shares.

Q. That suit is in your favor?—A. Yes, sir.

Q. Who are the defendants in that suit?—A. The defendants are the stockholders, managers, and corporation of the Credit Mobilier and Oakes Ames and John B. Alley.

Q. Are you acquainted with the history of this corporation known as the Credit Mobilier Company of America?—A. Yes, sir; I am acquainted with its history up to the time I spoke of.

Q. By what authority was this company chartered?—A. The Credit Mobilier corporation was the result of a charter obtained by a man named Duff Green from the Pennsylvania legislature, called the "Pennsylvania Fiscal Agency." It was subsequently changed by legislative enactment to the Credit Mobilier of America, and some little change made in its provisions. It was purchased by Thomas C. Durant from a man in Pennsylvania named Hall and George Francis Train. It was purchased especially with a view of building the Pacific Railroad. The Pennsylvania legislature made an amendment in the charter allowing a branch office to be in New York, and providing that it should be managed by what was called a railway bureau, all of whom need not be directors of the company.

Q. Do you know the organization of this Credit Mobilier Company—whether it was managed in the interest of and managed by persons connected with the Pacific Railroad?—A. It was obtained with that view.

Q. Can you state what use they made of this Credit Mobilier Company and the relation it held to the Pacific Railroad?—A. Yes, sir. The idea of the organization was to relieve the directors and shareholders of the Union Pacific Railroad Company from any individual responsibility in building the road and enabling them to share the profits in building the Union Pacific Railroad. That was the design. It was obtained to cover up anything that might have been done; to relieve individuals from responsibility. I was never a director or manager of the Credit Mobilier from its organization to the present moment.

Q. Your connection was simply as a shareholder?—A. Simply as a shareholder.

Q. How large a shareholder were you?—A. I have held as much as a thousand shares at a time. I am the holder in my own name of about eight hundred and fifty shares.

Q. These are shares aside from those in dispute between you and the company?—A. Yes, sir. As a stockholder, I have frequently asked to look at the books since the organization has been under its present management, but have never been accorded that privilege.

Q. When was the management changed?—A. In 1867; in May, I think. I think Mr. Dillon was elected president, and he, with Mr. Hazard and Mr. Alley, constituted the executive committee. These are the men who have the control and who do control, with autocratic power, everything connected with the institution. Just what suited Mr. Alley's particular convenience was done, and what did not suit him was not done.

Q. You claim two hundred and fifty shares of the original stock, and half as much more, making three hundred and seventy-five. Your claim is that, by a subscription made, you are entitled to these shares?—A. Yes, sir; by a subscription made the 3d of March, 1866.

Q. And these shares you have never received?—A. No, sir; nor any of their accretions.

Q. And you have a suit pending to recover these shares?—A. Yes, sir; that suit was instituted after a diligent effort on my part to obtain the shares from the company amicably.

Q. About what time was the suit commenced?—A. The papers were filed in November, 1868, I think, and the suit is still pending.

Q. What has become of the three hundred and seventy-five shares which you claim?—A. Mr. Ames must answer that.

Q. What is your information in reference to it?—A. They went into the hands of Mr. Ames—into the hands of Oakes Ames, trustee—and so stood recorded on the books of the Credit Mobilier, two hundred and fifty shares at one time and ninety-three shares, or whatever there was, subsequently.

Q. These shares appear to be assigned on the books to Oakes Ames, as trustee?—A. Yes, sir; that was to distinguish them from his own stock. He was a large holder of the stock of the company.

Q. And you understand these three hundred and seventy-five shares to be the shares you claim? Now, will you state what knowledge you have in relation to the disposition of these shares, or any of them, by Mr. Ames?—A. My knowledge is from Mr. Ames orally and from Mr. Ames in writing.

Q. Have you the writings you refer to?—A. I have the original of letters from him, and I have photographed copies made of them. I do not desire to part with the originals. The committee may examine them, and compare them with the copies, and I desire the originals to be returned to me. I now hand to the committee the original and photographed copy of a letter from Mr. Ames, dated January 25, 1868.

The letter was read and placed in evidence, as follows:

WASHINGTON, *Jan.* 25, 1868.

H. S. McCOMB, Esq.:

DEAR SIR: Yours of the 23d is at hand, in which you say Senators Bayard & Fowler have written you in relation to their stock. I have spoken to Fowler, but not to Bayard. I have never been introduced to Bayard, but will see him soon. You say I must not put too much in one locality. I have assigned as far as I have gone to 4 from Mass., 1 from N. H., 1 Delaware, 1 Tenn., 1 Ohio, 2 Penn., 1 Ind., 1 Maine, & I have 3 to place, which I shall put where they will do most good to us. I am here on the spot, and can better judge where they should go. I think after this dividend is paid we should make our capital to 4,000,000, and distribute the new stock where it will protect us, let them have the stock at par, and profits made in the future; the 50 per cent. increase on the old stock I want for distribution here, and soon. Alley is opposed to the division of the bonds; says we will need them, &c., &c. I should think that we ought to be able to spare them, with Alley and Cisco on the finance committee—we used to be able to borrow when we had no credit and debts pressing. We are now out of debt and in good credit—what say you about the bond dividend—a part of the purchasers here are poor, and want their bonds to sell to enable them to meet their payment on the stock in the C. M. I have told them what they would get as dividend, and they expect, I think, when the bonds the parties receive as the 80 per cent. dividend, we better give them the bonds—it will not am't to anything with us. Some of the large holders will not care whether they have the bonds or certificates, or they will lend their bonds to the company, as they have done before, or lend them money. Quigley has been here, and we have got that $\frac{1}{10}$ that was Underwood's. I have taken half, Quigley $\frac{1}{4}$ and you $\frac{1}{4}$. J. Carter wants a part of it, at some future day we are to surrender a part to him.

Yours, truly,

OAKES AMES.

Q. In whose handwriting was the original letter?—A. That is in Oakes Ames's handwriting.

Q. You are acquainted with his handwriting?—A. Very well; I have seen him write frequently; that is his handwriting.

Q. You received the letter—how?—A. I received it by mail. Let me explain that the last paragraph of that letter has no reference to the Credit Mobilier matter. That is on a different business entirely. That refers to the Alexandria Canal, Railroad, and Bridge Company, running between Alexandria and Washington.

Q. What other letters have you?—A. The second letter is dated January 30, 1868. I hand the committee the original with the photographed copy.

The letter was read and placed in evidence, as follows:

WASHINGTON, *Jan.* 30, 1868.

H. S. McCOMB:

DEAR SIR: Yours of the 28th is at hand, inclosing copy of letter from, or rather to, Mr. King. I don't fear any investigation here. What some of Durant's friends may do in N. Y. courts can't be counted upon with any certainty. You do not understand by your letter what I have done, & am to do with my sales of stock. You say none to N. Y. I have placed some with N. Y., or have agreed to. You must remember that it was nearly all placed as you saw on the list in N. Y., & there was but 6 or 8 m. for me to place. I could not give all the world all they might want out of that. You would not want me to offer less than 1,000 m. to any one. We allow Durant to place 58,000 to some 3 or 4 of his friends, or keep it himself.

I have used this where it will produce most good to us, I think. In view of King's letter and Washburne's move here, I go in for making our bond dividend in full. We can do it with perfect safety. I understand the opposition to it comes from Alley; he is on the finance com'ee, and can raise money easy if we come short, which I don't believe we shall, & if we do we can loan our bonds to the company, or loan them the money we get from the bonds. The contract calls for the division, & I say have it. When shall I see you in Washington?

Yours, truly,

OAKES AMES.

We stand about like this:

Bonds, 1st mortgage, rec'd on 525 miles, at 16 m	8,400,000
" " " " " 15 " " 48 m	720,000
" " " " " 100 " " 48 m	4 800,000
	13,920,000
10,000,000 sold & to sell to pay our debts	10,000,000
	3,920,000
80 p'r cent. dividend on 3,700,000 C. M. of A	3,000
	920,000
Gov't bonds received this day	960,000
Due for transportation 400 m., one-half cash	200,000
	2,080,000

In addition to this we can draw Gov't bonds for $\frac{2}{3}$ of the work done in advance of track, if we desire it.

Oakes Ames's list of names as showed to-day to me for C. M.:

Blaine, of Maine, 3,000.
Patterson, N. Hamp., 3,000.
Wilson, Mass., 2.
Painter, Rep. for Inq., 3.
S. Colfax, Speaker, 2.
Elliott, Mass., 3.
Dawes, " 2.
Boutwell, " 2.
Bingham & Garfield, Ohio.
Schofield & Kelley, Penn.
Fowler, Tenn.
FEB'Y 1, '68.

Q. This list of names is not in Mr. Ames's handwriting; in whose handwriting is it?—A. In my own.

Q. How came you to make that list?—A. I wrote those names as Mr. Ames read them to me from his memorandum-book. He sat one side of the table and I sat the other, in the office of the Union Pacific Railroad Company in New York, just as we sit opposite each other now at this table; when he read I wrote the names. This was early in February, 1868. My reason for writing that list of names was that I had before written a list which he had given to me, and in that list he had stated he had given a share to Senator James A. Bayard, of Delaware, the old gentleman, which I found that he had not done.

Q. Have you other letters from Mr. Ames?—A. I have other letters. I have only one more here, and I would prefer not to produce it now unless I am obliged to. I desire to say no more in this case than I am compelled to say for my personal vindication. This investigation is not of my seeking at all.

Q. If we are to inquire into your correspondence with Mr. Ames in reference to this subject, it will be our duty to learn all there is.—A. It is for the committee to say. I have only one letter here, and I have a motive for withholding it just now, which I do not object to expressing privately to you, gentlemen. I would like the committee to go through with their examination with other witnesses before this letter is brought in. I will bring it in after I have heard these other gentlemen testify. I would rather not do it now.

Q. I see that in this letter of January 30 reference is made to the letter Mr. Ames had received from you, inclosing a copy of a letter to Mr. King. Have you that letter?—A. Mr. Ames has that letter, I presume. I have not looked to see whether I have a copy of it or not.

Q. What Mr. King is that?—A. John L. King, of Springfield, Massachusetts, who was a shareholder and an acquaintance of all these gentlemen.

Q. The committee think whatever letters or writings on this subject are in your possession they ought to have now.

The WITNESS. Can I not be permitted to withhold it until these other gentlemen have testified?

The CHAIRMAN. We are not trying any case between parties. The committee desire you to produce the letter at this time.—A. This is the only letter I have here. I did want to withhold it, simply in reference to a statement made by Mr. Blaine yesterday. That is the entire reason I have for withholding it. Because in this letter, in addition to speaking of members of Congress, it gives Mr. Ames's view of the value of this stock, (at the time Mr. Blaine claims to have been offered the stock,) at a very much higher price than has been named in the newspapers.

Q. The letter which you produce is in Mr. Ames's handwriting?—A. It is. Here is the original, and I also have a photographed copy.

The letter was read and placed in evidence, as follows:

WASHINGTON, *Feb.* 22, 1868.

H. S. McCOMB, Esq.:

DEAR SIR: Yours of the 21st is at hand; am glad to hear that you are getting along so well with Mr. West; hope you will bring it out all satisfactory, so that it will be so rich that we cannot help going into it. I return you the paper by mail that you ask for. You ask me if I will sell some of my U. P. R. R. stock. I will sell some of it at par C. M. of A. I don't care to sell. I hear that Mr. Bates offered his at $300, but I don't want Bates to sell out. I think Grimes may sell a part of his at $350. I want that $14,000 increase of the Credit Mobilier to sell here. We want more friends in this Congress, & if a man will look into the law, (& it is difficult to get them to do it unless they have an interest to do so,) he cannot help being convinced that we should not be interfered with. Hope to see you here or at N. Y. the 11th.

Yours, truly,

OAKES AMES.

The WITNESS. I have some more letters which I did not bring with me, but I have sent my clerk to look them up, and ascertain whether they have any bearing on this subject. I brought these copies which I had photographed to be used in the suit to which reference has been made. I was away when this investigation was ordered, and had no opportunity to examine my papers after I received notice to come here as a witness.

Q. If you have other correspondence which has bearing upon this subject, we desire you to produce it.—A. I will do any thing that is demanded of me by the committee.

Q. State when you first had any conversation with Mr. Ames upon this subject.—A. Some time in the early part of January.

Q. Where was that conversation held?—A. In New York. I had been asked to sign a paper allowing Mr. Ames to take some stock without the purpose being specified. I signed the paper under protest, with the distinct understanding, expressed by all the persons present, that it would not intefere with my claim. That was done at a meeting of the seven trustees who were building the Union Pacific Railroad, under Oakes Ames's contract. The meeting was in New York, in a room occupied by Mr. Durant, on the corner of Cedar and Nassau streets. I did finally sign the paper under protest, and signed it without reading it. The purport of it, as stated, was to allow him to take certain shares of stock, but there was a distinct understanding at the time I signed it that it was not to affect my claim in any manner.

Q. Have you that paper?—A. They have it; I have not. I never had a copy of it.

Q. Are you able to state any more particularly the contents of that paper than you have done?—A. My recollection of the statement made was, that so much of the Credit Mobilier stock should be allowed to be taken by Mr. Durant and so much by Mr. Ames. I did not read it, as I have said. It was stated to me in general terms. They wanted the large stockholders to give their consent to these shares being so taken. This statement was made by these gentlemen at this meeting of trustees.

Q. At that meeting was anything said as to what disposition Mr. Ames was to make of these shares?—A. Not a word to me, that I heard at that time, other than what I have stated. I was the last signer on the paper, I think.

Q. About what time was this?—A. I could ascertain the time from the books of the company if I had access to them. I think it was early in January, 1868.

Q. This paper was signed by yourself and others?—A. Yes, by five or six.

Q. Do you remember the number of shares authorized to be taken by Mr. Ames in this way?—A. I think something like two hundred. I do not remember the exact number. I had refused peremptorily to sign the paper, and there was quite a wrangle or discussion in the meeting at the time. John B. Alley was present, and I remember that he was very suave in giving me to understand that it should not affect my claim. Mr. Ames also stated that it should not affect my claim.

Q. Do you understand that the stock taken by Mr. Ames was the identical stock you were claiming?—A. No, sir; I did not understand any such thing at that time. It was so much of the stock of the company. There was considerable stock in the treasury of the company at that time that would have given him his stock and me mine.

Q. Some time after that you had an interview and conversation with Mr. Ames in reference to that stock. How long after that did you have this conversation?—A. I was seeing Mr. Ames every few days. I was in Washington a good deal, and Mr. Ames was in New York a good deal.

Q. Do you remember where you had your first talk with him about it?—A. It was in the office of the Union Pacific Railroad Company in New York. The thing was brought to my attention, and I asked Mr. Ames what disposition he had made of this stock. He told me he had divided it among members of Congress.

Q. State all that he said.—A. I want to say here, in explanation of another thing, that a good many dividends had been paid on this stock of the Credit Mobilier of America up to the time of this transaction. I understood when I signed this paper that it would not include dividends which had been declared prior to that time. Yet Mr. Ames took with the stock all the past dividends, as well as those to be made in the future.

Q. Can you state in round numbers about what amount of dividends had been declared up to that time?—A. I think about 260 per cent. Mr. Ames states that he would not sell his own, although Mr. Grimes might sell some of his at 350, and this was about the time he claims to have sold this stock at par.

Q. Was this first conversation prior to the date of these letters?—A. O, yes.

Q. Now state as nearly as you can precisely the conversation between you and Mr. Ames in its details.—A. That would be a pretty hard thing to do. I do not know that I could give it in the precise words.

Q. State the substance of the conversation as nearly as possible.—A. Mr. Ames had shown me a list of names of members of Congress prior to this which I made a copy of as near as I could recollect. He stated to me how he had apportioned the stock.

Q. Have you that list here?—A. I have not. It was simply a rough memorandum, and I have not it with me. I think I have it among my papers.

Q. Did you make the memorandum from what Mr. Ames said?—A. I did not copy it from anything. I put it down from his personal remarks. Prior to the time of receiving these letters, in a conversation we had in New York, he had occasion to give me the names of the members of Congress to whom he had given this stock, and I took a memorandum of these names from memory immediately after that. That is the list of which I speak. The list I have produced here was read to me by Mr. Ames from a memorandum-book he had. I could not get the initials of the names, and I just put down the names as they were read. After he had read them he put the memorandum-book in his pocket.

Q. At the time you made this memorandum from what he had stated to you, what was the substance of the statement he made?—A. His statement was: In the first list which I made a memorandum of, he included Senator Bayard's name. When Mr. Ames told me that he was going to give the stock he had to members of Congress, some days after the paper was signed I asked him who he was going to give it to, and he gave me the names of some who are on this paper and of some who are not. He said to me at that time, I remember, that he had given stock to Mr. Wilson, of Massachusetts, Bingham, of Ohio, Speaker Colfax, and some others. I remember Mr. Bingham's name from his being here on the trial of Mrs. Surratt and of his being a prominent gentleman. I also remembered Mr. Wilson and the Speaker from the prominent positions they held. I had some little doubt about Mr. Ames doing what he said he was going to do, and I said to him that if he was going to give stock to these members of Congress, I would like him to give some to Senator Bayard, of Delaware, and to Senator Fowler, of Tennessee; also James F. Wilson, of Iowa, and William B. Allison, of Iowa, members of the House. I had known Mr. Bayard for many years. I knew he was incorruptible in anything pertaining to money. I knew that if he had given him any stock I should ascertain just the conditions on which he had been getting it. I called Mr. Bayard's attention to it subsequently. He did not understand it and wrote me for an explanation, which letter I received about the 14th of January, 1868, and immediately sent a copy of it to Mr. Ames. Mr. Bayard stated in his letter that he could not receive the stock if there was anything in connection with it that would come in conflict with his duty. I had told him that Mr. Ames had some stock to sell, and I stated that he was to pay for it if he got it. I sent a copy of this letter, as I stated, to Mr. Ames, but in Mr. Ames's subsequent letter to me he still apportioned one to Delaware. That is the reason which induced me to be particular in getting his list of names. You notice that he excludes Delaware in the list I have given you, though in the letters he brings in one for Delaware. I asked him whether, in putting down one to Delaware in this letter, he meant that he had given any to Mr. Bayard. He said "No, I gave that one to Senator Conkling, of New York; and that he gave a thousand dollars of the stock to him."

Q. Do I understand that you have now given the whole of this first conversation?—A. I am endeavoring to give you the first conversation after the meeting in New York, where these names were read out. But that conversation is somewhat interwoven with others, because I kept no record of the dates.

Q. Have you stated all that you remember took place in this first conversation you had with Mr. Ames?—A. I am not positive as to the date, because, as you understand, I had so many conversations with Mr. Ames. I talked with him on this subject a dozen times, and it was because of Mr. Ames's incorrect statements that I wanted to have something in writing. It was for that reason mainly that this correspondence occurred.

Q. Now, state a little more fully and particularly the transaction when you made the memorandum on this letter.—A. I made it early in February. I do not remember the date. It was very soon after I received the letter. Mr. Ames happened to be in New York, and I had his letter with me.

Q. You produced the letter to him?—A. Yes, sir; I produced the letter to him. That is the time he made the explanation about Mr. Conkling. He had previously talked about giving some of the stock to New York, to which I objected, and that is the reason I said in my letter "none to New York." I did not know Mr. Conkling, and was opposed to his having any of the stock.

Q. But you made this memorandum from something which Mr. Ames read there?—A. Yes, sir; he had a list of the names on a memorandum inside his pocket-book, which he took out and read from.

Q. Did you see the list?—A. I saw a list of names in his pocket-book, written in ink. He sat across the table from me, and I saw the list as I see now what he is writing.

Q. And as he read them you wrote them down?—A. Yes, sir; and that is the reason why I only wrote the last name in each case, because I wanted to follow him as rapidly as he read.

Q. This puts down Blaine, of Maine, at 3. Do you intend that to be $3,000?—A. Yes, sir; $3,000. That is par value for the stock, thirty shares.

Q. This memorandum puts down Wilson, Massachusetts, at 2. Is that $2,000?—A. Yes, sir; $2,000, or 20 shares.

Q. Did he state to you whether this stock had really been transferred to these men?—A. O, no; on the contrary, he stated that it was held by him as their trustee.

Q. What was his language, as nearly as you can remember, in relation to what arrangement had been made with any of them?—A. The statement that he made to me was that he had said to A. B. C., mentioning the names there, "you have $3,000 stock of the Credit Mobilier and the bonds will pay for it. The dividend in excess of the payment will be given to you." That is the reason I call it a gift, the stock being worth so much more in the market than the value it was sold for. It had just declared a dividend of 80 per cent. in bonds, which of itself was four-fifths of the par value of the stock.

Q. You say that the par value itself was paid out of the dividend declared?—A. That is it; and the par value only Mr. Ames paid back to the company.

Q. And what was divided beyond repaying this par value was a gift?—A. That is the point.

Q. Did Mr. Ames say how this was done?—A. He said he was to receive the bonds, convert them into money, and pay back the par value to the company. You understand that I never said any of these gentlemen got any stock whatever. I only state the information I received from Mr. Ames.

By Mr. McCrary:

Q. What was the value of the stock at the time, in your estimation?—A. Mr. Ames estimated its value about that time as 350, and he would not sell his at that price, although Mr. Grimes might a part of his at 350. My understanding was that it was worth about 600 or 700 a share, including prior dividends.

By Mr. Niblack:

Q. What Mr. Grimes was that?—A. Senator Grimes, of Iowa. He stood on the books of the Credit Mobilier as a subscriber to the stock from the beginning. Mr. Ames, however, was a half-owner of his stock. They owned it jointly. Mr. Ames collected dividends and divided them with Mr. Grimes. It was an honorable subscription made from the beginning, and before any dividends were paid. I knew Mr. Grimes well, and knew him to be an honorable, high-toned gentleman.

By the CHAIRMAN:

Q. At the time you made this memorandum on the letter did you have any further conversation on this subject with Mr. Ames?—A. I did. Mr. Ames being a large holder of the stock, I knew that while Mr. Alley was the nominal head, that he would follow, generally, anything that Mr. Ames positively directed him to do; that he would not do much that he did not assent to. I knew Mr. Alley very well, and I know perfectly well their relative positions. I therefore followed up Mr. Ames pretty close to get him to settle this claim of mine. He finally came out with the remark, "There is no stock for you. You consented to give it to me for members of Congress." That put the thing in a different position. If that was my stock, then I wanted him to be my trustee, instead of the trustee of these other persons.

Q. What did he tell you in reference to the disposition of that stock to members of Congress?—A. Nothing, except that he had given the stock—that he had appropriated it to them. He held it as trustee; and my understanding was that he apportioned the dividends to these members either in money or in bonds, to them or to some friends of theirs, in some way.

Q. Did you understand that other stock was given to any person except to those named in your memorandum?—A. I think he claimed that Mr. Brooks, member of Congress, got what was apportioned to him out of this amount. Mr. Brooks is the only member of Congress I know to have received any of this stock without a fair consideration.

Q. Are you speaking of stock obtained from Mr. Ames by him?—A. A portion of it; thirty-two shares came from him.

Q. Was this stock put into his hands?—A. I do not know. I think the stock Mr. Brooks received was given by Mr. Alley's direction, and not by that of Mr. Ames.

Q. Mr. James Brooks is a member of the present Congress; will you state what knowledge you have in relation to this stock?

WITNESS. Am I obliged to answer that question?

The CHAIRMAN. The committee desire you to answer it.

A. All I know in regard to Mr. Brooks's receiving any of this stock is this: I saw Mr. Brooks and Mr. Alley together several times, and heard Mr. Brooks pressing Mr. Alley to let him have fifty shares of the Credit Mobilier stock, and I heard him say to Mr. Alley that if he would accord him that privilege and give him the stock, he would take care of the democratic side of the House. Mr. Brooks was at that time either a Government director, or said he would have himself made a Government director, of the Union Pacific Railroad. I overheard such conversation between Mr. Brooks and Mr. Alley on several occasions; Mr. Alley finally consented to give him fifty shares of that stock, and it was transferred to Mr. Brooks, or to his son-in-law, Neilson. I do not know precisely when the transfer was made. Mr. Alley gave his pledge that Mr. Brooks should have the fifty shares.

Q. What is Mr. Neilson's full name?—A. Charles H. Neilson, I think. That was along in the fall of 1868.

Q. It was subsequent to these letters that you have produced?—A. O, yes.

Q. You understand that that fifty shares of stock went to Mr. Brooks, and that he had the advantage of them without making any payment?—A. Yes, sir; with all the accretions. The par value of $100 a share was paid out of the accrued dividends. I tried to follow this thing up myself by getting access to the Credit Mobilier books, but they were always sealed books to me. I was never allowed to look into them.

Q. Do you understand that the fifty shares which went to Mr. Brooks were a portion of the shares put into Mr. Ames's hands?—A. Only from Mr. Ames's statement that thirty-two shares of that amount put into his hands went to make up the amount which was to go to Mr. Brooks. That was a mere passing remark; whether it was true or not I do not know.

Q. You understood the remark to be made in accounting in part for the number of shares Mr. Ames had placed in his hands?—A. Yes, sir.

Q. State any other conversation you had with Mr. Ames in reference to his dealings with members of Congress on the subject.—A. This case has been going on several years. The counsel for Mr. Ames's side had demanded, before proceeding with my cross-examination, the production of Mr. Ames's letters. I evaded it for awhile, but finally I gave him a copy of one of these letters, but he was not satisfied with that. I insisted that these letters should not be made any part of the case on my side. But the counsel for Mr. Ames demanded that the originals should be made a part of the case in my suit. I visited Washington about April of this year, and had an interview with Mr. Oakes Ames at the Arlington House. I brought these letters, and all the letters I had from him. I stated the fact that I was obliged to produce these letters in the suit. I told him that I had no desire to produce them, but that his counsel refused to go on with my further cross-examination until the letters were produced. I said to him, "If you will give me, over your signature, an agreement that if I gain my suit you will account to me for this stock, I will surrender all these letters to you, and when I go back to Philadelphia will say to the counsel that I have not the letters, and I will keep no copies of them." Mr. Ames replied, exhibiting some petulance of feeling, "You can publish any letters you have from me; everybody knows that members of Congress are bribed, and everybody does it." That he said at the Arlington Hotel in this city. I then went back to Philadelphia and produced the letters, and that is how they came out. Up to that time I supposed Mr. Ames had some little consideration for his friends, and that he would try to shield them, but he seemed to be entirely indifferent, and said I could publish the letters. I did not see Mr. Ames after that until I met him in New York, at the Fifth Avenue Hotel, after the publication of these letters. We had a little spat between us at the time, and he and I have not spoken since.

Q. Have you stated the substance of all that has occurred on this subject?—A. I think so, unless a further examination may bring to mind something I have forgotten.

Q. Have you any knowledge in relation to transfers and arrangements about stock between Mr. Ames and members of Congress, except what you learned from him?—A. I have not, and I want to be distinctly understood as saying that I do not charge or know that members of Congress received any stock, or had anything to do with the stock, except what I learn from Mr. Ames himself. In making this statement I should except Mr. Brooks; also Senator Grimes, who bought his stock originally as I have stated; and I believe Mr. Hooper also had some stock, which he bought at the beginning.

Q. All the knowledge other than that which you have on this subject is derived from Mr. Ames?—A. Yes, sir.

Q. Have you any knowledge other than that derived from Mr. Ames, in relation to any member receiving stock in this company, from anybody?—A. I have not.

Q. Have you made any arrangement yourself, in any way, with any member of Congress?—A. Never for a dollar, either in stock of this or any other company, in money or any other consideration. I never did.

Q. Do you know that anybody else has had anything to do with that stock, except what you have stated as coming from Mr. Ames?—A. No, sir. I might say here, and it comes to my mind just at this moment, that I was in the office at New York when Mr. Ham was transferring some Union Pacific Railroad stock to a Mr. Kennedy, of Washington. Mr. Ham stated that Mr. Ames was transferring some of his trustee stock to Mr. Kennedy as trustee.

Q. Do you refer to J. C. Kennedy?—A. I do not know his name. He is a tall man, with iron-gray hair. He has a brother who is a banker or broker in New York. I do not know what bearing, if any, that had upon this subject.

By Mr. NIBLACK:

Q. At the time of this agreement authorizing Mr. Ames to receive a portion of that stock for distribution, did you understand that any of it was to be divided among members of Congress?—A. I did not.

Q. Did you ever afterward voluntarily or conditionally assent to any such disposition of it?—A. No, sir. I was never solicited. I knew very little about the transactions of the Credit Mobilier after the time I have referred to. It was managed in a secret kind of way, and these gentlemen can best answer for themselves for what passed.

Q. What I want to know is whether you ever assented to this disposition of this stock?—A. No, sir; I did not.

By Mr. MERRICK:

Q. I understand you to say that Mr. Ames represented that these members of Congress youhave named were to be paid from this general stock, which was to be contributed by the members of the company at large.—A. This stock apportioned was to be taken from the general treasury. You asked me if I could remember anything else. I do now remember something else very distinctly which I would like to state. Reference is made in one of Mr. Ames's letters to Durant's action in New York, and Washburne's move here. Mr. Ames wrote to me—I am not sure but he told me—that E. B. Washburne, of Illinois, in his place in the House had moved some kind of investigation into the affairs of the Union Pacific Railroad. I do not recollect the precise point. Mr. Colfax was in the chair as Speaker of the House, and by some parliamentary maneuver they blocked the game and defeated it. Mr. Ames called my attention to it, and asked me if I did not think that in Mr. Colfax's case the investment had paid. Reference to the records of Congress would fix about the day, and show what Mr. Washburne's motion was, and what Mr. Colfax did.

Q. You stated that you were solicited to sign a paper contributing a portion of the general stock to be used by Mr. Ames for distribution among members of Congress?—A. No, sir; I did not say that. I did not say I understood the purpose for which it was to be used. I said at the time it was presented to me for my signature, it was at a meeting of the seven trustees appointed to execute Mr. Oakes Ames's contract. I am not sure whether Mr. Oakes Ames's name was on the paper. Oliver Ames's name was on the paper, and several of the large holders of the stock were on it. The presentation of the paper to me was a matter of surprise. If the stock was to be sold properly, it could have been done by the officers of the company without any such agreement. It was competent for the president of the company to have sold any of the stock in the treasury, if it had been on a fair basis, without any such assent by the stockholders. But they wanted to have the consent of the large stockholders for a portion of the stock to be placed in Mr. Ames's hands, as I have stated.

Q. Was the use to be made of it discussed?—A. No; it was not specified; as I said, I had some angry discussion at that meeting with the trustees; I think all the trustees were present, and they assured me that this stock should not be chargeable against any of my stock; they gave me a general statement in regard to the paper, and I finally put my signature to it; I think the last on the paper.

Q. I understand you then that you gave your assent to that arrangement, whatever it was, without having disclosed to you what was the purpose for which the stock was to be used?—A. Yes, sir; I did not know what it was to be used for; they just asked me to sign the paper for a special purpose, without disclosing the purpose; I did not know what was to become of the stock; I was very careful to receive from them the assurance that it should not affect the stock claimed by me.

Q. When you came to learn from Mr. Ames that it was used for distribution to members of Congress did you remonstrate?—A. I did, most assuredly, and I told them I should demand that stock. This suit began in the fall of 1868; notice was served upon Mr. Ames about the 10th or 11th of November, 1868; in the original bill I made no reference to members of Congress.

By Mr. McCrary:

Q. What was the total amount of stock to be transferred to Mr. Ames under the original agreement?—A. I think, as far as I know, he got three hundred and forty-three shares; he was to have two hundred and fifty original shares with the accretions, making in all three hundred and seventy-five.

Q. Was the amount named in the paper you signed?—A. Not that I recollect; it was a very unusual and unwise thing on my part to sign a paper I had not read.

Q. Do you know whether it was all transferred to him at one time or not?—A. I think he got it at several different times; my recollection is that the first he drew was fifty shares, and then there was a second installment; I think I saw his name down for the first installment for fifty shares, or perhaps it was one hundred shares.

Q. Do you know of his drawing ninety-three shares at any one time?—A. No, sir; I was not applied to to sign the paper for that; in fact, it seems to me that he got a portion of this stock before that. I did not know at the time I signed the paper that there was another transaction of ninety-three shares; I do not know anything about that; it was a part of the same stock, I think, but I never had any conversation with Mr. Ames about it. I had no expectation of any intention to apply the stock I had claimed for this purpose until Mr. Ames said, as I have stated, "O, there is no stock to give you; you consented to my having the balance of that stock," or something of that kind.

Q. Have you given all the names of the members of the present House mentioned to you by Mr. Ames as having received shares of this stock?—A. There may have been more names on Mr. Ames's list than I have written here. These are all I was able to write as he read the names. I wrote them down as rapidly as possible. I did not ask him to repeat the list, for I was afraid he would not do it.

Q. Did I understand that he gave you another list?—A. He gave a list of names on another occasion prior to this time. He did not know that I took any memorandum of it.

By the CHAIRMAN:

Q. If you can find the first memorandum of names mentioned by you you will please produce it, and the committee also desire you to examine your other correspondence with Mr. Ames and produce any other letters on this subject you may have.—A. I will do what I can. I have not gone over my correspondence with Mr. Ames at all on this subject.

By Mr. NIBLACK:

Q. You referred to Mr. James A. Bayard, of Delaware, and spoke of a letter from him in regard to the matter. What has become of that letter?—A. Mr. Bayard's original letter I think I have among my papers. A copy of it was sent to Mr. Ames in Washington.

Q. I was requested by Mr. Thomas A. Bayard, the present Senator from Delaware, to ask the indulgence of the committee to have his father's letter produced.—A. I cannot produce it now; if I can find it I will furnish it with pleasure to the committee.

Mr. AMES stated that he did not wish to cross-examine the witness.

WASHINGTON, D. C., *December* 17, 1872.

The committee met at 10 a. m.; all the members present.

Mr. McMurtrie, counsel for Oakes Ames, read to the committee the direct testimony of Mr. Oakes Ames, which had been reduced to writing, as follows:

The charge is that I received from the Credit Mobilier two hundred and fifty shares of its stock for the purpose of corrupting members of Congress. That while I in fact paid the company the par value of the stock, yet its actual value at that time so far exceeded par that the difference was in reality a gift, and the subscription a mere sham to conceal the transaction. This charge is based on the testimony of Colonel McComb as to statements I made him and letters I wrote to him. In truth, the whole case lies in this short compass: In my efforts to raise capital and enlist friends and influence to enable me to carry out successfully a gigantic undertaking, by which I was ultimately compelled to ask an extension from my creditors, I had persuaded a number of persons to agree to take this stock, and when I applied for and got this little remnant of the unalloted stock the values had very materially changed. My object—and it was concealed from no one—in getting the stock was to fulfill my engagements at a time that the value was very different. Mr. McComb conceals that fact and invents another, viz, that the stock was got for *future* contracts or dealings; and the difference in value between the subscription price and the market-value he converts into a bribe.

To enable the committee to appreciate the facts I will go back a little. The last grant of privileges to the Union Pacific Railroad by Congress was by the act of June 4, 1864. After that not a favor even was asked, unless you see fit so to style the authority to remove an office to Boston to escape from a corrupt judge, (Barnard, the tool of James Fisk,) and the right as a national corporation to have our causes heard in the Federal courts.

I propose now to state the facts to which Mr. McComb has referred as they really existed. And it will be found that his whole story lies in suppressing facts of which he is as fully aware as I am, and which happily are known to many.

At the time this last subsidy, a reward for accomplishing the great national object of connecting the Pacific and the Atlantic by rail, was offered to the public, I had no connection with the enterprise, and no expectation of such connection. It was not until the persons who had undertaken it had halted and sought for assistance from me that I gave my mind to the subject. I and my brother embarked very largely. There were members of Congress who did the same. No one seems to have thought this was corrupt, and yet it will be seen the acts I am charged with are nothing more than this.

Those of us who were willing to aid this great enterprise were under the impression our acts were praiseworthy and patriotic. We certainly hoped we would make a profit, but we knew the risk was enormous.

To give those who were willing to risk the capital required to avail ourselves of the assistance or reward offered by Congress, it was necessary that we should be our own contractors, and thus receive for building the road what Congress offered to any one who would do so.

To avoid the responsibility, as partners, we purchased this charter of the Credit Mobilier, it being intended that this corporation should be the contractor, and we, as its shareholders, should receive the profits on the building. The profits were to be received in stock and bonds of the Union Pacific Railroad, which were paid on the building-contract.

It must be observed our profits were merely nominal or contingent. If the road was completed, and when completed could earn interest on the debt, and profits besides, then our profits would be great. If our road was not completed, or, when completed, unprofitable, not only would our profits be lost, but our capital likewise. When I tell you that one of our contracts required the actual expenditure of $47,000,000, while the resources were the original capital of the Credit Mobilier, all of which had been absorbed in prior construction—the bonds lent us by the United States land-grants and the bonds of our company, the whole value of which depended on our ultimate success—you will perceive why I was seeking for associates and assistance.

We wanted capital and influence. Influence not on legislation alone, but on credit, good, wide, and a general favorable feeling. If the community had confidence in our ultimate success, that success was insured. But if there was distrust or ill-will, the reverse was as certain. For unless we could get off our bonds and land-grants, to raise money to pay our way, we must certainly fail. When, then, I tell you in the light of these circumstances that I wished to enlist our public men as well as capitalists, to obtain their influence, have I not the right to ask you to infer that I meant a proper influence? Can I not appeal to the openness of my statements at the time and the utter absence of concealment on my part, that I intended nothing that ought to brand me with disgrace?

At the start a number of public men had embarked with us. As the work progressed I solicited such men wherever there was a chance of success. As our prospects brightened and the profit had become almost certain, I persuaded men whose means were small to take the risk, and this certainly on my part with the expectation that they would reap a profit. I engaged, as I supposed at least, with a number of persons in this way. Some asserted they had agreed to take the stock that I could not remember, and I find that some differ from me as to our arrangements. But it is very disagreeable to come in conflict as to past facts.

known only to the disputants. Nor is it material for me to name persons or go into details, for happily I can prove by a very considerable number of persons that every share of stock with which corruption is charged was obtained to enable me to fulfill these engagements. It is certainly true that those I had expected to take the stock I thus received and paid for declined doing so when they heard of the litigations that were pending. It was claimed by one of these litigants that all the capital we had subscribed in the Credit Mobilier and all our profits belonged to them.

Mr. McComb also asserted that this was his stock, and demanded a specific transfer and an account of all profits. And perhaps not the least motive was—what has culminated here—he charged that the object in issuing this stock to me was the corrupting of members.

The result was, most of these men declined the stock, and those who had long since paid me the price on my promise to get the stock, asked me to return the money, and I did so.

There was another motive I now recall that had an influence in this. A few among us, better lawyers than others, were convinced that we were all liable as partners in this immense undertaking. We had started as a corporation, and without that shield would never have been connected with it. Just before the $47,000,000 contract was made, a dispute among us resulted in the compulsory abandonment of the corporation and this contract was made with me, and by me put in trustees for the persons who were stockholders. A most serious litigation has now determined that the corporation was not the owner of this contract, but that we had really assumed the position of partners, acting by the agency of a trust. I will not trouble you with the details; they are so complicated that one court was unable to perceive this, and it required the judgment of the supreme court of Pennsylvania to make it clear that the contract was an individual property, and so were the profits. The question arose on an attempt to tax the profits divided, as profits and dividends of the corporation.

I must now go into the particulars relative to the issue of this stock to me. You were told that the stock was, in January, 1868, worth more than par. That is true, though the value stated by Mr. McComb is very much exaggerated. The best test is actual sales. These were made at 160 or thereabout.

When I desired to secure the stock to enable me to fulfill my previous engagements, not (as is falsely asserted) to purchase congressional influence, I applied to the company for the purpose. I was met by the objection that it would not be fair to let any man have the stock at par, because it would sell in the market for a higher price. I urged the fact that I had taken a great part of the responsibility of the work, and I had made many engagements, and that these had been beneficial in enlarging the number interested, and thus operating to our advantage. Mr. Durant asserted he was similarly circumstanced; that he had promised to procure stock, and was bound to do so. Mr. McComb also made the same assertion, and mentioned two or three persons that he had engaged to get stock for. It was said to him, what right had he to pledge the company's stock; and it was said his right was equal to mine. The committee seemed to think Durant and myself were entitled to some consideration, owing to the immense stock we always had had in the enterprise. It was then verbally agreed that Durant and myself should have all the unallotted shares to fulfill our engagements. The president of the company declined acting on Mr. McComb's verbal authorization, and required a written consent by the large stockholders. It was prepared and signed. It reads thus:

We, the undersigned, stockholders of the Credit Moblier of America, understanding that $65,000 of the capital stock of this company, held in trust by the president, has been promised certain parties by T. C. Durant and Oakes Ames, do hereby consent to and advise the transfer of said stock to such parties as they, the said Durant and Ames, have agreed upon and designated, say, to Durant parties $37,000, and Ames parties $28,000.

JOHN DUFF.
THOS. C. DURANT.
S. BARDWELL.
OAKES AMES.
OLIVER AMES.
JOHN B. ALLEY.
C. S. BUSHNELL.
SIDNEY DILLON.
H. S. McCOMB.

The undersigned, stockholders in the Credit Moblier of America, recommend the issue to Hon. Oakes Ames, trustee, of ninety-three (93) shares of the capital stock of this company at par.

T. C. DURANT.
C. S. BUSHNELL.
OAKES AMES.
OLIVER AMES.
C. A. LOMBARD.
S. HOOPER & CO.
S. BARDWELL.
JOHN DUFF.
WM. H. MACY.

Mr. McComb denies that he read it.

It can be proved that he was present at the discussion which led to it; that he heard my reasons for wishing it; that he heard it read more than once; that he was finally persuaded to sign it. The promise that he asserts was made is untrue. It is quite different from what I am informed he asserted when examined in the litigation. But it is quite impossible that he did not know what the paper was if he did not read it.

There had been a lengthy discussion, a verbal agreement, a refusal to act on that, a refusal on his part to sign a paper as a favor to Mr. Dillon, with whom he had quarreled, and then his signature. They can be proved by probably half a dozen, viz, the grounds of my demand and grounds of hesitancy.

These facts can certainly be proved by several witnesses. They have made the same statement under a judicial oath long before anything like this was anticipated. Mr. McComb's statement of my avowed purpose is simply false, and what I did avow was as innocent as my own subscription in the first instance. There is not a word of truth in this, and I never stated anything that McComb thought was intended to convey that meaning. He knew I had stated why I wanted the stock, and he immediately began writing to get me to give some that I had got to one of his friends. He had previously complained that I was trying to make this a local concern. In my letter I tried to point out the unreasonableness of his request; that I had less stock than was required to fulfill my promises; and to show him that, in making these engagements, I had endeavored to select the purchasers in all parts of the country.

In point of fact I endeavored to carry out the engagements for which the company allowed me to take the shares, fulfill prior engagements, or what I considered engagements. As I have stated, most of them declined taking the stock. Mr. McComb says I dictated a list of names for him to write down. It is not true. It is proved by the fact that I could not have mentioned the names as stated by him as persons connected, or expected to be, with that stock. It is, I believe, true that he did ask who was to get the stock, and I have no doubt I mentioned the names of some that I expected would take it, as I had promised to get it for them, and had endeavored to persuade them to invest in it.

While the statements of Mr. McComb are entirely false with regard to my alleged purpose and intent in disposing of stock to members of Congress, and I never gave him the list of names as stated by him, yet the fact is true, which I never tried to conceal from any one who had any right whatever to know, that I did agree to sell to several, and did actually deliver to some members of Congress, without as much as a thought then or now of any wrong or corrupt purpose on my part or theirs, a small amount of stock, and the names of such members I will gladly furnish the committee if they desire, and leave it to those gentlemen to say for themselves whether on my part, or theirs, there was the most distant thought at the time of any impropriety, any more than there would have been in their buying of me so many shares of national-bank stock.

I understand the committee as intimating that I was to state all the particular instances in which I had transactions with members of Congress in reference to the Credit Mobilier or the Union Pacific Railroad. For the purposes of this inquiry they may stand as one. And I understand the inquiry to have reference to all acts of mine which are of the character or supposed character of the particulars on which the charge is based.

My connection with the road began by a subscription to the Credit Mobilier in August, 1865. My determination to do so, of course, preceded that some short time.

I have pointed out the nature of the undertaking, and the necessity I felt to enlist all men of influence or public opinion.

I began by soliciting my intimate friends and men in Congress possessed of means, and capitalists in large cities. Those whom I persuaded to do so I have no difficulty in naming, for they have continued to act with me. But it is not so easy to recall others I failed to persuade. Senator Grimes, John B. Alley, and Samuel Hooper, of the House, were willing to go in, and subscribed very largely in all these cases. I offered to guarantee them against loss. I also distinctly remember applying to W. F. Weld, as his prophecy of ruin made an impression. I have been reminded, though I had forgotten it, that I had suggested it to Mr. Scofield when the organization was merely projected. Our capital soon proved inadequate, and it was increased, and with difficulty. It was again inadequate, and again increased, and this time obtained only with the aid of an enormous bonus.

During 1865-'66, and until late in 1867, there were neither dividends nor profits. During all this time I was constantly at work endeavoring to enlist others. Confident of ultimate success, and of the profit that would come, I held out every inducement, and made every representation that I believed to be justifiable for this purpose.

Precisely who I spoke to or who formally agreed to take shares, but desired to postpone the time of payment, it is quite impossible for me to recall. When the stock was obtained in 1868 there was a difficulty about this, and time has not aided me in this respect. But as the time approached for profits, the number of shares that remained, and with which alone I could fulfill many engagements I had made, or supposed I had made, was very small. I then applied and got the shares I have stated. The agreement says two hundred and eighty; my recollection is it was two hundred and fifty shares, and this is confirmed by the share list, which shows but two hundred and fifty were allotted to me.

From first to last I was influenced by the same motive—to aid the credit of the road.

It was not until December, 1867, that there was a dividend. All these were in bonds or stock. All looked very fair, but some of us knew there was a risk yet. It so proved. The road was not completed till May, 1869, and in March, 1869, some of us had to raise on our private credit several millions to enable us to complete the work. The contractors were unpaid and their men had struck, and our bonds and stock and the credit of the company discredited in the market.

But in the early part of 1868 our prospects were very flattering, and I was compelled, in distributing the few shares I could get, to disappoint many. But I strove to use them in a way that I thought most advantageous in spreading our influence everywhere.

I will now speak of the transactions with the individuals named in the letters produced by Mr. McComb in his testimony.

Mr. Colfax is one mentioned. I cannot remember which of us first mentioned the subject, but I know he wanted to get some stock. I am pretty confident he has paid me for it, though it was never transferred to him, nor can I remember having paid over to him any dividends. At the next session he said something about that thing being off.

Mr. Henry Wilson is another. There was a fund given Mrs. Wilson on the twenty-fifth anniversary of her wedding, and I was consulted about investing it. I recommended twenty shares of this stock for $2,000, and the money was paid me; some months afterward he objected to the investment, and I felt bound from what had occurred to take it off his hands, and return the money, which I did.

Mr. Patterson bought of this, thirty shares, and it was by his order transferred to a banking-house in New York.

Senator Grimes. I have stated all I can say respecting his connection with the business.

Mr. Blaine. You have heard Mr. Blaine's testimony in advance of mine and my acquiescence therein. He declined the stock, and nothing more needs be said.

Mr. Dawes. In December, 1867, he came to me to purchase a Cedar Rapids bond. I advised him to take the amount in stock of the Credit Mobilier, which I thought a better investment; that I would guarantee him 10 per cent. interest on his investment and take it off his hands at any time he wished me to. After making inquiries, he gave me $1,000 to invest in the stock. Some time after he came to me he asked what Larned meant by asserting that he and his friends were the owners of the Credit Mobilier. He then said he would rather not take the stock, and the contract was rescinded.

Mr. Bingham asked me to invest some money for him in such stocks or things that I knew would pay well. He furnished me about $2,500. I invested it in twenty shares of Credit Mobilier, and the balance in Iowa Falls and Sioux City Contracting Company stock. I settled up this matter with him in 1870, I think, and paid him the amount due, and took the stock off his hands at his desire.

Mr. Garfield. I agreed to get ten shares of stock for him and hold it until he could pay for it. He never did pay for it or receive it.

As to Mr. Boutwell, I offered him some of the stock, and there was some negotiation, but it resulted in his not taking the stock, nor did he receive any dividends.

As to Mr. Elliott, he never agreed to take any stock. I offered it to him, but he declined. I cannot, therefore, believe I ever mentioned his name to Mr. McComb, for I never had any reason to suppose he would buy it.

Mr. Kelley is another. I recommended him to buy, and he said he would like to, but had not the money to spare to pay for it. I told him I would carry it for him till he was able to pay for it. He never took the stock. My recollection is very indistinct as to this case of his. I made a loan to him of $1,000, I think, which he has never settled. He regards the stock as belonging to me. It being a transaction of long standing, and of small amount to me, I have never given it special thought.

Mr. Scofield. He frequently talked with me very early in the enterprise about having some stock in the Credit Mobilier, and I urged him to take some, as I did many others. At that time I had got a number of members of Congress to go on with me, Messrs. Grimes, Hooper, and Alley, as I have stated. It was perfectly notorious that I urged every member of Congress who I knew had any money to invest to do so, from first to last, until every share of the stock in the Credit Mobilier was taken. And none suspected any wrong until the enterprise proved to be a pecuniary success; on the contrary, everybody that did so was congratulated thoughout the country for their courage, enterprise, and patriotism. Mr. Scofield agreed to take ten shares. He afterward paid me par and interest and took a receipt. Subsequently he became dissatisfied with it, assigning that he had heard there was a personal responsibility and returned it. I took it back, as I had agreed to do with him, as in almost every instance I had done.

Mr. Fowler. I never sold any stock to him, and he never received any that I am aware of.

James F. Wilson, of Iowa, also bought and paid for ten shares, and so did Senator Allison, then a member of the House. Mr. McComb swears I told him I had given one to Senator Conkling. It is absolutely untrue. I never said so, nor did I ever agree to get him one, nor was he ever interested in the company.

I have now stated, I believe, the exact facts in relation not only to all those parties upon Mr. McComb's list of names, but also in relation to all sales of this stock to every member of Congress, with all the particulars of such sales, so far as I have now any recollection. I of course include under the word sales every transaction by which any member of Congress became entitled to a share.

As to what I said in my letter of January 25, I can add little to what I have stated. The letter of McComb, to which it was a reply, sought to get the stock allotted to me for the persons he named, because he had promised it to them. I endeavored to explain why I could not. I did speak to Mr. Fowler, but nothing came of that. I also showed him, McComb, that I had endeavored to select from those who had wanted the stock, persons scattered over the country; and I desired to go on, as we had done from the beginning, by making the number interested as large as possible. That these were intended as sales they were to pay for this letter shows. It did not occur to me there was any impropriety in selling them because the thing was a success, any more than it did when all was a speculation. In the letter to which mine of January 30, 1868, is a reply, we had been threatened with congressional investigations, and suits before Judge Barnard, whenever I would not agree to certain schemes, and he alluded to this, no doubt, because I would not let his friends have some of my stock. I had never been able to discover anything that could make me fear such investigation; certainly, I had none to fear, and I told him so. There is nothing in this letter that I have not given an explanation of the intention under which it was written, except the allusion to Mr. Washburn, and this I will explain in connection with my proposal in the letter of the 22d of February, for they belong to the same subject:

It had become tolerably well known to all the world that the road was likely to be a success, and those of us who had risked the chance had won a prize.

There appeared to be a disposition then to complain of the grants that had been offered without opposition.

There was first a complaint made by Mr. Washburn of the value of the land-grants. In view of this I desired that we should put it out of the power of any one to take from us what we had, in my view, paid the Government for. It was to get these land-grants as private property. I wanted them sold and the bonds divided. Mr. Alley thought we could not afford to do this; and the event proved he was right.

It was also complained that we were excessive in our charges for freight and transportation, not that we exceeded our legal right, but it was proposed to trammel that right. Being a mere private right I had always found it difficult to induce any one to take the trouble to look at the case. I did not want any assistance or privilege, but that our legal vested rights should not be taken from us. I thought we had fairly bought or earned them, and I knew if any one would examine he would see this. For this reason I wanted more shares to be issued; for I have found that there is no difficulty in inducing men to look after their own property. But no one seemed to think this was necessary, and it was never done.

As bearing on my belief of my fairness of intention and the absence of all evil purpose or design, I can state that when I wrote those letters to Mr. McComb we were in no sort of confidential relations, though our interests were largely connected. Before that time I had ascertained facts connected with him that would prevent me placing any confidence in him.

Before any publication of these transactions a threat of exposure was communicated to me. My informant will name the person. The price of secrecy offered was the compromising with McComb. Though perfectly aware of what I had done and my motives, so confident was I in my innocence of all evil design, that I refused to pay one dollar.

Since then, and after the testimony had been given by Mr. McComb, I was again offered to be relieved from all the difficulty and a withdrawal of all the charges if I would acknowledge that I held the stock in trust for Mr. McComb. I told Mr. Black, who made me this proposition, that I could not and would not do this, as it was not true.

Mr. McComb says, in his evidence, he offered to surrender these letters and deny he had any such if I would settle his claim, or something to that effect. He repeatedly made such offers, and I always refused to have anything to do with him after the charges he had made in the suit. He referred to these letters, and said they were very damaging. I told him to publish them if he chose. I knew I had done or said nothing that meant anything wrong to a fair mind. The remark he puts in my mouth, viz, that all members of Congress are bribed, &c., is entirely untrue. I said nothing of the kind to him.

The reading having been concluded, the examination of the witness was continued as follows:

By the CHAIRMAN:

Question. Is the committee to understand that you put this in as your testimony, and swear to the truth of it?—Answer. Yes, sir.

Q. It is said in this last paper that was read that they were compelled to abandon the Credit Mobilier Company. Do you understand that that company is still in existence?—A. Yes, sir.

Q. It is still existing as a corporation?—A. Yes, sir; but the $45,000,000 contract, as it was called, was not guaranteed by the Credit Mobilier. That company had nothing further to do with the building of the road after my contract, I think.

Q. Where is the office of that company, and where are its books kept?—A. In New York, I believe. The head office, I think, is in Philadelphia. I was never a director in the company, and never had anything to do with the books.

Q. Who is the president of the company now?—A. Sidney Dillon, I think.

Q. Where does he live?—A. In New York.

Q. Has your company a secretary?—A. Yes, sir; I think so.

Q. Who is the present secretary of the company?—A. I think Mr. Benjamin F. Ham.

Q. Does he live in New York?—A. Yes, he has his office in New York; but his house, I think, is in New Jersey.

Q. And the books of the company you suppose are in New York?—A. I suppose they are; I have no knowledge on the subject.

Q. Have you any knowledge in regard to the manner in which the books are kept?—A. No, sir; I do not think I ever saw their books.

Q. You do not know whether they had a stock-book as a corporation?—A. O, of course they had a stock-book. I wrote to Mr. Ham after these charges were made to send me a list of the stockholders of the Credit Mobilier, which he did. The stock-list of the Credit Mobilier is given in this printed pamphlet, (handing it to the chairman.)

Q. Here is a list of stockholders in this pamphlet under date of December 12, 1867, and another list under date of February 20, 1868. Are they the same lists that were furnished you by Mr. Ham, the secretary?—A. Yes, sir; I do not know whether there have been any changes or not. I think not.

Q. In this first list of December 12, 1867, I see the entry of Oakes Ames, trustee, ninety-three shares, and in the list of February 20, 1868, the entry of Oakes Ames, trustee, two hundred and fifty shares. Do you understand that the two hundred and fifty shares in the last list embrace the ninety-three shares in the first list?—A. No, sir; I do not. The two hundred and fifty shares and the ninety-three shares were the amount that I received under the vote of the company to be disposed of.

Q. Can you tell what time it was that these two hundred and fifty shares were assigned to you as trustee?—A. No, sir; I cannot.

Q. Do you understand that it was between those two dates—between December 12, 1867, the date of the first list, and February 20, 1868, the date of the second?—A. I cannot tell you. I cannot recollect. It is my impression that the ninety-three shares came after I had the two hundred and fifty shares.

The CHAIRMAN. It does not seem so from the two lists?

WITNESS. But I received them both I think.

Q. At the time that this last number of shares—two hundred and fifty—was assigned to you, was there at the same time an assignment of shares made to Mr. Durant?—A. I think so. They were voted to Durant at the same time that they were voted to me.

Q. That vote assigning the stock to you and Durant, did it exhaust all the stock of the company, except that which was held by other persons?—A. Yes, sir; that was all the company owned which had not been issued.

Q. Then this assignment of stock to you covered, of course, the two hundred and fifty shares which Mr. McComb claimed he ought to have? —A. Yes, which he claims now. They were either counted in my shares or in Durant's. Mr. McComb claimed two hundred and fifty shares out of those that were unallotted.

Q. Out of the stock which the company had to dispose of?—A. Yes, sir.

Q. In your statement you have referred to various transactions between you and several members of Congress in regard to their becoming owners of stock in this Credit Mobilier Company?—A. Yes, sir.

Q. I think that generally, and perhaps in all the cases, you have not given any date for these transactions?—A. No, sir. One of the things I can never do is to remember dates.

Q. Can you tell whether these transactions were all of them prior to the time when the stock was assigned to you.

WITNESS. What do you mean by transactions?

CHAIRMAN. What you have stated.

A. I have been talked to by a great many persons about getting an interest in that stock, and I had promised it to a great many. I presume that most of them, or perhaps all of them, were promised it before the stock was awarded to me. Perhaps some of them were promised it afterward; I cannot recollect positively as to that.

Q. Something has been said by Mr. McComb about a stock dividend, at one time, of half the amount of the original stock?—A. We increased our capital stock at one time to half the amount; that is from $2,500,000 to $3,750,000.

Q. That was an increase of the capital stock?—A. An increase of the capital stock.

Q. You do not understand that it was a stock dividend?—A. No, sir.

Q. You understand that the increased stock was to be disposed of to somebody?—A. Yes, sir.

Q. Would a man who has subscribed for any given number of shares in the original stock be entitled to any portion of this additional stock, unless he bought it and paid for it?—A. No, sir; he would be entitled to his *pro rata* of the increase.

Q. That is, he would be entitled to take it if he paid for it?—A. Yes, sir.

Q. So that a man who was the owner, say of one hundred shares of stock, would not be entitled to fifty shares more unless he chose to pay for them?—A. No, sir; he would be entitled to take fifty shares more and pay for them. If the stock was not all taken by stockholders the company would have what was left.

Q. Then all the difference in that respect, between those who were stockholders and those who were not, was that the stockholders were entitled to take the additional stock if they chose?—A. Yes, sir; but we could not get it all taken. I took my *pro rata*, but I had to dispose of it; I let Mr. Dana, of Boston, have $10,000 of it at 95; I did not consider it an object to take that additional stock, but I had to take it and got rid of it. I sold some of it to several parties at 95; I let them take part of my stock at par. But when I could not get rid of it at par I had to sell it at a discount. I refer to the additional stock which I was entitled to take.

Q. Were any of the two hundred and fifty shares that were assigned to you ever transferred on the books of the company to any member of Congress?—A. No, sir; I do not think there was ever any of it transferred.

Q. It continued to stand in your name?—A. Yes, sir.

Q. And does so still?—A. Nearly all of it, I guess—a good deal of it. Most of it stands in my name. I do not know but that some of it may have been transferred, but I cannot say. I have not seen the books of the company.

Q. Do you know how early any dividend was made on the Credit Mobilier stock?—A. I do not recollect any dividends being made on it until about January, 1868. I think that was about the first.

Q Do you recollect the amount of the first dividend?—A. No, sir; I do not.

Q. Do you recollect whether it was a dividend in money or in railroad stock?—A. I think the dividends have all been made, except one, in bonds and stock.

Q. Did the Union Pacific Railroad have any stock proper, aside from its bonds?—A. Yes, sir.

Q. And those dividends that were made, were they in the stock of the Union Pacific Railroad Company, or in its bonds?—A. In both.

Q. The Union Pacific Railroad Company had Government bonds, (so much a mile,) and then was authorized to issue its own bonds, secured by mortgage, so much per mile?—A. Yes, sir; to the same amount.

Q. Were the funds which were derived from the sale of those two classes of bonds kept separate and distinct?—A. No, sir.

Q. The proceeds of the sales of both of them were used in the construction of the road?—A. They were used in the construction of the road.

Q. Can you tell the amount of the first dividend that was made?—A. No, sir; I cannot.

Q. Mr. McComb says that in January, 1868, there had been several dividends, amounting in the aggregate to 260 per cent.; do you know whether the dividends at that time did amount to that?—A. No, sir; I do not. Probably that was in stock to come. I do not recollect.

Q. Now, in regard to these particular cases: In your statements with reference to Mr. Colfax, you say that you are pretty confident he has paid you for it, although the stock was never transferred to him?—A. Yes, sir; that is my recollection.

Q. Do you recollect when that payment was made?—A. No, sir; I do not.

Q. Can you give us any idea in respect to the time?—A. I suppose it must have been in December, 1867, or January, 1868.

Q. You think he paid for it?—A. Yes; that is my impression.

Q. You suppose that he paid the par value of it?—A. Yes, sir; I did not let anybody have it for less than par and accrued interest.

Q. Has that money ever been repaid to him, to your knowledge?—A. No, sir.

Q. You do not know whether it has ever been or not?—A. No, sir; he paid for the stock to me.

Q. Is he still an owner of that stock?—A. It never has been transferred to him. I do not know whether he or I own that stock.

Q. Do you understand that the money which he paid for the stock has ever been returned to him?—A. Not to my knowledge.

Q. And do you not suppose that it has been?—A. No, sir.

Q. Do you know whether he has ever received any dividends on it?—A. It is my impression that he has, but I am not certain.

Q. Did you pay him the dividends yourself?—A. I cannot recollect.

Q. If this stock stood in your name on the books, the dividends would have been paid to you, I suppose?—A. That would be a natural consequence.

Q. And can you recollect, do you recollect, whether you paid dividends to Mr. Colfax?—A. No, sir; I do not recollect; it is my impression that I did.

Q. Have you any idea of the amount you paid him?—A. No, sir.

Q. Or when you paid it?—A. No, sir.

Q. Do you believe that of the dividends which have been declared and paid on the stock Mr. Colfax has received his proportion?—A. I think he received some of the dividends.

Q. And the contract between you and him in reference to his having a certain number of shares of stock—can you recollect how many shares he was to have?—A. Twenty, I think. That is what I agreed to sell him.

Q. And you understand that in equity Mr. Colfax is now the owner of that number of shares?—A. I do.

Q. And is entitled to his dividends on it the same as any other stockholder?—A. Yes, sir.

Q. As to Mr. Wilson, of Massachusetts, you say that a certain amount of money was contributed to Mrs. Wilson, and that $2,000 of it was invested in twenty shares of this stock?—A. Yes.

Q. Can you tell when that was done?—A. That was done, I think, in December, 1867. I think that that money was received by her in the fall, and Mr. Wilson applied to me to know what would be a good investment.

Q. And these twenty shares were paid for by that $2,000?—A. Yes, sir; for Mrs. Wilson.

Q. And you say that some months afterward he objected to the investment and the money was returned to him?—A. Yes; he said the road would never pay anything.

Q. Do you know whether any dividends were paid on that stock while it was held by Mr. Wilson or Mrs. Wilson?—A. I do not think there were. If there were, the amount was paid back; I am sure of that. I guaranteed him 10 per cent. for his money when he went in, and when he went out my idea is that he took his money back, and that I paid him 10 per cent. on it for the time.

Q. And you think that neither Mr. Wilson nor Mrs. Wilson received any other benefit than to get 10 per cent. for their money while you had it?—A. Yes, sir.

Q. As to Mr. Patterson, you say that he bought thirty shares, and that it was transferred to a banking-house in New York for him?—A. Yes, sir; by his direction.

Q. You say, also, that he owned it, and you think some dividends were paid upon it. Does he still own it?—A. I do not know.

Q. The contract never has been taken back?—A. No, sir; not by me.

Q. That is, he either owns it now or has disposed of it?—A. Yes, sir.

Q. For aught you know he is still the owner of that stock?—A. I cannot give you any further information about it.

Q. I see in that list of stockholders the name of the Fourth National Bank of New York.—A. It was not to that bank that Mr. Patterson's stock was transferred; it was to his friends, Morton, Bliss & Co. I believe that they advanced the money to pay for it originally. His stock is not on that list. I do not suppose it was transferred to them. I do not know anything about it, however.

Q. You do not suppose it was transferred on the books to that firm?—A. That I cannot say; I have no knowledge of it.

Q. Do you know whether those thirty shares were ever, on the books of the company, transferred to anybody, or whether they still stand in your name?—A. I do not know. I have not seen the books of the company.

Q. But you understood that you had really parted with those thirty shares of stock for the benefit of Mr. Patterson, and that he, or somebody for him, was entitled to take dividends on them?—A. Yes, sir.

Q. And that that has continued down to the present time?—A. Yes, sir.

Q. The contract has never been rescinded?—A. Not by me.

By Mr. McCRARY:

Q. What Mr. Patterson is that?—A. Senator Patterson, of New Hampshire.

By the CHAIRMAN:

Q. You say, in reference to the transaction with Mr. Blaine, that you agree that the transaction was as he stated it?—A. Substantially so.

Q. In regard to Mr. Dawes you say that in December, 1867, he gave you $1,000 to invest in that stock?—A. Yes, sir.

Q. There never was any transfer of stock to him?—A. No, sir.

Q. You go on to say that some time after that he said he would rather not take the stock. What became of the thousand dollars which he gave you? Was it returned to him?—A. Yes, sir.

Q. Can you state about how long it was after this transaction in December, when he gave you the $1,000, until the time when the contract was rescinded?—A. No, sir; I cannot.

Q. Can you state whether Mr. Dawes ever received any dividends on that stock?—A. I am not certain; I cannot state it positively. I think that in the settlement with him he got his 10 per cent. and that the thing was settled up. Whether he received any dividend and paid the money back I cannot say.

Q. Do you think that he received any more money in that transaction than his $1,000 with 10 per cent. interest?—A. I think not.

Q. In reference to Mr. Bingham you say that he was to have twenty shares in the Credit Mobilier stock?—A. Yes, sir.

Q. And that it never was transferred to him?—A. No, sir.

Q. Can you state whether Mr. Bingham, during the time that that arrangement existed, received the dividends that were paid on that stock?—A. He did.

Q. You say that in 1870 the matter was settled, and that you took the stock off his hands?—A. Yes, sir.

Q. Do you know how much Mr. Bingham received?—A. He received what dividends were paid on his stock.

Q. The whole of the dividends?—A. Yes, sir.

Q. How much was paid back to him for the stock more than the par of the stock?—A. I bought his stock from him and paid him the market price for it.

Q. He received the stock at par, and when you took it back you paid the market price. That was the basis of the settlement?—A. Yes, sir; I think that the price of the Union Pacific stock I bought from him was nineteen.

Q. That is the stock which he had received as dividends?—A. Yes, sir.

Q. How was it with the twenty shares of Credit Mobilier stock that he had?—A. It is my impression that I settled the whole thing with him, and that he has no interest in any of it now. My recollection is that I settled with him, and paid him the whole thing, and bought his Credit Mobilier stock from him.

Q. What was the market value of that Credit Mobilier stock when you took it back?—A. We thought it worth from twenty to fifty cents. Somebody spoke the other day of selling it for five cents.

Q. In reference to Mr. Garfield, you say that you agreed to get ten shares for him, and to hold them till he could pay for them, and that he never did pay for them nor receive them?—A. Yes, sir.

Q. He never paid any money on that stock nor received any money from it?—A. Not on account of it.

Q. He received no dividends?—A. No, sir; I think not. He says he did not. My own recollection is not very clear.

Q. So that, as you understand, Mr. Garfield never parted with any money, nor received any money, on that transaction?—A. No, sir; he had some money from me once, some three or four hundred dollars, and called it a loan. He says that that is all he ever received from me, and that he considered it a loan. He never took his stock, and never paid for it.

Q. Did you understand it so?—A. Yes; I am willing to so understand it. I do not recollect paying him any dividend, and have forgotten that I paid him any money.

Q. In reference to Mr. Boutwell, you say that Mr. Boutwell never had any stock nor any dividend from you; you received no money from him and he received no money from you?—A. No, sir.

Q. And the same with reference to Mr. Elliott?—A. Yes, sir.

Q. In reference to this transaction with Mr. Kelley, you said that there was some talk between you and Mr. Kelley, and you recommended him to take some stock?—A. Yes sir.

Q. And that he never took it?—A. He did not.

Q. But you say you made a loan to him of $1,000, which he never settled; had that loan any connection with the stock of this company?—A. Well, he expected, you know, that we were going to have some dividends on the stock, and he came to me one day and said that he was pressed upon a mortgage and wanted to raise $1,000, and, said he, "I suppose that probably there will be some dividend on that stock;" told him I did not know. He wanted to know if I would loan him $1,000. I told him I would. I loaned him $1,000. He never has taken the stock, and never has had any dividends.

Q. And he never paid anything for the stock?—A. No, sir.

Q. All the money transaction between you and him was that you loaned him $1,000?—A. I think that that is, as nearly as I can recollect.

Q. In reference to Mr. Scofield, you say that he frequently talked with you very early in the enterprise, and that you advised him to take stock; that he agreed to take ten shares, and afterward took it, paying for it par and accrued interest; that subsequently he became dissatisfied with it, and returned it. Mr. Scofield was to have ten shares of this stock, and paid the par value on it?—A. Yes, sir.

Q. And afterward he became dissatisfied, and you took it back?—A. Yes, sir.

Q. And you repaid his money?—A. Yes; I think so.

Q. Did he receive any dividend during the time he had it?—A. I think he did.

Q. Do you know the amount?—A. No, sir.

Q. Did he retain whatever dividend he did receive?—A. It is my impression that he did; I am not certain; I cannot recollect all these transactions.

Q. You say that that was quite early in the enterprise; can you state what time it was?—A. No, sir; Mr. Scofield and I boarded together in 1866 and 1867, and had very frequent talks about this matter, and I urged him to take stock.

Q. Do you know at what time he did take it?—A. I told him a long while before, in 1866 and 1867, that I would get some of it for him.

Q. Can you tell at what time he paid you the money for it?—A. It was after the stock was awarded to me for distribution, in December, 1867; he could not have had the stock until after that.

Q. You received $1,000 from him?—A. Yes.

Q. When the contract was rescinded and the money was returned to him, what was done then?—A. I cannot recollect.

Q. Was there anything more than the $1,000 returned?—A. That I cannot recollect.

Q. Can you recollect at what time this matter was rescinded?—A. No, sir; several years ago.

Q. In regard to Mr. Fowler, you say he never had any stock?—A. He had not.

Q. He never paid anything nor received any stock?—A. No, sir.

Q. In regard to James F. Wilson, of Iowa, and Mr. Allison, of Iowa, you say they got ten shares each; they are the owners of those ten shares now, for aught you know?—A. No, sir; Mr. Wilson sold his.

Q. The contract never was rescinded between him and you?—A. No, sir.

Q. He received ten shares of stock and disposed of it as he saw fit?—A. Yes, sir.

Q. And the same with Mr. Allison?—A. I am not certain about Mr. Allison; I have not so distinct a recollection of that matter.

Q. He received the ten shares of stock?—A. O, yes; he received ten shares of stock and paid for it.

Q. What was the arrangement made with them by which they were to become stockholders?—A. That was before the time that the stock was awarded to me for distribution. They both said that they were promised fifty shares each, but I could only give them ten. Mr. Wilson said that he had been promised fifty shares of the stock and could only get ten.

Q. And they have continued to be owners of that stock, unless they have disposed of it to somebody else?—A. Yes, sir; Mr. Wilson disposed of his some time ago.

The Speaker, in connection with the question about Messrs. Wilson and Allison, remarked to the committee that, in the Forty-first Congress, there was an investigation in regard to the alleged sale of cadetships, which has led to serious proceedings in the House, and that the Committee on Military Affairs, which had the investigation in charge, acting on its own judgment, which was afterward affirmed in some form by the House, decided that it had no power, and that it was out of the pale of propriety for it to investigate the transactions of men who had been in Congress, but who had returned to civil life. He merely wanted to make the suggestion to the committee.

All the proceedings before that committee, in the Forty-first Congress, touching any members of the prior Congress, had been erased from the record, and no report made of it to the House.

The CHAIRMAN. It is very clear that we cannot deal with Mr. Wilson and Mr. Allison in any way, but perhaps we may with Mr. Ames.

Mr. MCCRARY. If we go on with the inquiry in regard to those ex-members, of course they must have a hearing, if they desire it.

The CHAIRMAN, to the witness:

Q. As to Senator Conkling, you say that he never was the owner of any stock, and that there never were any negotiations between him and you?—A. No, sir; he never had any stock and never paid for any, and never received any dividends from me to my knowledge.

The chairman handed to the witness the letters produced the other day by Mr. McComb, and the witness identified them as in his own handwriting.

Q. Were those letters written at the various dates they bear—A. Probably, unless I made a mistake in the date. They were intended to be correct.

Q. In the letter of the earliest date, January 25, 1868, you say that you have "assigned, as far as you have gone, to 4 from Mass.; 1 from N. H.; 1 Delaware; 1 Tenn., and 1"—as it seems to have been changed by pencil to "2 Ohio; 2 Pa.; 1 Ind., and 1 Maine." You were writing, I suppose, in reference to the stock of the Credit Mobilier?—A. Yes, sir.

Q. What did you intend by saying that you had assigned as far as you had gone? Do these figures refer to persons or to quantities?—A. To persons.

Q. They have no reference to the amount of stock, but to the number of persons in each State?—A. That is it.

Q. You say, "I have assigned as far as I have gone, to 4 from Mass." Now, who were the four Massachusetts persons to whom you referred?—A. I meant that I intended to give it out to four from Massachusetts.

Q. You say that you "have assigned" as far as you have gone?—A. What I meant by saying that I had assigned was, that that was my intention. For instance, I said that I had assigned one to Delaware, whereas I had never spoken at the time to Senator Bayard, for whom I had intended it. So, too, with Mr. Fowler, of Tennessee; but my intention was to assign stock to each of them. This letter was drawn out from me by a letter from Mr. McComb wanting me to give $5,000 in stock to Senator Bayard, of Delaware, and $5,000 to Senator Fowler, of Tennessee. This stock was given to me to distribute as I saw fit, and I was intending to give some to Senator Bayard and to Senator Fowler, that is, not to give it to them, but to sell it to them. That was the way that I intended to place the stock, but I had not so placed it.

Q. Then the real meaning of the letter is that that is what you had designed to do?—A. That is what I had designed to do. It was in answer to a letter from Mr. McComb, desiring that his friends should have stock. I think that Mr. Wilson, of Iowa, was one whom he mentioned.

Q. This letter says, "The 50 per cent. increase on the old stock I want for distribution here."—A. The old stock was the ninety-three shares that I got afterward. My recollection is this, that the fifty-eight shares were the number unallotted of the original stock, before it was increased 50 per cent. I did not get but ninety-three shares, while I should have got one hundred and twenty-five shares. That is my recollection of it.

Q. In the last part of this letter you say, "Quigley has been here."—A. That relates to another matter altogether.

Q. Mr. McComb was correct in saying that that has no reference to the affairs of the Credit Mobilier?—A. Yes; that is the truth.

Q. Now, in reference to this list of names in the letter of January 30, Mr. McComb says that the memorandum of the names was made by him by your reading these names from some memorandum-book or pocket-book where you had them entered. Now, will you state what you know in regard to that transaction?—A. I might have mentioned names that I intended to give stock to, as I say in the fore part of the letter—names of persons I intended to give this stock to.

Q. Did you have that list of names in a pocket-book or memorandum book, or did you read that list of names to him from any book or paper?—A. I cannot say. I may have had a memorandum of persons to whom I intended to sell stock.

Q. Do you recollect whether you had or not?—A. I am not positive Very likely I had a memorandum of persons on that list whom I did not sell stock to, and the amounts in the list are not the amounts that I gave, so that it could not have been taken from any list that Mr. McComb saw.

Q. On this list he says, "Oakes Ames' list of names a sho'd to-day to me for C. M., Blaine, of Maine, 3,000." Did you say anything to him about Mr. Blaine?—A. No, sir; I do not recollect; I may have mentioned the names that I intended to enlist and sell stock to.

Q. Do you recollect whether you mentioned Mr. Blaine's name?—A. I do not.

Q. He says that you gave him the name of Mr. Blaine as one of those who were to receive $3,000, or thirty shares?—A. That cannot be correct. Mr. Blaine's name may have been mentioned, but Mr. Blaine never was, in any idea of mine, to have more than $1,000.

Q. Was there any talk between you and Mr. Blaine about his having more than ten shares?—A. I have no recollection of it at all; I am very certain that there was not.

Q. "Patterson, of N. H., 3,000." Do you recollect whether you mentioned Senator Patterson's name to him?—A. I do not; I cannot recollect; I may have told him and I may have had a list of names of persons to whom I intended to sell stock; we did not mean to give away any.

Q. You do not mean to have us understand that you ever gave anybody any shares of stock?—A. No, sir; never.

Q. Did any member of Congress ever receive any shares from you except by paying for them?—A. No, sir; never.

Q. "Patterson, of N. H., 3,000. How many shares did Mr. Patterson have?—A. Thirty shares; that is correct.

Q. Mr. Patterson did have thirty shares?—A. Yes, sir.

Q. "Wilson, of Mass., 2,000." You have told us all that there was in regard to that?—A. Yes, sir.

Q. "Painter, reporter for Inquirer, 3,000?"—A. Yes, sir; he had thirty shares.

Q. He became a stockholder?—A. Yes, sir; he said he was promised more, and was very indignant that he did not get fifty shares.

Q. "S. Colfax, Speaker, 2?"—A. Yes, sir; that is according to my testimony.

Q. "Eliot, of Mass., 3?"—A. He did not have any.

Q. "Dawes, of Mass., 2?"—A. Mr. Dawes had ten shares.

Q. Did you tell McComb that Mr. Dawes was to have twenty shares?—A. No, sir.

Q. Was there ever any negotiation for his having more than ten shares?—A. No, sir. He never talked about investing more than a thousand dollars, which he wanted to buy a bond for, and I told him I thought that this was a better investment.

Q. "Boutwell, 2?"—A. Mr. Boutwell never had any. He was one of the men from Massachusetts to whom I intended to sell stock.

Q. Do you recollect whether you said anything to McComb about Mr. Boutwell?—A. I don't know what names I did mention to Mr. McComb. All that I know is that Mr. Boutwell was at one time intended. If I said anything to McComb about him it was about what I intended to do.

Q. State whether in any of those negotiations with members of Congress there was any purpose on your part of exercising any influence over them, or to corrupt them in any way?—A. I never dreamed of it; I did not know that they required it, because they were all friends of the road and my friends. If you want to bribe a man you want to bribe one who is opposed to you, and not to bribe one who is your friend.

Q. In the transactions that you had with them, had you any view of obtaining their influence, or aid, or efforts in Congress?—A. No, sir; all my idea was, to have enough people interested to look into the matter. We did not want any legislation from Congress. We did not know in 1867 that Jim Fisk and Judge Barnard were going to drive us out of New York, and we did not know that we would have to ask to have our office removed to Boston. I never made a promise to, or got one from, any member of Congress in my life, and I would not dare to attempt it.

By Mr. MERRICK:

Q. Had you promised to all these members of Congress mentioned in this written statement to procure for them stock of the Credit Mobilier?—A. I cannot recollect. There were so many who talked to me about getting an interest in it, when they began to think it was a good thing, I cannot recollect all the names; I do not know whether they had all spoken to me before; I know that several of them did.

Q. Can you specify any of those who did?—A. I do not know that I can.

Q. Please state which of them did, so far as you recollect.—A. I have no doubt that Mr. Scofield did, and Mr. Patterson, and Mr. Dawes, and Mr. Bingham, and Mr. Wilson.

Q. Any others?—A. I think that Mr. Colfax did. It is very difficult for me to remember dates.

Q. I was not asking the dates, but the names.—A. I have given the names as far as I recollect; I cannot be positive as to all of them; I remember distinctly that these were previous to that time, and it is my impression that most of them were, perhaps all of them, but I am not certain.

Q. Can you state how long it was before the time that the stock was awarded to you that you had these conversations with these gentlemen?—A. Probably a few months before, or at the session of Congress before—the summer before.

Committee adjourned till to-morrow at 10 o'clock.

WASHINGTON, D. C., *Wednesday, December* 18, 1872.

Committee met at 10 a. m.; all the members present.

Examination of Oakes Ames continued.

By Mr. MERRICK:

Question. In these letters, copies of which have been filed with the committee, of the 25th of January, the 30th of January, and the 22d of February, 1868, you refer to letters of Mr. McComb of the 23d and 28th of January, and the 21st of February, and your letters are replies to these letters. Have you the letters of Mr. McComb to which these are a reply?—Answer. No, sir; I do not think I have. I do not generally keep letters unless they are business letters of importance. There may be some of them among my own letters at Easton.

Q. These seem to be business letters?—A. Relating to this matter, yes. If I were showed my answers they would refresh my memory as to what they are answers to.

Q. Have you examined among your papers to see whether you have these letters still?—A. No, sir. My papers are at Easton, Massachusetts. I think it very likely I burned these letters, as I generally did letters that I did not consider important. I did not suppose anything in these letters would ever be considered as referring to bribery or anything of that sort, and I did not regard them as important.

Q. In your letters of January 30 you refer to a letter of Mr. McComb's of the 28th, inclosing a copy of a letter from, or rather to, Mr. King, in which you say, "I do not fear any investigation here." State whether you have that letter of Mr. King.—A. I cannot tell you. It is among my papers at Easton if I have it. I recollect very well the substance of the letters replied to in both cases.

Q. What did they refer to?—A. The first letter of Mr. McComb wanted me to dispose of some of this stock to his friend Senator Bayard and his friend Senator Fowler. I wrote back that I had seen Mr Fowler, but I had never been introduced to Mr. Bayard.

Q. You state in your answer referred to here, of January 28, 1868, "You say I must not put too much in one locality." In your letter of January 30 you say, "I do not fear any investigation here." Did the letter you received from Mr. McComb refer to any investigation, called for or threatened?—A. I cannot say. I presume not. I know it was frequently alleged in our New York consultations that there would be an investigation into the affairs of the Pacific Railroad, and I always said I would like to have an investigation. I knew that I had never done anything that I feared to have investigated. It was alleged that things had been done before I had any connection with the road, in connection with obtaining the original charter, which would not bear investigation. About that time C. C. Washburn made a speech in the House of Representatives, finding fault with the rates established, and wanting to have them investigated; charging that they were building a poor road; were trying to cheat the Government, and were charging a great deal too much in the rates established.

Q. Have you kept any memorandum or any entries of these various transactions with the different members of Congress, receiving stock from the Credit Mobilier or Union Pacific Railroad Company?—A. I do not know whether I have any memorandum or not. I suppose I probably did make a memorandum at the time.

Q. What have you done with these memoranda?—A. I do not know whether I have destroyed them if I made them. I have none here. My papers are all at Easton, as I told you before.

Q. Is it your habit, as a matter of business, in conducting various transactions with different persons to do it without making any memoranda?—A. This was my habit. Until within a year or two I have had no book-keeper, and I used to keep all my own matters in my own way; and very carelessly, I admit. I do not know that I have any memoranda relating to these transactions, and still I may have.

Q. Then your answers and statements in reference to these various transactions with members of Congress, contained in your written testimony, were from memory and not from any records, memoranda, or books?—A. From memory. I had no records or memoranda to refer to.

Q. What members of Congress requested you, during the last autumn, to return to them the money they had invested in Credit Mobilier stock?—A. I do not know that any of them asked me to return their money last autumn.

Q. I understood you to say in your statement that during last autumn you were asked by certain members of Congress to return the money they had given you, and did so?—A. I think you must be mistaken in regard to last autumn. What I referred to was before that.

Q. You do not know what members of Congress they were, if there were any, who made such a request of you last autumn?—A. I do not remember any who asked me to return their money.

Q. You say you do not know of any requesting you to return their money and cancel the sto.k during last autumn?—A. Some of them sent me stock they had received.

Q. Who sent you stock?—A. Mr. Allison sent me his stock.

Q. Is he a member of the House of Representatives?—A. Not now.

Q. What members of the present Congress asked you during last summer or autumn to return their money and take back their stock?—A. I do not think any of them asked that last autumn. I think you are mistaken in the time.

Q. What members of Congress at any time asked you to return the money invested by them and receive back the stock?—A. Mr. Dawes and Mr. Bingham.

Q. When did Mr. Dawes ask that?—A. After that suit was brought by Mr. McComb. I think it was in the autumn of 1868 or 1869. It was as long ago as that.

Q. When did you cancel the transaction with Mr. Bingham?—A. I think perhaps in 1870 or 1871.

Q. Did all these gentlemen pay you money for the stock you had assigned to them, or proposed to assign to them?—A. Not for what I proposed to assign to them. They paid the money for the stock assigned to them.

Q. Did any of them pay more than the par value of the stock?—A. Mr. Dawes paid the par value and interest, and so did Mr. Bingham.

Q. How much did Mr. Dawes pay you?—A. He paid me a thousand dollars and interest.

Q. How much did Mr. Bingham?—A. Two thousand dollars and interest.

Q. Was it two thousand or twenty-five hundred?—A. It was two thousand. Mr. Bingham gave me twenty-five hundred to invest for him, but five hundred related to another matter.

Q. Did you pay these gentlemen any dividends upon their stock?—A. Yes, sir.

Q. What dividends did you pay them?—A. I cannot recollect.

Q. Did you pay them all the dividends that had been declared?—A. I did not pay them any dividends, I think, after this suit was commenced.

Q. Did you pay them any dividends at any time?—A. Yes, sir.

Q. What dividends did you pay them?—A. I paid them what was received.

Q. Did you pay them all the dividends that had accrued up to the time of bringing this suit?—A. I think I did.

Q. This suit was docketed in November, 1868; did you pay them all the dividends that had been declared prior to November, 1868?—A. It is my impression that I did.

Q. Can you state what these dividends were?—A. I cannot.

Q. Was there a dividend April 1, 1867, of 50 per cent., payable in the first-mortgage bonds of the Union Pacific Railroad Company?—A. That could not have belonged to this stock. That was a long while before they bought it. That was a dividend declared previous to the time this stock was set apart.

Q. Did you pay them any dividends which were declared as early as July 1, 1867, a dividend of 100 per cent., Union Pacific Railroad stock?—A. No, sir; I think not. I think that did not belong to this stock at all. I have no such recollection.

Q. Did you pay them any dividend declared January 4, 1868, of 80 per cent., first-mortgage bonds of the Union Pacific Railroad Company, and on the same day a dividend of 100 per cent. Union Pacific Railroad stock?—A. I cannot say. I presume I did.

Q. Did you pay them a dividend declared June 17, 1868, of 60 per cent., cash currency, and the same day one of 40 per cent. Union Pacific Railroad stock?—A. I cannot tell you. I presume I did to those who had paid for their stock. Some of them never paid for their stock, and were therefore not entitled to the dividends.

Q. Can you distinguish among those you dealt with as to who paid and who did not pay, and as to who actually received the dividends?—A. I think Mr. Bingham had his dividends in full; and I think Mr. Patterson did.

Q. Did Mr. Dawes?—A. I think he had it up to the time he declined to take the stock. He declined early on account of this suit of Duff Green's, as they called it.

Q. Did you pay them a dividend declared July 3, 1868, of 75 per cent. Union Pacific Railroad stock, and on the same day a dividend of 75 per cent. first-mortgage bonds of the Union Pacific Railroad Company?—A. I presume I did.

Q. The same question is asked you in reference to a dividend declared September 3, 1868, of 100 per cent. Union Pacific Railroad stock, and the same day 75 per cent. first-mortgage bonds Union Pacific Railroad Company?—A. It is my impression that I did. I do not recollect. It depended on the conditions on which they took the stock. Some gave up their stock, and some did not pay, and, therefore, did not get their dividends, of course.

Q. And of all these diversified transactions you say you have no memorandum?—A. I have none here; I may have at home.

Q. Will you examine and see if you have such memorandum?—A. I will.

Q. Did you receive these dividends upon the two hundred and fifty shares and ninety-three shares spoken of, as declared at these respective times?—A. It is my impression that I did. I have no reason to doubt it.

Q. They were assigned to you, if I understand, upon your claim to the company that you had made arrangements with certain gentlemen to transfer these shares to them?—A. My statement is that people applied to me for stock, and that I promised to get them some if I could. I took this stock for the purpose of carrying out this arrangement as far as I could.

Q. Were or were not these dividends which you say were distributed to these gentlemen up to and including September 3, 1868, more than an equivalent to the sums of money they had paid to you as the price of the stock?—A. Yes, sir; I think they were.

Q. When these arrangements in reference to the transfer of this stock were rescinded between you and these members of Congress, were the dividends which you had paid them returned to you, or were they retained by them?—A. They were returned in some cases, and in some they have never been settled up yet.

Q. Be good enough to specify in what cases they were returned and in what retained.—A. That I cannot tell.

Q. Can you tell the names of any individuals who did return the dividends they had received?—A. I think Mr. Dawes did, and I think Mr. Scofield did.

Q. What was your motive in endeavoring to induce members of Congress to become shareholders in the Credit Mobilier and Union Pacific Railroad Company?—A. My object was to have associated with us men of influence and character who would investigate and see for themselves in regard to the rights and privileges of the Union Pacific Railroad Company.

Q. Investigate what?—A. Investigate the whole matter. There was a prejudice against the Union Pacific Railroad. It was charged that we were a set of scoundrels and swindlers, who had committed all kinds of crimes against the public.

Q. Did you represent or explain to these gentlemen, or did they know incidentally, when they subscribed for this stock, the arrangements you had made in reference to the Credit Mobilier and the relations in which the Credit Mobilier stood to the Union Pacific Railroad?—A. I do not know that I made any full explanation.

Q. And the character of the business transacted by the Credit Mobilier?—A. I suppose I told them the Credit Mobilier was a contractor to build the Union Pacific Railroad. I suppose everybody knew that who knew anything about it.

Q. You supposed the relations between the Credit Mobilier and the Union Pacific Railroad to be a matter of public notoriety?—A. Yes; everybody knew it. It was public.

Q. Were the terms and nature of the contract which is called the "Ames contract," which was assigned to trustees for building six hundred and sixty-seven miles of the Union Pacific Railroad, known to those who were concerned as owners of the stock of the Credit Mobilier?—A. I presume so. They would be very apt to know it.

Q. Would these members of Congress know it with whom you made arrangements to take stock in it?—A. I cannot tell you.

Q. But it was a matter of public notoriety for everybody to know; there was no secrecy about it?—A. None whatever.

Q. Had you any motives or purpose in soliciting the influence of these public gentlemen to take an interest in this Credit Mobilier and Union Pacific Railroad Company, to avert inquiry that might be raised by the Government of the United States into the manner of conducting the affairs of the Union Pacific Railroad?—A. No, sir; never. Such an investigation could not have been avoided if we had desired it. We had five Government directors whose business it was to sit with us in every meeting of the board, and it was their duty to protect the interest of the Government, which they did to such an extent as made the road cost us a great deal more than there was any necessity for.

Q. Did these five directors of the Union Pacific Railroad know of the contracts made with the Credit Mobilier in reference to building the road?—A. The contract was made with Oakes Ames; the Credit Mobilier had no interest in it.

Q. I mean the transfer of that stock to trustees.—A. Yes, sir.

Q. State whether the printed paper now handed to you is a correct copy of that contract.—A. I presume it is.

Q. The paper I handed you is an exhibit connected with your answers in the chancery suit heretofore referred to, and sworn to by yourself and others?—A. I presume it is correct. I do not know anything to the contrary. I could not answer fully without comparing it with the written interrogatories to which it was an answer. I cannot testify absolutely to the fact of its exactness, because I have not the original to compare it with.

Q. Have you ever looked over these printed copies that purport to be copies of the answers of yourself and others to interrogatories propounded to you on the part of the complainant in that chancery suit in Pennsylvania?—A. I cannot say whether I have this printed copy or not. My signature purports to be attached to it.

Q. If you cannot say now, I will ask you to take that paper and examine it before to-morrow.—A. I cannot say whether it is an exact copy without having the original to compare it with. I suppose it is correct. I have no reason to doubt it. I do not suppose the man would commit forgery in copying. There may be clerical errors. It seems to be substantially correct, and I am willing to admit that it is substantially correct.

Q. I ask you if, at or about the time when these transfers of stock were made by you to members of Congress, there was any threat or rumor on the part of the Government of the United States to cause an investigation to be made into the manner in which the affairs of the Union Pacific Railroad Company had been conducted?—A. No, sir; I do not know that there was. The matter of an investigation had been frequently talked over in New York, and I always said I was in favor of it.

Q. Were there any movements in Congress looking to an investigation as to whether the charter of the Union Pacific Railroad had been forfeited at that time?—A. Not to my knowledge.

Q. Or any movements in Congress looking to the ascertainment by the Attorney-General of the United States, whether or not illegal dividends had been made, and to cause re-imbursement thereof?—A. I think some time after this, I should say a year after this stock was assigned, Garrett Davis made such charges in a speech in the Senate.

Q. At the time this stock was assigned to you, or during your negotiations with members of Congress, were there any movements made in Congress, or any rumors or suspicions of movements to be made in Congress, looking to such results?—A. No, sir, not to my knowledge.

Q. Do you know when the first movement was made in Congress looking to the passage of the act of April 10, 1869, in the fourth section of which the Attorney-General was authorized to investigate whether the charter was not forfeited, and to ascertain if illegal dividends had been made, and to cause the re-imbursement thereof; also to see whether any of the directors of the road or agents had violated any penal law?—A. I think that grew out of the Garrett Davis speech to which I have referred, if I am not mistaken.

Q. I ask you if you know when the first movement was made in Congress looking to the passage of that bill?—A. I cannot tell you. I am the worst man to remember dates you ever saw. I recollect now there was such a resolution introduced into the Senate, and if I am not mistaken inquiry was made.

Q. The movement ripened into this law of April, 1869?—A. That is probably the time.

Q. You say there was no movement nor rumor that such a thing would be done during that winter and spring of 1868, nor was there any apprehension in your mind or the mind of others connected with the Credit Mobilier at that time that such movement would be made?—A. No, sir; not to my own knowledge. I always wanted an investigation, as can be proved by many witnesses. I wished to have an investigation. I knew I had done nothing wrong, nothing that was dishonorable, and I wished an investigation.

Q. Have you any knowledge as to whether James Brooks, of the House of Representatives, has been the owner, directly or indirectly, of any stock in the Credit Mobilier?—A. No, sir; I never knew of it.

Q. Or in the Union Pacific Railroad?—A. I think he is an owner of stock in the Union Pacific Railroad; if he was not he could not be a director.

Q. Does not the law expressly forbid Government directors from owning any of that stock?—A. He was at one time a Government director. He is now a stock director.

Q. You transferred some of this stock to Mr. Wilson, of Iowa; was he not a Government director of the Union Pacific Railroad at the time you transferred that stock to him?—A. No, sir.

Q. Was he a Government director afterward?—A. Afterward he was.

Q. Did he retain his stock in the Credit Mobilier after he was a Government director?—A. No, sir. I testified that he sold his stock in the Credit Mobilier and the Union Pacific Railroad before he left Congress. My brother bought it of him.

Q. Can you fix the time?—A. I cannot. It was before he left Congress.

By Mr. McCrary:

Q. Can you tell us when the Credit Mobilier was chartered by the Pennsylvania legislature?—A. No, sir; I cannot. I had nothing to do with the Credit Mobilier until 1865, I think.

Q. It was prior to 1865, then?—A. My impression is that it was an old charter that George Francis Train had control of. Mr. Durant bought it of him. Mr. Durant was one of the first stockholders of the Union Pacific Railroad. The object for which it was intended was that the individual stockholders should not be liable for the debts incurred, other than as they had paid for their stock. They did not want to be liable as general partners. Mr. Alley has been a director of the Union Pacific Railroad and a director of the Credit Mobilier, and you can get all that information from him.

Q. When did this corporation, known as the Credit Mobilier, become interested in the construction of the Union Pacific Railroad?—A. I think it had something to do with some of the early contracts, which are set forth in this paper presented here. There was the Hoxie contract, which, if I am not mistaken, was run by the Credit Mobilier. It was used in this way in some shape for a year or two before I had anything to do with it. I think the first contract for the Credit Mobilier was the Hoxie contract, and the dates of it, as given here, were August 8, 1864, May 12, 1864, and October 1, 1864.

Q. When did you commence your negotiations with public men, and influential men, with a view of interesting them in this stock?—A. When I first went in myself, some time, I think, in 1865. I urged on my friends to go in. I urged Mr. Alley to go in, and guaranteed him against loss. I induced Mr. Samuel Hooper, a member of the House, and Senator Grimes, and a great many others, out of Congress, to become interested. Every man of influence and capital that I could induce to go in I endeavored to induce. We wanted a great deal of money and a great deal of strength, and it was my object to associate in the corporation respectable and responsible men; men of character and standing, both in public and in private life.

Q. Did you solicit all these members of Congress to take stock?—A. No; I think most of them solicited me. Some of them I solicited. I solicited Mr. Scofield when I first went in. He and I boarded together. I did not consider that there was any impropriety in owning stock in any corporation, particularly when we did not want anything of Congress. We asked no legislation and expected none, and there had been nothing asked of or granted by the Government since that time that takes anything from the Government or benefits the Union Pacific Railroad. The only thing I ever asked was the removal of the office from New York to Boston in order to get rid of the injunction of James Fisk and others granted by Judge Barnard's court, and the right to transfer such causes to the United States court. That I did not consider as requiring bribery or the use of corrupt appliances. The gentlemen I am accused of bribing have always been friends of the road and have always voted for it, except Mr. Scofield. I think he voted against it. But I do not think that owning a thousand dollars of the stock would induce Mr. Scofield to violate his oath.

Q. Was this stock promised to these members of Congress in the fall of 1865?—A. No, sir; I think not. The stock of the company was all taken up as we supposed, but this amount of stock which we divided was in the hands of Mr. Durant, as I understand it. He had never paid for it, and the company made him transfer it to the corporation, which left that amount of stock for sale.

Q. What I want to get at is this. It seems from this agreement or consent of the stockholders that you and Mr. Durant were to make use of certain shares. Shares had been promised to various parties. I want to ask you if that promise was made as early as 1865; and, if not, when it was made?—A. I think not. I think not before the summer or fall of 1867.

Q. Was not stock promised to any members of Congress prior to the summer or fall of 1867 by you, or to your knowledge?—A. Some members of Congress owned it before this; and I think some members of Congress had spoken to me about it. I told them I would try to get some, but we had none to give them until the stock held by Mr. Durant, not being paid for, was transferred to the company. I had sold some of my own stock to parties.

Q. When was the act passed which subordinated the Government loan to that of the Union Pacific Railroad Company?—A. In 1864.

Q. Did any member of Congress hold any of this stock prior to that time?—A. I think not; I do not know of any. I had nothing to do with it till long after that time.

Q. When you received money from these gentlemen for stock was it assigned to them, or did it still remain in your name?—A. It still remained in my name; most of it.

Q. Why was it not assigned?—A. I don't know of any reason, except that when a man buys stock and keeps it there is no use of transferring it; when the suit of Mr. McComb was brought, they did not, any one of them, want to own the stock.

Q. Was it kept in your name because the transaction was such that they did not want it to be public?—A. No, sir; I had no such idea.

Q. How frequently were dividends declared upon the stock of the Credit Mobilier?—A. All the dividends that were declared were, I think, from December, 1867, until about July, 1868. I am not positive, but I think there has been no dividend declared since.

Q. How many within that time?—A. I cannot tell; three or four, I think.

Q. I see in this printed pamphlet before me what purports to be a list of dividends, and I wish to ask you if that list is correct. It is as follows:

April 26, 1866, 100 per cent. on Union Pacific Railroad stock.

April 1, 1867, 50 per cent. on first-mortgage bonds Union Pacific Railroad Company.

July 1, 1867, 100 per cent. on Union Pacific Railroad stock.

July 4, 1868, 80 per cent. on first-mortgage bonds Union Pacific Railroad Company.

Same day, 100 per cent. on Union Pacific Railroad Company's stock.

June 17, 1868, 60 per cent. on cash currency.

Same day, 40 per cent. on Union Pacific Railroad Company's stock.

July 3, 1868, 75 per cent. on Union Pacific Railroad stock.

Same day, 75 per cent. on first-mortgage bonds Union Pacific Railroad Company.

September 3, 1868, 100 per cent. on Union Pacific Railroad Company's stock.

Same day, 75 per cent. on first-mortgage bonds Union Pacific Railroad Company.

December 19, 1868, 200 per cent. on Union Pacific Railroad Company's stock.

A. I think that is correct, except as to the first three named, which were not dividends; I have no reason to doubt it. This list seems to reach to December, 1868.

Q. I do not understand distinctly your answer to Mr. Merrick's question as to how many members of Congress received these dividends upon that stock, and what members did not receive it, among those you have mentioned.—A. I think that all who paid for their stock received their dividends up to the time this suit was commenced; that is my impression.

Q. Who received the dividends?—A. Mr. Patterson, Mr. Bingham, James F. Wilson did, and I think Mr. Colfax received a part of them. I do not know whether he received them all or not. I think Mr. Scofield received a part of them. Messrs. Kelley and Garfield never paid for their stock, and never received their dividends.

Q. Have you mentioned all the members of Congress who took stock in the Credit Mobilier?—A. I have mentioned all that have been named here.

Q. Have you mentioned all who are members of the present Congress who took stock?—A. I think I have.

Q. Are you certain on that point?—A. There is no member of the House now whose name I have not mentioned.

Q. Have you mentioned all members of the past Congresses whose names were mentioned here before you commenced to testify?—A. Yes sir; that was my understanding of the instructions given me. I suppose Mr. Wilson's and Mr. Allison's names would not have been mentioned if Mr. McComb had not mentioned them.

Q. Had not a congressional investigation into the affairs of the Union Pacific Railroad Company and the Credit Mobilier, one or both of them, been threatened prior to January 30, 1868?—A. I do not know whether there had or not. It used to be talked about sometimes up there in New York. I do not know that I ever heard anything of it here.

Q. Was there or not an investigation by Congress referred to in your letter to Mr. McComb of January 30, 1868, in which you say, "I do not fear any investigation here?"—A. Yes, probably; I had nothing to fear from an investigation.

Q. Then a congressional investigation had been suggested prior to that time?—A. Up there in New York; not here that I know of.

Q. You say in the same letter that, in view of King's letter and Washburn's move, you go in for making the bond dividend in full. What did you refer to by "Washburn's move" here?—A. Washburn made an attack upon the Union Pacific Railroad, that we were charging too much fare; that our lands were enormously valuable, worth five to ten dollars an acre for the alkali regions on the plains; that they were not going to build the road so as to be good for anything; that the object was to get the Government bonds, and then abandon the road to the Government.

Q. Had Washburn said anything about an investigation?—A. I do not recollect that he had. He wanted to fix a rate of fare by law, beyond which we could not charge. He wanted us to be restricted to a certain amount. That was one of the things he claimed. I do not remember fully all he did claim.

Q. In your letter to Mr. McComb of January 25, 1868, you say you think that the dividends having been paid you ought to make the Credit Mobilier capital four millions, and distribute the new stock where it will protect you, &c. What do you mean by having stock placed where it will protect you?—A. Placed with men of character, property, and standing. I wanted that such men should own it and have interest with us.

Q. Did you have any reference to that protection which you might get from favorable legislation in Congress?—A. No, sir; we did not wish any legislation from Congress; we did not expect any. Congress in 1864 had given us all we asked. That was before I had anything to do with the road. We did not expect anything further.

Q. You speak in the same letter in regard to the 50 per cent. increase on the old stock that you wanted for distribution here. How did you propose to distribute that here in Washington?—A. To carry out my engagements for stock. That was in January. The $25,000 of old stock I had got was entitled to the increased stock when the increase of capital was made. It was applied to that stock, and there is where I got the ninety-three shares referred to. It was the increased stock on the two hundred and fifty shares assigned me.

Q. The stock list shows that you had the ninety-three shares before you had the two hundred and fifty?—A. I cannot help that. That is my recollection. I had both, at any rate.

Q. So you think the ninety-three shares is 50 per cent. additional stock on the two hundred and fifty?—A. Yes, sir. I should have had one hundred and twenty-five instead of ninety-three. I only got ninety-three.

Q. You speak of Alley and Cisco being on the finance committee. What finance committee do you refer to?—A. To the Union Pacific Railroad.

Q. You did not refer to any committee of Congress?—A. No, sir. Mr. Cisco was not a member of Congress. I supposed that they could raise money as members of the finance committee of the Union Pacific Railroad Company, if we came short.

By Mr. BANKS:

Q. What effect was produced on your mind, or that of the company, by the reports made by one of the Government directors in 1866 or 1867, representing that the road had been improperly built; that the structure was not sufficient to sustain the traffic?—A. The effect produced on my mind was simply that we had to make it perfect.

Q. Had it anything to do with this transaction?—A. No, sir; nothing whatever. Under a misapprehension in consequence of the report you allude to, the Government at one time withheld their bonds on the ground that the road was not built in the proper manner. I came to Washington at that time with my brother and gave bonds for I do not know how much, one or two million, that the road should be properly constructed.

By the CHAIRMAN:

Q. I understood you to say that Mr. Brooks you never understood was a stockholder of the Credit Mobilier?—A. Not to my knowledge.

Q. Do you know his son-in-law, Charles Neilson, in New York?—A. I do not know him. I know there is such a man. I have heard of him as being a son-in-law of Mr. Brooks, and a stockholder. I think part of the stock Mr. Durant distributed went to Mr. Neilson, as he had promised it. That, however, is only a matter of hearsay. I had nothing to do with it.

Q. You have no knowledge nor information that that stock was held for the benefit of Mr. Brooks in any way?—A. No, sir.

Q. You have no information that leads you to believe that that or any other stock was held for the benefit of Mr. Brooks by anybody?—A. I have no knowledge on that subject either way. I know nothing about that.

By Mr. NIBLACK:

Q. In this arrangement with members of Congress by which you sold them shares of stock, did you regard it as a private transaction between you and them, or were you acting on behalf of the Credit Mobilier of America?—A. I regarded it as a private transaction between myself and them. The stock was given to me to distribute as I pleased, to carry out my arrangements.

Q. Given to you without consideration?—A. No, sir; I paid par and interest; I gave my checks for the amount.

Q. Then the money paid for it by members went into your own purse?—A. Yes, sir; it was my private money.

Q. And when the money was refunded to them it was refunded by you and not by the Credit Mobilier?—A. Certainly. I had nothing to do with the Credit Mobilier. I paid for the stock par and interest.

Q. You received the stock as trustee; for whom were you acting as trustee?—A. I was not acting as trustee for anybody. I put it in that way to distinguish it from the stock I held for myself. I do not know why I stated it as trustee. In the examination last fall before the commissioner in Boston, I stated that I held it in trust. Mr. Bartlett asked me whom I was trustee for, and I replied that I was not trustee for anybody. I simply took it as trustee to distinguish the stock from that which I held before for myself.

Q. Didn't I understand that, in point of fact, you acted as trustee for several members of Congress to whom you sold the stock, allowing it to remain in your name?—A. It still remained in my name, but not as trustee. I do not know that I acted as trustee for anybody, and I was not authorized by anybody to act as trustee.

Q. When you received the dividends which you paid over to members of Congress, who had received their assignments of stock, did you receive the dividend in your own name?—A. Yes, sir; I received it and receipted for it on the books of the company, in my own name, I acting as the agent of these parties.

Q. You received the amount of the dividends in gross and distributed among your friends as you understood your arrangements with them, making it a private transaction between yourself and them?—A. Yes, sir; a private transaction.

By Mr. MERRICK:

Q. I have seen it stated that J. C. Kennedy acted as a co-trustee for these two hundred and fifty shares.—A. Yes, sir; that was one of McComb's statements.

Q. Will you state whether he did act as co-trustee?—A. Mr. McComb stated that he had seen on the books of the Credit Mobilier stock transferred to a man by the name of Kennedy, as trustee. I do not know a man by the name of Kennedy in Washington; I never saw him and never heard of him till now.

Q. You never had any transaction with him in connection with the Credit Mobilier?—A. No, sir; I do not know the man.

Q. You had no dealings with him at all in reference to the Union Pacific Railroad or the Credit Mobilier stock, either in respect to stock, dividends, or otherwise?—A. Never. I will tell you what Mr. McComb makes that out of. Geo. W. Kennedy was a book keeper of ours in Massachusetts. I bought some stock in his name as trustee. I do not think Mr. McComb ever saw him. He is not a large man, or a good-looking man, or a man with gray hair.

Q. What was your object in putting the stock in his name as trustee?—A. I cannot tell you. I had it all transferred to myself a long while ago.

Q. You had no object at all in putting it in his name as trustee?—A. No, sir.

Q. You did it as a matter of pure caprice?—A. Yes, sir.

Q. Did he have any knowledge of its being in his name as trustee?—A. Yes, sir; because he transferred it to me back again, and he had to sign his name in the same way.

Q. Did you name to him any purpose for which you transferred it to him as trustee?—A. Not that I know. I transferred it to him as trustee without his knowledge.

Q. And you did it without any motive whatever?—A. I do not know that I had any motive. A part of this stock stood in the name of those parties who did not take their stock, and a portion of the stock I transferred to him was that stock.

Q. A portion of this unclaimed stock which you demanded to meet your engagements?—A. Yes, sir; and it was transferred back to me a year ago or more.

By the CHAIRMAN:

Q. It seems by this list that the dividends on the Credit Mobilier stock began to be made as early as April, 1866, and there was another in

April, 1866 and 1867, and July, 1867. These two hundred and fifty shares of stock were transferred to you in December, 1867, as I understand you.—A. I cannot recollect. I think the stock was assigned to me in December, 1867.

Q. There had been three dividends made up to that time. Did these dividends go with the stock?—A. No dividends went with the stock except those declared after it was assigned to me.

Q. You did not understand that if you held the stock yourself you were entitled to any prior dividends?—A. No, sir.

Q. Did any of these persons who received stock from you, and who had made these arrangements with you, these members of Congress, did they receive any prior dividends?—A. No, sir.

Q. At the time these dividends were declared this stock was owned by the company itself, and the dividends therefore were not made upon that stock?—A. That I cannot tell. If they were made at all they were made to Dr. Durant. They stood in his name previous to that time, as I recollect.

Q. If any persons received this stock from you they took it with the same rights that you had and with no right to prior dividends?—A. Certainly.

The chairman stated that the question had been raised as to whether the counsel of Mr. McComb should be permitted to cross-examine witnesses in this investigation. The committee think that while Mr. McComb of course is not the prosecutor in this proceeding, yet the proceeding is founded upon transactions sworn to by Mr. McComb, and which in some way became public, and the inquiry being based upon that, the committee are to ascertain whether his statement is true or not. They think, therefore, they should have some means of determining the accuracy of testimony which may be given against him, and are of opinion that he should be permitted, through his counsel or otherwise, to cross-examine the witness.

Mr. BANKS. My reason for assenting to the decision of the committee, which the chairman has stated, was that so far as the parties are known to us Mr. McComb may be supposed to have information of the facts if there has been anything wrong in this transaction. If we exclude his testimony, or his inquiries, when rebutting testimony, it may be supposed that we have suppressed information within our reach. Therefore, not so much recognizing his right as a prosecutor in any way, but to get the full statement of the truth in this case, I assent to his being permitted to propound inquiries to witnesses, either by himself or his counsel.

Mr. MERRICK. It appears to me probable that Mr. McComb and his counsel may have sources of information, and that they may be able, by a cross-examination of Mr. Ames and other witnesses, to develop facts connected with this inquiry which have not been adverted to by members of the committee in their examination. In order that all sources of truth may be searched I think it expedient that Mr. McComb, by his counsel, shall have the privilege of cross-examining Mr. Oakes Ames, and of suggesting to the committee other facts to be inquired into which have not already been made the subject of inquiry.

Mr. ALLEY. With the permission of the committee I wish to say, you may remember, the other day, at the conclusion of Mr. McComb's testimony you invited me to cross-examine him. I did not do so for two reasons: I had not appeared here as counsel; I was summoned here as a witness, and I did not suppose it was proper for me to cross examine a witness. I did not know that course was to be pursued. I thought inasmuch as the committee had been raised it was eminently proper and right that you should allow the fullest inquiry, and the most thorough and searching examination. I am very glad, for one, that you have taken that course. I am, however, now in a position to have some interest in this matter, more than simply as a witness. I did not avail myself of the privilege you gave me the other day to cross-examine, for another reason, which was that I was so utterly taken by surprise, and so astounded, having come here merely as a witness, to be called upon in regard to so infamous a charge—infamous on my part if true, equally so on his part if not true—I was so astounded, I will not say disconcerted, that I was unable to respond to your invitation, even if I had deemed it proper. I would now like the privilege, before leaving the room, if it is not improper, to propound to Mr. McComb a question or two.

Mr. BLACK. It does interfere with the regular course of business of course. There are a great many objections I could urge to that course. I desire to put a very few questions to Mr. Ames, but before doing so I wish to define as carefully as I can what the position is that Mr. McComb occupies to this proceeding. He appears here solely as a compulsory witness, and in no other capacity. I do not ask for the right to cross-examine Mr. Ames, except as I am here simply as counsel in a case into which this runs more or less, another and a judicial tribunal. I do not propose to ask Mr. Ames any question concerning the subject-matter of inquiry here.

The CHAIRMAN. If you examine witnesses at all you must examine them under the leave we have given, and you must do it for the reasons we give. It cannot be done in reference to the other case. We have only ten or fifteen minutes before adjournment, and you can go on in that time if you desire.

Mr. BLACK. I do not want three minutes.

Examination by Mr. BLACK:

Q. Did Mr. McComb give a true history of the Credit Mobilier?—A. I do not recollect what account he gave.

Q. Then I will ask you, particularly, was it a Pennsylvania corporation?—A. I expect it was.

Q. Was the object of the organization, on the part of yourself and the other gentlemen who were associated with you, to reap the profits of building the road without personal responsibility?—A. I believe that was the original intention.

Q. What were these profits, and from whence were they derived?—A. They were derived from the Oakes Ames contract, I believe.

Q. Whence did the money come from that constituted the profits of making the road?—A. I suppose it came from the sale of bonds. The profits were what they got for building the road more than the actual cash cost of the road. I suppose they were entitled to a profit.

Q. They were derived from the sale of the bonds which took precedence of the loan of the United States?—A. I do not know that. I did not notice any distinction in the bonds. I suppose the company sold all the bonds of both classes, and that the proceeds of both were applied to building the road.

Q. A part of them constituted the bonds for which the income of the road was pledged?—A. Not that I know of.

Q. And a part from bonds which were a lien upon the lands of the company?—A. I believe they were issued after the company got in debt, and had to issue them to pay for building the last part of the road. That is my recollection.

Q. A part of the money was the proceeds of stock sold?—A. Not that I know of.

Q. None?—A. I do not know of any.

Q. Was the company solvent at the time these dividends were made?—A. Yes; I suppose so.

Q. Is it now?—A. I expect so.

Q. How much stock was issued?—A. I do not know. What has that to do with this transaction?

Q. Was there any money paid on that stock?—A. It was paid for at par, I believe. That was my understanding.

Q. You were of opinion at the time that this association was formed for the purpose of dividing what you call profits; that it was all right?—A. Certainly; and I believe we did it under the advice of Jerry Black. I believe we consulted him, did we not?

Mr. BLACK. No, sir; you did not do that under any advice of mine.

WITNESS. Well, you were counsel part of the time, and I suppose it was all right, that part of it.

Q. Did it strike you that it was entirely proper for a member of Congress to be concerned in that arrangement?—A. It did, sir.

Q. You thought that it was also right for you to take in, either by gift or sale, anybody else who desired to come in and who was a member of Congress?—A. Certainly. There is no law and no reason, legal or moral, why a member of Congress should not own stock in a road any more than why he should not own a sheep when the price of wool is to be affected by the tariff.

Q. That is your conviction now?—A. Yes, sir; and always has been.

Q. Were you not apprehensive that any one might take a different view on that subject?—A. No, sir; I was not. I did not know that anybody had a different view until the other day you told me that you thought it was wrong for a member of Congress to own a share of bank stock or any other security which could be affected by the legislation of Congress. You stated that we in New England were not as pure as you were in Pennsylvania; that you did not own a share of bank stock, and that you thought no member of Congress ought to Well, I am not so pure as that. I think a member of Congress has a right to own property in anything he chooses to invest in.

Q. Did it strike you there might be some incompatibility between your duty as a member of Congress, to guard the public money which was held by a corporation in trust for public use, and your interest as a member of a ring, organized of persons for the purpose of appropriating it to their own private use?—A. I do not know anything about any ring. I never went into any ring.

Q. We will not call it a ring—an association. Did you see anything incompatible between your position and an association such as that in which you were joined?—A. No, sir; I never did and do not now.

Q. Are you not aware that the propriety of that course has been very seriously questioned?—A. No, I am not. General Butler once, since I have been in Congress, questioned the right of any member holding bank stock to vote on a question in which national banks were concerned, and I suppose on the same principle any man owning a Government bond would have no right to sit in Congress.

Q. Are you not aware that in 1869 there was a discussion on this subject in the Senate, and that opinions were expressed inconsistent with those you now express?—A. I do not know. There have been all kinds of opinions expressed, in the Senate and House both, on all subjects.

Q. Were you not present in a debate in the Senate in April, 1869, in which Mr. Stewart, of Nevada, and many other persons participated, in which they thought the whole transaction a gross and stupendous fraud?—A. I think it very likely that such things were said in the Senate in 1869, and I do not know but Mr. Stewart may have said them.

Q. Were you not present when that discussion occurred?—A. I do not know. I heard debates probably about that time in the Senate. That was about the time, if I remember right, when we were trying to fix the terminal point of the two roads, and I think it was in relation to that.

Q. Was it not in regard to the other matter on which you stated that legislation was asked, namely, the removal of the place of business from New York to Boston?—A. I cannot tell you.

Q. And you do not recollect that you were present at the debate referred to?—A. I have been present when debates in the Senate have occurred on questions of that kind.

Q. You do not recollect a debate on this subject in which Mr. Stewart participated?—A. I remember something of such a debate. I cannot recollect what Mr. Stewart said. I think the debate you refer to was on the subject of fixing the junction of the two roads. He was speaking in the interest of the Central Pacific Railroad, and wanted to get the junction as far east as he could. That was nothing we asked from Congress, and it did not cost the Government anything except the time spent in debate. There was no subsidy of any kind connected with it.

Q. How much stock do you own in the Pacific Railroad now?—A. I cannot tell you; I do not remember.

Q. Can you not approximate it in conjecture?—A. I should think I owned 1,000 shares.

Q. How much did you pay for that stock?—A. Various prices.

Q. Did you get it directly from the company?—A. A part of it; but what has that to do with this investigation?

The CHAIRMAN. I should say that is one side of any inquiry we are in pursuit of.

Q. I want to ask you whether the Credit Mobilier was not discarded as machinery for transferring these profits to the partners who were associated together originally under that name?—A. I think it was.

Q. But the contract continued to be held by the seven trustees?—A. The Credit Mobilier was discarded, of course, as I testified yesterday.

Q. The object of the organization under the seven trustees was the same as the Credit Mobilier had been used for?—A. It was for the benefit of the stockholders of the Union Pacific Railroad Company, in order that every man might have what he was honestly, fairly, and justly entitled to.

Q. Then the partners who held that stock in the Credit Mobilier were entitled to exactly the same dividends out of the profits they would have received if the Credit Mobilier should continue to perform the functions which it was originally intended to perform?—A. You have seen the records, I suppose, and you can ascertain from that better than I can tell you. If you have not, you can have them; they are open to the inspection of everybody.

Q. I will ask you another question. Did that change in any way affect the right of the holder of Credit Mobilier stock to receive the dividends they would otherwise have been entitled to?—A. I am not lawyer enough to answer that question. I do not pretend to have any legal knowledge at all.

Q. Did you or did you not receive dividends yourself?—A. I received all the dividends that were given me, at all times. I was always willing to take dividends.

By the CHAIRMAN:

Q. Can you state whether they were divided to the stockholders of the Credit Mobilier?—A. I do not think it was intended they should be divided to the stockholders of the Credit Mobilier. But the same parties who owned formerly were entitled to receive stock under it. That is my idea. I am not lawyer enough to understand the distinction Mr. Black desires to make. I suppose he wants to entrap me in connection with the other case.

By Mr. BLACK:

Q. If you will receive my assurance of that fact, I have no such design. These contracts were made by you previous to the time when you got your stock?

WITNESS. What contracts?

Q. The contracts under which you subsequently agreed to hold this stock for members of Congress and others.—A. I did not say I had made any contracts with members of Congress.

Q. You had conversations with them about it, whether there was a contract or not.—A. I had talked with them and it was understood that when I got this stock I would give it to them.

Q. Was there no contract to give them stock?—A. No contract. I did not know I could get it. I had told persons who applied to me for stock that I would get it for them if I could.

Q. If you gave them this stock——

WITNESS. I did not give it to them.

Mr. BLACK. Understand me, if you please. When you gave it to them for a consideration had they a title to it which would give them the right to receive dividends before the stock was actually transferred to them?

A. I do not know how to understand your question. You want to know if I was under any obligation to supply them with this stock.

Q. What I want to know is whether they were entitled to the stock at any time before you actually received it for them?—A. I do not suppose I was under any positive obligation. I promised them I would get them some stock if I could.

Q. This, then, had no relation backward of the time when the stock was actually transferred?—A. I do not know. I said I promised before that I would get the stock if I could.

Q. The men you have mentioned as having received this stock, some of them have it yet, and some of them have given you the back dividends. What you have received back from these persons does not amount to as much in the aggregate as that paid on the whole three hundred and forty-three shares?—A. Not to the persons named. I sold some to other persons, not members of Congress.

Q. Can you state who they were?—A. I do not know that that has anything to do with this transaction.

Q. You decline to answer?—A. You have no right to ask me for the names more than you have to ask me whom I sold a dozen shovels to.

Q. Have you any portion of this stock as your own which you did not dispose of?—A. That is a question you have no right to ask me. This inquiry, I understand, is simply to affect the suit in Pennsylvania.

Mr. BLACK. I admit that, and I want to tell the committee that I have no other object in making any other inquiries, except in relation to that suit in Pennsylvania.

The CHAIRMAN. Mr. Merrick suggests that you told him a larger amount had been given to some men than you now admit. It was proper for Judge Black to ask you whether you parted with the whole of that two hundred and fifty shares, or whether some of it still remains in your hands.

A. I may, perhaps, have a little of it.

The following interrogatories and answers, having been admitted by the witness to be authentic, were placed in evidence:

J. T., 1868.—Supreme Court.—No. 19.

HENRY S. MCCOMB
vs.
THE CREDIT MOBILIER OF AMERICA, SIDNEY Dillon, John B. Alley, Roland G. Hazard, Charles M. Ghriskey, Oliver W. Barnes, Thomas Rowland, Paul Pohl, jr., Oakes Ames, Charles H. Neilson, Thomas C. Durant, John M. S. Williams, Benedict D. Stewart, John Duff, Charles M. Hall, and H. G. Fant.

Interrogatories to defendants.

1. State precisely what entries were made on the books of the Credit Mobilier of America by the treasurer or assistant treasurer or other officers of the company, so far as they relate to the contract or subscription of the plaintiff for account of H. G. Fant. On what books are those entries made? When were they made? Produce copies of the entries and append them to this answer.

2. Was or was not a list of the stockholders of said company made out by the company or its proper officer, on or soon after the 3d day of March, 1866? And does or does not the name of H. G. Fant stand next to the last on said list as the holder of two hundred and fifty shares? Was Fant the holder of any shares other than those mentioned in the plaintiff's bill as being taken for his account by the plaintiff?

3. Who were the stockholders of the said Credit Mobilier of America, on or about the 12th day of December, 1867? Append to your answer a list of their names, with the number of shares belonging to each, and state whether the name of Oakes Ames appears there, and as the holder of what number of shares. Is he there set down as the holder of 250 or 343, or any other number of shares as "*trustee*" for persons not named?

4. Who were the stockholders of said company on or about the 20th day of February, 1868? Append to your answer a list of their names, showing the number of shares held by each, and state whether the name of Oakes Ames does or does not appear on said list as "*trustee*" for 250 shares.

5. State whether copies of the several lists of persons who held stock in the said company on the 3d of March, 1866, the 12th of December, 1867, and the 20th of February, 1868, were or were not made out on or about those days respectively, by the proper officers or agents of the company, and delivered as authentic to the plaintiff and other persons. Did the books exhibit a true statement of the stock taken and held at those times, or were the said lists falsified by omitting therefrom the names of some stockholders, or by placing thereon the names of other persons who were in fact not stockholders? If the said lists or either of them were false and deceptive, what was the object of making them so?

6. Did or did not the same persons hold proportionally the same amount of stock in the Credit Mobilier of America and in the Union Pacific Railroad Company? Were not the leading and active managers of each company holders of stock in both? Append to your answer a list of the stockholders of the Union Pacific Railroad Company, as they appear from the books to have held the stock of the last-named company on the 3d of March, 1866, on the 12th of December, 1867, and on the 20th of February, 1868.

7. Did the Union Pacific Railroad Company make a written contract on the 8th of August, 1864, for grading, building, constructing, and equipping one hundred miles of the Union Pacific railway and telegraph, beginning at Omaha, with one Herbert M.

Hoxie, at $50,000 per mile, including all work and materials? Was said contract signed by Hoxie himself or by his attorney in fact? Who was Hoxie? Where did he live and what was his business, occupation, and employment at the date of said contract? Was he a man of property or capital, or at all able to meet the responsibilities of such a contract? Produce the contract with Hoxie referred to in this interrogatory and append a copy to your answer.

8. Did not Hoxie soon afterward, to wit, on the 30th of September, 1864, agree and bind himself in writing that he would transfer the said contract of 8th of August, 1864, to Thomas C. Durant or such person as Durant would direct? Was or was not the said T. C. Durant at that time vice-president of the Union Pacific Railroad Company? Produce the written contract last referred to between Hoxie and Durant, and append a copy to your answer.

9. Did or did not Hoxie, after the agreement with Durant, to wit, on the 4th of October, 1864, propose to the Union Pacific Railroad Company to extend the contract to the one hundredth meridian west longitude, at the same rate of pay, namely, $50,000 per mile? Was not this proposal accepted the same day it was made? Is not the one hundredth meridian 257½ miles (by the route of the railroad) west of Omaha? Produce the proposal herein referred to and a copy of the resolutions accepting it and append them to your answer.

10. Did Hoxie ever do or attempt to do any part of the work required by the contract, or furnish any of the materials or expend any money or time thereon? If yes, what and how much? Were not all the materials furnished and paid for by the Union Pacific Railroad Company, by and through the agency of its own officers? Or did the officers of said railroad company distribute the same work to other contractors? Did Hoxie ever receive or claim anything from the company for work done or materials furnished by him under his contract? If yes, how much and for what?

11. How much was the actual cost of the whole road and telegraph from Omaha to the three hundredth mile-post? Did not the proper officer make a report, or in some other form communicate to the Union Pacific Railroad Company and to the Credit Mobilier, that the cost of the first three hundred miles was $7,800,000, or $26,000 per mile on the average? Did not this include all expenses for surveying the route, furnishing iron and other materials, grading, laying, and building the road, putting up the telegraph, and equipping the road with sufficient rolling-stock? State separately how much was the cost of surveying, construction, stock, and iron, as nearly as you can from recollection or from records of the company. Was not a total of $26,000 a mile for all these together a very extravagant price, considering the nature and character of the work? Make a fair estimate of the cost, at economical prices, and say what would be a just compensation per mile for the construction of such a road.

12. Did not the vice-president of the Union Pacific Railroad Company make a contract with one L. B. Boomer, of Chicago, for the construction of 150 miles of the company's railroad and telegraph line west of the one hundredth meridian? Produce the contract referred to and append a copy thereof to your answer. Was this contract made in good faith and with the intention that the parties should fulfill it? If not, with what other intent, purpose, or object? Was the contract of Boomer ever carried out by him in whole or in part? Or was he ever called upon to perform it? Or was any attempt ever made by the company or any of its officers to compel performance?

13. Was there not also another contract made by one Williams with the said railroad company for the construction of 267$\frac{57}{100}$ miles of the same road, commencing at and running west from the one hundredth meridian? Was this contract made with intent that the contractor should execute it according to its terms? Was it in fact executed or carried into effect in any manner by the said Williams? What was the object of making or causing the said contract to be made?

14. Were not all the contracts referred to and inquired about in the preceding interrogations really and truly made for the benefit, use, and behoof of the Credit Mobilier of America? Were not one or more of them assigned by the nominal contractors to the said Credit Mobilier? Was not the contract with Williams assigned to said Credit Mobilier or its stockholders? Did not the stockholders receive and divide among them all the profits of all the said contracts; that is to say, the whole contract-price, after deducting therefrom the cost and expenses of the railroad company in surveying and constructing said railroad?

15. Was not a contract in writing made by Oakes Ames on the 16th day of October, 1867, and antedated as of August 16, 1867, with the Union Pacific Railroad Company, for the construction of 667 miles of the said railroad, beginning at the one hundredth meridian and extending westward? Were not all the previous contracts merged in that? What prices or compensation did the Union Pacific Railroad Company agree by that contract to pay for constructions, materials, and stock? Produce the said contracts and append a true copy thereof to your answer.

16. Was not this contract assigned on the day of its actual execution, to wit, on the 16th of October, 1867, to seven "trustees?" What were the names of the trustees? Were they not all stockholders of the Credit Mobilier of America? And was not the

assignment coupled with the express condition that the profits of said contract should be divided among the stockholders of the Credit Mobilier in proportion to the number of shares which they respectively held in that company? Produce the said assignment and append a copy thereof to your answer.

17. Was not the same contract upon the same terms extended so as to cover all the road which was to be built between the one hundredth meridian and the terminus authorized by the company's charter? Produce a copy of the contract making this extension, together with copies of all resolutions and other records of the acts done by both companies in relation thereto, and append them to your answer.

18. By whom and at whose expense, upon whose credit and responsibility, and with whose capital was the road built and stocked which Oakes Ames agreed to build and stock? What were the profits thereupon? How much did the contract price exceed the actual cost of the construction and equipment? To whom was the surplus paid?

19. Is not the following a true and accurate statement of the dividends or allotments made by the Credit Mobilier, or the trustees under the Ames contract, to and among the stockholders of the Credit Mobilier at the several times therein mentioned? If the statement be inaccurate in dates and amounts, state wherein and to what extent such inaccuracy is found, and furnish a correct statement according to your knowledge and the books of the company:

April 26, 1866, 100 per cent. in Union Pacific Railroad Company's stock.
April 1, 1867, 50 per cent. 1st mortgage bonds of Union Pacific Railroad Company.
July 1, 1867, 100 per cent. Union Pacific Railroad Company's stock.
January 4, 1868, 80 per cent. 1st mortgage bonds of Union Pacific Railroad Company.
Same day, 100 per cent. Union Pacific Railroad Company's stock.
June 17, 1868, 60 per cent. cash currency.
Same day, 40 per cent. Union Pacific Railroad Company's stock.
July 3, 1868, 75 per cent. Union Pacific Railroad Company's stock.
Same day, 75 per cent. 1st mortgage bonds of Union Pacific Railroad Company.
September 3, 1868, 100 per cent. Union Pacific Railroad Company's stock.
Same day, 75 per cent. 1st mortgage bonds of Union Pacific Railroad Company.
December 19, 1868, 200 per cent. Union Pacific Railroad Company's stock.

20. Was there not also another dividend of 14 per cent. declared and made payable either in gold or its equivalent in currency, or in Union Pacific Railroad Company's stock at 30 per cent.? Did not this purport to be for interest on the capital of the company, at the rate of 7 per cent. per annum for the years 1867 and 1868?

21. State whether any other dividends or allotments have been made since December 19, 1868? Whether the profits of the company's business have accumulated in its treasury since that time, and to what amount, and also whether its capital has been lost or diminished, or expended in part or in whole?

22. If the money, bonds, and stock referred to in the 19th interrogatory, were actually distributed to and among the stockholders of the Credit Mobilier, were they or were they not paid to them as dividends upon their stock in said company? If they were not called and regarded as dividends, by what other right or upon what other ground did the stockholders receive them? State also how it came to pass that the distribution was made only to stockholders of the Credit Mobilier, and to them always in exact proportion to the shares they held in its stock. Say whether this was or was not a mere accidental coincidence. If they were in fact dividends, but called or entered upon the books or receipted for by another name, or if they were made to assume another form, what was the object of giving to the transaction a false appearance?

23. Were the shares in the Union Pacific Railroad Company's stock, which were dividends allotted or given to the Credit Mobilier or its stockholders, regularly issued by the said company and certified as fully paid up? Were they, in fact, paid for by the Credit Mobilier or its stockholders? If yes, how much was paid for them? If no, what was the consideration for which they were given to the said last-mentioned company or its stockholders? Did the Credit Mobilier, or the trustees under the Ames contract, or the treasurer of either, give his or their check or draft to the Union Pacific Railroad Company for the price or value of the said shares, and receive the check or draft of the railroad company for the same amount, and thus pretend to be paying for the stock, when in truth and in fact no payment whatever was made? If the last question be answered in the affirmative, state what was the object of the sham.

24. State whether Oakes Ames is a member of the House of Representatives of the United States, and how long he has had a seat in that body. Are any other stockholders of the Union Pacific Railroad Company, or of the Credit Mobilier, members of Congress, and who? Were any of them members of Congress when the transactions referred to in the preceding interrogatories took place, or when the charter of the Union Pacific Railroad Company was passed, or when the said charter was amended and changed?

25. State who were the holders of the "certain actual and valid shares of the stock of said company," (to wit, the Credit Mobilier of America,) which are referred to in the 16th paragraph of the defendants' answer, and of which two hundred and fifty are

said in the same paragraph to have been "duly issued" by said company, and "held by lawful owners thereof," before the 3d day of March, 1866. Are the names of said holders on the list of stockholders made out 12th December, 1867, or on any other authentic list of the stockholders of said company, or are the said names to be found anywhere in the books or records of said company? If yes, on what list, book, or other record? If the said shares were valid and actual, duly issued by the company, and held by lawful owners for several years before Oakes Ames became trustee thereof, what was the object and purpose of the company or its officers in falsifying its records and lists?

26. Besides H. G. Fant, is there any stockholder named on any list or book of the company, whose name has disappeared from the more recent lists, and from the books as lately made up, except in consequence of regular transfers? Did any lawful holder of valid and actual shares duly issued, by said company, ever transfer such shares to Oakes Ames, or authorize them to be transferred to and held by him as trustee? If yes, produce the proper documents or records which show the fact, and append copies thereof to your answer.

27. Were not all the shares (three hundred and forty-three of them in number) which are now or have been held by Oakes Ames, trustee, given, granted, and issued to him directly by the said company, and registered in his name, on the mere motion of the directors; that is to say, without authority, direction, transfer, or power of attorney, from any previous holder, real or pretended? Does or does not the registry or grant of said shares to Oakes Ames purport on its face, or by any record of the company, to be in pursuance of any transfer or direction of a previous holder or holders?

28. At the time when said shares were transferred and issued to Oakes Ames, had they been paid for to the company by any person whatever, unless by the plaintiff or H. G. Fant? Did Oakes Ames himself pay for them at the time or before the time when they were registered to him? If yes, how much?

29. Were not the shares aforesaid given, granted and registered to Oakes Ames without any consideration previously paid, but with an express understanding between him and the board of directors that he should "*place*" them at Washington City according to his discretion, to suit the interests of the company? Did he or did he not afterward *place* them in the hands of several persons to the number of twenty-five or more, by agreeing to hold the title in his own name for the use of such persons? Did not the persons for whom he agreed to hold the said shares in trust receive from the company, either directly or through Oakes Ames, all the dividends which had accrued or been declared before the *placing* of the shares as well as afterward? What were the amounts of the back dividends on the 8th and 20th of January, 1868?

30. Mention the persons with whom these shares were thus *placed*, or to whom they were given, or for whom they are or have been held by Ames as trustee. State particularly the names of each beneficiary under said trust, the number of shares held or placed for his use, the State in which he resides, the amount of dividends he received along with the shares, and state at the same time how many of the said beneficiaries, and which of them, are, or were at the time of such *placing*, members of Congress. State also whether the company ever received from the said Oakes Ames or any other person for said shares more than 100 per cent.; or whether Oakes Ames ever received from his *cestui que trust* anything beyond that amount in payment for said shares. Was or was not this sum of one hundred dollars for each share paid out of the back dividends? Did not the back dividends at the time of the *placing*, as aforesaid, amount to much more than one hundred dollars per share? If yes, how much more? Were not the shares themselves and all the dividends beyond one hundred dollars per share essentially and substantially a gift?

31. Did not Oakes Ames, during the winter of 1867 and 1868, write from Washington to one or more officers and stockholders of the company, describing how he had *placed* a portion of the stock which he held in trust, to what States of the Union he had distributed it, and how much he still held for distribution to others? And did not the said Oakes Ames afterward at the company's office in the city of New York exhibit to the directors or some of them a memorandum-book containing a list of names to whom he had given or agreed to give shares of said stock? Produce the said letters of Oakes Ames, if you have them or copies thereof. Produce also the list of persons exhibited by Oakes Ames; produce all papers, records, or written documents showing the nature and character of these transactions, and append copies to your answer.

32. Did Charles H. Neilson receive thirty-two shares or more of the stock of the Credit Mobilier? Was not the same consideration paid for the said stock as was paid for the three hundred and forty-three shares given to Oakes Ames as trustee? Did not said Neilson receive said stock for and on account of James Brooks, his father-in-law, then or since a Government director of the Union Pacific Railroad Company?

33. When it was proposed among the directors of the company to give, grant, and register the said two hundred and fifty shares to Oakes Ames as a trustee for such person as he might himself designate, did not the plaintiff protest against such use of his

stock, and did he not then and there warn them that he was the owner of the two hundred and fifty shares subscribed for by him on account of Fant? And did not the said directors or managers, and Oakes Ames, in effect, give the plantiff a pledge that no stock of his should be so used, and that his right to the stock he claimed should not be affected by the said trust or by any act of said Ames, under or in pursuance of it?

34. Produce the "dividend statement" referred to in paragraph 25 of the defendants' answer, as made out on the 28th day of December, 1867, together with the receipts of the plaintiff and other stockholders; produce also the several other writings referred to in paragraph 26, and others alleged to have been subscribed by the plaintiff on the 4th of January, 17th of June, and 15th of July, 1868. If these papers be not in your possession or within your power and control, describe them particularly, so that they can be identified and produced by any person in whose custody they are. If you have them, append copies thereof to your answer.

SAMUEL G. THOMPSON,
WILLIAM STRONG,
J. S. BLACK,
Pro Plff.

McCOMB *vs.* THE CREDIT MOBILIER OF AMERICA. } S. C. January term, 1868. No. 19. Equity.

The answer of the Credit Mobilier of America and others, defendants, uniting herein, to the interrogatories filed in this cause on the day of December, 1869.

We each answering positively as to all our own acts and doings, and as to the acts and doings of all other persons, to the best and utmost of our knowledge or information and belief, do for answer as to so much of the said interrogatories as we are advised we are inquired to answer, say:

To the first. The only entries inquired of are in the journal, under the dates of March 3, 1866, and June 29, 1866, and they were, we believe, made at those dates. We have not the slightest reason to supect they were made at any other date.

"MARCH 3, 1866

	Cash	$25,000	
Dr.	To capital stock		$25,000

"For 250 shares, subscription of H. S. McComb, for account H. F. Fant, Virginia, and draft made on him this day for the amount.

"JUNE 29, 1866

	Cash	$25,000	
Dr.	To cash		$25,000

"For draft of H. S. McComb, for account subscription of H. G. Fant, March, 3, 1866, for 250 shares stock returned dishonored, and subscription canceled."

To the second. We never saw or heard of such a list, and we, on information, believe none such was ever made, and we know from the books of the company that no correct list could have been made out with H. G. Fant's name on it as a stockholder, as he certainly never was such. Nor was he ever entitled to become such, saving in the short interval between the subscription professed to be for his account and the return of the draft for the price, which was dishonored, acceptance of it having been refused by him. If such a list was ever made out with his name, and it was not done by fraud or mistake, it could only have been truly made in the expectation that he would carry out the contract of subscription made in his name. On the contrary, he rejected on the first opportunity by refusing to pay the price to the company, and the company assented to this and canceled the contract.

To the third. We annex a list of the stockholders on the 12th day of December, 1867, and the number of shares they held. Oakes Ames did not hold any shares as trustee on that day, but he did hold ninety-three shares as trustee on the 1st day of April, 1868, and it was added to a list of the stockholders of the 12th day of December, 1867.

To the fourth. A list is annexed. Oakes Ames does there appear as holding in trust ninety-three shares and two hundred and fifty shares.

To the fifth. We have no knowledge or information of any list made out the 3d day of March, 1866, or about that time, nor of any list made out about the 20th day of February, 1868. There was a list made out about the 12th day of December, 1867, and delivered to the trustees of the Oakes Ames contract, of whom plaintiff was one, to enable those to divide the profits agreeably to the terms of the contract, as hereinafter more particularly set forth.

The books do exhibit a true state of the stock at those times subscribed for and taken, excepting certain shares set forth and explained in answer to subsequent interrogatories; said lists were neither false nor deceptive, nor intended to be so, so far as we can learn or have any reason to believe.

To the sixth. The same persons were for the most part stockholders in the Union Pacific Railroad and in the Credit Mobilier of America—some persons who owned stock in one company did not own any in the other, and the proportion in which the two stocks were held by some differed from those of others considerably. Some of the most leading and active managers in one company were not managers in the other after May, 1867. Prior to that time, the more active men in either company were also active managers in the other. We have no authentic list of the stockholders in the Union Pacific Railroad at any time. The only lists that we know of that can be relied on are in the books of the company, which is not a party, and which we would not be allowed to copy if we were disposed to do so, for the purpose of answering this interrogatory.

To the seventh. We have no knowledge, such as is inquired of, of the contract with Hoxie referred to, except what is contained in documents of which copies are annexed. Who Hoxie was, where he lived, his business, occupation, and employment at the date of the contract, whether he was a man of capital or able to meet the responsibilities of the contract, we cannot say either from knowledge, information, or belief.

To the eighth. We believe he did make the agreement inquired of, and we annex a copy. T. C. Durant was vice-president of the Union Pacific Railroad.

To the ninth. We have no other knowledge on the subject inquired of than is contained in the paper, copies of which are annexed.

To the tenth. We believe that Hoxie never did anything under this, and that it was afterward assigned or became the property of the Credit Mobilier. That company thus becomes the contracting party, and executed the work under that contract.

To the eleventh. We cannot say, as we do not know, what was the actual cost of the road and telegraph from Omaha to the hundred-mile post, and have not materials in our own possession to determine this by, nor do we know of our own knowledge that any such report or estimate was made, though we deem it highly probable. We do not think $26,000 per mile was an extravagant price, considering the nature and character of the work and the risk that was run, but we are advised we are not bound to make an estimate such as is called for—it is a work none of us are competent to do, and would require an expensive outlay to employ an agent competent to do this; and we are further advised that there is no averment in the bill which shows that this is pertinent, or entitles the plaintiff to ask this discovery.

To the twelfth. We know nothing about the Boomer contract, except that such a contract was understood to be made by the vice-president of the railroad company without the knowledge of the company, and they never assented to it. As to the intent, purpose, or object of, we know nothing, and have no means of ascertaining. It was never carried out by said Boomer, in whole or in part, and he never was called upon to perform it, nor was any attempt ever made by the company to compel its performance.

To the thirteenth. There was a contract intended to be made with one Williams, and we believe it was of the character stated in the interrogatory, and we think that no work was done under it; but in consequence of disagreement among the parties in interest or other causes, it was abandoned, as we believe, before being completed and delivered. The object was to have a part of the road built under it.

To the fourteenth. We have already stated, as far as we know or believe, the facts in relation to all of the supposed contracts. The contract with Hoxie we believe was originally made with T. C. Durant, for the benefit, use, and behoof of the parties who associated and organized under the name of the Credit Mobilier of America, but it was a long time after said contract was made before it was assigned to the Credit Mobilier, and no other contract was ever assigned to that corporation; when the Oakes Ames contract was made all possible claims under previous supposed contracts of every description were assumed by him with an agreement to indemnify the company therefor, and upon the assignment of the Ames contract to the trustees, it was agreed with the Credit Mobilier that all profits arising from the construction of the road on the first hundred miles west of the hundredth meridian up to the 1st of January, 1867, should be received by them in final adjustment of their claims and expectations, and the same was accordingly paid them.

To the fifteenth. There was a contract made with Oakes Ames, by the Union Pacific Railroad Company, for the construction of nine hundred and sixty-seven miles of the road, west of the hundredth meridian. It was not antedated, but was dated and delivered on the 16th day of August, and was then in Mr. Ames's possession. Some new and additional but entirely unnecessary approvals thereof were made on the 16th day of October, 1867; but the contract between the directors and officers and Ames was made and executed on the 16th day of August. All prior, possible, previous contracts of every description were assumed by Mr. Ames, as before stated. From that time Mr.

Ames, and the persons associated with him in the undertaking, were the contractors—he the formal party, they, associated with him, though without any written arrangement, but relying on his undertaking to act for them, which he fully carried out to the end of the business.

A copy is annexed which shows what price and compensation the railroad company was to pay and did pay.

To the sixteenth. This contract was not assigned to trustees till the 16th day of October, 1867, for this reason: when the Ames contract was being negotiated, it was desired by many of those who were associated with him, and to be interested therein, all of whom were stockholders in the Union Pacific Railway, that after he got the contract he should assign it to the Credit Mobilier, and for this reason the parties who were to be associated with him had taken stock in the Credit Mobilier, with the design that this corporation should be the contractor for building the Union Pacific Railroad, and they desired this that they might secure themselves from personal liability as contractors beyond the capital they had subscribed to that corporation, and their respective shares in that contract were in the proportions they owned stock in the Credit Mobilier. But in May, 1867, the directors and officers of the Credit Mobilier were changed. This led to hostile feelings, and there were men who had large interest in the Ames contract and great influence in the Union Pacific Railroad who refused to acquiesce in the assignment of the contract for building the road to the Credit Mobilier.

After long-continued and most earnest negotiation a result was arrived at, to which all consented. The contract was assigned to trustees; the profits were to be divided among the same persons and in the same ratio as they would have been if the Credit Mobilier had been substituted for Ames. That company agreed to supply or procure the funds the trustees required in executing the contract, and was to receive interest. And they were also to guarantee the performance by the trustees and receive for this a commission. When this was settled a contract to that effect was executed, assigning the Ames contract to the trustees. A copy is annexed.

The names of the trustees appear in that paper; they were at first all stockholders in the Credit Mobilier; but one of these (Mr. Alley) retired, and in his place Mr. Duff was appointed, who was not and had not been a stockholder for a long time.

To the seventeenth. There was, as the document shows, an option given by Mr. Ames to extend the contract to the rest of this road, but it was not extended to the rest of the road. We know of no resolution or other record of acts done by either company in relation to the extension of the Ames contract.

To the eighteenth. So much of the road as Oakes Ames agreed to build and stock was built and stocked at the expense and upon the credit and responsibility and with the capital of the trustees and the persons for whom they were trustees; and also, with all the resources of the Union Pacific Railroad Company, and the aid given them by the United States, in loaning bonds secured on the road and the land-warrants.

The accounts of the expenditures connected with the construction are not so far closed as to enable us to state the cost of the construction and equipments. It can be stated as quite certain, however, that the profits will not exceed 15 per cent. of the price of the contract; many of us do not believe they will exceed 10 per cent. It depends on what can be realized on bonds and stock of the Union Pacific Railroad. The contract price was paid to the trustees as stated in the answer to the nineteenth interrogatory, and was by them applied as agreed; a part being divided among their *cestuis que trust*, as stated in that answer.

To the nineteenth. The statement annexed to this interrogatory is incorrect. The first three items were, either at the dates mentioned or about those dates, received by the Credit Mobilier in payment of debts due them by the Union Pacific Railroad, as contractor under the Hoxie contract. The stock of the company was sold and the cash went into the ordinary business; none of it was divided among its stockholders, nor could they have done so without impairing the capital. The bonds were used to pay premiums to persons who would subscribe additional cash capital. It was found to be absolutely necessary to have more capital, and no one would subscribe; to induce persons to do so a premium was offered and paid in these bonds. Even with this inducement there was difficulty in getting the subscriptions, and some stockholders refused to put in any more. None were used to pay dividends.

The next four items, under dates of January 4, 1868, and June 17, 1868, were never divided by or for the Credit Mobilier directly or indirectly. This stock and these bonds were paid to and held by the trustees under the Ames contract, and were by them distributed among the persons parties to the assignment who complied with the conditions of the assignment and trust, with an agreement, on their part, to restore the same, or the proceeds *pro rata*, if necessary to complete the contract—a contract which had not only never belonged to that company, but which the parties refused to allow that company to own or take, even as a trustee or agent, and the transfer of which to or for the use of the company was enjoined. They belonged, as did the contract out of which they arose, to their trustees and their *cestuis que trust;* the persons who, as individuals, were associated with Oakes Ames when he made the contract. The trustees who received and divided them were not trustees for the corporation, nor was the property or the profits thereof the corporation's nor had that company ever had any other connection with or relation to the Ames contract, and the profits derived from it, except the duty and the rights defined by the contract of the 16th day of October, 1867. That was the origin and definition of the right of the company, it is true, and this may have misled persons who have not taken the trouble to examine; the persons who received the profits from the trustees are described as stockholders in the Credit Mobilier, but they did not receive them from the company directly or indirectly, nor from property of the company, but from property that had been their own before the contract of the 16th day of October, 1867, was made, nor had the corporation ever at any time any right or power to control or direct the payment of these profits. In no possible sense were these dividends of the company. As to the last five items, under dates of July 3, September 3, and December 19, 1868, the same were allotted or distributed at or about those dates except the two items of September 3, which are mistakes, to the persons who became parties to the indenture of the trust and assignment of the Ames contract, and complied with the conditions thereof, and in that character, and not as stockholders in the Credit Mobilier.' It should, perhaps, be added, that in July, 1868, the trustees demanded an advance of the Credit Mobilier, as stipulated to be made by the agreement of the 16th day of October, 1867. That company was without means to perform their engagement, and without credit to obtain means, owing to litigation about their right to claim to be a corporation, and other questions which destroyed confidence. In consequence of this, the contract was rescinded, and the Credit Mobilier withdrew from all connection with the Ames contract.

September 3 is a mistake; there was, in fact, no dividend at that time. The value of these allotments was very much less than the nominal price attached to them.

To the twentieth. There was no such dividend or anything of the kind as that inquired of. The whole truth, as respects the subject referred to in this interrogatory, is this: In 1867 there was a settlement between the Union Pacific Railroad, through the trustees, under the Oakes Ames contract, in respect of the work done by the Credit Mobilier before the Ames contract took effect, and there was paid them on account thereof certain stock, which was sold, and the proceeds divided, making a dividend of 6 per cent. for 1866 and 6 per cent. for 1867; and there was no other dividend made by the company or for it, or out of its property, directly or indirectly, during those years.

To the twenty-first. No other dividends were made by the company except the dividend for 1866 and 1867, of 6 per cent. each, unless it be that an equalization of interest on new subscriptions can be so treated. If this is the legal effect of that act no one suspected it at that time, and in this the plaintiff participated.

There have been no profits on the business since August, 1867, for the simple reason the company did none. Its functions were gone by the refusal to let it take the Ames contract. Its capital is locked up in the obligations and property taken when executing the Hoxie contract and the work prior to the Ames contract. Its capital is certainly diminished; but to what extent will depend on what it can realize out of these assets.

To the twenty-second. The money, bonds, and stock referred to were allotted and distributed to and among the persons parties to the assignment in trust of the Ames contract, upon their compliance with the terms of the trust, as hereinbefore stated. They were not paid to them in the character of stockholders of the Credit Mobilier, but of that trust, although their proportions of profit were to be determined by the amounts of stock respectively held by them in the Credit Mobilier at the time of the creation of the trust. The reason that such distribution was made only to parties who were stockholders in the Credit Mobilier and in the proportion which they held in the stock of that corporation, was that it was originally expected by many of the parties that the Ames contract would be assigned to the Credit Mobilier, and all the parties to said trust and assignment were holders of stock in that corporation. When it was found that there was not a concurrence in the desirableness of transferring the contract to the Credit Mobilier, and the differences of opinion were reconciled by assignment of the Ames contract to the trustees, as before stated, then the relative number of shares of each, in the Credit Mobilier, was assumed as the basis of the respective interests of the parties. We are aware of nothing in any of the books that gives or is intended to give a false appearance to the transaction.

To the twenty-third. The shares of stock in the Union Pacific Railroad, which were received by the Credit Mobilier up to the date of the Ames contract, and those received by the trustees of that contract afterward, were fully paid, and by the parties receiving them, in this manner: That company and the said trustees were successively contractors to build the road as already stated, and by the contract they were obliged to receive the stock in payment of part of the sums due under their respective contracts. Thus, the Union Pacific Railroad, instead of paying one hundred dollars to the contractors, delivered them a share of stock, the *face* of which was one hundred dollars, and extinguished a debt of that amount by receiving this in satisfaction as a payment to their capital. It is believed the form generally observed was to exchange checks. It is believed no one having any conception of what constitutes reality will suggest there is anything looking like a sham in this. Probably no corporation whose stock is not above par but would gladly receive subscription to capital on the same terms.

To the twenty-fifth. The stock referred to was held in the name of Thomas C. Durant, who was the president of the corporation until the change of directors in May, 1867, and he alleged he held it for persons who had agreed to take it, but who had not paid in their subscriptions. The managers finding this was held without capital having been paid in, on inquiry were informed it was held for persons who had agreed to buy it, but had not yet paid in the price. They therefore required it to be transferred to the then president, S. Dillon, and so it stood in the name of Mr. Dillon until the time that the stock was transferred to Oakes Ames, as stated in their answers. The stock was issued and the capital paid in and received by the company. It was stated—and the company acted on this—that there were engagements to take this stock and that it was transferred in fulfillment of these engagements. Those who had engaged with Durant to take the stock had it transferred to him; and those who had engaged with Oakes Ames to take it had it transferred to him; or rather it was settled for and transferred by the company to those two, on the allegation of these gentlemen that they had made these engagements. Throughout the company dealt on the footing that this stock was held to meet these engagements. None of this stock had ever been bought by Fant or subscribed for by him, or for him, and if he had complied and taken shares it would have been other shares, which he would have received, that is, shares unallotted; and those were ultimately and after his failure to comply with his subscription subscribed for and taken by others.

To the twenty-sixth. No stockholder named on any list or book of the company that any of us have any knowledge of have had their names withdrawn or dropped. Nor have they disappeared from said lists or books except by transfers in the ordinary manner, so far as we know or believe. Fant was no exception to this. He never did become a stockholder, the plaintiff professed to have authority to subscribe for him, and to draw on him for the subscription price, but Mr. Fant refused to honor the draft, and the company acquiesced in his disavowal of the contract, and, as already stated, canceled the subscription.

We have already stated all that relates to the transfer of the shares to Oakes Ames as trustee. Durant was the actual holder for undeclared purchasers. He transferred them for Dillon, the president, and he by the direction of all parties, including the plaintiff himself, transferred them to Ames as trustee. The authorization signed by the plaintiff we append a copy of, as follows:

"We, the undersigned stockholders of the Credit Mobilier of America, understanding that $65,000 of the capital stock of this company, held in trust by the president, has been promised certain parties by T. C. Durant and Oakes Ames, do hereby consent to and advise the transfer of said stock to such parties as they, the said Durant and Ames, have agreed upon and designate, say to Durant parties, $37,000, and Ames parties, $28,000.

(Signed)

"JOHN DUFF.
"THOS. C. DURANT.
"S. BARDWELL.
"OAKES AMES.
"OLIVER AMES.
"JOHN B. ALLEY.
"C. S. BUSHNELL.
"SIDNEY DILLON.
"H. S. McCOMB."

"The undersigned, stockholders in the Credit Mobilier of America, recommend the issue to Hon. Oakes Ames, trustee, of ninety-three (93) shares of the capital stock of this company at par.

(Signed)

"T. C. DURANT.
"C. S. BUSHNELL.
"OAKES AMES.
"OLIVER AMES.
"C. A. LOMBARD.
"S. HOOPER & CO.
"S. BARDWELL.
"JOHN DUFF.
"WM. H. MACY."

There were no other documents or records connected with this than the ordinary transfer on the books.

To the twenty-seventh. We have already answered this interrogatory as fully as possible, saying that the ninety-three shares, being a portion of the additional capital due on the two hundred and fifty shares, were issued (on the request of the stockholders, including the plaintiff) to the holder of the said two hundred and fifty shares as already stated.

To the twenty-eighth. At the time when these shares were issued to Oakes Ames as trustee, he paid the company the par value for them in money. And exactly as much was paid, and in the same manner, as was paid for any other shares; and this payment was made in good faith; it was not paid out of money received from the company, nor from profits or dividends accrued; no such profits or dividends were ever paid to the holders of two hundred and fifty of those shares, nor on account of these shares until long after this payment of the subscription and issue of the stock. Mr. Ames received no share of profits or dividend on those two hundred and fifty shares until the 17th day of June, 1868, when the dividend then made by the trustees was paid to him. The dividends of December, 1867, and January, 1868, were paid him on the ninety-three shares, on the 8th day of April, he having paid for the shares on the 1st day of April.

To the thirtieth. Mr. Ames has not communicated to the company, and we have no knowledge who the parties were that proposed to purchase the shares of him or in his name. The company received $100 per share in cash for the stock, from Oakes Ames as from every one else. That amount Mr. Ames paid for the stock, and where he got the money we are unable to say, but certainly not out of profits received on these shares. He signed the obligations and agreements required by the trustees as "trustee."

We do not know and have no information what Mr. Ames received, if anything, from his *cestuis que trust.* The $100 paid the company certainly was not paid out of back dividends, as none such were paid except, as already stated, as to ninety-three shares. The receipt-book of the trustees shows that no dividends were paid on these two hundred and fifty shares until the 17th day of June, 1868, to Mr. Ames.

The back dividends did not, at the time Mr. Ames got and paid for the stock, amount to anything except as to the ninety-three shares, and these shares were not a gift or anything like it; but a sale at par in pursuance of old and existing contracts which it was believed the parties were entitled to have fulfilled, and no one pretended or supposed it was anything else, so far as we know.

To the thirty-third. When the proposal was made to make the two hundred and fifty and the ninety-three shares in the name of Oakes Ames, it was verbally agreed to by all parties, including the plaintiff, although known to be all the remaining stock of the company. The plaintiff at this time not only assented to and advised this transfer to Oakes Ames, but did not mention that he had any claim to any stock on account of any such Fant subscription, nor was any officer of the company at that period, nor until some time afterward, aware that any such claim or pretended claim or subscription ever existed. But subsequently one of the officers of the company refused to act in this matter on a verbal agreement, having had some disputes with the plaintiff when the written agreement (incorporated in the answer to the twenty-sixth interrogatory) was prepared and the plaintiff asked to sign it; he did not then pretend that he had any right, through Fant or otherwise, to this specific stock, though he knew these were the only shares remaining to be issued; but he said the president had not treated him properly when he informed him the first time, a few days before, of his claim, and had told him his claim was all bogus; and he would not even listen to him, and if treated in this manner he would grant no favors and sign no papers. When asked what he wanted, he stated he only wanted a fair hearing; and one of these defendants then stated he would undertake that he should be fairly heard, if he had any claim, if that was all, and the plaintiff then signed the paper by which all the stock not previously paid for and issued was handed over to Oakes Ames upon the agreement above stated, and afterward he, the plaintiff, joined in receiving the profits under the Ames contract, and signed the receipts to the trustees, in which very document the profits were allotted to Ames on these shares, and were received by him. In all these transactions he never protested against this use of the stock, never pretended it was his, and gave no warning or authority of the kind; and it is obvious that such conduct would have been absurd and contradictory, to have authorized stock to be transferred to strangers and yet protest and claim this same stock as his own; all that he did was to demand a hearing on his claim. From what we had heard and knew of it, we all regarded his claim as without a pretense of foundation, but were willing to listen to him if he wished to be heard, at least some of us; others were impatient at what they deemed a gross imposition attempted. No pledge was given, or anything said that he could torture into a pledge, that this stock should not be given to others, or that his rights to this stock should be regarded, for he never pretended any, and the only object of the whole business was to give authority to hand it over to Oakes Ames for others who were purchasers thereof. His claim was to a right to be considered in consequence of this Fant subscription. Certainly, however, he never pretended to a right to the stock he thus asked the company to issue to another.

To the thirty-fourth. We cannot annex a copy of the dividend statement made out as of the 28th day of December, 1867, as it has been mislaid; but we annex copies of the receipts signed by the plaintiff and all other stockholders. These were declared and paid by the corporation. We have obtained, and annex, the receipts of the dividends made by the trustees of the Ames contract on the 4th day of January, 1868, June 3 and July 3, and signed by the plaintiff on the days stated, opposite his signature.

SIDNEY DILLON.
JOHN M. S. WILLIAMS.
JOHN B. ALLEY.
JOHN DUFF.
C. S. BUSHNELL.
R. G. HAZARD.

Witness: E. H. ROLLINS.

STATE OF MASSACHUSETTS, *County of Suffolk, City of Boston, ss:*

The foregoing instrument, subscribed and sworn to by Sidney Dillon, John M. S. Williams, John B. Alley, John Duff, and C. S. Bushnell, and subscribed and affirmed to by R. G. Hazard, at the city of Boston, this 10th day of February, A. D. 1870, before me.

[SEAL.]

A. W. ADAMS,
Commissioner for Pennsylvania.

Before me, the subscriber, a notary public in and for the city of Washington, in the District of Columbia, personally appeared Oakes Ames, who, being duly sworn, says the facts set forth in the foregoing answers (excluding the answer to the thirtieth interrogatory, which this deponent has answered separately) are true.

OAKES AMES.

Sworn and subscribed before me this 14th day of February, A. D. 1870.

[SEAL.]

N. CALLAN,
Notary Public and Commissioner for State of Pennsylvania.

List of December 12, 1867.

Names.	Stock.	Names.	Stock.
Oliver W. Barnes	15	Fourth National Bank	750
Thomas C. Durant	4,915	Barton H. Jenks	500
Willie Davis Train	175	A. A. Low	100
L. Eugene French	20	J. B. Pigot	200
Charles A. Lombard	775	Harvey Sanford	125
Sidney Dillon, president	400	Henry Trowbridge	75
Sidney Dillon	1,005	Ezekiel H. Trowbridge	50
William T. Glidden	625	W. F. Day, cashier, in trust	100
G. M. S. Williams	620	Royal E. Robbins	200
R. G. Hazard	1,690	William A. Cummings	100
Oliver S. Chapman	412	Frank W. Andrew	100
Oliver Ames	4,680	S. H. Fessenden	50
C. S. Bushnell	410	Nathan Peck	100
William H. Macy	300	Pupont P. Foske	50
J. H. Scranton	5	Elizabeth Hazard	34
R. Griswold Gray	1,620	Elizabeth Hazard, jr	13
Joseph Nickerson	380	Anna Hazard	20
Benjamin Holliday	750	Mary P. Hazard	10
Benjamin E. Bates	500	Lydia Torrey	11
Frederick Nickerson	250	Anna Horner	1
John B. Alley	290	Sophia Vernon	1
Isaac P. Hazard	380	Henry Hotchkiss	150
Samuel Hooper & Co	750	William B. Bristol	50
Horatio Gilbert	185	Sylvester M. Beard	100
Cyrus P. McCormick	945	Ely Beard	100
David Jones	380	Gamaliel Bradford	100
Oakes Ames	1,955	Le Grand Lockwood	500
Elisha Atkins	622	John R. Duff	1,880
Ezra H. Baker	623	Samuel S. Dana	100
H. J. McComb	750	John M. Davies	500
Horatio J. Gilbert	137	Robert G. S. McNeil	5
Ezra H. Baker, jr	50	E. C. Moore	10

List of December 12, 1867—Continued.

Names.	Stock.	Names.	Stock.
Paul Pohl	6	John Smith	405
J. W. Grimes	380	Aaron Hobart, jr	25
Thomas Nickerson	150	Isaac Thacher	92
George Opdyke	712	James B. Johnston	200
Josiah Bardwell	710	B. M. Boyer	75
Josiah Bardwell, jr	300	Charles H. Neilson	100
C. C. Waite	80	Josiah Hedlea	100
B. D. Stewart	5	F. Skinner & Co	500
H. C. Crane	128	H. C. Crane, trustee	60
E. W. Gilmore	150	Charles H. Neilson	50
Rowland Hazard	300	Oakes Ames, trustee	93
John L. King	80		

HOXIE CONTRACT.

NEW YORK, *August* 8, 1864.

To the President and Committee on Contracts of the Union Pacific Railroad Company:

GENTLEMEN: I propose to enter into a contract to build and equip one hundred miles of your railroad and telegraph, commencing at Omaha City, complying, as far as practicable, to the general specifications hereunto annexed, upon the following terms and conditions, viz:

To proceed at once with the grading and bridging, and complete the same within the time required by the acts of Congress specified, and in such manner as will comply with the same; to assume all your contracts for ties, iron, and equipment—the company reserving the right, if they elect, to dispose of what iron they have, with the exception of, say, five hundred tons, which may be required to facilitate the grading, and also to dispose of the equipment not needed this season, except three locomotives and ten platform cars; but, in case they elect to do so, shall give me written notice of their intention prior to the 1st day of October next.

To build all necessary side-track not exceeding 6 per cent. in length of the main line, the contractor to have the right to change grades, provided the maximum grade shall not exceed that of the New York Central Railroad. Also to have the right to enter upon all lands belonging to said company for the purpose of obtaining material used in the construction of the road.

Should the company decide to Burnetize the cottonwood used for ties, they shall pay in addition sixteen cents for each tie, and for all other timber in like proportion.

The contractor shall not be required to expend in the construction of any one bridge over eighty-five thousand dollars, nor shall he be required to expend for the erection of station-buildings, machinery, machine shops, tanks, equipments, &c., more than five thousand dollars per mile, or five hundred thousand dollars in the aggregate, but the same shall be expended as directed by the engineer. The contractor to have the use of the road until the contract is completed. The work on the sections near Omaha, which have been let by the company, or which have been commenced, to be continued by them or transferred to me, as may be agreed upon hereafter, and the cost of the same to be charged to me in final settlement. Any excess in the cost of iron above one hundred and thirty dollars per ton at Omaha to be allowed by the company. Right of way to be furnished by the company. The expense of engineers engaged in the construction to be paid by the contractor. The company to pay for the same at the rate of fifty thousand dollars for each and every mile so completed. Payments to be made as the work progresses, upon the estimate of the engineers, in making which the engineer shall deduct from each section its proportion of the cost of equipment not then furnished, station-buildings, superstructure, and cost of telegraph; but all material delivered or in transit for the account of the company may be estimated for. The contractor to furnish money upon the securities of the company, as hereinafter provided for, in the construction of each section of the length required by the acts of Congress hereinbefore referred to, viz:

The company shall proceed to mortgage the land acquired from the Government at not more than sixteen thousand dollars per mile, bearing 7 per cent. interest, payable semi-annually in the city of New York, which bonds shall be receivable as the bonds of the company, at such prices as may be fixed upon from time to time as the cash price of the lands. The company to proceed to the preparing of the first-mortgage bonds, as provided for under the act, made and put on record, the mortgage securing the same, so that the bonds may be ready for issue as soon as the provisions of the law are complied with; and shall do everything necessary and requisite to obtain the Government bonds at an early day. In the mean time, if required, the company to execute certificates of an amount to correspond to the first-mortgage and Government bonds, changeable for the same upon the company's obtaining the United States bonds. Said certificates to bear interest, payable semi-annually, at the rate of 6 per cent. On these certificates I will advance, or procure to be advanced, the necessary funds to the company at the rate of 80 per cent. of their par value, and on the land-grant bonds, 70 per cent., reserving the right to dispose of them whenever the amount so advanced, including what may be due on construction, shall exceed five hundred thousand dollars, or whenever said advance shall have been made over five months, but not to do so for less than the prices above named. The company, in their option, to decide whether I take the bonds or any portion of them at the prices above named, in payment for advances and interest, if called upon to do so within thirty days thereafter. I will also subscribe or cause to be subscribed to the capital stock of your company five hundred thousand dollars. I will assume and pay such obligations or accounts as may have been certified to by the committee appointed by your board or executive committee for services and expenses, the company paying me the amount of the obligation so certified to and assumed. In making this proposition it may be well to state that I am connected with and agent for parties who have machines, oxen, and necessary outfit for prosecuting the work, and am prepared to commence at once, having sent cattle and tools to Nebraska.

H. M. HOXIE,
By H. C. CRANE,
Attorney.

H. M. HOXIE, Esq:

DEAR SIR: You will please go on with the work under the above proposition, and if the company do not accept it before the first day of October next, they will pay you upon the same terms and conditions for what work may be done, as shown by the estimates of the engineers, made as provided in this proposition, first giving you thirty days' notice that they do not accept.

GEORGE T. M. DAVIS,
Special Commttiee.

SEPTEMBER 23, 1864.

Above contract is approved and ratified.
[SEAL.]

JOHN A. DIX,
C. S. BUSHNELL,
GEO. T. M. DAVIS,
Special Committee appointed for this purpose May 12, 1864.

NEW YORK, *October* 4, 1864.

To the President and Executive Committee of the Union Pacific Railroad Company:

On condition that your company will extend my contract from its present length for one hundred miles, so as to embrace all that portion of the road between Omaha and the one hundredth meridian of longitude, I will subscribe, or cause to be subscribed, for five hundred thousand dollars of the stock of your company.

Respectfully, yours,

H. M. HOXIE,
By H. C. CRANE,
Attorney.

The above proposition is hereby accepted for and on behalf of the Union Pacific Railroad Company.

JOHN A. DIX,
C. S. BUSHNELL,
GEO. T. M. DAVIS,
Special Committee.

OCTOBER 4, 1864.

TRANSFER OF THE HOXIE CONTRACT.

Whereas the Union Pacific Railroad Company have made a contract with H. M. Hoxie, for the construction of one hundred miles of their railroad and telegraph, a copy of which is hereto annexed:

Now, therefore, this agreement between the said H. M. Hoxie, for himself, and as agent, party of the first part, and Thomas Durant, party of the second part, witnesseth: The said Hoxie, for and in consideration of one dollar to him in hand paid, the receipt of which is hereby acknowledged, hereby agrees to make over and assign to said Durant, or any party or parties he may direct, who will furnish the necessary funds to complete the same, all the unfinished portion of the above-mentioned contract, and all rights under the same, at any time when called upon by the said Durant, or his heirs or assigns, so to do, upon the payment according to the contract for all work done and materials on hand, said party of the first part to have five days' notice in writing, at Omaha, of the intention of the party of the second part to take a transfer of the contract.

The engineers shall proceed at once to adjust the accounts and make up the estimate of settlement for the work done according to the contract, which shall be completed as soon as practicable, but the party of the second part is to become responsible for all labor or demands of every kind or description pertaining to the contract after the expiration of the five days' notice; and from that time the party of the first part shall not be liable for any work done or material furnished. The party of the second part also to take at cost the oxen, shovels, picks, tents, and shanties on hand at the time they take possession of the work, and also to pay the party of the first part ten thousand dollars in the stock of the company, and five thousand dollars in cash; in consideration of which the said party of the first part shall, if required, take general supervision of the work until the expiration of one year from the 1st day of August last.

In witness whereof the parties have hereunto set their hands this 13th day of September, 1864.

(Signed) H. M. HOXIE,
(Signed) By H. C. CRANE,
Attorney.
THOS. C. DURANT.

[5-cent stamp.]

Agreement made this sixteenth day of August, 1867, between the Union Pacific Railroad Company, party of the first part, and Oakes Ames, party of the second part, witnesseth: that the party of the first part and Oakes Ames, party of the second part, witnesseth: That the party of the first part agrees to let and contract, and the party of the second part agrees to contract as follows, to wit:

First. The party of the second part agrees and binds himself, his heirs, executors, administrators, and assigns, to build and equip the following-named portion of the railroad and telegraph line of the party of the first part, commencing at the one hundredth meridian of longitude, upon the following terms and conditions, to wit:

1st, 100 miles at and for the rate of $42,000 per mile.
2d, 167 miles at and for the rate of $45,000 per mile.
3d, 100 miles at and for the rate of $96,000 per mile.
4th, 100 miles at and for the rate of $80,000 per mile.
5th, 100 miles at and for the rate of $90,000 per mile.
6th, 100 miles at and for the rate of $96,000 per mile.

667 miles.

Second. At least three hundred and fifty miles shall be, if possible, completed and ready for acceptance before the first day of January, 1868, provided the Union Pacific Railroad Company transport the material; the whole to be constructed in a good and workmanlike manner, upon the same general plan and specifications as adopted east of the one hundredth meridian of longitude. The party of the second part shall erect all such necessary depots, machine-shops, machinery, tanks, turn-tables, and provide all necessary machinery and rolling-stock, at a cost of not less than $7,500 per mile in cash; and shall construct all such necessary side-track as may be required by the party of the first part, not exceeding 6 per cent. of the length of the road constructed and to be constructed under this contract. The kind of timber used for ties, and in the bridges, and in its preparation, shall be such as from time to time may be ordered or prescribed by the general agent or the company, under the rules and regulations and standard as recommended by the Secretary of the Interior, of the date of February, 1866.

Third. Whenever one of the above-named sections of the road shall be furnished to the satisfaction and acceptance of the Government commissioners, the same shall be delivered into the possession of the party of the first part, and upon such portions of the road, as well as on that part east of the one hundredth meridian, now completed. The party of the first part shall transport without delay all men and material to be used in construction, at a price to be agreed upon by the party of the second part, his heirs, executors, administrators, or assigns, and the general agent, but not less than cost to the party of the first part.

Fourth. The party of the second part, his heirs, executors, administrators, or assigns, shall have the right to enter upon all lands belonging to the company, or upon which the company may have any rights, and take therefrom any material used in the construction of the road, and may have the right to change the grade and curvature within the limits of the provisions of the act of Congress for the temporary purpose of hastening the completion of the road, but the estimate and cost of reducing the same to the grade and curvatures as established by the chief engineer, or as approved from time to time by the company, shall be deducted and retained by the party of the first part, until such grade and curvature is so reduced.

Fifth. The party of the second part, his heirs, executors, administrators, or assigns, is to receive from the company and enjoy the benefit of all existing contracts, and shall assume all such contracts and all liabilities of the company accrued or arising therefrom for work done or to be done, and materials furnished or to be furnished for or on account of the road west of the one hundredth meridian, crediting, however, the party of the first part on this contract all moneys paid or expended on account thereof.

Sixth. The party of the second part, for himself, his heirs, executors, administrators, and assigns, stipulates and agrees that the work shall be prosecuted and completed with energy and all possible speed, so as to complete the same at the earliest practicable day, it being understood that the speed of construction and time of completion is the essence of this contract, and at the same time the road to be a first-class road, with equipments; and if the same, in the opinion of the chief engineers, is not so prosecuted, both as regards quality and dispatch, that the said party of the first part shall and may, through its general agent, or other officer detailed for that purpose, take charge of said work and carry the same on at the proper cost and expense of the party of the second part.

Seventh. The grading, bridging, and superstructure to be completed under the supervision of the general agent of the company, to the satisfaction of the chief engineer, and to be of the same character, as to workmanship and material, as in the construction of the road east of the one hundredth meridian. It is, however, understood that all iron hereafter purchased or contracted for shall be of the weight of not less than 56 pounds to the yard, and to be fish-bar joint.

Eighth. All the expenses of the engineering are to be charged to and paid by the party of the second part, except the pay and salary of the chief engineer and consulting engineer and their immediate assistants, and the expenses of the general survey of the route.

Ninth. The depot-buildings, machine-shops, water-tanks, and also bridges, shall be of the most approved pattern, and they, as well as the kind of masonry or other material used, shall be previously approved by the general agent and chief engineer of the company, and all tunnels shall be of the proper width for a double track, and shall be arched with brick or stone when necessary for the protection of the same.

Tenth. Payments to be made as the work progresses, upon the estimate of the chief engineer, in making which the engineer shall deduct from each section its proportion of the cost of equipments not then furnished, station-buildings, superstructure and cost of telegraph, but all material delivered or in transit for the account of the company may be estimated for.

Eleventh. Payments hereon shall be made to the party of the second part, his heirs, executors, administrators, or assigns, in cash; but if the Government bonds received by the company cannot be converted into money at their par value net, and the first-mortgage bonds of the company at ninety cents on the dollar net, then the said party of the second part, his heirs, executors, administrators, and assigns, shall be charged hereon the difference between the amount realized and the above-named rates, provided the first-mortgage bonds are not sold below eighty cents on the dollar, and if there shall not be realized from the sale of such bonds an amount sufficient to pay the party of the second part, his heirs, executors, administrators, or assigns, for work, as stipulated in this contract, and according to the terms thereof, then such deficiency shall be from time to time subscribed by the said party of the second part, his heirs, executors, administrators, or assigns, to the capital stock of said company, and the proceeds of such subscription shall be paid to said party of the second part, his heirs, executors, administrators, or assigns, on this contract.

Twelfth. On the first hundred miles on this contract, there shall be added to the equipment now provided for and intended to apply on this section, as follows, viz:

Six locomotives, fifty box-cars, four passenger-cars, two baggage-cars, and a proportionate amount of equipments of like character, to be supplied on the second section of one hundred miles after the same is completed.

Thirteenth. The amount provided to be expended for equipments, station-buildings, &c., shall be expended under the direction of the party of the first part, and in such proportion for cars, locomotives, machine-shops, station-buildings, &c., and at such points as they may determine. The party of the first part to have the full benefit of such expenditures, without profit to the contractor, or they may in their option purchase the equipments and expend any portion of said amount, provided at any point on the road, where they may deem the same most advantageous to the company, whether on the section on which the said reservation occurs or not.

Fourteenth. The telegraph line is included herein under the term railroad, and is to be constructed in the same manner and with similar materials as in the line east of the one hundredth meridian. The said parties hereto, in consideration of the premises and of their covenants herein, do mutually agree severally to perform and fulfill their several agreements above written.

This contract having been submitted to the executive committee by resolution of the board of directors, August 16, 1867, and we, having examined the details of the same, recommend its execution by the proper officers of the company with the Honorable Oakes Ames, the party named as the second part.

Resolutions passed by executive committee of Union Pacific Railroad, at a meeting held October 1, 1867:

Resolved, The foregoing contract between the Union Pacific Railroad Company and Oakes Ames, referred to the executive committee by a resolution of the board, August 16, 1867, to settle the details, be approved, and that the proper officers of the company be instructed to execute the same, subject, however, to the written approval of the stockholders of the company, as understood by the board of directors when the same was voted upon.

Resolved, That the option to extend this contract to Salt Lake be referred to the board, with a recommendation that the said option be accepted.

(Signed) OLIVER AMES,
C. S. BUSHNELL,
SPRINGER HARBAUGH,
THOS. C. DURANT,
Executive Authority.

TRANSFER OF AMES'S CONTRACT TO TRUSTEES, &c.

MEMORANDUM OF AGREEMENT, in triplicate, made this 15th day of October, 1867, between Oakes Ames, of North Easton, Massachusetts, party of the first part; Thomas C. Durant, of the city of New York; Oliver Ames, of North Easton, Massachusetts; John B. Alley, of Lynn, Massachusetts; Sidney Dillon, of the city of New York; Cornelius S. Bushnell, of New Haven, Connecticut; Henry S. McComb, of Wilmington, Delaware; and Benjamin E. Bates, of Boston, Massachusetts, parties of the second part, and the Credit Mobilier of America, party of the third part, witnesseth: That whereas the party of the first part has undertaken a certain large contract for the construction of certain portions therein named of the railroad and telegraph line of the Union Pacific Railroad Company over the plains, and over and through the Rocky Mountains, which will require a very large and hazardous outlay of capital, which capital he is desired to be assured of raising at such times and in such sums as will enable him to complete and perform the said contract according to its terms and conditions;

And whereas the Credit Mobilier of America, the party of the third part, a corporation duly established by law, is empowered by its charter to advance and loan money in aid of such enterprises, and can control large amounts of capital for such purposes, and is willing to loan to said party of the first part such sums as may be found necessary to complete said contract, *provided* sufficient assurance may be made to said party of the third part herein that such sums shall be duly expended in the work of completing said railroad and telegraph line, and that the payments for the faithful performance of said contract by said railroad company shall be held and applied to reimburse said party of the third part for their loans and advances, together with a reasonable interest for the use of the money so loaned and advanced;

And whereas said party of the third part fully believes that said contract, if honestly and faithfully executed, will be both profitable and advantageous to the parties performing the same, are therefore willing to guarantee the performance and execution of the same for a reasonable commission to be paid therefor;

And whereas both parties of the first and third parts have confidence and reliance in the integrity, business capacity, and ability of the several persons named as parties of the second part hereto, and confidently believe that said persons have large interests as well in the Union Pacific Railroad Company as in the Credit Mobilier of America, they will execute and perform the said contract, and faithfully hold the proceeds thereof to the just use and benefit of the parties entitled thereto:

Therefore it is agreed by and between the parties of the first, second, and third parts hereto as follows: that is to say, that said Oakes Ames, party of the first part hereto, hereby, for and in consideration of the sum of one dollar, lawful money of the United States, to him duly paid by the party of the second part, and for divers other good and valuable considerations herein thereunto moving, doth hereby assign, set over, and transfer unto the said Thomas C. Durant, Oliver Ames, John B. Alley, Sidney Dillon, Cornelius S. Bushnell, Henry S. McComb, and Benjamin E. Bates, parties of the second part, all the right, title, and interest of, in, and to, the certain contracts heretofore made and executed by and between the Union Pacific Railroad Company and the said Oakes Ames, bearing date the sixteenth day of August, 1867, for the construction of portions of the railroad and telegraph line of said company, to which contract reference is herein made, for them, the said parties of the second part, to have and to hold the same to them and their survivors and successors, forever, in trust, nevertheless, upon the following trust and conditions and limitations, to wit:

First. That they, the said parties of the second part, shall perform all the terms and conditions of the contract so assigned, in all respects, which, in and by the terms and conditions thereof, is undertaken and assumed and agreed to be done and performed by the said party of the first part herein named.

Second. That they, the said parties of the second part, shall hold all the avails and proceeds of the said contract, and therefrom shall re-imburse themselves and the party of the third part hereto, all moneys advanced and expended by them, or either of them, in executing or performing the said contract, with interest and commission thereon as hereinafter provided.

Third. Out of the said avails and proceeds to pay unto the parties of the second part a reasonable sum as compensation for their services as such trustees for executing and performing the terms and conditions of this agreement, which compensation shall not exceed the sum of three thousand dollars per annum to each and every one of the parties of the second part.

Fourth. To hold all the rest and residue of the said proceeds and avails for the use and benefit of such of the several persons holding and owning shares in the capital stock of the said Credit Mobilier of America, on the day of the date thereof, in proportion to the number of shares which said stockholders now severally hold and own, and for the use and benefit of such of the several assignees and holders of such shares of stock at the times herein set forth for the distributionof said residue and remainder of said avails and proceeds, who shall comply with the provisions, conditions, and limitations herein contained, which are, on their part, to be complied with.

Fifth. To pay over, on or before the first Wednesday in June and December in each year, or within thirty days thereafter, his just share and proportion of the residue and remainder of the said proceeds and avails as shall be justly estimated by said trustees to have been made and earned as net profits in said contract during the preceding six months to each such stockholder only in said Credit Mobilier of America who, being a stockholder in the Union Pacific Railroad, shall have made and executed his power of attorney or proxy irrevocable to said several parties of the second part, their survivors and successors, empowering them, the said parties of the second part, to vote upon at least six-tenths of all the shares of stock owned by said shareholders of the Credit Mobilier of America in the capital stock of the Union Pacific Railroad Company on the day of the date hereof, and six-tenths of any stock in the Union Pacific Railroad Company he may have received as dividend or otherwise, because or by virtue of having been a stockholder in said Credit Mobilier of America, or which may appertain to any shares in said Union Pacific Railroad Company which have been so assigned to him at the time or times of the distribution of the said profits as hereinafter provided; and this trust is made and declared upon the express condition and limitation that it shall not inure, in any manner or degree, to the use or benefit of any stockholder of the Credit Mobilier of America who shall neglect or refuse to execute and deliver unto the parties of the second part his proxy or power of attorney in the manner and for the purpose hereinbefore provided, or who shall, in any way, or by any proceedings, knowingly hinder, delay, or interfere with the execution or performance of the trust and conditions herein declared and set forth; and the above transfer and conveyance of said contract is made upon these further trusts and conditions, to wit:

First. That said parties of the second part, their survivors and successors, trustees as aforesaid, in all their acts and doings in the execution and performance of said contract, and in the execution of their several trusts and conditions herein set forth, shall act by the concurrent assent of four of their number expressed in writing, or by yea and nay vote, at a meeting of said trustees, either or both of which shall be recorded in a book of the proceedings of said trustees, kept for that purpose by their secretary, and not otherwise.

Second. Said parties of the second part shall keep an office in the city of New York, for the transaction of the business incidental to said trust. Meetings of said trustees may be held on call of the secretary on request of any two of their number; such call may be made personally or by mail.

Third. The said trustees shall appoint a competent person as secretary, who shall keep a faithful record of all their acts, proceedings, and contracts, in books provided for that purpose, and shall cause to be kept suitable books of accounts and vouchers of all their business transactions.

Fourth. The said trustees shall cause a monthly statement to be made, showing the amount due from the Union Pacific Railroad Company on account of work done, or equipment or material furnished under the contract, according to the estimate of the engineer of the Union Pacific Railroad Company, as provided in said contract, a copy of which statement shall be furnished to the Credit Mobilier of America.

And the above transfer and conveyance of said contract is made upon the further trust and condition:

First. That in case of the death, declination, disability by reason of sickness, or absence from the country for the space of six months, or neglect to fulfill the duties and obligations of said trust for the same time by either said trustee, the remaining or surviving trustees may declare the place of such trustees to be vacant, and fill such vacancy by vote, in manner aforesaid.

Second. That in case any one of said trustees shall willfully neglect or evade the performance of his duties as such trustee, or shall willfully attempt to hinder, delay, obstruct, or interfere with the execution or performance of said contract, or the due execution or performance of said trust or condition, according to the true intent thereof, or shall appropriate to his use or benefit any money or other valuable thing belonging to or appertaining to said trust-fund or property, he shall not be entitled further to act as such trustee or to receive any of the benefits of said trust, either as shareholder in said Credit Mobilier of America or otherwise.

The parties of the second part do hereby accept the said trust, and agree faithfully to execute and perform the same according to the terms, conditions, and limitations herein set forth.

The party of the third part, in consideration of these premises, hereby agree to advance, as upon a loan, to the said parties of the second part, their survivors and successors, all such sums of money and at such times as may be necessary to enable said trustees economically and promptly to execute and perform the conditions of said contract upon the call of said parties of the second part, their survivors and successors, such sums never to exceed in the whole the amount provided for in said contract to be paid by the Union Pacific Railroad Company for the execution and performance thereof, and to receive therefor interest at the rate of seven per centum per annum, payable semi-annually on each sum so advanced, until the same are repaid. And the said party of the third part do further agree for the consideration aforesaid, and for an amount equal to two and one-half per cent. on the amount to be by them advanced, to be paid to them as commission to, and do hereby guarantee unto the parties of the first and second parts the due performance and execution of said contract according to its terms and conditions, and to indemnify and hold harmless the said parties of the first and second parts of and from all cost, liability, loss or damage to them or either of them arising from or on account of said contract, and to the faithful performance of the agreements, contracts, and conditions hereinabove specified to be done and performed by each.

And this conveyance and transfer is made upon the further trust and condition—

That the trustees shall adjust and pay over to the Credit Mobilier of America such portion of the net profits of the work done and material furnished on the first one hundred miles west of the 100th meridian, as was done and performed prior to January 1, 1867.

In witness whereof, the party of the first part, the several parties of the second part, in their own proper persons, have hereunto set their hands and seals, and the party of the third part has caused these presents to be executed by its president, attested by its secretary, with the seal of said company, on the day and year above written.

(Signed) OAKES AMES.
THOS. C. DURANT.
OLIVER AMES.
JOHN B. ALLEY.
SIDNEY DILLON.
CORNELIUS S. BUSHNELL.
H. S. McCOMB.
BENJAMIN E. BATES.

Signed, sealed, and delivered and executed in the presence of—

(Signed) CLARK BELL.

THE CREDIT MOBILIER OF AMERICA, *by its President,*

SIDNEY DILLON.

Attest:

BENJ. F. HAM,
Assistant Secretary.

Receipt of dividend of Credit Mobilier.

NEW YORK, , 1868.

Received from the Credit Mobilier of America, certificate No. , for shares of the capital stock of the Union Pacific Railroad Company, and scrip for , of a share, in full payment of dividend, under resolution adopted December 28, 1867.

Receipt to trustees under Ames's contract of dividend paid by them to the stockholders of the Credit Mobilier, December 12, 1867.

Received of Thomas C. Durant, Oliver Ames, John B. Alley, Sidney Dillon, Cornelius S. Bushnell, Henry S. McComb, and Benjamin E. Bates, the sums set opposite our respective names in full of the dividends declared December 12, 1867, under and pursuant to the foregoing contracts, and payable on the 3d day of January, 1868, and we do hereby severally, in consideration of the amount so received by us, consent to and approve of the foregoing contracts, and agree severally to be bound by and conform to all the terms and conditions of said agreement, and we do hereby release the said Thomas C. Durant, Oliver Ames, and their associates, from all liability, personally or otherwise, by reason of their acts as parties to said foregoing triplicate agreement.

Receipt, &c., January 3, 1868.

Received of Thomas C. Durant, Oliver Ames, John B. Alley, Sidney Dillon, Cornelius S. Bushnell, Henry S. McComb, and Benjamin E. Bates, the sums set opposite our respective names in full of the dividend declared January 3, 1868, under and pursuant to the foregoing contracts, and payable the 3d day of January, 1868, and we do hereby severally, in consideration of the amounts so received by us, consent to and approve of the foregoing contracts, and agree severally to be bound by and conform to all the terms and conditions of said agreement, and we do hereby release the said Thomas C. Durant, Oliver Ames, and their associates, from all liability, personally or otherwise, by reason of their acts as parties to said foregoing triplicate agreement.

Receipt, &c., June 17, 1868.

Received of Thomas C. Durant, Oliver Ames, John Duff, Sidney Dillon, Cornelius S. Bushnell, Henry S. McComb, and Benjamin E. Bates, the sums set opposite our respective names in full of the dividends declared June 17, 1868, under and pursuant to the foregoing contract, and payable on the 17th day of June, 1868, and we do hereby severally, and in consideration of the amount so received by us, consent to and approve of the foregoing contract, and agree severally to be bound by and conform to all the terms and conditions of said agreement, and we do hereby release the said Thomas C. Durant, Oliver Ames, and their associates, from all liability, personal or otherwise, by reason of their acts as parties to said foregoing triplicate agreement.

Receipt, &c., July 3, 1868.

Received of Thomas C. Durant, Oliver Ames, John Duff, Sidney Dillon, Cornelius S. Bushnell, Henry S. McComb, and Benjamin E. Bates, the sums set opposite our respective names in full of the allotment declared July 3, 1868, under and pursuant to the foregoing contract, and payable on the 3d day of July, 1868, and we do severally, in consideration of the amount so received by us, consent to and approve of the foregoing contract, and agree severally to be bound by and conform to all the terms and conditions of said agreement, and we do hereby release the said Thomas C. Durant, Oliver Ames, and their associates, from all liability, personal or otherwise, by reason of their acts as parties to said foregoing agreement, or either of them, and we agree to pay such ratable sums as said trustees may call for, not exceeding the amounts so received, to enable them to complete the construction contract.

LIST OF STOCKHOLDERS, CREDIT MOBILIER OF AMERICA, FEBRUARY 20, 1868.

Names.	Stock.	Names.	Stock.
Oliver W. Barnes	15	J. B. Johnson	200
Thomas C. Durant	4,658	E. H. Baker, jr	50
George F. Train	175	H. C. McComb	1,250
L. E. French	20	Paul Pohl, jr	6
C. A. Lambard	150	J. W. Grimes	380
Sidney Dillon	1,005	G. Opdyke	712
W. T. Glidden	625	J. Bardwell	730
J. M. S. Williams	620	J. Bardwell, trustee	300
R. G. Hazard	1,680	C. C. Waite	80

Names.	Stock.	Names.	Stock.
O. S. Chapman	412	B. D. Stewart	5
Oliver Ames	4,680	H. C. Crane	128
C. S. Bushnell	510	R. Hazard	300
W. H. Macy	300	John L. King	80
J. M. Scranton	5	Fourth National Bank	750
G. G. Gray	1,300	A. A. Low	100
J. Nickerson	380	J. B. Pigot	150
Ben. Holladay	750	Thomas Nickerson	150
B. E. Bates	500	H. Sanford	125
F. Nickerson	250	H. Trowbridge	75
J. B. Alley	290	E. H. Trowbridge	50
I. P. Hazard	380	W. F. Day, Cashier, in Tr	100
Samuel Hooper & Co	750	W. A. Cummings	100
H. Gilbert	185	R. E. Robbins	300
H. I. Gilbert	137	T. W. Andrews	100
C. P. McCormick	945	S. H. Fessenden	50
David Jones	380	N. Peck	100
Oakes Ames	1,955	P. B. Foster	50
E. Atkins	622	Elizabeth Hazard	34
E. H. Baker	623	Elizabeth Hazard, Tr	13
Mary P. Hazard	10	Anna Hazard	20
Lydia Torrey	11	B. M. Boyer	75
Anna Horner	1	C. H. Nielson	100
Sophia Vernon	1	J. Hedden	100
H. Hotchkiss	150	F. Skinner & Co	250
W. D. Bristol	50	Thomas M. Stetson	30
S. M. Beard	100	H. Blood	7
E. Beard	100	A. G. Lathrop	10
G. Bradford	100	H. W. Gray	10
LeGrande Lockwood	500	J. Richardson	50
J. R. Duff	80	Oakes Ames, trustee	250
J. M. Davies	500	H. C. Crane, trustee	180
R. G. S. McNeil	5	W. H. Newbold, Son & Aertsen	400
E. C. Morey	10	H. A. Robins	100
Jno. Smith	405	J. Gardner, trustee	625
A. Hobart, jr	25	F. Skinner, trustee	250
I. Thatcher	92	W. B. Stevens, trustee	50

WASHINGTON, D. C., *Thursday, December* 19, 1872.

Committee met at 10 a. m.; all the members present.

H. S. McCOMB recalled for cross-examination.

By Mr. ALLEY:

Question. You stated in your testimony the other day that I ruled the corporation with autocratic power, or refused to allow you to see the books; that whatever I said or did was done, &c. Then you say, in another part of your testimony, that while Mr. Alley was nominally at the head, he followed generally anything that Mr. Ames positively directed him to do, and that he would not do much he did not assent to. Both of these statements cannot be true; which one of them is true?

WITNESS. Put your questions separately, and I will answer them.

Q. My question is, which statement is true?

WITNESS. Read the first statement and ask me, and I will answer fully in regard to it.

Q. I will ask you if you mean to say that I have refused to let you see the books?—Answer. I do most emphatically, not only once, but a number of times.

Q. When?—A. A number of times since you have been on the executive committee of the Credit Mobilier.

Q. And you say that you have not had the opportunity to see them?—A. Not with your consent.

Q. Nor in my presence?—A. Yes; I have seen them in your presence, but not with your consent.

Q. You say that I have ruled the whole corporation with autocratic power?—A. I did, and I repeat it.

Q. And you say you saw the books in my presence, but not with my consent?—A. I do; I saw them in your presence once or twice without your consent or your knowledge; at least I did not know that you saw me examining them.

Q. But in my presence?—A. You were in the room.

Q. How recently did I refuse to allow you to see them?—A. Ever since you came into the Credit Mobilier.

Q. How recently?—A. I have not asked you, probably, within three years. Do you want to know why?

Q. Not particularly. You say in your testimony that when you heard this conversation between Mr. Brooks and myself there was a distinct agreement and understanding that he should control the democratic side of the House?—A. I say this, and I want you to note what I say; I say that you and Mr. Brooks, in my presence on several occasions, were arranging that you should give him stock, and that he should give you service. I say that you spoke to him about his demand for stock. I say that he spoke to me about his pleading with you to give it; and I say that in this conversation I heard Mr. Brooks remark in substance that he could compensate the company fully for all the favor done in giving him this stock at par, and you dare not deny it. I say further that after that thing was done you spoke contemptuously of him. You said you had given it to him, and that you were compelled to; that is what I say.

Q. That is not answering my question.—A. It is answering your question fully.

Q. I ask you if, in that conversation, you mean to say that I required Mr. Brooks, or that Mr. Brooks agreed, to control the democratic side of the House?—A. Don't you put words into my mouth. The expression I stated I heard him use in this conversation was, that he would take care of the democratic side of the House.

Q. He being in Congress?—A. Yes; and a Government director at the same time, and the owner of one hundred shares of the Credit Mobilier stock besides this, which his son-in-law held at the time, although a Government director.

Q. You are sure of that?—A. Yes, sir; I am sure of that.

Q. He was a member of Congress at the same time?—A. Yes, sir; a member of Congress and a Government director, and I am sure he was a very pliant tool, and that you know very well.

Q. How long has he been a member of Congress?—A. I can tell you that by reference to the record.

Q. Do you know about the time?—A. I think he has been in Congress all of six or seven years; I am very sure that he was a member of Congress then, and a Government director besides.

Q. You think he has been a member of Congress six or seven years?—A. Yes, sir; dating from now back.

Q. And that he was a member of Congress at the time you allude to?—A. I say that is my belief.

Q. And the condition was, that he was to take care of the democratic side of the House?—A. That he was to take care of the democratic side of the House.

Q. Do you remember whether Mr. Brooks was elected to the Fortieth

Congress?—A. No, I do not. I do not keep the run of Congress. I am telling you what I believe is true.

Q. You are sure he was a member of Congress at this time?—A. Yes; I feel sure of that, so far as I know anything. Let me state myself clearly; my recollection is that Mr. Brooks has been in Congress ever since he has been connected with the Union Pacific Railroad; that is my recollection and belief; do you doubt it?

Q. I am not on the stand. You have no recollection about Mr. Brooks not being a member of Congress during this period?—A. Without referring to some record, I have no recollection of Mr. Brooks not being a member of Congress during this period. I do not know when he entered Congress, or anything further than I have said.

Q. You do not remember whether he was a candidate for the Fortieth Congress and was defeated, do you?—A. I do not recollect that. I do not know whether that was so or not.

Q. Now, I would like to know about the time that conversation took place?—A. These conversations, some of them——

Q. I want to know in regard to this particular conversation.—A. I cannot give you the date of this particular conversation; there were a great many of them.

Q. Cannot you state generally about the time?—A. I think in January, February, or March, 1868.

Q. You are sure of that?—A. I am sure of one of these months; I cannot give you the exact date; I cannot answer you as to precisely the day; but I have a memorandum which, after I have consulted, will enable me to answer you.

Q. Then it is your impression that the conversation occurred within the months you have named?—A. My impression is, that it was within the months of January, February, and March; and that the conversation occurred two or three times.

Q. And you know that Mr. Brooks was a member of Congress at that time?—A. I did not say that; I say that Mr. Brooks was a Government director at the time I saw you making arrangements about giving him stock, or that he was about becoming a Government director.

Q. Then he was not a Government director, and was not a member of Congress?—A. He was a member of Congress during some of the time I heard these conversations.

Q. Was he a member of Congress at the time I made arrangements to give him this stock?—A. I cannot give you the exact dates.

Q. You were quite sure a while ago that it was in January, February, or March?—A. I am quite sure that I heard these conversations in each of these months, and in the fall of 1867; I should say in November.

Q. You are willing to swear that these conversations took place, then, between the first of November, 1867, and the first of May, 1868, not confining you to any brief period?—A. I did not expect to be questioned in reference to this matter, and I shall have to refer to memoranda I have at home; I had no thought the matter of Mr. Brooks was what I was to be examined on.

Q. I merely want to ask you whether it was within the months referred to?—A. I cannot answer that now until I refer to memoranda which will show the exact facts. My recollection is, that in the latter part of 1869 or early part of 1868, Mr. Brooks took one hundred shares of Credit Mobilier stock and had it transferred to Charles H. Neilson, his son-in-law. I saw Mr. Durant pay him $6,000 in dividends or in excess of dividends, and at another time $8,000. I have, as I said, memoranda in regard to another circumstance by which I can fix the time when Mr. Alley and Mr. Brooks had the conversations referred to with regard to the fifty shares of stock, and I heard Mr. Brooks say in that connection, distinctly, that he would take care of the democratic side of the House. I noted it down at the time. I will tell you what led me to take an especial interest in these conversations between Mr. Alley and Mr. Brooks. While the negotiations were in progress Mr. Alley expressed great disregard and contempt for Mr. Brooks, and Mr. Brooks was about as free in his expressions of friendly regard for Mr. Alley. They both appeared separately to have about the same views of each other, but together they hobnobbed in regard to this stock, and it disgusted me with them both. The Union Pacific Railroad occupied three rooms in a building at the corner of Cedar and Nassau streets. The corner room on Cedar street was occupied by Mr. Durant. [Witness here explained in detail the relative location of each of the rooms.] There was a table in the second room, not so long as this, at which I was writing, when Mr. Alley and Mr. Brooks took seats at the opposite end of the table and discussed Credit Mobilier stock. Mr. Brooks was imploring Mr. Alley to give these shares to him, urging that he had rendered services which he thought were worthy of return. Mr. Alley thought it was a pretty good thing, and did not want to let it go. He wanted a finger in it himself, I imagine. They had several interviews, and I heard the conversations take place to which I have referred, when Mr. Alley awarded the stock, and said, "I guess we will have to let him have it." Mr. Brooks made the remark, distinctly, that he would take care of the democratic side of the House.

Q. Then, when these arrangements were made there was no significance in the remark unless he was a member of Congress?—A. Or expected to be.

Q. But you are not sure whether he was a member of Congress?—A. I say that is my recollection.

Q. Would there be any significance unless he was a member of Congress?—A. I cannot answer like that. He may have regarded it as for past services, or he may have taken care of the democrats outside of the House as well as in.

Q. Does your recollection confirm your remark, now, that he was a member of Congress?—A. My recollection confirms that, most emphatically, the remarks he made to you and the reply made by you was, "Well, I guess we will have to let him have it." But I cannot now give the date.

Q. You stated a moment ago, and were entirely certain, it was in January, February, or March, 1868?—A. I did not say that remark was made within these months. I said to you that you had conversations with him in these months.

By the CHAIRMAN:

Q. What is your best recollection as to when that remark was made?—A. My recollection is now that it was in the fall of 1867 or in 1868, running from January to July, 1868. I think it was certainly within those months. Mr. Brooks was very frequently in the office of the Union Pacific Railroad.

Q. Is not your recollection any narrower than that?—A. I would not like at this day to be positive as to the date of a conversation which occurred four or five years ago. I have data, as I have stated, that I can refer to which will fix it absolutely.

Q. If your recollection does not narrow it within smaller time than that, you can say so.—A. I can fix no month from recollection. I can fix very nearly the precise month from the data to which I have referred. There are circumstances connected with it which will refresh my recollection as to the date.

By Mr. ALLEY:

Q. You are, however, I understand you to say, ready to state most postitively, and almost certainly, that it was between the month of November, 1867, and the month of May, 1868?—A. I will say from July to July; from July, 1867, to about the same month, 1868.

Q. You are willing to say you are positive that it was within that limit?—A. I will tell you what will refresh my memory, so you may see there is nothing about it to conceal. My recollection is that this conversation took place and this promise was given to Mr. Brooks during the time Mr. Durant was in Europe, and he was in Europe two or three months. I can fix that time by memoranda I have. I do not know how long he was away, but I can ascertain that fact, and also ascertain whether Mr. Brooks was a member of Congress at the time or not.

Q. You say that a portion of that stock—thirty-two shares—came from Mr. Ames?—A. I said that Mr. Ames told me they took thirty-two of his shares to make up Mr. Brooks's complement. I did not say that any of it came from him.

Q. You say that Mr. Alley finally consented to give him fifty shares of Credit Mobilier stock, and that it was transferred to Mr. Brooks or his son-in-law, Neilson. When was that given and when was it transferred?—A. I have said that the agreement was made while Mr. Durant was in Europe. Mr. Alley kept from me, so far as he could, these records. To use a figurative expression, the records of the Credit Mobilier were sealed to me. Anything I got from these records I never got with his knowledge that I had obtained it, so that I did not have any opportunity to look and see when the transfer was made. I would like to say to the committee that bringing here the cash-books and ledger and all the Credit Mobilier books and laying them down on this table would enable me to answer a great many questions that I could not answer now.

Q. Then you cannot state the date of the transaction?—A. Not being an officer of the Credit Mobilier and not being present when the certificate was transferred, I cannot say as to the date.

Q. Can you not say whether the certificate was given to Mr. Brooks or Mr. Neilson?—A. My impression is that Mr. Brooks was, undoubtedly, too smart to take it in his own name.

Q. Yet you say here that I gave it to Mr. Brooks?—A. If I saw your pocket-book given into another person's hands I should still say it was your pocket-book.

Q. But you do not know whether it was given to Mr. Brooks or to Mr. Neilson?—A. You awarded it to James Brooks; whom you transferred it to I do not know.

Q. You have sworn here that this was in the spring of 1868; you had no hesitation then?—A. That was my recollection.

Q. Your answer to the interrogatory as to what Mr. Neilson's full name was, was "Charles H. Neilson, I think; that was along in the fall of 1868."—A. Well, I will be able to fix it by the data I have referred to.

Q. You are then asked, "It was subsequent to the letters you have produced?" and you respond, "O, yes."—A. The circumstance of its occurring during Mr. Durant's absence was not brought to my mind until this morning; I know now that the occurrence took place while

Mr. Durant was in Europe, and, therefore, I shall be able to fix the date by that circumstance.

By the CHAIRMAN:

Q. You understand that the one hundred shares of stock you speak of was really the property of Mr. Brooks?—A. O, yes; everybody about the office understood that.

Q. Did you know anything about the original subscription of that one hundred shares?—A. I would rather Mr. Durant would answer that question; I got my information from him, and I could only answer from hearsay.

Q. You did personally know that Mr. Brooks received dividends?—A. I did personally know of Mr. Brooks receiving dividends, and that Mr. Durant did not think he ought to have them. Mr. Brooks took at one time $6,000 and at another $8,000; that was prior to this fifty shares transaction. I was present in the room and heard Mr. Durant agree to give him the money, or the Credit Mobilier of America stock.

Q. Can you give us about the time?—A. I would rather Mr. Durant would answer that. It was after the organization of the Credit Mobilier, and after that while the Credit Mobilier transactions were being carried on at Nassau and Cedar streets; I did not count the money that was given in these settlements, you know. I only heard Mr. Brooks claim that there was so much money he ought to have. Mr. Durant said he would give it to him, but that he did not think he was entitled to it. I do not mean to say that I saw any money pass or anything of that kind.

Q. In regard to the fifty shares which you heard Mr. Brooks claim from Mr. Alley, did you understand that he claimed that as this 50 per cent. additional stock he would be entitled to as his original subscription?—A. No, because he would be entitled to that under the resolution of the company.

Q. He would then have been entitled to fifty shares?—A. Yes, sir. Allow me to say this: every man who stood on the books of the Credit Mobilier at the time the stock was increased was entitled to his percentage of increase. The increase was in this form: the directors of the Credit Mobilier, the large stockholders, Mr. Ames among the number, agreed to increase the stock to the extent of twelve hundred and fifty thousand dollars; it was two millions before. With that increase they gave a Union Pacific Railroad bond for each ten shares' worth the price of the stock, so that the person could sell his bond and pay for his stock if he chose to. For instance, if I had one hundred shares of Credit Mobilier original stock, that would give me fifty new shares and $5,000 of bonds; I would give my check for $5,000, get the stock, and with it $5,000 Union Pacific Railroad bonds.

Q. You understand that these one hundred shares of stock which stood in the name of Mr. Neilson was really Mr. Brooks's stock?—A. Certainly.

Q. And he would, therefore, be entitled to the blessed privilege of having fifty shares additional stock and the bond; do you know whether he ever did have that fifty shares?—A. I don't know that he ever did in his own name.

Q. Do you know whether the one hundred shares which stood in the name of Neilson ever received its fifty shares, to which it was entitled?—A. I do not.

Q. Do you know that these fifty shares which you say Mr. Brooks subsequently received was not the fifty shares he was entitled to by this arrangement?—A. I do not say anything of that kind at all. I only know this, that if he had a right to it he had no occasion to beg Mr. Alley to let him have it. He could have got it by demanding it without putting himself under obligations to anybody.

By Mr. ALLEY:

Q. You state that Mr. Brooks was at that time either a director or said he would have himself made a Government director. Now, if he was Government director at that time, what was the necessity of making himself so?—A. That Mr. Brooks can better explain than I can.

By Mr. BANKS:

Q. The idea is that you are not sure whether he said he was a Government director or would have himself made one?—A. Yes, sir; I know there was a good deal of trouble at that time as to who should be appointed. Mr. Ames wrote me a letter wanting to have a certain gentleman appointed. I wanted to have Senator Bayard appointed.

By Mr. McCRARY:

Q. Who is the Mr. Durant of whom you speak?—A. Thomas C. Durant, who was president of the Credit Mobilier, and was displaced by these people.

Q. Where is he now?—A. In New York, I think. Mr. Durant to my knowledge had taken proceedings or was about taking proceedings to make Mr. Brooks repay for those fifty shares of stock. I saw the papers as prepared, in which Mr. Brooks is charged with receiving fifty shares without consideration. I saw the papers in Mr. Durant's office as prepared by Mr. Tracy, his counsel. Mr. Durant told me he had taken the papers back, and included in them Mr. Ames, with his three hundred and odd shares, in the same bill.

(The witness subsequently presented to the committee the following letter, referred to in his testimony:)

WASHINGTON, *January* 14, 1868.

MY DEAR SIR: I received this evening your letter of this date informing me that Mr. Ames, of Massachusetts, had one or two thousand dollars of stock in the Credit Mobilier for me. My son, in a letter which I received this morning, informed me of your short conversation with him, and that it was to your friendly feeling I was indebted for the subscription to what you tell me is "a good thing." I am, however, utterly in the dark as to the nature and objects of this corporation, and you will oblige me if you will give my son as much information as you have in relation to them.

I do not know Mr. Ames personally, and must wait, of course, till he addresses me on the subject. I take it for granted that the corporation has no application to make to Congress on which I shall be called upon to act officially, as I could not consistently with my views of duty vote upon a question in which I had a pecuniary interest. Whether I become the owner of this stock or not, I am obliged to you for your intention to benefit me. As I must, of course, pay for any stock I get, please let my son have full information as to its prospective value.

Your communication I consider, as you have indicated, confidential, except as to him, and he and I are almost one person.

Yours, very truly,

J. A. BAYARD.

H. S. McCOMB, Esq.

WASHINGTON, D. C., *December* 19, 1872.

JOHN B. ALLEY, having been duly sworn, made the following statement:

I wish to say first with regard to Mr. McComb's statement about my agreeing to give Mr. Brooks fifty shares of the Credit Mobilier stock at his intercession, or as he now modifies it to Mr. Neilson, which is the same thing. I never had any conversation whatever of the kind referred to by Mr. McComb. I never gave nor sold a share of stock in the Credit Mobilier to Mr. Brooks, or to any other member of Congress. I never had any negotiations, or understanding, or talk with him or any other member of Congress, with a view to give him or sell him one single share or any number of shares of the stock of the Credit Mobilier. I do not know how I can better or more fully answer than by saying that neither directly nor indirectly, in any way, shape, or manner did I ever propose to give, or sell, or negotiate for, or have any understanding about, directly or indirectly, with Mr. Brooks or Mr. Neilson, by or through him or them, or any other party or person whatever. As to Mr. Neilson, I do not know him. I never saw him in my life, and never had any conversation with anybody from him or through him, directly or indirectly. There could not be a more thorough and entire fabrication from beginning to end than the statement of Mr. McComb.

By the CHAIRMAN:

Question. Right here, Mr. Alley, let me ask you in regard to the one hundred shares of Credit Mobilier stock, said to stand in the name of Mr. Neilson on the books of the Credit Mobilier; do you know anything in reference to Mr. Brooks having any interest in that one hundred shares of stock?—Answer. No, sir.

Q. Have you any information upon that subject?—A. None; except what I have obtained since this investigation came up. I talked with Mr. Brooks about it, and the only information I have on the subject is from what he told me. It seems that Neilson appears as a stockholder of the Credit Mobilier.

Q. You never had any knowledge or belief that that one hundred shares belonged to Mr. Brooks?—A. No, sir; I never had any reason to suppose that they belonged to Mr. Brooks other than this; when I come to that I will explain what was my understanding.

Q. Suppose you state it right here.—A. It will come in more properly at another point.

Q. So far as Mr. McComb's testimony goes in any way to implicate you, it was wholly about Mr. Brooks; and the committee want to know all you know, and to hear all you want to say upon that subject. Please state all you know in reference to ownership in that company by Mr. Brooks; whether he did or did not own any stock, and whatever passed between him and you upon the subject.—A. I have no knowledge whatever of Mr. Brooks ever owning one share of stock. Since this investigation commenced, and the charges were made, I asked Mr. Brooks what there was in any way, shape, or manner that could have given Mr. McComb any impression of that kind, or that I had anything to do with giving any stock to him or to his son-in-law, Neilson.

Q. We do not ask you what Mr. Brooks says about it. In all of your connection with this company, as an officer or stockholder, have you any knowledge of Mr. Brooks owning any of the stock of the company?—A. I have no knowledge whatever of his ever owning a share of that stock, directly or indirectly; none whatever.

Q. Did you ever have any conversation with him about his becoming an owner of shares?—A. No, sir, never; not a word.

Q. Do you know anything in relation to any of these dealings between Mr. Ames and any of the members of Congress, who have been named, in relation to shares in this stock?—A. I have something that I would like to say in relation to this matter a little further, in regard to Mr. Brooks, in order to show to the committee that from the very circumstances of the case it would be not impossible, but exceedingly improbable, that I should have had anything to do with him in any such confidential relations as this. Mr. McComb has very fully stated here that at that time my relations to Mr. Brooks were of an antagonistic character. I was politically opposed to him, and I was opposed to him in the management of the Union Pacific Railroad Company. His views did not correspond at all with mine. He was in favor of Mr. McComb and his party. I did not feel any confidence in their management. Consequently I stood in such relations to Mr. Brooks that I could not have done anything of that kind with propriety. Then, in addition to that, let me say that so far from wanting him to be a Government director, and giving him fifty shares of stock to induce him to become a Government director, I was opposed to his being appointed to that position, and did all I could to prevent his being appointed. I was in favor of another man, and for the reason solely that I have stated. I think Mr. Brooks is an able man, but he and I did not coincide in our views in regard to the management of the Union Pacific Railroad Company. After Mr. Brooks came in as a Government director and found how things were, he ascertained that my views and statements in regard to this man McComb corresponded with his own, afterward when he had some experience as a member of the board of directors, and he frankly told me so. Subsequent to that time, when he became a stock director, I was in favor of his election as such, and he has had no hesitation since that time in speaking of Mr. McComb about as I have done. It was a matter of notoriety that Mr. McComb's feelings toward me were as adverse as they could be. I have nothing further to say on that point unless the committee wish to ask me further questions.

Q. If you know anything in relation to any matters that have been spoken of here respecting Mr. Ames or any of those members of Congress, any one or all of the transactions referred to, you may state it.—A. I would like to go into the whole history of this Credit Mobilier business.

The chairman stated that that would be outside the sphere of this investigation.

The WITNESS. Then I will just confine myself to a statement of facts bearing upon this particular matter; but I am sorry the committee will not allow me to go into the whole history of the Credit Mobilier. I know that when Mr. Ames went into the Credit Mobilier it was his habit to try to get everybody into it. He came to me at that time. I was then a member of Congress, and as the circumstances in connection with it are rather peculiar, let me go back a little and state that when the bill was passed in 1864, Mr. Ames was on the Pacific Railroad Committee. You will remember that the feeling in the House in favor of a Pacific Railroad was intense, when the effective provisions making it practicable to build the Pacific Railroad became a law. In 1864, you will remember that nearly everybody was in favor of building the road on almost any terms. Mr. Lincoln, President of the United States, with whom I was intimate, said a great deal about it to me. He urged me to go for it. I did not like the provision in the bill about the lands, and said to Mr. Ames that I thought it was too good a grant altogether. Mr. Ames remarked that he thought it was none too good a bill. He said that the committee desired it very much, and everybody was in favor of the Pacific Railroad. He made this remark: "You would not do such a foolish thing as to put your money into it, even as good a bill as it is." I replied, "No, I would not." That bill was passed with the assent, I think, of every member of Congress from New England, and it received almost the unanimous sanction of Congress. Everybody in all parts of the country was in favor of it. Those who procured the passage of this bill thought the railroad under it should be put through. They went to New York and enlisted capitalists to the amount, perhaps, of half a million. After spending that half million it broke down substantially. The gentlemen who had subscribed came to the conclusion that they would rather lose what they had put in than to go further and risk their all. Mr. Ames came to me in August, 1865, and said, "These gentlemen have come on to see me. I have been looking this thing over, and I think it is a practicable scheme, and I want you to go in with me. I am willing to put in a large amount of money." I said to Mr. Ames, "No man nor body of men can build that railroad under that charter, with these provisions in it, with safety," pointing out the provisions in it to which I referred; that it was an utter impossibility; that no sane man would invest money in it, with the provisions to which I referred, which was a requirement in the charter that the books should be kept open until $100,000,000 had been subscribed, and that not a share of the stock should be sold at less than par. I told him that the literal fulfillment of that provision would prevent the road from being built. He replied, "I know that, because no body of men will take that responsibility. It involves the investment of at least $51,000,000, in order to enable the parties to get control of the road. Now, capitalists are generally very timid. At that time I knew that it would be absolutely impossible to get capitalists to invest $51,000,000 in an experiment. I thought everybody regarded it in that light. I conversed with members of Congress about it, and they agreed with me. When Mr. Ames suggested that he wanted me to go in with him, and said he did so because he regarded me as a capitalist, (he was very much mistaken in that,) and said he wanted my influence, my advice, and my assistance, he said, "I tell you that it is a great thing." He put his hand down on my desk in my counting-room. I said, "It is a great thing for the country, and I should be glad if I could, with safety, be associated with you in putting the enterprise through." He observed, "I believe it can be done, and I am going to tell you how. It will be impossible to build it under the provisions of that bill, but you can construct it by a contracting company, to which parties owning stock in the railroad can subscribe a limited amount and be in no danger of losing any more than they have subscribed. Now, my brother and myself are going to take hold of this, and, if you will take hold with us, I believe it can be put through, and there is no danger if it is properly managed." He explained then in regard to building sections of the road, and how it could be done safely by a corporation. He went on, "I am willing to put in with my family a million dollars, and I want you to put in $50,000. I want you to be identified with us. It can be made a safe thing to do and a reasonable amount of profit can be got out of it." His chief argument to me was of a patriotic character. The plan at that time struck me as hardly feasible. I said I did not want to go into it; that it was outside my line of business. He observed, "I want very much your influence, as well as your money. We shall want pecuniary aid, and there is every consideration with me why we want you to go in."

By Mr. NIBLACK:

Q. And did you go in? We desire you to make this general statement as short as you can.—A. I will not say another word on that subject. You will remember that this is a matter of very great importance to a very dear friend of mine, and therefore I desire to state very fully. We went into the Credit Mobilier; I put in $50,000 under Mr. Ames's persuasion; he persuaded a great many of us to go in in the same way; among others, Senator Grimes and Mr. Hooper, a member of the House; that is all I know about members of Congress. Mr. Hooper is a member of Congress now, and it is proper that I should mention his name; he went in at the same time and on the same ground that I did; it never entered his mind, as it did not mine, that there was any corruption in it. After the election of directors of the Credit Mobilier we went to New York and found standing in the name of Thomas C. Durant six hundred and fifty shares of stock which had not been paid for. We called Mr. Durant's attention to it, and asked him what it meant. He said that was for A, B, C. I do not think he mentioned any names to me. Perhaps he did and perhaps he did not. If so, I have forgotten. He said he held them in trust. We told him he must either pay the money for it, or the gentlemen for whom it was held must pay it. He rather declined. We told him that it must be put into different form, then; that it did not stand properly on the books. After considerable talking he transferred it to the company, and it was placed in the name of Mr. Dillon, president of the company, and stood for awhile. This was in the summer of 1867, according to my recollection. It was for sale during that whole time. It was expected, I suppose, that Mr. Durant would fulfill his promise to give it to the men whom he pretended to be carrying it for. They were not ready, as he said, to take it then. So it was carried along. It was very difficult to sell it; there was not much call for it. Mr. Ames had great faith in it, and believed it was a very great thing. When we were put in control and Mr. Durant was turned out, there was a great controversy and a great deal of ill-feeling, and, as you may say, a fight over the whole thing. Mr. Durant and his party said the Credit Mobilier should never have another contract. The Credit Mobilier had built over two hundred miles, and he said they should never have another contract, and they never afterward obtained a contract. While this condition was existing, everybody connected with the road supposed that the Credit Mobilier would keep on as it had begun, as the contracting party to build the road; but Mr. Durant said no. His feelings were enlisted; his pride and everything forbade it. He and his party tried, until there was an election in the fall, to prevent it. We all of us supposed, however, that the final result would be that it would be found for the interest of all the parties concerned to allow the Credit Mobilier to build it. These six hundred and fifty shares of stock still remained for sale. Mr. Ames was trying to sell it to everybody, especially to those who had influence, power, and money. He had a very heavy load on his shoulders. He felt that he had a big enterprise, and he was soliciting men from every quarter to come in. Finally, he told me one day that he believed this stock was going to be worth several dollars for one; that it certainly would if we got a contract to build the whole road. The capital stock of the company was then $3,750,000. If the company undertook to build the road it would be a long time, probably, before they would get enough out of it to make very handsome profits on their capital. One day he said to me he was going to let Henry Wilson have some of this stock, and remarked, "I believe it is a mighty good thing. I have offered him some. His wife, you know, has got some money to invest. Wilson is a good fellow, and I think it will be a nice thing. I have told him that if he or his wife will take a couple of thousand dollars of it, I will guarantee them against loss, if he will give me half the profits." I think he said he would take it back at any time and give him 10 per cent. on his money. A short time afterward Senator Wilson came to me and asked me what

I thought of it. I do not know that I should say particularly that he came to me. We were talking about it, and he asked me what I thought he ought to do. He said Mr. Ames had offered to guarantee it in the way I have stated. I told him he could not afford to lose anything, but that if Mr. Ames had guaranteed it it would be perfectly safe, of course, and I did not see why he should have any hesitation. He replied, "No; I shall take it." I supposed he did. I heard nothing about it for some time, until he came to me and wanted to know what this thing meant about the McComb suit at Philadelphia. He said that somebody had sent him a pamphlet in which there were charges of corruption, bribery, &c., made against Ames by this man McComb. I said to him, "You know who McComb is?" He replied, "Yes." It is not necessary for me to state what was said in regard to him. He had come to the conclusion that if it would be mixed up in a suit of that kind, or if there was to be a shadow or suspicion of any impropriety, he did not wish to remain in the company. I told him I did not see any impropriety in his owning twenty shares of stock, or in his wife owning it. It was a *bona-fide* transaction. It was bought with her own money, as I myself knew, because a sum had been made up by Mr. Ames, myself, and many other friends as a present to Mrs. Wilson, on the occasion of their silver wedding. Afterward I saw Mr. Ames, who told me about what Wilson had done. I told him I did not see any use in his giving it back; still if he chose to give up what honestly belonged to him, it was not for him to object. I remember using this illustration with Mr. Wilson: said I, "You say you have no belief whatever in these charges that Mr. Ames acted improperly in any way." He said no; that he offered him the stock, he knew, only to benefit him, (Wilson.) Then, said I, "Have you not the courage to keep that stock? Would you get frightened and return it to Mr. Ames if a pickpocket should cry 'thief' in order to get it himself?" I think that is the illustration I used. He said, "I do not know but you are right; but I do not want even a breath of suspicion against me. You know that if there is a man who is pure in regard to these things, it is myself. I am as poor as a rat, and always want to be, rather than have even a suspicion that I or my wife have made a thousand dollars out of a transaction wrongfully. What is that to me? I want it all taken back. I do not want to have anything to do with it; not that I have the slightest suspicion that Mr. Ames had any wrong intentions in any shape or manner, for I know he did not."

Q. Please get on as rapidly as possible. As you understood, the money was paid back to Mr. Wilson or Mrs. Wilson?—A. I have understood so since. I never heard any more about it till the charge was made in the newspapers this last fall. Then he told me that it was all paid back, and I suppose it was paid at the time.

By the CHAIRMAN:

Q. How long was Mrs. Wilson the owner of these twenty shares?—A. Some months, I should think. I do not know about that. I do not recollect, for it was a long time ago, and it has passed out of my mind.

Another case was that of Mr. Dawes. Mr. Dawes came to me and said he had been talking with Mr. Ames about the Credit Mobilier. He said that he went to Mr. Ames to buy a bond of $1,000 in one of his Iowa railroads. Mr. Ames had sold several thousand dollars of them, I think, to Governor Washburn. He said that he had been told that I was a director of this Credit Mobilier, and would know all about it; that he had understood that it was a good investment; if it was he would like to invest. Mr. Dawes is a moderately thrifty man, and has talked to me sometimes about his investments, which was very natural, as I was his colleague. When he came to me he said that he went to Mr. Ames to buy this bond; that Mr. Ames had said he had none he could let him have, but that he could give him something better than that, and that he then told him about the Credit Mobilier; that he asked Mr. Ames if he thought it was a good thing, and Mr. Ames replied it was, and that Mr. Alley could tell him all about it; that Mr. Ames had remarked that if he was not entirely satisfied with it he could bring it back and he would give him the money at any time. I told Mr. Dawes that that was perfectly safe, of course. He said he was going to take it, and he did take it. He told me afterward that his neighbor Larned, in Pittsfield, had said to him that the Credit Mobilier belonged to him, and that he was going to have a lawsuit about it, and was going to oust Ames, Alley, and all of us. He said to me, "What does it mean?" I told him it meant nothing. He did not like it at all; did not want to be in a company where there was to be such a suit as that. According to that man's statement there would be a pretty heavy litigation. He went off, and I heard no more about it till this affair came out in the papers. Then Mr. Dawes told me that he at that time gave it back to Mr. Ames, and he was very glad he did so, because of this fuss. I mentioned it to Mr. Ames, who told me that it was so. This was all there was of that case.

Then another colleague of mine, Mr. Boutwell, spoke to me. What he said to me precisely I do not remember. I understood that he agreed to take ten shares of the Credit Mobilier stock, and asked me about it. I told him what I had told Mr. Dawes and Mr. Wilson. He said he thought it was a very good thing. I said I did not think as well of it as Mr. Ames; but as he is very confident, and as he offered to return you your money if you are not satisfied, I should recommend it to you. He does that for everybody, for all his friends, which shows that he has very great faith in it. Mr. Boutwell replied, "Yes, I see he has, and think I shall take ten shares of it." I heard no more about that till this talk in the newspapers, when I asked Mr. Ames in regard to it, and he told me that Mr. Boutwell never had any of the stock; that he never took it; that for some reason, he did not know what, he never had had anything to do with it. There was nothing strange in Mr. Boutwell coming to Mr. Ames and to me to talk about investments in a small way. He is a man of moderate property, and thrifty in his management of it. He is as pure in his personal integrity as an angel in heaven, if you will allow the expression.

Now, in regard to Mr. Scofield. I remember he came one day and told me that Mr. Ames had been talking to him about the Credit Mobilier, and he asked me about it. He had an idea in his mind that there was a personal liability about it. I told him there was, and told him just the situation. At least I think I did when he came to me to talk about it. What the conversation was I do not now recollect particularly. I do not know about his case, only that he told me he was going to take some, or that Mr. Ames had agreed to let him have some of the stock. Whether he took it or not I did not know until this affair came out, when I went to Mr. Ames about it, and he said Mr. Scofield did take some. I believe these are all the cases of members of Congress I know anything about.

Without finishing the examination of this witness, the committee adjourned till January 7, 1873, at 10 a. m.

WASHINGTON, D. C., *January* 7, 1873.

The committee met pursuant to adjournment. All the members present except Mr. Banks.

The chairman stated that he had received a letter from Mr. Banks notifying him that it would be impossible for him to be present for several days.

The following resolution of the House of Representatives was laid before the committee:

FORTY-SECOND CONGRESS, THIRD SESSION.

CONGRESS OF THE UNITED STATES,
In the House of Representatives, January 6, 1873.

On motion of Mr. FRYE,

Resolved, That the committee of this House appointed to investigate charges of corruption in the matter of stock in the Credit Mobilier be, and they are hereby, instructed to continue such investigation without secrecy as to either their past or future proceedings; and that the testimony hitherto taken be made public.

Attest:

E. McPHERSON, *Clerk*.

SCHUYLER COLFAX, Vice-President of the United States, appeared, and, having been duly sworn, made the following statement:

I should like, if I may be permitted, to make a full statement of the whole matter so far as my name is connected with the subject of this investigation, and then to answer any questions which may be asked in the nature of a cross-examination.

Let me remark, in the first place, that what I am about now to read was written immediately after my informal appearance before the committee on the 16th of December last, and it is therefore entirely unaffected by anything that has been published since. I expected then to have been examined immediately after Speaker Blaine.

I may add that Mr. Ames will recollect, when I call to his mind the circumstances of the transaction, that he never paid me a dollar, or the value of a dollar, on any account whatever. I notice in the papers of this morning that Mr. Ames's mind, when he was before the committee as a witness, was unsettled in regard to the payment of dividends. I wish to repeat that I never did receive a dollar, or the value of a dollar, or any amount whatever from him, and I think Mr. Ames will recollect that I did not, when I recall to his mind these circumstances, which would of course impress themselves more on my mind than his, as it was a larger matter to me than to him.

I had expected, after the Speaker had testified, that I would be the next one invited before this committee. But, as this was not done, I asked the committee on December 16 to be allowed to testify, and that my testimony might be made public.

I state explicitly that no one ever gave, or offered to give me, any shares of stock in the Credit Mobilier, or the Union Pacific Railroad. I have never received, nor had tendered to me, any dividends in cash, stock, or bonds, accruing upon any stock in either of said organizations. And neither Mr. Ames, nor any other person connected with either of said organizations, ever asked me to vote for or against any measures affecting the interests of either, directly or remotely, or to use any personal or official influence in their favor.

I desire, however, to state all the circumstances through which probably my name came to be associated with this organization.

Five years ago, about the time of the holiday recess, I was conversing on the floor of the House with Mr. Ames in regard to the Pacific Railroad, in favor of the building of which I had previously made hundreds of public addresses. In the course of this conversation he asked me if I would not like to purchase some stock in the Credit Mobilier. Up to that time I knew nothing of its capital or profits; and I inquired of him as to its objects and the value of its stock.

As near as I can recall this conversation, after the lapse of so many years, I was informed by him that it was a legally incorporated company, composed of the principal stockholders of the Union Pacific Railroad, who were themselves building the road instead of letting it out to contractors, who always expected large profits for their risk and their advances of money for supplies. I told him after his explanation that it looked like a good and safe investment for one of limited means, and that I would be willing to purchase twenty or thirty shares at a fair price if I had the money. But I added frankly that I could not pay for them till two or three months afterward, as my housekeeping expenses in the opening months of the session were much larger than the average. He replied that he would contract to sell me twenty shares at par, if I would in addition agree to pay interest until final payment. I inquired what per cent. it would pay, and he replied that there had been large dividends, but as the road was pushed farther into the interior, the profits might not be so large, though they would be very surely remunerative.

The Union Pacific Railroad had no legislation that I knew of pending before Congress at that time, nor did I suppose there could be any in the future, as the last amendment to their charter authorizing the issue of first-mortgage bonds which should have priority of the Government lien had been enacted in 1864, over three years before this conversation. Inferring that any questions arising under their charter would be judicially settled, and supposing, at any rate, that I had the same right to purchase this stock as to buy stock in a national bank chartered by Congress, or in a manufactory, I told him that I would agree to purchase twenty shares at par and interest, to be paid for as soon as I had the money. Some weeks or months afterward, at the same session, I paid Mr. Ames about $500 in cash on this contract of purchase, being all the money I had; but received no dividend or certificate of stock, in whole or in part. My impression is that he told me that one or two dividends had been earned, but they were not in cash, and were as yet unadjusted. Certainly I did not receive any, and was not offered any in cash, bonds, or stock, then or since. A few weeks or months after this I heard a rumor that unpleasant controversies existed among the largest stockholders, which were certain to involve the organization in prolonged litigation.

The very day I heard this rumor I told Mr. Ames that no profits, present or prospective, could induce me to buy into a lawsuit; that I had never been, during all my life, a plaintiff or a defendant in a court of justice; that I must therefore recede entirely from the transaction between us, as I did not want stock of any kind, on any terms, that would make me a party to litigation. He assented to this, and nothing was said as to the money paid, my anxiety being not to get into a lawsuit. All these things occurred at the same session of Congress, five years ago, which closed in the summer of 1868. The next year, or the year after, Mr. Ames suspended payment, in consequence, as was said, of financial involvements connected with the Pacific Railroad, and his creditors gave him an extension on his liabilities. But, regretting his failure and its cause, I voluntarily told him to dismiss from his mind the small amount of money between us. I suppose, but for this, he would have repaid me the money I had paid him.

I may repeat, therefore, that neither stock nor bonds were given to me, nor offered to be given to me; that I have never received a dollar in bonds, stock, or money as dividends; that I did contract to purchase twenty shares of stock in the company at par and interest, but that, after a partial payment, I withdrew entirely from what I regarded as an uncompleted contract to purchase, from repugnance to being involved in litigation; and that, instead of being enriched by it one thousand or twenty thousand dollars, as has been charged, I am voluntarily out of pocket five hundred dollars, and have been for nearly five years.

By the CHAIRMAN:

Q. I may, perhaps, inquire whether you have any knowledge of ownership of stock in the Credit Mobilier by any member of Congress?—A. No, sir; Mr. Ames did not mention anything to me in regard to the sale of stock to members of Congress. I had made a good many speeches in my own State and many other States in favor of building the Pacific Railroad, and I asked him how the road was progressing, how it was being pushed into the interior, and out of that inquiry grew this conversation in regard to the Credit Mobilier on the part of Mr. Ames, as I inferred. I have no knowledge whatever of the ownership of stock in the Credit Mobilier by members of Congress at all except through the newspapers.

By Mr. MERRICK:

Q. Have you any knowledge of the relations between the Credit Mobilier and the Union Pacific Railroad Company?—A. No, sir; except so far as Mr. Ames and these conversations explained them to me. I had heard of the Credit Mobilier and of the Credit Foncier, as connected with the Union Pacific Railroad. I had known of them because persons had spoken about the Credit Foncier and the Credit Mobilier. I did not know what they were, except that they had some connection with this road. When Mr. Ames spoke to me about it I asked what the objects of the Credit Mobilier were, and, as nearly as I can recollect a conversation that occurred five years ago, he told me it was composed of the principal stockholders of the Union Pacific Railroad Company; that its object was to build the railroad, and I think he said they had received or would receive considerable profits, and perhaps very large profits, for the risk they ran and the advance of money made. At any rate the impression he gave me was that the principal stockholders of the road were themselves building it. The proposition seemed, as he stated it, to be a reasonable one. I did not know then that Mr. McComb was interested in it. I knew that Mr. Alley and Mr. Ames had the reputation of considerable wealth, and that their credit would enable them to purchase iron and other supplies, which I could not purchase without advancing the money. What I understood to be the object of the Credit Mobilier was to build the road within the subsidy proffers of the Government.

Q. Then you understood that the stockholders and officers of the Union Pacific Railroad Company were to contract with themselves as stockholders and contractors to build the road, and derive for themselves the profits under the contract for its construction?—A. Not quite so strong as that. The conversation was not exactly to that length by any means. I am free to say that, as I recollect my impression of the matter in 1865, I considered the project a natural one. If I had had the money to spare I should have put it in myself as one of the original stockholders of the Union Pacific Railroad, having so often urged others publicly to risk their money in its construction. I do not know that Mr. Ames went fully into the organization of the Credit Mobilier. I do not know that he told me what State had authorized its charter. I understood that they were to build this road instead of letting it out to contractors over the country, who would charge proportionate profits for the risks they incurred. I inferred from these statements, as I have said, that it would be a good investment for the reason that the men in it being known as gentlemen of wealth could purchase supplies at less rates than could have been done by others.

Q. Did he say that all the stockholders of the Union Pacific Railroad were stockholders of the Credit Mobilier?—A. He did not say that all of them were. I understood that the principal stockholders were.

Q. Did it occur to you at that time that there was any moral or legal impropriety in the stockholders of a railroad company making a contract with themselves to build the road?—A. I do not like to be called upon to settle moral questions for others. I can say for myself that it did not seem to be morally wrong. My impressions in regard to it were as follows: I had heard of railroads being built and the contractors paid in bonds furnished them at the low figures of 60 or 70 cents on the dollar, which the railroad ultimately had to pay for at par. In this way the roads had to pay 75 or 100 per cent. profit. As these gentlemen had put their money into an enterprise which was regarded by millions of people as an uncertain and dangerous one, they would evidently desire to build the road within the limits of the proffer made by the Government. Otherwise, if it had been let out to contractors and there had been a large deficit at the end, they and the other stockholders of the road would have had to meet it. I do not, however, as I have said, undertake to decide questions of ethics or law as to others, and on matters not within my knowledge. I did not think there was anything morally wrong in agreeing to buy this stock; and my impressions about it, whether right or wrong, were as I have stated.

I wish to say that, if any further testimony should be desired of me, I shall be ready to respond to the invitation of the committee at any time, without the formality of a summons. And I would also ask that Mr. Ames and Mr. McComb, who are both present, should cross-examine me now on any point that occurs to them.

[Both these gentlemen, being invited by the chairman to do so, replied that they had no questions to propound to Mr. Colfax.]

WASHINGTON, D. C., *January* 7, 1873.

Examination of JOHN B. ALLEY resumed:

Before resuming my testimony proper, I wish to make to the committee a very few observations.

I rejoice that these doors are thrown open to the public, and I hope the committee will see their way clear now to allow what I so earnestly plead for at the last meeting—the fullest and freest investigation into all matters having a tendency to throw light upon all questions connected with these charges.

It is hard for men who feel conscious, not only of deserving no censure, but, on the contrary, meriting great praise, to have their names inscribed upon the enduring records of the nation as guilty of purposes which, if true, should consign them to eternal infamy, without having the opportunity to show, in the fullest manner possible, every act and circumstance which, in their judgment, would establish their innocence. If this privilege is accorded, I think Mr. Ames will be able, not only to show his own honest intentions, but, also, that the cry of "Stop thief" was raised by *the thieves themselves*. If allowed to reveal to you the entire history of the Credit Mobilier and its whole connection with the Union Pacific Railroad Company, I shall exhibit, I am sorry to say, a sad and sorrowful record, but one in no way discreditable to that corporation or any of its managers, and which will, I feel certain, leave no impression on the public mind prejudicial to any member of the present House of Representatives, however it may affect others.

I am here not only at your request, but at the earnest solicitation of one of the most eminent lawyers of New England, distinguished as much for his sterling integrity as great capacity. He is the friend of Mr. Ames, and knows everything in connection with the history of the Credit Mobilier and Union Pacific Railroad Company. He said to me, "You know as well as myself all the facts in connection with these corporations, and remember them with more distinctness than any one." "And," said he further, "you and I know Mr. Ames to be a perfectly honest man; therefore I think it is your duty to go to Washington and testify in his behalf." I said I would go, and I feel that if the American people could know all the facts, instead of bestowing upon Oakes Ames one word of censure, they would far sooner erect a monument to his name in grateful recognition of his eminent services.

I came here simply as a witness, having been for several years out of the direction of the Credit Mobilier, and for a long time out of the Union Pacific Railroad Company. I have very little interest in either. I do not hold a single bond of any of their securities, and but a trifling amount of stock. I did not dream of any one charging me, or supposing I had ever bought, or sold, or given a share of Credit Mobilier stock to any member or members of Congress, as I never had bought or sold, negotiated or talked of negotiating, directly or indirectly, or given to or had any conversation with any member of Congress, or with any one else, with a view to selling or giving any stock to any member of Congress.

Imagine my astonishment, coming here as a witness, and finding myself charged with yielding to the entreaty of James Brooks, and consenting to his being given, by Mr. Ames, or the company, or both, fifty shares of stock, without consideration, for his congressional influence.

There seems to be a great mist hanging over the public mind in relation to this corporation called the Credit Mobilier. The honorable Speaker remarked, in his testimony, that everybody knows that the Credit Mobilier built the Union Pacific Railroad. I did not know it; but I *do* know that the fact is otherwise. The Credit Mobilier did not build but two hundred and forty-seven miles of the Union Pacific Railroad, and that was the first two hundred and forty-seven. The last eight hundred miles were built by other contractors, and the Credit Mobilier had nothing to do with it, directly or indirectly, except in guaranteeing a contract. The Credit Mobilier never made a dollar out of the Union Pacific Railroad. The Credit Mobilier has not paid 7 per. cent. on its capital, and its stock is not now, and has not been for a long time, worth sixty cents on the dollar. Its board of directors is now, and has been for five years, composed of men of the highest respectability and character. It has been plundered, swindled, and outraged more than any corporation I have ever heard of. But for the honesty and sense of justice of Oakes Ames, who, with rare magnanimity, (considering the treatment which he had received at that time from some of the largest stockholders,) let the stockholders all into his contract, and not only enabled us to save ourselves from loss, but make something handsome upon our investment.

In order, however, to do it, all had to sign agreements and become personally liable for the whole amount. When some of them found what an immense risk they were taking, they were not so earnest to get into it. This was the only contract in which anything was ever made. All others resulted in loss. The net profit of this enormous contract of $47,000,000, in compensation for its immense risks and prodigious labor, were between eight and nine millions of dollars, provided they sold the securities which they received in pay at their average market value before the first day of January, 1870, which was over seven months after the road was opened. Oakes Ames's individual interest in that contract was between five and six millions. He made less than a million, and he has got no one of his several millions which has cost him one-half of the effort, anxiety, and risk as this one has. He ought and would have made two millions if there had been no plundering, and the road had been well and economically managed in its construction. My interest in that contract was less than half a million. I have sold all the securities I have ever received on account of it, and know what I have made, and my books show $93,456. This was every dollar I ever made in the construction of that road. I have got no money that I earned harder or took more risk for. I aided the road and Mr. Ames nearly the whole time with capital to the amount of three-quarters of a million. But nearly all the losses, occasioned by plundering, cheating, and mismanagement, were borne directly or indirectly by the stockholders of the Credit Mobilier and the Union Pacific Railroad. The Government has not been wronged or cheated in any way that I am aware of. It has got all that it required, and all that was agreed to—a first-class road, thoroughly equipped. The Government has been well treated, thanks to the Ameses and their friends, and has got all that belongs to it. It made a better bargain and got more benefit than any other party or parties. It has the second lien upon the road for the loan of its credit, and the security is good.

I shall now submit my testimony in detail, and I hope without interruption, willing, then, to submit to any cross-examination, however searching, by the committee or any one else. Although some of it may appear irrelevant as I go along, I think you will find, when through, that I could have omitted nothing and given a proper understanding of the case, or said less in justice to Mr. Ames and all those members of Congress who are implicated with him in these charges of corruption and fraud; every fact I shall state and every declaration I shall make will be susceptible of the clearest proofs by documentary evidence and oral testimony as unimpeachable as would be that of John Marshall, were he living and present here to-day. It was found by Mr. Ames and others that the management of the Credit Mobilier and Union Pacific Railroad, both being managed by the same parties, Mr. Thomas C. Durant, (with Mr. McComb, director in the Pacific Railroad Company, as coadjutor and friend,) as president of the Credit Mobilier and vice-president of the Union Pacific Railroad Company, it may be said that he had both completely and entirely under his charge.

Mr. Ames and his friends and associates were greatly dissatisfied with the management, and felt that a change must be effected, or the road could never be completed to his and their satisfaction; Mr

Ames always contending that his sole object was, so far as pecuniary profit was concerned, to make whatever money he should make out of it by operating the road, and to attain this end the interests of the Government and his own were identical, and he was determined that it should be a first-class road, thoroughly equipped, as they had agreed with the Government that it should be. Durant, McComb, and their supporters believed that everything that could be made must be made in the construction of the road, and that whoever depended like Mr. Ames for profitable returns upon his investment in the future earnings of the road was, to use Durant's own expression, "a damned fool." Mr. Ames and his friends feeling that it was indispensably necessary (in fact self-preservation required it at that time) that they should get rid of Durant and company. While not able to turn them out of the direction of the Union Pacific Railroad Company at that time, they had the power to turn Durant and friends out of the Credit Mobilier. They did so, and elected seven directors of the highest character and respectability, three of whom were appointed on the executive committee. Mr. Sidney Dillon was elected president; Mr. Rowland G. Hazard, of Rhode Island, a distinguished and wealthy citizen of that State, and myself, together with the president, constituted the executive committee, upon whom devolved chiefly the administration of the corporation. Immediately upon being installed into office we discovered great irregularities. Enormous amounts of money had been used for purposes which we could not discover, called, I believe, a secret fund. We also found 650 shares of stock standing in the name of Thomas C. Durant, the circumstances of which I have already related. As I have said before, it had been the purpose of all the parties in interest to have built the road under contracts by the Credit Mobilier; but Mr. Durant and his friends declared that the Credit Mobilier should never have another contract of the Union Pacific Railroad Company. He and McComb and their associates in the board of direction in Union Pacific Railroad Company had sufficient influence and power to prevent being carried out the original design of building the road by and through a contracting company called the Credit Mobilier. Through the summer of 1867, from May to August, the two parties finding that nothing but loss would accrue to each under such a state of things, finally agreed that Mr. Oakes Ames could be trusted with a contract to any amount. It was proposed to give Mr. Ames a contract to build 667 miles of road, believing him to be a perfectly honest man, notwithstanding all the dissensions and opposition to him upon other grounds. All were perfectly agreed that he was perfectly honest and could be safely trusted with all their enormous interests. Accordingly it was proposed to him, which proposition he accepted, that he should build 667 miles, for which he should receive in the aggregate the sum of $47,000,000. It was thought by all concerned that it was a happy solution of the difficulty, and we believed no other man in the country who had millions to lose, as Mr. Ames had, could have been induced to assume such an immense responsibility. He took it, however, upon himself with only this condition being attached to it: that it should receive the assent of all the stockholders of the Union Pacific Railroad Company; other than that there were no conditions, and he would make no pledges. In reply to their solicitations he would only say, "I am an honest man; no man shall be cheated; all shall have what justly belongs to them." After the contract was given to him he then said: "I know that this contract in honor and honesty belongs to the stockholders of the Credit Mobilier. I will assign it to seven (7) trustees upon certain condition, and every individual member of that corporation shall be offered the opportunity of taking an interest in that contract, in *pro rata* proportion to his ownership in the stock." This he regarded as nothing but honest and just. In order, however, to obtain an interest in that contract they must all sign certain agreements, and they all became individually liable for the whole amount. That was agreed to by all parties. When we came into the direction of the Credit Mobilier we found, among other matters, that there was charged $41,000 for its charter of franchise, which only cost $1,600. We also found that, in the transfer of settlement of the Hoxie contract, there was charged an immense sum more than should have been, which went into the pocket of somebody to whom it did not belong. Then there were other vast sums claimed to have been spent as secret-service money in Washington. This included sums charged to that account by both the Credit Mobilier and the Union Pacific Railroad Company; how much to each I do not know; which was the only explanation ever obtained respecting this enormous deficiency. McComb, in his testimony before the court in Pennsylvania, says that Mr. Alley denounced Mr. Durant and called him dishonest, and told him (McComb) that he was not fit to be trusted with the funds of the corporation; that a committee was appointed to investigate, audit, and settle his accounts; and that Mr. Alley was the only man upon that committee who was not satisfied with his accounts. Now, this is not true at all. Mr. Oakes Ames, as well as myself, and I think some others, refused with me to sign the report. My recollection is that no one but McComb was entirely satisfied, and Rowland G. Hazard, one of the most eminent citizens of Rhode Island, who was upon the executive committee of the Credit Mobilier with me, brought a suit in the courts of Rhode Island charging Mr. Durant with the embezzlement of very large sums belonging to the Credit Mobilier and Union Pacific Railroad Company, for one or both, I am not certain which, and which he refused to account for. He would only explain that expenditure so far as one individual was concerned, and with him he had quarreled. That man was Thaddeus Stevens. He declared that he had paid him $80,000 in a roundabout way for getting bills through Congress. He refused to reveal the name of any other member. McComb was satisfied with his explanation, but Mr. Ames and myself were not, and I believe all our honest associates were entirely convinced, after that attempt of Fisk, Durant, and McComb to steal the road from us, that they were not only bosom-friends, but partners in a greater or less degree in every wrongful scheme from the inception of the enterprise to their dismissal from the direction. Neither Mr. Ames, Mr. Hazard, nor myself believed a word of the story about Mr. Stevens. We certainly should not have sanctioned it if it had been true, and we were not going by any means to allow it when we believed it false. Every circumstance within our knowledge forbids its belief: our opinion of Mr. Stevens, and the fact that at that time everybody almost of all parties, in Congress and out, were in favor of the bill, which destroyed all necessity or motive to bribe any one. The President, Mr. Lincoln, was ardently in favor of it, and in fact was willing to go for a more favorable bill, and told me that the capitalists of the country, if any such could be found, who would build the road under that bill, would immortalize themselves. Durant and his party finding themselves ousted from the Credit Mobilier corporation, and finding themselves and their friends the owners of only about one-fourth of the stock of the Union Pacific Railroad, resorted to a scheme or trick, in association with Jim Fisk, by which they hoped to wrest from its rightful owners the Union Pacific Railroad, and throw out these men who had invested their millions in it in good faith, without Fisk, Durant, or McComb investing an additional dollar in it, except, perhaps, $140, which Fisk invested. But their machinations and intrigues did not succeed. In order, however, to fully thwart them, we had to raise the enormous sum of $15,000,000 in a single day. Jim Fisk, McComb, and Durant came to grief in this attempt, and the result was Durant, McComb, and friends were put out of the direction. Some of them were finally re-instated upon a compromise, and this contract of Oakes Ames for the benefit of the stockholders of the Credit Mobilier as I have described went into effect. I was one of the trustees, at the earnest solicitation of Mr. Ames, of this contract. I served two or three months, when to the great joy of Durant and McComb, and to my own great relief, I was, with the consent of Mr. Ames, permitted to withdraw. After that I had nothing whatever to do with the construction of the road. During the summer of 1868, Jesse L. Williams, a Government director and an honest man, ever watchful of the interests of the Government, complained bitterly to Mr. Oliver Ames, the president, and others of the board, of the influence of Durant, McComb, and company, and did not feel satisfied with the way in which the road was being built, and pointed out certain defects which should be remedied. Mr. Ames assured him that he desired as much as himself that the Government should get a first-rate road. I asserted the same, and General Dodge, our chief engineer, also, and we three pledged ourselves to him that the interests of the Government should be protected, so far as in our power, and they should have a first-class road. That pledge, I think, Mr. Williams will testify was fully redeemed so far as we three were concerned. We were all four then in the West on the line of the road. On our return home we found that the executive committee had passed resolutions conferring full authority to act upon the line of the road upon Mr. Durant, the vice-president, amenable only to the executive committee, chiefly composed of his friends, practically ignoring the president and chief engineer; Mr. Oliver Ames, always honest and true, yet often yielding reluctantly to these men, as I thought, because of the excessive amiability of his nature. I denounced to Mr. Oakes Ames this action of the executive committee, and predicted the ruin of the enterprise if the management was to be given to such men as Durant and McComb; that the Government would be wronged and cheated, and that such men as himself would be plundered. Mr. Ames concurred with me. I need only add that the passage of that resolution did nearly bankrupt the company. In my disgust I wrote to Mr. Oliver Ames, the president, my view of the situation and his duty in the premises. This letter was as follows, and this is the original draught:

BOSTON, *July* 25, 1868.

DEAR SIR: I have been reflecting upon the resolution passed by the executive committee, and the action and evident purpose of some of our directors, and I must say that, dissatisfied and uneasy as you and others know I have been ever since I have been engaged with the road, I have never known anything in the action of these men that has alarmed me more than their present course. If our associates had been all of them like you and your brother, disposed and desirous to do right and doing justice to the stockholders and the Government, we should not now have been troubled with the injunctions and rascalities which, I fear, may injure us seriously.

You have acquiesced in and submitted to wrong; and to the view of outsiders even appeared to countenance and encourage it, until there is great danger, I think, of compromising your character by any longer acquiescing in their machinations and wrongdoing. I feel that we have a trust confided to us which, as honorable men, we are bound to administer in the interests of the stockholders, the Government, and the American people. The Government has been liberal and generous, and is entitled to protection in all its rights. We can afford and ought to give them a first-class road. I know that you are as strongly in favor of that as I am, and that you have always been.

We made strong pledges, and so did our chief engineer, General Dodge, to Mr. Williams, that no stone should be left unturned to accomplish that end, and by no vote or act of ours should anything be countenanced looking to any different result. Now, what do we find upon our return? The executive committee practically ignoring the board of directors, and no meeting of the board for four months; the chief engineer subordinate and insulted because he is fearless and honest and wishes to protect the rights of all; your authority very much impaired and crippled—in fact almost destroyed for the same reason. I have for many months struggled and battled for the right in the interest of the road and the rights of the Government conscientiously and industriously. I have countenanced measures and acquiesced in proceedings that I did not always like for the sake of peace. Yet notwithstanding, I have made myself odious and hated, almost beyond endurance, because I have stood up boldly and persistently for what I knew was right. For this they attempted to throw me out of the direction last spring, and almost succeeded, and at the next election will probably do so. But if we are to get along in this way I shall be glad to retire now. I feel that you and I both have endeavored to do right and countenance no wrong; but just as sure as we acquiesce and help these people to carry out their designs we shall be compromised and disgraced by their actions, as I fear we are already, to some extent. Now, I do not feel that there is value enough in the money we get to induce me to do what my judgment and conscience condemn. Now, Mr. Ames, I advise you, as a friend, and I earnestly implore you by every consideration of justice and right, and in behalf of your own honor and that of ourselves, to resist, by all the power which you possess, these encroachments upon your rights and ours. For one, I will stand by you and defend you with all the ability which God has given me. If you will, however, allow yourself to be subordinated by such men and the board of directors ignored, the rights of the stockholders trifled with, and our pledges to a beneficent Government trampled upon, then I must enter my solemn protest; and if such a state of things must continue, then let me retire from the contest.

Yours, truly,

JOHN B. ALLEY.

Hon. OLIVER AMES,
President of the Union Pacific Railroad Company.

We found six hundred and fifty shares of stock, as I have before mentioned, standing in the treasury unsold. Mr. Ames, supposing that it would finally be determined that the road should be built, as originally contemplated, by a contract with the Credit Mobilier, he believed that the stock of that company would be very valuable, and he urged his acquaintances to buy who had capital, power, or influence, as he had done from the time of his first connection with the enterprise. Probably not a week elapsed at any time through the whole period until every dollar of the stock was taken that he did not solicit his friends to purchase some of that stock.

After the matter was compromised and Mr. Ames had made the proposition to offer an interest in that contract to everybody who would take it, who owned stock in the Credit Mobilier Company, the stock of that company being thus made the basis by Mr. Ames of the right to an interest in his contract, immediately rose in value, and, from being a drug in the market at $100 per share, became of marketable value at $160 up to $200 almost immediately. Mr. Ames found himself somewhat embarrassed from having promised a great deal more stock than the company could issue. He and Mr. Durant had promised some seventy or eighty thousand dollars of stock, as they alleged, each claiming a right to sell, as had been their custom, and urging others to buy. It was finally agreed that this stock should be divided between Mr. Durant and Mr. Ames, Mr. Durant to have four hundred shares, I think, and Mr. Ames two hundred and fifty shares, I believe, and sold to them at par, although the stock was then worth at least $160, to fulfill engagements which they had previously made. It was upon this ground, and this only, the officers felt justified in disposing of stock at $100 when it was of far greater value. But the leading stockholders of the company, after hearing a statement of the facts, concluded that it was no more than justice required. Mr. McComb claimed that he had sold quite an amount, and that he was as much entitled to have his bargains recognized and confirmed as Mr. Durant or Mr. Ames. On the other hand, it was contended that Mr. McComb had no right whatever to promise any stock; that he had never interested himself in its sale, and I think the company had also no confidence in his representations, and they declined to issue to him any stock. But, upon his positively asserting to Mr. Ames that he had engaged some of the stock to several gentlemen, Mr. Bayard, of Delaware, Mr. Fowler, of Tennessee, and some other gentlemen, I have forgotten whom, Mr. Ames told him that he would do the best he could, and if possible he would make good some of these engagements. Finally, after this was agreed upon, the President refused to issue any of the stock to anybody unless he could be protected by the written consent and request of quite a large number of the largest stockholders. A large number of gentlemen, including Mr. McComb, joined in a written request to Mr. Dillon to issue this stock to Messrs. Durant and Ames, as had been agreed upon. Some time afterward, I think only a few days, Mr. McComb called the executive committee together and stated that he had a claim against the company for 250 shares of stock. He stated what the grounds of his claims were, and then asked the executive committee what they thought of his claim. The president told him that in his judgment it was so base and so fraudulent that, in presenting it, he had shown himself to be a scoundrel unworthy to associate with gentlemen, and he would not give such a bogus claim the slightest consideration. A few days afterward Mr. McComb threatened to bring a suit against the company if the claim was not allowed. He proposed, however, to refer it, and the president of the company said he should always be willing to refer a case rather than have a lawsuit where he thought there was the least semblance of a claim in justice and right; but where it was nothing but bogus and an attempt at blackmailing the company, he should never have his consent to refer such an infamous claim. Mr. McComb persisted in his demand, and finally commenced a suit in which he claimed that the company owed him 250 shares of stock, with all its accretions and dividends, and this stock which had been awarded Mr. Ames belonged to him, and in his bill he set forth that this stock was taken from him and distributed to members of Congress, without consideration, for corrupt and fraudulent purposes.

That bill was answered by the officers of the Credit Mobilier, by Mr. Oakes Ames, by several of the stockholders, and every statement which he made was flatly and fully contradicted upon these points. Then finding Mr. Ames and the company determined not to be black-mailed, he then resorted to threats of a little different character. He said that he had letters from Mr. Ames which he would expose, in which Mr. Ames stated that he had given this stock to certain members of Congress, the names of whom Mr. Ames had given in these letters, as the recipients of that stock which he had given them for nothing. Those letters would be produced, and Mr. Ames would be forever disgraced if he did not settle that suit. His counsel, Judge Black, called upon me, and had several conversations upon the subject, in which he urged with great force the necessity of Mr. Ames compromising this suit, and said that I, as the friend of Mr. Ames, ought to do everything in my power to save him from such terrible disgrace as the publication of these letters would occasion. I told him I did not believe a word of it, and I would not believe anything that McComb should state. I knew of my own knowledge that no stock had been given away to anybody. That much was false I knew. If he would say that he had seen the letters, and they were such as he described, I should feel that it might be possible that it was partially true; still it was so contrary to everything that I knew of Mr. Ames that I could not and I did not believe a word of it. Judge Black told me that although he could not say he had seen the letters, yet he had no doubt of it. I told the judge that never, with my consent, should that suit be compromised and the Credit Mobilier, as a corporation, made to suffer. While I had no belief whatever that Mr. Ames had done or would do any wrong in that direction, yet if he had, then upon himself must rest the consequences. I certainly should not shield him in any such business as that. Again he came to me and re-assured me that the letters were as he described. I told him that it was a black-mailing affair, and that the claim itself had no foundation in law, equity, or justice, and he knew it as well as I did; and he knew he had for his client an infamous scoundrel; and no man could know Oakes Ames as he did without feeling that he was a perfectly honest man. "Well," said he, "if you do not convey to Mr. Ames what I say, you will be doing great injustice to him." I told the president of the company; I told my colleague upon the executive committee, Mr. Hazard, what Judge Black said. They agreed with me that it was a story impossible to believe of Mr. Ames; that it was an attempt to black-mail the company and Mr. Ames, in which Judge Black was lending his aid, and under no circumstances would they consent to reference or compromise. When Mr. Ames was told what they said, he said to me and the executive committee that he had written no such letters; that it was impossible he could have written such letters, for the reason that if he had there would not have been a word of truth in them; that he had never given a member of Congress a share of stock; that he had never sold a share of stock to any member of Congress with any hope, expectation, or idea that he would thereby procure his congressional influence; and no man in Congress would say of him that they ever dreamed of such a thing. He utterly refused to do anything about it. Judge Black still insisted that McComb had these letters, and the names of the parties he said were inserted by Ames in the letters, and he understood that the names of Colfax, Boutwell, and Wilson were among them, also Mr. Garfield. He should be very sorry, he said, to expose Mr. Garfield, who was a particular friend of his. He said it would be found that these gentlemen and several others were stockholders who were also members of Congress. I told him very likely. I know there were some members of Congress who were small stockholders, but who they were I did not know, as I did not deem it important enough to inquire. He asked me if I did not think it wrong for Congressmen to own stock in our company. I told him, under ordinary circumstances, no worse than owning bank-stock. He said it was very wrong, in his estimation, for Congressmen to own bank-stock. He would not own it if he were a member of Congress. I saw Mr. Ames again and reported what Judge Black said; he then said to me, "Don't allow the judge or McComb to black-mail your company by any such threats, as I have never done anything wrong, and I know I have nothing to fear from any exposure of any transactions of mine in regard to this or any other company."

In justice to Judge Black, I ought to say that I do not indorse this opinion of Judge Black being a black-mailer. I told them, as I told the judge, I thought his judgment was entirely blinded by his prejudice against Ames, and that his client had grossly deceived him as to the facts.

Mr. Ames speaks in his letters to McComb rather complainingly of me, and said that I was the only person opposed to the distribution of profits. That was true; he referred to the dividends upon the contract. I was opposed to any such distribution; I believed that no profits or dividends should be given stockholders until the road was completed; I think all the honest stockholders would say now, as Mr. Ames frankly says in his testimony, that I was right and they were wrong; this, I believe, was the only instance in which Mr. Ames and I differed in our views of what was our duty to the stockholders and the Government.

These letters were written, not as they appear to be on the face of them, by a confiding friend, but to one whom he knew was not to be trusted. McComb and his party were continually scolding about Mr. Ames's determination to place all the power by distribution of stock and otherwise into the hands of his particular friends, and especially Massachusetts folks. Mr. Ames always disclaimed any such purpose, or having any sectional feeling; I have frequently heard him say, as he says in those letters to McComb and others, that he always endeavored to put it where it would do the most good; that we needed all the influence we could get in every quarter; but it never entered my head or the head of any one else but McComb's, that he had any improper design; he knew what McComb was from me a long time before those letters were written.

I met McComb, for the first time, when I went into the direction of the Credit Mobilier, and I was favorably impressed with his appearance; I knew that he had a bad name in the leather trade, which he and I had been engaged in all our life-time; my prejudices were against him, and so I told Mr. Ames; but his fine appearance and plausibility led me to feel that he had been slandered.

I inquired of a mutual friend about him—Mr. Jackson Shultz, one of the most prominent citizens of New York, and also in the leather trade—as worthy as he is distinguished, and well known, I suppose, to the committee. He told me that he thought that he must be a much better man than his reputation indicated; I expressed to him the same opinion. A short time after Mr. Shultz came to me and said that if I had taken any stock in McComb on the strength of anything he had said, he wished to take it back, as he would be sorry to mislead me; I asked him what caused him to say this; he told me that he had been talking with Mr. Dana, editor of the Sun, and he had requested him to say, in his paper, a good word for the Union Pacific Railroad, as he had some friends in the direction he would like to do a favor to. As he had assisted Mr. Dana to get up the Sun, Mr. Dana replied and said he would be glad to, and asked him who he had in that concern in whom he felt so much interest. He told him that Mr. Alley was a particular friend of his, and McComb he felt friendly to; Mr. Dana replied that he could not say anything in favor of any concern with such a man as McComb in its direction. Mr. Shultz asked what he knew against McComb; he said he regarded him as the most infamous scoundrel he knew, and that he ought to be in the penitentiary instead of the direction of that company. He had robbed and cheated the soldiers and the Government more than anybody could dream of, and the archives of the Government would show it. He said he had discovered his infamy when he was Assistant Secretary of War. Mr. Ames was told of this and put upon his guard. This, I think, was a long time before he wrote those letters to him. Shortly afterward a distinguished Senator came to me and wanted to know what we had that infamous wretch McComb as a director for. I asked what he knew about McComb. His reply was, "He ought to be in the State's prison. He had robbed the soldiers and the Government, as the records of the Government could show, and he being chairman of the Military Committee had occasion to know all about it." This information was given to Mr. Ames, so that it was impossible he could have had the slightest confidence in McComb when he wrote those letters. Mr. Ames, in one of his letters, speaks of fearing no investigation. The Union Pacific Railroad Company and the Credit Mobilier Company had been black-mailed in every conceivable way, by insiders and outsiders, until the two companies were robbed of immense sums for which they never received any value. They endeavored always to accomplish their purpose when any large scheme was involved, and it was resisted, by threats of exposure to the Government. The fright occasioned by these threats too often succeeded, because these men had embarked their millions, and a row with Congress, whether they were right or wrong, was sure to bankrupt the road, and most of the individuals engaged in it. I knew Durant to carry his threats so far once as to write a letter and put it in the post-office, directed to Elihu B. Washburne, accusing the companies of the greatest rascalities. Had this letter gone forward, you can realize the consequences. They found they had gone a little too far, and McComb said he could get that letter out of the post-office, as he knew the clerk well. The letter was got out of the office by McComb. Mr. Oakes Ames always claimed, I believe, that they had nothing to fear from investigations, and I cannot now recall to mind a single instance where I thought any such threat influenced his action; but there were others equally honest and true that did not possess quite his courage, and at that time he was not a director. This misapprehension in the public mind in regard to the Credit Mobilier, occasioned more than anything else by the blackmailing suit of McComb, which was commenced more than four years ago, beginning his suit with a false but sworn statement that the Credit Mobilier had been making fabulous dividends, counting by the million; that its officers and principal stockholders were robbing the Government and bribing Congress, whereas, since the dismissal of the Durant-McComb party, I think I may say that no corporation in the country has a set of directors, each and every one of whom, if I except myself, are well known to be, in the respective communities in which they reside, gentlemen of unusual high character and probity; and they defy any human being to show any wrong-doing by that corporation or any member of it toward Congress or the Government since they have been in charge of its administration, since the 19th May, 1867, to the present time. It (the McComb suit) has been the cause of great persecution, numberless law-suits, and severe losses, besides great vexation.

First, the Duff and Green suit, so-called, suing us for the franchise which they had forfeited, and these millions of profits McComb had sworn to, when the whole amount that that party ever invested in it was two old office-chairs and an old desk, and, I believe, a bogus check on a broken bank, by a failed individual! This, if possible, was more ridiculous than the Fisk claim. Fisk sued for millions, but he had actually paid, in clean cash, $240, and had a *bona-fide* interest to that amount. Next came the State of Pennsylvania, aroused by the sworn statements of McComb to millions of profits. Her law-officers could not be made to believe that any man could be so wicked as to make such statements, under the solemn obligations of an oath, that were entirely false. So they sued us for about a million for taxes upon these fabulous profits.

A Pennsylvania jury, reluctant to let such a large sum slip, seemed unwilling to believe the truth, and twice unjustly declared that we must pay up for taxes on profits which existed only in the imagination of McComb, so far as having any application of the Credit Mobilier Company. Twice the supreme court sent back the suit to the lower court, and the second time with a severe rebuke to the judge for his absurd rulings; then the case was dismissed, but a few months since. At last there comes now, growing out of the same false swearing, an arraignment of this company and Mr. Ames, charged with high crimes and misdemeanors for selling a few shares of stock as a favor to a few personal friends, some of whom happened to be members of Congress; but every man of them friends from the start, to their praise be it spoken, of this great enterprise in which he was engaged, therefore of all men needing no bribe to induce them to vote in that direction, especially when you consider that all required legislation, affecting in any way the interests of the road, had been obtained three years or more before, if you except perhaps one bill passed in 1866, which was not, however, in the interest of the Union Pacific Railroad, but against it, for which Mr. Ames himself voted, and when denounced for it by Mr. Durant as a fool for doing so, in my presence, as it damaged the company millions of dollars, Mr. Ames said in reply, "I thought it was right, and so I voted for it." Oakes Ames, with his millions to lose of his own money, periled all in this great enterprise, took upon his own broad shoulders one single contract of $47,000,000, when in all America there was not another man who would have done the same. For all this peril, anxiety, and abuse, he has realized less than a million profit, which he will tell you if you will ask him; and his brother Oliver, who was president of the road, upon my return from Europe in August, 1869, told me then, more than three months after the road was opened and a success, such was the pecuniary embarrassment of the road even then, and of such doubtful issue, he would give me half a million dollars if I would relieve him of his load and agree to hold him harmless. And how much worse was his brother Oakes's case!

One of America's most distinguished sons told me the other day, one who has lately returned from Europe, where he had been engaged in an important service for our country, that if our own people failed to appreciate the prodigious service which Oakes Ames had rendered the country, the thinking minds of all Europe were struck with admiration for his great courage and boundless energy, culminating in such a grand achievement.

Since your last meeting I have examined the books of the company, and learned from them and the officers of the company that the fifty shares of stock alleged by McComb to have been given to James Brooks, or his son-in-law, Neilson, by me or Oakes Ames, were fifty shares of stock, belonging by right to Neilson, as the owner of a hundred shares of original stock for which he paid $100 a share, and interest from July 1, 1867. He was entitled to it under the resolution of the company, allowing 50 per cent. increase, as well as all the other stockholders. He was entitled to it the company believed from Durant, who went to Europe and did not give it to him. The stock was demanded expressly upon that ground, that it belonged to him, and the president and treasurer issued a certificate to him for that reason only. It was the company's stock that was issued to him. I was not present, had nothing to do with it, and never knew anything about it until the other day, it so happened, but had I been present or consulted about it, I certainly should have consented to it, because he was entitled to it by right. Mr.

McComb was unfortunate under the circumstances in selecting me as the person to ascribe this transaction to. He might have selected almost any one else and made his perjury less apparent.

Mr. McComb. Before the committee proceed with Mr. Alley's cross-examination, I wish they would allow me to say a word, and to inject it right at this point.

The Chairman. The committee prefer to allow Mr. Alley to proceed with his testimony. If he has made any statements in the paper he has read not proper to be made, they can be stricken out hereafter.

Mr. McComb. I simply want, inasmuch as this proceeding is public, that the bane should go with the antidote.

The Chairman. It has been determined that the bane shall go first.

Examination by the Chairman:

We have here what purports to be interrogatories to the defendants in this suit of McComb against the Credit Mobilier of America, with the answers thereto.

Witness. These interrogatories and answers are not in the tax-suit, but in the other suit to which I have referred.

Question. On the sixth page of these interrogatories is what purports to be a list of dividends that were made on this Credit Mobilier stock.—Answer. Yes, sir; these are the dividends that Mr. Ames speaks of in his letter, and to which I was opposed.

Q. Do you understand that all these dividends were declared and paid as stated in these interrogatories?—A. Substantially, I suppose. I have not looked at them lately. [Paper handed to witness.] The dividend as mentioned under date of April 26, 1866, of 100 per cent. in Union Pacific Railroad stock, is, I think, not correct. Neither is that of April 1, 1867. That was not a dividend. The original capital of the Credit Mobilier was $2,500,000. An increase of twelve hundred and fifty thousand dollars was determined on, and it was very difficult to get the stock subscribed. No bonds had then been sold. They had no market-value. A good many of them were pledged in large sums, and large sums in small amounts. The company felt that some additional capital must be raised, and they voted to raise this twelve hundred and fifty thousand from the stockholders who would pay in 50 per cent. additional, and as an inducement to subscribe and pay in that amount they offered them a bond for every thousand dollars of additional stock subscribed. That is my recollection.

By Mr. Merrick:

Q. If I understand you, it was a premium rather than a dividend?—A. Yes, sir; it was not a dividend. The next dividend referred to here is July 1, 1867, 100 per cent., Union Pacific Railroad stock. That was not a dividend. My recollection of both these items is that the Credit Mobilier had subscribed for stock of the company for which they were to pay $100 a share. I think that some $30 a share had been paid in. The company subscribed for that stock, and paid on it $1 a share or something like that, assuming the liability to pay the balance. It was in no sense a dividend.

Q. Who assumed the liability to pay the balance?—A. The parties who took it. It was a subscription for stock on which $30 a share had been paid. They gave four dollars a share, I think, for it, and became liable, as I suppose, for the balance. This was a long time before I had anything to do with the Credit Mobilier. That was when it was under the supervision of Durant & Co.; that is as I understand the facts.

By the CHAIRMAN:

Q. Right here let me inquire in reference to the stock of the Union Pacific Railroad Company. What is the capital stock of that company?—A. The capital stock of the company is now about $36,000,000, as I recollect. The original bill of Congress required that $100,000,000 should be subscribed, and required books to be opened in the principal cities of the Union; the places at which they should be kept to be designated by the President of the United States. The President designated for New York the office of the company; for Boston the Merchants' Bank. The other places designated I do not recollect, but the books were to be kept open until $100,000,000 had been subscribed. Therefore, as I said to Mr. Ames when he called on me, as referred to in my other testimony, it was impossible to build the road under that bill; because, in the first place, to get control of the road there must be an actual subscription of $51,000,000, and no responsible men having money to lose would be willing to risk it in any such enterprise as an experiment.

Q. It would seem here that there had been considerable dividends in stock of that road. What I want to know is whether it amounted to anything in money value?—A. When Mr. Ames took this contract of $47,000,000, he was to take his pay in stock at par, and in bonds, I think, at par. I am not certain whether the bonds were to be sold or not. The stock was taken, I believe, at par, and paid for at par. At that time it was worth I hardly know how much. I think some of it sold at twenty cents on the dollar, but it had no real market value.

Q. How much stock was ever subscribed?—A. The whole of it was subscribed. By an arrangement with the trustees, to whom Mr. Ames's contract of $47,000,000 was assigned, they subscribed for this stock and paid for it at par.

Q. How much stock did they subscribe for?—A. A good many millions, and actually paid over the money. But there was due them this large amount as contractors, and they took their pay in stock, which was subscribed on the books at $100 a share, and paid for at $100 a share.

Q. That is, this company paid them on their contract?—A. Yes, although after this their profits were large, they were not in point of fact out of debt.

Q. Was there any money paid over for stock of the Union Pacific Railroad in the ordinary way of subscribing for stock and paying for it?—A. Yes, sir.

Q. How much?—A. That I could not now tell.

Q. Have you any idea of the amount?—A. I do not think there was any paid for in full, because in this way it was subscribed for and the assessments paid. I think the highest that was paid for any of it in money was $50 a share, and that was afterward bought up. I do not think there was ever any of that stock paid for in full, except in the way to which I have referred.

Q. Was this stock in the market? Did it have a market value?—A. It had not until a long time afterward. It had a market value, as I have said, previous to the $47,000,000 contract, and I figured it up in this suit at between eight and nine millions as the profit on this contract, taking the stock divided at the average market value at par during the period I have named. Large quantities of it were sold for 13. I believe it has been sold as low as 10, and my impression is that it has sold in the market as high as 46 or 47. But take the average value of the stock and the other securities, from May, 1869, to January,

1870, if they had sold all their securities, the profits would have been what I have stated. Mr. Ames and his brother have kept theirs. They have always, from the start, said that if they made any money out of it they should make it in the running of the road.

Q. Can you tell how much stock of the road Mr. Ames was to take on that $47,000,000 contract, and how large a proportion of that amount was to be paid in stock?—A. I do not think it was especially agreed upon, as to the amount of stock. That depended upon future events, I suppose, in regard to what the profits should be. The expectation was that a very large amount of it would have to be paid in stock, because they had nothing else to pay with. It ate up all their securities pretty much, except stock. The company came very near failing even at that time, and after January, 1870, they had to resort to all sorts of expedients to keep it afloat, issuing new bonds and paying premiums to people who would take the stock and bonds together.

Q. These dividends, or whatever is put down as dividends, are all in Union Pacific Railroad Company stock, or in first-mortgage bonds of the Union Pacific Railroad, with one exception. June 17, 1868, there is a dividend of 60 per cent. in cash currency.—A. My recollection is that that was a cash dividend.

Q. Was that the only cash dividend they made upon that stock?—A. That is my impression. I could not say certainly without reference to the books.

Q. All the other dividends, or whatever they were, were paid in Union Pacific Railroad stock or bonds?—A. Yes, sir; they were. They were too hard run to distribute Government bonds. They sold them almost before the ink was dry. That is my impression. It was a good while ago, but I think I am right about it.

Q. What was the market value of the bonds of the road itself? How high did they sell?—A. There were different prices. There was a great variation. They went up as high at one time, I think, as 102, and they have been sold down as low as 60 odd. There has been great fluctuation as there has been in the stock.

Q. Can you tell what was their value in the market about 1867 or 1868, about the time these dividends were made?—A. I think they were nearly up to par. Then there were certificates issued. I do not know whether there was more than one paid in certificates. Certificates were issued for bonds, payable in bonds when the company could spare them. All these dividends, I think, were declared a little too soon; as one gentleman expressed it, "they ate the calf up in the cow's belly."

Q. How did they become entitled to the bonds for these dividends made upon Credit Mobilier stock?—A. When these trustees took hold to build the road under the Ames contract, for instance, when they had gone a distance of a couple of hundred miles, a dividend would be declared of the supposed profits. There were six hundred and sixty-seven miles of road under this contract, and they had the privilege of one hundred and fifty miles more, which they did not take.

Q. They declared the dividends upon the presumption that so much profit had been earned?—A. Yes, and they ascertained, when they came to build the last one hundred and fifty miles of the six hundred and sixty-seven miles contract, that the building of the road cost them a good deal more than they got for it.

Q. But when they had built one hundred miles they knew how much it had cost and knew how much they were to receive for it?—A. Yes, and they declared their dividends.

Q. And the risk was whether they would continue to make a profit on the other portion of the road?—A. Exactly. The first portion of the road under this contract was much less expensive than farther along. I told them it was exceedingly unwise to declare dividends on the first sections; that they had better wait until the road was finished and then see what they had to divide.

Q. If I listened correctly to your written statement, you say that this contract called the Ames contract was for a portion of the road not built by the Credit Mobilier Company?—A. No, sir; the Credit Mobilier Company had nothing to do with it, nor with any contract, except for the first two hundred and forty-seven miles.

Q. That was not in the Ames contract?—A. No, sir; but Mr. Ames after he had received the contract, these men who had put in their money into Credit Mobilier stock, thought by right and justice they ought to have what profit there was in building the road, and that contract was assigned to seven trustees for that purpose. I was originally one of the trustees, but I got out of it very soon afterward.

Q. While the road was being built under that contract were not dividends declared upon the Credit Mobilier stock out of the profits?—A. No, sir; dividends, however, were declared to the persons interested corresponding with their amount of stock in the Credit Mobilier. But the Credit Mobilier corporation had nothing to do with it.

Q. Were these dividends declared upon the stock of the Credit Mobilier, or only upon the stock of certain shareholders?—A. Upon the stock that had come in, I think.

Q. Was it not assumed that the Credit Mobilier was really entitled to the benefit of that contract?—A. No, sir; the Credit Mobilier had nothing to do with it as a company. Mr. Durant declared in the most positive terms that the Credit Mobilier should never have another contract.

Q. But I understand you that the contract was assigned to certain trustees. What I want to ask is whether the advantages of that contract were not really in the shape of dividends upon the Credit Mobilier stock?—A. The Credit Mobilier stock was made the basis of the amount of dividends going to the persons interested, so far as these persons had signed a certain agreement.

Q. Was it confined to them?—A. Yes; confined entirely, with one or two exceptions. Where stockholders in the Credit Mobilier refused to sign the agreement, as I refused for a considerable time on account of the personal responsibility involved, they did not get their dividends.

Q. Were there not persons in the Credit Mobilier who were not included in the trustees' arrangement?—A. I think of only two or three.

Q. Did they get their dividends?—A. I think not.

Q. It was understood that these trustees held them for the benefit of whatever stockholders should come into this agreement?—A. Yes, sir.

Q And for nobody else?—A. For nobody else. Some were afraid of their personal liberty, and declined coming in. I delayed myself for some time, and I think Mr. Hazard was another. As I have said, I was opposed to declaring these dividends; but as one of the trustees I acquiesced in what was done.

Q. The division was made according to this stipulation in the assignment of the Ames contract to the trustees?—A. Yes; it is there stipulated that they should sign an agreement to give up their proxies in the Union Pacific Railroad. They all became liable personally for the whole amount. The stockholders in the Credit Mobilier were really losers in this venture of theirs in the Union Pacific Railroad. So far as the stock of the Credit Mobilier was concerned, any man who owned that stock would be very glad to sell it with all the dividends ever received upon it, for par and interest, and give something besides. I will mine, at any rate.

Mr. McCOMB. I will take your stock on those terms.

By Mr. MERRICK:

Q. You were not one of those embraced in this class of stockholders? —A. Yes; I held two hundred and ninety shares of that stock, and I signed the agreement. If you count in the profits made, under the trustees' arrangement, of course it was a profitable investment.

By the CHAIRMAN:

Q. What you mean, then, is, that taking the Credit Mobilier stock, without participation in the Ames contract, you would not make anything?—A. That is what I mean.

Q. And whatever was really made by stockholders of the Credit Mobilier was in consequence of the Ames contract?—A. Yes; so far as the construction of the road was concerned.

Q. Those who entered into that arrangement, and shared in the profits of that contract, got something?—A. Yes; I stated the amount made according to my calculations, taking the market value of the securities between May 19, 1869, and January 1, 1870.

By Mr. NIBLACK:

Q. Is the Union Pacific Railroad Company substantially controlled by the same men who built it?—A. I should hardly think it was. Mr. Ames is now a director, but was not during the building of it, and has not been till recently.

Q. Do the same class of men control the Credit Mobilier at the present time, and for three or four years past, who are now controlling the Union Pacific Railroad?—A. No, sir. They have scarcely anything to do with the Union Pacific Railroad. Mr. Hazard is on the executive committee, and Mr. Dillon is president of the Credit Mobilier. I believe Mr. Dillon is a director of the Union Pacific Railroad. I think he has a small interest in it, and if I am not mistaken Mr. Hazard has no interest in the Union Pacific Railroad at all.

Q. I understand, then, that the Credit Mobilier, as now organized, has no control in the management of the affairs of the railroad company?—A. No, sir. I think the directors of the Credit Mobilier have scarcely any interest in the Union Pacific Railroad. I do not know of but one who is in the direction, and he is Mr. Dillon.

Q. I ask because it appears in the commencement that the Credit Mobilier was purchased for the purpose of building the road.—A. Yes; but I have explained why it could not go on and build the road.

Q. An impression seems to exist in the public mind that the two are the same, identically, yet co-operating together.—A. No, sir; they are not.

Q. Are not the principal stockholders in the Union Pacific Railroad now the principal stockholders in the Credit Mobilier?—A. I should think not. I could not tell without examining the books. They were at one time substantially the same, but I think they are now different. Some of the largest stockholders in the Credit Mobilier, as I understand, do not own much stock in the Union Pacific Railroad. I own, as I have stated, 290 shares of the Credit Mobilier stock, but I own a very small amount, indeed, of Union Pacific Railroad stock, and scarcely any of their securities. I have not been in the direction for several years.

Q. In point of fact what has experience demonstrated in regard to the profits of running the Union Pacific Railroad by the men who own it?—A. There are three classes of bonds. The first-mortgage bonds, $27,000,000, I think; the land-grant bonds, reduced, I believe, to about $9,000,000, and the income-bonds of $10,000,000—I should say about $46,000,000 altogether. The road is running just enough to pay the interest on these securities from its net proceeds. The Government bonds are not included in this calculation. They are provided for in another way.

Q. In your statement you say that Mr. Durant and his party always insisted that anything to be realized from the road would be from the construction, not from its earnings.—A. Yes; there were always two parties on that question.

Q. What I want to inquire is, which party has proved to have been more nearly correct in that regard?—A. Mr. Ames and his party. I can speak, however, only for Mr. Ames himself, because I have had a great deal of talk with him about it. He has always contended that it is going to be a very valuable stock; that while it is not worth much now, its prospective value is very great; that the increase of traffic will be very great. He therefore keeps his stock and has not sold it. If it proves to be worth 100 cents on the dollar he has made a very handsome thing; if it proves to be worth nothing he will lose money.

Q. So far as your connection with the road gives you information, have you any reason to believe that the Union Pacific Railroad Company will ever be able to redeem the bonds the Government has given for its construction?—A. I think so. I think at the end of 30 years, the time the bonds have to run, ample provision will be made. If Congress and the Government so decide the money will be collected, I think, without any doubt; that, however, remains to be seen. The Government at the present time, in my judgment, has not been wronged a single dollar in any shape or manner; but those poor people who have put their money into the road, if it doesn't earn anything, will lose.

Q. I have understood that during a portion of the time the management of the Credit Mobilier regarded these bonds as a bonus to the railroad, to be divided among the gentlemen who control its direction; that the theory was that these bonds were so much clear to the company, without making any particular provision for redeeming them.—A. I do not think any Government bonds were ever divided to the contractors. The road cost too much. It was badly managed in its construction. The road actually cost about $69,000,000, as I recollect. I could tell you almost exactly by going into it.

Q. What amount of Government bonds have been received?—A. Twenty-seven million dollars, or in that neighborhood.

Q. You have not had much to do, I suppose, in connection with the Central Pacific Railroad?—A. I have never had any connection with it.

WASHINGTON, D. C., *January* 8, 1873.

Examination of JOHN B. ALLEY resumed.

By the CHAIRMAN:

Question. You saw what purported to be a list of the dividends in the printed pamphlet we had yesterday. Do you know whether that list included the dividends that were made from the profits of the Credit Mobilier, and whether these profits were divided among the stockholders of the Credit Mobilier?—Answer. I believe it does.

Q. As I understand, whatever profits were made out of that contract were divided among the stockholders, or only to those who came within that stipulation referred to?—A. Yes, sir; that was the condition of the contract.

Q. What I wanted to get at is whether this list of dividends includes the dividends from that contract to these individuals?—A. I think it includes all the dividends which were paid to individuals who were owners of the Credit Mobilier stock and who is in the stipulation; that is my impression.

Q. Do you know whether those dividends appear on the books of the Credit Mobilier as dividends made to that company?—A. No, sir; the Credit Mobilier never had anything to do with that in any shape or manner. They had no control or interest in it, and nothing whatever to do with it.

Q. It was not true, then, that a dividend was made by that company to its shareholders, and so appears upon the books?—A. Not at all, it was never so regarded. The dividends were made by these seven or eight trustees to the persons who came under the arrangement I have stated, and to nobody else, so far as I know.

Q. Do you know what was the market value of these Credit Mobilier shares in December, 1867, and January, 1868?—A. There was really no market value up to December, 1867. I know of a few shares being sold at 95, and some were offered as low as 75. But late in December, 1867, after Mr. Ames agreed to make the ownership in that company the basis of the right to subscribe or take an interest in this contract of his, they rose in value. I think the very last of December they brought 160, and before the end of January they brought as high as 200, and I believe later a few shares sold as high as 225. I do not know of any being sold any higher than that.

Q. All that rise you attribute to the fact that they were entitled to share in the Ames contract?—A. Yes, they would be if they came in under the stipulation.

Q. And they were entitled to come in?—A. They were entitled to come in if they chose to come in; that is to say, they were not entled to come, but they were allowed by agreement of Mr. Ames and the other parties interested, provided they signed the stipulation referred to.

Q. One shareholder had as good a right to come in as another?—A. O, yes, sir.

Q. Do you know how large a proportion of them had come in?—A. I think I stated yesterday that all came in with the exception of perhaps one or two; in fact, I rather think the whole stock was represented. Those who did not come in sold out their right.

Q. Practically, then, the dividends were divided upon the Credit Mobilier stock?—A. Yes, sir; it was the practical result in the end, because every man who owned that stock had the right to come in.

Q. I inquired of you the other day in regard to the persons who have been named here as congressional holders of stock in that company, and asked a question or two in reference to Mr. Brooks. It seems here that one hundred shares of the Credit Mobilier stock were standing in the name of Mr. Neilson. Do you know Mr. Neilson?—A. I do not. I never saw him.

Q. He is said to be the son-in-law of Mr. Brooks?—A. He is. I have no doubt of that fact.

Q. Do you know anything in relation to the purchase of that first one hundred shares of stock by Mr. Neilson?—A. No, sir; nothing except what appears upon the books.

Q. You have no personal knowledge as to who was the owner of that or who paid for it?—A. No, sir; only as I have stated, and from what appears on the books, that Mr. Neilson was the owner and was entitled to the additional fifty shares; which I never knew anything about, as I stated, until the other day.

Q. As I understand you, there was no negotiation and no conversation between you and Mr. Brooks in relation to these other fifty shares Neilson had?—A. None whatever. I never knew anything about it or heard anything about it until the other day.

Q. Have you any personal knowledge as to who paid for the fifty shares that Neilson had?—A. I have none at all only from what the books show, that Neilson paid for it.

Q. And for aught you know it was paid by Neilson?—A. For aught I know or presume it was paid by Neilson. I happened to be away at the time and knew nothing about the contract. He had a right to take that as an increase and to take it at par, and he availed himself of his right.

Q. You suppose the fifty shares which now appear in the name of Neilson are the fifty shares he was entitled to in consequence of the one hundred shares original stock owned by him?—A. The books show it, and the officers say it was so.

Q. You have no reason for knowing that it was not really Neilson's stock and paid for by him?—A. No, sir; I presume it was. I know nothing to the contrary. I never had any conversation with Mr. Brooks, and I never knew Neilson. As I said before, I never knew anything about this stock. It came, as I understood, from Mr. Durant. I can tell you what Durant told me if you desire it. I know nothing of my own personal knowledge.

By Mr. MERRICK:

Q. You stated yesterday that you had prepared the statement read to the committee upon the advice of one of the most eminent counsel of New England. Will you be good enough to say who that counsel was?—A. I did not say I prepared it under the advice of eminent counsel. I said I submitted it to him.

Q. Will you be good enough to state his name?—A. Mr. McMurtrie, of Philadelphia.

Q. The same gentleman who appeared here as counsel?—A. Yes, sir.

Q. Have you any personal knowledge of any of these transactions other than by conversation with Mr. Brooks, and that spoken of by Mr. Ames in his testimony?—A. Nothing, except in regard to the three gentlemen I named, Mr. Dawes, Mr. Wilson, and Mr. Boutwell; and I stated fully then all I knew in regard to them.

By Mr. MCCRARY:

Q. Do you know how much of the stock of the Credit Mobilier was disposed of to members of Congress?—A. No, sir, I do not. Mr. Ames's subscription, I believe, is on the books, and so is that of Mr. Hooper, Mr. Grimes, and myself. These are all I know of except what I have stated in regard to the three gentlemen just mentioned; and, as I said the other day, I only know in regard to them that Mr. Wilson agreed to take twenty shares, and Mr. Dawes ten shares.

Q. You do not know of any other members than those you have named?—A. No, sir; I never knew anything further until this investigation, and since then I have been informed from the same sources of information you all have.

Q. How much did you take at the beginning?—A. I took five hundred shares. It was not all my own, but it was my subscription. I was the owner of two hundred and ninety shares under this contract.

Q. You took it at par, I suppose?—A. Yes, sir.

Q. When did that stock rise in value above par, or was it worth more than par at the beginning?—A. No; it was hard work to get people to take it at first. I do not know that it could actually have been sold at par before early in January, 1868, and then it was sold at 160; and, as I said before, it went to 200 before the end of January. After that some of it was sold at 225. I do not remember of any being sold higher than that—it may have been.

Q. You say it was worth more than par after the 1st of January, 1868; was it sold to members of Congress at par after that date?—A. I do not know of any being sold to members of Congress. The time I have referred to when we had this meeting of prominent stockholders, officers of the company, &c., when Mr. Durant and Mr. Ames came forward and stated that they had sold to A, B, C, and D the six hundred and fifty shares of stock, was, I think, early in December. I am not certain as to the exact time, but I suppose the books will show. It was then stated that this stock had been agreed for some time before. I know Mr. Ames said he was a good deal embarrassed because some of the parties claimed they had bought more than he thought they had.

Q. Do you know whether these particular contracts which were to be carried out by the delivery of that stock were made by members of Congress alone, or by them and other parties?—A. I do not understand that it had anything to do with members of Congress particularly. I know nothing about any members of Congress except those I have mentioned, Mr. Wilson and Mr. Dawes.

Q. Do you know whether the stock was delivered to other persons besides members of Congress after that permission was given to Mr. Ames and Mr. Durant?—A. Not of my own knowledge. I suppose it was. I never made any inquiry in regard to it.

Q. Has any of the stock which stood in the name of Mr. Ames been transferred of record to any other persons?—A. That I do not know.

Q. You do not know whether it still stands in his name?—A. I do not know; I could not say; my impression is that it does, most of it, stand in his name as trustee.

Q. Can you explain why the transfer was not made if the stock was actually sold to the parties, and why it was kept in Mr. Ames's name?—A. That I do not know.

Q. That is not the usual mode of transacting that kind of business, is it?—A. It is frequently done with responsible men. Mr. Ames is a very responsible man, and a person holding a certificate from him would be just as safe as if the transfer was actually made on the books. In the State of New York, I believe, such a certificate carries the stock with it just the same as if it were entered upon the books. Of course with those who hold stock temporarily it is a matter of convenience. In respect to the Union Pacific Railroad stock I am confident that not more than two-thirds of it stands in the name of the parties who really own it.

By Mr. MERRICK:

Q. They have certificates delivered to them with a blank power of attorney, I suppose?—A. Yes, and as I understand this was delivered to Mr. Ames in the same way. Mr. Ames stated at the time that to distinguish it from his other stock, as a matter of convenience, he wanted it put in his name as trustee. I do not know of any other reason, and I do not suppose there was any other reason than that. I, however, had nothing to do with the transfer; I was not an officer of the company, and had no occasion to inquire particularly in regard to it.

Q. It seems that most, if not all, of this stock, standing in the name of Mr. Ames as trustee, really belonged to other persons; what kind of evidence of ownership had these other persons?—A. I do not know; I understood from the testimony here that he gave in some instances a receipt for the money with a promise to transfer the stock at some future time, and his receipt was just as good to them as a certificate of stock, and would perhaps obviate the personal-liability difficulty. That, however, I only state as an inference; I do not know what his reasons were; I only know the facts I have stated.

Q. The persons whose names stand upon the books of the company would be the ones to draw the dividends of the company if dividends were declared?—A. Certainly.

Q. And Mr. Ames drew the dividends on the stock which stood in his name as trustee?—A. I presume so, or he may have given orders to the men to whom it belonged; I do not know anything about that.

By Mr. McCrary:

Q. The Union Pacific Railroad was built largely if not exclusively by the bonds and subsidies and land-grants of Congress?—A. O, no, sir; not by the bonds at least. As I stated yesterday, the road cost sixty-eight or sixty-nine millions, and only received twenty-seven millions of bonds from the Government. Very few lands were sold, or the title to them obtained so they could be sold, until the road was completed. They never realized much from their land-grant until the road was completed. They found when they came to finish it they were very deeply involved, and they had to raise a good many millions. Mr. Ames himself furnished quite a number of millions in the way of taking securities, &c., and I suppose it is well known here that he finally broke down; he took such a load that he could not stand up under it.

Q. Did you or not regard the success of the enterprise, the value of the Union Pacific Railroad stock, and also of the Credit Mobilier as depending very much upon the friendly or unfriendly legislation of Congress toward the road?—A. No, it never entered my head when I went into it that there would be any more legislation required, and I believe that none was required or obtained which had anything to do with the pecuniary matters connected with the road in any way. The Fisk raids, &c., occasioned the company to go to Congress for authority to keep itself out of the New York courts.

Q. Was there not a good deal of talk about investigating the affairs of the Union Pacific Railroad Company by congressional committees at various times?—A. Yes, sir; and no honest man in that company had the slightest objection to such an investigation.

Q. Would not an investigation, or even a threatened investigation, most likely have affected unfavorably the value of the securities of the road?—A. It very likely would; but that did not make any difference to those men who went into it and expected to make their mony out of the earnings of the road. As Mr. Ames very well knows, I said to him a great many times that, so far as an investigation was concerned, for one I would like to have it; and so far as he was concerned, as he intended to keep his stock and make his money out of the earnings of the road, it did not make any difference to him what Wall street thought about the stock. As I have before stated, I do not think that either

Mr. Ames or his brother have parted with any considerable portion of their stock in the road.

Q. You did not consider, then, that you had any interest whatever in the vote for or against an investigation, if one had been proposed?—A. So far as I am concerned there has never been a day that I would not desire the fullest investigation into this whole matter. The people of the country would have been better satisfied by it, especially after there was so much misunderstanding in regard to the matters of the road, growing out of the McComb suit.

Q. Did you regard it as important to have the office of the company removed from New York to Boston?—A. Of course. Judge Barnard had granted an injunction, and Fisk seemed to have full control of his court. Fisk came to me the very day the injunction was put on and said, "I will agree to settle this thing for $100,000, and relieve you entirely." I said to him that never with my consent should the company pay a dollar in any such way; that all the interest he had in the concern was $240. He replied, "It is a mere matter of dollars and cents, and if your company does not do it I will damage you a million." I said to him I did not care what the consequence was; the company would never with my consent pay him anything whatever. He did damage the company, I suppose, to the extent of several millions.

Q. Then I understand you to say that the Union Pacific Railroad Company was largely interested in the bill providing for the removal of its office to Boston?—A. The Union Pacific Railroad Company I think felt that it was a matter of life and death to them to get out of the clutches of the corrupt New York courts.

Q. Would you, then, or not, regard a member of Congress who had stock in that company as interested in that question?—A. He would be interested, of course, as he would be in legislation affecting national banks, if he was the owner of national-bank stock; he would have no improper interest that I can see. The whole country saw the necessity and justice of that action of Congress, and subsequent events have certainly shown that it was impossible for property or life even to be very safe in the city of New York under the jurisdiction of these courts. The directors of the company were arrested. I was arrested for one. Oliver Ames, the president, was arrested, and the officer was told not to take bail for him, but to put him in jail. One of the parties went down and swore before Judge Barnard that he resisted the injunction by violence, and upon that statement Judge Barnard told the officer not to take bail for him, but to confine him in jail. I was present at the time and know that Oliver Ames never lifted a finger. The moment the injunction was served he left the chair. He is one of the most amiable men living. That is a specimen of the proceedings which were resorted to.

Q. I understand you to be of opinion that because you had a good case it was perfectly proper for an interested party in your favor to decide it?—A. I did not say that.

Q. Is not that the effect of your statement?—A. No, sir; I do not think so. You may be the owner of ten shares of national-bank stock; there may be a raid upon national banks such as to require action upon the part of Congress, and whether your ownership of that stock would give you such an interest as to make it improper for you to vote upon the question would be a matter about which you would have to be your own judge. The coming into possession of the stock without anticipating any such proceeding certainly would not augur any impropriety in voting for the measure, as I regard it. There may be difference of opinion, however, as to the propriety of a member voting under these circumstances. I was not in Congress at the time of the legislation for the removal of the Union Pacific Railroad office to Boston, and do not know whether any member interested voted upon it or not.

Q. What was the decision of the Secretary of the Treasury concerning the payment of interest on the bonds of the United States granted to the Union Pacific Railroad Company?—A. His decision was, I think, that all the Pacific Railroad companies should pay interest upon the bonds that were loaned to them. That is my impression.

Q. Did the Union Pacific Railroad Company pay in accordance with that decision?—A. They did not. They came to Congress for relief, and the law appeared to be so plain to all the parties in interest that they were able, I suppose, to convince Congress. I never knew a lawyer of any standing, who examined the question, come to any other conclusion.

Q. You regarded that as an important subject of congressional legislation, for the interest of the company, did you not?—A. I should say so. At that time I had very little interest in the company; I think I was not then a director. Of course everybody can see that it was a very important matter to the interest of all concerned. I thought Congress decided rightly, and if I had been a member I should have so considered it.

Q. If you had been a member at the time this act was passed in reference to the payment of interest, would you have regarded it as a question upon which you could properly vote?—A. I hardly know. It is not a matter I have given any thought to; I have never had any occasion to have any opinion about it. There were no members of Congress at that time who had any interest amounting to anything.

Q. I am requested to ask you a question, which you can answer or not, as you please. Did you not get, or have put into your possession, or under your control, a hundred thousand dollars in money after Secretary Boutwell's ruling in reference to the interest due on the Union Pacific Railroad Company's Government bonds for the purpose of influencing legislation upon that subject?—A. I am very glad to answer that question or any other question any gentleman may choose to put concerning this matter. So far as I am concerned, I am prepared to challenge investigation by anybody. No, sir; I never had a dollar put into my hands and never spent a dollar, directly or indirectly, for any such purpose.

Q. Were you here in Washington urging the passage of that bill about the time it passed?—A. No, sir; I think not. That bill passed March 3, 1871. I do not think I was in Washington after the 1st of February of that year. I can ascertain that fact definitely and inform the committee at a future day if they desire.

Q. You say there was no purpose in the distribution of this stock by Mr. Ames, so far as you know, to secure friendly action in Congress?—A. No, sir; I never supposed any such thing, and do not believe now he had the slightest idea of influencing legislation by letting his friends have a few shares of that stock. No conversation I ever had with him would lead me to suppose he ever dreamed of anything of the kind.

By Mr. MERRICK:

Q. It has been stated that the Union Pacific Railroad cost altogether sixty-eight or sixty-nine millions. What was the length of that road?—A. I think one thousand and fifty or one thousand and eighty miles; speaking from recollection.

Q. When you give the amount stated as the cost of the road, do you include the cost of construction only, or the cost of construction and equipment?—A. Of construction and equipment. A great deal of it was spent foolishly, as I thought. I was constantly protesting against it.

Q. Did the cost of construction actually exceed $27,000 a mile?—A. Yes, sir; the entire cost, as I said, was nearly $70,000,000, including equipment and everything. What the cost of equipment was I do not know.

Q. It has been suggested to me that the actual cost of construction was $29,221,000, and the cost of equipment about $7,000,000, making in all $36,221,000. Is that or not a correct statement according to your recollection?—A. I should say not. I have stated what the cost was. It ought not to have cost as much as it did; but I think the cost could not have been less than $54,000,000 or $55,000,000, to say the least. My statement of the cost of course includes the profit which was made on the contract with Mr. Ames.

Q. Do or not the books of the company show what has been the actual expenditure for construction?—A. I presume so; they ought to, and no doubt they do. I think I could have taken that road and built it, equipped it, and done everything that was done, for inside of $50,000,000. I do not think I could have done it for $36,000,000, because there was necessarily an enormous expense attending the construction of the first two or three hundred miles. There were no railroads across the State of Iowa, and the rails had to be carried across or sent around up the river at a monstrous expense. There were heavy losses and expenses that could not be avoided. Then out in that country there was inevitably always a large amount of plunder. In crossing the mountains, too, there were items of expense perfectly fearful. For instance, ties were made to cost $5 apiece which should not have cost but forty cents. But the Government never was robbed or cheated; it was the parties who undertook to build the road, who put their money into it, and who ought to have got out of it whatever there was.

Q. You have spoken of the price of Credit Mobilier stock; did you sell any of your shares of Credit Mobilier stock?—A. Yes, sir.

Q. At what price did you sell?—A. I sold mine at 200, I think.

Q. Did that include the dividends, or was it exclusive of the dividends which had been declared and collected before the date of sale?—A. My impression is that it included all dividends which had previously accrued. I never got any dividends on it. I sold it in January, 1868.

Q. To whom did you sell?—A. I sold to Peter Butler, of Boston, for himself, as I supposed at the time. I understood afterward that he bought it for Mr. Bardwell, of Boston. I believe he and Mr. Bardwell had a joint interest in it.

By Mr. NIBLACK:

Q. I understood you to state yesterday that there were two classes of stockholders in this Credit Mobilier, one interested in the Ames contract and the other not, and that the stock represented in the Ames contract was much more valuable than the other stock?—A. No, sir; I did not say anything of that kind. I stated that, so far as the Credit Mobilier stock was concerned, the corporation never made a dollar out of the Union Pacific Railroad Company; that it had never paid 7 per cent. interest on its par value; that its stock was not now, and had not been, for a long time, worth sixty cents on a dollar, and that statement applied to all classes of the Credit Mobilier stock.

Q. Then I understand you to say that the stock Mr. Ames distributed among his friends, by allowing them to purchase it at par, was regarded as a very good investment at the time?—A. A very great privilege, because the stockholders of the Credit Mobilier were permitted by Mr. Ames to become interested in his contract in *pro rata* proportion to their ownership in the Credit Mobilier, on signing an agreement making themselves personally liable.

Q. And all those who received any of the two hundred and fifty shares given to Mr. Ames as trustee participated in the benefits of that contract?—A. Yes; and some of them took Mr. Ames's receipt instead of a transfer of stock, supposing, I imagine, that they would not be personally liable on the contract unless they signed the agreement. All the stockholders of the Credit Mobilier, as I have stated, had the right to an interest in the Oakes Ames $47,000,000 contract on signing the stipulation, but the Credit Mobilier itself, as a corporation, had nothing whatever to do with that contract.

By Mr. MERRICK:

Q. If there was a profit made on that six hundred and sixty-seven miles covered by the $47,000,000 contract, how is it that the cost of construction of the road itself exceeded $68,000,000?—A. The sum I stated of $68,000,000, or $69,000,000, covered the entire cost of the one thousand and eighty-three miles of road.

Q. Do you know how much money Oakes Ames really put into Credit Mobilier stock; how many shares he subscribed and paid for?—A. I do not; the books will show. He paid $100 a share into the treasury, to my personal knowledge, for every share of stock issued to him.

Q. Did you not state yesterday that Mr. Ames put in $6,000,000 or $7,000,000?—A. No, sir; I said that he had an individual interest in this contract of between five and six million dollars, and that my own individual interest in the contract was less than $500,000.

WASHINGTON, D. C., *January* 9, 1873.

Examination of S. M. MCCOMB continued.

The CHAIRMAN stated that he had expected Mr. Ham, secretary of the Credit Mobilier, to have been present this morning for examination as a witness, but information had been received that he was detained, and would be for several days, on account of the sickness of his wife. The committee desired to have the books of the Credit Mobilier, in the custody of Mr. Ham, present before calling other witnesses, and unless Mr. McComb was prepared to produce other papers to which he had referred in his previous evidence and to give further testimony, the committee would adjourn until Monday.

Mr. MCCOMB said that upon reflection he had concluded not to make any reply to anything that had been said or could be said by Mr. Alley, preferring to let his life answer Alley's statement. If future developments should render any further statement necessary, he would be glad to avail himself of the permission of the committee.

Mr. MERRICK. You stated that you had other papers you could produce.

Mr. MCCOMB. I have, and, if the committee wish, will produce them now. When I left here before, it was to refresh my memory as to the particular time a conversation occurred between Mr. Alley and Mr. Brooks; and I stated that it occurred while Mr. Durant was in

Europe. That fact was very strongly impressed on my mind. I can now say that Mr. Durant left New York for Europe on the 8th day of January, 1868, and returned the 5th day of March, 1868, being gone fifty-seven days; and the time this transaction occurred between Mr. Brooks and Mr. Alley, for the fifty shares of stock put in the name of Neilson, was between these two dates.

By the CHAIRMAN:

Question. Can you fix the date any nearer than that?—Answer. No, sir. The difficulty the other day was in being able to fix the precise time of those conversations. I could not fix the precise date. These conversations were very frequent.

Q. If you have any impression yourself as to what portion of the period between the 8th of January and the 5th of March this conversation occurred, you may state it.—A. No, sir; I have not. It was in his absence. The whole thing impressed itself upon my mind as being taken advantage of in his absence. Mr. Durant had, a few days before, I think on the 26th of December, 1867, transferred to Mr. Brooks, or rather sold to him, if you please to term it so, one hundred shares of the Credit Mobilier stock for $100 per share, and had given with it $20,000 of Union Pacific Railroad stock, and $5,000 first-mortgage bonds, for which Mr. Brooks gave his check for $7,000, and his draft for $3,000, payable the 22d of January, 1868. Then, a few days after the 26th of December, and before the 8th of January, 1868, Mr. Brooks claimed from Mr. Durant $6,000 more of bonds and $6,000 more of stock, which was given him; that was the payment referred to in my testimony, making 370 per cent. received, besides the stock of the Credit Mobilier itself, for $10,000.

Now, I may say that I have refreshed my recollection on the question of Mr. Brooks being a member of Congress. I find that Mr. Brooks was a member of Congress in the fall of 1867, and in the spring of 1868, during the time of this transaction. I also am able to state that Mr. Brooks was appointed a Government director of the Union Pacific Railroad Company by President Johnson, the 23d of October, 1867, two months and three days before he got this transfer of Credit Mobilier stock, for one year, and re-appointed the 11th of March, 1868, until the 11th of March, 1869. Therefore, he was a Government director and a member of Congress during the period of these transactions. I have searched the records of Congress for information in regard to whether Mr. Brooks was in Congress, and I have also a letter of Mr. Crane, about this stock transaction.

Q. The committee propose to examine Mr. Crane as a witness, and you, therefore, need not produce his letter. In regard to this transaction in December you speak of, have you any personal knowledge; were you present, or is it something you have learned from others?—A. I was in the office when Mr. Brooks and Mr. Durant were talking. This conversation between Mr. Brooks and Mr. Durant occurred subsequent to my signing the paper which these gentlemen presented. I heard the conversation with reference to Mr. Durant giving or selling Mr. Brooks the one hundred shares of Credit Mobilier stock.

By Mr. MCCRARY:

Q. What do you know personally about Mr. Brooks paying for it; and how do you know it?—A. I do not know of his paying for it myself, except by looking at the books of Mr. Durant with the entries of Mr Crane on them. I did not see Mr. Brooks make the payment.

By Mr. MERRICK:

Q. You speak of seeing the books of Mr. Durant; do you mean the private books of Mr. Durant, or the books of the Credit Mobilier?—A. I mean the private books of Mr. Durant, kept by Mr. Crane. The stock was transferred by Mr. Crane. Mr. Crane held the stock, and it was transferred, by Mr. Brooks's direction, to Mr. Neilson, on the books of the Credit Mobilier.

Q. Was this the general stock of the Credit Mobilier that Mr. Durant controlled as an officer of the company, or some of the stock he himself held?—A. It was presumed to be a part of the six hundred and fifty shares, testified to by Mr. Ames, held in trust for specific parties.

Q. It was a part of the stock Mr. Durant claimed should be transferred to him in order that he might comply with his contracts with various parties?—A. That is what I understand the letter of Mr. Ames to refer to, wherein he was to take three hundred and eighty shares to keep himself or give to his friends.

By the CHAIRMAN:

Q. In this conversation between Mr. Durant and Mr. Brooks, was anything said, that you remember, about the shares being transferred to Mr. Neilson?—A. I do not think there was. These conversations were very frequent with us all. It was the exciting time which has been testified to by Mr. Ames, with the Credit Mobilier. It was very shortly after the organization of this trusteeship for the execution of the Ames contract, and there were meetings almost every day. Mr. Brooks was at that time a Government director, and consequently a good deal about there. I would not like to undertake to give words or expressions.

Q. Was there anything said that you remember as to whether this stock was to be given in his name, or in the name of Mr. Neilson?—A. Nothing as between him and Mr. Durant.

Q. Do you remember the precise time when this increase of 50 per cent. of Credit Mobilier stock was made?—A. It was made in April, 1867, some time before the Ames contract, and the rights under it were by order of the board only allowed to stand for ninety days. Notice was served upon each shareholder that his option to take his 50 per cent. increase would expire in ninety days.

Q. In regard to those one hundred shares which Mr. Brooks, or somebody, received by virtue of this transaction, in December, 1867, how could that subscription of one hundred shares entitle a man to fifty additional shares under this increase?—A. It did not entitle him to fifty per cent. increase, and it did not entitle him to anything.

Q. Then you claim that his taking the one hundred shares did not entitle him to the fifty shares?—A. No, sir; that right had expired long anterior to that. General Dodge got one hundred shares of Credit Mobilier stock along about this time, and he has never got an increase upon that, or been allowed to get it, or claimed it, that I know of, by virtue of having one hundred shares of original stock. The one hundred shares were held in the name of his wife; not in his own name.

Q. Do you know anything of Mr. Allison, of Iowa, being the holder or owner of any shares of Credit Mobilier stock?—A. I do not, and I thought he was not, as I stated the other day, until Mr. Ames said he was.

Q. Have you any knowledge whatever of his owning any Credit Mobilier stock?—A. None whatever.

Q. If you have any further papers to produce, you may present them now.—A. I will do so whenever desired. I did not know that I was to be examined to-day, and haven't them in my pocket.

JOHN B. ALLEY made the following statement in regard to his testimony of yesterday:

I wish to answer further to a question put to me yesterday. My testimony in answer to the question "Were you here in Washington urging the passage of that bill about the time it passed?" was "No, sir; I think not. That bill passed March 3, 1871. I do not think I was in Washington after the 1st of February of that year. I can ascertain that fact definitely, and inform the committee at a future day if they desire." I wish to say now that I have ascertained that it was as I supposed. I was not here after the 1st of February. I came to Washington January 22, and was here and in the vicinity until the 30th of that month. I was not here again until not far from that time the following January. I have been in the habit, ever since I left Congress, of making visits to Washington in January, and I was here then as I stated.

By Mr. MERRICK:

Q. Were you a member of Congress in 1867 or 1868?—A. No, sir; I went out at the close of the Thirty-ninth Congress, which expired the 3d of March, 1867.

Q. You had no connection with the Credit Mobilier stock before your term in Congress expired?—A. Yes; I subscribed to this Credit Mobilier stock in August, 1865, as I stated in my testimony, for five hundred shares.

The committee adjourned until Monday next at 10 a. m.

WASHINGTON, *January* 13, 1873.

HENRY L. DAWES, a member of the United States House of Representatives, having been duly sworn, made the following statement:

I have been ready at all times, whenever it should be desired by the committee, to make a full statement of whatever connection I have ever had with the Credit Mobilier, and regret that I have not had an earlier opportunity. I was never the owner of any of the stock of that corporation, yet I did agree to take ten shares of that stock, but the agreement was rescinded before the stock was transferred to me, and it never was transferred.

At the commencement of the session in December, 1867, I had due me at the Sergeant-at-Arms' office $1,000 of my salary, that I had then no occasion to use. I asked a colleague of mine, Mr. Washburn, with whom I was rooming at the time, what I could best do with it, and he advised me to purchase with it a bond of the Iowa Cedar Rapids Railroad, of Mr. Oakes Ames, saying that he had been purchasing of him a large amount of those bonds for 90 cents on the dollar for his bank, and he thought it an excellent investment. I accordingly went to Mr. Ames, and asked him to sell me such a bond as he had been selling Mr. Washburn. He replied, that he had not got any of these bonds then, for he had sold them all, but that he had something else as good, and he thought better. He would let me have for my $1,000, 10 shares of Credit Mobilier stock. I said to him, I did not know anything about that stock, and asked him to tell me about it. He replied, "It is a Pennsylvania corporation, which has the contract to build the Pacific Railroad; it is a good thing, and I think it will make money out of it. At any rate I will guarantee you 10 per cent. on your money, or if you don't want your stock at any time, I will pay you back your money and 10 per cent. interest." I told him I would think of it and let him know. I then inquired of Mr. Alley about this stock, and he said it was good stock, but he did not think it was as good as Mr. Ames thought it was. On my telling him that Mr. Ames offered to guarantee me 10 per cent., he said that I was safe enough then, and I made no further inquiry, but went to Mr. Ames and told him that I would take the stock. He said he could not transfer it to me then, but that it was at his home; that the first time he went home he would get it transferred to me and let me have it. I thereupon paid him over the $1,000, and took his accountable receipt for it, he saying at the time he gave it to me, that if at any time I got sick of it he would take it back and pay me back my money and 10 per cent.

Before he went home I had occasion to go home to Pittsfield, and while there Mr. Edward Learned, a friend and neighbor of mine, who was then, I believe, an officer in the Kansas Pacific Railroad, came into my office and told me of a suit which Duff Green had commenced, or was about to commence, in the Pennsylvania courts against Mr. Ames and his associates to get possession of the Credit Mobilier charter, claiming that it belonged to him and his associates, and had been wrongfully taken possession of by Mr. Ames and those connected with him. When I returned to Washington I told Mr. Ames what Mr. Learned had said to me, and told him that I did not want any such stock. He replied, "Well, you need not take it. I will pay you back your money and 10 per cent. interest if you prefer." I told him that I did. He thereupon settled with me in that way, allowing me interest and paying me back the money. In the mean time, and before I went to Pittsfield, he had paid me a dividend once; I do not know how much it was, but I think it was about 35 per cent. Whatever it was I allowed him in the settlement, he paying me over the balance only. This was the end of the transaction. The stock was never transferred to me at all. I have had no other transaction with the Credit Mobilier or the Union Pacific Railroad.

Neither during this transaction, nor before it, nor since its close, have I entertained any thought or purpose in connection with it; nor was anything ever suggested to me in that connection in any way, directly or indirectly, having reference to any offical conduct of mine in or out of Congress. Nor did anything in connection with it pass between me and Mr. Ames or any other person, other than would naturally have passed had I purchased of him the Iowa railroad bond I endeavored to get, or had I purchased any share of national-bank stock, or a United States bond, either of him or of any banker outside of Congress. Before and up to that time I do not remember to have heard the Credit Mobilier mentioned, or any measure touching the Pacific Railroad since the legislation of 1864, under which it was then being constructed; nor did I know of Mr. Ames's dealings with any other person in or out of Congress.

In closing the statement of all that did occur in this transaction, I desire to add that, although I have never desired or sought to conceal in any way anything that I have done in this matter, I have never made or authorized any public statement in reference to it before to-day, feeling that I could patiently wait until your committee should call upon me for this statement; nevertheless, there did get into print, without my authority or knowledge, a private note written by me to a friend in New

York, thanking him for voluntarily and on his own responsibility denying the statement in the New York Sun that Mr. Oakes Ames had, for corrupt purposes, given me stock in the Credit Mobilier. I desire to make that note a part of this testimony, in order that all I have said, as well as all that I have done in reference to this matter, may become a part of this statement.

The note is as follows:

PITTSFIELD, MASSACHUSETTS, *September* 11, 1872.

MY DEAR SIR: I thank you for denouncing as a false libel the charge of the New York Sun, so far as I am concerned. Neither Oakes Ames, nor any other man, dead or alive, ever gave me, directly or indirectly, a penny of the stock of the Credit Mobilier, or of any other corporation in this world. I never owned a dollar of any stock or any property of any kind that I did not pay the full value of, with my own money, earned with my own labor.

Truly yours,

H. L. DAWES.

By the CHAIRMAN:

Question. This sum of $1,000 you let Mr. Ames have was about the beginning of the session of Congress?—Answer. I am not entirely certain that it may not have been before the end of the previous session, but I do not think it was. I am sure it could not have been later than the first week in December, 1867. I have no memorandum, and cannot tell you the date. I think it was when I came back here at the beginning of the session of 1867.

Q. You say the dividend was paid to you during the time of the transactions between you and Mr. Ames. Can you date the time the dividend was paid?—A. It was between the first of the session and the time I went home. It could not have been more than a few weeks after I paid the money. It was before the conversation to which I referred with Mr. Learned.

Q. How soon after you returned was this matter closed up?—A. Immediately; within a week. I went right back and told Mr. Ames I could not take it.

Q. If I understood the reading of your statement, the result of the thing was that during the time Mr. Ames had the $1,000 he paid you ten per cent. interest?—A. He paid at the rate of ten per cent. interest, deducting out of the amount the dividend I had received. He did just as he told me in the beginning he would if I preferred; that is, that he would allow me ten per cent. for my money.

Q. Did Mr. Ames say anything or did you know anything in relation to the market value of this stock at the time?—A. No, sir; all I knew at the time was that it was good stock—at least that Mr. Ames thought the company would make out of this contract with the Union Pacific Railroad. He told me that he would guarantee me ten per cent., and I felt safe. The option was all I desired.

Q. The dividend you received you supposed to have been declared on the stock after the time you made this arrangement?—A. Yes, sir.

Q. Did you understand that you were entitled, if you took the stock, to any accrued dividends?—A. No, sir; I was to take it from the time, as I supposed.

Q. Did Mr. Ames say anything to you in relation to dividends that had been previously made upon the stock?—A. No, sir; he did not.

Q. I think you say in your statement you had no knowledge or transactions between Mr. Ames and any other member of Congress?—A. No, sir; I did not know of his dealings with anybody else. I did not inquire in regard to anybody else, and the first I knew about anybody else was at the time I saw it in the papers last summer.

By Mr. MCCRARY:

Q. The only paper you got from Mr. Ames was a receipt?—A. That was all.

Q. And that was canceled and delivered up?—A. That was delivered up.

Q. That stock you never saw?—A. No, sir.

WASHINGTON, D. C., *January* 13, 1873.

CHARLES H. NEILSON, sworn and examined.

By the CHAIRMAN:

Question. State your residence and occupation.—Answer. I reside in the city of New York. I am an insurance broker and adjuster of marine losses, also a dealer in stocks; that, however, is separate from my regular business.

Q. Are you son-in-law to the Hon. James Brooks, member of the House of Representatives?—A. Yes, sir.

Q. State whether you are the owner, or have had at any time in your possession any stock of the Credit Mobilier Company?—A. I was the owner of 100 shares of the original stock of the Credit Mobilier, and subsequently of 50 shares more. I have here the receipt of the original 100 shares Credit Mobilier stock, dated December 26, 1867, and another certificate of stock, 50 shares in the same company, dated February 29, 1868.

Q. Of whom did you purchase these first 100 shares?—A. The first 100 shares was an original subscription to the company, as I understand it.

Q. Did you sign for any number of shares?—A. I do not recollect that I signed for any number of shares.

Q. State the negotiation or transaction by which you became the owner of those 100 shares.—A. The Hon. James Brooks, my father-in-law, put me in the way of being the owner of it, and loaned me the money, $10,000, to pay for it. The dividends that have come from it have all come to me. I have received them all and have got them all.

Q. State what you did in reference to the purchase of that stock.—A. I stated that Mr. Brooks put me in the way of possessing it and loaned me the money.

Q. That is rather the result than the process. Did you do anything yourself about the negotiation?—A. No, I had no information personally, and could not have got any myself.

Q. All the business was done by Mr. Brooks?—A. Mr. Brooks told me that he could not go into it himself, but that he had the chance to put me in and he did so. This was the conversation. He advanced me the money or advanced the money for me. I do not recollect which.

Q. Did you yourself actively have anything to do with that transaction?—A. Nothing except by receiving and receipting for the stock. I authorized him to advance the money for me.

Q. How did you get the certificate?—A. I do not recollect. I got the fifty shares directly from the company. The other was so long ago that I cannot state how I got it.

Q. State whether this was delivered to you by the officers of the company or whether Mr. Brooks brought it to you.—A. I do not remember distinctly; to the best of my recollection I received it from the company.

Q. Just how you came into possession of it you cannot state ?—A. I do not remember distinctly.

Q. You previously had a conversation with Mr. Brooks about it, in which Mr. Brooks said he would advance the money if you became the purchaser ?—A. He said he would take care of it.

Q. And he did, as you suppose, pay the amount ?—A. I know that I got the certificate and received the dividends; that is all I know about it positively.

Q. You never paid for the stock directly to the company yourself ?—A. Not to my present recollection. I do not recollect that I did for the one hundred shares. I have been in there very often to collect dividends, but I do not recollect that I ever went there to pay for that stock.

Q. How was the matter arranged between you and Mr. Brooks in reference to paying the $10,000 ?—A. The arrangement was simply that he advanced the money and I presume paid the company. That is all I know about it. He told me that he would advance the money or take care of it. He gave me the certificate, I think, and I collected the dividends and kept them all myself. They are all mine. In other words, it was done for my benefit.

Q. Has this $10,000 which Mr. Brooks advanced to you been in any way adjusted between you and him ?—A. I have an open account with Mr. Brooks, and have given my collateral security for the amount of the loan.

Q. When was that security given to Mr. Brooks ?—A. As fast as money came into my possession that I could use in that way I gave it to him.

Q. Did you give security to him at the time the money was advanced ?—A. No, I did not think it was necessary.

Q. You never gave any note or bond for the money ?—A. No, I do not think that it is customary between father and son.

Q. It has remained as a matter of account between you ?—A. Precisely. I have never given him any note or any bond for the money—that is, my individual bond.

Q. The matter then remains unadjusted between you and him ?—A. It remains unadjusted up to this time.

Q. How soon did you begin to receive dividends upon this one hundred shares of stock that you received ?—A. I could not tell that from memory; it was very shortly afterward; I could not recollect the date.

Q. Can you state the amount of dividends you have received upon it ?—A. Not accurately. I can state, approximately, that I received about eight hundred and twenty-two shares, I think it was, of Union Pacific Railroad Company's stock in the aggregate, and then some first-mortgage bonds to the amount of about $20,000, par value—that is, twenty one-thousand-dollar bonds. That is what I recollect. I am not sure about it.

Q. What would be the par value of the Union Pacific Railroad stock you received ?—A. Of eight hundred and twenty-two shares, the par value would be $82,200, but it never sold for anything like that. It sold as low as $9 a share at one time.

Q. What was its market-value at the time you received it ?—A. I do not think it was on the market. It was on the broker's board, but I did not hear of any sales.

Q. How long a period of time was covered by these dividends; when did you receive the last dividend ?—A. I could not remember. I gave receipts for all I received.

Q. Have you received any dividends in money?—A. I have received one dividend, if I mistake not, of $9,000.

Q. Was that $9,000 on the one hundred shares, or $9,000 on the entire one hundred and fifty shares?—A. That I do not recollect. My memory is clear that I received one dividend of $9,000 in money.

Q. Can you state what time that was?—A. No; I cannot.

Q. These dividends of stock which you received are dividends on the one hundred shares?—A. The eight hundred and odd shares of stock, I think, must have been dividends on the one hundred and fifty shares. I am speaking of all I received altogether on the one hundred and fifty shares.

Q. Have you repaid any portion of the $10,000 that Mr. Brooks advanced you?—A. Yes; since I received it; although he did not demand it, I went and gave the $9,000 dividends to his agent. I have received other money beside from him. I have an open account with him. I have borrowed money, and he has given me money from time to time.

Q. Now, state what the transaction was in which you received the second certificate of fifty shares by which you became the owner of that amount of stock.—A. I went to the company and got it and paid for it.

Q. That is, by yourself?—A. I did it, together with Mr. Sidney Dillon. Dillon was there, and I saw him and got the money from him, and gave collateral security. He loaned money to me individually.

Q. Had Mr. Brooks anything to do with the purchase or obtaining these last fifty shares of stock?—A. Nothing whatever. I think he was out of town at the time.

Q. He furnished none of the money to pay for it?—A. Not to my knowledge. I obtained it from Mr. Dillon.

Q. Did you say Mr. Brooks was away?—A. He was not in town, I recollect, because I remember going to see him that evening, and he was away. I think he was in Washington.

Q. Had Mr. Brooks nothing to do, in any manner, about the negotiation or payment for that fifty shares of stock?—A. Nothing. I know that he told me that I was entitled to fifty shares of stock, and that I went there and asked for it and got it.

Q. Did he tell you you were entitled to fifty shares of stock by virtue of your having one hundred original shares?—A. Yes, it was in consequence of that. It was an increase of the capital stock by which the holders of original stock were entitled to the increase.

Q. Was there any question made, when you went to claim these fifty shares, as to your right to it?—A. I went first and did not get it. The second time I went I got it without any question.

Q. Whom did you see the first time?—A. I do not know the name of the gentleman. It was somebody behind the desk. I told him I had come for fifty shares I was entitled to.

Q. What did he say?—A. I have forgotten exactly what he said. I know I did not get it at the time. It was unsatisfactory in some way.

Q. Who was the man you had the transaction with at the time you received these last fifty shares?—A. Mr. Dillon, who was president of the company at the time, I believe. I gave him collateral security for more than the whole loan.

Q. He was the officer of the company from whom you received it?—A. Yes, sir.

Q. He not only loaned the money to pay for it, but he acted as officer on the part of the company to let you have the stock?—A. I do not know whether I got it from him or whether I got it from the desk. It is a long time ago, and I do not recollect all these details. He was the only one I had any words with, any conversation in relation to it.

Q. Has that loan been adjusted between you and Mr. Dillon?—A. I have not adjusted that loan with Mr. Dillon.

Q. You gave him security?—A. He has the security and I have his receipt.

Q. In what form?—A. In Union Pacific Railroad Company bonds I had in my safe. I deposited them with him as collateral security for the loan. Whether the loan has been taken up yet I do not know. I did not take it up myself.

Q. Nobody has taken it up for you to your knowledge?—A. Not to my knowledge.

Q. The last fifty shares of stock you received in February. Did you have that stock at par?—A. I think I gave over par for it. I think it was 104. I will not pretend to be accurate about it. It was over par, and I think it was four per cent. premium.

Q. Were you entitled upon that last fifty shares of stock and did you receive any accrued dividends that had been declared before the date of the certificate?—A. Not at that time. I do not know whether I received any subsequently. I received all that was to my credit on the books of the company, but I have not examined the books since to see whether I was entitled to more than I got or not.

Q. Do you know whether you did get any dividend prior to that receipt?—A. That I do not know. I never took the trouble to examine.

Q. But with these last fifty shares you say Mr. Brooks had no connection in any form?—A. Not with the purchase in any form.

Q. Has he had since in any way?—A. Not in any form whatever.

Q. And all he had to do with the first one hundred shares of stock was to loan the money to pay for it?—A. That was all. Whether he has taken up my loan on the fifty shares or not I do not know.

Q. You have never employed him to do it?—A. I have never employed him to do it. I authorized him generally to take care of everything, and let me know if there was anything for me to do.

Q. You have no knowledge that he has done anything in reference to the fifty shares?—A. No knowledge.

Q. You have never made any request of him to do it?—A. Never any request.

Q. If he has done anything in reference to it, it is by virtue of some general authority he has to act for you?—A. Yes, sir.

Q. I suppose you are aware that the question has been made whether this stock was yours, or the stock of Mr. Brooks, although standing in your name. What we want to ascertain is whether, in point of fact, it is yours, or whether, in point of fact, it is the stock of Mr. Brooks.—A. In point of fact, that one hundred shares of stock and the supplemental fifty shares are mine, and the dividends have been all collected by me, and they are mine still; all the profits coming from the Credit Mobilier are mine.

Q. You say that Mr. Brooks has no ownership, and has had no ownership in any way in these shares, but simply advanced $10,000 to purchase the first lot for you. He had no interest or concern in it except as loaning that amount of money?—A. Nothing beyond that.

Q. Was there any understanding that he was to have any profit or advantage from it?—A. No. On the contrary, the understanding was that it was to be mine.

Q. In regard to the $10,000 advanced to pay for it, was it understood that it was to be a loan of money to you, and that you were to repay it?—A. Nothing was said about repaying it at the time. He simply said he would advance it to me.

Q. Did you understand that it was a loan or a gift to you?—A. Not a gift, but a loan.

Q. And you understood that you were to repay it?—A. Yes, and I did repay $9,000 in money, and he has security for the balance, with the general open account between us.

Q. What security does he hold of yours?—A. First-mortgage bonds of the Union Pacific Railroad Company.

Q. These you received in the way of dividends?—A. Yes, I received them in the way of dividends.

Q. Did you own any other stock in the Union Pacific Railroad except what you received in the way of dividends?—A. I never did.

By Mr. MERRICK:

Q. Did you approach Mr. Brooks for the purpose of getting him to secure this stock, or did he mention the matter to you personally?—A. Mr. Brooks originally mentioned the matter to me.

Q. Can you remember the substance of what he stated?—A. It was to the effect that there was a chance there for me to make money, and that he would put it in my way, and had the power to do so.

Q. He had the power to put your name in?—A. It is so long since that I cannot be certain. I cannot recollect these conversations as far back as 1867.

Q. Did he explain to you how he could put your name in?—A. He did not make any explanation. He simply said to me that he did not care to hold any himself. That was all he said. It was a speculation. He told me he could put me in for one hundred shares.

Q. Did you advance any money at any time to him?—A. I never advanced him any money before I received the stock.

Q. Was this a sort of gift, an advancement to you as a matter of fatherly generosity?—A. It was an advance in the form of a speculation for my account.

Q. Did he explain to you that there would be any money necessary to pay for it?—A. He did not say anything of that. He said he would take care of it for me.

Q. He never inquired where the funds were to be raised by which he was to be paid?—A. No, sir; he left that entirely to me.

Q. Did you understand that payment could be made by the dividends arising from it?—A. There was no understanding of the kind with me.

Q. Was Mr. Brooks at that time an officer of the Union Pacific Railroad Company?—A. I do not know. I do not recollect. The records will show, I suppose.

By Mr. NIBLACK:

Q. You were at that time a son-in-law of Mr. Brooks?—A. Yes, sir.

Q. It has been stated to the committee, I do not recollect from what source, that your subscription of one hundred shares to this Credit Mobilier was not made in time, so as to entitle you, as a matter of right, to the increase of fifty per cent. at par; that is, the arrangement by which stockholders were entitled to this increase of fifty per cent. had expired some months before the date of your first certificate in December, 1867, and therefore that you could not have obtained these fifty shares of additional stock as a matter of right from the company. Have you any knowledge or recollection on this point?—A. No knowledge or recollection. I know nothing about it.

Q. Have you any recollection of any difficulty in getting it upon that ground?—A. There was no ground given to me at first; the answer was simply unsatisfactory, that I must call again, or words to that effect. I went subsequently and got it.

Q. And you understand that you got it as a matter of right under some arrangement with the company?—A. That was my understanding; that I was entitled to it as a matter of right.

Q. Do I understand that you paid for the fifty shares?—A. I have somewhere a receipt for the money paid out, I think at 104; I know I paid a premium; I do not recollect the exact payment.

By the CHAIRMAN:

Q. Do you know whether Mr. Brooks had any agency in getting these last fifty shares?—A. I do not know. He did not say anything to me about it.

Q. You went once to the office and called for fifty shares, but did not get it. You were told to call again, or had some put-off of that kind; did you make any application, or say anything, to Mr. Brooks upon the subject of these fifty shares?—A. I did. I told him I went to collect it, but could not get it at the time. I was told to call again; he told me to go and get it.

Q. He stated that you were entitled to it?—A. He stated I was entitled to it.

Q. Did you understand at the time you made application, and did not get the stock, that there was going to be any question or difficulty in your obtaining it?—A. I did not suppose there would be any difficulty. Mr. Brooks came, I think, where I was living and told me there was fifty shares of stock I was entitled to.

Q. This was before you went the first time?—A. That was before I went the first time.

Q. Was that the first knowledge you had that you were entitled to fifty shares?—A. Yes.

Q. Did you have any conversation as to who you were to pay for the fifty shares?—A. Not at all with him. He left that entirely to me. There was nothing said about paying for it that day.

Q. There was nothing said about his advancing it?—A. No; not for the fifty shares.

Q. There was nothing said as to how you were to raise the money for the fifty shares?—A. No; nothing said about it.

Q. Did you understand whether Mr. Brooks had anything to do with it; whether he interfered, whether he had personally any interview in reference to getting it?—A. Not to my knowledge.

Q. You mean us to understand that Mr. Brooks had nothing to do in any way or form about getting the fifty shares?—A. Nothing to my knowledge.

Q. Have you any reason to suppose he had?—A. No reason that I could fix upon.

Q. You have no reason to suppose that Mr. Brooks had anything more to do about getting the last fifty shares than anybody else?—A. No reason, any more than he came to me and said, or wrote to me, that I could get that fifty shares of stock.

Q. Can you tell at what time it was you got that information from Mr. Brooks; how long before you got the stock?—A. That I do not recollect.

Q. Did you understand that he wrote to you, or that you got this information from him in consequence of any negotiation with anybody?—A. No; I had no such understanding.

Q. It was a mere statement of fact that you were entitled to fifty shares additional stock because you were the owner of these one hundred shares?—A. That was all.

By Mr. MERRICK:

Q. How long after you got this information before you got the stock?—A. I think it must have been several weeks.

Q. Was the stock dated at the time you got it?—A. That I don't know. I did not look at the certificate to see what the date was, or whether it corresponded with the time I received it or not.

Q. Did you recollect what time you got it?—A. I do not recollect that.

Q. You borrowed some money from Mr. Dillon *at that time*, and pledged with him for the repayment of the money on certain bonds of the Union Pacific Railroad, which you had derived as dividends?—A. Yes; some in my possession; some of my own bonds.

Q. Which you had derived as dividends on the previous shares?—A. I never had any but my own bonds.

Q. But they were derived from dividends previously declared?—A. Previously declared—yes.

Q. How many bonds did you deposit with him, do you recollect, for that five thousand dollars?—A. About enough to cover the amount and a little margin over, enough margin to cover it. I think I gave him the certificate. The certificate, however, was not of any value except upon my indorsement on the back of it, which I see it has not, so that I must have given him other security.

Q. You did not give him a certificate then?—A. I gave him bonds. The certificate was worth no more than blank paper until my name was indorsed upon the back of it. I have a memoranda which will show exactly what I gave him.

Q. Have you got the memoranda with you?—A. I have not.

By Mr. McCRARY:

Q. Can you tell the committee how many dividends you received upon this stock?—A. No, I cannot; it is such a length of time. My memory is not good enough to enable me to state.

Q. I find here a statement of dividends running from July, 1866, to December, 1868; look at this list and state whether you received all these dividends.—A. If this is an accurate statement, I presume I must have collected all. I do not recollect.

Q. Do you mean to say you collected those which had accrued before you got your stock?—A. I collected all I was entitled to—all that the company gave me. That is all I can remember about it.

Q. Can you tell how much you realized upon that stock in the way of dividends?—A. Do you mean in the way of money?

Q. How much money and how much bonds?—A. I know I received eight hundred and odd shares of railroad stock and a cash dividend of nine thousand dollars. I do not recollect any other cash dividend.

Q. From whom did you collect the dividends; from what officer?—A. I think it was from Mr. Ham. Generally speaking, I do not recollect any other man.

Q. What position did he hold?—A. I think he was secretary, and he may have been treasurer.

Q. Did you in all cases collect directly from him personally?—A. That

I cannot say. I do not know whether I did or not. I do not recollect.

Q. Did Mr. Brooks collect any of the dividends and pay them over to you?—A. He never collected a single dividend. He could not do it without my authority, and I never gave him any such authority.

Q. Did any person collect them for you?—A. No; I collected them personally.

Q. In regard to this additional fifty shares, which you got by some arrangement with Mr. Dillon. How much money did you borrow from Mr. Dillon?—A. Over five thousand dollars. Five thousand and some hundreds. I have forgotten the exact amount.

Q. Upon what time was that borrowed?—A. No time fixed; it was a call loan.

Q. Do you know whether that loan is still unpaid?—A. I have not paid it myself.

Q. Have you any knowledge as to whether any other person has paid it?—A. I have no knowledge.

Q. Have you any information upon that subject at all?—A. No information. I have never spoken to Mr. Brooks at all about it, and he was not called upon to pay it.

Q. That loan was of the same date as the certificate of 50 shares?—A. I do not know whether it is or not. It was dated when I received the money and paid it over.

Q. Which was about February 28, 1868, about the date of the certificate?—A. I presume so.

Q. He gave you a receipt?—A. He gave me a receipt showing the money he had loaned me, and also the collateral I had furnished him.

Q. He did not give you a receipt for the stock?—A. I do not know that that was necessary.

Q. Did he give you a receipt for the money he had loaned you?—A. He gave me a receipt for the bonds I gave him for the loan, stating that it was collateral on that loan. That was the only receipt he gave me.

Q. So expressed upon its face?—A. So expressed upon its face.

Q. Have you that receipt?—A. Not with me.

Mr. MERRICK. You will please procure it and produce it before the committee.

By Mr. MCCRARY:

Q. Mr. Dillon has never called on you for a settlement of that money?—A. He has never on me.

Q. And you have never spoken to him on the subject?—A. No, sir.

Q. And have no reason to believe that it is settled?—A. I have not spoken to him about it, but it may have been settled.

Q. Have you any reason to believe that Mr. Brooks settled it?—A. No. If anybody has settled it, it must have been through or for Mr. Brooks.

Q. You said that you paid Mr. Brooks $9,000?—A. Yes; on account of that loan.

Q. Have you let him have any of the stock or receive any of the dividends?—A. No. No stock is in his name and none has been transferred to him.

Q. Have you paid Mr. Brooks any other money on that account?—A. I have given him nothing else except the bonds as collateral for the loan.

Q. What bonds have you received?—A. Union Pacific Railroad bonds.

Q. Did you turn over to him all the bonds you received in the way of dividends?—A. I do not recollect what I turned over to him at the time. He could not have had them all back. I gave some to Mr. Dillon, and I must have retained some myself.

Q. Did you give Mr. Brooks all the bonds except those you turned over to Mr. Dillon?—A. That I do not know. I gave Mr. Brooks enough to cover his loan, and I gave Mr. Dillon enough to cover his loan.

Q. Have you any bonds now in your possession?—A. I have; they are all mine.

Q. Are they in your possession?—A. Some are in the possession of Mr. Dillon.

Q. Have you any others except those you have hypothecated with Mr. Dillon?—A. I do not think I have. I think I have given all the bonds I have to Mr. Dillon and Mr. Brooks.

Q. Then if Mr. Dillon has turned over to Mr. Brooks the bonds you gave to him, Mr. Brooks has received all the bonds paid you in the way of dividends?—A. If he has, I suppose Mr. Brooks himself must have transferred the loan to his own account.

Q. Then I understand you to say that you have not now in your possession any of the dividends upon this stock, unless these bonds are with Mr. Dillon?—A. Nothing in my actual possession; they are hypothecated on other loans.

Q. You do not know whether Mr. Dillon still holds these bonds or not?—A. I cannot say; I do not know.

Q. Are you certain you received but one cash dividend upon the stock?—A. I do not recollect any other; it must have been very small, if there was any other, and made no impression upon me.

Q. According to this statement of June 17, 1868, there was a cash dividend of 60 per cent.; is that the one you refer to?—A. That is the one I refer to. It makes nine thousand dollars on the one hundred and fifty shares.

Q. Were not the first-mortgage Union Pacific Railroad bonds equivalent to cash?—A. They were not par in value, I think.

Q. What were they worth?—A. I do not know what they were worth at the time—somewhere in the neighborhood of 75, perhaps not so much. I do not think it was over that.

Q. What kind of bonds did you leave with Mr. Dillon?—A. They must have been first-mortgage bonds.

Q. Some of your dividend bonds?—A. I think so; the memoranda-receipt will show.

Q. You did not leave with him any Pacific Railroad stock?—A. No.

Q. What have you done with the Union Pacific Railroad stock received in the way of dividend?—A. I have it in my own possession, with the exception of three hundred shares, which I sold.

Q. I understood you to say that you had nothing in your possession except the bonds you left with Mr. Dillon?—A. I did not say I had no stock. I said no bonds. I said, on the contrary, I had over eight hundred shares of stock, which, with the exception of three hundred I sold, I still have.

Q. What you have left in your possession as dividends, then, is Union Pacific stock?—A. Yes.

Q. What is that stock worth?—A. To-day? I do not know. It fluctuates. One day it is forty or thirty-eight, and the next day it is down to thirty-five. I have not heard what the market-value is to-day.

Q. It is between thirty and forty, then?—A. That is too wide a margin; probably about thirty-five or thirty-six.

Q. Has Mr. Brooks ever said anything to you about the settlemei of your account with Mr. Dillon?—A. Not to my recollection.

By Mr. NIBLACK:

Q. According to your statement you are still the owner of somethin over five hundred shares of the Union Pacific Railroad stock?—A. Ye: sir.

Q. Is that stock in your own name?—A. It is in my own name an in my own possession. It is not hypothecated; I have it.

Q. Has it been in your own name ever since it was issued?—A. I has ever since it was issued. It has never been changed.

Q. Then none of your stock has ever been in the name of Mı Brooks?—A. Not one share of it.

Q. You received this stock as dividend from this Credit Mobilier?- Yes, sir.

By Mr. MCCOMB:

Q. I understood you to say a moment ago that fifty shares of th Credit Mobilier stock you received by virtue of your ownership of th first one hundred. Am I right in that?—A. That is what I said.

Q. Do you know when the increase of Credit Mobilier stock was mad entitling the holders to that increase?—A. I do not know the exac date.

Q. Did you get any notice from the Credit Mobilier corporation o any person that you were entitled of right to take an increase of you stock?—A. I may have done so, but do not remember.

Q. Do you not know that they served a written notice upon ever holder of the Credit Mobilier stock to that effect?—A. I do not kno that they did. I am not aware of it. I do not know many of the stock holders.

Q. From whom did you get the first hundred shares of that stock?— A. I explained all a moment ago to Judge Poland.

Q. Not with sufficient clearness, however. To whom did you pa your money for the first hundred shares?—A. I was unable to get that except through the influence of Mr. James Brooks, and he advance the money.

Q. Did he pay for it?—he must have paid for it.—A. I do not kno the fact.

Q. Did you know to whom he paid it?—A. I do not know. It wa paid and charged to my account, and the money must have been paid

Q. But not to your knowledge by you?—A. I did not pay it mysel with my own check.

Q. When you went to the office to get the stock, you found it alread paid for, and standing in your name?—A. Standing in my name, yes according to the understanding.

Q. To whom did you make application for the first hundred shares?— A. I do not know; it was the person I applied to in the Union Pacifi Railroad office.

Q. There are a good many persons there, are there not?—A. Ther are a great many there. I do not know which I applied to. There ar several gentlemen to whom I have applied on different occasions.

Q. Who are these several gentlemen?—A. Mr. Crane I have some times been there to see.

Q. What about?—A. I do not know. I have talked with him.

Q. Talked with him about this stock?—A. Not especially this stock.

Q. Had you any other business there except this?—A. No.

Q. You do not know what you talked about?—A. I do not remember.

know that I did not consider it a matter of sufficient importance to ake a memorandum of. I got my dividend, but I have collected larger vidends than that, frequently, on other transactions.

Q. When you got your certificate of one hundred shares, did you get dividend ?—A. I do not recollect whether I did on that day or not.

Q. Can you tell whether you did within two weeks of that ?—A. I unnot.

Q. When did you get dividends on your stock ?—A. I got them at urious times, distributed over years.

Q. You do not remember when you got the first dividend ?—A. There as one near the time I got my certificate of Credit Mobilier stock.

Q. You do not know whether you got it on that day or six months ter ?—A. I do not remember the time.

Q. Do I understand you that the dividends were distributed over ears ?—A. Over more than one year.

Q. Do you or not know that the original holders of Credit Mobilier ock received every dividend from the first declared, which was in pril, 1866, whether retrospectively or prospectively ?—A. I do not now about that. I do not know what all the holders did.

Q. Do you know whether you got that ?—A. I only know that I colcted all the dividends they would pay me.

Q. When you made application for the first certificate of stock you ceived, did you not at the same time get a memorandum, made out in gular form, with a description of stocks and bonds already accrued as vidends ?—A. I could not swear that I did.

Q. Did you not sign a book receipting for your dividends ?—A. I ways signed a book for receipts.

Q. Did you not sign a book without getting something ?—A. No, I ever did sign any book without receiving something for it.

Q. Do you recollect, when you gave the first receipt, what you reived ?—A. I do not remember.

Q. Do you know whether you got anything ?—A. I got something for or I would not have given the receipt.

Q. You do not know that you received stock and bonds which had ccrued; you do not know anything about that ?—A. No, sir.

Q. You say you got notice to go for this additional stock from Mr. rooks. Has Mr. Brooks given you a chance in other things ?—A. He is put me in other good things.

Q. Did you ever receive chances from him in the Atlantic and Pacific elegraph Company ?—A. No, sir; he never put me in any telegraph mpany.

Q. From whom did you get notice about the fifty shares of stock ?— Mr. Brooks told me I was entitled to fifty shares of stock.

Q. To whom did you make application for that stock ?—A. To one of e gentlemen in the office, I do not remember which. The only three knew in the office were Mr. Dillon, Mr. Crane, and Mr. Ham.

Q. What did you understand by Mr. Brooks having power to put you to this concern ?—A. I understood him exactly as I stated, that he uld put me into a good thing if I wanted to go in. That was my derstanding, that he would give me a chance and put me in the way making a good speculation.

Q. You say you got the money to pay for this additional stock from r. Dillon, president of the company; that you received the bonds hich you gave him at that time as collateral ?—A. I did not say that. gave him, as collateral, bonds which I had received long before.

Q. As dividends on the one hundred shares ?—A. Yes.

Q. Then you got dividends from the time you received the first stock until the time you collected the fifty shares?—A. I must have done.

Q. But you are not sure you did so?—A. Perfectly sure.

Q. You did not recollect it just now?—A. I did not recollect the date, whether it was the 16th or 18th of any month. I recollect getting the dividends.

Q. Do you recollect from whom you collected them?—A. I think it was from Mr. Ham; I will not be sure.

Q. Do you not know that the dividends were paid by Mr. Crane, and not by Mr. Ham?—A. No, sir; I do not know that.

Q. Do I understand you to say now that all the dividends you received on your Credit Mobilier stock were paid you by Mr. Ham, in 1868?—A. I did not state that.

Q. From whom did you get that?—A. I said I did not recollect. I got them from Mr. Crane or Mr. Ham. I think I collected from both of them.

Q. Then you say you have collected Credit Mobilier dividends from Mr. Ham?—A. I did not say that. I said from Mr. Crane or Mr. Ham; I do not remember which.

By Mr. McCrary:

Q. I see by this list of dividends that the last one mentioned was paid December 19, 1868. Can you tell us whether any dividend has been made since that upon the stock of the Credit Mobilier?—A. I do not remember.

Q. You cannot fix the date of the last dividend you received?—A. I cannot fix the date of it.

Q. Nor tell the year you received them?—A. No. I have had a great many transactions of the kind, and I cannot swear as to the dates of everything I have done.

Q. You cannot recollect whether you collected any in the year 1869?—A. I cannot recollect.

By the Chairman:

Q. I am requested by Mr. Brooks to ask you whether there was ever any understanding in any way or form that Mr. Brooks should realize any benefit from your shares of the Credit Mobilier?—A. Not the slightest understanding. On the contrary, it was the understanding that I was to receive all the benefit. That was the understanding between Mr. Brooks and myself.

Washington, D. C., *January* 14, 1873.

The Chairman stated that Mr. Brooks had yesterday requested the committee to send to the War Department and get the records of some military investigation in regard to Mr. McComb. He also gave the names of several witnesses whom he desired to have summoned. The committee understand the purpose of Mr. Brooks in making this request to be to prove that Mr. McComb had something to do with some other transactions which were not creditable. They consider that this would not be competent evidence, and therefore declined to go into it.

Mr. Brooks said that the allegation of Mr. McComb before the committee was that Mr. Alley gave Mr. Brooks fifty shares of Credit Mobilier stock upon condition that he should influence democratic members of Congress. Mr. Alley denied that charge, and no proof of it was alleged except the statement of Mr. McComb. If the allegation had made any impression or lodgment upon the mind of the committee he desired the testimony referred to from the War Department for the purpose of impeaching the credibility of Mr. McComb as a witness, and to throw more light upon the question as to whether the committee should believe Mr. McComb or should believe Mr. Alley.

The CHAIRMAN stated that the committee understood that to be the object of offering the evidence, and have ruled that if produced it would not be legal evidence for that purpose.

Examination of CHARLES H. NEILSON continued.

By Mr. SMITHERS, (counsel for Mr. McComb:)

Q. Judging from the report I have seen of your testimony yesterday, you stated that you borrowed from Mr. Dillon the sum of upward of $5,000. Am I right in that statement?—A. The sum was fifty-two hundred and some odd dollars.

Q. Will you be good enough to state how long you knew Mr. Dillon anterior to that?—A. I was introduced to Mr. Dillon, I think, some six months before that. I am not sure of the date.

Q. Was that introduction a casual one?—A. Not casual.

Q. By whom were you introduced to him?—A. By Mr. Brooks.

Q. Had you, or not, had frequent interviews with Mr. Dillon afterward, or were they casual merely?—A. Merely casual.

Q. Can you give me any information as to how many times you had met Mr. Dillon between the time of your first introduction and this investment of money?—A. I cannot recollect.

Q. Were they frequent or infrequent?—A. Infrequent, comparatively speaking.

Q. Then, if I understand you, Mr. Dillon was a comparative stranger?—A. What do you mean by a comparative stranger? I would know him if I met him on the street.

Q. Had you had any other business operations with him?—A. No business operations with him specially.

Q. No business operations specially. Had you any generally?—A. I had none.

Q. When this money was advanced, where was it advanced?—A. At Mr. Dillon's office.

Q. At the office of the Credit Mobilier?—A. At the office of the Credit Mobilier.

Q. How was it advanced—how paid—what form was it put in?—A. I cannot recollect the exact form, whether he gave me a check for it or not.

Q. You do not know, then, how it was advanced?—A. Not precisely. It was so long ago, and I did not take any memorandum of it.

Q. When was this security, if any, given to Mr. Dillon to repay him?—A. I gave that security for the loan in the ordinary way.

Q. When?—A. It was the 3d of March, 1868.

Q. At the time when you received the money from him?—A. At the time when I received the money from him.

Q. What was that security?—A. I have a memorandum of it in my pocket, if you would like to see it.

Q. A memorandum made at the time?—A. Made at the time.

Q. The committee would probably like to see it.—A. This is the memorandum to which I referred in my testimony yesterday. It reads: 'March 3, 1868. Received from Charles H. Neilson certificate 298, for

20 shares; 299, for 30 shares; capital stock U. P. R. R. Co., and first-mortgage bonds, as collateral for the loan of $5,233.33. Sidney Dillon."

Q. When was this stock transferred to you?

The WITNESS. Which stock do you refer to?

Q. When were the fifty shares transferred to you?—A. On the 29th February.

Q. Did you, on the 29th of February, receive a certificate for this stock?—A. No, sir; I did not.

Q. When did you receive the certificate?—A. When I paid for it.

Q. Then the certificate was made out before you borrowed the money?—A. The certificate is dated before I borrowed the money.

Q. Was it made out before?—A. I am not an officer of the company, and not a transfer clerk, and do not know. It was dated the 29th of February. That is the only guide I have.

Q. How came you to adopt the plan of borrowing money from Mr. Dillon?—A. I went to him and asked him on the spot.

Q. When; on that day?—A. On that day. That was the first of the negotiation which I made with Mr. Dillon.

Q. Had the certificate been made out in your name, previously dated the 29th of February?—A. The certificate was made out in my name, dated the 29th of February.

Q. How long before that had you any knowledge in relation to these fifty shares?—A. About the same time; in the latter part of February.

Q. Your knowledge, if I understand you correctly, came through the suggestions of Mr. Brooks?—A. My impression is that he told me I was entitled to more stock there.

Q. Had you any specific information, or did you inquire as to the operation of the Credit Mobilier and to your rights under it?—A. I have made no inquiry as to my rights under it.

Q. You knew nothing of those rights, except as derived from Mr. Brooks?—A. Nothing except as derived from Mr. Brooks. I was told I was entitled to fifty shares.

Q. That information came from Mr. Brooks originally?—A. From Mr. Brooks. I wish to say that I was summoned here at 10 o'clock Saturday night, and came on Sunday night, without going back to my office, or looking over any papers I had on the subject.

WASHINGTON, D. C., *January* 14, 1873.

J. A. GARFIELD, a member of the United States House of Representatives from the State of Ohio, having been duly sworn, made the following statement:

The first I ever heard of the Credit Mobilier was some time in 1866 or 1867—I cannot fix the date—when George Francis Train called on me and said he was organizing a company to be known as the Credit Mobilier of America; to be formed on the model of the Credit Mobilier of France; that the object of the company was to purchase lands and build houses along the line of the Pacific Railroad at points where cities and villages were likely to spring up; that he had no doubt money thus invested would double or treble itself each year; that subscriptions were limited to $1,000 each, and he wished me to subscribe. He showed me a long list of subscribers, among them Mr. Oakes Ames, to whom he referred me for further information concerning the enterprise. I answered that I had not the money to spare, and if

I had I would not subscribe without knowing more about the proposed organization. Mr. Train left me, saying he would hold a place open for me, and hoped I would yet conclude to subscribe. The same day I asked Mr. Ames what he thought of the enterprise. He expressed the opinion that the investment would be safe and profitable.

I heard nothing further on the subject for a year or more, and it was almost forgotten, when some time, I should say, during the long session of 1868, Mr. Ames spoke of it again; said the company had organized, was doing well, and he thought would soon pay large dividends. He said that some of the stock had been left or was to be left in his hands to sell, and I could take the amount which Mr. Train had offered me, by paying the $1,000 and the accrued interest. He said if I was not able to pay for it then, he would hold it for me till I could pay, or until some of the dividends were payable. I told him I would consider the matter; but would not agree to take any stock until I knew, from an examination of the charter and the conditions of the subscription, the extent to which I should become pecuniarily liable. He said he was not sure, but thought a stockholder would be liable only for the par value of his stock; that he had not the stock and papers with him, but would have them after a while.

From the case, as presented, I probably should have taken the stock if I had been satisfied in regard to the extent of pecuniary liability. Thus the matter rested for some time, I think until the following year. During that interval I understood that there were dividends due amounting to nearly three times the par value of the stock. But in the mean time I had heard that the company was involved in some controversy with the Pacific Railroad, and that Mr. Ames's right to sell the stock was denied. When I next saw Mr. Ames I told him I had concluded not to take the stock. There the matter ended, so far as I was concerned, and I had no further knowledge of the company's operations until the subject began to be discussed in the newspapers last fall.

Nothing was ever said to me by Mr. Train or Mr. Ames to indicate or imply that the Credit Mobilier was or could be in any way connected with the legislation of Congress for the Pacific Railroad or for any other purpose. Mr. Ames never gave, nor offered to give, me any stock or other valuable thing as a gift. I once asked and obtained from him, and afterward repaid to him, a loan of $300; that amount is the only valuable thing I ever received from or delivered to him.

I never owned, received, or agreed to receive any stock of the Credit Mobilier or of the Union Pacific Railroad, nor any dividend or profits arising from either of them.

By the CHAIRMAN:

Question. Had this loan you speak of any connection in any way with your conversation in regard to the Credit Mobilier stock?—Answer. No connection in any way except in regard to the time of payment. Mr. Ames stated to me that if I concluded to subscribe for the Credit Mobilier stock, I could allow the loan to remain until the payment on that was adjusted. I never regarded it as connected in any other way with the stock enterprise.

Q. Do you remember the time of that transaction?—A. I do not remember it precisely. I should think it was in the session of 1868. I had been to Europe the fall before, and was in debt, and borrowed several sums of money at different times and from different persons. This loan from Mr. Ames was not at his instance. I made the request myself. I think I had asked one or two persons before for the loan.

Q. Have you any knowledge in reference to any dealings of Mr. Ames with any gentlemen in Congress in reference to the stock of the Credit Mobilier?—A. No, sir; I have not. I had no knowledge that Mr. Ames had ever talked with anybody but myself. It was a subject I gave but little attention to; in fact, many of the details had almost passed out of my mind until they were called up in the late campaign.

By Mr. BLACK:

Q. Did you say you refused to take the stock simply because there was a lawsuit about it?—A. No; not exactly that. I do not remember any other reason which I gave to Mr. Ames than that I did not wish to take stock in anything that would involve controversy. I think I gave him no other reason than that.

Q. When you ascertained the relation that this company had with the Union Pacific Railroad Company, and whence its profits were to be derived, would you have considered that a sufficient reason for declining it irrespective of other considerations?—A. It would have been as the case was afterward stated.

Q. At the time you talked with Mr. Ames, before you rejected the proposition, you did not know whence the profits of the company were to be derived?—A. I did not. I do not know that Mr. Ames withheld, intentionally, from me any information. I had derived my original knowledge of the organization of the company from Mr. Train. He made quite an elaborate statement of its purposes, and I proceeded in subsequent conversations upon the supposition that the organization was unchanged. I ought to say for myself, as well as for Mr. Ames, that he never said any word to me that indicated the least desire to influence my legislative action in any way. If he had any such purpose, he certainly never said anything to me which would indicate it.

Q. You know now, and have known for a long time, that Mr. Ames was deeply interested in the legislation on this subject?—A. I supposed that he was largely interested in the Union Pacific Railroad. I have heard various statements to that effect. I cannot say I had any such information of my own knowledge.

Q. You mean that he did not electioneer with you or solicit your vote?—A. Certainly not. None of the conversations I ever had with him had any reference to such legislation.

By Mr. MERRICK:

Q. Have you any knowledge of any other member of Congress being concerned in the Credit Mobilier stock?—A. No, sir; I have not.

Q. Or any stock in the Union Pacific Railroad?—A. I have not. I can say to the committee that I never saw, I believe, in my life a certificate of stock of the Union Pacific Railroad Company, and I never saw any certificate of stock of the Credit Mobilier, until Mr. Brooks exhibited one, a few days ago, in the House of Representatives.

Q. Were any dividends ever tendered to you on the stock of the Credit Mobilier upon the supposition that you were to be a subscriber?—A. No, sir.

Q. This loan of $300 you have repaid, if I understood you correctly?—A. Yes, sir.

By Mr. MCCRARY:

Q. You never examined the charter of the Credit Mobilier to see what were its objects?—A. No, sir; I never saw it.

Q. If I understood you, you did not know that the Credit Mobilier had any connection with the Union Pacific Railroad Company?—A. I understood from the statement of Mr. Train that its objects were connected with the lands of the Union Pacific Railroad Company and the development of settlements along that road; but that it had any relation to the Union Pacific Railroad, other than that, I did not know. I think I did hear also that the company was investing some of its earnings in the bonds of the road.

Q. He stated it was for the purpose of purchasing land and building houses?—A. That was the statement of Mr. Train. I think he said in that connection that he had already been doing something of that kind at Omaha, or was going to do it.

Q. You did not know that the object was to build the Union Pacific Railroad?—A. No, sir; I did not.

WASHINGTON, D. C., *January* 14, 1873.

BENJAMIN F. HAM sworn and examined.

By the CHAIRMAN:

Question. State your residence and occupation. Answer. I reside in the State of New Jersey. My business is in New York. I am engaged, passively, in building railroads.

Q. Have you been in any way connected with the Union Pacific Railroad Company or the Credit Mobilier?—A. Yes, sir; as auditor of the Union Pacific Railroad Company and assistant secretary of the Credit Mobilier.

Q. How long have you been auditor of the Union Pacific Railroad Company?—A. From January, 1867, until October, 1870.

Q. You do not hold that position now?—A. No, sir; I do not.

Q. How early were you connected with the Credit Mobilier?—A. Early in 1867.

Q. Do you hold that position still?—A. I hold it now, but have not held it during all that time. I resigned the position in December, 1868, and received the appointment again in May, 1870.

Q. During that period of time, were you in any way connected with that company?—A. Simply as clerk.

Q. You were in the office of that company?—A. No, sir; the office was removed from place to place during that time.

Q. Have you now the custody of the books of the company?—A. Yes, sir.

Q. Have you brought here such as the committee directed you to bring?—A. They have been brought to the city, and I expect the Express Company to deliver them here every moment.

Q. I am requested by Mr. Alley to inquire whether a portion of the books were not in Philadelphia?—A. A portion of them were in Philadelphia, and it was necessary for me to telegraph to have them sent here. A portion of them I brought with me from New York.

Q. State whether you are familiar with the list of the stockholders of that company.—A. Yes, sir.

Q. Do you know Charles H. Neilson of New York?—A. I have met Mr. Neilson. I do not know whether I would recognize him if I would meet him now.

Q. Do you or not know whether his name appears as one of the shareholders of the company?—A. It does for one hundred and fifty shares.

Q. Have you any knowledge of the actual ownership of these shares, as to whether they belonged to Mr. Neilson or anybody else?—A. I supposed they belonged to Mr. Neilson. I know of nothing to the contrary.

Q. Have you ever known Mr. Brooks to have any interest in these shares?—A. I have no such personal knowledge.

Q. Have you ever known Mr. Brooks to have anything to do with these shares?—A. I do not know distinctly that he ever had.

Q. Have you ever known of any negotiations between Mr. Brooks and any officer of the company in reference to these shares?—A. I have no personal knowledge of any such negotiations.

Q. Do you know to whom the dividends declared upon these shares have been paid?—A. To Mr. Neilson.

Q. What are the books you have present?—A. I have the stock-ledger, the five certificate-books, and the letter-book.

Q. Is this the only stock-ledger the company has?—A. It is the only stock-ledger.

Q. Turn to the entry of Mr. Neilson's stock and state what it shows.—A. It shows the date of issue December 26, 1867. It shows the number of the certificates, the number of shares, and the receipt for the certificate of Mr. Neilson. It shows also that it was transferred to him by Mr. Thomas C. Durant.

Q. Then this stock before that time stood in the name of Mr. Durant, and was transferred by him to Mr. Neilson?—A. Yes, sir.

Q. What does the stock-ledger show in regard to the fifty shares increase? What do the words "new subscription" mean?—A. That means that he bought fifty shares additional of new stock, which was issued to him directly. That stock had not previously been in the name of any one; he took it directly from the company.

Q. Did you understand that he was entitled to take fifty shares of new stock in consequence of his ownership of the previous one hundred shares?—A. That was my understanding.

Q. When was the new stock authorized?—A. In February, 1867.

Q. And this issue of fifty shares was in March, 1868. It has been stated here that the time for taking this new stock was limited; that there was some short period of time within which the owners of original stock had the right to take additional shares, and that that time had expired long before this transaction?—A. The resolution adopted allowed the stockholders to take additional shares, as I recollect, within ninety days, but, after that period had expired, by general consent, it was extended. There were several large stockholders who had not then paid for their subscriptions.

Q. You mean, then, that the resolution was not regarded in its limitation, but that every man who was the owner of original stock was allowed to take, even at a later period, additional stock?—A. Yes, sir.

Q. Mr. Neilson was in that way allowed to take these fifty shares?—A. Yes, sir.

Q. It is stated here that he paid something in addition to the par value of this stock; that he paid $5,233 for the fifty shares. Can you explain what that premium was for?—A. This stock was issued the 1st of July, 1867, and every man who took stock subsequent to that date paid interest on this additional, and the $5,000 paid by Mr. Neilson was to adjust his interest account.

Q. This certificate of stock is dated February 29, 1868; how comes it that the date on the stock-ledger is the 3d of March?—A. I cannot explain, although the entries are in my handwriting.

Q. The entry on the ledger is supposed to correspond with the date of transer?—A. Yes, sir, with the transfer of the certificate; there must have been some mistake in the entries. I cannot account for it myself.

Q. Was this first one hundred shares, which stood in the name of Mr. Durant and then transferred to Mr. Neilson, really the stock of Mr. Durant, or did it belong to the company?—A. Mr. Durant had paid for it.

Q. Then you suppose that Mr. Neilson, or whoever paid for that stock, paid Mr. Durant instead of paying the company?—A. I suppose so; I know they did not pay the company.

Q. There is nothing, then, on your books to show that the payment was made by him; the payment was made at the time the stock was transferred to Mr. Neilson?—A. No, sir; the stock stood in the name of Thomas C. Durant, and the certificate came to me with the request that I would transfer it to Mr. Neilson.

Q. You have no knowledge by whom the payment was made, whether by Mr. Neilson or by anybody for him?—A. No, sir.

Q. In relation to the payment of the last fifty shares of stock, was that payment made to you?—A. Yes, sir.

Q. Have you the book here that shows in reference to them?—A. The cash-book, which I expect here every moment, will not show who I received it from, but it will show the date of its reception.

Q. Do you know whether Mr. Neilson paid it himself or whether anybody paid it for him?—A. I do not remember anything about it; when the cash-book is here it will show the date, and will show the money as coming from Mr. Neilson; whether it was really received from him I cannot say.

Q. Turn now to the name of Mr. Durant, as trustee, in the stock-ledger.—A. I do not think any of that stock was taken by Mr. Durant as trustee; I think it was taken in his own name, or in the name of H. C. Crane as trustee. Here is Mr. Durant's individual account. One of the certificate-books seems to be gone. I thought they were all here. I can show you, however, the particular certificate from which this stock was taken. I see that one certificate for three hundred and fifteen shares was canceled; of that, two hundred and fifteen shares were issued to Mr. T. C. Durant, and on the same day one hundred to Mr. Neilson.

Q. Do you say there was no stock standing in Mr. Durant's name as trustee?—A. I think none of it was issued to Mr. Durant as trustee.

Q. Then two pages are all there is on the stock-ledger, referring to Mr. Durant's account of stock?—A. Yes, sir; some of the stock apportioned to Mr. Durant was issued to H. C. Crane. Mr. Crane is private secretary, and that stock was issued to him as trustee.

Q. Then the stock held in the name of Mr. Crane was held for Mr. Durant?—A. That was the understanding; I do not know anything about it.

Q. Turn now to the page containing the entries of Mr. Crane's stock. —A. Yes, sir; the only stock that now stands in his name is one hundred and fifty-three shares; twenty-five shares appear to have been issued to B. M. Boyer, as trustee of Mrs. Boyer, and the balance was issued to Mr. Crane under date of September 12, 1866.

Q. Now, turn to the account of stock of Oakes Ames, as trustee, and state how much appears on that account.—A. Three hundred and thirty shares now appear in his name; three hundred and forty-three shares was the amount originally stated, but thirteen shares have been transferred; ten shares were transferred to H. J. Gilbert, of Boston, and three shares to R. D. Bush, trustee.

Q. Do you know who he is?—A. Yes, sir; he lives in New York.

Q. Do you know for whom he is trustee?—A. That belongs to my son; Mr. Bush holds these three shares as trustee for my son.

Q. Do you know whether or not a portion of the stock standing in the name of Mr. Ames, as trustee, has ever been sold to anybody, except the thirteen shares?—A. I do not.

Q. Have you ever had any information from him that anybody was the owner of any portion of that stock, except as to these thirteen shares?—A. No, sir.

Q. Have you any knowledge in relation to his having contracts for any portion of it with anybody?—A. Nothing except a general knowledge, such as people would get from the papers and from his own published testimony.

Q. I mean knowledge derived from your personal knowledge?—A. No, sir; I have no personal knowledge.

Q. Have dividends been declared upon this stock standing in the name of Mr. Ames, as trustee, the same as upon other stock of the company?—A. They have.

Q. Can you state to whom these dividends have been paid?—A. They have been paid to Mr. Ames, as trustee.

Q. Have you any knowledge as to what was done with the money?—A. No, sir; I have not.

Q. Can you state how this stock came to stand in the name of Mr. Ames, as trustee, or who he is trustee for?—A. I have no personal knowledge on that subject.

Q. Do you know, from your connection with the business, why it was that this amount of stock was different from the rest of the stock Mr. Ames held, and why it was put in his name as trustee?—A. Because he requested it to be issued in that way; if he had requested it to be issued to Oakes Ames I should have issued it to him.

Q. Was this stock paid for to the company by Mr. Ames at the time he received the certificates?—A. Yes, sir, except that some of it was paid for before he received the certificates.

Q. The stock has all been paid for to the company by Mr. Ames and he has received all the dividends upon it?—A. Yes, sir, all the dividends the Credit Mobilier ever made.

Q. Have you here a book showing the dividends that were made?—A. That book will be here shortly; however, there was but one dividend made by the Credit Mobilier. I paid that myself.

Q. When was that made?—A. I should prefer to take the books as the dates. It was 6 per cent. interest each year for two years, made in Union Pacific Railroad Company stock at $30 a share.

By Mr. BLACK:

Q. Payable in gold, was it not, or in stock at $30 a share, at the option of the stockholders?—A. No, sir; in stock only.

Q, That is the only dividend that appears upon the books of the Credit Mobilier?—A. Yes, sir, this is the only one.

By Mr. MERRICK:

Q. I see that three hundred and forty-three shares were transferred to Mr. Ames in small parcels of ten and twenty share certificates; can you explain why it was not transferred in gross in one certificate?—A. Because Mr. Ames requested it, and I always issued at the request of parties in such amounts as they desired.

By the CHAIRMAN:

Q. Do you remember whether he gave any reason for that request?—A. No, sir.

Q. Did you understand why he wished to transfer it in small sums?—A. I supposed he held the stock for different parties and that it was in that way and for that reason, so that he might give them their certificates.

Q. Do you not know whether Mr. Ames said so?—A. No, sir; that is what I presumed. I presume that he had the certificates issued in small lots, so that he could give the stock to the parties for whom he held it.

Q. But you do not know it from him?—A. No, sir.

Q. This is the only stock-ledger of the company?—A. It is the only stock-ledger.

Q. It will show the name of every person who has been an owner of stock in the Credit Mobilier?—A. I think it will show the name of every person to whom certificates of stock have been issued.

By Mr. MERRICK:

Q. I suppose this stock was like other stocks of incorporated companies, transferable upon indorsement and power of attorney?—A. Yes, sir; I think that is the usual mode of transfer, with the name in blank.

Q. And the parties to whom it passes intermediately are not noticed at all in your certificate-books, although it may have passed from hand to hand a dozen times?—A. No, sir; we should have no knowledge of that. I think the stock is seldom transferred on the books of the company in New York, except when dividends are to be declared or for the purpose of an election. The parties in whose name the stock stands when the books are closed for the dividends are the parties to whom the dividend is paid.

Q. So that the man whose name appears on your stock-ledger when the dividend is declared is the man to whom you pay the dividend, although another person may be the owner of the stock?—A. Yes, sir.

Q. Suppose he gives a blank power of attorney to the party who owns it; will you not transfer the stock to him?—A. The party in whose name the certificate stands on our books is the party who will collect the dividends. For instance, I sold the other day one hundred shares of Northwestern stock standing in my name, and the party to whom I sold it had to come to me to get his dividend or a power of attorney from me to collect the money.

Q. Do I understand you if A holds twenty shares, upon which a dividend will be declared next July, and those twenty shares are transferred a half a dozen times, that the ultimate holder must hunt up the man in whose name it stood on the books and get his authority before he can draw the dividends?—A. Yes, sir. He must get his authority or a power of attorney, unless he has had it transferred before the books were closed. If that has been done, it will appear upon the stock-ledger in the name of the proper owner, but the certificate must have been surrendered. He can then draw the dividend in his own name.

Q. How much time does the letter-book which you have produced here cover?—A. It is the only letter-book I have in my possession, and the only one I know of.

Q. This seems to commence February 23, 1867. Does it extend to the present time?—A. Yes, sir.

Q. Are you in the habit of keeping copies of your letters?—A. Yes, sir; but we seldom write any letters. The company is not doing any business.

Q. Then this book embraces all the letters that have been written for the company from its commencement to the present time?—A. It embraces all written by me and all handed down to me by my predecessors. It is the only letter-book I have, or have ever seen, belonging to the company.

Q. Who has the custody of the books and papers which show the transactions in the Oakes Ames contract?—A. I presume Oliver Ames has charge of them. That, however, is a presumption on my part. I had nothing to do with that.

Q. Do you know who originally kept the account under that contract?—A. Mr. Crane did originally, but I presume they have been turned over to Oliver Ames, as chairman of the trustees.

By the CHAIRMAN:

Q. The dividends that have been made, except the one you referred to, have been made through the intervention of these trustees, and do not appear at all upon the books of the Credit Mobilier?—A. No, sir; they do not appear upon their books.

Q. All the letters in this book, except a few of the earliest, were writen by yourself?—A. Yes, sir.

Q. Was there anything in this correspondence that relates to the transactions in regard to these shares that stand in the name of Neilson?—A. No, sir.

Q. Was there anything in any of them in reference to the shares issued to Mr. Ames in his name as trustee?—A. There may be something of that kind. I frequently wrote letters to Mr. Ames.

Q. I see here notices sent to various parties that they must come in by a certain time and take their additional 50 per cent. of stock or it would be canceled?—A. Yes, sir; but, as I stated, that notice was not enforced.

Q. The name of Mr. Brooks does not appear on your books as a holder of stock?—A. No, sir.

Q. Does the name of Mr. Dawes, of Massachusetts; Mr. Garfield, of Ohio; Mr. Scofield or Mr. Kelley, of Pennsylvania?—A. No, sir.

By Mr. MERRICK:

Q. Can you explain how it was that these fifty shares appear dated February 29, and not paid for until the 3d of March?—A. I do not know. This book may be in error. Mr. Neilson did not get the stock until he paid for it. There is some mistake in these entries which I cannot now account for.

Q. Is it in accordance with the course of your business that the stock should be issued before it was paid for?—A. No, sir; he did not get it until he paid for it. Perhaps when I get the cash-book I will be able to explain the discrepancy. It may have been issued on the 29th of February, and not delivered until he paid for it on the 3d of March. Sometimes the president of the company was absent when I had directions to issue stock, and the certificate may have been written, dated, and remained two or three days for the signature of the president. I cannot tell where the discrepancy occurred.

Q. You may have delivered it at a subsequent date, I suppose, while the certificate itself was antedated?—A. Yes; that might be done if it had been issued as I said, and kept in my possession waiting for it to be paid for, or for the signature of the president, it would appear to be antedated.

By Mr. McCrary:

Q. You issued these additional fifty shares yourself?—A. Yes, sir.

Q. Did Sidney Dillon have anything to do with it?—A. I presume as president of the company he directed it and he signed the certificate.

Q. Do you know whether he furnished the money to pay for it?—A. No, sir; that would be a personal matter, of which I would know nothing.

Q. You do not know of any loan he made to Neilson at that time?—A. No, sir; that would be a personal matter that I should not know about.

Q. You know nothing personally about the dividends paid after the Ames contract was entered into?—A. No, sir.

Q. Do you know that the profits were divided among the holders of the Credit Mobilier stock?—A. For a time they were. Afterward they were divided among certain individuals.

Q. Were these certain individuals the same as the holders of the Credit Mobilier stock?—A. They were the same as the holders at that date. The transfer of stock on the books of the Credit Mobilier, after that date, did not convey any interest to the Oakes Ames contract.

Q. Why was the Credit Mobilier abandoned after the Ames contract was entered into?—A. Mr. Durant can tell you the whole history of that better than I can. Any statement I could make about it would be merely from hearsay.

Q. Do you know how many dividends were made after you went into the Credit Mobilier?—A. No, sir; I do not recollect.

Q. This one, declared by the Credit Mobilier as a corporation, you paid yourself?—A. Yes.

Q. And you say you paid Neilson his share in person?—A. The certificates of the Union Pacific Railroad stock were issued to Mr. Neilson on the company's books, I presume, and their books will show who receipted for them.

Q. You do not remember the particular transaction, then, of paying that dividend to Neilson?—A. No; I do not.

By Mr. Niblack:

Q. You had no official or personal connection with the trustees of the Ames contract?—A. No, sir.

Q. Have not many persons confounded in their minds the profits made upon that contract and the profits made upon the Credit Mobilier stock?—A. I presume so.

Q. Who can best inform the committee in regard to the operations of the trustees of the Oakes Ames contract?—A. Mr. Crane can inform you in regard to that.

Q. Was the change made from the Credit Mobilier, as the contractor, to the trustees for the purpose of avoiding the payment of the Pennsylvania State tax?—A. Yes, sir; I believe so.

Q. But the stockholders continued to receive the same dividends they would have received if the Credit Mobilier had been the contractor?—A. That is involved in the history of the Ames contract, which Mr. Alley or Mr. Ames can tell you better about than I can. I know simply in regard to the transactions of the Credit Mobilier corporation. Mr. Crane, or Mr. Ames, or Mr. Alley can give you the facts in regard to the execution of the Ames contract.

Q. Do your stock-books show that any members of Congress are stockholders of the Credit Mobilier?—A. Yes, sir; they show that Samuel Hooper was interested as a member of the firm of Samuel Hooper & Co.; that B. F. Boyer was interested, and Mr. Grimes and Mr. Alley were.

Q. Was Mr. Boyer an original subscriber to the stock, or did he purchase the certificate afterward?—A. He purchased afterward. Mr. Grimes, Mr. Hooper, and Mr. Alley were among the original subscribers.

Q. None of these received any part of the stock that stood in the name of Mr. Ames, as trustee, to your knowledge?—A. No, sir; that stock Mr. Ames still holds in his own name, as trustee, except the two small certificates to which I have referred.

Q. You stated that the time during which parties holding original stock were allowed to take additional stock was extended by common consent; is there any official action on record making the extension?—A. No, sir.

Q. Did anybody besides Neilson get stock after the time had expired?—A. I think several parties did.

Q. Will you give us the names of any others?—A. I think Mr. G. G. Bray received his, and he was a very heavy stockholder.

Q. How long after the time had expired elapsed before Neilson took his additional stock?—A. It was over six months. I see several parties on the books who took their additional stock after the expiration of the ninety days.

By the CHAIRMAN:

Q. I see in the letter-book, here, a letter from yourself to Mr. Ames, dated January 20, 1868, which letter is as follows:

"JANUARY 20.

"DEAR SIR: Your letters of the 14th and 18th were received this p. m. The one of the 14th was addressed Boston instead of New York. Draft of $3,105 is received, as stated. I have transferred to Oakes Ames, trustee, the remainder of the Credit Mobilier stock of $22,000; have made two certificates of thirty each, six of twenty each, and four of ten each. I inclose herewith one of twenty and one of ten, as desired by you, and will forward others when desired. There is no stated time for the meetings of the Credit Mobilier of America. There will be one whenever Mr. Hazzard and Mr. Alley are both here. I wrote you Saturday in regard to bonds, &c. Our sales to-day amount to 105. We have $350,000 cash on hand; are paying our paper when we can get 7 per cent. off; have used over half of the first thousand bonds as collateral.

"Respectfully,

"BENJAMIN F. HAM.

"Hon. OAKES AMES, M. C.,
"*Washington, D. C.*"

What explanation have you to the reference here made to dividing this stock up into small certificates?—A. It was at Mr. Ames's request.

Q. Does this letter give you any further information in relation to why that was done?—A. No, sir. I suppose he was about to dispose of it.

Q. Then you made the certificates in that way by Mr. Ames's direction, and, as you supposed, for convenience of delivery?—A. Yes, sir.

I supposed for the purpose of enabling him to deliver it to different individuals.

Q. I see another letter in this letter-book, dated January 31, 1868, which reads as follows:

"JANUARY 31.

"DEAR SIR: Your letter of the 27th is received, with contents as stated. The parties should pay 7 per cent. from July 1, 1867, to date of payment. I inclose herewith certificates for ten shares, as desired by you. The transfer of 300 to H. S. McComb, I do not understand what it is for. If it is on account of the 500 Credit Mobilier, you will know.

"Respectfully,

"BENJAMIN F. HAM,
"*Assistant Secretary Credit Mobilier of America.*

"Hon. OAKES AMES,
"*Washington, D. C.*"

Do you preserve all the letters you receive?—A. No, sir; this Credit Mobilier during the time I was out of office was pushed around from one place to another, and many of the papers were lost. During the James Fisk raid, the company was transferred to New Jersey, Pennsylvania, and to other places, and many of the papers were lost.

Q. Do you suppose you could produce the letter of Mr. Ames, under the date 29th January?—A. No, sir; I do not.

Q. Have you any recollection whether he stated in that letter what he wanted the certificates for?—A. I know that he did not state what they were for. I suppose he wanted to dispose of them from the fact that I wrote him that he ought to collect 7 per cent. from July 1, 1867.

Q. And that interest you suppose made up the premium on the fifty shares of Neilson's stock?—A. Yes, sir; he paid interest from the 1st of July, 1867, in the same way.

Q. Do you know anything in relation to how these shares stood in the market in December, 1867, and January, 1868?—A. After this subscription was first made, the stock could have been bought at 90; I could have bought it at 90 myself.

Q. How long did it remain at ninety?—A. I think for two or three months—from January until May, 1867; still it was not upon the market.

Q. In December, 1867, and January, 1868, what was it selling for?—A. There were no sales that I knew of, and knew the price. The rates were so high that parties who sold and the parties who purchased would not state what was paid.

Q. Do you know that any sales were made?—A. Some transfers were made, but not to exceed a thousand shares.

Q. Can you give any opinion as to the value that holders of this stock placed upon it in December, 1867, and January, 1868?—A. They considered it very valuable.

Q. Was there any general opinion among them as to how valuable it was?—A. They all considered it valuable, and did not wish to part with it.

Q. Do you know what Mr. Ames or Mr. Alley considered it worth?—A. No, sir.

Q. What did you consider it worth yourself?—A. I should not have wanted to pay the prices at which it was held by various parties.

Q. What prices?—A. From two to three hundred.

Q. Do you think you would have lost anything if you had purchased at that price?—A. I think if I had held on to all the dividends received until this time, with the stock and securities, I should not have made anything.

Q. The value of the stock itself has gone down, you mean?—A. Yes, sir.

Q. The first-mortgage bonds of the Union Pacific Railroad Company have not depreciated in value?—A. They were selling at 85 yesterday.

By Mr. BLACK:

Q. It seems that a number of the stockholders or directors of the Credit Mobilier authorized Mr. Ames to receive two hundred and fifty shares at one time and ninety-three shares at another time. Were you present at the time when that was done on either occasion?—A. I do not think it was done at a meeting of the stockholders.

Q. Were you present when it was done by a certain number of stockholders, who were directing the affairs of the company?—A. I think it was done by signing an agreement to that effect. I may have seen some of the signatures put on.

Q. Did you ever hear any of the conversation which led to it?—A. No, sir.

Q. Do you know whether Mr. Ames, or anybody else there present, agreed that the shares thus given to him as trustee should be distributed?—A. No, sir.

Q. Do you know of any intention of their being distributed at Washington, among members of Congress or other persons here, or whether he was to distribute them elsewhere?—A. There was nothing said to me on that subject.

Q. Nor for what parties they were put into his hands?—A. No, sir; I was simply a clerk in the transaction.

Q. Did Mr. Ames pay anything for these shares at that time?—A. He paid for them before he took them. He paid for them at different times.

Q. When the entry was made upon the books of the Credit Mobilier of the transfer to Oakes Ames of the three hundred and forty-three shares—two hundred and fifty and ninety-three—was he put down generally as the owner of that gross amount, or was there any entry made as to who was the owner of the different lots of ten, twenty, thirty shares, &c.?—A. No, sir. And there was no entry made until the cash was received.

Q. And the cash was not received until he directed them to divide them in that way?—A. No, sir.

Q. And he took them there at different times?—A. Yes, sir.

Q. Was there ever a list of stockholders made out?—A. Certainly; several lists. Every year one.

Q. Wherever he is put down as a trustee for other stockholders, he is put down for that amount of three hundred and forty-three shares?—A. Yes, sir; except that in November, 1868, he transferred the ten and three shares, as I have stated. With that exception the three hundred and forty-three shares have remained on the stock-list in his name as trustee.

Q. Then he is supposed to have disposed of these different lots before he took the certificates for them, and he took the certificates only to get the money from the persons he had sold them to?—A. I presume not. I suppose he put them into his own pocket. He gave me his own checks for the money, and usually upon Boston banks.

Q. Of course it was his own money when he got it, no matter how he got it. Did Oakes Ames receive all the dividends made, or allotments divided to the different stockholders, the same as anybody else did? That is, did these three hundred and forty-three shares receive the same amount of dividend that anybody else got on the same number of shares? —A. They received the same number of dividends that any other like amount of Credit Mobilier stock received.

Q. Did any other stockholders of the Credit Mobilier receive a larger share in proportion out of the profits of the railroad company?—A. The profits of the Oakes Ames contract Mr. Crane can explain fully to you. He can state whether Mr. Ames received the same profits as any one else. I had nothing to do with it.

Q. Can you state whether Mr. Ames received all the profits that accrued upon these three hundred and forty-three shares of Credit Mobilier stock?—A. No, sir.

Q. Do you know whether he had been receiving the dividends which had previously accrued on the three hundred and forty-three shares?—A. He had; yes, sir.

Q. You say that Mr. Durant was the owner of the stock which was assigned to Neilson, and that he held it in the name of Crane?—A. No, sir. The stock was in Mr. Durant's name. The stock was never in the name of Crane.

Q. Do you know how he got that stock?—A. The identical certificate from which it was transferred was a part of the original subscription.

Q. Do you know by what authority, or for what reason, or in pursuance of what agreement the fifty shares were directed to be transferred from Mr. Durant to Neilson?—A. They were never transferred at all; they were new stock. They had never been issued to anybody.

Q. By what authority were they given to Neilson, by whose direction?—A. By the authority of the parties in interest. I certainly would not have issued the stock without authority.

Q. Who were the parties in interest?—A. The heavy stockholders.

Q. Did they direct it to be done in writing?—A. I think they did.

Q. Have you that writing with you?—A. I have not. As I said, many of the papers, during the time while I was not secretary—when they were lost—they were scattered. The books were in the office of Mr. Barnes, some of the time, in Philadelphia. They were kept there quite a time.

Q. Kept there to avoid judicial process?—A. To avoid judicial process in the State of New York.

Q. Who were the signers of that paper?—A. I cannot remember.

Q. Have you any idea whose names were affixed to it?—A. I think Mr. McComb was one. [Mr. McComb. I was not.] I do not recollect positively what names were on it.

Q. Was Oakes Ames's name on it?—A. I do not think he signed it, and I do not think Oliver Ames signed it.

Q. Who were the heavy stockholders?—A. Mr. Durant was one of the heaviest. I think Oliver Ames was second; and Oakes Ames was a very heavy stockholder.

Q. Is the paper you now refer to the one which specifically authorized the transfer of the fifty shares?—A. Yes, sir; that is as I understand.

Q. When these shares were issued, which were accretions of the stock which had been previously taken, were they not accompanied with a bond of $1,000 for every ten shares?—A. They were ordinarily accompanied with a bond; that is, the parties holding original stock, who received the 50 per cent. additional, received a $1,000 bond for every $1,000 of shares.

Q. Which bond would pay for stock?—A. Not quite, because the bonds were not worth par. The bonds at par would pay for the stock.

Q. They were the first-mortgage bonds of the company?—A. Yes, sir.

Q. Who were at that time the executive committee of the Credit Mobilier?—A. I should prefer to look at the records. I think Mr. Alley, Mr. Hazzard, and Mr. Dillon were the executive committee.

Q. Do you take your directions in your official conduct from them?—A. Yes, sir.

Q. Would you have considered yourself authorized to issue any stock, or doing anything else of as much importance as to issue this stock, without their direction?—A. Not without the direction of the executive committee or the direction of the president. I would have done anything Mr. Dillon, the president of the company, directed.

Q. Was that after the Credit Mobilier ceased to be used as a corporation by the Union Pacific Railroad, or before?—A. It was after the Credit Mobilier had anything to do with the construction of the road.

Q. Then what authority would Mr. Dillon, as president of the company, have to direct you, when the whole business was in the hands of the seven trustees?—A. The business of the Credit Mobilier was never in the hands of the seven trustees. The contract made with Oakes Ames was in the hands of seven trustees. The business of the Credit Mobilier was not in their hands; it was conducted by itself, and by its proper officers.

Q. Had these corporate officers any control in the Pacific Railroad afterward?—A. It had control over the issue of its own stock.

Q. What value had that stock apart from the profits it would make out of that contract?—A. It had no value except that the assets were worth something.

Q. The assets amounted to the par value of the capital?—A. No, sir; a portion of that par value had been divided; it had not all been retained. In taking this new subscription the company had to buy these bonds of the Union Pacific Railroad Company and pay for them with their own money. They paid them out to their new stockholders; consequently the new stock did not net the Credit Mobilier anything. They bought them, and paid 85, the market price.

Q. The bonds they divided under the new subscription was not called a dividend, was it? It was based on the new subscription?—A. Yes; it was not called a dividend.

Q. Whom did they buy the bonds from?—A. From the Union Pacific Railroad Company.

Q. And paid for them out of the capital stock?—A. Paid for them out of the money they received for the new subscription.

Q. They divided these bonds, after buying them out of their own capital? That was a corporate act done by the Credit Mobilier?—A. Yes, sir.

Q. And yet the Credit Mobilier has made no dividend except two of 6 per cent. each?—A. They did not make the allotment of bonds under the new subscription as a dividend; it was a part of the subscription. There was an agreement in the subscription that these parties who took the stock should receive the bonds. There was no regular dividend resolution passed by the company.

Q. Was it not in fact a dividend, regular or irregular?—A. You might call it so.

Q. Do you say that the assets of the company have been exhausted in this way?—A. No, sir; I do not say that the assets of the company have been exhausted.

Q. How nearly have they been exhausted? How much of the capital has been disposed of in this way?—A. It would be difficult to say what the assets of the company amount to now.

Q. Let me ask you whether you could or could not have issued that fifty shares of stock to Neilson without special direction or instruction either from the president of the Credit Mobilier or the executive committee of that institution?—A. I could not have issued it without the signature of the president. All the stock-certificates bear his signature.

Q. Had you, or any other subordinate of the company, a right to sell that stock to anybody? Was it up for sale? Were the books open for receiving subscription?—A. No, sir.

Q. Then any issue of these fifty shares must have been the result of some special agreement between the authorities of the company and the person who received them?—A. Yes, sir.

Q. But you say you do not know what the nature of the agreement was?—A. No, sir; the agreement might have been made known to me at the time.

Q. Do you say it was, or was not, made known to you?—A. It may have been made known to me, and I may have been instructed to issue it on account of the desire of the principal stockholders.

Q. Who would give you such instructions?—A. Mr. Dillon, the president, or Mr. Hazard, or any one else having authority.

By Mr. MERRICK:

Q. Let me ask whether, when you delivered this stock to Neilson, you delivered to him also the bonds of the Union Pacific Railroad Company, according to the general arrangement under the new subscription?—A. I will state that as soon as I receive the cash-book of the company. This was four or five years ago, and I do not remember.

Q. It would have been in accordance with the course of dealing of the company in this matter to have issued such bonds to Neilson at the moment of delivering to him the certificate of his stock?—A. Yes, sir.

By Mr. BLACK:

Q. When it was concluded to discard the corporate machinery of the Credit Mobilier in this business and substitute the seven trustees, did that make any difference in the right of the stockholders of the Credit Mobilier to receive the same dividends which they would have been entitled to if no such transaction had taken place?—A. I presume it did not.

Q. The stock of the Credit Mobilier continued to be transferable as before?—A. Yes, sir.

Q. And the transferring of stock carried with it, of course, the right to receive the dividends which would otherwise be received on the stock?—A. The dividends were paid upon stock-lists furnished by me.

Q. Just as they would have been if they had been declared by the corporate authorities of the Credit Mobilier?—A. Yes, sir.

Q. Was there any difference in the arrangement of the whole matter, except in the mere personal material by which it was done, the mere organism of the association?—A. Yes, sir; there was a decided difference. I was assistant secretary of the Credit Mobilier, keeping these books and accounts, and they had nothing whatever to do with the Oakes Ames contract.

Q. Was Mr. Alley generally at the meetings of the executive committee?—A. Not necessarily. It only took two to make a majority of the executive committee.

Q. Was Mr. Alley generally one of the majority?—A. No, sir; sometimes Mr. Hazard and Mr. Dillon acted, and sometimes Mr. Dillon and Mr. Alley.

Q. Was Mr. Alley the principal man or the leading man among them?—A. Mr. Alley had a good deal of influence.

Q. Do you know whether he did not take such a supervision of the affairs of the company there as to make it almost necessary for him to know everything that took place, at least in regard to every important transaction that took place?—A. No, sir; I do not know that it did become necessary.

Q. Was it not his duty, as a member of the executive committee, to see to everything of very great importance?—A. The duties of the executive committee were to transact all the business that the board of directors could transact. They were not required to do it, but they had the power and the authority to do it.

Q. Did not the possession of that power and authority require them to exercise it properly and carefully?—A. That is a legal question, and I am not a legal man.

Q. You might know enough of law for that without being hurt. Did you ever see Mr. Alley looking over the books?—A. Not very frequently.

Q. Did he ever ask you when he came back what had been done?—A. These things occurred six years ago, and I can hardly remember every circumstance.

Q. Did he call upon you for an account of your stewardship?—A. An account of my stewardship was annually rendered at the annual meeting of the corporation.

Q. Was that all?—A. If he asked me for information, I always gave it to him. I do not think Mr. Alley ever required of me any specific information in writing.

Q. Did he not take a very lively interest in all these transactions?—A. He took a lively interest in the Credit Mobilier. He was a heavy stockholder, and I suppose he took more interest because Oakes Ames and Oliver Ames were among the heaviest stockholders.

Q. What business was the Credit Mobilier interested in besides this?—A. It never had any other business, except that it is just now trying to dissolve its corporation capacity, and surrender its charter.

Q. You referred to a paper, signed by certain of the heavy stockholders, authorizing these fifty shares to be issued to Mr. Neilson. Now, I want you to recall, if you possibly can, the names sent to that paper. State the names of some of the other signers.—A. That is beyond my recollection. I cannot recollect.

Q. Did you recall what was contained in the body of the paper?—A. My idea of it was, that it was simply a request that the stock should be issued.

Q. Was not the reason stated there why it should be issued, the consideration for its being issued, and for whose benefit it was; was it not there set forth that it was to be for the benefit of Mr. Brooks?—A. I do not think it was. It may have been. I cannot tell without seeing the paper.

Q. Was there any recital in that paper of a previous contract between Mr. Durant and Mr. Brooks, or between Mr. Alley and Mr. Brooks?—A. There was no contract between Mr. Alley and Mr. Brooks recited;

there may have been between Mr. Durant and Mr. Brooks, or Mr. Durant and Mr. Neilson. There was nothing between Mr. Alley and Mr. Brooks.

Q. How long had you the custody of these papers?—A. I had them until December, 1868.

Q. Why, among other things ordered to be produced before this committee, did not you produce that paper?—A. I could not produce anything that was not in my hands.

Q. Would you not have been bound to produce it if you had had it?—A. I would have produced everything in my possession.

Q. Why did you not produce these?—A. Because I had not possession of it.

Q. Did you look and search for it?—A. Yes, sir.

Q. Where is it?—A. That I cannot say.

Q. Where are the letters and other papers of the company generally?—A. As I have said, many of the papers were lost. At the time of the Fisk suit, some of the books were lost, and I cannot reproduce them.

Q. How lost and when?—A. I cannot state how. I surrendered them in December, 1868, to Mr. Dillon, the president of the company. They were removed from the office to the Union Pacific Railroad, at 20 Nassau street, and what became of them I cannot say.

Q. Do you know by whose order they were removed?—A. They were removed by order of Mr. Dillon.

Q. Where?—A. That I cannot say. They went traveling. A part of them went to Mr. Barnes, in Pennsylvania.

Q. That was because others wanted to get a sight of these papers? They went traveling to avoid letting those who were interested in them see what they were?—A. No, sir; they went traveling to avoid letting people who had no interest in them see what they were.

Q. Did not a court of justice order them to be produced?—A. No, sir; not while they were in New York. If there was an order, they were out of the jurisdiction of the State when the order was made.

Q. Was it you who locked up the safe, and carried away the combination?—A. Yes, sir; but they were not in the safe.

Q. You had carried off the papers before you carried away the combination?—A. Yes, sir.

Q. These papers, and a good many papers, are running before the same pursuit still?—A. No, sir; Mr. Fisk is dead.

Q. But the public is said to have about as lively an interest now in getting at these papers as it had then. Is not this paper concealed now for the same reason it was concealed then?—A. In the first place, I deny that the public has a lively interest in this matter. I think it is only a few newspapers who take a lively interest in it.

The CHAIRMAN suggested this was getting too elementary for the purposes of this investigation.

Q. Do you not know that Mr. Dillon has these papers or has the control of them?—A. No, sir; I do not. I do not think Mr. Dillon could tell you anything about where they were.

Q. Were they not taken and destroyed, that they might never be seen by anybody?—A. No, sir; I do not think they are destroyed.

Q. They were taken and taken care of, then?—A. Yes, sir.

Q. Then does not somebody know where they are?—A. That I cannot state. I have no knowledge.

Q. Do you know where the stock transfer-book is?—No, sir; I do not. That is one of the books that disappeared.

Q. Disappeared how?—A. I do not know how.

Q. You mean to say you saw it disappear?—A. I mean to say that I saw it in December, 1868, and have never seen it since.

Q. You knew where it went to?—A. No, sir; I did not.

Q. Did you destroy it?—A. No, sir; I did not.

Q. Do you know who did?—A. No, sir; I do not think it has ever been destroyed, but I do not know where it is.

Q. What do you think has become of it?—A. I never have an opinion in regard to a matter I have no opinion about. I do not speculate.

Q. Did you keep a blotter?—A. No, sir; there never was any blotter kept in the office.

Q. No such thing?—A. No, sir.

Q. Never any blotter or scratcher or journal?—A. We kept a journal——

Q. Or book of any kind, in which you put down the daily proceedings of the company as they occurred?—A. We kept a journal, in which we enter the records of the company. That journal I purpose producing here within a few minutes. That is a book of original entry.

By the CHAIRMAN:

Q. You think there was a paper signed by somebody, authorizing the issue of fifty shares of stock to Neilson?—A. That is my impression, sir.

Q. You refer only to these fifty shares?—A. I would not say it referred only to these fifty shares. It may have had several items.

Q. What is your judgment about it?—A. I should say it had several things. For instance, there was some stock issued to General Dodge about that time, and that may have been in it.

Q. Do you think it was?—A. That I do not know, and I should hesitate to state what I do not know.

Q. What I want to know is, whether the best memory you have about it is, that it applied only to these fifty shares of stock issued to Neilson, or whether it applied to other stock?—A. I think it applied to some other things; that is my recollection about it.

Q. And to stock of other people?—A. Yes, sir.

Q. Did this agreement or partition which the company made to every man who signed for any number of shares of the increased Credit Mobilier stock, giving them an equal amount of Pacific Railroad bonds, apply also to the original subscription of stock?—A. It did not apply to the original stock, only to the increase. The original stockholders did not have a bond for each thousand dollars of stock. It was only the persons who had the 50 per cent. increase who received the bonds.

Q. Was all this fifty per cent. increase taken by the men who held the stock originally?—A. They either took it or sold it to other parties whom they procured to take it.

Q. If a man holding original stock transferred that stock to somebody else, it was understood as transferring the ——— he himself would have had?—A. Yes, sir. Men who were stockholders at the time the 50 per cent. subscription was made were the men who received the increase of stock and the bonds accompanying.

Q. It seems that Mr. Durant was the owner of these one hundred shares of stock Mr. Neilson first had in December, 1867. Did Mr. Durant ever receive the 50 per cent. increase for that stock?—A. I presume he did. I do not know how that is.

Q. If Mr. Durant had already received the 50 per cent. on this stock, would Neilson or anybody else acquire the right from him to receive it over again?—A. He would not acquire any right except such as the parties in interest might choose to confer.

Q. If Mr. Durant had received the additional stock, and received the one thousand dollars for each ten shares of it, what right would he have, by transferring a portion of the stock, to give somebody else authority to take as many more shares, and for as many more bonds?—A. There might be no right in it, and yet it might have been done for the parties in interest.

Q. Then it would have been a mere piece of favoritism if it was—if it was not a proceeding growing out of the original understanding?—A. It would be, unless the parties in interest considered that Mr. Durant had the right to make that arrangement.

Q. Suppose this hundred shares which Durant transferred to Neilson had been all the stock he owned, he would have received on that the 50 per cent. increase of the bonds?—A. Yes, sir.

Q. And then, when he sold that one hundred shares of original stock to Neilson, Neilson, in virtue of this arrangement of the company, would not be entitled to take any additional stock or bonds?—A. No, sir.

A. And you would not be authorized to issue it to him?—A. No, sir.

Q. What right would anybody, except the stockholders, have to authorize Neilson to receive fifty additional shares and five additional bonds?—A. None, until they obtained the consent of the stockholders. If they could get the consent of the larger stockholders, the stock would be issued.

Q. Do you know whether, in point of fact, Durant had received additional stock upon all the original stock he owned?—A. I presume he did.

Q. In the case where a man who was a stockholder, and who had neglected, within the time fixed, to take his additional stock, was it not treated as a matter of course to issue it to him afterward, without requiring the special consideration of the president of the board?—A. There was no resolution of the executive committee in regard to that matter.

Q. You say that really this vote, limiting the time within which the increase of stock could be taken to ninety days, was practically annulled, and that the old stockholders were allowed to take this additional stock whenever they called for it?—A. Yes, sir.

Q. In a case of that sort, where a man did not receive his additional stock, would you have required the special direction of the president or executive committee to allow him to take it whenever he called for it?—A. Yes, sir. I could not have issued it without the certificate of the president.

Q. Would you have issued it and received the money from him?—A. No, sir. I should have refused the money without the direction of the president.

Q. You would not have required it as a matter of course that he was to take it?—A. No, sir; not after the time given in the notice had expired.

Q. Do you mean to say that, after the time did expire, it was by the special license of the men who controled the company that the additional stock was allowed to be taken?—A. Yes, sir.

Q. Do you know of any other case, except this one, in which a man was allowed to take fifty per cent. increase of stock for which fifty per cent. had already been taken by somebody else?—A. No, sir; I do not. The stock-list was not full, and they were willing the stock should be issued to the full limit of $3,750,000.

Q. Was not the original $2,500,000 all taken?—A. No, sir; it was not all taken at the beginning.

Q. Therefore, if every man holding stock took his fifty per cent. additional, there would still be stock remaining?—A. Yes, sir; there would still be stock remaining. These ninety-three shares given to Mr. Ames were the remainder left over of the $2,500,000 which had not been taken.

Q. I understand you, then, that when Neilson took these last fifty shares, he took them directly from the company, and received $5,000 of Union Pacific Railroad bonds?—A. No, sir; I do not understand that. I say he may have received the bonds. When I get the books here, I can tell you positively.

Q. According to the course of business he would have received it?—A. I presume he did not receive it.

Q. Do you remember of any case where a subscriber did not receive the bonds?—A. No, sir; I do not.

Q. How would the cash-book say anything about that?—A. Every time the parties took stock and bonds, I had to buy the bonds.

Q. Then there would be a corresponding entry, under the date of issuing the stock, of the purchase of the bonds?—A. Yes, sir.

Q. He would pay over his money for the stock in the same way, whether he received his bonds or not? But if he received his bonds, you would have some account on your books of getting the bonds for him?—A. Yes, sir.

By Mr. ALLEY:

Q. You have spoken of bonds being given with this stock, and stated that the market-price of this stock was 85 cents on the dollar of its par value. Do you remember that when the subscription was made for the increase of the capital stock to $3,750,000, that the company were very much embarrassed; that there was no market value for the bonds; and that, if sold at all, it would have been at a rate far less than 85?—A. The bonds had not been upon the market. They were pledged as collateral for money the company was borrowing at the rate of 50 cents on the dollar; that is, two for one.

Q. What do you think they would have brought in cash at that time?—A. They would not have brought 85 cents, because they were not known.

Q. At the time the capital stock was increased, were all the stockholders, or nearly all of them, willing to take it even upon these favorable terms?—A. Some of them did not take it for a long time. I think Mr. McComb refused to take his at the time, and I do not think he ever took it in his own name. He probably procured somebody else to take his stock.

Q. Do you remember that I declined for some time to take mine?—A. Yes, sir.

Q. Do you remember that it was in consequence of the affairs of the company taking a more favorable turn some time afterward that some of the stockholders did come and take their stock, and that the company determined that it would be unjust to those stockholders who had not availed themselves of their privilege not to be allowed to take their stock, and therefore the arrangement was that they should all be served alike?—A. Yes, sir.

Q. Are you the custodian of the books, and have you been all the time since I have had any particular connection with the Credit Mobilier?—A. Not all the time.

Q. Were you not, with the exception of the period during the Fisk raid, when the office of the company was removed?—A. Yes, sir.

Q. It has been stated here that one gentleman was refused by me the right to look at the books—that he never, by my consent, could get a sight at them. Did you ever know me to oppose at any time anybody seeing the books?—A. I have no recollection of it.

Q. Were the books, to your knowledge, ever refused access to by any stockholder of the company who asked to look at them?—A. That I cannot tell. There may have been such instances.

Q. But certainly not by my direction?—A. Certainly not by your personal direction. There may have been a general direction.

Q. In relation to this stock that was issued to Neilson, you have stated, I believe, that it was issued to him by virtue of the right which he had to the increase of the 50 per cent. Is that so?—A. I suppose that was the case.

Q. Do you know whether it was done by my direction in any way, or that I knew anything about it?—A. I cannot say that you knew anything about it at the time.

Q. Have you no knowledge that I ever knew anything about it?—A. No, sir; I have not.

Q. Do you think I ever knew anything about it?—A. That I could not say. I would not want to answer in that way.

Q. Do you remember whether my name was on that paper requesting the president to issue that stock to Mr. Neilson?—A. I do not think it was.

Q. At the time of this raid, when these books were concealed, was it in consequence of the Fisk suits, and the breaking open of the safe for the purpose of putting the property of the company into the custody of Judge Barnard, that that proceeding took place?—A. It was previous to the appointment of Mr. Tweed as receiver.

Q. Was it not in anticipation of that?—A. Yes, sir; it was entirely on account of that suit.

Q. It was not to keep the books or papers from any of the stockholders or from any proper suit?—A. No, sir; it was not.

Q. That was a suit which was so annoying and perilous to the rights and interests of the company as to induce them to come to Congress for relief from these New York courts, and get their authority to remove the office of the company to Boston?—A. It was.

By Mr. BLACK:

Q. Was this increase of stock before or after you became treasurer?—A. It was before.

By the CHAIRMAN:

Q. At what time was it that these books and papers were removed from New York?—A. I think it was in December, 1868. I could not state positively.

Q. From that time you had not the custody of the books or papers until 1870?—A. Not until 1870.

Q. Do you know in whose custody the books and papers were kept during that period of time?—A. A portion of the time they were in the custody of the secretary, O. W. Barnes.

Q. He lived in Philadelphia?—A. A part of the time, and a part of the time in New York.

Q. What portion of them were in Philadelphia?—A. I do not know but they were all there. I did not know where they were. I know that

I had hard work to get them again, and that I did not succeed in getng all of them.

Q. Do you know where any of these missing books and papers of the company, which you have not produced here, are?—A. No, sir; if they were in my possession, I should have produced them.

Q. Have you no information as to where they are?—A. No, sir.

Q. Have you any belief where they are?—A. No, sir; I have not.

Q. Can you give to the committee any clue, of whom they shall inquire, or where they shall make search for them?—A. No, sir; I do not know anything about them.

Q. Have you endeavored to find them all?—A. Yes, sir; I have made inquiry and examination in various places.

Q. Have you made examination in all the places where you supposed there was any likelihood that you would find them?—A. Yes, sir; I have.

Q. And you protest here that you are unable to get them, and do not know where they are?—A. Yes, sir.

Q. And that you are not able to give any information as to where they can be obtained other than you have stated?—A. No, sir.

By Mr. McCRARY:

Q. Do you say they went into Mr. Dillon's hands?—A. Yes, sir; but he would not know anything about them. He paid very little attention to the matter.

Q. Did you ever inquire of him?—A. Yes, sir.

Q. Do I understand that most of the papers in the case of the Oakes Ames contract have passed into the hands of Oliver Ames?—A. I think so. Mr. Crane can answer that.

By Mr. BLACK:

Q. When you parted with these books, did you take a receipt for them?—A. No, sir.

Q. Did you pass them over into the formal custody of any one?—A. No, sir; they were in the safe which was handed right over.

Q. The same safe that was broken open?—A. No, sir; it was the vault that was broken open. This was just an iron safe that was not in the vault.

Q. Do I understand you that this increase of stock was ordered before you took possession?—A. This increase of stock was ordered in February, 1867. My appointment was in May, 1867. I had nothing to do with the books of the Credit Mobilier previous to that.

Q. Had you everything to do with making a settlement with Mr. McComb for the increase of the stock?—A. I could tell you that by referring to my cash-book. I cannot tell now. If he paid his subscription previous to me, it did not come to me.

Q. Did he pay everything that you ever demanded from him?—A. I do not know that I ever demanded anything at all. It would not be necessary to demand it. It was his option to take it or not as he saw fit.

Q. State whether these books were demanded by the court in Pennsylvania in the case of McComb against the Credit Mobilier.—A. I believe they were.

Q. Where were they at the time the demand was made?—A. They were in New York.

Q. Where they have been since that time?—A. In Pennsylvania a portion of the time.

Q. Did you make any answer in the case of that demand for the books?—A. Yes, sir; I made answer in that case.

Q. In which you stated what?—A. The main point of the answer was that they would be unsafe in the hands of the referee. Another answer was that we expected to be required to produce the books in another case. We expected to have to use them here.

Q. Did you state that you were using them every day and could not spare them?—A. That may have been in the notes; but it was not a prominent point.

Q. That you could not spare them from your every day's use?—A. I would not say whether that was in the answer or not.

Q. Were they not then in the city of Philadelphia?—A. They were not then in the city of Philadelphia. They were taken there some time afterward. I took them there myself.

By Mr. MERRICK:

Q. Can you tell us who were the directors or managers of the Credit Mobilier in 1867 and 1868?—A. Mr. Dillon, Mr. Hazard, and Mr. Alley were the principal managers from May, 1867. There were four other directors in Pennsylvania.

Q. Was Mr. Oliver Ames a director and manager?—A. No, sir; he never has been.

Q. Was Oakes Ames?—A. He never has been.

Q. Was T. C. Durant?—A. Not since May, 1867.

Q. Was John J. Cisco?—A. No, sir.

Q. H. S. McComb?—A. No, sir.

Q. Was Sidney Dillon?—A. Yes, sir.

Q. Was B. E. Bates?—A. No, sir.

Q. Was John B. Alley?—A. Yes, sir.

Q. Was Charles A. Lambard?—A. No, sir.

Q. Was Ebenezer Cook?—A. No, sir.

Q. Was John Duff?—A. No, sir.

Q. Can you state who were the other directors?—A. I remember Mr. Barnes, Mr. Stewart, and Mr. Neilson.

Q. Were these persons, who were directors and managers, necessarily stockholders?—A. No, sir; not necessarily. A man might be a director and not a stockholder.

Q. What was the fact in regard to that?—A. These men were generally stockholders at the time. At the present time some of the directors do not hold any stock.

Q. Do you know who were the directors of the Union Pacific Railroad at that time?—A. No, sir.

By the CHAIRMAN:

Q. What entries have you in regard to the issuing of the ninety-three shares of stock to Mr. Ames as trustee?—A. I have here an entry of $9,300 received from Oakes Ames as trustee.

Q. Which shows that he paid for the ninety-three shares?—A. Yes.

Q. You stated that you could tell by reference to the books whether Mr. Neilson, at the time he received the last fifty shares of stock, received bonds at the same time. You will please turn to your entry and state what the fact is.—A. The entry shows that Mr. Neilson received fifty shares of stock, for which he paid $5,000, and also two hundred and forty-odd dollars, which was carried to the interest account. He received no bonds with that stock.

Q. Did he receive the bonds subsequently?—A. No, sir; nor subsequently.

Q. You stated, I think, that if he had received the bonds there would be an entry of your purchase of them from the Union Pacific Railroad?—A. Yes, sir; but there is no entry of any having been received on that day, nor from the 27th of February to the 15th of October, 1868. This bond account closed the 15th of October, 1868, and it appears there is no entry anywhere of his having received these bonds.

Q. I notice that the name of Charles H. Neilson is written over an erasure in this entry?—A. Yes, that is written over an erasure, and that is my own handwriting. Something has been written there and erased, but I do not know what it was.

Q. Have you any recollection whatever in relation to it?—A. No, none whatever.

Q. The erasure is in the name in both cases where it appears?—A. Yes, there is an erasure, and the name of Charles H. Neilson is written over the erasure.

Q. Are these entries posted on some other book?—A. Yes, posted upon the book called the capital-stock book.

Q. Have you that book here?—A. Yes, sir; it shows simply that $5,000 cash was received March 11. No name is given. I want to explain that these books were not written up by me as the transactions occurred. They were written up subsequently, at my leisure.

Q. Were they written from other memoranda; and if so, what?—A. Yes, from the check-book.

Q. Will the check-book show what was written and erased?—A. No, sir. It will show whether I received a check or currency.

Q. How can this entry have been made from the check-book, if the check-book will not show that?—A. It was written from the check-book and from memoranda. It was written up very close to the time the transaction occurred.

Q. Would you carry transactions of this sort in your memory?—A. I had the check deposited or the money deposited, whatever it was, and I had the certified entry here.

Q. Any other memoranda?—A. No, sir. Let me explain that during most of this time I had other business, and that I would have gladly been out of this concern if it had not been for some of the gentlemen connected with it.

Q. You have no recollection at all in reference to these erasures?—A. None whatever.

Q. As that erasure was in the place where the name should be written, would not you naturally infer that some other name was written in the place of Neilson?—A. No, sir; I would not. I might have written in something else.

Q. But it would have been a name, would it not?—A. No, sir; I might have written in a description there by mistake.

Q. Would you have written the description in the place where the name belongs?—A. Yes, I might have done so.

Q. Do you not think it was probable, if you made a mistake, that it was in writing in some other name?—A. No, sir; I do not think so. It may have been that.

Q. Would you not infer from the appearance of this that the name Neilson was not written at the same time that the other portions of the entry were?—A. It is very likely; it may not have been.

Q. And you think you would not naturally have written some other name in that place?—A. It is very probable it may have been some other name.

Q. Is not that the only explanation you can give of the erasure?—A. The appearance is that I did write some other name there.

Q. In your entries of this sort, that is the place for the name?—A. That is the way I have written these entries. There were very few transactions in the course of the month, and a man who is not in the habit of writing up these books except occasionally, would be very likely to make mistakes.

Q. The other portions of the writing upon these lines seem to be a part of the original entry.—A. Yes, sir.

Q. And the erasure, and the writing of the name of Neilson, seem to have been at a subsequent period to the original entry.—A. Yes, sir.

Q. And you are sure you have no memory upon the subject?—A. No, sir; I have not.

Q. All you can state about it is what appeared upon the face of the entry?—A. That is all.

Q. You have no idea what was written there, prior to the name of Charles H. Neilson?—A. No, sir.

By Mr. BLACK:

Q. You do not know when the erasure was made?—A. It was very soon after the original was written.

Q. Why do you say that?—A. Because I have not written anything in those books for two years at least. My brother has been keeping them.

Q. Do you find any other place where a name has been erased and a new name put in these books?—A. Yes, sir.

Q. Were you in the habit of making mistakes of that kind, and doing it over again?—A. Yes; I did not pretend to keep these books as nicely as I would have done if it had been my principal business. Here is an entry in which G. M. Dodge was originally written. The name was erased, and Anna Dodge was substituted, because the stock was issued in her name.

Q. There is good reason for that change. General Dodge, I suppose, was the owner of the stock, and wanted it placed in his wife's name, and therefore had the change made?—A. Yes, it was changed to the wife of General Dodge.

Q. Didn't the same reason cause you to make the other erasure?—A. I do not think it was.

Q. Did you not originally put in the name of Mr. Brooks?—A. I cannot say; I may have done so. I do not recollect it.

Q. And did you not make the change by the direction of somebody else?—A. If I wrote in the name of James Brooks, I had no authority to do it, for the stock was issued to Charles H. Neilson. I did not make the change by the direction of anybody. I put in Mr. Neilson's name as a matter of course, when the stock was issued to him.

Q. You are satisfied you made the change without the instructions of anybody?—A. Without the instructions of anybody.

Q. Why would you change the books of the company without instructions from anybody?—A. Because I kept the books.

Q. Is not the erasure of a name and the substitution of another name the falsification of your record?—A. That depends altogether upon how the courts would take such things, I suppose. I am not legal enough to know what the courts would do.

By Mr. BROOKS:

Q. Did I ever give you any request or direction to make any entry in that book in any form?—A. No, sir.

Q. Did you ever know me as the owner of any stock in the Credit Mobilier?—A. No, sir.

Q. If I had given you any direction to make any such erasure as that, would you have made it?—A. I think I would have made it if you had given me any instructions. I made the erasure because it was entered wrong.

Q. Is it possible that you could have entered my name as the owner and then have substituted Mr. Neilson's for it?—A. It is possible, of course, that I might have done so.

Q. Have you the least recollection of having done it?—A. No, sir; I have not.

Q. Everything is possible; is it probable that you would have done it?—A. From Mr. Neilson's intimate connection with you it may even be probable; I would not say it was not.

Q. Would you have changed the entries in that record if you had put in my name there instead of that of Mr. Neilson?—A. I should have made a mistake if I had written your name there, because the stock was issued to Neilson.

Q. Would you not have been as likely to have written some other name as to have written mine?—A. I cannot say whether I should or not.

Q. Is it not probable that Mr. Neilson's name being often pronounced Nelson you may have misspelled the name and corrected it?—A. I do not think that is possible. That would have required very little erasure to have done that. In this case the whole name is erased.

Mr. BROOKS. I want to say that is the first time I ever heard of the thing in any form.

By Mr. MCCRARY:

Q. Do your books show the persons who received first-mortgage bonds in connection with the addition of stock that was issued?—A. Yes, sir.

Q. And they show that Mr. Neilson did not receive his?—A. They show he did not receive his.

Q. Do they show that any other one received first-mortgage bonds on that stock at as late a date as that?—A. No, sir; nobody received first-mortgage bonds upon that particular stock at all. He must have taken the stock just as it was and paid for it.

Q. Had Mr. Durant any first-mortgage bonds to dispose of in connection with the stock he controlled?—A. Mr. Durant took the first-mortgage bonds on all his subscriptions and the increase, the same as every other stockholder.

Q. Was the fifty shares of Neilson considered a part of Durant's increase?—A. I cannot say as to that.

Q. I understood Mr. Crane to say that Mr. Neilson got his first-mortgage bonds and fifty shares of additional stock from Durant. Do the books show that?—A. No, sir; the books do not show his transaction in regard to his original subscription, because he got the stock from Mr. Durant.

WASHINGTON, D. C., *January* 14, 1873.

HENRY C. CRANE sworn and examined.

By the CHAIRMAN:

Question. State your residence.—Answer. I reside at Yonkers, but do business in the city of New York.

Q. State if you have been connected in any way with the Union Pacific Railroad Company?—A. I was director for a short time.

Q. For what period of time?—A. The books will show. I do not recollect.

Q. During the time the road was being built?—A. Yes, sir.

Q. Were you a shareholder of that company?—A. Yes, sir.

Q. And a stockholder of the Credit Mobilier?—A. Yes; I bought some of the stock; I did not subscribe for it.

Q. At what time did you become the owner of shares in the Credit Mobilier?—A. Shortly after the company removed to New York. The books will show.

Q. As early as it had anything to do with the Pacific Railroad?—A. About the time of the commencement.

Q. Were you an officer of that company?—A. I was assistant treasurer of the Credit Mobilier.

Q. From what time to what time?—A. From about the date of its removal to New York until the time Mr. Ham took possession of the office.

Q. Then you preceded him in office, occupying the same position that he did?—A. I was assistant treasurer. I was not secretary.

Q. Do you know anything in relation to Mr. Neilson becoming the owner of one hundred shares of that stock in December, 1867?—A. Yes, sir.

Q. State what you know about it.—A. The 24th of December, 1867, James Brooks paid a check of $7,000, and a draft, due the 22d of January, 1868, for $3,000, and my impression is that I delivered to Mr. Brooks, or somebody for him, $5,000 first-mortgage bonds of the Union Pacific Railroad Company, and transferred to Mr. Neilson two hundred shares of the Union Pacific Railroad stock and one hundred shares of Credit Mobilier stock.

Q. Now, state to the committee all you know in reference to the negotiation for that stock. How did it come to you?—A. That is all I know about it. I received, as I stated, $10,000, and at the request of Mr. Brooks transferred to Mr. Neilson one hundred shares Credit Mobilier stock and two hundred shares Union Pacific Railroad stock, and on the same day, December 24, gave to Mr. Brooks five bonds of the Union Pacific Railroad stock.

Q. Was this the stock that belonged to Mr. Durant?—A. It was. I was Mr. Durant's attorney and confidential clerk. This was his stock; it was not mine.

Q. Do you know anything in connection with the negotiation for the purchase of that stock?—A. I do not know anything about it.

Q. Did you hear any conversation between Mr. Durant and Mr. Brooks on that subject?—A. I have no recollection of any conversation at all about it.

Q. Did Mr. Brooks say anything in relation to the ownership of this stock, whether it was for himself or Mr. Neilson?—A. I have no recollection about it. I have told you all I know about it.

Q. You say that you received Mr. Brooks's check and draft for the aggregate sum of $10,000?—A. Yes. I find by reference to my deposit-book that Mr. Brooks gave me a check on the Fourth National Bank for $7,000. I have no recollection about it otherwise.

Q. You say you delivered to him $5,000 first-mortgage bonds of the Union Pacific Railroad, and two hundred shares Union Pacific Railroad stock. What was that for?—A. My memorandum says it was earnings on the one hundred shares of Credit Mobilier stock.

Q. Was that accrued dividends?—A. I should say so.

Q. These one hundred shares received then was no part of the increase of 50 per cent.?—A. Not at all. I transferred the stock by Mr. Durant's direction. I was told to receive from Mr. Brooks $10,000, and he gave me his check and draft, as I have stated; and by Mr. Brooks's direction I transferred it to Mr. Neilson—the one hundred shares of Credit Mobilier stock and the other securities, as I have stated.

Q. What was the value of Union Pacific Railroad stock then?—A. There was none in the market. I know nothing about its value. I have no recollection of its price.

Q. What was the value of the bonds then?—A. The Credit Mobilier paid 85 for bonds. I think they had not been marketed at all then.

Q. They were worth at least 85?—A. I think they were worth 85.

Q. Was the $10,000 paid by Mr. Books considered by the company an equivalent for the one hundred shares of Credit Mobilier stock, $5,000 Union Pacific Railroad bonds, and $20,000 Union Pacific Railroad stock?—A. Mr. T. C. Durant gave them; the company had nothing to do with it.

Q. Did you have anything to do with Mr. Neilson about it?—A. I transferred the railroad stock to Mr. Neilson, who went to the Credit Mobilier and got his stock. I had nothing to do with it.

Q. Was Mr. Neilson present the 24th of December when the drafts were delivered to you?—A. I do not think he was.

Q. He subsequently got his stock from both companies?—A. The books will show. I do not think I saw him at all. I do not think he was there when Mr. Brooks gave the check.

Q. All you know in reference to it, then, is that the books show that the stock was transferred to him?—A. Yes, sir.

Q. Do you know anything in relation to the fifty shares of stock Mr. Neilson subsequently received?—A. I know nothing about it.

Q. Nothing in reference to the payment of it?—A. No, sir.

Q. Had you anything to do with the business of the Credit Mobilier after Mr. Ham came into the office?—A. Nothing at all. That ended my connection with the company.

Q. But after that you were connected with Mr. Durant?—A. All the time, and am still.

Q. Have you any knowledge in relation to this assignment of stock to Oakes Ames, which stands on the books in his name as trustee?—A. Nothing except that I know it stands there.

Q. Have you any knowledge how it came to be there in his name as trustee?—A. I cannot tell you anything about it.

Q. Have you any knowledge of his disposing of any of that stock, or agreeing to dispose of any?—A. I know nothing about it.

Q. This draft or check you had from Mr. Brooks you received from him personally?—A. My impression is that I received it from Mr. Brooks himself.

By Mr. MERRICK:

Q. Have you any knowledge of any transfer of Credit Mobilier stock by Mr. Durant to any other person, or to any member of Congress?—A. I do not think I have.

Q. Have you any knowledge of any member of Congress being the owner in trust or otherwise of Union Pacific Railroad or Credit Mobilier stock?—A. I only know, and that by the books, of but one case I believe the books show that I had some stock in my name as trustee, and that I transferred twenty-five shares of that to Mr. Boyer, who I believe was a member of Congress.

Q. You did not hold stock as trustee for any other member of Congress?—A. No, sir; nor for him.

Q. You do not know whether Mr. Durant held, as trustee, for any member of Congress, or transferred stock to any member of Congress?—A. I cannot tell you.

By the CHAIRMAN:

Q. This stock which stood in your name was really Mr. Durant's stock?—A. Yes.

Q. When it was transferred to Mr. Boyer it was really transferred from Mr. Durant?—A. Of course. It was not my stock.

Q. You never did own it?—A. No, sir.

By Mr. McCRARY:

Q. What was your official connection with the Credit Mobilier?—A. Assistant treasurer in New York.

Q. This transaction with Mr. Brooks was dated when?—A. December 24, 1867.

Q. I understood you to say that you were transacting business for Mr. Durant personally.—A. All this business of Mr. Durant's has been done by me for years.

Q. You mean, then, that in this transfer you were directed by Mr. Durant?—A. I suppose so. Of course it was his business, not mine.

Q. What were one hundred shares of Union Pacific Railroad stock worth at that time?—A. That I cannot tell you.

Q. Give us the best estimate of its value you can.—A. I have no way of estimating what it was worth. It may have been worth 50 and it may have been 30.

Q. What were the first-mortgage bonds, Union Pacific Railroad, worth?—A. They sold at 85.

Q. What was the Credit Mobilier stock worth?—A. I should say it was worth considerable about that time; there was a dividend to make on it then.

Q. And these other securities, given to Mr. Brooks, were a part of that dividend?—A. The memorandum I have says $20,000 stock; $5,000 bonds were given as the earnings for those one hundred shares of Credit Mobilier stock.

Q. How much was Mr. Durant receiving for the $10,000 paid by Mr. Brooks?—A. Ten thousand dollars.

Q. Nothing more?—A. No, sir.

Q. How much did Mr. Brooks receive in return?—A. One hundred shares Credit Mobilier stock; $25,000 securities of the Union Pacific Railroad Company.

Q. Total how much?—A. That depends on the value of the securities. If the Union Pacific Railroad stock was worth 50, the amount for two hundred shares would be $10,000. If the bonds were worth 85, the amount for them would be $4,250.

Q. What, then, would be the profit to the purchaser of those one hundred shares of stock?—A. The amount received would be $25,000 Union Pacific Railroad securities, and the market-value of one hundred shares of Credit Mobilier stock. I do not know how much, but I think it was a pretty good trade.

Q. Did Mr. Durant make many trades of that kind?—A. I do not think he did.

Q. Do you know of any particular reason why he made this one?—A. No, sir; I know nothing about it. I only know I had directions to do what I did.

Q. You had direction to transfer the stock to Mr. Neilson?—A. Yes, sir.

Q. Did you get this direction from Mr. Durant?—A. No, sir.

Q. From whom?—A. From Mr. Brooks.

Q. Who directed you to make the transaction in the first place?—A. Mr. Durant.

Q. He directed you to receive from Mr. Brooks $10,000, and to transfer all these securities?—A. Yes; and afterward, by Mr. Brooks's direction, I transferred the stock to Mr. Neilson.

Q. Can you tell us how many dividends have been paid upon this Credit Mobilier stock in all?—A. I could not without reference to the books.

Q. Were any paid in 1869?—A. I am not certain. The books will tell all about that.

Q. What books?—A. The books of the contractors for the Oakes Ames contract.

Q. Where are they?—A. I do not know where they are; I suppose in Boston.

Q. Have you not a pretty distinct recollection about the number of dividends paid?—A. I have not. I know there were several dividends, amounting to quite a large sum.

Q. You hold some of the stock?—A. Yes, sir.

Q. Have you no recollection as to how much you collected?—A. No; I know I got as much as everybody else. I was careful to know that, I can tell you. I cannot give you the details. They are all on the books in plain writing. There was no secret about it. There were several dividends; one made in January, 1868; I remember this. They came along pretty thick.

Q. Refer to the list of dividends now shown you, and see if you remember them as there stated.—A. I cannot tell anything about that. If I had the books I could tell you exactly how many dividends were made. I know the last one named in this list is right.

Q. Do you remember any since the last date in that list?—A. No; not since the last date.

By the CHAIRMAN:

Q. Do you know whether this stock, transferred from Mr. Durant to Mr. Neilson, was really Mr. Durant's stock?—A. I think it really was. I think he paid for it.

Q. Can you give us any reason why he should sell this stock at par, with all its accretions, at that time?—A. No, sir.

Q. What I want to get at is, whether this was Mr. Durant's property which he was selling for the best price he could get, or really the stock of the company which they chose to let somebody have.—A. It was Mr. Durant's stock, which he had a right to do what he pleased with. I do not know anything about it.

Q. Do you know any reason why he should give so large a return for that $10,000?—A. I do not know of any reason. Mr. Brooks and he were on friendly terms. I do not know of any reason why he should have given him that chance.

Q. Do you know anything about the relations between Mr. Durant and Mr. Neilson?—A. I do not know whether Mr. Durant knew Mr. Neilson. I do not think I had ever seen him until that transaction.

By Mr. NIBLACK:

Q. In speaking of the dividends which the Credit Mobilier made, you refer to the Credit Mobilier proper, and not to the trustees of the Ames contract?—A. I am speaking of the dividends which came from the Ames contract.

By the CHAIRMAN:

Q. Mr. Ham has said there never was but one dividend made by the Credit Mobilier to his knowledge. Did you hear what he stated upon that subject?—A. I did.

Q. Did he state correctly?—A. I think it very likely he did. You may call it an allotment or a dividend; it makes no difference as to what term you use. They got the securities. I think his statement is correct.

Q. The issuing of one bond for every thousand dollars of additional stock of the Credit Mobilier does not appear on the books as a dividend?—A. No; it was a resolution on the books by which parties were induced to take the increase of stock.

Q. It was to sharpen the appetite of the subscribers?—A. Their appetite did not need much sharpening.

By Mr. SMITHERS:

Q. You speak of a draft having been given by Mr. Brooks in part payment for the one hundred shares of stock. Was that draft paid at maturity?—A. It was in this way: Mr. Brooks had made a loan to Mr. Durant, which matured the 22d of January, and this draft was applied in part payment of the loan.

Q. On whom was the draft drawn?—A. That I have not said; my impression is that the draft was made on himself. I think I paid $6,000 on the loan, $3,000 of which was covered by this draft.

By Mr. BROOKS:

Q. Do you know how much money I loaned Mr. Durant?—A. Yes, sir; October 19, 1867, you loaned him $25,000 for three months. This obligation matured the 22d of January. You had as security for it four hundred and fifty shares of Credit Mobilier stock collateral, and we paid you 10 per cent. interest for the money. When that matured, or rather two days before maturity, we reduced that $25,000 loan to $19,000 and gave three hundred and ninety shares Credit Mobilier stock as collateral. That matured the 23d of April, and I paid 10 per cent. interest on that. The 30th of January we had $43,000, for which you had seven hundred and fifty shares of Credit Mobilier stock as collateral. This matured the 3d of May, 1868, and you had 10 per cent. interest. I then reduced the amount to $40,000, and paid a thousand dollars as commission, and 10 per cent. interest. That matured August 5. The 5th of August the amount was made $45,000, for which you had 7 per cent. interest and commission. That matured October 7. October 7 the note was renewed at $45,000, at 11 per cent. interest, running until January 8, 1869, when I think it was paid off.

Q. Was that anything beyond the current rates of interest on Mr. Durant's paper?—A. It was fully as much as we paid any one.

Q. You paid that to others?—A. I do not recollect. We may have; we used a great deal of money.

Q. Was there anything unnatural, considering Dr. Durant's great want of money, that he should sell one hundred shares of Credit Mobilier stock at par?—A. I do not think he was obliged to sell it at par. I should say he could have got a good deal more for those one hundred shares of stock.

Q. It may have been worth more at the time of delivery; was it not contracted for some time before?—A. I know nothing about that. I recollect that about that time we sold two hundred and fifty shares at 160.

Q. Let me ask you, in connection with that if, in the testimony of Mr. Durant taken in the Fisk suit, he does not swear that the highest he ever sold this stock was 136?—A. I know nothing about that. I have testified in regard to a sale that I do know about.

By the CHAIRMAN:

Q. Can you state the name of the party to whom the sale was made at 160?—A. It was made to John B. Alley. That was in January, 1868. I think the stock was really worth 200 at that time.

By Mr. BROOKS:

Q. Was not Dr. Durant very desirous to obtain money on his paper?—A. We have always used a great deal of money; his transactions were very large.

By Mr. MERRICK:

Q. Was there any difficulty in getting purchasers of Credit Mobilier stock at rates above par?—A. I should not think there would be for parties who knew anything about it.

By Mr. BROOKS:

Q. You spoke of a check of mine of December 24, for $7,000, and a draft of $3,000; how do you know that was not in payment of the loans I had made?—A. I made the entries myself. They state what the checks were for.

Q. Have you the books here?—A. No, sir; but I know that this check and draft were in payment of Credit Mobilier stock.

Q. You are sure that was not in payment of the loan?—A. I am very sure.

Q. You say I received five bonds at that time?—A. That is my impression.

Q. Did you get a receipt for them?—A. No, sir; it did not require any receipt.

Q. Are you in the habit of delivering bonds to a third party without taking a receipt?—A. If you paid the money I considered the stock as belonging to you. It was, by your direction, transferred to Mr. Neilson; I know nothing about that. I have stated the transaction simply as I know it.

Q. Did Mr. Neilson ever give you any receipts for his dividends?—A. O, yes. All the dividends that were paid out of the Oakes Ames contract I paid and took receipts from the parties.

Q. You always took receipts from Mr. Neilson?—A. I did, unless the dividends were paid on his order.

Q. Did you ever give them to me?—A. No; I had nothing to do with you on this stock. It being in Mr. Neilson's name prevented you from collecting it anyhow. It was impossible for you to collect the dividends while the stock was in Mr. Neilson's name.

Q. What creates the impression on your mind that I received five bonds—what could the five bonds have been received for?—A. I find in my cash-book that I was to transfer two hundred shares of Union Pacific Railroad stock to Neilson and one hundred shares of Credit Mobilier stock to Neilson and deliver five bonds. There was no need of any receipt, and there would be no record except in the cash-book.

Q. With whom were your transactions in behalf of Mr. Durant with me in regard to these loans?—A. With Mr. Kingsley, your book-keeper

Most generally you came with him if you were in town. The transactions were done with you and the checks for interest given to your order.

Q. Then my indorsement must have been on them?—A. Not always. When you were out of town, Mr. Kingsley would take them. I have some checks to your order and some to Mr. Kingsley's.

Q. These five bonds were part and parcel of the delivery of the one hundred shares of Credit Mobilier stock?—A. Yes; they are so entered on my book. I took a copy of the entry, and if you want me to I will read it.

Q. I understand that you delivered one hundred shares, and also delivered two hundred shares of stock and the bonds, but the why and wherefore you do not know?—A. I do not, except that it was part of the trade between you and Dr. Durant.

Q. Are you quite sure you were cognizant of the transactions between Dr. Durant and myself?—A. I know the transactions—yes, sir.

Q. Are you very sure of that?—A. I have had charge of his business for sixteen years or eighteen years. All the money that has been paid upon the checks I have drawn.

Q. May he not have made contracts without your knowledge?—A. There may have been matters outside of his legitimate business, of course, that I do not know about.

Q. You only know in regard to real money transactions, but nothing of the circumstances surrounding them?—A. Nothing at all.

By the CHAIRMAN:

Q. If you have a copy of the entry in the books to which you refer with you, you will please read it to the committee.—A. I have it here, and it reads as follows:

Memorandum of loans.

October 19, 1867, $25,000, 10 per cent., 450 Credit Mobilier of America, due January 22, 1868.

January 20, 1868, $19,000, 10 per cent., 390 Credit Mobilier of America, due April 23, 1868.

January 30, 1868, $43,000, 10 per cent., 750 Credit Mobilier of America, due May 3, 1868.

May 2, 1868, $44,000, 7 per cent., $1,000 commission, 750 Credit Mobilier of America, due August 5, 1868.

August 5, 1868, $45,000, 7 per cent., (certificates,) 50 Union Pacific bonds, due October 7, 1868.

October 7, 1868, $45,000, 11 per cent., (certificates,) 50 Union Pacific bonds, due January 8, 1869.

Cash-book:

December 24, 1867.—Stock account Credit Mobilier of America for transferring to J. Brooks's son-in-law one hundred shares stock at par, with the five bonds Union Pacific Railroad Company, and two hundred Union Pacific stock as earnings on the stock, $7,000 cash; draft, due 22d January, $3,000=$10,000.

Check-book:

Deposit, December 24, 1867, Fourth National Bank, James Brooks, $7,000.

Check-book, Fourth National:

Bills payable, January 20, 1868.—J. Brooks on account note due this day, cash.	$3,000
Draft	3,000
	6,000

Renewed for $19,000.

January 20, 1868.—To interest account on J. Brooks's note	$474 74
Charge bills payable	25,000 00
Credit bills payable	19,000 00

January 20, 1868, 3 months.

By Mr. BROOKS:

Q. You say the draft for $3,000 was drawn on myself?—A. I think it was, but have nothing to show. It was paid in settlement of the loan in January.

By the CHAIRMAN:

Q. Were the rates of interest paid by Mr. Durant to Mr. Brooks upon these loans as high as the ordinary rates of interest for money in New York?—A. I should think they were. I have not examined, however, to ascertain that fact. I looked over the books to see what I paid.

Q. Was Mr. Durant using very considerable amounts of money about that time, and paying as good rates of interest to others?—A. I presume so.

WASHINGTON, D. C., *January* 14, 1873.

THOMAS C. DURANT sworn and examined.

By the CHAIRMAN:

Question. State your residence and occupation.—Answer. I reside in New York, and I am railroad contractor and builder.

Q. Were you a stockholder of the Union Pacific Railroad?—A. Yes, sir.

Q. One of the original stockholders?—A. I was an original stockholder and a subscriber to a very large amount of the stock of that company.

Q. Were you also a director of that company?—A. I was also a director.

Q. Have you been ever since its organization?—A. I was director and vice-president of the company from the time of its organization until the last rail was laid.

Q. Can you state the time when you ceased to be a director?—A. I think it was in May or June, 1869.

Q. Since that time have you had any connection with the Union Pacific Railroad as an officer?—A. No.

Q. Were you a stockholder of the Credit Mobilier?—A. I was.

Q. One of the largest?—A. The largest, and president from the time it took an interest in the Hoxie contract until the contract was executed. I was president until May, 1867.

Q. You were president of that company from the time of its organization as a contractor of the Union Pacific Railroad until May, 1867?—A. Yes, sir.

Q. Did you continue to be an officer of that company in any capacity after that time?—A. No, sir. The connection of that corporation with the Union Pacific Railroad Company ceased at that time, except to guarantee the Oakes Ames contract.

Q. Were you one of the board of trustees to whom the Ames contract was assigned?—A. Yes, sir.

Q. Do you continue to be one of those trustees up to the present time?—A. Yes, sir.

Q. Did these trustees keep books and records of their proceedings in regard to these transactions?—A. They did.

Q. Have you these books?—A. I have not; I have certified copies of them.

Q. Of everything?—A. I do not know whether I have of everything. I think the books were sent to Boston.

Q. In whose custody are they?—A. They were sent to the president of the board of trustees, Oliver Ames.

Q. Is he now president of that board?—A. He is chairman of the board. I think he gave an order for them to be sent there. I am not positive about that.

Q. It seems that at one time there was a quantity of this Credit Mobilier stock assigned to Oakes Ames, three hundred and forty-three shares. Do you know anything in reference to that transaction?—A. I think there is a resolution on the books of the railroad bureau of the Credit Mobilier, or of the board of directors, giving a certain amount of the stock to Mr. Ames and myself. I have here that resolution authorizing the transfer of $65,000 of the Credit Mobilier stock to Mr. Ames and myself, at par and interest, in accordance with the request of a large majority of the stockholders. This resolution is dated January 4, 1868.

Q. That resolution was adopted at that date, was it?—A. It was adopted at that date, and passed by the committee of the Credit Mobilier, Mr. Dillon, Mr. Alley, and Mr. Hazard being present.

Q. Do Mr. Dillon, Mr. Alley, and Mr. Hazard constitute the whole of that executive committee?—A. I do not know who the executive committee were.

Q. Who was president of the company at that time?—A. Sidney Dillon.

Q. This resolution refers to stock held in trust by Mr. Ames with various parties. Can you tell us what that means?—A. I cannot. I suppose it refers to the stock of the company. I had nothing to do with the company at that time, and I never saw the resolution till some time afterward.

Q. Who the various parties were he held it for you do not know? A. I do not know.

Q. Did you have anything to do with these transactions, or were you present at the time the transfer was made?—A. No, sir; I was not.

Q. What does the expression "as agreed upon by Thomas C. Durant and Oakes Ames" mean?—A. That, I presume, refers to the agreement previously made to distribute the stock on hand to certain parties.

Q. Were you present when that paper was executed?—A. I think it was presented to me, and that I signed it, to distribute some of the stock on hand.

Q. Have you any record or copy of that paper?—A. No, sir.

Q. You do not know where it is?—A. No, sir.

Q. Have you ever had the custody of it?—A. I never had.

Q. After that resolution was there some stock transferred to you?—A. Yes, sir.

Q. What amount?—A. I do not recollect; I suppose one-half of it.

Q. For what purpose was it transferred?—A. To enable me to fulfill engagements I had made before that time to let various parties have stock. Most of them I agreed with before I left the presidency of the company, in 1867.

Q. Can you name any persons you had such engagements with?—A. I think I had engagements for seventy-five or eighty thousand dollars' worth of stock, which I had to carry out to a large extent from my own stock. I transferred to Mr. Lockwood, I think, five hundred shares, and to Mr. Barton Jenks, of Philadelphia, I think, some three hundred. I had engagements which I was obliged to comply with, and which I did out of my own stock, as I stated.

Q. Do you know what amount of stock was transferred to Mr. Ames under that arrangement?—A. I do not know. I can easily ascertain. I think some $30,000 worth.

Q. Do you know anything in relation to the persons to whom Mr. Ames was to transfer that stock; for whom he received it?—A. I do not know. It was his own stock, his own matter.

Q. Did you learn anything from him, Mr. Ames, in reference to whom it was for?—A. I heard Mr. Ames speak of it two or three times; I heard him say that he had offered it to different parties; he had a list of names that I remember; Mr. Colfax was one; I do not know who else; I did not pay any attention to it.

Q. Do you remember any other names besides that of Mr. Colfax?—A. I do not; Mr. Colfax's name struck me, he being a prominent man; that is how I came to remember that name.

Q. Do you remember whether the list contained the names of other members of Congress?—A. I think it did.

Q. But you do not remember who they were?—A. No; I was under the impression at the time that there were several gentlemen he talked with, but that he was getting the stock for himself.

Q. State whether on or about the 26th of December, 1867, you sold or transferred one hundred shares of stock.—A. Yes.

Q. Will you state whether Mr. Neilson was one of the men with whom you had engagements?—A. I never had any conversations with Mr. Neilson.

Q. Did you know him?—A. I may have known him by sight; I do not know whether I should recognize him if I were to see him to-day.

Q. Had you any arrangement with Mr. Brooks?—A. I had, but this was entirely a business arrangement between Mr. Brooks and myself, which was settled between us in that way, and settled without any regard to his being a member of Congress; in fact, I had no idea of any further legislation ever being wanted at that time, and no idea of any service that was to be rendered, or had been rendered, in Congress by him.

Q. State what the transaction was between you and Mr. Brooks.—A. In the early part of 1867, or late in 1866, the Credit Mobilier executive committee made propositions to the Union Pacific Railroad. At that time the Union Pacific Railroad was owing some money. The Credit Mobilier proposed to take securities of the railroad company to the amount of $6,000,000, embracing some of their first-mortgage bonds, which had never been sold in the market, and some land-grant bonds, and I think some stock, for which the company was to go on building a portion of the road. At that time they had no contract with the Union Pacific Railroad. They proposed having an increase of capital stock of 50 per cent. on the amount of original stock, and giving the different stockholders the right to come in within a given time and subscribe for the stock. These bonds were taken from the Union Pacific Company at 85. In order to get subscriptions for this additional stock, as the Credit Mobilier had no contract on hand, (it had finished its contract,) all its assets were not sufficient to furnish much inducement to new stockholders to come in, they agreed to give for each two thousand dollars of new stock a thousand-dollar bond, for which they paid 85. Or it may be a thousand-dollar bond for each thousand dollars, or ten shares of the stock. I always regarded it as virtually watering their stock so much. The stock was increased 50 per cent., and the amount paid on the increase was returned less 15 per cent., taking the bonds at 85, which the Credit Mobilier paid for it. That was the first sale of bonds, I think, the Union Pacific Railroad Company made. About that time many parties in interest were desirous of placing a portion of the stock, and it was about that time I had my first conversation with Mr. Brooks relative to the affairs of the Credit Mobilier. Mr. Brooks thought he would be able to place four or five hundred thousand dollars of these securities, and I offered him, if he would do so, or could do so, a commission of 5 per cent. I went with him, I know, to one party, C. K. Garrison. Mr. Brooks told me at various times that he was trying to place it, and said that he would like to take fifteen or twenty thousand dollars of it himself. Afterward he spoke of having devoted considerable time to the matter, and asked me if I could not give him this stock so that it would date back. That I could not do under the circumstances. The stock had become valuable. Still he wanted his fifteen or twenty thousand dollars of it, and it was pretty difficult to get hold of it then. Everybody who had ever talked about it wanted it then. I finally arranged it with Mr. Brooks to give him one hundred shares of Credit Mobilier stock at par, and with the one hundred shares to give $20,000 Union Pacific Railroad stock and $5,000 Union Pacific Railroad bonds. I preferred to do that rather than to give him what he claimed, two hundred shares of stock. About that time he had been appointed Government director, and very properly suggested that he could not and would not hold the stock, being a Government director; in fact, I think an act of Congress prohibited the Government directors from holding any of the stock of the Union Pacific Company, and it was transferred to Mr. Neilson, by his instructions, without ever being in his own name.

Q. Have you had any negotiation with Mr. Neilson on the subject?—A. O, no.

Q. The whole transaction was with Mr. Brooks?—A. The whole transaction was with Mr. Brooks. At that time I had no idea that we should ever be before Congress for anything; and the transfer of this stock had nothing whatever to do with any past or future services in Congress.

Q. From whom did you receive payment for the one hundred shares?—A. Mr. Brooks made the payment to Mr. Crane, I think. Mr. Brooks made no concealment of the matter at all. He mentioned Mr. Neilson, and stated that he did not wish to have it transferred to his own name.

Q. Did you understand that this was really to be transferred to Neilson as Neilson's stock, or that it was to be transferred to the name of Neilson for the benefit of Mr. Brooks?—A. I knew nothing of it, except that it was transferred to Mr. Neilson.

Q. From the negotiation you had with Mr. Brooks did you understand that the stock really became the stock of Mr. Brooks when you made this transfer?—A. I did not know whether he had sold it, or what he had done with it.

Q. You had nothing to do with Neilson?—A. O, nothing at all. I did not see Neilson.

Q. Did you ever have anything to do with Neilson?—A. The only time I ever had anything to do with Neilson was after I had returned from Europe, when he came and asked about the dividends on the fifty shares. I asked him what fifty shares; that he had no business with any fifty shares; that I had settled up everything he was entitled to.

Q. Upon the one hundred shares you transferred to Mr. Brooks had you taken the 50 per cent. addition to which you were entitled?—A. I think so. I transferred my own stock—stock that was transferred to me from the company in the same way that my other stock was. I have a copy of the transfer-books here, I think.

Q. What I want to get at is whether each original stockholder was entitled to take 50 per cent. additional stock ?—A. Yes, sir, within a certain time.

Q. Had you taken all the additional stock to which you were entitled on the stock you had ?—A. I think so ; on all the stock that stood in my name.

Q. When you transferred the one hundred shares to Mr. Neilson, did he acquire any right to purchase fifty additional shares ?—A. No ; the time had passed.

Q. And you had received the increase also ?—A. If it stood in my name I had.

Q. But it did stand in your name, did it not ?—A. It did.

Q. So that no right passed over to him to have that additional stock ?—A. O, no.

Q. Do you know anything in regard to his receiving fifty shares of stock subsequently ?—A. I do not. I was absent in Europe when he received it.

Q. Mr. Neilson did subsequently receive fifty shares of stock ?—A. I saw one hundred and fifty shares in his name on the books, instead of one hundred.

Q. Do you know whether, when he received that fifty shares of stock, he received an equal amount at par of Pacific Railroad bonds ?—A. I do not. I presume he did not.

Q. Why do you presume that ?—A. Because I think they had paid out all the bonds. I suppose the fact can be very easily stated from the books.

Q. You suppose he did not receive it, then, because he was not entitled to receive it, not receiving the stock as an increase on the one hundred shares ?—A. He would not be entitled to it ordinarily. I do not know what promises Mr. Ames may have made to him.

Q. Did Mr. Brooks say anything to you in relation to this, when he paid for the stock, that he was advancing it as a loan to Mr. Neilson ?—A. He said nothing about it. I was under the impression that Mr. Brooks intended to take the stock in his own name, but that afterward his official relations to the company changed, and he had to dispose of it, so that when he came to the office of the company to pay for it, it was not placed in his name.

Q. Until the negotiation was completed the only knowledge you had was that Mr. Brooks was taking it for himself ?—A. That was all. When the transaction commenced between us, I would have been very glad to have had him take it, and offered him 5 per cent. to place it. But the value of the stock increased very suddenly. The moment the Oakes Ames contract was executed, there were $4,000,000 of profits on hand. The stock of the Credit Mobilier suddenly became very valuable, and everybody who had any sort of claim for it came forward and wanted it.

Q. But to outsiders, who had no claim, you would not have sold the stock at par ?—A. No ; but everybody I had ever talked with came forward and wanted it then.

Q. How much did you consider the stock worth then ?—A. I do not know what it was worth at that time. I think I made a sale or option about that time at 160, and it was worth a much higher price then, as I supposed.

Q. Was that the stock you sold to Mr. Alley ?—A. Yes, sir.

Q. The transfer of that was on the 20th December, according to the books ?—A. Yes. It carried with it a dividend which was made on the 12th or 13th of December. The books were about to be closed, and everybody wanted to get the stock in his own name in order to draw the dividend.

Q. Do I understand that you sold this stock to Mr. Alley at 160?—A. I gave him a call for it at 160. I think it was worth 200 at the time, or more, when the transfer was made.

Q. You understood that you parted with that stock to Mr. Brooks?—A. Yes, and simply to settle what he claimed as an obligation. There was some difference of opinion as to how much he was entitled to, and I preferred to give him less stock and give him a bonus with it.

Q. Can you state from memory the amount of dividends which had been paid upon the Crebit Mobilier stock in all?—A. I cannot; no, sir.

Q. Have you books here that will show that?—A. I have the trustees' receipts for dividends, which will show. These books contain the dividends made upon the Ames contract, and give the receipts of each party receiving the dividends.

Q. This book shows the first dividend was December 12, payable the 3d January, 1868. That was a dividend upon those one hundred shares of stock you transferred to Neilson on the 26th December?—A. The receipt will show.

Q. The book shows that Mr. Neilson received this 12th of December dividend of $6,000 Union Pacific Railroad bonds on one hundred shares, and $3,000 Union Pacific Railroad bonds on fifty shares?—A. Yes; he was entitled to whatever dividends there were on the stock standing in his name before the books were closed. I repeat that this was a settlement in the nature of a compromise with Mr. Brooks, by which I gave him fifteen or twenty thousand dollars in value rather than all the stock he claimed. The stock was worth intrinsically twice its par value, from the fact that it carried with it the right to participate in the profit of the Ames contract.

Q. The next dividend seems to have been declared January 3, 1868, payable the same day?—A. Yes. The stockholders in the Credit Mobilier were, by virtue of an agreement signed by them, entitled to share in the profits of the Ames contract. After they had signed the agreement, they all came in as co-partners, every man being liable for the entire amount, although he may have had but a single share of stock.

Q. On the 3d of January Mr. Neilson seems to have received $2,000 Union Pacific Railroad bonds on his one hundred shares, and $1,000 on the fifty shares. The other dividends following were on the 10th of January, the 8th of April, and the 17th of June, when he received a cash dividend of $9,000?—A. Yes; by the terms of agreement between the Oakes Ames contractors and the Pacific road, the Credit Mobilier was to guarantee the contract and receive 2½ per cent. commission on its advances of money to the trustees in case they wanted it. The trustees pushed forward the road pretty rapidly, and soon called upon the Credit Mobilier for a million dollars. They did not respond, and the agreement was canceled with the Credit Mobilier.

Q. This paper dated October 15, 1867, agreeing to the Ames contract, you understand to have been signed by Mr. Neilson?—A. Yes; it was assented to by all the stockholders.

Q. You understand that the stock represented by these signers embraced the entire stock?—A. Yes.

Q. State whether the dividend declared December 29, 1868, payable January 1, 1869, for three hundred shares, was Union Pacific Railroad stock.—A. That is Union Pacific Railroad stock.

Q. Was this the last dividend?—A. That is the last dividend ever made.

Q. Were all these dividends made by the trustees of the Ames contract?—A. Yes; and they embrace more than the actual profits on the Ames contract.

Q. I understand that considerable work had been performed before the Ames contract was executed?—A. There was a contract known as the Hoxie contract, which the Credit Mobilier extended to the one hundredth meridian, 249 miles. The Oakes Ames contract was for 667 miles. The Oakes Ames contract was assigned, if I remember, in October, 1867. I think the road had then 500 miles built.

Q. Had there been dividends upon the Credit Mobilier stock before it went into the hands of the trustees?—A. The Credit Mobilier took a contract, I think, at $50,000 a mile, but were obliged to take a larger portion of the stock than was specified under the contract, because the Union Pacific Railroad had not money to carry it on. I think on the first of that stock which they took they paid 30 per cent., and sold it to the stockholders at 71; the arrangement being that they would pay 1 per cent. on it and be subject to a call of 70 per cent. Afterward the arrangement was that the parties who had taken stock should pay for their stock in full. I think there were two dividends on the Credit Mobilier stock at 6 per cent. Then, if I recollect, there was an adjustment of interest. After they put in Mr. Dillon as president they made an adjustment. Some of the stockholders had come in late, and it was not considered fair that they should come in at the full rate, and they adjusted the rate of interest at 12 or 14 per cent. from the time they put their money in, so as to give them a starting point.

Q. Did the stock you sold to Mr. Neilson or Mr. Brooks have the benefit of all these dividends?—A. That was all long passed. They only got what this book shows. It was the Ames contract which made the stock valuable; but it was always supposed that they would get some sort of a contract.

Q. You have spoken of your obligation to Mr. Brooks. It was your understanding that by virtue of that obligation he was to have some stock?—A. Yes, sir.

Q. Something has appeared in reference to money transactions between you and Mr. Brooks. Had it any reference to this?—A. None at all. At one time I was using considerable money, and borrowed from Mr. Brooks. Afterward the company were paying much higher rates than I could pay, and Mr. Brooks loaned his money to the company.

Q. The obligation you felt under to Mr. Brooks had no reference to your money dealings with him?—A. Not at all. I could not have told whether there was $5,000 or $75,000 between us. All that was in the hands of Mr. Crane.

By Mr. MERRICK:

Q. This was, then, a personal sale of yours to Mr. Brooks to enable you to raise money?—A. No, sir; I could have taken a very much larger amount for the stock and securities which went with it. It was simply an unsettled account. Mr. Brooks had been very active in trying to place stock, and I preferred to give him this stock and securities rather than to give him the stock he claimed.

Q. Do you know of any Credit Mobilier stock having been transferred by any person whatever to members of Congress?—A. No, sir; except as shown on that list.

WASHINGTON, D. C., *January* 15, 1873.

Examination of THOMAS C. DURANT continued.

By the CHAIRMAN:

Question. State whether the Pacific Railroad stock and railroad bonds were to go with these one hundred shares of stock which you made a contract for with Mr. Brooks.—Answer. That was entirely in consequence of the contract.

Q. You made the contract?—A. Yes, and I gave less Credit Mobilier stock than was claimed.

Q. If you had sold him or sold anybody one hundred shares of that stock, and there had been no special agreement for bonds or railroad stock, they would not have gone with it?—A. O, no, sir; the time had gone past for all that.

Q. It was entirely, then, by virtue of your contract with Mr. Brooks that this railroad stock and the bonds went with the Credit Mobilier stock?—A. Yes, sir; Mr. Brooks claimed more stock, and, as a compromise of a disputed claim between us, I agreed to give him that. The bonds and stock were not a dividend of the Credit Mobilier; they were simply a compromise of a disputed claim. It was pretty difficult then to get the stock, and I preferred he should have more securities and less stock. This was not any dividend. The dividend-books will show the dividends.

Q. Do you know anything with reference to the original subscriptions to the Credit Mobilier stock?—A. Yes, sir.

Q. Have you a list of the early subscribers—the first subscriptions made?—A. Before I answer that question, I will make a statement which will enable you to understand the answer better. The Credit Mobilier was a charter for what was called the Pennsylvania Fiscal Agency; some parties had subscribed for stock enough to organize the company, and had paid, I think, 1 or 2 per cent. on the stock, but there had never been anything done until the charter passed into new hands, at the time we made the second subscription, which embraced all the stock. I think I can give you from the books of the company the first subscription, and also the second, which is probably what you want.

Q. I mean the subscription after it was contemplated to have some connection with the Union Pacific Railroad?—A. Yes, sir; I have that here. I have a notarial copy of it, but this will answer the same thing here. This gives the conditions of the subscription—the original subscription by virtue of which the Credit Mobilier had anything to do with the road. The conditions of that subscription were that the railway portion of the company should be managed by a railway bureau to consist of five members. After these subscriptions were made it was suggested to increase the number to a committee of seven.

Q. Do you know a man by the name of Alexander E. Laing?—A. I think there is a man by the name of Laing in New York.

Q. Do you know him?—A. Yes, sir.

Q. Had he any connection with this matter in any way?—A. No, sir.

Q. Do you know whether he was a subscriber to this stock in any way?—A. I think I can explain what there is about him. Some parties were interested in this Pennsylvania Fiscal Agency when I first went into the Credit Mobilier. They had taken a few shares of stock before the branch was established in New York, under the amended charter. I sent Mr. Train to Philadelphia. We wanted it for a stock operation, but we could not agree what was to be done with it. Mr.

Train proposed to go on an expanded scale, but I abandoned it. I think Mr. Train got some subscriptions; what they were I do not know; they were never collected and returned to the company. These are all the subscribers to the Credit Mobilier.

Q. That paper gotten up by Train you have not?—A. No, sir; it never amounted to anything; he may have got some subscriptions prior to the one you have, but he never returned them to the company; he placed some stock afterward. All the connection the Union Pacific Railroad had with the Credit Mobilier through the contract was an accidental matter entirely; the company attempted to build the road themselves until they exhausted their means. They then made what was known as the Hoxie contract, but that soon exhausted the means of the friends of the enterprise. They then started a subscription paper to see if they could raise $1,600,000 to enable them to carry on the contract, as a margin to complete the first section of the road. The subscription reached the amount of $1,600,000, and 25 per cent. was paid in. On the next call for an installment on the subscription the parties would not pay up. They were generally capitalists, and while they were willing to risk the money they had put in, they would not risk their whole fortunes, and it was then suggested that we would get some corporation in which the individual liability would only reach the amount subscribed. We fell upon this corporation, and the parties transferred their subscriptions to it. I have a list here somewhere of the original subscriptions, with the Hoxie contract and all.

Q. Have you anything here which will show the dividends declared by the Credit Mobilier prior to the Ames contract?—A. I think we have the books of the company, or copies of them, here, and if you have an expert he can make them up in half an hour. Their dividends were light.

Q. If you have a book, showing precisely what the dividends were, the committee would be glad to get it.—A. The original book is in the other committee-room.

By Mr. MERRICK:

Q. Be good enough to tell me what other directors, officers, and principal stockholders of the Union Pacific Railroad Company, besides yourself, were also directors, stockholders, or managers of the Credit Mobilier.—A. I think there was none, unless it was Mr. Bushnell and Mr. McComb. The Hoxie contract extended 247 miles, to the one hundredth meridian. That the Credit Mobilier guaranteed to complete in the fall of 1866. Through the Credit Mobilier taking some of their stock at a low price, and dividing or selling it to its stockholders, other parties became interested as stockholders in the Union Pacific Railroad Company. They were not original subscribers, but through their interest in the contract with the Credit Mobilier they became stockholders in the Union Pacific Railroad Company. After that contract was completed they claimed, being then large stockholders in the railroad company, the right of sitting in the board, and several of these parties were elected as members of the board.

Q. Can you state which were so elected?—A. I think Oliver Ames, Mr. Duff, and Mr. Dillon were, and several others whose names I do not recollect. Mr. Oakes Ames was a stockholder in the Credit Mobilier, and also a stockholder in the Union Pacific road. At the time of this election there was a collusion between these parties who were in both corporations. I perhaps should not say collusion, but they became a majority of the directors. At first there was no contract; the contract of the Union Pacific Railroad Company with Mr. Hoxie was transferred to the Credit Mobilier.

Q. After the transfer of the Hoxie contract, and before the Ames contract, a majority of the directors and principal stockholders of the Credit Mobilier became also directors of the Union Pacific Railroad Company?—A. I do not know that I can say a majority; several of them did. It was subsequent to the Hoxie contract and anterior to the Oakes Ames contract. They made no contract with the Credit Mobilier afterward. They passed a resolution shortly after these gentlemen came in, extending the Hoxie contract at $50,000 a mile, and ordered the Union Pacific Railroad Company to pay that sum to the Credit Mobilier. I put an injunction on them on the ground that we were the interested party in both companies, and had no right to make a contract with ourselves. That resolution was rescinded and they afterward made a contract with J. M. S. Williams, of Boston. Mr. Williams agreed to transfer the contract to the Credit Mobilier if he got it. I put an injunction on that arrangement, which has never been dissolved. Then came the contract with Oakes Ames. In the complaint I made, I, as a matter of policy, agreed to consent to anything that all the stockholders would agree to, and that contract was made provisional on its receiving the assent of all the stockholders of the Union Pacific Railroad Company.

Q. Was Oakes Ames a director at that time, or a large stockholder of the Union Pacific Railroad Company?—A. He was a stockholder, not a director.

Q. And also a stockholder in the Credit Mobilier?—A. He was; he was not a director. This contract was not let to the Credit Mobilier; it was let to Oakes Ames, and assigned to seven trustees.

Q. I will ask you if you can state to the committee what was the original contract between you and Mr. Brooks out of which this ultimate settlement grew, resulting in the transfer of 100 shares, to which you deposed yesterday.—A. It was in the fore part of 1867—in the spring of 1867. The Union Pacific Railroad were considerably in debt. I think they owed then four or five million dollars. The Credit Mobilier made a proposition to them through their executive committee, to take about $6,000,000 of their securities. I will read the proposition if you wish. It is as follows:

To the executive committee of the Union Pacific Railroad Company:

GENTLEMEN: The Credit Mobilier of America propose to purchase of your company $3,000,000 of land-grant bonds at 80 per cent. of their par value; $2,060,000 of first-mortgage bonds at 85 per cent. of their par value; $750,000 of the certificates of the company convertible into first-mortgage bonds, at 80 per cent. of their face, the said certificates to bear 6 per cent. interest until the first-mortgage bonds are issued and exchanged.

They will loan, or procure to be loaned to the company, $1,250,000 on four months' time, at the rate of 7 per cent. interest per annum, and 2½ per cent. commission, with first-mortgage bonds as collateral security at 66⅔ per cent. of their par value.

Payments on purchase and loans to be made as follows, viz: 25 per cent. on or before February 22, 1867; 25 per cent. on or before March 15, 1867; 25 per cent. on or before April 5, 1867; 25 per cent. on or before April 25, 1867.

The company to proceed at once to issue the said land-grant bonds; and if requested so to do by the Credit Mobilier, shall issue certificates convertible into the said bonds prior to their being issued.

This proposition is made on the express condition that your company pay as soon as practicable the balance due on account of contract east of the one hundredth meridian, but which time shall not extend beyond the time of the several payments herein specified in the purchase of bonds, and the further condition that the present contract for which this company is the agent shall be extended so as to include 100 miles westward from the one hundredth meridian as follows: The said 100 miles to be completed to the acceptance of the Government commissioners for the sum of $42,000 per mile.

The same quantity and kind of material to be used and the work to be of the same general character as the work on the last 100 miles east of the one hundredth meridian, with the same guarantee as to cost of iron and price for Burnettizing timber or ties.

Turnouts, side-tracks, and station-buildings to be made adequate for the present business of the company as now proposed by the engineer in charge; should more be required, the company to pay for iron and superstructure.

The hotel at North Platte station to be completed according to the plans and specifications adopted.

Turn-table, engine-house, with ten stalls, blacksmith and repair shop, with stationary engine suitable for the purpose, two lathes, and other tools in proportion, which have been decided as necessary for the immediate requirements of the company; water-tanks at the points heretofore designated by the engineer in charge; also two locomotives and fifty flat cars.

The running of trains on the road to be under the control of the contractors' superintendent; the contractors to pay the cost of transporting material used in construction.

Payments to be made on the monthly estimate of the chief engineer, which estimates are to be made as in the former contract; contractors to assume all liabilities incurred by the company on account of the construction of said 100 miles.

By order of the committee:

BENJ. F. BUNKER,
Assistant Secretary Credit Mobilier of America.

NEW YORK, *February* 13, 1867.

The executive committee of the Union Pacific Railroad Company accepted that proposition of the executive committee of the Credit Mobilier, and the Credit Mobilier, in order to carry it out, immediately increased their capital stock to $1,200,000, and in order to induce their old subscribers to come in and put in more money, they offered a portion of these bonds which they had purchased to each shareholder to come in. The entire proposition was never carried out fully.

Q. I am not asking you about that. I am asking you for the date of this contract with Mr. Brooks.—A. It was about the date of the one I am speaking of, the payments on which were due between February and April, I should say, of 1867. At that time the stock was of doubtful value.

Q. You need not go into these matters; I want you to answer the specific question. The original contract out of which this arrangement with Mr. Brooks grew was between February and April, 1867?—A. Yes, sir; perhaps earlier. Mr. Brooks took a great deal of interest in the enterprise, and began by looking about to see what could be done. He did not succeed in raising much money among his friends, but he spent a good deal of time, and finally said he thought he would take some of the stock, say from $15,000 to $25,000. The stock afterward suddenly became valuable.

Q. Then, if I understand you, Mr. Brooks took an active interest in carrying out the proposition or arrangement which you have read from this paper, and thereupon he claimed from you the privilege of becoming a stockholder in the Credit Mobilier?—A. You may call it a privilege if you choose; we were very anxious to get anybody to take it then at par.

Q. Upon that request of his, was there any specific arrangement on your part to let him have any of your stock?—A. He wanted to take between $15,000 and $20,000.

Q. There was no agreement, then, as to any specific amount?—A. Except for $15,000 or $20,000.

Q. Was that all that occurred at that time?—A. On several occasions he referred to it.

Q. That was the basis of his claim?—A. Yes, sir.

Q. You and he differed about his demand, and this settlement was the compromise?—A. A compromise by giving him this bonus. He wanted $20,000, and claimed he was entitled to $20,000 of the Credit Mobilier stock.

Q. And what did you do?—A. I do not know. I had several conversations with him, and finally made a settlement as I have stated.

Q. Did you concede his claim or deny it?—A. I conceded his claim by compromising it.

Q. Did you before the compromise?—A. I thought he did not fix a sum sufficiently definite.

Q. What was your position?—A. My position was to get off with letting him have just as little as I could.

Q. He claimed that he was entitled to $20,000 of stock, and out of that grew the compromise?—A. I gave him a bonus, as I have stated, and ten shares of Credit Mobilier stock.

Q. Was his claim such that he looked to you to give it to him individually, or was the contract you made to be liquidated between him and the company?—A. I was president of the company at the time it was first talked of, and, I supposed, was the only one to dispose of any stock, if there had been any to sell, for the company.

Q. How did it happen, if you were president of the company, and acted only in the character of president of the company, that you made a promise by which you in your individual character made this ultimate adjustment with him?—A. I had to settle most of these agreements out of my own stock. I was not president at time of settlement. I got from the company what they would allow me, and had to make it up out of my own stock.

Q. Did you consider yourself as personally obligated for this arrangement made by you as president of the company?—A. Certainly I did. I had taken $600,000 of the stock, which was increased to $900,000. I had spoken to a great many parties, and most of them were willing to take it after it had got to be a good thing.

Q. Were there any other members of Congress than Mr. Brooks, within your knowledge, concerned in the stock of the Credit Mobilier?—A. Here is a list of the stockholders and the dividend-book.

Q. I do not suppose their names appear upon the dividend-book at all. Were they interested in any way?—A. If they were interested, they must appear, unless they held in the name of others, of which I would have no knowledge.

Q. Had you any such knowledge, directly or indirectly?—A. No, sir, except what appears on the books.

Q. Have you any information from other sources which would enable the committee to arrive at a knowledge of such transactions?—A. I am sure I do not know where Mr. Ames placed his stock. I only know what I saw on the books.

Q. You have no information, as I understand, from other sources, which you could communicate to the committee that would enable them to ascertain any connection on the part of any other member of Congress with the Credit Mobilier?—A. The stock that stands in the name of Mr. Ames, as trustee, I claim belongs to the company yet, and I have a summons in a suit in my pocket waiting to catch him in New York, to serve the papers.

By Mr. NIBLACK:

Q. It seems that B. M. Boyer, a former member of Congress from the State of Pennsylvania, was one of the stockholders whose name appears on the books. How did he become a stockholder?—A. I met Mr. Boyer on an excursion over the road in 1866, about the time we were finishing up the first contract. Mr. Boyer said he thought he would like to invest a few thousand dollars in the enterprise if he could make more than his interest out of it; that he had some Government bonds that he could dispose of to raise the money. I promised him some stock. He applied several times for it. I rather hesitated in giving it to him, fearing that as he was embarking in it on my advice, and as things looked rather blue at that time, he might be disappointed. At any rate, I did not give it to him till several months afterward.

Q. How much did you let him have eventually?—A. I think it was fifty shares. He took it at the same price we were then trying to sell it at to other parties.

Q. At about what period did he become the owner of this stock which was transferred to him?—A. He was virtually the owner from the time I promised it to him. He made arrangements to send me the securities as soon as I notified him I wanted them.

Q. About what time did you transfer this stock to him?—A. I think it was transferred to him in December, 1867. I am not positive of that. We closed up all our obligations as far as we could as soon as the Oakes Ames contract was made.

By Mr. McCRARY:

Q. How much stock in all was put into your hands to distribute?—A. I think about a quarter of what I had promised. When the first injunction was put on the Union Pacific Railroad against letting a contract to themselves, I was vice-president of one company and president of the other. Of course after that they had no further use for me in the Credit Mobilier Company. I had promised this stock at that time, a portion of it, in fact all of it. There was a balance of my subscription unissued, and, though it was paid for, they issued these six hundred or seven hundred shares, and the certificates were left with the assistant treasurer to be used to fill my contracts. After I left the presidency of the company, the new officers demanded of him the certificates, and I was therefore unable to meet my obligations with it. I allowed the stock to be transferred. I told the assistant treasurer in my telegram to let them do anything they wanted to, and he wrote a letter, which is here in this book.

Q. Can you state the amount?—A. I forget the amount.

Q. Was there any other stock left in your hands besides that $60,000?—A. None for that purpose.

Q. You say you had not promised any of that stock to any member of Congress except Mr. Brooks and Mr. Boyer?—A. Not that I know of; everything is on this list; whenever I delivered or settled for any stock, this list covers the entire matter.

Q. Did you make any promise to any of the members of Congress besides these two?—A. I do not remember of any. If I did, it will appear on some of the books.

Q. You did not hold in your own name stock for any member of Congress?—A. No, sir; I held no stock as trustee, I am quite positive. I think I should recollect it if I had. We were through with legislation long before the Credit Mobilier came up. We had no idea we should ever come to Congress for anything again.

Q. Were you not apprehensive of a congressional investigation?—A. I was not.

Q. Do you know whether any of the parties interested were?—A. At the time we had these injunctions I insisted on not going into a contract unless it was assented to by every stockholder. There was some difference of opinion about requiring the assent of every stockholder, which grew into quite a little quarrel, when I made the remark that I was tired of law, and that I proposed to go to Congress, and get them to say whether they would allow this company to contract with themselves without the assent of stockholders. I had written such a letter, and mailed it to Mr. Washburn. Several gentlemen then said they would not go into a contract without the consent of all the stockholders, and they received my order to go to the post-office and get my letter. I think Mr. McComb, Mr. Bushnell, and Mr. Crane went and saw the postmaster. They ransacked the mail and got the letter out.

Q. Was it regarded by the gentlemen connected with the Union Pacific Railroad and the Credit Mobilier as exceedingly important that there should be no investigation by Congress?—A. I think not; we were advised by eminent counsel that we had vested rights, and we had no reason to fear any interference on the part of Congress. We had no reason to fear anything except little quarrels among ourselves.

Q. You appear, however, to have induced the parties to come to your terms by a threat of congressional investigation?—A. No; I am simply stating the history of this matter. I believe at that time Mr. Washburn offered some resolution in the House. This was in 1867. An investigation would not have amounted to anything. It only raised the question as to whether the board should protect the minority as well as the majority of stockholders. That was the only question that would have been raised.

Q. What was the value of the securities you let Mr. Brooks have besides the Credit Mobilier stock?—A. I considered it in the light of a business transaction. It was just the same as letting him have a hundred shares and buying the other hundred at about 200 per cent.; that was about the way I figured it.

Q. I will understand you better if you will give the value of the securities in dollars and cents.—A. I considered that if he took two hundred shares they were worth double their par value, and I preferred to give him these securities, which then had only a nominal value, and in place of giving him two hundred shares to give him one hundred of the Credit Mobilier.

Q. I would like to know what the securities were worth.—A. The bonds were worth 85; it is difficult to tell what the stock was worth.

Q. How much was two hundred shares of Union Pacific Railroad stock worth?—A. Credit Mobilier was worth $200 per share. I have been told that a good deal of the Union Pacific stock has been since sold as low as 9. I know of no sale at that time. I think the Credit Mobilier did once make a price, and got their stockholders to take it when it could not have been done outside at 30.

Q. That would be $6,000 for the Union Pacific Railroad stock. What would be the value of $5,000 first-mortgage bonds at 85?—A. At 80—and they have sold at about 80—the amount would be $4,000. Taking an average price for the stock, it would be $9,000 altogether, and a thousand dollars better for me than if I had given him the two hundred shares of stock.

Q. Do you know of any property among the assets of the Union Pacific Railroad Company, or the Credit Mobilier, being used in any way to influence legislation in Congress?—A. No, sir; none of the assets.

Q. Do you know of money being so used?—A. Nor money.

Q. Do you know of any influence being procured in that way?—A. We consented to give up a valuable portion of our franchise. I did not know at the time how that could influence members of Congress, but we found that we were meeting with opposition. Mr. Ames came to me and told me we could not carry the bill with that branch on it, and we waived the Sioux City branch and consented to lose it.

Q. That was not in the interest of any particular member of Congress?—A. I do not know anything about that. I think you will find that the Credit Mobilier is made a scape-goat for other things.

Q. Do you know of any other person besides Mr. Brooks who received a similar bonus for taking stock in the Credit Mobilier?—A. It was not a bonus for taking stock; it was a bonus to settle a claim for stock. The subscribers to the $1,200,000 additional stock received the bonds.

Q. The same bonds that Mr. Brooks received?—A. The same kind of bonds. They received a bond for every ten shares. They paid for the stock at par, and loaned the Credit Mobilier an equal amount on four months' time, which enabled the Credit Mobilier to pay two and a half millions to the Union Pacific Railroad Company, and help them out of their difficulty at the time.

Q. What you did with Mr. Brooks was substantially what the company had done with other parties before, was it not?—A. If Mr. Brooks had been a subscriber, and had taken originally one hundred shares of stock, he would have been entitled to ten bonds of that stock. If he had had one hundred shares of the increased stock he would have had ten bonds with it; but this transaction with Mr. Brooks was a matter of settlement, having nothing to do with what he would have been entitled to in the Credit Mobilier. Mr. Brooks wanted two hundred shares; I did not want to give him but one hundred; I gave him one hundred, and gave him $9,000 worth of securities, according to your estimate of them.

Q. Can you explain why the first five mortgage-bonds and two hundred shares of Union Pacific Railroad stock are entered in your book as earnings of the stock of the Credit Mobilier?—A. That is simply a term used to identify the stock. It must be credited to something. I had received the bonds under my right acquired by the increase of stock in the Credit Mobilier, and you may call it earnings or call it what you like; the object was simply to keep track of the investment on the books.

Q. Do you not think it would have been more correct to have entered it as given in settlement of a compromise with Mr. Brooks in accordance with the facts?—A. The paper you have is a memorandum. It amounts to the same thing nearly, and it is about what he would have received if he had held the original stock and purchased the same amount of Union Pacific stock other shareholders did. I discover now, for the first time, that in my estimates for compromising I made a mistake of $500, which made him $500 better off than if he had received the original stock and the securities he would have had turned over to him in consequence.

By Mr. BROOKS:

Q. Do you remember how far back our business acquaintance commenced? Have you any memorandum to which you can refer?—A. I have no memorandum which will show that.

Q. What is your impression as to the date?—A. I think in 1866 or 1867.

Q. Do you remember the date of our going out on an excursion over the road?—A. That was in 1866. I had forgotten you were on that excursion.

Q. You knew me at that time?—A. I had known you many years before that. I thought you referred to these transactions.

Q. I mean general business transactions; did they commence in 1866 or before?—A. O, yes; they commenced as early as 1864. I could not tell you the date without looking at the books.

Q. You spoke, or rather the chairman did, of contracts with me in 1866 or 1867; what kind of contracts do you mean, verbal or conversational?—A. Conversational contracts.

Q. Talks?—A. Talks in 1866 and 1867.

Q. Did I or not make a great effort with you among capitalists in New York to get the stock of the Credit Mobilier taken, in order to go on with the work on that road?—A. I so stated. You thought you could place $500,000 of the stock—that was when we had the increase.

Q. Did I not go with you to see Commodore Garrison on that subject?—A. Yes.

Q. And George Law?—A. No.

Q. Did not your engineer go with me to see George Law?—A. I do not know. I know you made great efforts to place that stock.

Q. Did I not send representatives of Mr. Vanderbilt to see you?—A. I do not know. You made efforts to have the stock taken, and devoted considerable time to it.

Q. Did anybody at the time take it?—A. No; I do not believe you got a dollar taken.

Q. Did they give any reason why they did not take it?—A. I did not converse with any of them except Mr. Garrison.

Q. Did they not say it was too distant an enterprise, among savages, in an unknown country?—A. That was the objection made everywhere nine times out of ten.

Q. Was it essential that the Credit Mobilier stock should be taken, in order to carry on the Union Pacific Railroad?—A. Yes.

Q. Were not the finances of the railroad company in such a condition that, if the Credit Mobilier had not come forward and advanced the money, the road would have gone to the wall?—A. Yes.

Q. Would you deem it patriotic or unpatriotic on the part of a public man to exercise all his influence among capitalists to induce them to invest their money for that purpose?—A. Certainly; and that was the feeling of everybody. Everybody wanted the road to go on.

Q. I made great efforts to induce capitalists to do that, did I not?—A. Yes, sir.

Q. I could have had any amount of the stock of the Credit Mobilier if I had chosen to take it at that time?—A. You could have had $500,000 at that time. That was the amount you tried to place.

Q. Having done all that I did, was it not natural, when the stock became valuable, that I should prefer to have some of it?—A. Yes; but if you had not said anything about it before, you would not have got it.

Q. Would the capitalists of New York touch the Credit Mobilier or Union Pacific Railroad stock at all in 1866?—A. Some of them did and some of them did not. A majority would not touch it, from the time of its taking the contract up to that time, and it was up-hill work all of that time.

Q. What was the nature of the Government surveys which had been made?—A. The Government surveys were of no use whatever. Their estimates and their routes were almost impracticable. The road would have cost so much that nobody would have touched it then.

Q. Did or did not their surveys exhibit almost insurmountable obstacles in carrying on the road?—A. They did.

Q. Did not these Government surveys frighten most of the capitalists in New York from engaging in the enterprise at the time?—A. Yes, sir. I am as venturesome as anybody, but I would not have invested a dollar if I had not known a better route.

Q. How was a better route discovered?—A. I made surveys at my own expense.

Q. What were the discoveries you made in that unknown country?—A. In the last year of Mr. Jefferson Davis's term as Secretary of War a party was sent out.

The CHAIRMAN suggested that this had not much to do with the investigation.

WITNESS. I will only say, then, that an examination eight or ten years previous satisfied me that there was a good route through the mountains. Previous to the organization of this party, I dispatched five parties of engineers to survey the mountain passes.

Q. Did or did not the pass over the Laramie Mountains largely lessen the expense of constructing the road?—A. The information I got gave me more confidence than I could inspire in anybody else; that is the amount of it.

Q. The chairman has used the word "contracts." Was there ever any general understanding on the subject, and did you or did you not feel that I had rendered services to the public in all the efforts I had made to induce capitalists to embark in it?—A. You certainly did; you did not succeed in placing the stock, but you created a favorable impression among gentlemen who would not otherwise have taken the subject into consideration.

Q. Was there any contract other than that sort of transaction?—A. There was no contract.

By Mr. NIBLACK:

Q. State whether the Union Pacific Railroad, or men connected with that enterprise, were called upon to assist in the senatorial election in 1866 in the State of Iowa.—A. I do not recollect. I did assist myself. I had a large interest in Iowa, personally, and during the canvass I assisted.

Q. It has been stated to me that you gave a check for $10,000 to assist in that election.—A. No, sir; I did not. I gave two checks of $5,000 each to assist in that election.

Q. Can you explain the history of these checks, and state for what purpose they were given?—A. For the purpose of securing the election.

Q. Whose election?—A. Mr. Harlan's; for the purpose of securing the influence of some newspapers. I do not know how it was applied. Moses H. Grinnell subscribed in my name, during my absence, to the general republican committee, $5,000, to aid in Grant's election. That seemed to be pretty well past, to object when I returned, and I paid the subscription.

Q. It has been suggested to me, also, that it had been urged upon you very strongly to give Senator Carpenter an interest for congressional influence; do you know anything about that?—A. No, sir; I do not recollect. I am sure I did not do it. Mr. Harlan had been an old personal friend. My personal intercourse with him had continued fifteen or twenty years. He lived on a rival line of railroad through Iowa to one in which I had long been interested, to be sure, but he understood the wants of the State, and, besides, he had been in Washington long enough to know how to care for the interests of the State here.

Q. He was at that time Secretary of the Interior?—A. I believe so; he was not in Congress at that time.

WASHINGTON, D. C., *January* 15, 1873.

C. S. BUSHNELL, having been duly sworn, made the following statement:

I come here voluntarily, without a summons, for the purpose of offering the information I have, in the interests of all parties, and especially of the stockholders of the Credit Mobilier, who are entitled to the information I can give. I was a trustee under the Oakes Ames contract. I was, with Mr. Durant, a managing director of the bureau of the Credit Mobilier. I was an original incorporator of the Union Pacific Railroad Company, was connected with its original organization, and know its whole history down to the present time.

During 1865 and 1866 the principal management of the Credit Mobilier was in the hands of Dr. Durant, myself, and J. M. S. Williams, our treasurer. We succeeded in completing the road to the one hundredth meridian in the fall of 1866, but it left us in debt three or four million dollars, which we were carrying, with our friends, at a large and expensive rate of interest. We had repeated meetings of the parties in interest, and consultations as to how we could raise the money to pay off this debt and go on with the road. Finally, in the sping of 1867, at the Fifth Avenue Hotel, the parties in interest of the Credit Mobilier settled on a plan which has been prosecuted. We called upon the stockholders of the Credit Mobilier to increase their subscriptions 50 per cent. A part of them were willing to take it. Others would not take it or have anything to do with it.

There was placed in my hands about $500,000 of this stock, to place with outside parties. I went to work very vigorously to place it, because of our financial necessities. In New Haven I appealed to the directors of the banks and to the heaviest capitalists there, and succeeded in placing about a hundred thousand dollars; not, however, without first giving them a personal written guarantee against loss if they would take it. In this way I induced the Trowbridges and other parties in New Haven to take a hundred thousand dollars' worth of stock. I succeeded in placing in New York one hundred and fifty thousand dollars more of the stock. The company gave it to me at 95 to place, and it was placed at 97½, and in some instances at par.

While I was thus engaged, Mr. Ames was doing his best to place stock, and did place a large amount of it. Where he was placing it I did not inquire, so long as he turned the money into the treasury of the company.

That, however, was not sufficient to help us out of our difficulties. That twelve hundred and fifty thousand dollars only went a small way toward helping us out, and the question came up, what could we do? They finally referred to the matter of selling the bonds we had on hand. We had sold the Government bonds at 90, and had four or five millions of first-mortgage bonds on hand, which we had sold none of. I thought we could sell some of these bonds. Most of the others thought we could not sell the bonds until a portion of the road had been finished and was doing a paying business. I insisted that the bonds could be sold to help us out of our difficulties, and they finally appointed me an agent to sell the bonds. As I said before this, the stock of the Credit Mobilier was sold from 95 to 97½ to par, and they wanted me to take it for almost any price. We appointed advertising agents, and advertised largely in all the leading papers in the United States. I sent advertisements to every leading city, and the result was that in five or six months we succeeded in selling ten millions of the bonds, which placed our finances in a very different condition.

In the mean time we had discovered that, instead of the route where we had expected to build the road, by crossing the Black Hills we could save millions of dollars in expense.

So that, within a few months, from these two causes, the stock of the Credit Mobilier came right up from less than par to 160, then 200, and then a great deal higher.

The work was pushed on, and that fall it was completed to the base of the Black Hills.

We came together again, and Mr. Ames met us, and discussed the question of dividends. We had made a great deal of money. He said that he had promised, during the spring, in our dark days, some two or three hundred shares of stock, and that the parties were fairly entitled to it. I knew that he had done it. During the spring he had placed a great deal of it, and I had done the same. He asked us to sign a paper or an agreement that he might have this stock and fulfill his promises made in the spring. I had no hesitation in signing that agreement. The view I took of it was, that if parties in Congress or out of Congress had taken that stock they ought to be proud of it. If these parties had agreed in the dark days of the spring of 1867 to take the stock, I held that after we had sold eight or ten millions of dollars, and the expense of construction had been reduced four, five, or six million dollars by the change of route, these parties were entitled to the stock. I justify my act in the signing of that agreement, authorizing Mr. Ames to fulfill his pledges, which he said he had made to deliver this stock, just as unhesitatingly as I did when I got Mr. Ames in 1865 to help us. I did not think there was any delicacy in asking Mr. Ames in 1865 to advance a million or two of dollars, and when he got other friends in Congress to aid in the enterprise, I thought he had induced them to do an act that every man in Congress or out of Congress ought to be proud of. There is no act of my life which I look upon with so much satisfaction, and I think my children will be proud of it to the last generation. And when I see my stock, through a misapprehension, depreciated to almost nothing, I think it is time to set forth the true history of the case.

I have now a letter in my pocket from one of our banks, where I had sent fifty thousand dollars of that stock as collateral, within a week, saying they will have nothing to do with the iniquity. The stock of the Credit Mobilier is worth to-day, or should be, 75 or 80, and yet you could not borrow five thousand dollars on a hundred thousand of it, simply because there has been a misunderstanding of what certain parties have done or agreed to do. I say that members of Congress who agreed to take this stock in the spring of 1867 were entitled to take it, and if I were a member of Congress, and had received such a pledge, I would demand it.

By the CHAIRMAN:

Question. At the time this stock was put in the hands of Mr. Ames to fulfill his promises or agreements in reference to these shares, did you learn of any persons he had made these arrangements with, or was under obligations to?—Answer. I do not think I did. It is possible he may have given me names; I do not remember. I believed his word when he said he had promised it, and it was nothing to me whom he had promised it to.

Q. Do you remember the name of any member of Congress with whom he had made arrangements?—A. I have no doubt the names were mentioned. I do not remember them.

Q. You may have seen in the newspapers the names of Mr. Colfax,

Mr. Blaine, Mr. Wilson, Mr. Kelley, Mr. Scofield, Mr. Garfield, Mr. Bingham, and others. Do you remember whether any of these persons were named?—A. I do not remember that he gave me the names at all; and if he did not, I should not have asked him for them.

Q. Have you any knowledge whether Mr. Ames did, in point of fact, distribute any stock to any of these gentlemen, or to any member of Congress?—A. I have not.

Q. It seems that Charles H. Neilson, of New York, a son-in-law of Mr. Brooks, had some of this stock. Are you acquainted with him?—A. No, sir.

Q. It seems that in December, 1867, he became the owner of one hundred shares, which were transferred to him by Mr. Durant. Have you any knowledge in reference to that transaction?—A. Not in reference to the immediate transaction. I know that Mr. Brooks did all he could to place the stock; that he did all he could to help us along in our emergencies.

Q. Did you, or not, know anything in relation to conversations which took place between Mr. Durant and Mr. Brooks in relation to his becoming a stockholder?—A. No; I was not present at all at any such conversation that I remember.

Q. Among the stock that was distributed, do you know of any that went to a member of Congress?—A. No, sir. I distributed more than anybody else, but it was mostly in New Haven and New York.

Q. Did you have any conversation yourself with Mr. Brooks in relation to his becoming a stockholder in the company, or taking stock himself?—A. No, sir.

Q. You knew he was actively at work in getting stock taken?—A. Yes, sir.

Q. But you know of no arrangement or conversation in relation to his becoming a stockholder?—A. Not a word.

Q. Subsequently Mr. Neilson became the owner of fifty shares more by direct subscription to the company itself, in February, 1868. Have you any knowledge in reference to that?—A. Nothing except what I have seen in the testimony.

Q. You had no knowledge at the time in reference to it?—A. No.

Q. And you have now no knowledge except such as you have derived from the public prints?—A. That is all.

Q. Did the stock you placed at 97 carry any bonds with it?—A. No, sir.

Q. How far out was the road built before the Ames contract was made?—A. Before the Ames contract was executed, the road was constructed beyond Sidney a considerable way.

Q. Was it or not built out beyond the Black Hills you speak of?—A. O, no, sir. It was built a little over 300 miles from Omaha.

Q. Was it not built to the summit of Black Hills?—A. No, sir. I went out on the line of the road to Sidney in the month of July, 1867. I came home, and was sick about four months. While I was sick, the Oakes Ames contract was executed, and they could not have gone more than fifty or sixty miles beyond Sidney at the time this contract was executed.

By Mr. NIBLACK:

Q. I understand, then, your proposition to be that these members of Congress who had taken or agreed to take Credit Mobilier stock made a mistake when they denied that they had any interest in this company?—A. I would like to make that a little clearer. We were placing that stock during the spring of 1867. This increase of stock of which I have spoken came before Congress met in the fall. When these gentlemen met in the fall the stock had gone up to 160 or 170. In the mean time, we had got into a pretty sharp contest between Mr. Durant and our Boston interest. It is barely possible that these parties whom Mr. Ames had promised stock were frightened about some trouble growing out of a lawsuit. If they were not, I think they were very foolish gentlemen for not taking the stock, and requiring or allowing Mr. Ames to fulfill his obligation to them.

Q. You think that, instead of denying that they had an interest in the company, they ought to be proud of having taken an interest?—A. Certainly I do. Mr. Hooper and Mr. Ames had taken their stock two years before. I do not think they are ashamed of having taken that interest and of being prominently connected with building the Pacific railroad, and why members should be, who agreed to assist two years afterward, I cannot comprehend.

By Mr. McCrary:

Q. You reside in Chicago?—A. No, I reside in New Haven.

Q. You were not subpœnaed here?—A. No; I came here voluntarily, for the purpose of doing what I could to get rid of the prejudice in regard to this Credit Mobilier interest. I hold over $100,000 worth of it, which is being depreciated to nothing by this unfounded prejudice against it.

Q. The refusal of the bank to take your stock as collateral was what occasioned your coming here?—A. No; that was a mere incident.

Q. You think the holder of stock in the Union Pacific Railroad Company, or the Credit Mobilier Company, would be a disinterested party in legislation affecting the interests of the company?—A. We never wanted any legislation after 1864. We got a bill through then which gave us all the legislation we required, and we only asked to be let alone.

Q. You considered it rather important to be let alone, did you not?—A. Yes, I did; and I thought we had a right to be let alone; we had fulfilled our part under this legislation faithfully.

By Mr. Niblack:

Q. According to your statement, as a holder of Credit Mobilier stock, you are entitled to damages for depreciating your stock?—A. I do not think of bringing any suit for that purpose. This is not the first time we have suffered. We have suffered seriously both before and since we have fulfilled our obligation.

By Mr. McCrary:

Q. Did you not solicit some legislation in regard to moving your offices from New York to Boston?—A. I did not; I was for fighting it out on that line in New York, as we have done since, and won.

Q. Was there not some legislation in regard to the decision of Secretary Boutwell concerning the interest in which you were largely interested?—A. I believe there was; I believe Congress set Secretary Boutwell right.

Q. Do you think a stockholder in your company would be a competent person to decide that question?—A. I do; the same as the holder of national bank stock would be to decide a bank question, or as a dealer in wool would be to decide a tariff question.

Q. Was there not a good deal of trouble about the terminus of the Union Pacific Railroad Company, which had to be settled by Congress? A. I never asked anything of Congress. I was in favor of adjusting the difficulty between ourselves.

Q. There was trouble, however, which was settled by Congress?—A. Yes, sir.

Q. The two companies had built their roads side by side, for some distance, had they not?—A. Yes.

Q. That was a serious question, involving serious consequences to the company?—A. It cost us a good deal of money in constructing the extra line of road.

Q. You think a stockholder in either company would be entirely disinterested upon that question?—A. I do not think the question should have come to Congress at all. I proposed to settle it without coming to Congress, and I think we never should have come to Congress on the subject.

By the CHAIRMAN:

Q. Did the stock of the Credit Mobilier go above par prior to the execution of the Ames contract?—A. I do not think its rise was based alone on the Ames contract. There was a distinct understanding that the contract was to be given to Oakes Ames a considerable time prior to the execution of the contract.

Q. Then, in point of fact, the contract had been agreed upon some time before it was reduced to writing. Did that stock go above par until that agreement was made which resulted in the Ames contract?—A. It was about that time that the stock appreciated.

Q. Was it not true that the making of that contract, and a knowledge of the profit to be derived from building the road under that contract, was the cause of the stock suddenly advancing in value?—A. No, sir; it was distinctly understood, long before that time, that the parties who had put their money into the Credit Mobilier were, in some shape, to have the profits of building the road. It was that fact, and it was also the prior fact that we had sold ten million dollars of bonds, and found an easier route over the mountains, that appreciated the stock.

Q. How early in the fall of 1867 was the stock above par?—A. Early in the fall.

Q. What do you think was the fair market-value of the stock; what would it have sold for among people who understood about it in December, 1867?—A. I remember one sale at $165, in the fall of 1867. I do not remember the exact date.

Q. To whom was that stock sold?—A. I understood it was sold by Mr. Alley at $165. I think it was sold by Mr. Alley to Peter Butler for account, as I understood, of Mr. Bardwell.

Q. You understood that this stock, which was put into the hands of Mr. Ames for the purpose of fulfilling engagements, was to comply with the obligations made by him as far back as the spring of 1867?—A. Yes, sir; when we were placing this stock.

Q. Did you understand Mr. Ames was going to part with that stock to members of Congress, or anybody else, with whom he had no previous understanding, at par, as late as December, 1867?—A. Not at all—not a share of it. He distinctly stated that he simply wanted to fulfill engagements he had made in the spring of 1867.

Q. It was no part of the understanding of stockholders who put this stock into his hands, that he was to make sales of it to persons with whom he had no interest of that kind?—A. Not the least.

Q. The object was to enable him to fulfill contracts and obligations he had made as far back as the previous spring?—A. Yes, sir; I would not have consented to have given it to him on any other terms than that.

Q. Do you suppose the other stockholders would?—A. I cannot speak for others. I do not think Mr. McComb would have consented to give it to him on any other terms.

Q. At the time this stock was put into the hands of Mr. Ames, while he was getting the consent of Mr. McComb and others for that purpose, was it then known that the stock was worth more than par?—A. Yes, sir.

Q. And they would have consented that Mr. Ames, should have it to sell to parties with whom he had no contract at par?—A. Certainly not.

Q. The company could have realized more for it?—A. Certainly; a part of it would have belonged to me, and I would not have parted with my share of it on any such terms.

By Mr. MERRICK:

Q. What right in the interests of the company would any one have had to allow gentlemen to take this stock at its par value, in the spring of 1868, where there had been no previous contract made for it?—A. I cannot see what possible object Mr. Ames or anybody else could have had in parting with the stock, if there had been no prior obligation. I cannot understand any motive or consideration for such a proceeding.

Q. No motive connected with the general advancement of the legitimate interests of the road?—A. I felt something like the expression in one of Mr. Ames's letters to Mr. McComb, that if a *bona-fide* promise had been made for the stock to Congressmen, and we did not comply with it, they might go back on us, if any question came up affecting our interest.

By Mr. BROOKS:

Q. Do you know whether I loaned the company considerable money to enable them to go on with the road?—A. You always stood by us in our dark days, when you were a member of Congress and when not a member of Congress.

WASHINGTON, D. C., *January* 16, 1873.

J. W. PATTERSON, a Senator of the United States, from the State of New Hampshire, having been duly sworn, made the following statement:

GENTLEMEN OF THE COMMITTEE: I have had no transactions with the Union Pacific Railroad, or with Mr. Ames, which, in my judgment, call for investigation, or which any respectable business man would think of criticising; still, I am glad to respond to your invitation to be present this morning, and with your permission will give you a brief, but complete, statement of all there is to this matter, so far as I am concerned.

I entered Congress after all the land-grants and subsidies to the Union Pacific Railroad had been made. The only legislation which has arisen since in respect to it, the wisdom and policy of which any one questions so far as I know, is the act of 1864, which passed during my first session in Congress. I was not as well informed in respect to the merits of this great work as I am now, but I have never regretted the vote I gave at that time. I then had but a slight acquaintance with Mr. Ames, having never seen him before I entered Congress. At a later period we were thrown together and brought into the relations of a somewhat intimate friendship.

Near the close of 1867, when no man could have anticipated any further legislation upon this subject, and since when, if we except the transfer of the office of the company to Boston, there has been none, unless giving a construction to a previous act, on a question raised unexpectedly by the Secretary of the Treasury, may be so considered, Mr. Ames came over to the Senate and proposed to sell me thirty shares of stock in the Credit Mobilier. He represented at the time that he did this as a friend, looking to my interest.

I asked him to explain to me what the Credit Mobilier was, and he did so. I then asked him if it was proper stock for a member of Congress to hold. He said he thought it was, as they did not expect to ask for any further legislation; and, to give strength to his view, he mentioned several distinguished gentlemen of acknowledged integrity who had either taken or proposed to take stock in the company. I then inquired if he thought it would be a profitable investment. He replied that he did, or he should not have offered it to a friend. I said I should be glad to take some of the stock, but could not then, as I had no money. "When you get some money which you wish to invest," said Mr. Ames, "come to me, and you shall have the stock."

At that time I purposed to take the stock, and doubtless Mr. Ames expected I should; but I never found it convenient to take it before I concluded it was not best to take it, and so the purchase was not consummated, and I never received, directly or indirectly, nor did any one ever hold for me in trust, one penny's worth of stock of the Credit Mobilier.

I have been thus explicit because I have been misrepresented in respect to this thing, and not because I see any breach of propriety or personal integrity in a Congressman's purchasing or holding this more than paper, wool, legal-tenders, bonds, bank-notes, bank-stock, or any other species of property liable to be affected by legislation, but upon which legislation was not anticipated at the time of the purchase.

On two occasions, subsequently, I purchased of Mr. Ames stock and bonds in the Union Pacific Railroad, which were placed in the hands of a friend in New York for sale. My friend sold them at a fair profit. For this stock and bonds I paid the full market price in money honestly earned by myself. These transactions were *bona-fide* purchases, and not exchanges of stock or distributions of dividends. It was a small investment, but reasonably profitable, and I regret it was not larger, as it was both honest and honorable. I doubt if there is any member of Congress who would deny the right or the propriety of such purchase to-day.

This is the whole of my connection with Mr. Ames or with the Union Pacific Railroad.

I have never purchased or received any property of any kind which had any connection, direct or indirect, with my vote or political influence.

By the CHAIRMAN:

Question. Can you state the time you made the purchase of the Union Pacific securities spoken of?—Answer. At two different times, as nearly as I can recollect. One was some time in the summer of 1869, and the other, if I remember correctly, in 1871.

Q. In about what amount, substantially?—A. I purchased, all told, about three hundred shares of stock. I cannot recollect the exact amount of bonds. I placed them in the hands of my friends to sell them.

Q. You never held, I understand you, any of this Credit Mobilier stock?—A. Never.

Q. Were you ever treated as being the owner of it by Mr. Ames?—A. I did not so regard it.

Q. The stock which came into your possession was not received as dividends?—A. I do not so regard it. I bought the stock with my own money.

Q. How long were you the holder of it?—A. A very short time. I put it into the hand of my friend in New York, who sold it.

Q. Upon the stock you held, did you receive any dividends during the time you held it?—A. No, sir.

Q. Whatever you made on that was a profit on the sale of it. Do you remember at what price Union Pacific Railroad stock was held when you purchased it?—A. I cannot remember; it was quite low. The last time I purchased of Mr. Ames was about the time they undertook to injure his credit, and the stock went down. Mr. Ames can remember the date probably better than I can. That was about the time I made the last purchase.

Q. Before it was sold the stock was in better credit?—A. Yes, sir.

Q. Can you state somewhere near the variations in price between the purchase and sale?—A. It was sold for 37, I think, or somewhere in that region. What it was worth at the time I bought it I do not recollect. I know I bought it at the market price, whatever it was selling for at the time, but I do not recollect what that was, nor do I suppose it material that I should, as I state that I had the stock.

Q. The negotiation in relation to your becoming an owner of Credit Mobilier stock was broken off by you?—A. It was never consummated by me.

Q. If you had insisted upon that stock, Mr. Ames would have let you have it?—A. I have no doubt about that.

Q. Can you state what the considerations were which led you to think it best not to become the owner of it?—A. I had not the money to buy it, was the trouble about it. If I had had the money within any reasonable time after this conversation, I have no doubt I should have got it, but I did not happen to have the money.

Q. Do you know of any dealings between Mr. Ames and any other member of Congress in relation to the stock of the Credit Mobilier?—A. No, sir; otherwise than at the time Mr. Ames came to see me as I stated. He mentioned the names of two or three gentlemen who, he said, either had or he expected would take stock.

Q. Do you remember who they were?—A. I think he mentioned Mr. Colfax, Mr. Wilson, and I think Mr. Boutwell.

WASHINGTON, *January* 16, 1873.

HENRY WILSON, United States Senator from Massachusetts, sworn and examined.

By the CHAIRMAN:

Question. The committee wish you to state in reference to any negotiations or transactions between you and Mr. Ames, in relation to the Credit Mobilier.—Answer. I have no written statement to make. I received your invitation yesterday. I came here this morning in response to it, and am ready to answer any questions or make any statement of the facts in the case. Mr. Ames did not come to me to offer any of his stock. We boarded at the same house, and often sat at the same table. I had some time before purchased of him two railroad mortgage bonds of Iowa roads; one was a bond of the Cedar Rapids road, and the other, I think, was the Chicago and Nebraska road. They paid 7 per cent. interest, and were bought for 90 cents on the dollar. They were purchased for my wife, and with her money, which had been presented to her on the 27th of October, 1865, the twenty-fifth anniversary of our wedding. During my absence from home, and without my knowledge, my neighbors and acquaintances in the eastern portion of my State made extensive arrangements to celebrate our silver wedding. I was sent for to come home. There was a large gathering from my town, from Boston, and other portions of the State. Many small presents and testimonials were presented to my wife, and a silver service was presented by my townsmen to myself. Before the company separated, a package was presented to my wife, I think by Governor Claflin, which was found to contain $3,800, with a letter and list of subscribers, containing a request that she would accept it as a gift to herself. The subscriptions ranged from fifty to two hundred dollars each, and were made by such men as Governor Claflin, Mr. Sumner, and Amos A. Lawrence. Mr. Ames was down for $200 and Mr. Alley for $100.

This money, given to my wife, I determined should be sacredly hers, and that I would never receive a dollar of it. I was the more resolved on this course because a paper in New York had criticised its acceptance. One thousand dollars of it had been invested by my wife on my advice, where it was all lost. At the time I was in debt several hundred dollars, but as soon as I could I refunded the money she had lost through my advice. In December, 1867, or early in 1868, my wife or myself spoke to Mr. Ames about purchasing one or two more of the Iowa Railroad bonds. Mr. Ames had not then any more of those bonds to sell, but could sell her stock that he believed would be of more value, which he said was the stock of the Credit Mobilier. I knew nothing of its origin, its history, or its value, and would not have given fifty cents on the dollar for it. I told Mr. Ames that I believed that much of the money put into the Pacific Railroad would be lost; that I had, years before, spoken and voted in favor of building the road, as a measure of great national importance, though I believed much money would be lost in its construction. Mr. Ames said that he would guarantee the stock, and that it should pay ten per cent. on condition that he should have one-half of the excess if any, and that Senator Grimes had bought some of the stock on the same conditions. I asked Mr. Alley's advice. Mr. Alley said that Mr. Ames valued the stock higher than he did, but that it was a safe investment with his guarantee. My wife and myself concluded that $2,000 of her money should be so invested; and a few weeks afterward the money was paid to Mr. Ames, and a receipt or paper was taken, with the promise that he would sell her twenty shares of the stock. The stock was never delivered, and neither myself nor wife ever received or saw a share of it.

Before accepting Mr. Ames's offer, I asked him if any more legislation for the Pacific Railroad would be required, and he assured me that there would not be. I told him I had made it an inflexible rule of action never to buy any property that might be affected by legislation, nor to use any information I had, as a public man, in making investments. I do not say it is wrong for other members of Congress to own stocks in banks, railroads, manufactories, or to purchase land or the public securities. Every one must judge for himself in those matters. My position was a peculiar one. Having learned in early life that a poor man cannot do what a rich man can, and that a lawyer can do what an unprofessional man cannot do, I made up my mind, when I came here, that

I would purchase no property that could be affected by legislation. I knew, when elected, that I should come here, if not under temptation, under the liability of being watched and criticised. I came into the Senate from a mechanic's shop. I had a home that cost me about $4,000. I was doing a small business, and soon found that I must leave the Senate or abandon it. I closed my business, paid my debts, gave my wife a deed of my home, and had less than $1,000 left, with no profession, no capital, no business, no partnership. Compelled to live with the strictest economy, I applied rules of action to myself that I did not apply to others who had professions, or capital, or business associations; and during nearly eighteen years, the only investment I have made has been the purchase of a house-lot in the town I live in, for $150, which I sold four or five years afterward for $400.

Some months after Mr. Ames received the money, I saw something in the papers concerning differences among the managers of the Credit Mobilier and of the Pacific Railroad. I asked Mr. Alley and one or two other gentlemen what those reports meant, and whether legislation would not grow out of those controversies. I told him that I should regard the transaction as incomplete; that I should have the receipt given up and the money returned. I said the same to Mr. Ames. He laughed at me, and thought I was doing a very foolish thing, but said he would take the receipt and return the money. A short time afterward he did so. The amount of profit on the transaction, including interest and dividend, was $814. This, with the original investment, belonged to my wife. That amount, on settlement, was allowed by me to Mr. Ames, so that in reality there was received from him the amount which was originally paid him. The $814 my wife received came from my own earnings. Mr. Ames said there would be due, he thought, some stock dividends when the account was made up, but I declined receiving it, and would have declined had the dividends amounted to $10,000. I regarded the bargain as incomplete, and resolved not to consummate it. I did not know or suspect that there was anything wrong in the transaction; but I was as resolved to have nothing to do with it as I should have done had I known it to be an infamous transaction.

Q. I understand you your wife received from Mr. Ames $2,000 and ten per cent. interest?—A. My wife, who was present when the settlement was made, received $814 more than was paid, but the profits came from me rather than from Mr. Ames, and I am, therefore, $814 poorer, and shall be till I die, for advising my wife to purchase that stock, as I never received any part of the $3,800 given at our silver wedding, or the income from it. When she died, in May, 1870, she gave this money to her own kindred, and $1,000 to the church of which she was a member, for the benefit of poor women. She lost $1,000 of the money given at the silver wedding by an investment which she made in accordance with my advice. That amount, as I said, I made up to her out of my own earnings, and the profit also she received from the transaction with Mr. Ames; so that I am now, and ever shall be, $1,814 poorer than I should have been had nothing been given her, and the investment with Mr. Ames had not been made.

Q. At the time you settled up this business with Mr. Ames and the money was paid back, you mean that the dividends from the Credit Mobilier were $814?—A. I mean that the dividends and interest amounted to $814.

Q. Mr. Ames only paid the money and interest to your wife, and you made up the additional sum, so that she should lose nothing by failing to receive the dividends?—A. I made it up to her by making the account square with Mr. Ames at the time of settlement, so that, in the aggregate, nothing was received from him, and what she made came from me. When this transaction had been completed, I do not think I was the possessor of property to the amount of $1,000.

Q. Do you remember the time when this transaction was closed with Mr. Ames?—A. I am not certain to a day, but I think it was in the month of November or December, 1868; it might have been a few weeks later.

Q. Do you recollect what it was about the Credit Mobilier which disturbed you?—A. I cannot; I saw something in the newspapers which gave me anxiety, and made me think that there might be something that I did not understand about it, or that might bring the road before Congress for legislation. I did not know anything about the Credit Mobilier, how it transacted its business or made its money. I had no doubt of my moral or legal right, or the moral or legal right of my wife, to invest the little she had in Government securities, bank, railroad, or manufacturing stocks, or in any other property in which others invested. I have no doubt, either, of the legal and moral right of any member of Congress to do so. But, as I have stated, my own circumstances and situation were peculiar. Entering Congress a poor man, with no capital, no business, no profession, and no occupation out of Congress by which I could make anything beyond my salary, I felt sensitive in regard to money transactions. I came into Congress in the beginning of 1855, and when the war opened I had saved, by the most rigid economy, about $3,000; and when the war closed my liabilities were many hundred dollars greater than my assets. I raised two regiments and two batteries at considerable expense; I had served several months with General McClellen, always paying my own expenses; I was chairman of the Committee on Military Affairs, and my rooms were continually thronged by officers and soldiers, and I can truthfully say that no soldier ever asked me for money who did not receive something, unless he was intoxicated. So that when my wife's money was given to Mr. Ames I was not worth a thousand dollars; and I would sell all I have to-day, my humble home excepted, for $3,500, and that I have earned during the last four years in writing for the New York Independent. In this transaction with Mr. Ames, I have done nothing which I did not feel that, as a member of Congress and a man, I had a perfect right to do; nothing to be palliated or excused; nothing I am called upon to apologize for to my fellow-men or my country; nothing I must take into my closet and ask God's forgiveness for. In making the investment with Mr. Ames, though the money was not mine and its profits would not be mine, I was actuated by no improper motives; and the moment I saw there was a bare possibility I might have made a mistake, the transaction was canceled, and that, too, at a sacrifice of $814. I am not regardless of the good opinion of my fellow-men; nor am I insensible, though I have been in public life for a third of a century, to the criticism of a portion of the public press. Conscious of my innocence, I feel outraged at the charges which have been made against me, and I believe no greater wrong was ever perpetrated than has been perpetrated on many honorable gentlemen, who could not be influenced by the Pacific Railroad, or all the railroads of the country.

By Mr. NIBLACK:

Q. Let me ask whether this odium which has been created in the public mind has not, to some extent, arisen from mistakes which some gentlemen have made in endeavoring to conceal their connection with it.—A. I cannot say as to others, but I will speak for myself. When the charges first appeared in the papers, I was in Hartford attending a public meeting, and a statement was put in my hands to the effect that I had been given by Mr. Ames two thousand shares of the stock of the Credit Mobilier, which was said to be worth, when I received it, $560,000; that I was a very rich man, and could afford to vote for the Pacific Railroad. A statement was made on my authority that I never owned a dollar's interest in the Pacific Railway or any of the Pacific Railways, either in stocks, bonds, contracts, &c. That statement was absolutely true, for I had had none of the stock of the Credit Mobilier given me, never saw any of the stock, and never had any interest in it, or benefits from it. I intended at once to publish an explanation, like the one I have made to-day. Before doing so, I consulted one or two gentlemen connected with the road, who said that I had done nothing demanding an explanation; that there was a lawsuit pending, and that, under those circumstances, I should say nothing, as it might injure them.

Q. On the supposition that it was an entirely innocent transaction, was it not a mistake for the persons whose names were mixed up with it to attempt to cover it up?—A. Every gentleman must judge of that for himself. I was never more innocent of wrong motive and intent than in this transaction; and it may have been a mistake for me to have acted on the advice of others rather than on my own judgment. I think mistakes have been made in this matter.

Q. (By Mr. Ames.) Did you not ask me, when I suggested this stock to you, if we expected to want any legislation in Congress upon the subject, and did I not answer that we did not want any?—A. I have stated that I was very explicit on that point.

Q. (By Mr. Ames.) I recollect that you were very particular about making the inquiry.—A. You told me that you wanted nothing; that all the legislation your road required had been passed years before. If there had been any question on that point, I should never have consented that my wife's money should have been so invested. You told me that you had sold some of the stock to Mr. Grimes, and that you had guaranteed it; but I did not then know that any other members of Congress had purchased any.

Q. (By Mr. Alley.) I have heard it stated that the Washington correspondent of the Boston Traveller has published in his correspondence that it was believed here that I was carrying some stock for Senator Wilson; will you be good enough to state whether there is any truth in such an intimation?—A. I saw that statement in the papers. I seldom complain of any criticism I see in the press, but when I saw this imputation I went to this young man and asked why he should write such a thing of me. He replied that he had heard some one state some such thing, and he had sent it as a matter of news to his paper. Neither you nor Mr. Ames, nor any other human being, holds now or ever held anything for me in regard to the Credit Mobilier or the Union Pacific Railroad. Mr. Ames told me, when the settlement was made, that there would be, he thought, some stock coming; but I told him I would not receive it; that I considered the bargain an unconsummated one, and would back square out of it without receiving any benefit from it; and I did so, as I have already stated, at a personal sacrifice.

WASHINGTON, D. C., *January* 16, 1873.

JOHN A. BINGHAM, a member of the United States House of Representatives from Ohio, having been duly sworn, made the following statement:

It is due to myself and to the House that I state all my transactions with Mr. Ames. The first of these was in March or April, 1866. Confiding in the integrity and financial judgment of Mr. Ames, and after consulting and advising with him, I at that time paid as capital stock into the Hubbard Silver Mining Company, of which Mr. Ames was the president and John B. Alley treasurer, $2,000. This company was organized under the laws of Massachusetts, and had no connection with the Credit Mobilier or the Union Pacific Railroad Company, nor with congressional legislation. The investment has returned me nothing, and is a total loss. In December, 1867, Mr. Ames advised me to invest in stock of the Credit Mobilier, assuring me it would return me my money with profitable dividends. I told him I knew nothing of the company nor did I know anything about dealing in stocks. He proposed to invest my money for me in the stock and account to me for the dividends. I agreed to invest $2,000, and about the 1st of February, 1868, paid him $2,000, for which he then gave me his written agreement to account to me for the dividends and proceeds of twenty shares of Credit Mobilier stock, stating therein the nominal value of Union Pacific Railroad stock then represented by it and to be accounted for by him. Afterward, in 1868, and upon his advice, I agreed with Mr. Ames for $1,000 of the stock of the Iowa Falls and Sioux City Construction Company, on account of which I paid him $650, and for which he gave me a written agreement to account to me for the same.

I never received or held any stock of the Credit Mobilier or of the construction company or of the Union Pacific Railroad Company from Mr. Ames or any one else. Mr. Ames was the only person known to me in these contracts. I contracted with him in good faith, as I then believed and still believe I lawfully might, and upon his assurance that the investment would return me large profits. I had then no question of my right to contract and to take the proceeds of my contracts. I no more doubted my right so to do than before that, in 1865, I doubted my right to buy, as I did then buy and pay for, thirty shares of the stock of the Harrison National Bank, located at the place of my residence.

In 1868, and a short time after I had paid Mr. Ames the money in consideration of which he gave me the Credit Mobilier agreement, he delivered to me two bonds of the Union Pacific Railroad Company, $1,000 each, at 95 cents on the dollar, and on account of which I paid him $300, and for the residue thereof, $1,600, he indorsed a credit on his agreement held by me. All subsequent dividends or payments were in money or the Union Pacific Railroad stock, the stock being charged by Mr. Ames to himself, at its nominal value, on the face of his agreement held by me, and the money indorsed thereon as a payment. In the summer session of 1870, I requested Mr. Ames to close these contracts with me, as I wished to use my money. He consented to settle, and did settle in December, 1870, as I recollect, the Credit Mobilier contract, and took it up, accounting to me for the Union Pacific stock dividends therein stated at their nominal value, and which nominal value was stated at about $8,500. He estimated the stock at not more than 19 cents on the dollar, or $190 to the $1,000, making in all $1,615, for which sum he gave me a memorandum, and which sum he paid about February or March, 1871, amounting, with interest, to $1,630.14. I wish to say here that I accept Mr. Ames's statement made to the committee, that he in his settlement with me in December, 1870, adjusted the value of the Union Pacific Railroad Company stock at 19 cents, or $190 on the $1,000. My recollection was and is that he adjusted it upon the basis of 18 cents, or $180 upon the $1,000, but I accept his statement in that regard. Since that settlement, I have had no interest, direct or indirect, in the Credit Mobilier stock, or in the stock of the Union Pacific Railroad Company. I sold the two railroad bonds, as my bank account shows, 23d August, 1869, at 88¼ cents on the dollar. In February, 1872, Mr. Ames settled and took up the construction contract and paid the balance thereon of $728.07. I have had no further transactions with Mr. Ames. Owing to the fact that all payments by Mr. Ames, before the settlements, were indorsed upon the contracts held by me and the account thereof not otherwise kept, I cannot state the payments with any greater accuracy than I have, but I do not hesitate to say that the aggregate amount received on these two contracts was about $6,500, and I am certain that on the final settlement of both contracts as above stated, I received in all $2,358.21, and that this sum is more than one-third of all that I realized in all my transactions with Mr. Ames. From the inception to the close of my business with Mr. Ames, I had no intimation that any other member of Congress had any contracts or dealings with him in relation to Credit Mobilier or railroad stocks; nor that any other member had any interest therein, except Mr. Hooper, of Massachusetts.

I did not, at any time during the continuance of these contracts, hear of any controversy between Mr. Ames and Mr. McComb, or any other person, about the distribution of the stocks of Credit Mobilier. I never heard any intimation that Mr. Ames was dealing in this stock corruptly, until September and October last, when such charges appeared in the public press. I never supposed Mr. Ames contracted with me for corrupt purposes, or on account of any person but himself. I know that I had no corrupt purpose in contracting with Mr. Ames. I never gave a vote for or against any measure in Congress, but as I believed to be just and right and in strict accordance with my sworn duty. I never made or authorized any publication denying or explaining any of these transactions. I had done nothing that in my judgment required either apology or explanation. When the accusation was made that the stock was a reward for votes for the act of 1864, which subordinated the United States lien on the Pacific Railroad to the lien of the company's bonds, &c., I knew that my answer was in the records of Congress, which show that I was not a member of Congress at that time. I had nothing to do with the passage of the act of 1864. When the accusation was made that the act of 1869 was only "a good done" the Union Pacific Railroad Company, I knew that the act would repel the slander. I make it part of my testimony. I supported it. After sixteen years of service in Congress, I leave it with no more property than I had when I entered it, save what I legitimately earned during the term of the Thirty-eighth Congress, and when I was not a member.

I have inquired of one of the members of the committee whether there is in the room a copy of the statute of 1869 to which I have referred. I desire that it may be incorporated into my testimony, that I may stand upon it before the people of the country. I desire that it may be so incorporated for the purpose of repelling the malicious slanders of a licentious press. The act in question, I think, is to be found in 16 Statutes at Large, page 56. I may say now in general that this statute provides for the continued organization of the Union Pacific Railroad

Company by authorizing an election of a board of directors at Boston, and having so provided, it saves expressly the rights of the United States. It provides that the President of the United States shall withhold subsidy bonds to a sufficient amount to secure to the United States the full completion of said road as a first-class road. It further provides that if the subsidy bonds remaining were not sufficient security, that requisition shall be made on the company for a sufficient amount of bonds to insure the full completion of the road, and that the Attorney-General shall take the necessary steps to enforce the requisition in the courts of the United States if need be. It further provides that inquiry shall be made by the Attorney-General whether either of these companies have forfeited their charters and franchises, and that he shall also make inquiry whether these companies have issued illegal dividends upon their stock; and also to investigate whether any of the directors or agents of these companies have violated any penal law, and, if so, institute proceedings.

I believe that I have now stated all that occurs to me which it is possible for me to state to put the committee in possession of the whole matter touching this business. I am, however, ready to answer any questions they may please to ask me. I ought to state before going further that in what I said upon the impulse of the moment in characterizing the press I did not intend to include the general press of the country, and perhaps very few of the journals of the country would come within the designation I gave. I referred to such journals of the country as had originated the false charge that a price had been paid to me as a bribe for my congressional action, and fixed it at $20,000. There is no color of truth in it.

By the CHAIRMAN:

Q. In your statement you say about the 1st of February, 1868, you agreed to invest $2,000, and that you paid Mr. Ames $2,000; that he gave you a written agreement to account to you for all the dividends and profits of twenty shares of Credit Mobilier stock. Have you that agreement?—A. No, sir. The agreement was a continuing contract by which Mr. Ames was bound to account to me, and on which the payments from time to time by him made were indorsed. When it was settled he took it up. I have no copy of it. It was exactly what I have stated.

Q. You have stated in your manuscript all you can state in regard to the stock?—A. I have, and I have not a doubt that I have also stated substantially the legal effect of the agreements with Mr. Ames.

Q. Did you understand from Mr. Ames at that time whether there were already declared dividends upon the stock?—A. I understood nothing from Mr. Ames in regard to it, except what was necessarily implied from the statement incorporated in the agreement to which I have referred in my written statement. He was to account for the value of the amount then received in Union Pacific Railroad stock therein stated at its nominal value.

Q. Do you now know whether there had been prior to this agreement dividends declared upon the Credit Mobilier stock, and in the stock or bonds of the Union Pacific Railroad Company?—A. I do not except what you might infer from the transaction. I have no recollection of it. I had entire confidence in Mr. Ames's statement that the investment would return large dividends, and I have stated that some short time after the contract was entered into he had given as a dividend bonds which represented, as I understand, a larger amount than was due, and he required me to pay back $300, which I did I ought to say further that what has been stated in the papers, of this stock being worth 300 per cent. premium, is a statement that by my experience and settlement is without any foundation in truth. Anybody who will take the trouble to compute the money I paid Mr. Ames from the first transaction I had with him in the mining stock, and compute the amount I received on both contracts as I have stated, will see that I received very little, if any, more than a return of the actual money ventured in these several transactions, with 10 per cent. interest. I do not intend, however, to take anything from the statement I have just made further than to notice that the statement I have heard of 200, 300, 400, and I think at one time 700 per cent. premium, or dividends, is not in accordance with my experience.

Q. In the settlement you made with Mr. Ames did he take back the mining stock which you purchased of him?—A. I hold the certificate for that yet, but there is nothing of any value in it.

Q. You own all in that investment that anybody owns, do you not?—A. I own all anybody does; if it is of any service to Mr. Ames he is welcome to it. It is not worth a farthing, and never was.

Q. When you made this settlement, was there any reckoning in any way about the mining stock?—A. Nothing. There was nothing in it to reckon.

Q. You did not include the money you had paid for it?—A. Certainly not. I do not mean to be understood that these two contracts had anything to do with the mining contract.

Q. How much did you actually receive from Mr. Ames in your settlement, or at any time, out of the $2,000 you paid him?—A. I have stated exactly the amount received on the final settlement of Credit Mobilier contract. It was $1,630.14. I have stated that I received in all, on the Credit Mobilier contract and the Construction Company's contract, about $6,500. That statement is substantially correct.

Q. For the Union Pacific Railroad stock; Mr. Ames kept the stock and paid you for it?—A. Certainly; he was bound by his contract to account to me for it. He entered it, from time to time, upon the face of the agreement, at its nominal value. At one time he took up that agreement on account of its interlineations, rewrote it, put upon the new one the amount already indorsed, and took up the old one.

Q. We have learned from the books and papers which are here that at one time there was a money dividend declared upon this stock; was that paid to you?—A. I have said distinctly in my statement to the committee that he accounted to me for dividends in money and Union Pacific Railroad stock and bonds. The money dividends were reported to me and indorsed by Mr. Ames on the contract held by me. The stock dividends were also charged on the face of the contract to be accounted for by him.

Q. Do you mean that Mr. Ames kept the money dividends himself and indorsed it upon the face of the contract?—A. No, sir; I never intimated that Mr. Ames kept any money dividends. I intend to make myself explicit upon that point. The money that was paid to me was indorsed on the contract as a payment by him to me, as already stated by me. What he paid me is all I know of money dividends.

By Mr. MERRICK:

Q. You say that you paid him $2,000 in money originally, and that the aggregate received from all sources connected with this Credit Mobilier business was about $6,500?—A. I stated that I afterward invested $650 in a contract with him for $1,000 stock of the Iowa Falls and

Sioux City Construction Company. I stated in addition that I settled for the Construction Company contract in the winter of 1872, and that I received for that on that settlement a balance of $728.07, and I stated that all the money I received from Mr. Ames on both these contracts was about $6,500.

Q. That is, upon the investment of $2,650, you received in the aggregate about $6,500?—A. That is just what I believe to be the truth as to the amount received on both contracts in all. The payments were indorsed upon the contract just as I would indorse payment upon the back of a promissory note.

Q. Were you the draughtsman of this act of April, 1869, which has been referred to?—A. I think not. My recollection is that I either reported from the committee or offered a resolution in the House for the purpose of enabling the railroad company to continue its organization substantially, as I remember. Whether that passed the House I do not know. My recollection now is, that the joint resolution to which you refer came from the Senate, in lieu of the one I have referred to, and that I called it up in the House and urged its passage, as I then believed, and now believe, it was my duty to do, in the interest of the United States.

Q. You advocated and supported the measure, and it was passed?—A. I most undoubtedly supported it; there was not much advocacy about it. There was a little excitement in the House, as there always is when any bill is proposed to be passed, and you understand, as I do, that under such circumstances the best thing to do is to stop debate and pass the bill, if it be just and needful.

Q. Have you any knowledge of any dealings by Mr. Ames with any other person, or with other members of Congress, relating to this Credit Mobilier stock?—A. My recollection is, that I stated that during the continuance of my contracts with Mr. Ames I had no information from any source that I can recollect that he had any dealings with any member of Congress about the stock except myself. I had no knowledge of any other member of Congress being concerned in the Credit Mobilier except Mr. Hooper. Since this noise made in the papers about the affair, I have heard from Mr. Ames that he had dealings with other members. All this information has come to me since the publications in September last, and since Congress met. I had no communication with him on the subject, or other members charged, until Congress met in December last.

By Mr. McCRARY:

Q. I understand that Mr. Ames induced you to take the silver-mining stock?—A. Yes. I do not wish to cast any reproach on Mr. Ames about that business. I think he wanted to do me a kindness. I said that after consultation and advice with Mr. Ames, in whom I had entire confidence, both as to his integrity and financial judgment, I did invest in that stock; and I had greater confidence in it from the fact that he was president of the company.

By Mr. AMES:

Q. I did not advise you to take it, did I?—A. I cannot say whether you did formally or not. The fact that you consulted with me about it I have stated, and the fact that you had embarked in it yourself, and was president of the company, I considered very strong advice.

By Mr. McCRARY:

Q. When he offered you this Credit Mobilier stock, had you the impression that it was to enable you to make up for your loss on the silver-mining operation?—A. I cannot say that. I will not say that Mr. Ames did it with that view. I will state he said it would not be right that I should lose the money I had invested in that. But I did not hold Mr. Ames responsible at all for the loss in the silver-mining operation.

Q. Was it not, however, one of the objects you had in going into this Credit Mobilier transaction to get even for the loss sustained?—A. I cannot say that I formed any opinion of that sort in my mind. He would be a very bold man who, five years afterward, would undertake to recall the secret operations of his own mind. I think it would be a very natural reflection, having lost $2,000 and interest, that, if I had an opportunity afforded me of making up that loss, I had better be about it. Still, I will not swear that that was the course of reasoning in my mind five years ago.

By Mr. NIBLACK:

Q. It is suggested that this enterprise of yours in the mining stock originated from Mr. Alley rather than from Mr. Ames.—A. As to that, I do not know. I recollect generally that Mr. Alley was very active about it. As to how it originated I do not know. Mr. Ames boarded at the house with me, and I had the most unlimited confidence in his integrity and financial judgment. I asked him about it, and he thought it was a wise thing for me to do, and, considering that he was president of the company and was taking stock himself, I thought it was safe for me to do it.

By the CHAIRMAN:

Q. You do not consider yourself now as having any interest in the Credit Mobilier?—A. I have sworn to the committee, and I repeat it, that, from the time of the settlement in December, 1870, and of the taking up of the obligation by Mr. Ames, I had no interest at all in the Credit Mobilier; I never held or received a certificate of stock, and, by the terms of the contract, was not entitled to any. We closed the whole matter, and it became merely a money-balance represented by a written memorandum which he gave me, and afterward paid me, as already stated.

By Mr. McCRARY:

Q. You regarded the act of 1869 as not in the interest of the Pacific Railroad Companies?—A. I certainly did consider that it was in the interest of both the companies, and it is very clear on its face that it was in the interest of the United States. I may just as well add here, from information I had at the time, without intending to reflect upon any tribunal, that the interests of the United States, without some sort of legislation, could not then have been protected, for the reason that the State courts would intervene to prevent the Union Pacific Company from re-organizing.

By Mr. MERRICK:

Q. Did the Attorney-General institute a proceeding under the fourth section of that resolution?—A. I do not know. It is reasonable to presume that what the law required to be done was done.

The act of April 10, 1869, above referred to by the witness, is as follows:

JOINT RESOLUTION for the protection of the interests of the United States in the Union Pacific Railroad Company, the Central Pacific Railroad Company, and for other purposes.

Be it resolved by the Senate and House of Representatives of the United States of America in Congress assembled, That the stockholders of the Union Pacific Railroad Company, at a meeting to be held on the twenty-second day of April, eighteen hundred and sixty-nine, at the city of Boston, (with power to adjourn from day to day,) shall elect a board of directors for the ensuing year; and said stockholders are hereby authorized to establish their general office at such place in the United States as they may select at said meeting: *Provided,* That the passage of this resolution shall not confer any other right upon said Union Pacific Railroad Company than to hold such election, or be held in any manner to relinquish or waive any rights of the United States to take advantage of any act or neglect of said Union Pacific Railroad Company heretofore done or omitted whereby the rights of the General Government have been or may be prejudiced: *And provided further,* That the common terminus of the Union Pacific and the Central Pacific Railroads shall be at or near Ogden; and the Union Pacific Railroad Company shall build, and the Central Pacific Railroad Company pay for and own, the railroad from the terminus aforesaid to Promontory Summit, at which point the rails shall meet and connect and form one continuous line.

SEC. 2. *And be it further resolved,* That to ascertain the condition of the Union Pacific Railroad and the Central Pacific Railroad, the President of the United States is authorized to appoint a board of eminent citizens, not exceeding five in number, and who shall not be interested in either road, to examine and report upon the condition of, and what sum or sums, if any, will be required to complete each of said roads, for the entire length thereof, to the said terminus as a first-class railroad, in compliance with the several acts relating to said roads; and the expense of such board, including an allowance of ten dollars to each for their services for each day employed in such examination or report, to be paid equally by said companies.

SEC. 3. *And be it further resolved,* That the President is hereby authorized and required to withhold from each of said companies an amount of subsidy bonds authorized to be issued by the United States under said acts sufficient to secure the full completion as a first-class road of all sections of such road upon which bonds have already been issued, or in lieu of such bonds he may receive as such security an equal amount of the first-mortgage bonds of such company; and if it shall appear to the President that the amount of subsidy bonds yet to be issued to either of said companies is insufficient to insure the full completion of such road, he may make requisition upon such company for a sufficient amount of bonds already issued to said company, or in his discretion of their first-mortgage bonds, to secure the full completion of the same. And in default of obtaining such security as [is] in this section provided, the President may authorize and direct the Attorney-General to institute such suits and proceedings on behalf and in the name of the United States, in any court of the United States having jurisdiction, as shall be necessary or proper to compel the giving of such security, and thereby, or in any manner otherwise, to protect the interests of the United States in said road, and to insure the full completion thereof as a first-class road, as required by law and the statutes in that case made.

SEC. 4. *And be it further resolved,* That the Attorney-General of the United States be, and he is hereby, authorized and directed to investigate whether or not the charter and all the franchises of the Union Pacific Railroad Company have not been forfeited, and to institute all necessary and proper legal proceedings; also to investigate whether or not said companies have or have not made any illegal dividends upon their stock, and if so, to institute the necessary proceedings to have the same re-imbursed; and also to investigate whether any of the directors or any other agents or employés of said companies have or not violated any penal law, and if so, to institute the proper criminal proceedings against all persons who have violated such laws.

Approved, April 10, 1869.

WASHINGTON, D. C., *January* 16, 1873.

Hon. WILLIAM D. KELLEY, a member of the United States House of Representatives from Pennsylvania, sworn and examined.

By the CHAIRMAN:

Question. Will you state to the committee, in your own way, whether you had any negotiations or dealings with Oakes Ames in reference to the stock of the Credit Mobilier?—Answer. I have no written memorandum and am here simply to answer such questions as the committee may put to me. I met Mr. Ames casually. I know it was casually for I came out of the hotel at which I was boarding, and found him waiting apparently for a car, which was also my business, on the F street line. We fell into conversation; he congratulated me upon having become rich enough to have a thousand dollars to waste, which led to some conversation about my financial affairs, not then in the most flourishing condition. They are very much better now, I am happy to say.

In that conversation I stated that my name had been improperly advertised as a subscriber to the stock of the Credit Foncier which was about to be organized by George Francis Train, to which subscription Mr. Ames had referred.

At this distance of time I do not pretend to repeat the conversation verbatim, but I remember the substance of it pretty accurately. Mr. Ames said to me that while that was a speculative thing, he felt disposed to let me have an investment which would be of a better character, and spoke of the Crédit Mobilier, of which I thought I knew something from the fact that it was chartered by my own State some years before I became a member of Congress, and the provisions of the charter of which I had discussed somewhat with my professional brethren, both in my office and in the court-room while waiting for trials or arguments. I had never discussed it before the bench of judges, but in that informal way. He said to me that the dividends had been pretty large; he did not know whether they would be so large in the future, but he regarded it as a good investment, and having heard a statement of the condition of my affairs, he proposed to carry ten shares, or a thousand dollars of it, on these terms, viz, that I should allow him seven per cent. interest on a thousand dollars, and any dividends the stock might earn would be carried to my account, and if it should pay for itself with seven per cent. down to the time at which it should so pay for itself the stock should become mine. If it should not pay for itself, but pay more than seven per cent., the difference should be mine. I said to him I did not see how I could lose anything by that operation. I regarded it as one between two friends, one of whom was in affluent circumstances and the other seriously embarrassed, while holding property which, if he could hold on to, would insure a competence; and when we parted it was with the understanding that the arrangement had been assented to by both parties.

Now, as to the date of that conversation: When this investigation arose, I challenged my memory in vain for an occurrence by which to fix it, even approximately. The 14th of last month I received a printed circular which I have upon my person, from New York, signed by John J. Cisco, John A. Dix, and others, reminding me that I was a subscriber to the stock of the Credit Foncier, and requesting my attendance at a meeting of the subscribers, Friday, the 20th of December. The postmark shows that it was mailed at New York, the 14th. I immediately addressed Mr. Cisco a note, of which the following is an extract:

"Now, my d ar sir, may I ask you to do me what, at this moment, will be a marked personal favor, inasmuch as it will enable me to fix, approximately, another date which it may be important to fix, and which I have no other means of ascertaining? Will you have the kindness to furnish the date of the subscription to the Credit Foncier obtained by Mr. Train in this city? An immediate compliance will oblige," &c.

I have never received an answer to that communication, but if it is desirable that the committee should learn, they will probably be able to be more fortunate than I in that behalf. The conversation between Mr. Ames and myself was subsequent to the publication of that subscription, because it began by his reference to it. There is only one other date in the whole affair that I am able to fix approximately, and I will come to that directly.

After the interview in question some time, how long I do not know,

Mr. Ames said to me, on the floor of the House of Representatives, that, owing to some embarrassments, which he did not explain, that contract could not be carried out. I think he said the embarrassment arose from the fact that the whole matter was in litigation.

Thus ended all connection of mine with the matter. During that time, nor subsequently, have I received directly or indirectly any money, stock, or bonds as dividends of the Credit Mobilier, or any interest in stock of Union Pacific Railroad or bonds. I have never to my knowledge seen a share of the stock in Credit Mobilier or in the Union Pacific Railroad Company. I have never owned but one Union Pacific Railroad bond, and that was purchased for me by my attorney as a temporary investment, with the balance of a fund awarded me by the city of Philadelphia as compensation for damage done me on opening Hutton street, not due to the mortgage creditor, and which I instructed him in my absence from the city to put into a ten per cent. income bond of the Union Pacific Railroad, as an investment until the next mortgage or judgment creditor should come around for something that I was not ready to pay.

I had previously to this, on the basis of my personal credit, borrowed from Mr. Ames $500, stipulating to pay him up about a certain time in which I did pay him. I subsequently borrowed from him a thousand dollars. This was before this Pacific Railroad or Credit Mobilier question had brought Mr. Ames into temporary embarrassment, and I fix that fact by this other one, that when, after a temporary absence from the House, he returned to it, I said to him that it grieved me to have to say that I could not return him that thousand dollars, and was very glad to hear him say that it would not distress him to withhold it; that he had been pretty seriously embarrassed, but that he had something else than that thousand dollars to look to.

I have given you, as nearly as I can remember, all that I know on this question.

You have put a question to other witnesses which makes it proper, at this point, for me to say that Mr. Ames did not intimate to me that any other member of Congress or any Senator had invested in or proposed to hold any of this stock. When I parted with him that evening, I supposed the conversation to have been a purely personal one, touching his interest and mine, and involving no question of legislation, and further that, knowing that the Credit Mobilier had been chartered, as I thought improvidently if not unconstitutionally, by the State of Pennsylvania, although I believe the courts have decided otherwise in the interim, and that it was chartered, not for the construction of the Union Pacific Railroad, but of railroads in the South and West, I did not suspect that it had confined its operations to one enterprise generally. In the course of the conversation with Mr. Ames, he spoke in general terms, imparting no definite information, as to past dividends, but said they might not be so good in the future. My recollection is that he intimated that the value of the stock would depend upon future contracts. Now, whether I knew it was for the construction of the Union Pacific Railroad, I am not able to say. I do not know what I did, but I do say this, that if I had known the fact, I should not have felt any hesitation or any doubt as to my right, or any doubt as to the propriety of my making that purchase; and I go further and say that, after what Mr. Ames said to me, that if I had had the ability to draw a check for one thousand dollars, I would, perhaps, have made more definite inquiry than I made when the offer came to me on such terms; but I have no doubt I would have drawn my check and taken the certificate for a thousand dollars of stock. I would doubtless have regretted it, in view of the facts that have since been disclosed; but, in reviewing the whole field, I cannot see that any member of Congress was precluded from making a purchase of that stock more than he would be from buying a flock of sheep, the value of which could be affected by a change of the tariff on wool or woolen goods. You cannot get a Congress of which none of the members shall be interested in any of the votes that must be taken. You cannot touch legislation that will increase or retard immigration without affecting the poor interest I hold in land that was, when purchased, suburban, but is rapidly becoming the central portion of Philadelphia.

My self-respect will not permit me to believe it was proposed to buy my legislative action with the profits I should make on an investment of a thousand dollars; nor can I believe that such an investment would be made suggestive of any such result, as it is widely known that it is now largely more than one-fourth of a century since I began, under the impulse of Asa Whitney, to agitate the question of a Government grant for a railroad across the continent.

I have with me in Washington a copy of a petition that I am known by the old residents of Philadelphia to have circulated in the early period of my professional life in 1845-'46, and to have spent much time in procuring signatures to, asking Congress to grant a strip of land sixty miles wide in aid of the construction of a railroad from the base of Lake Michigan to the waters of the Columbia River and Puget Sound.

In the year 1846 I entered upon a movement for the purpose of convening a meeting which became respectable and influential, but which required six months' labor to give it character—which meeting was held at the Chinese Museum, over which the then mayor of the city presided, at which Josiah Randall, esq., the father of my colleague, Samuel J. Randall, spoke with me in favor of the Government making such a grant, at which Asa Whitney also presented his views; all of which, in the month of June, 1871, I brought to the attention of the people of Philadelphia in an address at the Academy of Music, several of the officers of which meeting had, more than a quarter of a century ago, acted as officers on the occasion to which I have referred.

I therefore say that neither my self-respect will permit me to believe that I was sought to be bought by that operation which I believed was purely personal, having no reference to any such thing, or that Mr. Ames was stupid enough to invest his money with any such view in one who, for more than a quarter of a century, had been an enthusiast in the work for the promotion of which he was supposed to be purchased.

Q. This conversation you had with Mr. Ames in regard to your becoming the owner of ten shares of the Credit Mobilier stock was during the session of Congress?—A. I think so. I have no doubt of the fact. I was leaving the Ebbitt House or one of the newspaper offices—I cannot tell which—and joined him at the junction of F and Fourteenth streets, to take a car.

Q. Have you an idea in relation to the time of the year it was, whether it was winter or summer?—A. My impression is that it was cold weather. I remember very well the place and the incident. I remember having the thought for a time that I was to become the owner of ten shares of this stock; but I cannot fix the date or any approximate date by any circumstance that occurs to me except the one to which I have referred.

Q. The conversation grew out of the fact that you had subscribed to this Credit Foncier?—A. That I had subscribed, or that it was alleged that I had subscribed.

Q. The stock of this company, before its charter was transferred to New York, was rather fancy stock than otherwise, was it not?—A. I think it was, under the auspices of its commencement; I do not know what it may become under its present managers.

Q. The conversation you had with Mr. Ames resulted in the agreement on your part to take ten shares?—A. Yes, sir; and I wish it to be distinctly understood that it was not my fault that I did not get it. I supposed I had contracted for ten shares of stock.

Q. Were any dividends ever paid to you on it?—A. No, sir; I received nothing from it.

Q. The result of the money transaction in reference to the Credit Mobilier stock, then, was that you neither paid Mr. Ames anything nor received anything on that account?—A. Yes, sir.

Q. The question has been raised by somebody in regard to that thousand dollars; I understand that you had borrowed $500, which you repaid, and that subsequently to that you borrowed $1,000 of Mr. Ames?—A. Yes, sir. I assume it to be subsequent, because that puts the case most strongly against me.

Q. State whether the borrowing of that thousand dollars from Mr. Ames had any connection in any manner with the Credit Mobilier stock.—A. I am here reminded of what Judge Bingham said on the uncertainty of speaking of what may have been passing in a person's mind so long ago, and of all the considerations that may have entered into his motives.

Q. I am simply inquiring whether it was any part of that transaction in reference to the Credit Mobilier.—A. No; I was pressed for money; I went to Mr. Ames and asked him to loan me $1,000. I explained to him my embarrassment to a sufficient extent to induce the loan. It had, so far as I can remember, in my mind no possible reference to the Credit Mobilier; while I think it not impossible it may have had in his. If he still supposed I was to get the stock, he may have supposed the loan would be adjusted ultimately in connection with it. How that was I cannot say. I did not propose anything of the kind.

Q. To your recollection, was anything said between you and Mr. Ames at the time you borrowed the thousand dollars in regard to the contract of the Credit Mobilier?—A. No, sir; when the publication in regard to this matter first came to my attention, I was away from the excitement of Congress, in the Rocky Mountains. I have challenged my memory in vain for anything as being connected with the obligation of the loan and the receipt of the money. If I had received it in connection with the Credit Mobilier transaction, I should not, when Mr. Ames fell into what seemed to me financial misfortune, have gone to him to express my regret at being unable to repay him then.

Q. If you had received that as a payment upon the Credit Mobilier stock, you would not have been troubled about your inability to pay it back?—A. No, sir. I have tested that matter in my own mind in another way. I have asked myself the question, if that fund were garnisheed by a creditor of Oakes Ames, and on the other hand by a creditor of the Credit Mobilier, what would be my answer in court, as between the two, which I owed the money to. It would be a negative answer to the interrogatories of the creditors of the Credit Mobilier. It would be an affirmative answer to the interrogatories of the creditors of Oakes Ames. In that case the parties would be indifferent to me.

Q. Have you any recollection how long it was after this arrangement or contract between you and Mr. Ames before you learned from Mr. Ames that for some reason he could not fulfill the agreement to let you have the stock?—A. Upon my word, I have not. I have given you the only two points by which I can fix any approximate dates in the transaction.

Q. Do you remember what Mr. Ames said in regard to the probable earning or dividends of the Credit Mobilier?—A. I think he said they had been pretty large in the past; that they would not be likely to be so large in the future. I am confident he said it would be very good stock.

Q. Do you remember any particulars in regard to this statement of dividend to you?—A. There was nothing definite between us. It was a conversation at a casual meeting on the curbstone. I had no money to invest. I was really assuming no responsibility, and I did not inquire with that particularity I should have done under other circumstances. I supposed the whole transaction to be a friendly one. But as to my right to make the purchase, being a member of Congress, no question occurred to me; and I claim, as I have said, that I had a perfect right to make it.

Q. You say that in that conversation there was no reference made to any action of Congress upon the action of the Union Pacific Railroad?—A. Not the slightest.

Q. Have you any knowledge in relation to any transaction between Mr. Ames and any other member of Congress?—A. None except what I have gathered since these publications have been made, and the matter had almost passed from my mind until, on the 12th of September, when between Cheyenne and Fort Saunders, a Chicago paper was put into my hands on the train, which contained a statement from the New York Sun in regard to this matter, in which I was put down as having received two thousand shares of stock in the Credit Mobilier.

By Mr. MERRICK:

Q. Did you vote for a joint resolution, which has been referred to, of April 10, 1869?—A. I was unfortunately out of the House when it passed. I certainly should have voted for it. It was one of those acts which, strange to say, had the support of both sides. While it continued the organizations of the railroad company, it gave additional guarantees to the Government. I supposed the measure would not be passed without some discussion, and had gone to the Senate for a short period; when I returned the resolution had passed.

By Mr. NIBLACK:

Q. Let me ask, inasmuch as this loan has not been paid, whether it is your habit to allow loans to run for that length of time without any settlement?—A. I am very much obliged to you for asking that question. When I was elected to Congress I believed myself to be in very easy circumstances. I soon found myself in extreme embarrassment, arising from three causes.

[The witness here stated in detail the circumstances of his own financial embarrassment, extending through several years of time, in which, but for the indulgence of friends in permitting interest to run into principal, he must have been stripped of all his property.]

By Mr. MCCRARY:

Q. You were to pay Mr. Ames nothing on the stock he agreed to furnish you, except the dividends that should accrue?—A. No; in case the dividends amounted to but 7 per cent., he was to receive and retain them; but if they amounted, in addition to the 7 per cent., to the par value of the stock, the stock was to be transferred to me as a compliment on the part of Mr. Ames. I had no suspicion of the transaction having any political significance, or of its being connected in any way with public affairs.

Q. There was no obligation to pay anything at all to Mr. Ames?—A. No, sir; nor was there any obligation on his part to deliver anything to me unless the stock should earn more than 7 per cent. After the earnings amounted to more than 7 per cent., they were to be applied in payment of this stock until it was all paid for, if they should be sufficient.

Q. If it had been stated to you that the purpose of Mr. Ames was to place that stock with members of Congress, in order to have friends in Congress and prevent investigation by Congress, would it have presented a different question for your consideration?—A. If any such consideration had been presented, that would have concluded me, of course, but I took it for granted that a man who has been here through all this railroad legislation, advocating almost every measure which has been adopted for the encouragement of railroad enterprise, standing upon such a record for more than a quarter of a century as a uniform and fast friend of railroad extension, and who never has owned a share of railroad stock, except some five shares in a Pennsylvania railroad and a small interest in a street railroad in Baltimore—I say, the idea that a man with such a record was to have his integrity assailed by a contingent interest in ten shares of Credit Mobilier stock did not occur to me. During all this period of railroad legislation, if I had been disposed to have perverted my position to a source of relief from my embarrassment, I think I might have done so successfully, and have covered it up. Certainly, if it had been suggested to me that this stock was being put into the hands of members of Congress for any such purpose, I should have spurned it and the man who offered it.

Q. Have you read the letters of Mr. Ames to Mr. McComb which have been published?—A. Yes, sir; but until I read them, I did not conceive it possible that any suspicion of my integrity could be suggested by this operation.

Q. If you had known the character of these letters, would you have purchased the stock?—A. If I had read the letters, I certainly would not have purchased the stock; at the same time, I do not think Mr. Ames, (I cannot believe it of him,) and I do not believe Mr. Ames meant to imply that he was buying gentlemen in Congress to the support of any proposition by the possible gain they might have on ten or twenty shares apiece. The idea of drawing strength to the company by such proposition implies a depth of stupidity that I cannot attribute to Mr. Ames.

Q. You do not mean to be understood that it is immaterial whether members have a personal interest in matters of legislation or not?—A. Not at all. I mean to say you cannot get a Congress in which all the members will have no such remote interest in legislation as I have referred to.

Q. You refer to cases where the interest of the Government is also the interest of the individuals particularly concerned. You do not mean to say where the private interest of individuals might not come in contact with their duties as members of Congress?—A. Certainly not; I could mention one instance in which my own personal interest was very palpably in opposition to the legislation which I advocated. I am the owner, to a certain extent, of an interest in the street railroads of Baltimore, which have a hard contract with the city of Baltimore. Under the internal-revenue law, assessing a Government tax of 2½ per cent. upon the gross earnings of the company, they were permitted to re-imburse themselves by charging an additional cent for each passenger, which, in this instance, was receiving a cent on their part to re-imburse an outlay of a sixteenth part of a cent. During the existence of that law, they paid me dividends, but regarding, as I did, the tax on transportation as most prejudicial to the interest of the country, I was active, as the members of the Committee of Ways and Means will bear witness, to the extent of my ability, in laboring for its repeal. The result is, unhappily for my interest in the Baltimore street-railroads, that, having paid dividends during the existence of the tax, it does not pay any for the last six months. There is none for January. It seems to me, therefore, that the natural tendency of a personal interest in a matter of legislation would be to induce members to lean against their personal interest than otherwise.

By Mr. MERRICK:

Q. Does not a rule of the House forbid a member voting upon a measure in which he has a personal interest?—A. Yes; but as inasmuch as my personal interest was against the course I took, I did not feel myself bound by the rule.

By Mr. MCCRARY:

Q. Would you regard a stockholder in the Union Pacific Railroad or Credit Mobilier competent to vote upon that bill which subordinated the Government loan to the first-mortgage loan of the company?—A. This question as to what should be the standard of action in such cases is one that each member must decide for himself, and I think it should be left, as it is by parliamentary law, to the judgment of each member, subject to the criticism of his peers and his responsibility to his constituents. I can only say that, for myself, if I had held such an interest at the time the bill you referred to passed, I certainly should not have felt free to vote in favor of it.

WASHINGTON, D. C., *January* 16, 1872.

GLENNI W. SCOFIELD, a member of the United States House of Representatives from Pennsylvania, having been duly sworn, made the following statement:

For many years I have been in the habit of investing in bonds or stocks whatever surplus, however small, I might have from year to year. In December, 1866, I bought of Mr. Ames some bonds on the Cedar Rapids and Missouri Railroad. In December, 1867, I spoke to him about getting more. He suggested that I should take this Credit Mobilier stock. He explained that it was a contracting company, incorporated by the legislature of my State, and he would like to have some Pennsylvanians in it. In a brief way he explained its object. He said he would sell me some at par, with interest from some former period, at my own risk, or he would guarantee that it would pay 8 per cent. if I would give him half it earned above that sum. I told him I thought I would take one thousand dollars of it. I told him I would get the money and see him again. Before anything was done, however, I was called home by severe illness in my family, and did not return until some days after New Year's. Some time after, when I met Mr. Ames and spoke about getting him the money, he said he thought I was too late; as I did not give him the money he supposed I had abandoned it, and he thought it was all sold, but I could give him the money then, and he would ascertain and get it if he could. I gave him the money and took his receipt.

This was the last of January. He subsequently informed me that he could get the stock, but it was in a larger block, and he would have to get it divided.

Either at this time or soon after, I told him I had concluded not to take the stock. We talked the matter over, and I finally agreed to take some of his railroad securities instead. Some balance was settled in money, and I gave him his receipt. This was during that same session of Congress, more than four years ago.

I do not recollect of any legislation pending or in prospect at this time that Mr. Ames was interested in. I was not in Congress when the subsidies to the Pacific roads were granted, and I voted against the act of 1864 giving the company's mortgage priority. The legislation that came up two or three years after was based upon facts subsequently developed, and could not, therefore, have been anticipated by me. Nothing was said about legislation, and certainly it was not thought of by me.

By the CHAIRMAN:

Question. Will you state the time when this matter was adjusted between you and Mr. Ames finally?—Answer. I have stated that it was during that session of Congress. I fix it as during that session of Congress, and I fix it at that date from two or three facts which I could state.

Q. What were the securities that you finally received from Mr. Ames?—A. I think ten shares of Union Pacific stock and a bond of a thousand dollars, and that I paid him $230 in addition to the one thousand dollars he had received. In fact, I paid him more than the thousand at first. There was a small premium charged upon the stock. I am able to fix the amount which I first paid definitely. It was $1,041.

Q. Was that sum made up by the interest spoken of from some previous date?—A. I cannot say whether it was in the shape of interest or premium. I know from my accounts that that was the amount.

Q. Were any dividends received on this stock by you?—A. During the time he had my money, I think no dividends were declared by the company. If there were any, I have no recollection of receiving them in that form. I got back no more than I gave Mr. Ames, and I think there was no dividend paid me. If there was any, it was allowed in the final adjustment.

Q. Do you remember whether, in this conversation or negotiation between you and Mr. Ames, he said anything in relation to the then market-value of this Credit Mobilier stock?—A. I do not think he did. If the value now talked about was correct, I had no idea of it at any time.

Q. You had no idea then that the stock was worth two or three times its value?—A. No, sir.

Q. Have you any knowledge in relation to Mr. Ames's dealings with other members in reference to stock in the Credit Mobilier?—A. He told me in December, as an evidence that the investment would be a safe one, that Mr. Hooper, Mr. Grimes, and Mr. Alley were interested in it.

Q. Did you understand from him that these gentlemen were men who were early in the enterprise—who went into it at or about the time he did?—A. I do not know that he told me that.

Q. Did you learn anything from him in relation to the efforts he was then making to dispose of any of the stock to members of Congress?—A. I did not. This conversation was accidental. It began on the street, I think, while walking down from the Capitol—we boarded together—

and was continued at the table. I had boarded with Mr. Ames considerably since I had been in Congress.

By Mr. MERRICK:

Q. You say that finally an arrangement was made between you and Mr. Ames, by which, instead of taking the Credit Mobilier stock, you were to take certain bonds. What bonds were they?—A. The bonds of the Union Pacific Railroad Company. I took one bond of a thousand dollars, and ten shares of Union Pacific Railroad stock, and paid him the difference. I paid him $230, I think, over and above what I had paid before. That is my recollection. I think I paid him $200 in money, and cut off one of the coupons on the bond. I never had the Credit Mobilier stock at all, and never considered myself as having any interest in the corporation. I gave him $1,041 to see if he could get me some, but he never did get me any. He gave me a receipt for my money, which I returned him when I took the railroad securities.

Q. These railroad securities amounted to how much?—A. At par they amounted to $1,000 stock and $1,000 bonds.

Q. Do you still retain them?—A. No, sir; the next spring I had some stores burned, and began in the summer following to rebuild. I also began to sell my bonds and stock piecemeal, as I had bought them at different times, and I sold the bonds and the stock during that season.

Q. You say that Mr. Ames explained to you the object of the Credit Mobilier?—A. Very briefly.

Q. Did he explain to you that the Credit Mobilier was owned chiefly by the men who were directors and most largely interested in the Union Pacific road?—A. No; he told me that they had a contract from the Union Pacific.

Q. Were you not aware that the members and directors of the Union Pacific Railroad Company were also engaged in the management of the Credit Mobilier, and were making contracts with themselves, through the form of a corporation called the Credit Mobilier?—A. I do not know that he did or did not.

Q. If you had known that the directors of the Union Pacific Railroad were making contracts with themselves in the character of stockholders and managers of the Credit Mobilier, would you have become a participant in that transaction?—A. I cannot say that I had then an idea that such was the fact, and I cannot say now what my course would have been. "Avoid the appearance of evil," is an injunction that, I think, sometimes rogues are more careful to observe than honest men.

Q. You had none of this stock in your own name? Was any of this stock assigned to any member of your family?—A. No, sir.

By the CHAIRMAN:

Q. Do you remember what was the value of the Union Pacific Railroad stock at the time you received the ten shares from Mr. Ames?—A. I remember about what we called them. My impression is that the stock had no market-value. The bond had. I think we called the bond worth 97 and the stock 30.

Q. The money you had paid him to obtain Credit Mobilier stock you used to purchase these securities?—A. Yes, sir.

By Mr. MCCRARY:

Q. You sold the stock in 1869?—A. I cannot say positively when I sold the stock. It was in 1869 that I commenced selling my securities. I have no memorandum of the sales. It was about that time.

Q. There was no legislation in Congress while you held it concerning the Pacific Railroad?—A. I do not think of any. If there had been any, the interest was too small a matter, $200 or $300 of it—it might go up or down a little in price—to influence anybody's vote. I do not think the idea would ever have occurred to me.

By Mr. MERRICK:

Q. You do not remember when the resolution of Mr. Washburn was introduced, somewhere in 1867 or 1868, looking to an investigation into the affairs of the Union Pacific Railroad Company?—A. I do not remember.

By Mr. NIBLACK:

Q. You stated, I think, that Mr. Ames wanted to get prominent Pennsylvanians into the enterprise?—A. I think he wanted to have some Pennsylvania men in it, because it was incorporated in our State and must have its headquarters in our State.

Q. Did he assign any other reason than that it was a Pennsylvania corporation?—A. I do not remember that he did.

Q. Did he mention any other prominent Pennsylvania men who were interested in the corporation?—A. I do not know that he mentioned the name of anybody holding stock. He mentioned, I think, the names of two men by way of inquiring of me something about them. They were men unknown to me, and not in public life. I think the name of one of them was Stewart, but I have forgotten.

WASHINGTON, *January* 18, 1872.

B. F. BOYER, of Philadelphia, Pennsylvania, having been duly sworn, made the following statement:

I appear voluntarily before the committee without a summons, because I have been mentioned in the testimony as the owner of stock in the Credit Mobilier while I was a member of Congress. I desire that I may be examined in relation to my purchase of that stock. I have nothing to conceal concerning it. I took the stock in my own name and have so held it ever since, as the books will show. I held seventy-five shares as my own and twenty-five shares as trustee for my wife, making one hundred shares in all. I always regarded it as a legitimate stock operation, and never denied having made the investment. It did not interfere with my duties as a member of Congress. I entered Congress in 1865, and retired four years afterward. During that time neither the Credit Mobilier nor the Union Pacific Railroad required any legislation by Congress that I know of. The land-grants and subsidies to the Union Pacific Railroad had all been voted before I became a member of Congress, and the legislation relating to the postponement of the payment of interest on the Government bonds took place after I had left Congress. I am not conscious of ever having voted, while in Congress, for any measure in the interest of either the Credit Mobilier or the Union Pacific Railroad. I invite the most critical examination of my record. The investment in Credit Mobilier stock was recommended to me by Dr. Thomas C. Durant, who was my personal friend, and with whom I agreed for the purchase of one hundred shares at par, at a time when the success of the enterprise and the profits dependent thereupon were by no means certain. This was in the winter of 1866. The stock was not actually transferred to me until long after I had agreed to take it. There was some difficulty and delay in obtaining all I had agreed to take. At first seventy-five shares were paid for and transferred to me in December, 1867, and, some time afterward, the additional twenty-five shares, which I had transferred to me as trustee for my wife. This completed the original contract between Dr. Durant and myself.

I had no idea of wrong in the matter. Nor do I now see how it concerns the public. No one connected with either the Credit Mobilier or the Union Pacific Railroad ever directly or indirectly expressed, or in any way hinted, that my services as a member of Congress were expected in behalf of either corporation in consideration of the stock I obtained, and certainly no such services were ever rendered. I was much less embarrassed as a member of Congress by the ownership of Credit Mobilier stock than I should have been had I owned stock in a national bank, or in an iron-furnace, or a woolen-mill, or even a holder of Government bonds; for there was important legislation while I was in Congress affecting all these interests, but no legislation whatever concerning the Credit Mobilier. I can therefore find nothing in my conduct in that regard to regret. It was, in my judgment, both honest and honorable, and consistent with my position as a member of Congress. And as the investment turned out to be profitable, my only regret is that it was no larger in amount.

By the CHAIRMAN:

Question. Was this a purchase by you from Dr. Durant, or did you understand yourself to be a subscriber to the stock of the company?—Answer. I did not inquire particularly in what way, or from whom, I was getting the stock. I contracted to purchase it, and I was satisfied when it was transferred to me in a regular way.

Q. The negotiation you made for it was wholly with Dr. Durant?—A. It was wholly with Dr. Durant.

Q. And this arrangement, or contract for it, was made early in the winter of 1866?—A. Yes, sir; as early as 1866. I was ready to pay for it long before the stock was ready to be transferred.

Q. You understood that this Credit Mobilier was in some way connected with the Union Pacific Railroad?—A. Yes, sir.

Q. That they were really contractors for building the road?—A. I understood they were contractors for building the road.

Q. And that its dividends of money, if made at all, would be upon the profits of building the road?—A. Yes, sir.

Q. Do you remember at what time the seventy-five shares of stock were transferred to you?—A. Yes, sir; it was in December, 1867.

Q. And the form of your getting that was by transfer from Dr. Durant?—A. I do not precisely remember how that was. I remember the stock was transferred to me through Dr. Durant.

Q. That is, you understood that the stock you received had stood in his name before that?—A. Yes, sir; that was my understanding.

Q. In your negotiations with Dr. Durant in reference to this, did you understand it was a purchase from him, or that he was acting on behalf of the company?—A. I was not very particular about that. So I got the stock in a legitimate way, I thought it did not matter whether I received it from him, as a part of the stock standing in his name, or whether I received it directly from the company, and at this time I cannot precisely say how the certificates read. I thought at the time it made no material difference.

Q. When did you pay for the stock?—A. I paid for the stock at the time it was transferred.

Q. You paid for seventy-five shares at the time you got the certificate for the seventy-five shares?—A. Yes, sir.

Q. Your agreement was for one hundred shares?—A. My agreement was for one hundred shares.

Q. How did it come to pass that only seventy-five were transferred?—A. It was explained to me at the time that there had been more stock promised than there was stock to supply, and it was not until a considerable time afterward that Dr. Durant transferred to me twenty-five shares.

Q. So that the original contract, made between Durant and you, was made more than a year before it was executed fully?—A. Yes, sir.

Q. Do you remember the time of the transfer of the twenty-five shares?—A. I do not remember the precise time of the transfer of the twenty-five shares, but I think it was not until 1868.

Q. Had you received any dividends upon the twenty-five shares prior to the time you got a certificate for them?—A. No, sir; I think not.

Q. Do you remember at what time in 1868 it was?—A. No, sir; I cannot state at this time at what period in 1868 it was; but if that is important, I have memoranda to which I could refer, and inform the committee, I think, with precision. I have not it with me.

Q. This twenty-five shares you subsequently received to make up the one hundred you got as a fulfillment of the original agreement?—A. Yes, sir; and in no other way.

Q. Did you receive the same dividends upon the twenty-five shares as upon the seventy-five?—A. I think the dividends were accounted for and paid to me, and I was charged with interest on the par value of the stock.

Q. That is, you paid interest upon the price of the stock, so as to make it the same as if you had taken it at the time it was contracted for?—A. Yes, sir.

Q. You understand in point of fact that you got the same dividends upon the twenty-five shares as upon the seventy-five?—A. Yes, sir.

Q. Can you state the gross amount of dividends you received upon all the stock?—A. I cannot just now state the gross amount of dividends which I received altogether. I have no doubt that I received the regular dividends as other stockholders did, and I presume the committee have information before them which will enable them to say how much that was. It may not be improper for me here, however, to state that the actual value of the dividends received was not as great as it seemed to be, or as it has been ciphered up to be, in the newspapers. I sold all the Union Pacific Railroad stock which I received as dividends at about thirty-one dollars a share. The stock previously to that had been down, I think, as low as nine or ten dollars in the market.

Q. Did you sell the bonds you received?—A Yes, sir; I sold the bonds, I think, for less than par.

Q. Do you remember at about what price you got for the bonds?—A. I sold the bonds at different times and for the current prices in the market at the time.

Q. Can you state at about the range of prices you got for them?—A. I think for the first bonds I sold I received par or nearly so. I think that other bonds were sold for considerably less.

Q. Did you know anything in relation to the sales of stock or contracts for stock between Mr. Durant and any other men who were in Congress?—A. No, sir; I do not, except from hearsay.

Q. What source of information do you refer to as hearsay?—A. I refer to what I saw in the newspapers and what I heard in conversation with persons professing to know something about the Credit Mobilier transactions. But I have no information which comes from such a source as to make it reliable as testimony before this committee.

Q. Had you any information about the time you were making a contract with Mr. Durant of any dealings he had with others?—A. I understood there was a transaction between Mr. Brooks and Dr. Durant, but I have no knowledge of Mr. Brooks ever having taken any stock in his own name.

Q. Did you know about that, or had you information about it, before this became a matter for public comment?—A. Yes, sir; I had information at the time that Mr. Brooks had obtained some stock for his son-in-law.

Q. Did you get it from Mr. Brooks or from Mr. Durant?—A. I think I got it from both.

Q. If you heard Mr. Brooks say anything in reference to it, we would be glad to have you state it.—A. I remember when Mr. Brooks was appointed a Government director in the Union Pacific Railroad Company that I asked him how he could consistently accept that position, and he informed me that he did not hold any stock in the road.

Q. Did he go on then, in reference to the stock he took, and state to you how it was done?—A. No, sir; except that he did not own a share of stock in the road. This was at the time of his appointment as a Government director.

Q. Do you remember at what time it was that he was appointed?—A. It was during the administration of President Johnson. I have some occasion to remember the occurrence, because there were some parties who suggested to me the propriety of having me appointed a Government director in the Union Pacific Railroad Company, and I declined, on the ground, I thought it was incompatible with my position, and that I would not transfer my stock in the Credit Mobilier for the purpose of putting myself in a position to take an appointment.

Q. In that conversation, did Mr. Brooks say anything in reference to how he had qualified himself?—A. No, sir; he simply said that he was not the owner of any stock so as to disqualify him for the place.

Q. Did he say anything in reference to his son-in-law, Neilson?—A. He did say his son-in-law, Neilson, held stock.

Q. Did he go into any explanation of how it was done?—A. No, sir. I did not solicit and he did not volunteer it.

Q. Do you know of any other member of Congress who received stock from Mr. Durant, either in his own name or in the name of anybody else?—A. No, sir. I have no reason to think that any other persons did than myself and Mr. Brooks, if Mr. Brooks did.

Q. Did you know anything in relation to the dealings of Oakes Ames with members of Congress in reference to stock?—A. No, sir; upon that subject I have no knowledge whatever. I had no negotiations with Mr. Ames for any stock myself, and I do not think I ever conversed with Mr. Ames upon the subject until after I had become a stockholder.

Q. Did you then learn anything in relation to his having made contracts or sales of stock to members?—A. No, sir; I was not curious upon that subject. I asked no questions and Mr. Ames did not volunteer any statement.

Q. Never, at any time, did you get any information from him?—A. No, sir; not that I remember.

By Mr. MERRICK:

Q. You stated that you had no information directly which would be evidence before this committee such as you have detailed. Have you any information which would, if communicated to the committee, put them upon the track of ascertaining direct legitimate evidence touching this matter?—A. No, sir; I have no knowledge which would shed any further light upon the transaction than I have learned by the published testimony which you already have before you.

Q. When did you leave Congress?—A. I left Congress in 1869, at the close of the Fortieth. I was in Congress four years during the Thirty-ninth and Fortieth Congress. The Fortieth Congress expired the 4th of March, 1869.

Q. You were not in Congress at the time of the introduction of the joint resolution of April 10, 1869, affecting the relations of the Union Pacific Railroad Company with the United States?—A. No, sir.

Q. Do you remember any agitation in Congress prior to that time in 1868, looking toward an investigation into the affairs of the Union Pacific Railroad?—A. I remember that there was some agitation—I think the introduction of some resolutions, which were referred to the Pacific Railroad Committee.

Q. Do you recollect at what time these resolutions were introduced, and by whom?—A. No, sir; I do not; they never seemed to amount to much.

Q. Do you remember whether they were introduced by Mr. Washburn?—A. I do recollect now, that Mr. Washburn, of Wisconsin, made a raid in Congress, on one occasion, on the Union Pacific Railroad, and introduced some resolutions. That was in 1868, and while I was in Congress.

Q. At about what time was the transfer of these twenty-five shares of Credit Mobilier stock to you?—A. I do not remember the time. I do remember very distinctly that I never voted to smother any investigation in reference to the Union Pacific Railroad. I may say here that I do not altogether approve of some of the management connected with the Credit Mobilier, as well as the Union Pacific Railroad, but being a director in neither, I considered myself as having nothing to do with it.

Q. Was there any attack of notoriety, in connection with that road, while you were in Congress in 1868?—A. I do not remember much attack outside of Congress.

Q. I mean in Congress.—A. I do not think it created much excitement.

Q. I do not speak of it as a matter of excitement, but as a matter of notoriety, that such a movement was in agitation?—A. It could not help but be notorious in Congress, because it was in the published proceedings.

WASHINGTON, D. C., *January* 18, 1873.

JAMES F. WILSON, having been duly sworn, made the following statement:

Having noticed in the papers that my name has been connected with the Credit Mobilier stock, I am now prepared, with the consent of the committee, to make a statement. I wish to state here that probably my case is somewhat peculiar. Both Mr. Ames and Mr. McComb are present, and I desire them to pay attention to the statement I now make, inasmuch as when I have concluded what I have to say I wish to ask each of them a question.

I once bought and paid for ten shares of the capital stock of the Credit

Mobilier of America. The par value of the shares was $100 each—in all, $1,000.

The purchase of said stock came about in this way: When Mr. Oakes Ames was engaged in soliciting subscriptions to the stock of said company he asked me to subscribe $5,000 of it, which I declined to do. I heard nothing more of this stock until some time in the year 1868—the exact time I cannot state, but certainly not earlier than May—when I met in this city Mr. H. S. McComb, (with whom I had been acquainted for sêveral years, and against whose character I never had heard any reproach,) who, during a conversation had between us, asked me if I held any Credit Mobilier stock. I told him that I did not; that Mr. Ames had once asked me to subscribe for $5,000 of it, but that I had declined the offer. Mr. McComb replied that I could get that stock yet, and that he wished I would do so. I told him that I knew but little about it, and inquired its value. He said that would depend somewhat on circumstances, but that I need not hesitate because of that; that he thought I could get it at par, and that he would take it, furnish the money to pay for it, and allow me an advance which would have been a liberal compensation for the negotiation. He then related the circumstances under which he had subscribed for a number of shares; that he had made the subscription in good faith; that the company refused to recognize his subscription, and were trying to cheat him out of his rights under it; that he was determined to have the stock, and that, if he could not get it quietly and peacefully, he should enforce his rights at law; that he did not want to have or make any unnecessary trouble about it, but that he would not be cheated out of it; that he was willing to do anything for peace short of surrendering his rights; that to go to law would lead to strife, delay, and expense; but that he would go through with it all if driven to it. The impression which he made on my mind was that if he could get the stock, even by indirection, he would rather do that than resort to the courts; and in this connection he said that there was other stock in the same position as that which he said I could get, and that therefore there was no reasonable excuse for the company treating him as they had done.

As a result of this conversation, I had an interview with Mr. Oakes Ames. I inquired of him if there were not $5,000 of Credit Mobilier stock that I could have. He said, "No; you declined to subscribe for it, and it has been disposed of." I replied that I had been informed that that amount or more was undisposed of, and that I could have fifty shares. He repeated that the stock was disposed of, and that whoever told me what I had stated was mistaken.

I communicated the result of this interview to Mr. McComb, who said that it was just like Ames; that if he could take care of himself and his friends, everybody else might whistle for their rights; and said, "See Ames again, and tell him that there is no mistake about the matter, and that I (McComb) know there is not."

I did see Mr. Ames again, who said that Mr. McComb's statement was not true, and repeated his former statements. I then asked him if it could not be arranged so that I could get the stock. He replied that he did not believe that it could be, but that he was soon going to New York and would see what could be done.

Some time afterward Mr. Ames told me that he had arranged for ten shares for me at par and 7 per cent. interest ex prior dividends; that that was the best and most he could do then, but he would see if he could do any more. I took the ten shares and asked him to arrange for the rest if he could. But no more was arranged for, and when I subsequently told Mr. McComb he said, "Well, that is another of his tricks; he don't want to do any better, but if you insist on it he will;" and that he (Mr. McComb) wanted the stock on the "ground-floor," just as the rest had had theirs. I had talked so much to Mr. Ames that I concluded to await his movements; that anything further would look too much like importunity. But, as I have stated, he never arranged for any more stock, and the ten shares were on my hands. I held the stock until some time in the winter of 1869, when I sold it, the reasons for which I will state.

A good deal of contention had sprung up among the parties interested in the Union Pacific Railroad Company and the Credit Mobilier relative to the management of the affairs of said company, and an effort was to be made at the meeting of the stockholders of the Union Pacific Railroad Company in March, 1869, to change a part of the board of directors. My opinion was asked for concerning the rights of stockholders in the Union Pacific Company to vote shares held by them regardless of a proxy, which was said to run with the stock under the terms of the contracts and agreements existing between said company, the Credit Mobilier, and certain parties designated as trustees. In order to enable me to understand the question submitted, copies of certain papers were placed in my hands, (some of which I have now in my possession,) and among which was the contract between Oakes Ames, of the first part, T. C. Durant, Oliver Ames, John B. Alley, Sidney Dillon, C. S. Bushnell, Henry S. McComb, and Benjamin S. Bates, of the second part, and the Credit Mobilier of America, of the third part; an agreement between the aforesaid parties of the second part, in which they bound themselves to vote their own stock and that for which they held or should hold proxies, (which was represented to embrace all issued or to be issued under the Oakes Ames contract,) in the manner provided in the agreement, and some other papers not bearing directly on the question submitted.

I examined the question, and gave an opinion to the effect that holders of Union Pacific stock could vote their own shares, regardless of the proxy running with it; that the affairs of the corporation could not be tied up in the hands of a few individuals in the way attempted by the terms of said contracts and agreements; and that the scheme of the Credit Mobilier was one which might render every officer and director of the Union Pacific Company, who was a party to it, accountable to the latter company for the profits accruing to him from the construction contracts.

Down to the time these papers were placed in my hands, I knew almost nothing of the organization and the details of the Credit Mobilier, or of the value of its stock, but then saw that there was abundant ground for future trouble and litigation; and as one of the results, sold out my interest, and have at no time since been in any manner interested in the Credit Mobilier, nor did I at any time or in any manner have any interest of any kind or character in said company other than as hereinbefore stated.

So far as Mr. Ames is concerned, his action was the result of my application to him for the purchase of the stock. My action was induced solely by the conversation had with Mr. McComb, who was actuated, as I understood, by what he denounced as a gross injustice practiced on him by the company; and it was well known to both of them, as it was to everybody, that my connection with Congress would end with my then term.

The reports of the testimony given before this committee, as published in the newspapers, show that Mr. McComb has testified that he had requested Mr. Ames to let me have some Credit Mobilier stock. Not one word of this ever came to my knowledge from him, Mr. Ames, or any other person, except as I have related in this statement.

And I desire here to recall the fact that when the transaction above related occurred, the whole country resounded with praises of the energy manifested by the constructors of the Union Pacific Railroad. They had pushed the work with great vigor, and under great difficulties. In March, 1868, the chief engineer, in reviewing the difficulties attending the construction, told the country that, "During the past two years the road had been built through an Indian country with all the tribes banded together and hostile; our best and ablest men had been killed; our cars, stations, and ranches burned; our men driven off, and our stock stolen; graders and track-layers, tie-men and station-builders, have had to sleep under guard, and have gone to their work in the day-time with their picks and shovels and their mechanical tools in one hand and the rifle in the other, and they have often to drop the one and use the other." * * * "The graders went to their work as soldiers, stacked their arms by the cuts, and worked all day with hostile bands of Indians in view, ready to pounce upon, kill, and scalp any unlucky or negligent person who gave them an opportunity." Down to this time the interest on the bonds advanced by the Government had been paid by the company; and with only about four hundred miles of road completed there had been saved to the Government in the cost of transportation, for the year 1867, over $1,500,000. Every person seemed satisfied with what was being done, and astonished at the results produced. These facts, together with the recognized high character of most of the gentlemen connected with the enterprise, were sufficient to justify any person unlearned in the data which those versed in the secrets of the Credit Mobilier, in purchasing stock in either company. And it will be remembered that the praises of what was being done swelled on until they burst forth in the ringing of bells and the firing of cannon all over this country, when, in the spring of 1869, it was announced that the last spike had been driven, and that the tracks of the Union Pacific and Central Pacific Railroads had been united, and that an iron way spanned the continent from ocean to ocean.

The completion of the road brought to the surface the contentions and quarrels among the parties who held the power and the secrets of the Credit Mobilier. These developed the facts which now give direction and tone to the public judgment; but they are not those with which to measure the motives and actions of men who acted under the former state of facts. What I did was under the former state of facts, with no suspicion that they were not true and would not continue true to the end. The very fact that Mr. McComb threatened to carry his claim to the courts for adjudication was of itself calculated to prevent any suspicion of fraud or wrong in the affairs of the company; for such a suit would of necessity bring to light the whole history of the operations of the company.

I wish to say, in conclusion, that when I entered Congress, in 1861, I did so as the Representative of a constituency unanimously in favor of the construction of a railroad to the Pacific. My predecessor had been chairman of the Committee on the Pacific Railroad. To his efforts in favor of the construction of such a road, more than to any other one thing, he owed his last election to Congress. My district at that time embraced nearly one-half of the State of Iowa, and extended from the Mississippi to the Missouri Rivers. I desired to secure the location of the road so as to have it commence on the western boundary of my district, and thus secure connection with it for the Iowa roads then projected and in course of construction. The bill of 1862 secured this result, and I supported it earnestly. I supported the bill of 1864, believing the representations made as to its necessity to be true; I worked as efficiently as I could to promote the interests of the section of the country I was representing. I was the pronounced friend of such legislation as would tend to develop that great western country. I regarded the Pacific Railroad as the greatest of all measures proposed to effect that result. I believed that it would hasten the construction of the several roads projected through Iowa, and thus secure to our people at an early day the facilities for transportation so much needed to promote the growth, settlement, and prosperity of the State. The result proves that my judgment in this respect was not at fault. Consider what that country was a decade ago in comparison with what it is now, and I ask for no more perfect justification of the support which I gave to the measures of legislation which have produced the result.

I now wish to ask Mr. Ames, who I believe is under oath, whether the statement I have made, so far as it relates to him personally, is true.

Mr. AMES. It is true. You told me that I had promised you five thousand dollars. I replied that I had given you the opportunity, and you refused to take it. So far as relates to me, the statement is correct.

Mr. WILSON. I now wish to ask Colonel McComb, who is also under oath, whether the statement I have made in reference to him is correct.

Mr. McCOMB. Emphatically so, so far as I have any knowledge.

Examination of Mr. WILSON.

By the CHAIRMAN:

Question. Do I understand that you claimed of Mr. Ames that he was under any obligation to you in consequence of his promise?—Answer. O, no; none whatever. I supposed Mr. McComb was talking to me about the $5,000 stock which Mr. Ames had asked me to take when he was getting the original subscriptions.

Q. All there was of that transaction was, that Mr. Ames wanted you to subscribe $5,000 of that stock, and you declined?—A. I declined then.

Q. You did not consider Mr. Ames under any obligation, legal or moral?—A. None whatever.

Q. And you did not in your subsequent conversation with him, which resulted in your getting ten shares, claim that he was under any obligation in consequence of that first promise?—A. None whatever. I wish to state here—it is recalled to my mind by a question put by Judge Merrick in regard to action in Congress—it is recalled to my mind, that I proposed two amendments which were embodied in the act of 1864. I do not think after a while, when the benefits to be derived from this great improvement shall be fully understood by the country, that my action, or the action of any gentleman who supported that measure, is going to hurt his reputation. When the bill of 1864 was pending in the House, I had reason, as I supposed, to suspect there was an intention of constructing the Kansas line and leaving out the construction of the Omaha route.

I prepared the amendment to that bill, which I placed in the hands of one of my colleagues, Mr. Allison, and asked him to introduce it, providing that the company should not receive bonds for the road west of the one hundredth meridian until it should be completed to the one hundredth meridian. My object was to secure a connection with the Omaha line for the Iowa roads, and it did secure that object.

Another amendment was to secure the Government lien for transportation, and if I had the act here I would call your attention particularly to that provision. An amendment was offered by me for that purpose, providing that notwithstanding there might be a foreclosure under the first mortgage, the lien of the Government for transportation should still remain and be enforced under the act of 1862. That amendment was adopted, and became a part of the bill, and so far as the act of 1864 is concerned, that is the only thing which saves the Government lien for transportation in case of the foreclosure of the first mortgage.

Q. What do you mean by a transportation lien?—A. There is a section in the act of 1862 that gives the Government, for its transportation over the road, the right to retain out of the money earned for transportation by the company the sum earned by transportation for the Government.

Q. The substance of what you want the committee to understand is that provided the first mortgage is foreclosed, and the road should go into the hands of the mortgagees, the Government would still retain that right?—A. Yes, sir; that was my purpose, and if you will notice the debate in the House, when Mr. Washburn made his very bitter speech in 1868, to which reference has been made, he referred to this amendment of mine in 1864 as saving to the Government its transportation then.

Q. Do you, or did you know, at the time you had this negotiation with Mr. Ames, the value of Credit Mobilier stock?—A. I did not; and I wish to state here, in regard to that, that it was a very difficult thing to ascertain what was the value of the stock. Those who, as I say in my statement, possessed the secrets of the Credit Mobilier, kept them to themselves; and I never was able to get any definite information as to what the value of the stock was.

Q. This conversation you had with Mr. McComb was about what time?—A. In 1868, and I think not earlier than May, according to my best recollection. It was after this alleged distribution of stock, that I have seen published in the papers, to other gentlemen in Congress. I think it was months after that.

Q. Did Mr. McComb say anything in regard to the value of it?—A. No, sir; I asked him about it, but, as I said in my statement, he replied that that would depend upon circumstances. He said to me, "You need not hesitate about the stock; I will pay you for it, and pay you an advance, which will compensate for your negotiation."

Q. Did Mr. Ames in the conversation you had, which resulted in your getting ten shares, say anything about it?—A. No, sir.

Q. You had that stock at par?—A. No, sir. I had it at par and 7 per cent. interest; and my recollection is that I paid interest on it for seven or eight months, probably from the fall of 1867 until the time I got it. I have here, as I state, the contract between the parties and the assignment of the Ames contract. The contract is dated October 15, 1867, and I suppose the interest I paid must have been from the date of the contract until I paid for the stock, or it may have been even further back from the first of July.

Q. Was anything said by Mr. McComb or Mr. Ames to you in relation to any dividends that had been declared on it?—A. No, sir.

Q. Did you afterward learn what dividends had been declared?—A. No, sir; I did not. I learned of one, because there was one dividend that when I paid for the stock he accounted to me for. I do not remember what that was.

Q. You did not receive any dividends that had been declared to the time you purchased?—A. No, sir; except as I have stated.

Q. Do you remember what dividends you did receive prior to the time you purchased?—A. I received none of the others, because, as I have stated, this negotiation ran on pretty close to the close of the session of 1868, and when I came back my attention was called to the questions in reference to which I stated that I gave an opinion. I therefore received none of the dividends, but just sold the stock carrying the dividends with it.

Q. Do you remember what price you sold it for?—A. No; I do not remember. I authorized a gentleman to sell the stock, and it was afterward accounted for to me in a statement of accounts between us, the other matters of the account having nothing to do with the Credit Mobilier or the Union Pacific Railroad Company.

Q. Have you any memory in regard to it?—A. My impression is that that stock made me a profit in all of about $3,000.

Q. Do I understand you that you received no dividend at all, but sold it with the right to the purchaser to receive all the dividends?—A. Yes, sir; it carried all the dividends there were with the stock after my purchase, except as I have already stated.

Q. So that what you got out of it you got by the sale?—A. Yes, sir; that is it.

Q. Did you happen to know anything in relation to the holding of stock by any other members?—A. No, sir; I did not; my knowledge in this respect is all secondary. The first I heard of it was the charge published in September last in the political campaign, published originally in the New York papers.

There is one thing I want to say here, and I do not know that I shall have a better opportunity. I have been Government director of the Union Pacific Railroad for three years, and I wish to put in now my protest against the impression which seems to be getting over the country, that the investment the Government has made in this road is a loss On that question I have given my views and the views of the other Government directors in the report filed in the Interior Department. In that report we make some recommendations as to some change in the management of the affairs of the company, and I believe that with those changes made that road has sufficient capacity to pay back to the Government every dollar the Government has invested. This report is in my own handwriting, signed by myself and my co-directors, and I protest against the impression being made in the minds of the people of the country that the Government is to lose all the money it has put into that road, leaving out of the question the benefit it has already derived and is to derive in the future from the reduction of the cost of transportation.

Q. You had a certificate of ten shares?—A. No, sir. When I settled with Mr. Ames for the stock, I told him to send me a certificate, and he said he would do so. But it had not been sent to me before the winter of 1868-'69, when this question arose on which I gave my opinion, as above stated, and I said to Mr. Ames, "Just let it stand, and I will sell it as it is standing on the books of the company," and it was so sold.

Q. You never did have a certificate?—A. No, sir; for if it was ever made out in my name, it never came to me.

Q. You never transferred it to anybody?—A. No, sir.

Q. You suppose that if it had been transferred to you it would have been necessary for you to re-transfer it?—A. Of course it would have been necessary.

Q. And if it had been so transferred your name would appear on the books of the company?—A. If it had I should have re-transferred it; but I never did.

By Mr. NIBLACK:

Q. How could you sell it if you had no certificate—what evidence of ownership had you?—A. I sold it through General G. M. Dodge. General Dodge was the chief engineer of the company. He was going to New York in the winter of 1869. I authorized him to sell my interest in this ten shares of Credit Mobilier stock. The sale was made and the statement returned to me in our settlement of accounts afterward.

Q. You suppose that somebody in whose name the stock previously stood made the transfer?—A. I suppose so. I requested to have the certificate of stock made out and sent to me, but it was never done—neglected, as I suppose a good many other things are neglected, by Mr. Ames.

Q. Did you understand whether it was a personal sale by Mr. Ames, or whether he was acting on behalf of the company?—A. I knew nothing beyond this; when Mr. Ames came back from New York, as I have said, he told me he had arranged for these ten shares of stock, and I requested him to have the certificate made out and sent to me. It was then, as I recollect, pretty far along in the session of the last Congress I was a member of. I did not have any idea in the whole transaction that Mr. Ames, Mr. McComb, or anybody else was trying to influence my action as member of Congress. They knew, everybody knew, that I was a friend of this enterprise. Under the same state of facts I would do over again everything I did in connection with it.

Q. When did you become a Government director?—A. Some time in 1869, I think in the fall of 1869.

Q. Your sale of stock was not made with a view to that appointment?—A. Not in any way whatever. It had not the remotest relation to it. When I got an insight into the secrets of the Credit Mobilier, I did sell out and had no other connection with it.

By Mr. MCCRARY:

Q. Do you remember what time it was that Congress adjourned in the summer of 1868?—A. My recollection is that it was some time in July; I do not remember the exact date.

Q. Your conversation with Mr. McComb was then a month or more before the adjournment?—A. It may have been. I said it was certainly not earlier than May; that is my belief. It may have been in June. I am confident, from circumstances that I can bring to my mind, it could not have been earlier than that, and therefore I said in my statement, not earlier than May, 1868.

Q. Was your investigation into the affairs of the Credit Mobilier at the time you gave your opinion? Was it in the course of the vacation or after your return to Washington?—A. After my return to Washington, when they were organizing the movement made for the March meeting of 1869, when they changed the directors of the company. The whole thing was a mere matter of legal opinion. Some of the stockholders were restless under that proxy, and they wanted to know what power they had over their stock regardless of the proxy.

Q. You refer to the stockholders who had signed that paper to which reference has been made?—A. I do not know as to that. They were stockholders in the Union Pacific Railroad Company, and claimed the right to vote their stock regardless of the power of the seven trustees and the proxy given to them.

Q. Have you any means of fixing the date of that opinion?—A. No, I have not. It was in the winter of 1868–'69.

Q. Do I understand you to say that you considered yourself as obtaining these ten shares of stock from Mr. McComb?—A. Yes, sir; that was the purpose for which I went into the negotiation. I was negotiating the stock for Mr. McComb, and I suppose this is the first intimation Mr. Ames has had of that fact.

Q. What was the reason Mr. McComb did not take it?—A. He said to me, "If you will insist you can get the whole of it, and I want the stock on the ground-floor; that is, carrying all the dividends and everything." And this the ten shares did not do, as I understood.

Q. And you made your profit on it?—A. Yes, sir; much to my gratification. I did not know really when the stock was left on my hands whether I had made a profit or loss, but I had made the contract with Mr. Ames in my own name, without bringing in Mr. McComb at all, and I was not going to play the part of the amateur sportsman, who, on being taunted with shooting at a calf and missing it, replied that he was not certain whether it was a calf or a deer, and that he shot to hit if it was a deer, and to miss if it was a calf.

Q. Then you said nothing to Mr. Ames that you were getting it for Mr. McComb?—A. No, sir; that would have closed the whole transaction, of course. Mr. Ames, as I have said, acted solely on my statement. If he was around bribing anybody, I do not suppose it would have entered his mind to bribe a person who, from the start, was as true a friend to the Pacific Railroad legislation as a person could be.

Q. There was no legislation in Congress concerning the Pacific Railroad while you held that stock?—A. None that I recall.

By Mr. McComb:

Q. I want to ask the witness whether he thought I had backed down from my contract.—A. I thought that you considered I had not obtained the stock on the terms you wanted it. You insisted that you wanted it on the ground-floor, carrying everything with it. The negotiation had failed in anything further than the ten shares, which were not obtained on those terms.

Q. It was no bad faith on my part?—A. No; no particular bad faith. I would have been very glad at the time if you had taken the stock off from my hands, for I did not know whether there was profit or loss in it. You said if I would insist on it with Mr. Ames I could get it all. I do not think you and I met again until the latter part of the winter of 1869. Of course if I could have known all that everybody knows now I should not have had anything to do with the stock. I did not know it, and I still insist that, under the facts I had in my possession, I would do the same thing over again.

By Mr. McCrary:

Q. I understand you that Mr. McComb insisted that he should have the prior dividends, but that he did not make claim to them until you had your interview with Mr. Ames?—A. He may have supposed I knew all about it. I knew nothing about dividends or anything else as to what the stock was worth.

Q. Do you mean to be understood that, when you made your arrangement with Mr. Ames, resulting in the ten shares—that you understood that you were getting them for Mr. McComb?—A. Undoubtedly I understood that.

By Mr. AMES:

Q. And you understood that you were getting all the dividends you would be entitled to have on the ten shares of stock?—A. As I stated to you when you came back from New York and said you had arranged for ten shares at par, with the stock-dividends, and when I reported that to Mr. McComb, it was the first idea I had about the stock as to whether there had been any dividends or anything of that sort.

By Mr. MCCRARY:

Q. You discovered there had been a misunderstanding with Mr. McComb—perhaps a mistake—that he understood it one way and you another?—A. That was all. It was a mere business blunder; that was all there was of it.

Q. Do you know anything about the original subscription made by Senator Grimes to the Credit Mobilier stock?—A. Yes, sir; I do know about that. I was in Senator Grimes's room when Mr. Oakes Ames came in and requested Senator Grimes to make a subscription to the Credit Mobilier stock. I do not remember the amount. I think it was twenty or twenty-five thousand dollars he wanted him to take. Mr. Grimes said he would not do it. That while he had money, he did not want to go into anything he did not know about. They talked about it probably for half an hour, and it was in this same talk that Mr. Ames asked me to take five thousand. Mr. Ames said, we have got to have good people to go into it. We have got to raise the money, and I want you to go in. If you will go in I will agree that you shall have your money back and at least 10 per cent. interest if you will divide with me the profit there is over 10 per cent. Mr. Grimes replied, "I am satisfied with 10 per cent. for my money, and if you will guarantee that rate of interest I will take it, and divide the profits above that with you." I thereupon understood Mr. Grimes took the stock.

Q. Do you know whether Senator Grimes declined to vote upon questions touching the Pacific Railroad?—A. No; I have no knowledge on that subject at all.

Mr. SMITHERS stated that during the absence of Judge Black, and of any one representing Mr. McComb, Mr. Alley had presented to the committee a statement which he (Mr. Smithers) had not seen, but which, as he understood, Mr. Alley had submitted to counsel before presenting, and which contained personal reflections upon Mr. McComb, having no proper connection with the matters before the committee for investigation. The committee had very properly declined to permit Mr. Brooks to place before them the matters to which he alluded in the War Department, and he had understood that the statement first presented by Mr. Ames to the committee was, on motion of Judge Black, returned to Mr. Ames and a portion of it stricken out. He submitted now to the committee, as a matter of justice to Colonel McComb, the propriety of supervising the statement of Mr. Alley and erasing from it matters purely personal to Mr. McComb, and which are unjust to him.

The CHAIRMAN stated that the committee would take the matter under consideration.

WASHINGTON, D. C., *January* 18, 1873.

GEORGE W. KENNEDY sworn and examined.

By the CHAIRMAN:

Question. State your residence and occupation.—Answer. I reside at Easton, Massachusetts, and I am book-keeper for Oliver Ames & Sons.

Q. For how many years have you been with that firm?—A. Nearly ten years.

Q. Are you, and have you ever been, the owner of stock in the Credit Mobilier?—A. No, sir.

Q. Is there any stock in that company standing in your name?—A. Not that I am aware of.

Q. Had you never any information that there was stock standing in your name on the books of that company?—A. No, sir.

Q. Not from Mr. Ames?—A. No, sir.

Q. Did Mr. Ames never inform you at any time that there was a quantity of stock standing in your name?—A. No, sir.

Q. You have never received the dividends from any such stock?—A. No, sir; I think I should have remembered that.

Q. You were aware that both Oakes Ames and Oliver Ames were stockholders in that company?—A. Yes, sir; I believe so.

Q. Do you know anything in relation to sales of stock or disposition of stock by them?—A. No, sir.

Q. Did you ever hear Oakes Ames say anything upon that subject as to whom he sold stock?—A. Not that I know of.

Q. By the books of the company that have been produced here it seems that thirty shares of the stock of that company stand in your name. You have never known that fact?—A. No, sir.

Q. Mr. Ames never asked your permission to be a nominal holder of stock?—A. Not that I know of. It may be possible.

Q. If it does appear upon the books that thirty shares of stock were standing in your name, you do not know how it came to be there?—A. No.

Q. If the books show shares standing in your name, they belong to somebody else besides yourself?—A. I suppose so. I have no objection to taking it.

Q. You never purchased any, nor paid for any, and have no knowledge now that any was transferred to you?—A. No.

By Mr. MERRICK:

Q. Have you any knowledge at all of transactions of Mr. Ames in his dealings with the Credit Mobilier stock?—A. No, sir; I do not know that I have any positive knowledge.

Q. You seem to discriminate as to positive knowledge and other sort of knowledge. What knowledge have you at all, whether positive or otherwise?—A. I do not know that I have any knowledge.

Q. Are you sure you have no knowledge?—A. I do not know that I have any knowledge.

Q. Are you certain about that?—A. I do not know whether I am certain or not.

Q. Can you call to your mind anything in relation to transactions of Mr. Ames in connection with the Credit Mobilier stock?—A. No, sir; I do not know that I can in any special case.

Q. Do you know of any general case?—A. No, sir; I do not know of any.

Q. Nothing either general or special?—A. No, sir.

Mr. AMES. I do not think the witness understands your question. My idea is that he thinks you are asking about stock as trustee. He had no knowledge about any such stock.

Q. I asked you very distinctly if you knew of any dealings with Mr. Ames in reference to the stock of the Credit Mobilier with other persons, or any contracts or engagements with Mr. Ames to transfer stock to other persons, or to hold it for them.—A. I do not know that I have any positive knowledge of any such transaction.

Q. Have you any knowledge, positive or otherwise?—A. I have an impression that I have seen certificates of his for amounts of stock in the Credit Mobilier.

Q. Is that all you know about his dealings in Credit Mobilier stock—the possibility that you have seen certificates in his name?—A. All I know about it is this: that a number of years ago Mr. Ames wished me to assist him in his accounts. I was at that time employed by the firm, and I had not much time to devote, but I did a little for him. In fact, I attempted to keep some books, but I found it was more than I could attend to, and I gave it up. I kept his note accounts for him. I think I have seen, on some of his books, transactions, but I do not remember positively what they were.

Q. Transactions in reference to what?—A. Transactions in reference to Credit Mobilier stock. It was a long while ago; I have had nothing to do with these books for two years or more, and it has passed my memory.

Q. Can you recollect anything whatever, in reference to these entries and accounts that you saw in his books, touching the Credit Mobilier stock?—A. No, sir; nothing that I am sure about, at all. I never trust these things to memory. What I do I put in black and white.

Q. Have you any memory at all touching it?—A. No, sir; no positive memory; nothing that I could swear to, at all.

Q. State the best of your impressions of his dealings in Credit Mobilier stock, and transactions with other persons.—A. I think I saw, on his books, two or three entries made, of parties I supposed to be members of Congress; I am not sure of it.

Q. State to the committee what you can recollect about your impressions touching these entries.—A. I remember but very little about it.

Q. Be good enough to tell what you remember.—A. I remember nothing that I can swear to.

Q. You have just now stated that you had some recollection in connection with persons who were members of Congress.—A. I have seen so much in the newspapers about this matter that I have got it mixed up; I do not think I could separate it.

Q. You cannot separate your business transactions as a clerk for Mr. Ames from what you have read recently in the newspapers?—A. I never understood myself to be a clerk for Mr. Ames; I did a little writing for him; I kept his note-book.

Q. Do I understand that to be your answer, that there is nothing you can swear to?—A. Nothing that I can swear to positively.

Q. Have you any impression whatever, and if so, what is that impression, derived from the books as to the Credit Mobilier stock?—A. My impression is that some members of Congress, or people I supposed by the entries were members of Congress, had some of the stock.

Q. Be good enough to state, so far as your impressions enable you to state at all, who these members of Congress or any of them were.—A. I think Mr. Patterson was one.

Q. Can you state any impressions you have derived from those entries touching Mr. Patterson?—A. I think he paid some money for some stock; I should judge so from the entries. I did not see him pay the money.

Q. What other entries did you see in reference to any other member than Mr. Patterson?—A. Well, sir, I do not remember. I think I have seen three or four names that have been circulated in the papers, but the only one I seem to remember distinctly, and I do not remember certainly about him, was Mr. Patterson.

Q. Do you recollect seeing Mr. Garfield's name?—A. Not that I know of.

Q. Have you any impression at all in reference to Mr. Garfield?—A. No, I do not think I have.

Q. Have you any impression or recollection in reference to the name of Mr. Colfax?—A. I think I saw something I supposed was intended to refer to him.

Q. Can you tell us what that something was, so far as you recollect it?—A. No, sir; I remember only generally, that I recall to my memory having seen their names in the papers—that I saw three or four of them.

Q. Did you see anything in reference to Mr. Dawes, of Massachusetts?—A. No, sir; I think not. I am not sure of it.

Q. Did you see anything in reference to Mr. Wilson, of Massachusetts?—A. I think I did.

Q. What did you see there?—A. I do not remember. I only recollected generally that I saw some of those names.

Q. In what sort of books were these entries that you saw? Have you no impression where these entries were made, in what character of book, and what character of entry?—A. I think it was in some small book that Mr. Ames carried, that he took memoranda of notes from.

Q. What sort of a book?—A. I think it was a little memorandum-book in which he kept an account of his notes.

Q. Notes that were due to him?—A. Notes that he got discounted.

Q. In the book, then, in which he kept an account of the notes he had discounted from time to time, there were entries of names of these gentlemen of whom you spoke, to the best of your recollection?—A. I think I saw something of that kind.

Q. Can you give us any idea of the character of the entries?—A. No, sir.

Q. Were they brief memoranda?—A. Very brief.

Q. Did they contain the name and the amount of stock opposite the name?—A. I do not remember; I have simply an idea of seeing something of that sort. My business does not make any calls upon my memory; I put down whatever I have in black and white.

Q. You say that your memory is so defective that you cannot distinguish between knowledge you had some years ago, derived immediately from your connection with Mr. Ames, and that received from the papers you have read?—A. No, sir.

Q. You think you are certain that none of this Credit Mobilier stock stood in your name?—No, sir; it did not.

Q. You have never received a certificate?—A. Not that I know of.

Q. Do you know where those books of memoranda are now, which you had charge of, and kept at that time?—A. No, sir.

Q. They were Mr. Ames's private books?—A. Yes, sir.

Q. Have you seen, in the course of your employment as clerk of Oliver Ames & Sons, any books or accounts, or papers, relating to the Credit Mobilier?—A. There is an account on the books of O. Ames & Sons, representing Oliver Ames's subscription to the Credit Mobilier, amounting to some four thousand or five thousand shares.

Q. Or any books or accounts relative to Mr. Ames's contract in the Credit Mobilier?—A. No, sir; not that I know of.

Q. You have no knowledge in reference to that subject?—A. Only that I had charge of the stock-certificates. That is all I remember to have seen.

Q. Have you ever derived any information by conversation with Mr. Ames, or heard him say to others in your presence anything touching contracts of members of Congress, or others, in regard to the Credit Mobilier or Union Pacific Railroad?—A. No, sir.

Q. Then I understand you to say, under the obligation you have taken to tell the truth and the whole truth touching this entire matter, that you have no knowledge, direct or indirect, in regard to Mr. Ames's dealings with members of Congress, or other persons involved in the Credit Mobilier, besides what you have told?—A. I do not remember anything more than I have stated.

By Mr. SMITHERS:

Q. You spoke of a book in which these entries were made. What sort of a book, as near as you can describe it; was it a small book?—A. It was a small book.

Q. Was it a book which Mr. Ames carried in his pocket?—A. I should think he could.

Q. Was it a pocket memorandum, containing the matters of which you have spoken?—A. My impression is that it was something of that kind.

Q. It was such a book, then, as Mr. Ames carried in his pocket, in which he noted bills and notes to be discounted and other matters of that kind. It was in a book of this description that you say these entries in relation to members of Congress you have spoken of were made?—A. Yes, sir.

Q. The committee have inquired of you especially in relation to whether you had any shares of Credit Mobilier stock. Will you be good enough to say whether you had any shares of Union Pacific Railroad stock standing in your name?—A. Yes, sir; there were some.

Q. By whom were they transferred to you?—A. By Mr. Ames, I think.

Q. Were they your own—or what was the character of the transfer? Did you pay any consideration for it?—A. No, sir; I did not.

Q. Do you remember how many shares of Union Pacific Railroad stock stood in your name?—A. I think there were between six and seven hundred.

Q. They were transferred to you by Mr. Ames without consideration?—A. Yes, sir.

Q. Be good enough to state whether they were transferred in one parcel or in various parcels to you.—A. My recollection was that there were a number of smaller certificates put into one and transferred to me.

Q. Your recollection is, the stock which before stood in his name in small certificates was consolidated into one certificate and transferred to you?—A. Yes, sir.

Q. Did you or not retransfer that stock to Mr. Ames?—A. I did.

Q. You say that this large number of shares were transferred by Mr. Ames to you, without consideration, in one transfer or block?—A. I think so.

Q. Upon the retransfer to him were they transferred in one block or in smaller lots?—A. I do not remember; in fact, I am not certain that it was transferred to me all in one certificate.

Q. You had no interest in the matter as I understood?—A. No, sir.

Q. While they stood in your name it was really the stock of Mr. Ames?—A. So I understood it.

Q. And subject directly to his order. You acted under his direction?—A. Yes, sir.

Q. When you transferred it to him was it in one lot or in smaller parcels?—A. I am not certain about that at all. I remember I transferred it back.

Q. Does your memory serve you whether you transferred it to Oakes Ames individually or to Oakes Ames trustee?—A. I am not certain; I do not remember at all.

Q. Do you know for what purpose this stock was thus transferred to you and retransferred by you to Mr. Ames?—A. No, sir; I do not.

Q. Then your knowledge as to that is simply confined to the fact that such stock was transferred and retransferred, but what the object was and for what purpose it was done you do not know?—A. I do not know.

WASHINGTON, D. C., *January* 18, 1873.

C. K. GARRISON sworn and examined.

By the CHAIRMAN:

Question. You live in New York?—Answer. Yes, sir.

Q. Had you ever any connection with this company called the Credit Mobilier of America?—A. Not to the amount of $1, directly or indirectly.

Q. Or with the Union Pacific Railroad Company?—A. Not to the amount of $1, directly or indirectly, in stock or otherwise.

Q. The subject this committee are investigating is in reference to dealings with members of Congress in stock of the Credit Mobilier, by Mr. Ames or anybody else. Do you know of any members of Congress being the holders of the stock of the Credit Mobilier?—A. No, sir; I do not. I have no personal knowledge on the subject. I am entirely ignorant, so far as any dealings with members of Congress are concerned, in either of these stocks.

Q. Do you know anything in reference to James Brooks, of New York, in this connection?—A. I know nothing of my own knowledge in regard to any member of Congress or any Senator or any Government officer in this conneceion.

Q. Had you ever any conversation with Mr. Brooks, or did you hear Mr. Brooks say anything in reference to shares in that company?—A. Mr. Brooks brought Mr. Durant to me and introduced him to me. Mr. Durant desired me to take an interest in the Union Pacific Railroad, in its stock, or in this company. I had also been approached before that by another party—no one connected with the Government. After considering the matter I declined to go into it. I understood then that Mr. Durant wished to dispose of a certain interest to New Yorkers, and visited me for that purpose.

Q. Can you state about the time when this interview occurred?—A. I cannot. It was about the time the Credit Mobilier was created, as I understand it. I may be mistaken, but that is as I understand it.

Q. Was there ever any application made to you by Dr. Durant to take stock in this Credit Mobilier?—A. I believe not, to the best of my recollection.

Q. Did Mr. Brooks make application to you to take stock in it?—A. No; he simply introduced Mr. Durant to me.

Q. Did you ever hear him saying anything in reference to his having stock himself, or his son-in-law having stock?—A. No; the only information I have on that subject is the publications purporting to come from this investigation.

Q. With Mr. Brooks you never had any conversation, and never heard him say anything on that subject?—A. Mr. Brooks may have said some time subsequently that he thought I made a mistake in not going in and taking that interest I was solicited to take.

Q. Did he tell you why?—A. No; he took it for granted, I suppose, that I knew it had turned out to be a good thing.

Q. In that connection, did he say anything in relation to the stock that he had, or that his son-in-law had?—A. No; the first information I had about Mr. Brooks or his son-in-law (I did not even know he had a son in-law by that name) was the information I have from this investigation in the public journals.

Q. You are not aware that either he or his son-in-law held or contemplated holding any such interest?—A. No; I had no such knowledge from Mr. Brooks or anybody else.

Q. You had no knowledge in relation to any member of Congress having that stock?—A. No; the only information I have is from the newspapers since this investigation. I made up my mind not to go into the investment for reasons satisfactory to me.

By Mr. MERRICK:

Q. You have been familiar with Mr. Brooks for many years?—A. Yes, sir; I know him very well, personally.

Q. Did he or not ever endeavor to induce you to become the owner of Credit Mobilier stock apart from this introduction of Durant?—A. I think not. I had been approached during the presidency of General Dix, originally, to go into the Pacific Railroad, not by General Dix, but by a man named Stewart, who came to me several times, as I suppose, on the solicitation of somebody. I declined, and I had good reasons for declining, to go into the Credit Mobilier. My reasons were simply that I supposed if there was any money made in it, the chances were that it would be taken away from the parties, and that if they had any loss we would have to stand it. That was the real reason I did not go into it.

Q. What was the reason you supposed it would be taken away?—A. I merely supposed that if the parties who were going into it in the manner they went into it made anything, they would be liable to suits and annoyances, and perhaps might become personally responsible.

Q. Suits from whom?—A. From different individuals who might be holders of the stock. This was my reason. I did not at my time of life wish to hazard what I had for the purpose of possibly making a little gain.

Q. Had you any information of any probable suits?—A. No, sir; nothing more than a mere suspicion on my part.

Q. Why should there be any suits in this more than any other corporation?—A. I thought that the parties going into the Credit Mobilier might be liable in consequence of being the same parties connected with the Union Pacific Railroad Company.

Q. You remember knowing the fact that they were the same?—A. I suppose that was the general understanding. I had that impression, and consequently I did not think I could afford to take the chances. I did not know that that would be the case, but at my time of life I thought I could not afford to take the chances.

Q. I understand you to state very distinctly that you have no information, direct or otherwise, by conversation with Mr. Brooks, or otherwise, touching his connection with the Credit Mobilier, or Union Pacific Railroad Company?—A. Nothing further than I have said. The showing I had was very good, but I thought I could not afford to take the risk.

WASHINGTON, D. C., *January* 20, 1873.

SIDNEY DILLON sworn and examined.

By the CHAIRMAN:

Question. You reside in New York?—Answer. Yes, sir.

Q. Have you been connected with the Union Pacific Railroad Company as a stockholder or as an officer?—A. Yes, sir; I have been a director of the Union Pacific Railroad, and I was on the executive committee.

Q. Are you still a director?—A. I am.

Q. Have you been connected also with the Credit Mobilier as a stockholder?—A. I have.

Q. And as an officer?—A. As president.

Q. Are you now president of the company?—A. I am.

Q. And a director?—A. Yes, sir.

Q. Have you been connected with the company since it had any connection with the Union Pacific Railroad Company?—A. I think I was not connected with it in its first stages.

Q. Not connected with it when it first began to have any connection with the railroad company?—A. No, sir.

Q. How early had you any connection with the Credit Mobilier?—A. I can hardly give dates; it might be a year after its organization.

Q. Were you a stockholder in that company prior to the time when they increased the stock 50 per cent.?—A. I was.

Q. And you owned some of the original stock?—A. Yes, sir.

Q. To how large an amount?—A. Not very large. I am sorry to say that this morning I cannot give you the exact amount. I was not one of the large stockholders.

Q. Do you know anything in relation to the transaction by which a considerable number of shares were put into the hands of Mr. Durant and Mr. Ames for the purpose of enabling them to fulfill arrangements they had made in reference to the stock of that company?—A. I know that was done.

Q. Were you present at the time it was done?—A. I think I was.

Q. Do you remember that a paper was drawn up and signed by some of the principal shareholders, authorizing that to be done?—A. I do.

Q. Were you one of the signers of that paper?—A. I think I was.

Q. Do you remember what was said on that occasion by Mr. Ames and others, in reference to who the persons were that he was under obligations to, or that he desired stock to fulfill his obligations with?—A. I do not. I only understood that they had made certain agreements or obligations, and that this amount of stock was required to fulfill that obligation.

Q. Do you remember any persons that Mr. Ames said he was under obligation to?—A. I do not think that question came up at that time.

Q. Do you remember whether anything was said in relation to there being members of Congress with whom he had any negotiations for stock?—A. I think he said there were some members of Congress. I am not certain; it was a thing that I did not attach any consideration to at the time, except that there was that amount of stock that he called for to fulfill his engagements. I think there was some allowance made, but who or what or how, I do not remember any names.

Q. Do you remember whether the names of Mr. Wilson or Mr. Colfax or Mr. Garfield were mentioned?—A. I do not think there were any names mentioned to me at the time at all.

Q. Do you remember to whom any of this stock was given by Mr. Durant, or to whom he was under obligation, that he wanted the stock to enable him to fulfill?—A. I do not know, unless he may have said to me, and I am not positive of that. I have been trying to recall to my memory about these things since they begun to be talked of, but it seems to me that he said he was under obligations to Mr. Brooks. I will not swear positively that he did, but it just runs in my mind that he did.

Q. Is it your impression that Mr. Brooks was one of those named?—A. It is my impression, but I would not swear positively.

Q. Do you remember what he said in relation to the extent of his obligation to Mr. Brooks; for how large a number of shares?—A. No, sir; I do not.

Q. Do you know anything in relation to the negotiations between him and Mr. Brooks at that time?—A. No, sir.

Q. Had you known that Mr. Brooks had any connection with the enterprise, or of his making efforts to get people to take stock in the company?—A. I had not.

Q. You had known nothing in relation to Mr. Brooks's efforts in connection with the company?—A. I always knew that Mr. Brooks was a firm friend. He would come into the office occasionally, back and forth. That is all I know about it.

Q. What you knew was that he was a supporter and advocate of the Pacific Railroad?—A. Yes, sir.

Q. Had you any knowledge in reference to the transfer of these 100 shares to Mr. Durant?—A. I have no knowledge.

Q. It seems that 100 shares were transferred to Mr. Durant, which he had transferred to Mr. Neilson, Mr. Brooks's son-in-law. Do you know Neilson?—A. Yes, sir.

Q. You say you have no knowledge of how it was done, or why they were transferred to Neilson instead of Mr. Brooks?—A. No, sir.

Q. Did you hear anything said by Mr. Brooks, or by Mr. Durant, in reference to that?—A. I never changed a word with Mr. Durant about it, if I recollect right, except I think I heard him make mention that he had got to let Mr. Brooks have some stock. That is my impression.

Q. Had you any knowledge in relation to the subsequent transaction by which 50 shares were transferred or issued directly by the company to Mr. Neilson?—A. Yes, sir.

Q. Will you state what you know in reference to that transaction?—A. About the time of the transfer of the 50 shares, Mr. Durant went to Europe. He was formerly the president of the Credit Mobilier and the vice-president of the Union Pacific Railroad Company. After his leaving for Europe, Mr. Brooks came in one day and said to me, "Mr. Neilson has received of Durant a certain amount of stock." I think he named 100 shares, and there was an increase on the Credit Mobilier stock at a certain time. (That is the only way I knew how these things took place.) If Mr. Neilson got 100 shares prior to that time, he would be entitled to 50 shares more. Mr. Brooks said to me that he considered him entitled to those 50 shares. After talking some little time with him, I said to him I would consult a majority of the stockholders of the Credit Mobilier, and, if they thought well of it, I would recommend, according to his statement, that he should get it. I did consult with quite a number of the stockholders, and I not only consulted, but I took the precaution to get up a paper whereby quite a number of the stockholders of the Credit Mobilier sanctioned the proposition to issue the 50 shares more. I made that fact known to Mr. Brooks, when he said to me—I cannot word the exact phrase he used—the substance of it was that he would transfer any interest he had to Mr. Neilson. That was the purport of it. The stock was so transferred to Mr. Neilson, and in due time he came to get the 50 shares. This occurred a long time ago, and I had forgotten it entirely. If I had been asked by the committee at the first stages of the talk on this subject, I would have said I had no recollection about it. But, upon due reflection, it seems to me that when Mr. Neilson came for the stock he borrowed some money of me, I think about $5,000, to pay for the additional stock. As far as keeping any account, it is all on the books of my clerk. I am in a large business, in railroad business generally. I will say to the committee, at the present time, they must pardon me if I do not give the dates, for the reason that I never take care of them. I have men I trust all these things to, to bring them up when the proper time arrives. I leave it for them to take care of the details.

Q. Now, to go back a little; did Mr. Durant pay for the stock which was transferred to him by the company?—A. He did, as I understand it.

Q. I understand the one hundred shares of stock arranged for, and which was, in point of fact, transferred to Neilson, was first transferred to Mr. Durant?—A. That is as I understand it.

Q. Do you understand now, that, by Mr. Neilson becoming the holder of one hundred shares, he was, in point of fact, entitled to fifty shares additional?—A. I did understand it so, and I understand it so now, that he was entitled to fifty shares.

Q. Did you also understand that, upon these same shares Mr. Durant had, he had had the privilege of taking the additional 50 per cent.?—A. I did not understand it so at the time I had this conversation with Mr. Brooks. About the fifty shares, I think he said there had been some little talk between him and Durant, he asking Durant for it, or something of that sort; that there was some misunderstanding. I had made up my mind, when he came for the fifty shares, that it was a small matter not fully understood, and that, when Durant returned from Europe, the thing would be fixed up satisfactorily all around. That is the way I felt at the time.

Q. If Mr. Brooks or Mr. Neilson was entitled, by the ownership of the one hundred shares, to the 50 per cent. increase, what was the necessity of getting up a paper, and getting the authority of the principal shareholders?—A. The necessity was that, while Mr. Brooks said, (and I took his statement,) that Mr. Neilson was entitled to this, I felt that if I got a majority of the shareholders to agree to it I should be sustained in what I did; that I was pretty near right.

Q. If you had been entirely clear that he was entitled to fifty shares, you would not have supposed there was any necessity to get the consent of the stockholders?—A. If the one hundred shares had been bought from the Credit Mobilier, and held as stock belonging to him, I would not have been obliged to have gone to the stockholders to get their consent. But, as it came from prior stock, which, as I understood, Mr. Durant had laid aside, or called his, to distribute among others, I considered it discretion upon my part to do what I did.

Q. The point is, if you had supposed it to be clear that he was entitled to fifty shares, you would have issued them to him as a matter of course?—A. Exactly so.

Q. Have you that paper which was gotten up and signed at the time?—A. I have not.

Q. Or any copy of it?—A. I have not.

Q. Have you any knowledge in relation to what has become of the paper?—A. I do not know where it is. I say again, although I am president of the Credit Mobilier at the present time—that noble Credit Mobilier—yet I have not a paper belonging to it. I have trusted them entirely to our secretary to get whatever there was; there were not a great many papers.

Q. The proper place for this paper, if it is in existence, would be in the possession of Mr. Ham, your secretary?—A. Yes, sir.

Q. Was the paper ever in your possession?—A. I think it was in my possession at one time, and that it was either sent or I took it to Boston to get the names of parties who were interested—some of the Boston stockholders.

Q. Have you any recollection what you did with the paper?—A. I think it was placed, with the other papers, in the hands of the secretary.

Q. Have you ever made any search among your own papers, and had your attention called to it to look for it?—A. I had my attention called to it by my summons to this place, but I find I have no papers of the Credit Mobilier in my possession.

Q. Have you looked among your papers to be satisfied?—A. I am satisfied I have not got it.

Q. State as well as you can from memory what the substance was.—A. I cannot word it, and I cannot recollect the substance, except that it was a paper by which they conceded or agreed that Mr. Brooks was entitled to have fifty shares. I cannot say how it was, for I have not seen it for several years.

Q. It was giving their consent to your allowing this claim of Mr. Brooks for fifty shares?—A. Yes, sir.

Q. How much did Mr. Neilson pay for that stock?—A. My impression is that he paid par and interest, whatever it was.

Q. Interest from the previous July?—A. I think interest from the time; the interest which had accrued upon it.

Q. Do you remember the time when the certificate of stock was issued to Neilson?—A. I cannot tell from memory; I have nothing to refresh my recollection with; I have not seen the books.

Q. Was it as late as the 26th February, 1868?—A. The books will show; I cannot say. You must not ask me for dates.

Q. Before the 26th February, 1868, various dividends had been declared on the Credit Mobilier stock. Did they not begin to declare large dividends on that stock as early as December, 1867?—A. I never knew they ever did declare large dividends on the Credit Mobilier stock.

Q. Dividends under this trusteeship of the Ames contract?—A. There were dividends under the trustees.

Q. The point I want to get at is this: was Mr. Brooks or Mr. Neilson, or whoever became the owner of the fifty shares transferred to Neilson, to be entitled to all the dividends that had been previously declared, or only the dividends declared after it was issued?—A. I cannot tell you now.

Q. Do you know what was the value of this Credit Mobilier stock—what it sold for in the market, or what any had been sold for prior to that time?—A. I could not say what it sold for prior to that time. It sold at different times for different prices.

Q. Do you remember what prices it bore at any time?—A. I think it has been sold for 140, and I think some has been sold as high as 200.

Q. Do you think that was as early as the winter of 1867-'68?—A. I cannot give you the dates; you will pardon me.

Q. At the time the negotiation you had in relation to the issue of these 50 shares, was all with Mr. Brooks?—A. Yes, sir; and Mr. Neilson.

Q. Did you have any negotiation at all with Neilson or on that subject until he came to pay for it?—A. Nothing at all that I recollect.

Q. Had you seen Neilson or had any conversation with him until he came to get the stock?—A. I think not.

Q. Did Mr. Brooks say anything to you as to who would pay for it, or how it was to be paid for, and when?—A. I think he did not at first; when it was decided that he was to have fifty shares I think he then said to me that he gave his option or interest, or whatever you might call it—that he transferred it or gave it to Neilson.

Q. Did you know then, or did he tell you then, that the one hundred shares had been transferred to Neilson?—A. I did not then know whether it stood in Neilson's name or in Brooks's name.

Q. Did you suppose Mr. Brooks was negotiating with you on his own account or in his own behalf?—A. I did not suppose anything about it; I took it as he said that it was thus and so; I supposed he was telling me what was true at the time.

Q. At the time this paper was signed do you know whether Mr. Brooks's name or Mr. Neilson's name was used in the paper?—A. I do not.

Q. Did you write the paper yourself?—A. No, sir; I did not.

Q. Do you know who did?—A. I should think it was written by the secretary, Mr. Ham; still, it may have been written by our attorney, Judge Emmett, or by Mr. Hammond, or Mr. Pomeroy. I would sometimes—whenever a paper was wanted—go to our attorney and ask him to draw up something that would answer the purpose, but who wrote this I do not know.

Q. It was not a paper that required much legal formality?—A. No; it was not.

Q. State as well as you remember whose names were attached to that paper.—A. I think Oliver Ames's name was. I will not swear positively. I think Mr. Atkins and Mr. Glidden, of Boston, signed it, and Mr. Williams.

Q. Did Mr. Alley?—A. I do not think Mr. Alley's name was on it, or that Oakes Ames's name was on it. There were several in Boston. I cannot recall their names. If I could see a list of the Boston stockholders I could give you their names. There were quite a number.

Q. Were these gentlemen privy to the negotiation, or did they sign it on your representation?—A. They signed it on my recommendation.

Q. You say that when Mr. Neilson came to get the certificate of stock he then wanted to borrow the money to pay for it?—A. He asked me to loan him some money.

Q. Was that the first that you heard in reference to his wanting to borrow money?—A. That was the first time I had heard of it.

Q. Mr. Brooks said nothing to you in relation to paying for it, or how you were to pay for it?—A. Not that I recollect.

Q. You loaned the money to Mr. Neilson, $5,000 and the interest?—A. Yes, sir.

Q. Did he give you a note or obligation for the money?—A. I hardly know what he did give me at the present time. He gave me something which was satisfactory to me; I cannot now say what. Almost all these transactions I make in loaning money or borrowing money are done directly through my secretary. If I say I want to borrow $5,000 or $50,000, if I can get it, I place the securities in his hands, and he goes and gets it. And if I loan $5,000 or 50,000, I say to him, get such and such collaterals and give the money. I may not be right; but I trust a great deal to my subordinates.

Q. Do you remember what was said between you and Neilson in reference to security to you for the money?—A. I think this, that I ordered my secretary to let him have $5,000, or about that amount, and that he offered to give me—it is just in my mind at this time—some Union Pacific Railroad securities, or Credit Mobilier securities, or something like that; I cannot tell just what the security was.

Q. Has that money been repaid to you?—A. I cannot say. I think it has. I could tell by an examination of my accounts. I cannot tell now.

Q. Did you look at your books or accounts before you came here to see if that loan was still outstanding?—A. I did not.

Q. Is it your belief now that it has been paid?—A. It would be very strange if it has not been paid. I think it has.

Q. Have you any recollection when, how, or by whom it was paid?—A. That would not come to my knowledge unless I made special inquiry. It would come to my office if it was paid; my secretary would say to me that the negotiation had been closed; but I should not keep it in my head all this time; I would not try; on the contrary, I would try to keep it out of my head as much as possible. I wish to state to the committee all I know about it; but, as I have stated, I am very forgetful about dates and such things, and you must pardon me for it.

By Mr. NIBLACK:

Q. Is there not somebody in your office who could tell?—A. I think I can find it in due time. I could ascertain when it was paid, or whether it was paid at all, or not.

Q. You could ascertain more from your books than from memory?—A. Yes, sir; I think I can ascertain, and I will endeavor to do so.

Q. In relation to this increase of stock, we have understood from witnesses that when the increase was made, every stockholder who subscribed to the increase was entitled to the same amount in Pacific Railroad bonds. If he took a thousand dollars of stock he was entitled to a thousand dollars of bonds?—A. I think that was the case.

Q. How was it in relation to these fifty shares which Mr. Brooks or Mr. Neilson had?—A. Well, sir, I cannot tell you how it was in relation to that. If either had those one hundred shares prior to the time the increase was made, he would be entitled to the fifty shares increase.

Q. That is, if Mr. Brooks or Mr. Neilson was entitled to come in and take the fifty shares increase, he would also be entitled to the same amount of Union Pacific Railroad bonds?—A. If it showed so on the books. It would if Mr. Durant had the stock standing in his own name at the time the increase was made. He would be entitled to the increase of stock and to the bonds; I say, "if"—I do not know, and do not say, whether he was or not.

Q. Do you know whether in the talk or negotiation that occurred when you got up this paper for the signatures of the stockholders that point came up? Whether it was talked of that Mr. Brooks and Mr. Neilson were or were not entitled to the additional fifty shares, and whether they were also entitled to the $5,000 of railroad bonds?—A. I do not think it was discussed. I do not remember that it was talked of at the time.

Q. But you say if he was entitled to have the stock by virtue of his being the owner of the one hundred shares when the stock was increased, he would have been entitled to the Union Pacific bonds?—A. In other words, if that one hundred shares had been placed on the books in the name of Mr. Brooks or Mr. Neilson prior to the time of the increase, he would have been entitled to take that increase and to have the bonds; but if it was in the name of Durant at that time, and Durant had come in and taken that increase, and I had let him have the fifty shares, then the question comes up whether Mr. Brooks would have had the bonds, or whether he would not have to fall back on Mr. Durant for the bonds. That is all there is of it, for they could not both have had the same bonds and the same stock.

Q. Do you know whether in point of fact Neilson did receive $5,000 Union Pacific Railroad bonds with the fifty shares?—A. I do not know; I cannot tell you.

Q. Have you any further knowledge of Mr. Ames parting with any of those shares assigned to him?—A. I have not.

Q. You do not know to whom he sold them, or transferred them?—A. No, sir.

Q. You have no knowledge from him on that subject?—A. No, sir.

Q. I understand that in the negotiation you had with Mr. Brooks in regard to the proposed increase of stock which he claimed that he was entitled to, you do not remember whether Brooks, Neilson, or anybody else's name was mentioned? The question in negotiation was whether they should have the stock?—A. When Mr. Brooks came to me he said he was entitled to so much stock, but when he found that it was going to be given to him by the majority of the stockholders of the Credit Mobilier, he then said directly in substance that it was to go to his son-in-law, and not to him.

By Mr. BANKS:

Q. Let me ask you if, when the claim was made for the increase of Credit Mobilier stock by anybody else, that claim was decided by you as president, or by a majority of the board of directors?—A. It would be decided generally by the executive committee.

Q. Then the paper you speak of was a substitute for the order of the executive committee. If they had been present you would have submitted it to them, and you would have had no occasion to go to the stockholders?—A. Probably in order to save myself from possible censure I would have still gone to the stockholders of the Credit Mobilier. Although the executive committee have the power of the board of directors, it has always been my course in life to consult the stockholders as far as possible—the large stockholders, particularly—to avoid seeming to take an arbitrary course which would be distasteful to them. I therefore took this precaution to get a large number of the stockholders to sign this paper, so that in case it should be not in strict accordance with the regular course of proceeding I would have something to fall back upon.

Q. Then if the board of directors had been in session when the claim was made you would have submitted the matter directly to them?—A. I do not know. I might have got a paper signed whether there was a meeting of the board of directors or not. That was my general way of doing things.

By Mr. McCRARY:

Q. You were president of the board of directors at the time the stock was called for by Mr. Brooks?—A. I think so.

Q. Did he or you suggest getting up the paper?—A. I cannot tell; I think Mr. Brooks had not anything to do with it. I do not know that he did. I don't recollect that there was any conversation between him and me in regard to the matter at all.

Q. He applied to you, as I understand, for fifty shares additional to the amount of the whole, and you declined to issue it until this paper was signed?—A. Yes, sir; I think I took it into consideration after his talk with me, and after due consideration I took this course upon my own suggestion.

Q. Did you announce to him that you had come to the conclusion to have the signatures of a majority of the stockholders?—A. I do not recollect that I had any conversation with Mr. Brooks about it.

Q. Did you take the paper yourself to the stockholders?—A. I cannot say for certain whether I did, or whether I sent my secretary. I got the names of certain parties on it.

Q. Do you know whether Mr. Brooks applied to any of the stockholders, urging them to sign?—A. I do not. I do not know that he knew what I was trying to do. I think I said I would consult either the executive committee or the stockholders, or somebody, and see him again. I think I passed him off in some such way.

Q. I understood you to say that it was after you had obtained the consent of a majority of the stockholders that Mr. Brooks told you that he had assigned the stock to Neilson?—A. I think it was. I would not be confident, it was so long ago. It was, I think, after he knew that he was to get it.

Q. If that be the case, then, Mr. Neilson's name was probably in the paper which was signed?—A. I do not recollect that it was in it at all. I want you to understand that I am not explicit or certain whether it was before or after the paper was signed.

Q. You don't know, then, whether that paper was an agreement that fifty shares might be issued to Mr. Brooks or Mr. Neilson?—A. I think it was to Mr. Brooks; that is my recollection. I think Mr. Brooks said that was his right, and when he found he could get what he called his rights, it was then stated to me that it was for Neilson. I cannot give his exact words.

Q. Was there not a good deal of discussion and controversy as to the right of Mr. Brooks to these fifty shares, about the time of getting up that paper?—A. No; I do not think there was.

Q. Did not stockholders object to it and refuse to sign the paper?—A. I do not think any one refused that I talked with about it.

Q. Did you know of any one refusing?—A. I do not know; there may have been a refusal. I do not know whether there was or not.

Q. You did not hear Mr. Alley make any objections to issuing the fifty shares?—A. I did not ask Mr. Alley about it.

Q. You do not know of any conversation between him and Mr. Brooks about it?—A. No, sir; I do not.

Q. You do not know in whose name the original one hundred shares stood on the books?—A. No, sir; I do not.

Q. You must have supposed it stood in the name of Mr. Brooks at the time when he applied for the additional fifty shares?—A. I do not know whether it was in Mr. Brooks's name, or Neilson's name, or in anybody else's name. I took him to be the first owner. I supposed the statement he had made was true, but I went about getting it fixed up.

Q. And that statement was, that by virtue of his holding one hundred shares he was entitled to fifty additional shares? Did you look at the books to see whether there were one hundred shares standing in his name?—A. I do not think I did. I never looked at the books. Whatever I took, I took from my secretary in words.

Q. Would you have taken the steps you did to secure Mr. Brooks the additional fifty shares if you had not believed at the time that he held the one hundred original shares?—A. I would not have taken the steps I did if I had not considered he was entitled to fifty shares.

Q. If the books at that time showed that the one hundred original shares stood in the name of Neilson, you would have considered Neilson entitled to the additional fifty shares?—A. I should have been required to find out whether Mr. Brooks had transferred that stock to Neilson before I should have done anything.

Q. You do not know whether that stock stood in Mr. Brooks's name on the book, and whether it has since been changed?—A. No, sir; I don't.

Q. If the books should show that some name had been erased where the name of Neilson appears, the Neilson substituted, would you say that it had probably been done since the fifty shares were issued to Mr. Brooks or Neilson?—A. I could not say that. There might have been a mistake on the books, and there might have been erasures.

Q. Would you not have remembered it, if you had looked at the books and found the stock at that time standing in the name of Neilson?—A. I say I never looked at the books to see whether Mr. Brooks's or Neilson's name was there. I took the statements made verbally to me by my secretary.

Q. If your secretary had told you that the stock stood in the name of Brooks, and that Mr. Brooks applied for the fifty shares to be issued in the name of Neilson, would not that fact have made an impression on your mind that you would have remembered?—A. I could not say that it would. In the hundreds of thousands of dollars of business we were doing then, I do not think the details of a little transaction of fifty shares would have impressed itself upon my mind so that I should be likely to remember it.

Q. How did Mr. Brooks apply for the stock?—A. I do not remember that.

Q. Do you remember you took steps to secure it for him?—A. I do.

Q And do you remember that you got up a paper in order that he might obtain it, and got the names of the stockholders on the paper?—A. I do.

Q. You remember the ground on which he was entitled to it was because he owned one hundred shares, or because he said he owned them, and if your secretary had told you that Mr. Brooks was applying for fifty shares as an increase of stock standing in the name of Neilson, another man altogether, would you not have remembered it?—A. I suppose I would.

Q. Then the presumption is that the stock stood in the name of Mr. Brooks, and not in the name of Neilson, at that time?—A. No; I do not presume that. If I knew I would tell you.

By Mr. MERRICK:

Q. Do you recollect whether the paper which was drawn up in reference to the fifty shares, which you have just spoken of, included the transactions of any other parties than this specific one of Neilson?—A. I do not think it did.

Q. It applied explicitly to this transaction in reference to these fifty shares, and embraced no other?—A. I think that is the fact; I am not certain.

By the CHAIRMAN:

Q. Did you have more than one interview with Mr. Brooks on the subject of these fifty shares?—A. I might have had; I almost think I had two; I am not certain.

Q. Where were these interviews?—A. I think the first interview was in the Union Pacific Railroad office.

Q. Was that and the Credit Mobilier office kept together?—A. They were in the same building, in adjoining rooms.

Q. Have you any special memory as to the room it was in?—A. I think I met him in the hall or entry-way between the two rooms; I am not certain about that. I know it was in the building at one time when we had a conversation on the subject. I think he asked me at another time what I thought about it, or if I had done anything about it, or something of that sort.

Q. Have you any recollection who were present in the rooms at the time of either of the interviews?—A. I do not. I think it likely the proper officers and clerks about the building.

Q. Have you any recollection whether Mr. Alley was about there on either occasion?—A. He was not there. That is to say, that he was not there that I recollect. I do not recollect seeing him there, and I do not think he was there.

Q. Do you recollect whether Mr. McComb was there either time?—A. I do not recollect whether he was there or not.

Q. In these conversations that you had with Mr. Brooks, did he say anything in relation to what he could or would do provided he had these fifty shares? Did he say anything about his connection with Congress, or about his being a Government director? Did he hold out any inducement to you to let him have the stock as to any supposed influence he could exert?—A. No, sir; there was no talk of that kind at all at the time. He got it wholly upon the ground that it was his right.

Q. He said nothing in regard to any influence he could exert in favor of the company, either in Congress or as a Government director, in any way?—A. No, sir.

Q. Do you know whether any argument of that sort was used by him or anybody else to any of the shareholders?—A. I do not.

By Mr. BROOKS:

Q. If I had not held the one hundred shares, but they had been in the name of Neilson, to whom would the fifty shares be transferable by right?—A. At the time of the increase, if the one hundred shares had been on the books in the name of Neilson, the fifty shares would have been issued by right to Neilson.

Q. When I made some remark about this one hundred shares carrying with it the right to the additional fifty shares, did I not put it on the ground that it was involved in an agreement with Mr. Durant; that it was part of the legacy of the one hundred shares purchased?—A. I considered it so, and you did say that the one hundred shares carried with it the right to fifty shares.

By the CHAIRMAN:

Q. You stated that Mr. Brooks assigned these shares to Neilson. Were these shares in the possession of Mr. Brooks?—A. I did not mean that. I meant to be understood that the rights were assigned or transferred to Neilson. I am not a lawyer, and I cannot give the phraseology I wish to. What I meant was, that the right to these fifty shares had been in some way transferred to Neilson.

By Mr. BROOKS:

Q. Did you ever know of Mr. Brooks receiving any dividends from any of the shares entered upon the books of the company?—A. No, sir.

By Mr. SMITHERS:

Q. What is the name of the secretary who you say is familiar with the monetary part of this transaction?—A. B. F. Ham.

Q. Was Mr. Ham your private secretary and the secretary of the Credit Mobilier?—A. For this specific purpose, he was.

Q. Then, the facts of which you speak and of which you are ignorant, you suppose to be in the possession of Mr. Ham?—A. Yes, sir; I do.

Q. Do you mean us to understand that Mr. Ham attends to your private business?—A. I mean you to understand that in the early part of the Credit Mobilier transactions he did some of my private business. I was not in my own office; my office being in another street and in another place. I now believe and understand that the transaction of that business was done by Mr. Ham, by my order, for me.

By the CHAIRMAN:

Q. You stated, when I inquired what securities you got for the money you loaned Mr. Neilson, or whether you had any, that your secretary would know; did you mean Mr. Ham?—A. He is now my secretary in the office I occupy at No. 50 Wall street; that is, he is one of my secretaries; I have two or three. If I have a railroad contract, I have a secretary to attend to that. If I have a little contract, or bond transaction in the city, I have another man who attends to that expressly, and they have quite enough to do. Mr. Ham has to attend to that branch of my business.

By Mr. SMITHERS:

Q. The object of my question was to specify in relation to this information as to the persons who could give it.—A. I think B. F. Ham is the person could give you that information.

By Mr. NIBLACK:

Q. Mr. Ham testified the other day that he did not know about this.—A. He might not know it here; but he might know it after looking over my papers in New York. I have stated, as far as I understand, all about it.

By Mr. SMITHERS:

Q. Your impression is, if I understand you, that if this money was repaid, which you loaned, Mr. Ham would be the proper person to give the information in answer to that question?—A. That is my impression at this moment. It was repaid, no doubt.

Q. Do you remember whether, at the time the loan was made, there were any other papers executed between you and Mr. Neilson?—A. I do not.

Q. Do you remember whether, in fact, he pledged Union Pacific bonds in security for the loan?—A. I think there was some hypothecation of some sort; I cannot tell what it was.

Q. These are matters which would be in the possession of your secretary?—A. He may have transferred that transaction over to my other secretary. I don't know how that is, and I cannot answer, as the matter stands, any further now on that point.

Q. Do you remember whether at the time you executed or gave to Neilson a receipt for the money which he paid you for these shares of stock?—A. I do not recollect the transaction; I cannot recollect it.

By Mr. McCRARY:

Q. You do not know what has become of the Credit Mobilier?—A. I do not know, except that they are in the office of the secretary. There was, as perhaps some of you have known, quite a raid made on our books and papers for a year or two.

Q. You do not know who made way with them and got them out of the New York courts?—A. If there are any lost I do not know where they are. My secretary has been sick; I telegraphed to him on Saturday to know if he could come on with me here. I desired he should be here and straighten this thing up to your satisfaction. He replied that he was sick in bed. I should have been here last week if my own family had not been sick, and another reason was that I wanted him here with me.

Q. What was your business originally?—A. I am a contractor of railroads.

Q. On what railroads have you been a contractor?—A. I noticed some time ago a history of my life, in which I see I have been a contractor on about thirty railroads.

Q. Mention some of the largest of them.—A. I was on the Western Railroad, from Boston to Albany. I had some large contracts on that road, which I finished up in 1846. I was on the Rutland and Burlington Railroad, the Vermont and Massachusetts Railroad, the Connecticut River Railroad, the Philadelphia and Erie, the Hartford and Springfield Railroad, and several large railroads in that section. I am now interested strongly in a road called the Canada Southern, running from Buffalo to near Detroit, with an extension to Chicago, and likewise with an extension from Detroit to Toledo. I have just now taken a contract in the city of New York with Mr. Vanderbilt for sinking track, to the amount of about $5,000,000. I was also a contractor on the Northern Central Road.

Q. State whether in your connection with these railroads at different times you had any different book-keepers and secretaries.—A. I had different men for the different works I was engaged on.

Q. Is it, then, in your power, or would it be in the power of any man, to keep the run of these transactions in detail?—A. I am not a detail man. I have some secretaries who have been with me ten or fifteen years. I get good men; pay them well for it, and they keep my accounts up pretty close, and bring my dealings into such shape that I can understand very easily whether they are about right without going into the exact details. I have no time, and I cannot do it.

Q. In relation to the Credit Mobilier operations, I understand Mr. Ham was your secretary?—A. Yes, sir.

By Mr. ALLEY:

Q. Had I anything to do with that transaction with Mr. Brooks in any shape or manner? Did I ever give him any information or have any conversation with him in reference to it to your knowledge?—A. I don't know what conversations you may have had with him; you did not in my hearing.

Q. Were you ever spoken to upon the subject by me?—A. I do not think I was.

Q. You have no recollection of my ever having said anything or done anything about it?—A. I have not.

Q. You feel quite sure that my name is not on that paper?—A. I cannot say certainly; I do not think it is.

Q. It has been stated here that I had a great deal to do in the Credit Mobilier—more than anybody else; in fact, that I was captain, mate, and all hands. Was I as frequently present at the office in New York, and did I have as much to do with it, as Mr. Hazard?—A. Whenever I could catch you and Mr. Hazard together, I consulted you both. I considered that one was the same as the other. I think as Mr. Hazard was in New York oftener than you, I met him oftener than you, or than with both of you together.

Q. Was he not in New York much more frequently; in fact, three times oftener than I was?—A. I do not know; I think he was there oftener at that time.

Q. So that you think he had more to do with these matters than I, for the reason that I was less frequently there?—A. I think we met oftener together and consulted. The committee of three were not very often together, if you recollect; when any two, yourself or either of us, met, we constituted a majority to do any business.

Q. It was a committee of three?—A. Yes.

Q. Had the executive committee anything to do at all with this matter of Mr. Brooks as far as you remember?—A. I do not think it had.

The CHAIRMAN. We wish you to make such an examination that will enable us to have all the light you can give us in relation to the fifty shares of stock, the security you took, and when and by whom the loan was paid.

The WITNESS. I will endeavor to furnish it so far as I can.

WASHINGTON, D. C., *January* 21, 1873.

THOMAS C. DURANT recalled and examined.

By the CHAIRMAN:

Question. I think you stated the other day that you had copies of the books kept by this trusteeship of the Oakes Ames contract?—Answer. I had up to the time of the last dividend.

Q. Have you a copy of any of the books of the Credit Mobilier?—A. I have copies of them up to 1867. The original books are, however, here in Washington.

Q. It was said by Mr. Ham that the transfer-book had been lost?—A. I have a copy of the transfer-books up to 1867 or 1868.

Q. Was the stock that was put into your hands at the same time Mr. Ames had a certain number of shares given to him, to enable you and him to fulfill engagements which you had made—was this the stock which you had to distribute, and transfer to the persons with whom you had engagements?—A. Certainly it was, I think with one exception; and I think I settled that one claim.

Q. Do you remember these transfers appeared upon this copy of the book you have?—A. All the transfers I made appear upon that book.

Q. The book you have will show all the transfers that were made by you?—A. Yes. sir.

Q. Do you know whether any of the persons to whom you made these transfers held the stock for the benefit of any member of Congress?—A. I think not; I have no idea they did.

Q. You had no reason to suppose or believe that any member of Congress had any interest in any of the stock you parted with, except in the cases you have named?—A. I had not.

Q. Have you a list of the persons to whom you transferred stock?—A. Here is a list of persons to whom I transferred this stock.

Q. Do you remember the time this stock was assigned to you?—A. I do not; I claimed the stock early in 1867, on my promises.

Q. You received the stock for the purpose of enabling you to fulfill your engagements, at the same time this was assigned to Mr. Ames?—A. My engagements were to the extent of some seventy or eighty thousand dollars. I transferred much of it from my own stock, and when they gave me this, it was some of it used to replace the stock I had transferred.

Q. Was the portion you received from the company transferred to you at the same time the assignment of shares was made to Mr. Ames for the same purpose?—A. Yes, I presume it was at the same time. They were closing up their books then.

Q. Do you remember when that was?—A. I think these transfers were made in the month of December, 1867.

Q. Then all the transfers you made of that stock to fulfill your engagements would be subsequent to that date?—A. Not necessarily, because it was to replace the stock I had previously delivered. The books will not show the dates of the transfer on my part. It is customary in New York, among brokers, to receive certificates of one hundred shares of my stock transferable and payable on the indorsement of a blank power of attorney, and the certificates may pass from hand to hand to half a dozen owners before any transfer will be made on the books of the company.

Q. The paper you have given me shows that the only transfer after January 1, 1868, is to Henry Blood. Here is J. B. Johnston, who, under date of December 11, is down for two hundred shares.—A. That was collateral for a loan; it was not a sale.

Q. December 20, J. B. Alley two hundred and fifty shares.—A. That was the same call given on December 12 or 13. The circumstances under which that was made were these: When the trustees were discussing the matter of declaring the first dividend, Mr. Ames was very anxious the dividend should be made, but Mr. Alley was for delay. Mr. Bushnell remarked to me that Mr. Alley had sold out his stock pretty largely, and that Mr. Ames had promised stock; that they were short of stock; that they had sold at high prices; that nothing could be done with Alley until he had got his stock back again. We adjourned the trustees for twenty minutes, and I sold Mr. Alley a call at 160. When the trustees met again, Mr. Alley voted for the dividend.

Q. Was that intended to be a real sale?—A. O, yes. He called for the stock, and it was transferred to him the 20th December.

Q. It was, then, a real sale?—A. It was a real sale, under the circumstances that I have mentioned.

Q. B. M. Boyer's name is given here at seventy-five shares; you have already spoken of that. The next, under date of December 26, is C. H. Neilson, one hundred shares. We also have an account of that. The next is, December 27, H. C. Crane. That also you have testified to.—A. Yes, sir.

Q. Was that a sale of the number of shares given from you to Mr.

Crane?—A. My impression is now that I had it transferred to him for the purpose of enabling me to transfer it to meet some of these obligations I had incurred. I had transferred them all out of my own stock, and he held this stock for me.

Q. Is it still standing in his name?—A. I think it has been transferred to me.

Q. This was not a sale, then?—A. No.

Q. Have you any recollection of the purpose for which this transfer was made to Mr. Crane?—A. I think he took it in the way I have stated. If any obligations had not been fulfilled he would have transferred the proper amount of stock to the parties. The transfer-books will show to whom it has been transferred.

Q. Did he hold it for the benefit of any member of Congress?—A. No one whatever.

Q. The next on the list is J. Bardwell, two hundred and fifty shares.—A. Yes; Mr. Bardwell, of Boston. I sold it to him.

Q. That was a real sale?—A. That was a real sale; yes, sir.

Q. Have you any reason to suppose that Mr. Bardwell did not make the purchase for himself on his own account?—A. I am not positive, but he told me Mr. McComb had an interest in it.

Q. Had any member of Congress any interest in it?—A. O, no; it was his own investment.

Q. He holds it yet, as you suppose?—A. I suppose he does. I know nothing to the contrary.

Q. The next on the list is December 26, J. Hedden, one hundred shares.—A. He is a broker in Wall street. He holds the stock yet.

Q. Do you suppose or believe him to be the real owner of it? Was it a purchase for himself?—A. Certainly; he has always had his dividends. He has been unfortunate in business, and I understand it is among the assets of his creditors.

Q. December 31, J. B. Piggot, one thousand shares.—A. That was collateral security on a loan. That has been returned to me.

Q. That is now your stock?—A. That is my stock; yes, sir.

Q. January 9, Henry Blood, seven shares.—A. That was an interest Mr. Blood had, with I don't know whom. He was one of the original subscribers, and some of his stock stood in my name. He is a Wall-street man.

Q. This list covers all that appears on this copy of your transfer-book?—A. I think so. I had it made from the original book.

Q. You believe this covers all the transfers you have made to anybody; and you believe you have made no transfers since then?—A. No, sir; I think I have not.

Q. At the same time this stock was assigned by the company to you and Mr. Ames, and divided between you, to enable you to fulfill your engagements, did that assignment to you cover all the stock of the company except what was held by private stockholders?—A. I think it did. I have the names of the stockholders. I think it covered nearly all. This is that six hundred and fifty shares of stock which, in May, 1867, after I put the injunction on the Union Pacific Railroad against contracting with the Credit Mobilier, by direction of the Credit Mobilier, was changed, to carry out the obligations I had made. They had credited me for the money paid for the stock, and they owed me these six hundred and fifty shares to carry out my obligations. I left the transfer with the assistant treasurer, with instructions to issue the certificates to meet these obligations. After the administration was changed, it was surrendered to the company, and notice given in writing that it was subject to the obligations I had already made. That was in May, 1867.

Q. This increase was voted when?—A. The increase was voted either late in 1866 or early in 1867. The first payment was payable in February, 1867.

Q. Do you believe that the shares assigned to you and to Mr. Ames covered all the stock the company had after the increase was made, except what was held by private shareholders at the time?—A. I have no means of knowing of my own knowledge. At the time I understood it covered the entire amount within, perhaps, one hundred and fifty shares. Of that I think one hundred shares was assigned to General Dodge, and I do not know but Neilson had the other fifty. I am not sure that he did. I asked the question once, and was informed he did. I don't know of my own knowledge.

Q. At the time of the negotiations between you and Mr. Brooks, which resulted in this agreement that he should have one hundred shares, was anything said between you and Mr. Brooks in reference to whether that one hundred shares would be entitled to fifty shares additional?—A. At the time I commenced talking with Mr. Brooks it was before the increase. At the time I made the settlement with Mr. Brooks, it was after the increase had all gone by.

Q. This last time was when you had the talk with him which resulted in settling upon the one hundred shares. Was anything said in that settlement with Mr. Brooks whether after obtaining the one hundred shares he would be entitled to 50 per cent. increase?—A. I do not recollect that there was. It was, as I supposed, a settlement of the whole thing.

Q. You did not understand that he was to have another fifty shares at all?—A. I did not so understand.

Q. Whether Mr. Brooks understood it so or not, you do not know?—A. I do not know what Mr. Brooks understood; I certainly understood distinctly that it was a compromise of the whole matter, and the time had gone by for the increase.

Q. Do you think Mr. Brooks so understood it at the time?—A. I supposed he was satisfied at the time with what was done.

Q. From the negotiation, or from what was said between you and Mr. Brooks upon the subject, had Mr. Brooks any right to understand that he was entitled to fifty shares additional?—A. I do not think he had. He had previously claimed more stock; he had talked of a larger amount, I suppose for the purpose of getting the best compromise he could.

Q. You understood that compromise ended that claim?—A. I did, so far as I was concerned.

Q. And you understood that he had no claim on the company for more stock?—A. I did.

By Mr. McCrary:

Q. Was General Dodge chief engineer of the Union Pacific Railroad?—A. He was chief engineer; yes, sir.

Q. And had been for how long?—A. I do not recollect. I think since 1865. I can tell you by reference to the dates.

Q. Do you know anything about his having contracted for some stock while he was chief engineer, and before he was a member of Congress?—A. I do not.

Q. You do not know anything of a contract under which he got this stock?—A. I do not.

Q. The only members of Congress on your list were Mr. Boyer and Mr. Alley?—A. Yes, sir.

Q. When did you make your original contract with Mr. Boyer?—A. In the fall of 1866.

Q. Was he then a member of Congress?—A. I suppose so. It was on the excursion in the fall of 1866, to which I have referred.

Q. He was a member of Congress at the time of this excursion?—A. He was.

Q. Do you remember whether he was a member of the Pacific Railroad committee?—A. I do not think he was.

WASHINGTON, *January* 21, 1873.

JAMES BROOKS, a member of the House of Representatives, having been duly sworn, made the following statement:

Mr. McComb having sworn in the early part of this investigation that I was the only member of Congress within his knowledge to whom had been given Credit Mobilier stock to influence or bribe other members, and that fifty shares had been thus given me without consideration, I, naturally enough, when thus outraged, felt indignant and denounced him as a perjurer. Mr. Alley having since sworn that there is not one word of truth in this part of Mr. McComb's fabrication, and this having been confirmed by Mr. Ames's testimony, I ought, perhaps, to let the case rest, and I should let it thus rest, but for persistent efforts here to impair the testimony of both.

The following letter from the Acting Secretary of the Interior shows my first official relations with that board:

"WASHINGTON, *January* 20, 1873.

"SIR: Hon. James Brooks, of New York, was commissioned a Government director of the Union Pacific Railroad for the term of one year from the 3d day of October, 1867, and the oath of office filed by him in this Department was taken March 23, 1868.

"Respectfully, your obedient servant,

"B. R. COWEN,
"*Acting Secretary.*

"Hon. L. P. POLAND,
"*Chairman, &c., &c., House of Representatives.*"

It will thus be seen that for nearly six months I declined to take the oath of office. My hesitation arose mainly from the fact that there was discord in the board, and while that existed I did not want to be in it. When this discord was over, in compliance with a promise I had made to act, I took my seat in the board, to the apparent satisfaction of all the hitherto discordant parties. The sacrifice was something to me, for, in this official position, I could not be a stockholder in the Union Pacific road, and if I became a stockholder in the Credit Mobilier, though another corporation, in another State, I subjected myself to misconstruction. Hence, I was compelled to renounce a right to purchase at par from T. C. Durant two hundred shares in the Credit Mobilier, a right belonging to me, as testified by him, in 1866, or early in 1867, *before I was a member of Congress*, and which did not become valuable until December, 1867. I said, therefore, to Mr. Durant, as he has already testified, that, as a Government director, I could not, and would not, exercise my right to purchase the two hundred shares, then above par, but would transfer the right to C. H. Neilson, my son-in-law, to whom, as a stock operator, the right would be valuable. Mr. Durant made no objection, save as to the number of shares to be transferred, and has stated that he compromised on that by selling to Mr. Neilson one hundred shares, with five Union Pacific bonds in addition, and a certain number of shares of Union Pacific stock, which were immediately entered upon the books, as seen by the record, in Mr. Neilson's own name. I did not then receive, and have never since received, one cent of profit from the transaction, in my own or in another name. I have never receipted for, or had any dividend, or allotment, in any form, from any shares entered on the book in Mr. Neilson's name, either directly or indirectly. I did not give Mr. Neilson the money to purchase the stock, deeming it wiser to make him pay me back than to give it to him. I advanced the purchase-money as a loan, as he testifies, and only as a loan, and held him responsible for paying it back as soon as he could. Hence, probably, as Mr. Crane testifies, although I have entirely forgotten the transaction, I acted for Mr. Neilson in paying Mr. Durant, in part, three thousand dollars, by a draft, to be deducted from a loan due me January 22 by Mr. Durant, and, in part, seven thousand dollars, by a check. If there be any error or wrong in so public and natural an act, I am incapable of seeing it. If I had been plotting for concealment, as insinuated, I certainly should not have given my right to purchase to a son-in-law, but to some "dummy," to some "John Doe," or "Richard Roe," whose connection by marriage could not be traced to me in all the books of a great national corporation.

The fifty additional shares purchased by Mr. Neilson himself, on or about February 29, 1868, were necessarily sold to him by virtue of my agreement with Mr. Durant, and upon a statement of the fact to the company, it was conceded that the fifty shares belonged to him, upon his paying for them the par value, with interest from July 1, 1867. I never spoke to Mr. Alley, nor he with me, upon this subject, as sworn by Mr. McComb. Our relations were never confidential, and he never gave me these fifty, nor any other shares, with or without consideration, either for myself, or to influence or bribe democratic members of Congress. Now, in setting forth this statement of facts, I do not wish apologetically to convey the idea that I declined the ownership of Credit Mobilier stock because I was a member of Congress, for if I had never been named a Government director, I should probably have been the owner of a large amount of that stock up to this day. I have as much right to own paper stock as live stock—as sheep, or spindles, or lead, or iron mines, or barley, or lumber, or steam-engines, or founderies, with two or three thousand tariffed articles, largely endowed by congressional legislation; and no constitutional quorum can ever be got in either House of Congress, if members are to own no species of stock, alive or dead—agricultural, manufacturing, or commercial—when these interests are to be legislated upon.

From April 6, 1866, to March 4, 1867, I was not in Congress, and during that time, as a private citizen, whenever I had leisure, I exerted all the influence tongue or pen could give me to interest capitalists in the building of the Pacific Railroad, borrowing money for it, and loaning it money, at great risks, too, which led then, when I was not a member of Congress, as Mr. Durant shows, to his promising me the right to purchase some of his shares in the Credit Mobilier; and what he states I here reiterate, that the business transactions between us were in no way to influence Congress or legislation, but were the natural business transactions between man and man. Now, I have only to add that

I have never been asked to give or have given a vote in Congress that was unjust to the Government, or for the profit of the Union Pacific Railroad. Nor have I, as charged by Mr. McComb, asked democratic members of Congress to vote for the road, and I do not remember ever to have spoken to any democratic member upon any legislation relating to the road.

All I have done was, when not a member of Congress, to accept an offer Mr. Durant made, to sell me, at par, certain shares of the Credit Mobilier stock, and, when not a Government director of the road, to transfer to Mr. Neilson the offer made me when not a Congressman.

If this be a wrong, moral, social, political, or constitutional, it is not written in any code I have ever read or heard of.

By the CHAIRMAN:

Question. Were you a stockholder in the Union Pacific Railroad?

The WITNESS. When?

The CHAIRMAN. Ever.

Answer. I am now. I was obliged to be a stockholder when I became a stock director.

Q. How early was that?—A. I do not now remember; the records will show. It was six months or a year after I was removed as a Government director. I can tell you by a memorandum which I have here. I was removed as a Government director July 15, 1869. The election of directors occurred, I think, in March, 1870, and I must have then become a stockholder, as the laws of the company did not allow any one to become a director unless he was owner of stock.

Q. You purchased stock for the purpose of having the necessary qualifications to be a director?—A. I did.

Q. Prior to that you had not been a stockholder in the company?—A. No, never; not a share.

Q. How early was the conversation between you and Mr. Durant, when you were promised two hundred shares of stock?—A. It was in 1866. My impession is, early in 1866.

Q. You do not know when the connection of the Credit Mobilier and the Pacific road commenced?—A. I do not know when that connection commenced; the records will show the date.

Q. Did you have a conversation with anybody else except Mr. Durant in reference to taking stock in the Credit Mobilier?—A. I made great efforts with capitalists in New York.

Q. I mean in reference to taking stock yourself; did you have a conversation with any one upon that subject other than Mr. Durant?—A. I co-operated with Mr. Durant. I worked with him and others to induce capitalists to take stock in the Credit Mobilier.

Q. In regard to taking stock yourself in the Credit Mobilier, did you have any conversation with anybody except Mr. Durant on that subject?—A. I do not remember anybody else. Mr. Durant was the principal head of the road, or, perhaps, up to nearly that time, was almost the road himself.

Q. He was then president of the company?—A. Vice-president. I think John A. Dix was president; but Mr. Durant was the principal man at the head.

Q. Did you understand that you had a definite contract with him for a specific number of shares which you were to take?—A. I might have had any number of shares of Credit Mobilier stock prior to December, 1867.

Q. The great difficulty then was to get anybody to take it, was it not?—A. I could not get anybody to take it. I could have had any number of shares I wanted.

Q. Did you understand that you had a distinct agreement with him that you were to take a particular number of shares?—A. It was my option to take the shares or not. If the shares were under par, as they were a large proportion of the time, some of the time selling as low as 92, I did not want them, but when the stock went above par I did want some; before that I could have bought 1,000 shares at any time at 92.

Q. You were under no obligations to Mr. Durant to take any of the stock unless you wanted it?—A. No; it was what is called in Wall street on "option."

Q. You understood that your agreement with him was such that you had a right to take a specific number of shares agreed upon; did you, or was there simply a general talk?—A. I think it was two hundred shares. Mr. Durant's memory is better than mine. I seldom have any such things on my mind when not in New York. I have no reason to doubt the accuracy of his testimony that it was two hundred shares.

Q. When did the negotiations take place between you and Mr. Durant in reference to settling this matter?—A. It must have been before he went to New York, in December, I think, in 1867.

Q. You then claimed the fulfillment of this contract?—A. I claimed the fulfillment of it at that time; for the first time the shares went above par; I think early in December.

Q. How early do you think the shares began to be above par?—A. I think, as near as I can recollect, that on the 1st of December, 1867, it would have been difficult to borrow money on these shares, they were below par; but for some reason I never very well understood, perhaps the Oakes Ames contract—and let me say here I never heard as much about the Oakes Ames contract before as I have here—for some reason they became rapidly more and more valuable about this time.

Q. At the time you had this negotiation, which ended in the settlement of one hundred shares, what was your idea in regard to the value of the stock?—A. I think they were worth then about 130 or 140; that was my impression at the time.

Q. Do you remember whether that question was discussed between you and Mr. Durant?—A. I do not remember; Mr. Durant is a man of large business, and does not talk much in making his settlements.

Q. Did you learn at the time that for some reason it had become for your interest to call for this option?—A. I did.

Q. You learned from your conversation with him that the stock had for some reason become suddenly valuable, and that people were more anxious to take it than they had been?—A. I did.

Q. How early in that conversation with Mr. Durant did Mr. Neilson's name come in?—A. At the very start; as I have already stated, my official relations with the Government, if I accepted the position which had been tendered me, would give rise to misunderstanding and misapprehension if I were the owner of stock in this company. I thought I had the right, being a Government director, to hold this stock, but as I could not have done so without danger of being misunderstood and misrepresented, I would not hold it.

Q. The law prohibited a Government director from holding stock in the Union Pacific Railroad, did it not?—A. It did not prohibit me from holding stock in this company. I think I had the legal right, as I said, to hold it; but I was a journalist, and I did not want to subject myself to misconstruction as a public man, and therefore I threw away the right to hold the stock.

Q. You knew the Credit Mobilier had some connection with the Union Pacific Railroad?—A. Yes, sir, and that was the motive that made me refuse to hold the Credit Mobilier stock.

Q. And you think this was announced to Mr. Durant from the beginning of your negotiations with him, which resulted in this settlement?—A. It must have been. I see, by the entries that have been made, Mr. Neilson's name is not only upon the Credit Mobilier books, but upon the stock-books of the Union Pacific Railroad Company; that his name was there originally, and that the stock was issued directly to Mr. Neilson.

Q. It is undenied that the stock when transferred from Mr. Durant was transferred to Mr. Neilson. What I desire to know is, when Mr. Neilson's name came into the negotiations you had with him?—A. It must have been when we were talking on this subject. If I had not been a Government director, I probably should have been the owner of a large amount of Credit Mobilier stock. I said to him that I would not subject myself to misconstruction by owning a single share of it, and in accepting the position as Government director, I renounced my right to own any of the stock of the Credit Mobilier.

Q. You agreed with Mr. Durant that the result of this settlement between you and him was, that you were to take one hundred shares instead of the two hundred that you claimed?—A. Yes, sir; that was the result of the settlement. It was not a settlement which was satisfactory to me.

Q. And in order to compensate for not having one hundred more, he put in twenty-five thousand nominal value of the Union Pacific Railroad securities?—A. Five thousand of bonds, I think it is; he swears to it.

Q. And two hundred shares of Union Pacific Railroad stock in addition to the five thousand bonds?—A. Yes, the stock at a nominal value. I do not remember what its value was, because it never came into my hands; it passed immediately to Mr. Neilson.

Q. I am not talking about the value of it. The question I ask is, whether that was a part of the settlement between you and Mr. Durant, in connection with these one hundred shares?—A. It was, I presume.

Q. Was the receiving of these bonds and shares of stock what induced you to forego any claim to the additional one hundred shares?—A. It was in the power of Mr. Durant to do what he thought was right; I had only to accept what he thought was proper. I had no written contract or obligation from him.

Q. Did you have any conversation with Mr. Neilson upon the subject prior to this time?—A. Yes, I had told him what I should do.

Q. Do you remember how long prior to this statement or agreement?—A. I do not remember; it must have been on or about that time.

Q. The conversation in connection with this transaction was that, whatever this contract or privilege was worth in purchasing, the one hundred shares of stock with the other securities at par was a gift from you to Mr. Neilson?—A. Yes. I had not at the time any idea of its value; I had no conception when they were being transferred to him; I did not form an idea of this prospective value.

Q. You did understand at the time that the stock was worth more than par?—A. It was worth about 130, as I supposed, at the time, but it rose to all sorts of value; it went up as the Northwestern stock did the other day, from 100 to 300, up and down in all directions.

Q. Do you recall any conversation with any of these gentlemen—with Mr. Ames or Mr. Alley—in regard to the value of the stock at that time?—A. I never had any conversation with Mr. Ames or Mr. Alley about it; they were not my political friends. I felt angry and excited against them both at that time, because they had both just voted to turn me out of Congress.

Q. Do you remember in relation to hearing of sales of stock about that time?—A. I never gave it the least attention. After the stock was transferred to Mr. Neilson, I knew nothing about it.

Q. Did you before?—A. No; nothing.

Q. Did you hear of the sale from Mr. Durant to Mr. Alley?—A. Nothing, until it was mentioned here the other day.

Q. Did you make any inquiry to ascertain in relation to the value of it otherwise than in the conversation you had with Mr. Durant?—A. No; I knew it was above par, and that was all I wanted to know.

Q. When was it that the arrangement was made between you and Mr. Neilson, by which you were to advance the money to pay for this stock?—A. It was on or about the time of this transfer to him.

Q. Was anything said between you and him in regard to the security he was to give you for advancing the money, or whether you were to be secured at all?—A. I do not think there was. He was a man of property; he is my son-in-law; I have loaned him $10,000 or more very frequently.

Q. Do you remember whether you took any obligation from him in any way, showing that you advanced the money?—A. I do not think I did; he was my son-in-law; if he behaved badly I had him in my power, in the benefit he might or might not receive from my will. I knew that he had every motive to act properly toward me, and we have had the same sort of transaction frequently since.

Q. Did you make any charge of this money on your books, or keep any memorandum of it, as you remember?—A. I do not remember; my business is done pretty much in this loose kind of way. I cannot say whether I did or did not.

Q. Are you not in the habit of having some books in which you keep your business affairs?—A. Not my own affairs.

Q. What I want to know is, whether you have the account charged in any form.—A. I do not know. I do not think I have. It is a thing I should not be very apt to recollect if I had.

Q. Have you made any search or any examination to see whether you have anything of the kind?—A. No, sir; I have not.

Q. Did you say to Mr. Neilson that you should require some security or collateral from him for the payment of the money?—A. I do not remember that I did. I did not deem it necessary, and I do not suppose I did.

Q. Did he give you any security?—A. I do not remember whether he did or did not.

Q. If he did, you have no memory what it was?—A. I have not any memory what it was, and no memorandum.

Q. Has this $10,000 which you advanced to pay for the stock been repaid to you by Mr. Neilson?—A. Yes, sir.

Q. Can you state when?—A. A large portion of it was soon after the transaction. It must have been in February, March, or April, that a large portion was repaid to me.

Q. Was it paid at one time?—A. No, not at one time.

Q. Do you remember how much was paid at one time?—A. I do not.

Q. Can you tell when the balance was paid?—A. I do not remember.

Q. Did you have any other money transaction with Mr. Neilson?—A. Several others.

Q. Do you know if there was an account kept between you and him?—A. I have never kept any account beyond a general record, from the mere fact that I look upon him as my son-in-law, and I have always been very loose in keeping my accounts with him.

Q. You think you are not able to produce any account that existed between you and him in reference to this other money transaction?—A. I think I might be able if I were at home, by looking and searching among my papers.

Q. Have you made any such search in reference to that?—A. I have not. We have unsettled accounts, loose accounts, I think, in regard to other things.

Q. Do you remember whether this stock transaction between you and him was settled up and treated as a distinct transaction, or did it simply go into your general accounts?—A. I think it was settled up, or nearly settled up, eighteen months or two years ago.

Q. In a general settlement between you?—A. No, I think as to that particular transaction. There may have been some balance. I gave but very little attention. I never draw a check if I can avoid it.

Q. Was the first payment made by Mr. Neilson toward the $10,000 you advanced him $9,000?—A. He states that it was, and he is probably correct.

Q. Did you learn from him that it was the sum of $9,000 he had just drawn as a dividend upon the stock?—A. I never asked him upon the subject. It would not have come to me, but would have been deposited with my cashier and put in the bank.

Q. Do you remember about the transaction?—A. I remember that he got a large sum soon after.

Q. You do not suppose the payment was made personally to you?—A. I know it was not made to me.

Q. You have no recollection that you received from him anything to hold as collateral for this payment?—A. I may, and may not; I do not recollect. I should not have demanded collateral.

Q. If you did receive any collateral at all from him, it was something voluntarily proffered. You required no collateral?—A. I required no collateral. I never have required it, and should not for any loan to Neilson, unless I was apprehensive that he was engaged in some dangerous speculations; and then I would require double, triple, enough to prevent him from going in. He is a stock-broker, and I have assisted him from time to time.

Q. Have you any memoranda as to whether these 5,000 of Union Pacific Railroad bonds was together with the 20,000 Union Pacific Railroad stock, and whether either was ever in your hands?—A. I passed everything over to Mr. Neilson. I never touched a cent of the proceeds of the transaction.

Q. Do you remember whether these bonds were actually in your possession?—A. If they were, it would have been only long enough for him to go to my place, or for me to go to his place.

Q. Do you think these bonds could have been placed with you as security for the payment of the amount you advanced to Mr. Neilson?—A. My impression is that they were not. I never asked him for any collateral.

Q. Do you believe you ever held them at all?—A. No; I believe I never held them at all.

Q. And that you never had a certificate for Union Pacific Railroad stock?—A. I know I never did. I speak confidently in regard to that. I would not touch it. I was about to accept the position of Government director, and I would not touch a share of the stock of the railroad company.

Q. What I want to ask is, whether you ever had in your possession a certificate for Union Pacific Railroad stock, without its being transferred on the book?—A. I do not think I did. I am quite sure of that. I could never have had any in my possession, because, when I made the transaction with Mr. Durant, nothing was given on the stock-book. Mr. Neilson must have gone to the officer in charge and got it. I am confident it was never in my hand.

Q. Now, sir, as to the fifty shares of Credit Mobilier stock; at the time of this negotiation and settlement between you and Mr. Durant, was there anything said between you and him in relation to your being entitled, or Neilson being entitled, to fifty shares additional stock?—A. I knew very little of what was doing in the interior of the Credit Mobilier. When I arranged with Mr. Durant for these one hundred shares, I believed they carried with them whatever privileges or rights anybody else had; that these shares carried the same rights that any other stock had.

Q. You thought the fifty shares was an accretion that belonged to the original stock?—A. I learned at that time or soon afterward that this accretion was made, and that whoever held the early shares, the shares in the first issue of the Credit Mobilier stock, was entitled to one-half in addition.

Q. Did you understand at the time you were having your negotiation with Mr. Durant, that the negotiation ended in the adjustment by which one hundred shares were to be given?—A. The adjustment only related to what was on the face of it.

Q. Did you understand at that time that it would entitle you to fifty shares more?—A. I do not think I knew at the time anything about the accretions.

Q. Therefore you did not think, and there was no conversation in regard to any additional stock?—A. I do not think there was any conversation between Mr. Durant and myself on the subject. I think he is right in that. I do not know anything about the Credit Mobilier, and did not know what its interior operations were.

Q. Can you tell from whom, and when, you did learn in reference to these fifty shares additional?—A. I learned it from a conversation with Mr. Dillon.

Q. Did you inform Mr. Dillon how Neilson came to get the one hundred shares?—A. I did.

Q. You understood at that time that the shares were not directly from the company to Neilson, but from Durant?—A. I thought they ought to come from Mr. Durant; that it was an inheritance from him from my agreement with him.

Q. Did you explain that to Mr. Dillon?—A. I did.

Q. Do I understand that Mr. Dillon said that the manner in which you or Neilson came by that stock carried with it the fifty additional shares?—A. Mr. Dillon thought so, and his only hesitation was whether they were to come from Mr. Durant's portion or from the company. Mr. Dillon never doubted the right; it was only as to what source it was to come from.

Q. Did you have any conversation with others upon the subject?—A. I do not remember having any conversation with any human being upon the subject, except the president of the company, Mr. Dillon.

Q. Did Mr. Dillon say whether the company had more stock or other stock in its possession?—A. I did not enter into particulars with him, nor he with me.

Q. Did he make any question or scruple in regard to your right?—A. I do not think he did. I never understood that he did.

Q. Did he say anything to you about getting a paper and getting people to sign it?—A. Nothing to me. I never heard of there being any such paper till I heard of it here for the first time.

Q. Did he say anything about the necessity of getting a number of the stockholders of the company to agree to it?—A. Nothing. Mr. Dillon was a man of immense business, and spent very little time in talking.

Q. Do you remember whether you had more than one interview on the subject?—A. I do not remember more than one. There may have been two. I would not swear positively as to the number of conversations.

Q. Where were they?—A. It may have been in the office of the Union Pacific Railroad Company.

Q. You say that you had no conversation with anybody else connected with the company about it, except Mr. Dillon?—A. I do not recollect any conversation with anybody else. I certainly had none with Mr. Alley, for reasons I have given before. I never had any conversations with him on the subject, nor with Mr. Ames.

Q. Do you remember when you had this conversation, whether one or more, with Mr. Dillon, in the office, as to who was present, or whether anybody was present?—A. I do not remember.

Q. Do you remember seeing Mr. McComb about there at any time when you were there?—A. I never talked freely before McComb. I always guarded my tongue in his presence.

Q. You knew McComb?—A. Yes.

Q. Had you known him for some time?—A. I have known him about the Pacific Railroad.

Q. So that if Mr. McComb had been present, and you had seen him, you would have known who he was?—A. O, yes.

Q. Have you any memory whether you did see him about the office on this occasion?—A. I never saw him when I was talking with Mr. Dillon on that subject—never.

Q. You say the only question between you and Mr. Dillon upon this subject was as to where the additional stock should come from?—A. He did not dispute the right to it at all. He did not make any issue even as to where it was to come from. I only inferred from his conversation that the trouble in his mind was as to what fund the accretion should come from.

Q. Did you learn from Mr. Dillon that those persons who were entitled to this additional stock were also entitled to receive bonds of the Union Pacific Railroad to the same amount?—A. I knew nothing about the Credit Mobilier after I became a Government director of the road, or made up my mind to become one. I knew nothing of its dividends transactions.

Q. Did you ever know that the persons who were entitled to take fifty per cent. additional stock were entitled to have the same amount of Union Pacific Railroad bonds?—A. I did not know the particulars. I knew it brought a large profit; in what form I did not know, and I carefully avoided knowing.

Q. We have learned that there was such a right.—A. And I have also learned it with you here for the first time.

Q. The only idea you had was that the stock was worth more than you paid for it?—A. That was the only idea I had about it.

Q. After you had this conversation with Mr. Dillon, how did you first learn that these fifty shares had been transferred to Mr. Neilson?—A. I do not remember how I first learned it. It may have been from the general conversation about the office. My impression is that it was from some of the subordinate officers of the company, some of the clerks; that I first learned it.

Q. Was there anything said between you and Mr. Dillon as to how these shares were to be paid for ?—A. I understood they were to be paid for at par.

Q. Did you have any conversation with Mr. Dillon as to how that payment was to be made at par ?—A. I did not. I had no interest in the payment. I had no conversation upon the subject.

Q. Had you any conversation with Mr. Neilson in relation to the fifty shares of stock prior to the conversation with Mr. Dillon about it ?—A. I told Mr. Neilson he had that right in connection with his original one hundred shares.

Q. Was that before your conversation with Mr. Dillon, or afterward ?—A. Probable before.

Q. How did you learn that fact yourself ?—A. I probably learned it from the clerks of the company, who gave me the first information as to the hundred shares being entitled to fifty additional.

Q. You think you told Mr. Neilson of his right in this respect before you had this conversation with Mr. Dillon ?—A. That is my impression.

Q. Was Mr. Neilson aware that he had such a right until you told him ?—A. I do not think he was ; I do not think he knew much about the stock in any form or way. Let me remark here that stock operators frequently buy stock without knowing anything about it in any form ; they have all sorts of transactions without knowing anything about the details.

Q. Do you know whether Mr. Neilson had any connection with the Credit Mobilier stock in contemplation until you made this arrangement for him in regard to the one hundred shares ?—A. I do not. I think he had some conversation with me before upon the subject. I do not remember what it was. He is a stock operator, and is constantly conversing upon the subject of stocks of almost every kind, so that I have no doubt he talked about the Credit Mobelier.

Q. Do you know whether he had ever had any dealings in the Credit Mobilier stock as a broker ?—A. I do not know. I know but very little of his stock operations except when he comes to me for information or advice.

Q. Did you have any knowledge as to how these fifty shares of stock were paid for ?—A. No ; I only knew they were paid for.

Q. Did you have anything to do with the payment yourself ?—A. I had nothing whatever to do with the payment, and do not know in what manner the stock was paid for.

Q. Did you say anything to Mr. Dillon in relation to his letting Neilson have the money to pay for it ?—A. Not at all.

Q. When did you first learn that Mr. Dillon had advanced the money to pay for it ?—A. Not until after this investigation commenced here.

Q. Do you know whether Mr. Dillon has ever been repaid that money ?—A. I do not. I think he has ; not to my knowledge, however.

Q. Do you know whether you paid him ?—A. I never did pay him.

Q. If nobody has paid him but you, he has not got his pay ?—A. I do not know that.

Q. Mr. Neilson says he has never paid him.—A. Mr. Dillon says he thinks he did. It is a question of memory, therefore, between the two.

Q. You think you never had any connection in any way with making that payment?—A. I am sure I never did. I know I never did personally.

Q. Do you think if the payment had been made out of your funds, so that Neilson would have to account to you for it, it would have come to your knowledge?—A. I think so. If that were the case, I should think he must have paid him out of that $9,000.

Q. I understood Neilson to say that $9,000 was paid to you.—A. He says so. It is a question between him and Mr. Dillon. I know nothing about it.

Q. Do you think Neilson was mistaken in saying he paid that $9,000 to you? He could not have paid it to you and Mr. Dillon both.—A. I cannot say. I have not my cash-book here. I expected to have received it by express this morning.

Q. You think some of your books may give you more definite information upon this subject than you now have?—A. My cash-book would show what was received by my cashier. I never transact any such business personally unless in exceptional cases.

Q. You feel very confident that the $5,000 which Mr. Dillon advanced to pay for this stock has never been repaid by you?—A. Yes, sir. The securities Mr. Dillon got from Mr. Neilson were worth more than $5,000, and it may be that he has paid himself out of them. I do not know anything about it. I did not pay it personally, and I know nothing about it.

Q. And you have no clerk who would have paid it out of your funds without your knowledge?—A. I do not think he did. I say, again, that my cashier attends to all this business for me. He makes the entries and draws the checks, so that, without my cash-book and check-book, I speak very blindly upon the subject.

Q. We do not question your memory; we only want to know what the facts are from your memory.—A. Mr. Dillon has promised the committee that he will ascertain. It was entirely a transaction between him and Mr. Neilson.

Q. I understood you to say you have never derived any advantage or benefit from the one hundred shares or the fifty shares?—A. Not one cent, in any form or shape, directly or indirectly.

Q. And that neither money, stock, nor bonds came to you as dividends?—A. Nor allotments, nor advances, nor anything whatever.

Q. If any bonds went with the fifty shares' accretions, they never came to you?—A. They never came to me. I am so explicit upon that point because, when I started out, or made up my mind to accept the position of Government director, I made up my mind to have nothing to do with the stock or securities of the road, or the Credit Mobilier, in any way whatever, and I never did.

Q. Then the entire benefit or advantage to be derived from that stock, in bonds, railroad stock, money, or in whatever form the dividends were made, beyond the amount you advanced to pay for it, was intended by you as a gift to your son-in-law?—A. Yes, sir.

Q. Did you ever know of any transaction between Mr. Durant and any member of Congress?—A. I never knew of any.

Q. Did you ever know of any transaction or dealings between Mr. Ames and any member of Congress in regard to this Credit Mobilier stock?—A. I never did, and I never heard of his having any until I read the publication last fall in the New York Sun.

Q. You have no knowledge in any form upon that subject except what has been published in the newspapers?—A. None whatever.

By Mr. MERRICK:

Q. You spoke of the value of this stock as about 130; did you include in that valuation or exclude from it the bonds and Union Pacific Railroad stock which accompanied it?—A. The whole of it. I think I heard through the testimony in the Fisk case of some sale at 136. That included all dividends and allotments as I understood; and that I supposed to be about its value at the time. I had no conception of the magnitude of the transfer when I handed this stock over to Neilson, and I never did have any until I got it here.

Q. At the time of this adjustment between you and Mr. Durant, had you received the appointment of Government director of the Union Pacific Railroad Company?—A. Yes; I had been tendered the appointment. I had not then accepted it, as I stated.

Q. You say you did not take your oath of office as such until the March following?—A. Not until the March following.

Q. I understood you to say you had made up your mind not only not to have anything to do with Union Pacific Railroad securities, to touch or handle them, but also to know nothing in reference to Credit Mobilier stock?—A. Yes, after I became a Government director, I say that so far as these transactions through my son-in-law were concerned, certainly.

Q. Did you make up your mind both in regard to Union Pacific Railroad stock and Credit Mobilier stock?—A. Yes. Let me say right here, that in 1867, and until the first of 1868, I felt that the Union Pacific Railroad had gone to the wall. Mr. Durant had put into the enterprise $800,000 which he had made as a contractor on Iowa roads, and he had gone to the length of his tether; but little help could be got in New York for it. Nobody else would touch it. He went to Boston, and in Boston found Mr. Ames and Mr. Alley and some other gentlemen there, who were rich men. They went into it, for the first time, and increased the means and resources of the enterprise materially; but they were soon exhausted. I saw drafts coming from the contractors which were only met with the utmost difficulty and at high rates of interest. The first-mortgage bonds of the Union Pacific Railroad Company were held nominally at 85, but you could not borrow money on them from the banks at 40. The banks would throw them out as having little or no value, and the whole concern was supposed to be gone up, until the establishment of the Credit Mobilier, and until these gentlemen put their capital into it in that form, because they would not be liable as individuals for the drafts that might be made by contractors or speculators. They must have some machinery to intervene between the railroad and the personal liability. For some time scarcely anybody would touch the Credit Mobilier stock in New York. It was under par. Money could not be borrowed on it; and it was only in December, 1867, that it began to have character among moneyed men. Then it went up to double; it went up and down with all sorts of valuations. I was desirous of seeing the road built, I cared not at what expense. My only purpose as a Government director was to see that a good road was built, that the money of the Government was expended properly, and that the company got no more of the bonds of the Government than they were entitled to for the road built. At that time, what these gentlemen made or lost out of the transaction did not concern me. I was interested as a Government director, to see that a good road was built, and that the interests of the Government were properly protected in it.

Q. You considered it no part of your duty to ascertain whether proper prices were being paid for the work done?—A. I had nothing to do with the prices. My only care as a Government director was to see that the road was built, and that the money or lands received from the Government were properly and faithfully expended on the road.

Q. Did you, or not, know that those gentlemen were making contracts with themselves?—A. I did not; I knew nothing of the contracts, nor of the nature of them.

Q. Did you, or not, as a Government director, regard it as a part of your duty to see that the contracts for building this railroad were made with proper and responsible parties and for fair prices?—A. I know at the time that the contracts were for what you might term fair and reasonable prices. There could be no contracts made at such prices as railroads are built for in the East. There was great doubt and trouble as to whether the contractors would get their pay, and they charged high prices for everything, and had to pay high prices. Ten, twenty, and thirty per cent. was charged for money obtained from New York banks. I think the bank at Omaha must have realized twenty or thirty per cent. for the drafts cashed there, because they were uncertain whether the drafts would be cashed in New York. The prices paid for material that I heard of staggered me. There was a desperate struggle between the Union and Central Pacific, as to which should make their road the farthest; they worked at unseasonable periods of the year. Sections of the road were built, when they never ought to have been built, in mid-winter. Sometimes they built temporary tracks upon the snow, which would go down, of course, with the approach of mild weather. Sixty dollars a bushel was paid for corn, and five dollars apiece for ties. They paid enormous sums of money for iron. They were compelled to buy all the iron to build the road in our own market, and they were compelled to buy it of Pennsylvania companies, and give Pennsylvania prices for it, under the law of Congress. They paid ten and twenty dollars a ton more for iron than they could have purchased it for elsewhere. Everything was on an enormously large scale of expenditure, necessarily, in order to make the road. My associates in the Government directorship were Mr. Williams, of Pittsburgh, George Ashmun, of Massachusetts, and the late Vice-President Wade, of Ohio. All our efforts were expended in endeavoring to see that the money of the Government and that derived from the mortgage of the road, authorized by the Government, was used in good faith to construct the road. They got the bonds from the Government, and issued their own bonds, and from the proceeds of these they built the road.

Q. You did not consider it any part of your duty to protect the interests of the stockholders of the Union Pacific Rrailroad Company, and to secure for them the cheapest possible construction of the road, consistent with its being properly and well done?—A. I think, as far as I knew at the time, their contracts were let at as favorable rates as they could get to build a road in that wilderness country. There was no timber from Omaha to the Platte. The ties had to be brought from some point on the Missouri. They were cottonwood ties, and had to be burnetized. The expense of transportation was enormous. There was no railroad transportation across the State of Iowa, and everything had to be brought up and down the Missouri River, and the iron by way of New Orleans. Everything was done on the most extravagant scale of expenditure, and the road could not otherwise have been built. They had exhausted all their resources and all their means, at the time of which I speak, from the sale of Government bonds and of their own first-mortgage bonds. With the Central Pacific Company the case was somewhat different. The Central Pacific had double subsidies; they had subsidies from the Federal Government, and they had subsidies from the State of California. But the Central Pacific was compelled to transport its rails for building its road via the Panama Railroad at an immense expense, or to send them by way of Cape Horn. In their struggle to build the road quick, both companies made the work more than it otherwise would have cost, but the Government gained by its rapid completion. The road was, in fact, completed seven years before the time limited by Congress; and large amounts of money were saved to the Government in consequence, in the transportation of troops, munitions of war, and supplies to feed the soldiers in Montana, New Mexico, and everywhere through all that country. Large sums were also saved on the enormous prices before paid by the Government for the transportation of the mails; so that the additional amount paid for the construction of the road, under the circumstances I have stated, will have been saved to the Government in the matter of its transportation. This was the reasoning of the Government directors—of such men as Ashmun, Williams, and Wade, and the other gentlemen who occupied these positions, and was the reason on their part for not criticising these contracts in detail.

Q. In your explanation in the House, the 18th of December, if I remember correctly, you allude only to the transaction in regard to the fifty shares, making no reference to the transaction of the one hundred shares; can you suggest to us why that was?—A. Because Mr. McComb had specially charged before the committee that Mr. Alley had specially *given* me these fifty shares. I therefore alluded to that, and that only. In the same speech I promised, if I remember right, to allude to the subject again hereafter. I consumed the whole hour, if you remember. I would very gladly, if the rules had permitted me, have gone into the whole transaction.

Q. Was it your purpose at that time to have made a full explanation?—A. Certainly. There never was any secret about it. The fact was notorious to Mr. McComb and everybody else. In the Pennsylvania suit the one hundred shares had been set down to Mr. Neilson. There was no concealment about it. Why I confined myself to the fifty shares in that explanation was in order to make the issue in the House where he had made the issue in committee. He spoke only of the fifty shares given to me, and I therefore confined myself to the fifty shares.

Q. Was not that speech made to produce the impression upon the House and in the country that that was your entire vindication?—A. No. I should have been a great fool, with the records of the Pennsylvania suit and the records of the Union Pacific Railroad Company accessible to everybody, to have sought to do any such thing. In that speech I say, "I might dwell upon this, as I shall perhaps, at some time hereafter, take occasion to do." I expected at the proper time, here in this committee or elsewhere, to unfold the whole transaction, and for that purpose I challenged investigation, and asked the committee to riddle me from beginning to end.

Q. You had already in your mind then, in your speech in the House, to have gone into the whole matter of the one hundred shares?—A. Yes, but I did not want then to bring any other issue into the discussion than the distinct issue made by Mr. McComb. I did not want to make any other issue than to pronounce what he had said in committee, in regard to the transaction of the fifty shares, untrue.

Q. Was not substantially the issue before the committee, your entire relations in relation to the purchase of and dealings in this Credit Mobilier stock?—A. No; the issue was in reference to the fifty shares.

That had been reported in the newspapers, and was the only issue then presented. I therefore limited myself exclusively to the fifty shares.

Q. The committee had been raised to inquire into all the dealings of members in this stock?—A. I knew the committee would bring me before them, and that the whole transaction of the one hundred shares would necessarily be gone into. There was never any concealment about the one hundred shares. It was all set out, as I stated in the Pennsylvania suit two years before. It was as accessible to the public then as now. I could not have had any motive of concealment, then, in refraining from going into it in my explanations in the House.

By Mr. NIBLACK:

Q. You say that, having transferred your right to the one hundred shares to Neilson, you resolved to know no more of it, and to take no more interest in it; did you take any interest in it afterward in securing for him the additional fifty shares?—A. To get his rights.

Q. You therefore did feel interest enough in the matter to see that he got the fifty shares he was entitled to?—A. Yes; what I mean is, that I took no interest in the dividends or allotments or payment of bonds.

Q. Do you remember, when you talked with Mr. Dillon upon the subject, whether you claimed that you had a right to the additional fifty shares, or that your son-in-law had that right?—A. I claimed that my son-in-law had the right, through my settlement with Mr. Durant, when the one hundred shares were given, that it was a hereditary right that went with the one hundred shares.

Q. Inasmuch as you placed that right in your son-in-law, under the circumstances of your being appointed a Government director, you relinquished a very great advantage to yourself?—A. I did; I had not any conception of how much I did relinquish; I had no idea of its magnitude.

Q. Do you not now think, under all the circumstances, it would have been better to have relinquished your claims on Mr. Durant entirely, and to have foregone all the right you had in regard to your option to take the stock?—A. It is true that reputation, even when unjustly assailed, is worth more than money. I therefore answer, certainly, if that is what you mean by your question.

Q. What I meant is this: is it not better to do directly what you attempt to do, than to do what seems to have some indirection about it?—A. I asked myself at the time, shall I sell this stock for what I supposed it to be worth and take my profits now? And I said, no; they will say you have made this money out of the Credit Mobilier. Shall I leave it in the company? I did not think it was just to me. I deemed it wise, therefore, to transfer it to my son-in-law. My first impulse was to sell it and to receive the profits myself. I did not do that. I thought it would subject me to more imputation than to take the course I have taken.

Q. Placing it upon that ground, do you not think that transferring the stock to your son-in-law, and at the same time giving your checks and drafts for the payment of the stock, would be likely to give rise to as much suspicion as though you had taken it in your own name?—A. It never occurred to me when I made so plain a transaction as that; as to the question of being a member of Congress, I considered I had a right to be interested in stock of any kind.

Q. The point in the public mind, as far as we are able to gather it, is that the appearance of this transaction indicates that it was done in the name of your son-in-law, for your benefit.—A. That is the turn it takes, and it has the plausibility of the stock being in Mr. Neilson's name.

Q. And that, at the time you became a Government director, you had paid for the stock out of your funds, which seems to furnish a fair basis for the theory, at least, that Mr. Neilson held the stock for your own benefit.—A. If I had not supposed I was honorable and upright in the transaction, I should have placed the stock in the name of some unknown man instead of my son-in-law. I felt that I was doing right, and I did not care what sort of an investigation Congress or anybody else made of me; and I care nothing now. I know that it was a just transaction, an open transaction. As I have said, I considered myself as having a perfect right, as a member of Congress, to own stock in the Credit Mobilier, but that I could not as a Government director of the Union Pacific Railroad Company; after I accepted the appointment, I thought I could not hold the stock without giving just cause for suspicion.

Q. Do you not think now under all the circumstances it would have been better for you to have taken the stock in your own name than to have taken it as you did?—A. The Credit Mobilier had so close a connection with the Union Pacific Railroad, that as a Government director of the Union Pacific Railroad I would not own the stock at all. Let me ask you, was it right or wrong for me to hold United States stocks during the war?

Mr. NIBLACK. That is a question I will not go into now. There is some question as to the propriety of a member of Congress holding any securities which are likely to be affected by the legislation of Congress. That is a thing we cannot very well determine here. I am free to say that as a member of Congress I have refrained from holding any national-bank stock or Government bonds as an investment.

The WITNESS. Do you suppose it is democratic for a man to own nothing? If that is to be the doctrine, I am afraid the democratic party will never get any more votes.

Mr. NIBLACK. I do not know that the democratic party will get any more votes anyhow.

The WITNESS. I have been the owner of bank stock and am now; and yet my whole record shows that I have always voted against those institutions in every form.

Mr. NIBLACK. I do not want to go into that. I simply want to afford you the opportunity of making whatever explanation you desire of the transaction, in which there seems to be question in the mind of the public as to good faith on your part.

The WITNESS. What would you have done if you had had a right like that, which had suddenly become very valuable?

Mr. NIBLACK. I do not know. I have never been placed in that position.

The WITNESS. I could have given it to Mr. Ames, Mr. Durant, and others, by leaving it in the company. I could have taken it out when I became a Government director and sold it for thirty or more per cent. profit. Instead of that, Mr. Neilson has sworn, as I have sworn, that I had nothing whatever to do with the dividends, allotments, or accretions from the stock. I suppose I have done my share of abusing people, in my day, through the newspapers; but it does not pay, and the newspaper men who descend to this sort of abuse, through misstatements of facts, will find they will lose in the end in character more than they will gain. Let me add here that I have property which I must invest in something. I cannot allow it to remain idle. I have invested it at various times, in stocks and bonds of railroads, a portion in coal mines in Iowa, and in various securities. I could not allow it to lie idle. If it did not earn more than two per cent. it would be better to let it go on increasing. What am I to do? I invested in Government bonds during the war. Some people thought that patriotic. I did not. I did it as a business matter. If I bought Government securities when they were depressed, and made a profit on them when they advanced, was I right or was I wrong?

Mr. NIBLACK. What I wanted was simply to ask you whether you now deemed it wise to have transferred this stock, under the circumstances, to your son-in-law?

The WITNESS. It would have been more prudent, if I had intended anything wrong, to have placed it in the name of John Doe or Richard Roe; I did what I did as an honest, open transaction. I have never desired to conceal anything; I have never concealed anything. My duty to myself was never personally to receive any profit from the transaction, and I never have.

By Mr. McCRARY:

Q. Your objection to holding stock was your appointment as a Government director, and not because of your being a member of Congress?—A. Yes, sir.

Q. You are not aware that this $10,000 of stock ever stood in your name on the books?—A. I am sure it never stood in my name; I never heard of its being in my name, and I never had any suspicion of its being in my name on the books of the company.

Q. Did Mr. Neilson ever turn over to you any bonds or receive any dividends?—A. No.

Q. Do you know that he repaid you the $10,000 you advanced for the purchase of the stock?—A. He swears that he gave me $9,000 in cash, and $1,000 afterward. I do not recollect how that was. We have running accounts and running memoranda of accounts.

Q. You have no recollection of his turning over any first-mortgage bonds in payment of the loan?—A. I have not.

Q. You have no particular recollection of anything, except the payment of a large sum of money, which he paid you at one time—$9,000?—A. I do not think he paid me that personally; he paid it when I was absent in Washington here.

Q. You have no book from which you can tell precisely when and how he paid you for that loan?—A. I do not know. I keep a sort of book—a pocket memoranda-book—like the one I have in my hand, and at the end of the year, if there is anything valuable in it unadjusted, so far as my personal matters are concerned, I put it into another one.

Q. You are confident you never received any more than $10,000 and interest on that transaction?—A. I never did.

By the CHAIRMAN:

Q. The committee would be glad to have you examine your cash-book, bank-book, and any memoranda you have which will show anything in reference to dealings between you and Mr. Neilson bearing upon this subject.—A. I will do so. It has been charged that this stock was given me to influence my vote in Congress. Sometimes I voted on the matters affecting the Pacific Railroad, and sometimes I did not; I have generally refrained from voting in regard to every matter in which I had a personal interest. I desire to call the attention of the committee to an act that has been talked of a good deal in connection with this matter. On December 16, 1867, I made a speech in the House against the bill for changing the time for the annual meeting of the stockholders of the Union Pacific Railroad Company, which speech is published in the Congressional Globe. The bill was introduced, as was understood, in reference to a raid Fisk was making on the Union Pacific Railroad Company. He got an injunction, through Judge Barnard, to prevent the directors from being elected. It has been stated here that the company came here and desired to change the time of the annual meeting of the stockholders. If you look at the Congressional Globe of December 16, 1867, you will find that I opposed that action with all the vigor and force I could at the time. I called the attention of the committee to this particular item, in order to show that any interest people supposed me to have did not influence my action, having made a speech against a bill the company wished to have passed.

By Mr. MERRICK:

Q. You were then a member of Congress at the time you received and transferred to Mr. Neilson the one hundred shares?—A. I was at the time, but not when I first had the right to have one hundred shares. I was not a Government director. I was out of Congress for nearly a year before that. There are other statements, as regards my action, which I will volunteer here now, having hope that the committee would put some question to me, to bring out facts in connection with the Fisk raid, out of which grew the act changing the annual meeting of the stockholders. It will be remembered that Fisk had broken up the board of directors in New York. While they were in session, Fisk, with a deputy sheriff, came in with an injunction from Judge Barnard, by virtue of which, if discharged, all were to be put in prison. I advised them to go to prison and take the consequences of it, and not to pay the least attention to his injunction. I think they would have followed my advice but for the impression they had that I had privileges from arrest such as are supposed to belong to a member of Congress. This was not true. I would have gone to Ludlow street jail with them if they had taken my advice. I think they made a great mistake in not going to jail. This transaction, this raid upon their money-chest, I know cost the road a million, some of them think as much as $3,000,000. It certainly injured their credit very much.

By Mr. SMITHERS:

Q. I find in the Globe of December 18, 1872, a portion of the speech to which you referred, delivered in the House of Representatives in 1867, referring to this transaction, in which is this sentence: "I have asked of him to let me have the use of his shares of Credit Mobilier, and that he has done." I ask whether that is correctly reported?—A. The phrase "to let me have" should be "to loan me." You will find the expression is correct in that way.

Q. The sentence is correctly reported, then, except that the word "let" should be "loan?"—A. Yes.

Q. I wish to ask you what that transaction was in which he loaned you these shares?—A. He simply loaned me his certificate of fifty shares, which I exhibited in the House.

Q. Then the loan that you refer to of the shares was simply a loan of the certificate, for the purpose of exhibiting it to members in debate?—A. That is all. I asked Mr. Neilson to loan me the certificate made in his name, all these fifty shares. There was, of course, no transfer to me on the books, or anything of the sort.

Q. You meant, then, his certificate, which constitutes his evidence of ownership; you do not mean to loan these shares themselves?—A. Only the evidence of ownership. I did not mean to loan the shares. I sent to him in New York, and asked him to send me the certificate, for the purpose of exhibiting it in the House, which he did.

WASHINGTON, *January* 21, 1873.

Senator J. W. PATTERSON, having been recalled at his own request, made the following statement:

GENTLEMEN: A committee of the Senate would have the right and would be obligated, when there were sufficient grounds of suspicion, to investigate my conduct and satisfy itself whether or not I had been improperly or corruptly influenced in my official conduct; but here I appear by courtesy, and must plead, as my excuse for troubling you, the necessity of defending myself against an unjust suspicion of having been improperly influenced in my legislative action. This, as I understand it, is the legitimate and the only legitimate inquiry before your committee. What property, and how much property, I may purchase is a private matter, not open to legislative investigation unless the circumstances of that transaction indicate that I have been improperly influenced by it as a legislator.

When last before you, I stated that on two occasions I bought stock and bonds in the Union Pacific Railroad. I should with as little hesitation have stated that I had bought stock in the Credit Mobilier if I had understood that to be the fact, for I see no reason why a member of Congress might not with equal propriety own stock in either, or be corrupted as readily with one as the other.

Members of the House have owned stock in the Credit Mobilier from the first, and drawn their dividends upon it, whose integrity and official propriety have never been questioned, though they have exercised their right to vote whenever the Pacific Railroad has been before them. They who purchased this stock after all legislation had passed, and whose votes and influence could not have been affected in a solitary instance, cannot be less innocent, and should have been saved the cruel humiliation of this public scandal.

My object in coming before the committee this morning is to state or explain a little more fully than I did when first before you a point on which I find I differ from Mr. Ames's present position.

In my testimony of Wednesday, I stated that I made two purchases of stock and bonds of Mr. Ames, and I read that statement to him before presenting it to the committee. He said it was correct except in a single point. I believed it correct in every point, and therefore gave it to the committee.

I will state the case. It is in relation to the first purchase. We are agreed on the second.

More than a year after I had been offered stock in the Credit Mobilier, having some money to invest, I placed it in the hands of Mr. Ames, without a thought that the stock of the Credit Mobilier, represented as so profitable, was in the market, and with the understanding, on my part certainly, that he was to secure for me stock or bonds in the Union Pacific Railroad, and dispose of the same in such time and way as he could realize the most for them. On one occasion, and I have no recollection of any other, he paid me some money, which I then supposed, and now believe, came from the sale of stock or bonds which he had purchased and held for me. A day or two since he came to my room and said he had again been called before the committee, and showed me for the first time a memorandum, in which he had credited me with thirty shares of stock in the Credit Mobilier and two dividends on the same.

Supposing I was to receive stock or bonds, or their proceeds, and never having received anything else, I thought I had got what I paid for; but Mr. Ames, it seems, not wishing me to suffer from my ignorance of the mysteries of Pacific Railroad management, had put me down for stock in the Credit Mobilier, and assigned me what I received as dividends on the same.

So far as this investigation is concerned, it is a matter of indifference to me whether his understanding or mine is correct, for, in either case, it was simply an investment for profit, and had no connection, in thought or act, with legislation; but if he is right, somebody owes me a few thousand dollars, which if they will have the goodness to cash, I shall find my venture more profitable than I had any reason to expect.

I have volunteered this statement, because, if Mr. Ames is correct and I am wrong, it is due to myself that I, and not another, should make the correction.

I still maintain, however, that my understanding of the transaction is the correct one, and have reason to think that Mr. Ames at one time entertained the same view.

I have two letters, gentlemen, which I had not thought to make public, but, as they seem to confirm my position, I am sure Mr. Ames will justify me in making them a part of my statement.

Before reading the letters, let me give a word of explanation.

Near the close of the last session of Congress, a gentleman came to me and said that Hon. E. H. Rollins, who was a competitor for my place in the Senate, was reporting that I was an owner in the Credit Mobilier, and that he should use it against me in the canvass. Meeting Mr. Ames, I repeated what I had heard. He wrote a letter to Mr. Rollins, in which he denied that I owned stock in that company, and came over to the Senate and showed it to me. I said it was entirely satisfactory. On reaching Concord I found that, among other false and malicious stories concocted to injure my public reputation, this was afloat. I denied, as I do to-day, that I had ever owned any of the stock, but stated, as I have testified to you, that I had bought stock and bonds in the road. To confirm my statement, I telegraphed to Mr. Ames, at his home, to send me a copy of his letter to Mr. Rollins. My telegram reached him in Washington. Not hearing from him as quickly as I desired, I wrote him, and at length received replies, both to my telegram and my letters, which, with your permission, I will now read, so far as they relate to this subject:

"WASHINGTON, D. C., *June* 9, 1872.

"DEAR SIR: I have your telegram asking me to give you the substance of the letter I wrote Rollins. You saw the letter; I added nothing to it after you saw it, and it is the only letter I have written him.

"The substance of it was that I heard he was making charges against you, or representing you as holder or owner of stock in the Credit Mobilier, and that there were wrong and improper influences in relation to it.

"I wrote him that I *did not think you ever had any of the stock;* and if you had, there was no more impropriety in it than owning bank stock.

"Yours truly,

"OAKES AMES.

"HON. J. W. PATTERSON."

"NORTH EASTON, *June* 12, 1872.

"DEAR SIR: I wrote you from Washington in reply to your telegram.

"I have your letters of the 8th and 12th this evening here on my arrival home from Washington.

"I stated in that letter the substance of my letter to Rollins.

"You saw the letter I wrote him, and there was nothing in that but the truth; and that Mr. Rollins should say that the Credit Mobilier of America was a fraudulent concern, and that those engaged in it perpetrated a fraud on the country, community, or its stockholders, is simply an untruth. The stockholders of that company contained some of the best men of the country, and Mr. Rollins knows it. Such men as John J. Cisco, General Dix, William H. Macy, M. Dillon, McCormick, James Brooks, and many others of New York, Glidden & Williams, Ezra Baker, Elisha Atkins, John Duff, Samuel Hooper, F. Gordon Dexter, Hon. John B. Alley, Oliver Ames, and myself, and many others, and I am proud to say that I was a stockholder in it, and that there is and was nothing wrong in holding the stock, any more than in owning bank or railroad stock, and Mr. Rollins should be ashamed to make such charges *if you had been a stockholder and manager in the company, as you was not.* If Mr. Rollins can find nothing against you worse than being a stockholder in the Credit Mobilier, you must be the purest man in New Hampshire or in the United States Senate.

"Trusting that you will not suffer because you are accused of being a stockholder with me, *and not realizing the profits*, I am yours, truly,

"OAKES AMES.

"Hon. J. W. PATTERSON."

I have only to add that I have never received any certificate of stock or other evidence of ownership in the Credit Mobilier, and am not enough of a lawyer to know how I could draw dividends on what I did not own.

With this explanation I am done with this examination. Of the outrage done to the fair fame of men who have lived without reproach for half a century, by driving them into the gaze of the public with a scourge of epithets which should be laid upon the lowest criminals with caution; of the torture inflicted upon men, sensitive of their good name, by subjecting them to legislative inquisition without sufficient reason, I may take occasion to speak elsewhere; but here I close, simply remarking, if such things are to continue, all decent men will leave public life, as I do, with pleasure, and not with regret.

By the CHAIRMAN:

Q. If I understood the substance of your statement the other day, it was that you never purchased any stock of the Credit Mobilier, but that you did purchase stock and bonds in the Union Pacific Railroad Company?—A. Certainly, I say that now.

Q. What was the precise form of the dealings between you and Mr. Ames? How was the business done?—A. The conversation of which I spoke about the Credit Mobilier was in 1867. More than a year after that I went to Mr. Ames, having some money, not being a business man myself, and asked him to invest it for me. He being a business man, I gave him the money to invest. My understanding was that he was to invest it in the stock and bonds of the Union Pacific Railroad Company, and to make the most of it he could for me.

Q. What was the amount?—A. Three thousand dollars.

Q. Was anything said at the time about the Credit Mobilier?—A. No, sir; I have no recollection of a word being said.

Q. Was anything said about the stock and bonds of the road?—A. Yes. He thought the bonds would appreciate in value, and also that the stock would be a good investment.

Q. The amount of money you let him have was to be invested in the stock and bonds of the Union Pacific Railroad. Did you ever have any bonds delivered to you? Did you ever receive any bonds?—A. Yes, sir; and at one time I put my bonds into the hands of a friend in New York, and also the stock I had, except the stock which Mr. Ames sold for me.

Q. You had, then, a certificate for some stock?—A. I had a certificate for three hundred shares of stock. I do not remember the amount of bonds. My friend in New York did all the business for me; I had very little to do with it.

Q. Have you kept any money-account of the dealings between you and Mr. Ames?—A. No, sir; I generally put down such things in a little pocket memorandum-book, which is frequently destroyed. I do not know whether I have anything of that kind or not. If I have, it is at my home in New Hampshire; it is not here.

Q. The sales that were made by this gentleman in New York were by a member of the firm of Morton, Bliss & Co.?—A. That was the firm that made the sales for me.

Q. And whatever you put in their hands to sell was Union Pacific Railroad securities?—A. Yes, sir.

Q. Did you ever have a certificate of stock in the Credit Mobilier?—A. No, sir.

Q. You never received any transfer of it or made any transfer?—A. I never received it, haven't got it, and never transferred it.

Q. And you never supposed you had any sort of interest in the stock?—A. No, sir; I supposed I had stock and bonds in the railroad; not any in this company.

Q. Can you give an idea of the gross amount, nominal value, of the stock and bonds you received for your $3,000?—A. As I stated before, I can give you the amount of stock. As to the bonds I cannot state it, because, except what Mr. Ames sold, I put it in the hands of friends.

Q. And you do not know what amount they sold for you?—A. I do not now. I could easily ascertain. There is no question about the fact; I had it, and it was sold.

Q. And they never sold any Credit Mobilier stock for you?—A. No, sir; they did not.

By Mr. NIBLACK:

Q. While I recognize the seeming indelicacy of asking in regard to private transactions, they have been so often referred to in the statements gentlemen have voluntarily submitted, that it seems necessary in order to explain the entire transaction. I want to ask you whether you did not borrow the money you gave Mr. Ames to invest from a friend in this city, Ex-Mayor Emery?—A. Never; not a penny of it.

Q. Do you remember having a conversation with Mr. Emery in regard to this investment?—A. Not in the least; no, sir.

By Mr. MERRICK:

Q. Did Mr. Ames pay any dividends on this investment?—A. He states that he paid dividends; I understand that he accounted to me for Union Pacific Railroad stock he had bought and sold; he understands it differently.

Q. Can you state what amount you received?—A. It was five or six years ago. I should think it was $2,000 or $3,000.

Q. Did he pay you more than once?—A. I have no recollection now of more than one payment. He says he paid me twice.

Q. What was the character of the subsequent investment you speak of?—A. Simply that I bought some bonds and some stock.

Q. What sort of bonds and stock?—A. The bonds and stock of the Union Pacific Railroad.

Q. What was the amount of them?—A. I have just stated to the chairman that I could not give the amount of bonds.

Q. I mean the amount of money you invested in the purchase?—A. I think $4,000.

Q. Was that money had of your own, or of money you borrowed for investment?—A. I have no recollection of borrowing any money for the purchase of bonds.

Q. You would know it, if you had borrowed money for that purpose?—A. I would be very likely to remember it. This is a matter, however, that occurred four or five years ago.

By the CHAIRMAN:

Q. In this last transaction, you say that you invested so much money and that you received so much in bonds and stock coming from that purchase?—A. I did.

Q. Mr. Ames had nothing to do with the negotiation or sales of these securities?—A. No, sir.

Q. The difference between you grows out of the first transaction?—A. Entirely.

Q. You say that you let him have some money, which he invested in some way, and that he disposed of the securities?—A. Of the bonds and stock; yes.

Q. You did not understand then, and do not now, so far as you have any knowledge or memory about it, that that had anything to do with the Credit Mobilier?—A. No, sir; not as I understood it. Mr. Ames understands it differently. He thinks that it was the stock of the Credit Mobilier I bought, and that what he paid me was the dividends on that stock; that is the reason for my explanation here to day—I thought I would rather do it than to have him to do it. I want a correct understanding of the matter.

By Mr. AMES:

Q. You paid me $3,000 in January, 1868?—A. I do not recollect the date.

Q. February 14, I paid you $2,223, proceeds of a dividend on the $3,000 I invested for you in January; is not that correct?—A. It is your statement. I understood it to be a sale of bonds, as I said before.

Q. And I delivered to you thirty shares of Union Pacific stock at the same time?—A. I have no recollection about that.

Q. January 19, I paid you a dividend of $1,800, which was a dividend of 60 per cent. cash upon $3,000 invested in Credit Mobilier stock; I suppose that is correct?—A. That is the memorandum you showed me, and which I have just been explaining.

By the CHAIRMAN:

Q. Do you make any question but that you received the amounts of money from Mr. Ames?—A. I have stated that I received money from him once. I do not recollect about the other occasion referred to. I do not contradict Mr. Ames's statement. I say that I do not recollect it. When I received it, I supposed the money had come from a sale of the Union Pacific Railroad securities, purchased for me.

By Mr. AMES:

Q. What I want to get at is whether you deny having received of me these amounts for some purpose or other?—A. No; I do not deny it nor affirm it.

Q. Do you mean us to understand that you have any doubt as to the fact of receiving these sums, as noted down by me?—A. I mean to have it understood precisely as I stated it; I do not recollect it. That I received some money of you once, I admit. I do not recollect the other.

Q. But how it was derived is the issue between us. What I want to understand is whether you deny having received these amounts?—A. I do not deny it, because I do not recollect it.

Mr. AMES. The difference, as I understand, between Senator Patterson and myself is, that, as I stated in my testimony, my understanding was that Mr. Patterson purchased thirty shares of Credit Mobilier stock and received the dividends that I have mentioned in my testimony. Mr. Patterson in his testimony stated that he never purchased any Credit Mobilier stock of me and received no dividends. That is the only difference between us. If Mr. Patterson admits that he purchased the stock, or bargained for it, and received the dividends, that makes my statement correct. If he does not admit that, there is the point on which we differ.

By the CHAIRMAN:

Q. Mr. Patterson says that he had at one time, but long before the payment of this money, some talk about purchasing some Credit Mobilier stock. I understand him now to say that, at the time he paid over the $3,000 in money, he did not understand it was for Credit Mobilier stock, or that he was to receive dividends on it. He thought it was for the purchase of, or investment in, the stock and bonds of the Union Pacific Railroad. Now what was that transaction? What was said between you, Mr. Ames, and Mr. Patterson, when he received the money?

Mr. AMES. My understanding was that I took the $3,000 to buy stock of the Credit Mobilier for him. That was my understanding.

By the CHAIRMAN:

Q. What was Mr. Patterson's understanding?—A. I suppose he understood it in the same way.

Q. What was the talk between you?—A. We did not talk anything about the Credit Mobilier.

Mr. PATTERSON. What did we talk about at that time?

Mr. AMES. We didn't talk about anything of that sort.

By the CHAIRMAN:

Q. What was the date of this transaction?—A. January, 1868.

Q. You had had a conversation before upon that subject?—A. Yes, sir.

Q. How recently before?—A. I cannot tell you. I cannot remember dates.

Q. That transaction was here in Washington?—A. Yes.

Q. Do you remember any conversation, and can you tell the committee what was said between you and him at that time in reference to Credit Mobilier stock?—A. I cannot remember anything further than that I was to get $3,000 of Credit Mobilier stock for him, at par, with interest charged from July 1, 1867, to the time he took the stock, which interest amounted to $105. He paid me $3,000. When I received the first dividend of 80 per cent., the 14th February, I sold the bonds at 97, making $2,380. I deducted the $105 interest, and paid Mr. Patterson over the balance of the dividend, $2,223.

Q. Was the stock ever transferred to him?—A. I think none of the stock was transferred. It is my recollection that I handed him a certificate of stock. He says I did not, and his memory is better than mine. If I did not, then I have lost one certificate of thirty shares.

Q. I understand that, to make up the account of stock you should have, these thirty shares are gone?—A. Yes. I do not know that Mr. Patterson had it. I do not wish to insinuate that he had it at all.

Q. Have you now any memory of delivering it to Mr. Patterson?—A. It is my recollection that I delivered thirty shares of stock and thirty shares of Union Pacific Railroad stock at the same time I paid the first dividend.

Q. Have you examined the books of the company to see if that transfer was made?—A. I do not think the certificate of stock given to me as trustee has been transferred on the books. I held over two hundred shares, that I now have in my pocket-book in small certificates.

Q. Upon the books which were before the committee no stock appears to stand in Mr. Patterson's name?—A. I do not think any of that stock held by me as trustee has been transferred, except the ten shares I referred to, to Mr. Gilbert, and three shares to Mr. Ham.

Q. Your supposition is that you delivered a certificate of stock to Mr. Patterson, and that he has it yet?—A. That is my impression; I do not say that I did. I do not pretend to recollect. I may be mistaken.

Q. Do you feel certain, or anything like certain, in reference to it?—A. That is my impression. I do not want to say I am certain when Mr. Patterson says the contrary.

Q. Is that your belief?—A. That is my belief.

Q. Where was it done?—A. Done here in Washington.

Q. You think that was delivered to him at the time the thirty shares of Union Pacific Railroad stock were transferred to him?—A. Yes, I believe so, at the same time with the thirty shares of Union Pacific Railroad stock.

Q. What was the date of that?—A. I think it must have been some time in February, 1868.

Q. You claim that you received the money from him in January?—A. The $3,000 were received by me in January.

Q. Have you the date?—A. I have not it here; no, sir.

Q. Now, what was it understood that money was to be invested in; and how much, and what precisely did you pay or deliver to Mr. Patterson?—A. I delivered, on February 14, $2,223 in money, as I have stated.

Q. How was the money received by you?—A. I got it from the sale of his bonds.

Q. And these bonds were dividends on his stock?—A. These bonds were dividends.

Q. They were paid over to you because the stock stood in your name?—A. I collected the dividends on the whole amount that stood in my name.

Q. Go on and state just how much you received, and how much you paid to Mr. Patterson.—A. I have stated that the first payment that I received was 80 per cent. in bonds, which on $3,000 would be $2,400. I sold the bonds at 97, netting $2,380. I paid to Mr. Patterson, the 14th

February, $2,223, which, with the amount of $105 for interest on the $3,000 from July, makes up the amount of the dividend. Then in June I paid him a dividend of 60 per cent. in cash, $1,800.

Q. That was declared as a cash dividend?—A. That was declared as a cash dividend. I received the money and paid it over to him.

By Mr. MERRICK:

Q. In addition to that you delivered to him the thirty shares, on the 14th February, of Union Pacific Railroad stock?—A. Yes; it was the first dividend on the Credit Mobilier. I am not sure about the date when I delivered the stock, but it was about that time. It might have been when he paid me for the stock in January.

By the CHAIRMAN:

Q. The stock was received as a dividend?—A. The Union Pacific Railroad stock was received as a dividend on the stock which he purchased.

Q. Is that all you received on that $3,000?—A. When this suit of McComb was brought up I think I held most of the dividends in Union Pacific Railroad stock belonging to the different certificates held by me for various parties, and that I consolidated a large number of them, six hundred odd shares, belonging to these different parties, in one certificate, which I put in the name of Mr. Kennedy, as trustee. A year or more afterward he transferred it back to me, and I hold it now. Then something like a year and a half ago I settled with Mr. Patterson, and paid him what dividends in Union Pacific Railroad stock belonged to his thirty shares of Credit Mobilier stock.

Q. How much did you pay him then, do you remember?—A. I think, as near as I can recollect, his thirty shares gave him about one hundred shares of Union Pacific Railroad stock in all. I paid him this, and the balance of what was due beyond the thirty shares already referred to.

Q. Have you any idea what the amount was?—A. I gave him the stock.

Q. Did you ever pay him any more money than you have stated?—A. I cannot recollect that I ever did.

Q. Did Mr. Patterson receive the full amount of the dividend declared on the thirty shares of Credit Mobilier stock?—A. It is my impression that he did.

Q. When you settled with him was it understood that he was the owner of these thirty shares or that you were to have them? What was your understanding?—A. I thought they belonged to him. I had purchased them for him.

Q. You think that he was the owner of $3,000 of the Credit Mobilier stock upon which you drew the dividends and accounted to him for?—A. Yes, sir.

Q. You understood that he was the owner of thirty shares?—A. That was my idea. If I have not delivered to him all the dividends I am bound to account to him for it.

Q. Now, in this subsequent transaction, whatever may have been said, you supposed he understood it in that way?—A. I judged he did.

Q. Can you tell anything that was said between you and him upon the subject during this period?—A. I do not know that I can, now, anything in particular. I settled with him and gave him the dividends.

Q. You did not suppose there was any question between you but that it was Credit Mobilier stock; that he purchased thirty shares and received the dividends. You supposed that was clearly understood between you?—A. I did. I do not know that I had any conversation with him as to how it stood. I now suppose that Mr. Patterson, from his stand-point, understood it differently.

Q. When did you first learn there was any misunderstanding between you in reference to this transaction?—A. Not until recently.

Q. Mr. Patterson has shown some letters here from you last summer?—A. There were charges made against Mr. Patterson that he was the holder and owner of Credit Mobilier stock. My letter simply was that he never appeared upon the books of the company as the holder of stock.

Q. That is the way you reconciled the statement of your letter with the facts?—A. That is the way my letters read.

Q. You did not mean to say, or to be understood as saying, that he never had any interest in Credit Mobilier stock?—A. No, sir.

Q. But simply that his name did not appear upon the books as a stockholder?—A. Yes, sir; that it did not appear as a stockholder.

Q. Do you think that is a fair, gospel interpretation of your letter?—A. That is as I understood it. Mr. Patterson was very anxious that I should write him something to repel the slanderous abuse heaped upon him, and what I wrote I understood to be strictly true.

Q. It was literally, as a formal statement, true, I suppose?—A. Yes, it was literally true.

Q. Do you think a man would understand from these letters exactly what the transaction was?—A. He would by inquiring further.

Q. He would not understand exactly without inquiring further?—A. That would depend upon how much he knew before.

Q. You say you wrote that for what reason?—A. I wrote that to repel the charges made against Mr. Patterson of his owning improperly that Credit Mobilier stock. I did not think there was anything improper in owning it. I never felt ashamed of owning it. I never felt that I had done anything wrong, or that anything wrong could be made out of it.

Q. You did it out of consideration of the tenderness of his conscience?—A. Yes, sir.

Q. Did you have any conversation with Mr. Patterson about the time of writing these letters as to what the facts were?—A. No, sir.

Q. Was anything said between you to the effect that you were to write a letter that would be literally true and still not be in spirit in accordance with the facts?—A. What I said was that his name would not appear upon the books of the company as a stockholder, and that is all there is of it.

Q. If he could make anything out of that statement you had no objection?—A. I had no objection.

By Mr. MERRICK:

Q. Did you suppose at the time that you and he thoroughly understood each other on the subject?—A. I did suppose he knew all about it. I did not know that there was anything lacking in his information. I did not suppose there was; it seems there was. Of course, Mr. Patterson had nothing to do with it, except from what I told him, and he may have got a wrong impression from my statement. It seems that I make statements that are not wholly understood, and write letters that are not understood. I did not suppose there was anything wrong in saying in my letter, "four shares to Massachusetts," and I do not understand yet what there is.

By Mr. NIBLACK:

Q. If I understand, according to your interpretation, you received from him $3,000, and delivered to him thirty shares of Credit Mobilier stock, with the dividends and proceeds of the stock, amounting at the time of delivery to thirty shares of Union Pacific Railroad stock and 80 per cent. in bonds; that you afterward delivered a cash dividend in June, and an additional dividend in Union Pacific Railroad stock, a year and a half ago?—A. Yes, sir; when we settled up the matter.

Q. What do you say the additional dividend of Union Pacific Railroad stock was?—A. I think he had in all one hundred shares.

Q. About seventy shares in addition to the thirty?—A. Yes, sir; to close up the transaction.

Q. I understand you to say, and to have said from the start, that you regarded the Credit Mobilier stock as legitimate for any one to invest in, as a fair, honest corporation, for legitimate purposes?—A. I do.

Q. Then why the necessity of covering up any such investment?—A. There was no necessity; I do not know that I have covered up anything.

Q. Why, then, the necessity of carrying the stock in your name, instead of transferring it to those you sold it to?—A. There was no necessity of doing that; it did not make any difference. It was a matter of convenience for the parties holding these small amounts, some living in Iowa, some in New Hampshire, and some in New York, to have the dividends drawn and paid over to them. It would be very inconvenient for them to come to New York to draw personally the dividends on the little amounts held by them.

Q. Where, then, the necessity of apparently concealing the ownership and allowing the public to infer that these small owners did not own the stock; why not let it be understood that the stock stood in the name of the proper owners, if it was a fair, just, and honest transaction?—A. I certainly so considered it; and in this matter I did what Mr. Patterson wanted. I wrote these letters covering a certain point, and saying nothing more about it.

Q. In your letter to Mr. McComb you did not give the names, but simply gave the names of the States?—A. He did not ask for names; he said I was giving too much to eastern men.

Q. Still the letter seems to have an air of mystery connected with it?—A. That is what my friends say; that I never ought to be trusted to write a letter; that I never conceal anything.

Mr. PATTERSON. As I have already stated, so far as I am concerned, I would just as soon have it understood with the public that I own stock in the Credit Mobilier as that I owned any other stock. I have no feeling on that subject at all. I think it was equally honorable as a business transaction. I simply state the matter as I understood it. I never did receive—and I say it under the most solemn oath—one share of Credit Mobilier stock in my life.

By the CHAIRMAN:

Q. And you did not understand that Mr. Ames was holding it for your benefit?—A. No, sir; I understood I was buying the stock and bonds of the Union Pacific Railroad Company.

Q. You did not understand really that you were equitably entitled to the earnings on this Credit Mobilier stock?—A. No, sir; Mr. Ames says it; if that were the truth, I do not care a fig about it. I would just as lief it should be stated in that as in any other way.

Q. But you did not understand it so?—A. I did not understand it so, and that is all there is in reference to these thirty shares of stock. I have no recollection of ever receiving thirty shares, and I do not believe I ever did at the time he speaks of.

Q. It was in January or February, 1868, then, that you received the shares of railroad stock of which you speak?—A. I received the shares in this last transaction; there is no doubt about that. There is no question between Mr. Ames and myself about that.

Q. You have no recollection of ever disposing of the thirty shares of Credit Mobilier stock?—A. I never did that, I know; I am absolutely positive about it.

Q. Have you made any examination to see whether thirty shares of Credit Mobilier stock were entered on the books of the company in your name?—A. No, sir; I have never examined about it. I have taken no pains about and care nothing about it.

Q. You have no recollection of receiving thirty shares of Union Pacific Railroad stock as far back as 1868?—A. No, sir.

Q. Have you any account of sale of it from Morton, Bliss & Co.?—A. No, sir. I want to say one word further in relation to these letters. I went to Mr. Ames and saw him in the House and stated to him the charge which was in circulation. I said to him, "You know that it is not true;" and I asked him to write a letter. I did not indicate to him what to write. A little after that I was in my seat in the Senate, when Mr. Ames came over and showed me a letter he had written at his own option and in such language as he pleased. I said to him that it was satisfactory.

Q. You supposed the letter expressed the honest truth as you understood it?—A. I did, and that is my understanding now. I did not suggest at all what he was to write. I did not understand that he held in trust any stock for me.

Q. That letter of Mr. Ames you understood to be simply and literally true upon the face of it, honestly and substantially true?—A. True in every sense.

By Mr. AMES:

Q. In your final settlement of Union Pacific Railroad stock you received all your dividends on the Credit Mobilier stock; if not at the time they were declared, you received them afterward?—A. I received all that I understood to be my due for the money I had paid; that I do not question at all. I put that stock into the hands of Mr. Morton, who sold it. I am now speaking of the thirty shares you say I received in February, 1868. I never received in February, 1868, shares in the Credit Mobilier or shares in the Union Pacific Railroad Company. That I am positive about.

By the CHAIRMAN:

Q. Whatever you did receive, in money, bonds, or anything else, you did not understand it was a dividend upon the Credit Mobilier stock?—A. No, sir; I supposed Mr. Ames had very kindly bought the stock and sold it for me, and had made for me a little money in the transaction.

Q. You supposed it was an investment in the stock and bonds of the Union Pacifice Railroad, and had no idea there was any Credit Mobilier in it?—A. I have said that several times.

Q. You are not the owner now, as I understand you, of any Union Pacific Railroad stock?—A. No, sir.

Q. And if you did receive thirty shares in 1868, you never sold it?—A. No, sir.

By Mr. MERRICK:

Q. Is Mr. Ames still the owner of certain stock for you?—A. Not to my knowledge; all our transactions have been settled up. He has nothing for me; if he has I should be very glad to accept it.

By the CHAIRMAN:

Q. I understand, Mr. Ames, that the second purchase was a regular purchase of Union Pacific Railroad securities?—A. There was no Credit Mobilier about it.

Re-examination of Mr. AMES:

Mr. AMES. There is a statement in one of these letters which I wish to correct. I said, in one of the letters, that General Dix and Mr. Cisco were stockholders in the Credit Mobilier. I have been informed since writing the letter that they never were stockholders. I supposed they were stockholders from the fact that one was president and the other treasurer of the Union Pacific Railroad Company. It seems I was mistaken, and I wish to make this correction.

By Mr. NIBLACK:

Q. If I have understood you, Mr. Ames, you have insisted from the beginning of this investigation that this Credit Mobilier was an honest corporation; that there was no impropriety in a member of Congress, or anybody else, holding stock in it?—A. I hold there is no more impropriety in it than holding property in anything else.

Q. Then I will ask you what is your explanation of the sensitiveness which has been shown by members of Congress and others on the subject of having any connection with it?—A. It was in consequence of the slander and abuse heaped upon the Credit Mobilier. They became frightened; they thought it might affect their re-election, and they wanted to slip out of it the easiest way they could; I know of nothing else. I cannot see anything wrong in the transaction, and I do not think any of these gentlemen did.

Q. If there is nothing wrong in it, why not come out boldly and make an explicit acknowledgment to the country of their connection with it? Why this apparently general effort to conceal?—A. That I cannot explain. Here are Mr. Boyer, Mr. Wilson, and Mr. Bingham, who have come forward and stated frankly their connection with the Credit Mobilier, and who did not appear to feel ashamed of it.

Q. Why, without referring to individuals, have others taken a different course?—A. I do not know other than I have stated.

Q. Why did not this letter of yours to Mr. McComb state the names of individuals?—A. I do not know what the letter was in reply to. If a man sends you, or any member of Congress, a document in relation to which you have no particular interest, you throw it in the waste-basket; we cannot preserve all the letters we receive.

Q. Why could you not naturally, as you would in speaking of any other transaction almost, say you had given Mr. Patterson so much, or Mr. Bingham so much, without referring to them by their States?—A. I might have done that just as readily as to have written what I did, but it would have taken me longer to write it. Mr. McComb was talking about the location of it. He thought I was placing too much in one locality. He did not call for names. I was showing him that I had scattered the stock over several of the States, as I had been trying to do from the beginning. I was endeavoring to get people everywhere to invest in it.

Q. I understand you to say that you understood Senator Patterson to be a holder in this stock last June, when you wrote these letters?—A. That was my impression; he denies it.

Q. Would not the reading of these letters carry the impression that he was not the holder of shares in it, although you regarded it as a perfectly legitimate transaction?—A. I wrote these letters to help Mr. Patterson, and put it in that shape for that purpose. He says he had not any stock, and it did not stand in his name.

Q. Was not that an admission, on your part, of impropriety?—A. It was a little sort of a dodge, I admit, but there is no admission that there is any impropriety in holding the stock, and I never considered that there was. These gentlemen were so sensitive about the slanders heaped by everybody on the Credit Mobilier that they wanted to dodge and avoid it all they could. I did not consider it anything wrong, and never have.

By the CHAIRMAN:

Q. You considered it a kind of skulking on their part?—A. I did.

By Mr. NIBLACK:

Q. Why did you consent to help them, then?—A. Because I am kind hearted, and want to help everybody.

Testimony of Mr. AMES.

By the CHAIRMAN:

Q. Now, Mr. Ames, let me put one general question to you. In your letter of January 25 or 28 you speak of "Washburn's move" here, which, I suppose, means in Congress. Can you tell us what it was you referred to?—A. Mr. Washburn, if I recollect right, was complaining, and said there was complaint in Nebraska about the rates of freight on the Union Pacific Railroad, and he wanted to fix a rate by congressional legislation—something like that. I know that it was for our interest while the road was being built, and before it was completed. We required all the transportation we had to carry our railroad-iron and other material. All the freight we carried for private parties was a damage and a nuisance to us. We were building the road rapidly, and we wanted all the transportation we had to send forward our iron, ties, &c. The rates he proposed to fix, let me say, were a great deal higher than we are now charging. That was the substance of this "move;" there was nothing else.

Q. The "Washburn's move" that you refer to in this letter was his proposition, in some form to have Congress fix the price of freights?—A. That was my impression.

Q. Do you remember whether he had inroduced a bill or a resolution before that?—A. I do not remember.

Q. Which Mr. Washburn do you refer to?—A. C. C. Washburn. He is in the city now; I met him this morning. You can call him, and he can tell you himself what his "move" was.

Q. Was this Mr. Washburne the Mr. Washburne who offered the resolution for investigation?—A. I am not sure. I think I have that resolution here. It is as follows:

"UNION PACIFIC RAILROAD.

"Mr. WASHBURNE, of Illinois, by unanimous consent, offered the following resolution; which was read, considered, and agreed to:

"*Resolved*, That the President be requested to transmit to this House the report of the special commissioners to examine into the character of the work on the Union Pacific Railroad, and to inform the House what attempts, if any, have been made on the part of said railroad company to obtain money from the Government for building said road without having constructed the same in conformity to existing law; and also to further inform the House the amount of bonds issued to said railroad company, and if a sufficient amount has been retained in the hands of the Government to guarantee its completion as a first-class road, in further accordance with the existing law."

There is nothing in this, however, in regard to an investigation by Congress, and this I notice was offered by Mr. Washburne, of Illinois, and not by C. C. Washburn.

Q. This, then, is not the resolution you refer to?—A. No; and I do not know as I can tell you just what I did refer to. I have no recollection what it was.

Q. At what time was it that Mr. Washburn introduced his bill to regulate the fares of the Pacific Railroad?—A. I cannot tell you. I think the resolution he introduced was prohibiting the railroad charging more than twice the rates of roads east of the Mississippi.

Q. Can you tell whether that was what you referred to in your letter?—A. I cannot tell you; one of these resolutions probably.

Q. Do you now remember any communication between you and Mr. McComb, whether you said anything or wrote anything to Mr. McComb about Mr. Colfax?—A. I am very sure I did not. If he has any letters on that subject let him produce them. I have no recollection of anything of the sort, and I never heard anything of the sort until I heard his testimony.

Q. Did you ever, in your own mind or judgment, see any such beneficial working of your stock in Mr. Colfax?—A. I never did.

Q. Did you ever have any idea that Mr. Colfax, in his action as Speaker, was influenced by any such motives?—A. No, sir; I never saw anything of the sort, and never believed anything of the sort, and I do not believe I ever said a word of anything of the sort to anybody. I repeat that if Mr. McComb has any of my letters, he can produce them. He is at perfect liberty to produce any letters I ever wrote him, and I would be glad if he would produce all I ever wrote him. I am not aware of writing or doing anything wrong or dishonorable at any ime.

Mr. McComb. All I want to say in reply is, that I have a perfectly distinct recollection of a conversation with Mr. Ames explanatory of that expression in that lettter; that I asked what it meant, and that Mr. Ames replied, in substance, as I have stated. If I can find another letter on the subject I will bring it.

Mr. Ames. Produce the letter.

Mr. Brooks. Before the committee adjourns I wish to say that I have received my check-book from the express company.

The Chairman, (after examining the book.) The important fact to be got at from this check-book is whether you paid the $10,000. I see here no check for that amount.

Mr. Brooks. I stated in my testimony that I did not recollect it, but I accepted the statement of Mr. Crane. He is an accurate, reliable man, but on getting my check-book I do not find any such checks referred to by him.

The Chairman. I understood Mr. Neilson to state that you paid it?

Mr. BROOKS. He says I advanced it to him. He paid it himself. I have no personal recollection about it myself, but the check-book shows there was no such amount drawn. I had no doubt when Mr. Crane made the announcement that it was my transaction, although he knew nothing of my affairs with Mr. Durant. He is a man of truth, and I would not impugn in any way any statement made by him, but my check-book shows an entirely different state of things. It is a question merely of who paid the amount, and there is no check for $1,000, no check for $5,333, and no check of $7,000.

WASHINGTON, D. C., *January* 21, 1873.

H. S. McCOMB recalled and examined.

By the CHAIRMAN:

Question. In your testimony before the committee on a former occasion, in answer to some question which does not appear in this account of it, (I think published in the New York Tribune,) you are made to state as follows:

"You asked me if I could remember anything else. I do now; *I remember something else very distinctly which I would like to state;* reference is made in one of Mr. Ames's letters to Durant's action in New York and Washburne's move here; Mr. Ames wrote to me—I am not sure but he told me—that E. B. Washburne, of Illinois, in his place in the House, had moved some kind of an investigation into the affairs of the Union Pacific Railroad; I do not recollect the precise point; Mr. Colfax was in the chair as Speaker of the House, and by some parliamentary maneuver they blocked the game and defeated it; *Mr. Ames called my attention to it,* and asked me if I did not think that, in Mr. Colfax's case, the investment had paid; *reference to the records of Congress would fix about the day, and show what Mr. Washburne's motion was, and what Mr. Colfax said.*"

That purports to be your testimony before the committee; is it correctly stated?—Answer. That is substantially what I stated, according to my recollection.

Q. I want now to ask you whether you have made examination to see if you have a letter from Mr. Ames that contains anything on that subject.—A. I have looked over his letters and made a selection of some important ones, which were placed in one parcel, and some unimportant ones, which were placed in another. I handed both packages to my wife, and as I was leaving home to come to Washington, on Sunday night, she handed me the bundle of unimportant ones, which I brought along and have here with me.

Q. Have you examined the letters you received from Mr. Ames sufficiently to be able to say now whether you saw this statement in writing and whether Mr. Ames wrote it to you?—A. I have not the package of important letters here. I have letters dated July 13, July 17, and July 18. I remember to have had a conversation with Mr. Ames upon that subject.

Q. At the time you made this inspection and selection of letters received from Mr. Ames for the purpose of bringing on such as you regarded important, did you read them all?—A. I did not. I avoided reading them.

Q. How could you tell whether they were worth bringing until you had read them?—A. When I saw a remark in one of them that I did not care to speak of here I avoided reading the letter. I simply saw a name and I did not care to look any further into the letter.

Q. That may not be exactly fair treatment to us, although there might be something in it that we ought not to know.—A. I think, perhaps, that is the case—not affecting myself, however.

Q. Did you look over the letters you have from Mr. Ames enough to satisfy yourself whether the declaration of Mr. Ames about Mr. Colfax was in a letter to you?—A. I did not, and I have not since I made the statement originally to the committee.

Q. Have you any clearer recollection about it now than then as to whether this communication was in writing or verbal?—A. I remember a verbal communication. I have no better recollection as to the written one than I had when I made the other statement.

(The chairman stated that these questions were propounded to the witness in consequence of a letter received from Mr. Colfax requesting that he might be further examined in regard to the statement in his former testimony referred to.)

By Mr. NIBLACK:

Q. Were you not mistaken in the reference you made in that extract, which has been read, to E. B. Washburne, of Illinois; was it not C. C. Washburn, of Wisconsin?—A. If I recollect, in my original statement I gave the name of E. B. Washburne, as my impression. It was the Washburn to whom Mr. Durant wrote that letter which was taken out of the post-office in New York.

Q. They were both in Congress, but I presume it was C. C. Washburn to whom you referred. Can you tell us any better now than you could then the precise thing Mr. Ames referred to, either in his letter or conversation?—A. The reference I gave then is the best I can give. I said then that if you will refer to the records of Congress of the spring of 1868 you will see what the proceeding is that I refer to.

By the CHAIRMAN:

Q. We are asking you now what you refer to.—A. I referred to the statement in Mr. Ames's letter. I did not read the congressional proceedings.

Q. Can you state any more fully what Mr. Ames said about Mr. Colfax and what was done in Congress than you did before?—A. I think it was on a bill called the rate bill, prescribing something in reference to the rates of freight on the Pacific Railroad; that is my recollection about it. It was something in regard to a proposed investigation, or upon the subject of rates.

Q. Is it your impression that it was some bill in relation to the price charged for fares?—A. My impression is that it was a subject before Congress which the Union Pacific Railroad Company felt to be of considerable importance to them.

Q. Do you think it was upon the subject of making some reduction in their fares or rates?—A. I would not be certain about the particular thing.

Q. We want to ascertain if you can tell us what it was that Mr. Ames referred to in regard to Mr. Colfax, and which needs to be investigated for the vindication of Mr. Colfax as a fair presiding officer.—A. I should be very glad to assist in vindicating him or any other gentleman whose name is brought into this investigation. This is no contest between any of these gentlemen and myself. My recollection of Mr. Ames's statement was this: that in speaking of "Mr. Washburne's move," he said that by some parliamentary rule or move Mr. Washburn was choked off from offering his resolution, or by which the bill was gotten out of the way. That is the substance of my recollection, and whether it was the rate bill or some other bill or resolution, I cannot answer.

Q. I want to get what Mr. Ames said to you. I want to ascertain fully, if possible, what it was Mr. Ames referred to in that conversation. —A. Perhaps Mr. Ames may have some recollection himself. He wrote in his letter what it was best to do in view of "Washburne's move." Perhaps he can tell what move he referred to.

Mr. AMES. That will not prove that I said anything about Mr. Colfax. If Mr. McComb has any letters I hope he will produce them. I wish every letter I ever wrote to Mr. McComb may be produced.

The CHAIRMAN, (to Mr. McComb:)

Q. If I understand you right these letters which you understood to have some reference to this business you did not bring?—A. As I stated, I handed two packages of letters to my wife, as I frequently did when I came home in that way. You observe that I have not been in my office to transact business since the commencement of this investigation. I have gone home Saturday night and returned Sunday night. When I came away I asked her to give me the package of letters, and she handed me one of the packages. I did not look at the package until two or three days after I reached here, when it turned out she had given me the wrong one. I will look for the other when I go home.

Q. Cannot you send for it before you go home?—A. I can send on my clerk.

Q. Have you now any clear impression as to whether this communication from Mr. Ames was in writing, or a mere verbal statement?—A. I won't under the solemnity of an oath say that the statement was in writing. I recollect the original statement, and I think it was both written and verbal. I remember very distinctly the verbal one.

Q. Now state that conversation just as fully as you remember it. Let us know just what the statement was.—A. My recollection is this: that Mr. Ames met me in New York, and that he referred to this "move" in a conversation we had. I asked him what "Washburne's move" was. Mr. Ames replied, in regard to Mr. Colfax, "Didn't that pay," or "Didn't that stock pay;" some such expression as that. That was about the substance of it. I will not pretend to tell the identical words.

Q. Give us all that Mr. Ames indicated to you; of course you cannot remember his words.—A. That is just about the substance; my recollection is very general of the conversation that took place; the impression made upon me being that it referred to the rate bill, but I am not positive about that.

Q. Have you any idea of the time when that was?—A. No, sir; only that it was in the spring of 1868; taking in the months in which this correspondence was occurring, of January, February, and March, I could not give a nearer approximation to the date than that. We were meeting very frequently. We were having pretty lively times in our Union Pacific affairs. It was in the spring following our entrance upon the Oakes Ames contract, and the organization of trustees. We were getting our contracts out for iron and other material for the rapid prosecution of the work. There was a very busy time.

Q. But what was it Mr. Colfax had done or decided as Speaker; can you state it with any more definiteness?—A. I cannot give it with any more definiteness.

Q. You understood it was something that headed off Mr. Washburne. —A. That was my understanding.

Q. And the idea of Mr. Ames was, that the interests of the company might be advanced by the distribution of stock?—A. Yes; but this matter of Mr. Washburne was more particularly impressed upon my mind when Dr. Durant threatened to write to Washburne and have a general *exposé* of the whole affair, and did actually write the letter.

Q. Can you tell when it was?—A. I cannot. I know that with Mr. Bushnell and Mr. Crane I thought it was not wise to create any greater storm, and we went to the post-office and got the letter out.

Q. That was after the quarrel growing out of entering into contracts and getting an injunction?—A. No, sir; it was in the spring of 1868.

Q. What was that quarrel of Mr. Durant about?—A. It was a general distrust of each other. That was about the substance of it. Mr. Durant was not pleased with Mr. Ames and his friends particularly. Mr. Durant and myself always considered Mr. Alley the mar-plot of the concern.

Q. What did you differ about?

The WITNESS. Who differ about?

Q. You that disagreed?—A. I had nothing to do with any congressional action in any way. I did not come here to see anybody in connection with any Union Pacific Railroad interest. Mr. Ames would come on to New York fresh from Congress, and there had been wranglings between him and Dr. Durant, which finally became of sufficient importance to induce Dr. Durant to write that letter to Mr. Washburne.

Q. Was there discussion among these parties in New York in reference to anything which might take place in Congress?—A. I think it was in reference to some preliminary action in New York as well.

Q. Was not the quarrel, as Mr. Durant says, about making a contract for building the road? He says he objected to the stockholders of the Union Pacific Railroad Company contracting with themselves to build the road, and that he got them enjoined on that account.—A. No; I will tell you what I think it was. I think it was in reference to the change which was proposed in the election for directors for the Union Pacific Railroad Company, and the disposition of what was known as the Ames party to go back on their agreement. I think the election of directors was fixed by the charter of the company for October. Mr. Alley had come down here to Washington and procured a change of time of holding the election until March, or had threatened to come, or something of that kind.

Q. What I want to know is when it was that Mr. Ames said this to you?—A. It was immediately after he wrote that letter which has been placed in evidence. If you will tell me the date of that letter I will tell you the time.

Q. That letter is dated the 25th or 28th of January, 1868.—A. Then it was some time in February. It was subsequent to the writing of that letter.

Q. You think it was pretty soon after that date?—A. I think it was within a month or six weeks after.

Q. And did you understand him to refer to something that had just taken place?—A. I did in his letter and in his conversation. I think his conversation was explanatory of the letter.

Q. You put the two things together, and think it was something about "Mr. Washburne's move" which was mentioned in the letter?—A. Yes, sir; it was that, whatever that was.

By Mr. AMES:

Q. Was this conversation in New York?—A. I think it was.

Q. In February, 1868?—A. I think it was in February or March, 1868. I do not recollect the exact time.

WASHINGTON, D. C., *January* 22, 1873.

OAKES AMES recalled and examined.

By the CHAIRMAN:

Question. The committee wish to inquire a little more in detail in relation to these various gentlemen in Congress whose names have been connected with this matter. We will begin at the beginning. Will you state to the committee in reference to the conversation that took place between you and Mr. Colfax in regard to the Credit Mobilier stock?—Answer. I cannot recollect the exact conversation. I agreed to get for Mr. Colfax twenty shares of Credit Mobilier stock.

Q. Do you remember what time that agreement was?—A. No, sir; I do not.

Q. Do you think it was about the commencement of the session of Congress of 1867–'68?—A. I think it was.

Q. You agreed to get for him twenty shares Credit Mobilier stock; what further was done?—A. I got the stock and received a dividend on it of 80 per cent. in bonds. I went to Mr. Colfax and he gave me a check for the balance to pay for the stock account and for the bonds. He gave me a check for $534 and some odd cents.

Q. Did you sell the bonds?—A. I sold the bonds.

Q. He was to have the stock at par?—A. Yes, at par and interest.

Q. Can you give us the date of his check?—A. I think I can; I think the check was dated March 5, 1868, and was for $534.72.

Q. How did you keep your accounts?—A. I kept them on scraps of paper.

Q. And this paper you have in your hand is the original memorandum made at the time?—A. No, sir.

Q. What is that taken from?—A. From my memorandum made at the time. The check I got from the Sergeant-at-Arms. He gave me a check on the Sergeant-at-Arms for $534.72.

Q. Did you deliver the stock certificate?—A. No, sir; I don't think I delivered to him any stock, either the railroad or Credit Mobilier.

Q. This check which he gave you paid for the Credit Mobilier stock?—A. Yes, sir.

Q. Were there dividends on that stock afterward?—A. There was one dividend. There were other dividends in stock which I never delivered to him. There was a dividend in cash, in June, which I did pay to him.

Q. How large was that?—A. Twelve hundred dollars.

Q. Have you any receipt or voucher for that?—A. No, sir; I gave him a check on the Sergeant-at-Arms, and it is charged to me there.

Q. And you got this date from the Sergeant-at-Arms' book?—A. Yes; I never delivered to Mr. Colfax anything else, and never received anything from him except that time. He paid me for the balance of the stock, and I paid him a cash dividend.

Q. Have you ever offered him the railroad stock you received as a dividend?—A. Never.

Q. Has there ever been a conversation between you and him on the subject?—A. None at all.

Q. Did you hear Mr. Colfax's statement when he was before the committee the other day?—A. I did.

Q. What do you say in reference to that statement about his making a present to you of $500, saying that you might keep the $500 he paid you?—A. He made some remark of that sort to me.

Q. Will you state what was the whole conversation?—A. I cannot remember that at all. He made some such statement, that he was sorry for my misfortune, or something like that.

Q. How late was that?—A. That was about two years ago—about 1871.

Q. What is the amount of the stock you held that you received as dividends?—A. I cannot tell you. I have never footed it up. I have never done anything about the stock since these suits were brought up by McComb. I hold it for all these parties until that suit shall have been determined.

Q. Why was not this certificate of stock delivered to Mr. Colfax, when the adjustment was made in which he paid for it?—A. I do not know of any reason at all.

Q. Do you remember any conversation between you and him about it?—A. No, sir. I supposed, as I have stated, that the dividends on these small amounts would be paid in New York, and that it would be inconvenient for the parties holding the stock to collect them in person. I am only stating that, however, as my supposition.

Q. At the time you had this conversation with Mr. Colfax, two years ago or thereabouts, was anything said between you and him in reference to the ownership of the stock?—A. Not a word to my recollection.

Q. What did you understand him to mean by not calling on you? Did you understand that he had no right to call upon you for the $534?—A. I do not know. If I did not deliver him the stock, certainly I should pay him back again.

Q. Did he call upon you to deliver the stock?—A. No, sir; I do not think he did.

Q. Have you ever refused in any way to deliver it to him?—A. No, sir.

Q. You have held the stock ready for him at any time, if he wanted it?—A. Yes, sir.

Q. Have there ever been any dividends upon this Union Pacific Railroad stock?—A. No, sir.

Q. There was nothing to pay anybody upon that stock?—A. No, sir.

Q. You have had no conversation with Mr. Colfax in reference to that stock, as to whether he wanted it or did not want it?—A. No, sir; not to my recollection.

Q. There was nothing said about the stock at the time you had this conversation with him two years ago?—A. I do not recollect of it at all. I do not think there was.

Q. At the time you paid him $1,200, or gave him a check upon the Sergeant at-Arms for that amount, did Mr. Colfax understand that this was a dividend on this Credit Mobilier stock?—A. I suppose so; I do not know; I so understood it. That is what it was; whether he understood the matter is more than I know; I do not know that I gave him any explanation. I gave him the check.

Q. Have you any doubt that you told him what it was?—A. I cannot remember. When I suppose a man knows a thing I don't tell him over again.

Q. Do you remember whether he made any inquiry as to what it was?—A. I don't remember anything about what was said at all.

Q. You supposed that it was understood that it was a dividend you had received upon that stock?—A. I supposed so.

Q. Has he ever repaid you that $1,200?—A. Not to my knowledge. It did not belong to me.

Q. You never made any claim upon him for it, and did not suppose you had any right to?—A. No, sir.

Q. These $534 that were paid you, you did not suppose he had any right to call upon you to pay back?—A. I did not suppose so; I understood that I sold him $2,000 worth of stock. The first dividend, 80 per cent. in bonds, and that check for $534, paid for the stock. That was my supposition.

By Mr. MERRICK:

Q. In what order of time were these two dividends paid, of $1,200 and $500?—A. He paid me $500 in March, and I paid him $1,200 in the June following.

Q. Were there any other different transactions between you and Mr. Colfax to which these payments could refer at all, except this Credit Mobilier?—A. No, sir.

Q. What memoranda or entries have you in reference to this transaction?—A. I made a little memorandum at the time, I suppose, which I handed him; when I don't remember.

Q. Have you any memorandum with you?—A. No, sir.

Q. Have you made a memorandum of it at all?—A. Yes; I took a copy of the memorandum I made and brought with me. When I went home you asked me to look over my books. I did, and found I had received $534 from Mr. Colfax, and I found I had charged him with $1,200 in June.

Q. Have you the memorandum made at the time?—A. No, sir; not here; I have a memorandum which I took from that.

Q. What was the character of the book in which the memorandum was made?—A. It was in a small pocket-memorandum, and some of it on slips of paper.

Q. It was not entered in journal form?—A. No; it was simply a small memorandum-book. These things were closed up at the time here, and they were not entered upon my books at home.

Q. Is what you have here a copy of your memorandum made at the time?—A. Yes, sir; that contains the names I took from my books.

Q. The only entry in this in reference to Mr. Colfax is the $534. The $1,200 was not put on this memorandum?—A. No, sir.

Q. The extracts you have here from your memorandum-books are from the memorandum-book referred to by Mr. Kennedy in his testimony?—A. I presume so.

By the CHAIRMAN:

Q. Both these entries were made in this book, the $500 to pay the balance of the stock, and the $1,200 which were paid in June by a check on the Sergeant-at-Arms?—A. Yes; they were both on that book. I have looked it over to see, and I have looked over the Sergeant-at-Arms' book to see if my entries were correct, and I find they are.

By Mr. MCCRARY

Q. Did Mr. Colfax tell you at any time that he had concluded not to take the stock?—A. I have no recollection of it, unless it was in that conversation to which he has referred. I have no recollection of it.

Q. Have you any recollection of informing him of the litigation that had sprung up in regard to it?—A. I think I did; I think I told them all.

Q. You do not remember what he said when you informed him of that?—A. No, sir.

Q. Did you not understand that this sale of stock to Mr. Colfax was rescinded; that the trade was given up, and that he relinquished the stock to you?—A. Not unless he meant to be understood so in the conversation when I came back. I did not consider it given up. I did not consider that I had any right to withhold it.

Q. Was there anything of the kind said between you?—A. I cannot recollect; it might have been said, but I cannot recollect it.

Q. Have you ever been re-imbursed for that $1,200?—A. No, sir.

By Mr. COLFAX:

The chairman of the committee states that I may examine the witness in reference to these accounts between us, as when I gave my testimony I asked him to examine me. I want to give notice in advance that although it is difficult to prove a negative, yet I think I will be able to prove that I did not receive the $1,200 referred to. I assert that no such amount and no dividend was given to me. I desire the fact to be borne in mind while I am asking these questions. In my testimony I spoke of your asking me to take the stock; that you explained to me you thought it was a good and safe investment; that I said to you I could not pay then; that you replied I could have the twenty shares at par, if I would agree to pay interest until it was paid for—is that correct?—A. Yes, sir.

Q. This was about the opening of the session of 1867–'68, as you stated to the chairman to-day, and as you previously stated in your examination in general?—A. I think so.

Q. That was December. My recollection is that it was just before the holiday recess. Then you say that on the 5th March I paid you $534.72. That is the time—the 5th March?—A. That is my recollection.

Q. Did I offer to pay you, or did you give to me, or ask me to pay you that?—A. That I cannot tell you. I suppose I handed you a statement showing the balance due, and that you gave me the check.

Q. Do you swear that you did hand me a statement?—A. No; I will not swear to it.

Q. Did you not tell me at the time that there were more dividends that had been earned but which were unadjusted?—A. I told you there had been a dividend of 80 per cent. in bonds, and I gave you the proceeds of that in part payment of the stock. There had been also a dividend of 100 per cent. Union Pacific Railroad stock, which I did not give you.

Q. When was that dividend of stock declared?—A. In February, I believe.

Q. Did I ask you to buy bonds and pay for them?—A. No. sir.

Q. Why, then, did you prefer to buy bonds and not buy stock?—A. I did not buy bonds. I received the bonds as dividend on your stock and sold them.

Q. You sold the bonds without asking me anything about it, although they were mine?—A. I sold the bonds at 97.

Q. Without any authority from me?—A. I suppose so.

Q. Why did you sell stock without authority from me?—A. I have not sold it.

Q. That $534.72 which you say I paid you included interest on $2,000 from December to March, about three months?—A. I charged you interest on the $2,000 Credit Mobilier stock, $86.72.

Q. That is interest from when to when? That is the first I have heard of that amount of interest.—A. It is interest from July, 1867, when the stock was assigned, until you paid the money.

Q. Yet my contract for the stock was in December?—A. Yes, sir.

Q. And you say I paid you interest on the stock back to July, and you so state to the committee?—A. I do not know that I have so stated to the committee. I have made no statement in your case in regard to that before.

Q. Can you show me this private memorandum-book in which you have these amounts charged against me?—A. No; I cannot; I have not it here.

Q. Did you show it to me?—A. No; I think I showed you a statement, showing that the balance to pay for the stock was $534.72, and that you gave me a check for that amount, which check is now charged to you on the books of the Sergeant-at-Arms, $534.72; and I have it on my memorandum-book, crediting you that amount.

Q. My recollection in regard to that matter is exactly as I stated then. It appears that interest on the $2,000 was charged to me from July until March.—A. Until you paid for the stock—yes.

Q. And you sold the bonds, although they did not belong to you, and without asking my consent?—A. Yes; as I stated.

Q. You did not sell the stock?—A. No, sir.

Q. And you regarded me as the proprietor of that Credit Mobilier stock?—A. Certainly; you paid me for it; it belongs to you; it has never been returned.

Q. You stated in your first testimony, "I cannot remember which of us first mentioned the subject, but I know he wanted to get some stock, and I am pretty confident he has paid me for it, though it was never transferred to him, nor can I remember having paid over to him any dividend. At the next session he said something about that thing being off." Please state what I said to you the next session about that thing being off, and how it happened to come up in conversation?—A. I cannot remember anything further than I have stated.

Q. What did you say when I said something to you about that thing being off?—A. I don't recollect that I said anything. I do not remember the conversation any further than that you said you called the thing off.

Q. Why was it to be off?—A. I don't know.

Q. Do you remember whether you said anything to me that there was to be a litigation in regard to the stock?—A. I do not remember. I guess I informed you some time before that about litigation. I think so.

Q. You cannot remember what it was I said to you about the thing being off?—A. I cannot.

Q. And you cannot remember what you said?—A. No, sir.

Q. Then, if that is the case, why in your cross-examination did you say you did not know whether you or I owned that stock?—A. I do not think I said so.

Q. Did you say that you sold me the stock, and that I paid you the balance on it?—A. Yes, sir.

Q. But you cannot remember what I said to you about being "off," or what you said. Yet you testified in your cross-examination that you did not know whether you or I was the owner of that stock; and subsequently you said you thought I was the equitable owner?—A. All I know is what you said about it there in your testimony. I do not recol lect any such conversation, but I was willing to have it go as you stated.

Q. Mr. Ames says that he derived that information from my testimony, yet I read his statement from a paper published Tuesday morning, January 7, and I testified on the morning of January 7. Mr. Ames, therefore, must have obtained the information before I testified, and I think he will correct that now. I do not think he will say he had that information from my testimony before this committee.—A. I do not know. You may have said it to me before. I got it from you.

Q. I testified before this committee: "The very day I heard this remark I told Mr. Ames that no profits, present or prospective, could induce me to buy into a lawsuit; that I must therefore recede entirely from the transaction between us, as I did not want stock of any kind, on any terms, that would make me a party to litigation. He assented to this, and nothing was said as to the money paid, my interest being not to get into a lawsuit." Do you remember anything of that transaction?—A. No, sir.

Q. You do not remember my saying that I did not want to buy into a lawsuit?—A. I do not now.

Q. You don't remember that, when I said I wanted to be "off?"—A. No, sir.

Q. Is it not probable that I based my desire to be off upon this litigation?—A. I cannot tell; you may have said so. I cannot remember. I do not say that you did not base it on that.

Q. Now, after I had testified, I asked you to cross-examine me. You said that you did not desire to do so. I ask you now whether you did not state, that afternoon, to a gentleman, after you had heard me testify, that you believed my statement was substantially correct?—A. I don't remember saying that.

Q. Will you testify that you did not say that?—A. I do not recollect that I did.

Q. Mr. Crounse, Washington correspondent of the New York Times, telegraphed to the Times that Mr. Ames had said to him my testimony was substantially correct, and Mr. Crounse stated to me that Mr. Ames so told him.

The WITNESS. When was that?

Mr. COLFAX. The 7th of January. Now, when I testified on the 7th of January, and asked you to cross-examine me, if the statement I made was not correct, why did not you contradict me then?—A. I had not examined the records then; I had not refreshed my recollection.

Q. The subject had been discussed all over the country, and your attention must have been called to it.—A. My minutes were at home, and I had not examined them until I went back home.

Q. You say that you paid me $1,200 by a check on the Sergeant-at-Arms?—A. I did.

Q. Where was I when you paid me?—A. I do not know; I cannot say. The check is in the Sergeant-at-Arms' room.

Q. Now, when I asserted, in my testimony, that I had never received a dollar from you, why did not you contradict me then, and say to the committee that you had paid me a check of $1,200?—A. I was not in a position to contradict you, because I had not examined my minutes and refreshed my recollection.

Q. Did I not tell you the first of the present session that I wanted you to tell the whole truth about the matter?—A. Well, I think I have done so.

Q. Why not have done so at first? Why didn't you tell it when I was here and gave my testimony? Why didn't you state that you had paid me $1,200?—A. I did not want to dispute you.

Q. You say that was the only cash dividend in 1868 upon this stock?—A. I think the only cash dividend.

Q. In Mr. Durant's testimony there is a statement that there was a cash dividend of 30 per cent., July, 1868.—A. I think not.

Q. Mr. Durant states also that there was a bond dividend during that session. What did you do with the bonds belonging to me?—A. There are bonds belonging to you now.

Q. You did not sell all the bonds then?—A. No; there are bonds that belong to you now, bonds that belong to your stock, and that you are entitled to.

Q. Where is what I am entitled to now?—A. I hold it.

Q. Have you ever offered it to me?—A. No, sir; I am waiting for the result of this suit.

Q. Have you ever told me anything about it?—A. I suppose I told you about it in 1868, when I told several others.

Q. You do not think you told me, do you?—A. I do not know whether I did; I suppose I gave you a statement.

Q. Now, in regard to this thing being off, you say you got that from my testimony?—A. It must have been from a conversation with you since we have been here the present session. I called upon you at your room.

Q. Did you not, at the time I said I wanted this thing to be off, learn, as the reason, that I did not want to buy into a lawsuit; and did not you say that you would buy it back?—A. I do not recollect.

Q. Did you not proffer me some small sum of money, and say to me, "Take it, and consider it bought back?"—A. I may have done so.

Q. Did I not tell you I wanted the whole thing off; that I did not want to buy into a lawsuit?—A. I do not remember.

Q. Do you not remember that you stated to me that you would regard it as bought back?—A. I do not remember that I did.

Q. You testified a few moments ago that there was some remark made by me about my giving up these $500?—A. That you told me at your room before I testified.

Q. You testified in answer to a question of Judge Poland about your recollection of that fact that there was some such remark as giving up $500, and of my being sorry for your misfortune. Do you remember where this conversation occurred?—A. I think it was at Wormley's.

Q. I mean the conversation about giving up the $500, and that I was sorry for your misfortune.—A. You told me that you said so, and I presume you did or I would not have so stated.

Q. You believe I said so. Did I not say it to you on the floor of the Senate after you had failed?—A. I do not know.

Q. Did you not tell me that the stock had gone down to 10 cents on the dollar, and that you had had an extension by your creditors?—A. Everybody knew that.

Q. You remember that conversation?—A. It is very likely. I recollect seeing you over there in the Senate, but what was said I do not remember. I do not dispute that you said so.

Q. You understood that I said this $500 could go?—A. I do not know that I understood that till this winter.

Q. Then why did you state to Judge Poland that you did?—A. I supposed so; I got it from you.

Q. Then you were testifying partly from my recollection and partly from your own. Did you have any other checks on the Sergeant-at-

Arms at the same time you gave me this one for $1,200?—A. Yes, sir.

Q. You do not remember where you paid me this $1,200 check?—A. I suppose it was in the House. The Sergeant-at-Arms paid it.

Q. Was it paid to my order?—A. It was payable to "S. C. or bearer."

Q. Paid to me by the Sergeant-at-Arms?—A. I think so. It is in his possession as a voucher for the money, and my books show that I gave you the check at that time for $1,200.

Q. Is it not more probable that you got the money on that check yourself, as we had had this talk about being off?—A. This check was given a long while before I had any talk about being off. The check was given in June, 1868.

Q. My recollection is that the talk we had about being off was in the summer of 1868, at the same session at which you say the check was given.—A. There had been no litigation then.

Q. Was it not in regard to prospective litigation that we were talking?—A. No; I did not know anything about any litigation or suit until after June.

Q. You are positive that you paid me this check for $1,200?—A. I am positive I gave you the check.

Q. And then I ask you again, why did you not say so when you testified in December?—A. I testified that I had paid you the dividends.

Q. You stated in your first examination that you could not remember having paid me any dividends. Then, in your cross-examination, you said that possibly you might have paid me, but you were not certain.—A. Yes; now I am certain.

Q. Then this transaction had passed out of your mind, so that you were not certain then?—A. I could not remember the amount at all until I had examined my books. I examined my books when I went home, and when I returned to Washington I compared my memorandums with the checks the Sergeant-at-Arms had on file; and I found my check for $1,200 filled out "S. C.," which corresponded with the memorandum I had on my book.

Q. You have stated in your testimony that two of the gentlemen you have referred to, J. F. Wilson and Judge Bingham, got all of their dividends, stock, and bonds?—A. Yes, sir.

Q. Why did I not get mine?—A. I settled with them a year afterward, and I am ready to settle with you.

Q. Did you ever tell me you were ready?—A. No; I did not tell you; I was waiting for the decision of this suit by McComb. I did not want to be mixed up with anybody else in that suit.

Q. After this conversation, in which I told you to never mind the $500, did you not regard it as off?—A. No, sir; I supposed I had to pay the $500. I did not know who had the certificate, you or I.

Q. You knew very well that you had it in your possession, did you not?—A. I do not know that I did. I find now that I have it in my possession, and after my return home.

Q. Did I ever see a certificate of the stock?—A. I do not know.

Q. Did you ever give me one?—A. I think not.

Q. Did you ever give me a share of Union Pacific Railroad stock?—A. No, sir.

Q. Did you ever give me a bond of the Union Pacific Railroad Company?—A. No, sir; I sold the bonds and accounted to you for them.

Q. You sold them without my authority?—A. Yes, sir.

Mr. COLFAX. I want again to state to the committee, as I before stated, that I do not remember ever having received one dollar from Mr. Ames, and I hope to be able to prove that fact. I think there is a mistake in the statement Mr. Ames makes.

By the CHAIRMAN:

Q. Are we to understand, in relation to this matter between you and Mr. Colfax—and we want you to testify from your recollection, whether you understand—that this contract about the Credit Mobilier stock was ever rescinded?—A. I do not recollect it.

Q. Do you now remember anything in connection with any conversation between you and Mr. Colfax in relation to putting an end to it, or being off?—A. Nothing except a casual remark. There never has been any negotiation about having it off, or any agreement about it.

Q. What do you think that remark was—just what he said?—A. I have no particular recollection of it.

Q. Have you any recollection?—A. I do not think I have. I think what I did was what I got from him this winter.

Q. Then you yourself have not now any recollection of this thing?—A. No distinct recollection; no, sir.

Q. Have you any impression of any such thing being said between you and him?—A. I do not think I have until this winter. I am willing to have it go any way Mr. Colfax pleases, to call it off or call it on.

Q. The question is as to what occurred at the time. State again the whole transaction.—A. All I can state is, that I agreed to sell Mr. Colfax, or get for him, twenty shares of Credit Mobilier stock, at par and interest from July, 1867. In February we had a dividend of 80 per cent. in bonds, which I sold at 97 and paid Mr. Colfax the proceeds, which left a balance due of $534.72, for which he gave me his check.

Q. You do not mean that you paid the money over to him that you got from the bonds?—A. No; I deducted that from the price of the stock.

Q. You deducted from the price of the stock the proceeds of the bonds, and he gave you a check for the balance; that is that transaction?—A. That is the transaction.

Q. And subsequently when you got the money dividend you paid that money by a check on the Sergeant-at-Arms?—A. That is what my books show.

Q. Have there been any other money dividends on that stock at any time?—A. No, sir; there has been a certificate for bonds.

Q. But the amount you paid Mr. Colfax in June was the money dividend?—A. Yes, sir; it was his dividend in money. The stock dividend I still hold; the Credit Mobilier stock I also hold, although he has paid me for it.

Q. There has been no conversation between you and him, that you know of, as to whether you were to keep the stock or deliver it to him?—A. No, sir; unless he considers this casual remark of calling the thing off as rescinding the contract.

Q. That remark you say you have no remembrance of?—A. I had not when I testified before.

Q. Have you now?—A. No, sir; except what I heard here.

Q. We have heard that; we want to know what you remember about it.—A. I have no recollection about it.

Q. I have here, which has been handed me, a printed list, taken from a New York paper, in one column of which, under date of July 8, 1868, there is a cash dividend of $3,000; was any cash dividend declared in

July, 1868, upon the stock of the Credit Mobilier?—A. Not that I know of. I do not think that is correct; still it may be.

Q. Have you any recollection that there was any cash dividend declared upon this stock—one in June of 60 per cent.?—A. I have not. I think the other was in bonds or certificate for bonds. The bonds were not delivered, and they were afterward changed to income bonds. The company never had the bonds. That is my impression. I think the statement in that printed list is a mistake.

By Mr. COLFAX:

Q. Do you remember this conversation with Mr. Crounse in which you stated that I was substantially correct when I testified the 7th January?—A. I have no recollection of it.

By the CHAIRMAN:

Q. Do you remember any conversation with Mr. Crounse upon that subject?—A. I do not.

Q. Do you remember saying to him or anybody that the account given by Mr. Colfax was a correct account of the transaction?—A. No, sir.

By Mr. MCCRARY:

Q. You do not recollect anything about talking with Mr. Colfax in regard to repurchasing the stock from him for a nominal consideration?—A. I do not know that I remember it; still I may have done so. It would be difficult to remember everything I have said to gentlemen in the last six years.

Q. You held the stock as his trustee?—A. I have that stock in my own name as trustee; it was in a certificate with other stock. I do not consider myself as a trustee for anybody. The stock belongs to these parties, and they can have it whenever they ask for it.

Q. Do you desire to have it in your individual capacity and not as trustee?—A. No, sir; the stock I have taken back has never been changed. I have never transferred any stock on the books of the company since I took it for these parties.

Q. You might be called on to account for this stock in your name as trustee if it remains in that way.—A. I cannot help that.

Mr. Colfax stated that he desired the committee to call one or two witnesses in regard to some points in the above testimony.

The following is the memorandum from which the witness testified in ralation to Mr. Colfax:

S. C., DR.		CR.	
1868.		1868.	
To 20 shares stock C. M. of A	$2,000 00	March 5. By cash	$534 72
To interest	86 72	Feb. 14. Dividends of bonds: U. P. R. $2,000.80, $1,600, less 3 per cent	1,552 00
June 19. To cash	1,200 00	June 17. By dividend collected for his account	1,200 00
	3,286 72		3,286 72

By the CHAIRMAN:

Q. I now wish to ask you in regard to Mr. Wilson, of Massachusetts. —A. That statement heretofore made by me is correct. As I said before, I took the stock back from him and settled with him.

Q. You have heard Mr. Wilson's statement here?—A. Yes, sir; and it is substantially correct. My recollection is that my books show that I settled with him, took the stock back, and squared it up as he says.

Q. Mr. Wilson says that $2,000 of the money given to his wife he paid over to you for twenty shares of that stock?—A. Yes, sir; that is correct.

Q. That during that time, and during the time I held it, and before it was given up, there was a dividend?—A. Yes, sir.

Q. That he refused to receive that dividend and only received back $2,000 with 10 per cent. interest?—A. I think he received the dividend in the first place, and that in the settlement he paid it back.

Q. I understood him to say that the only amount he received in the settlement was the $2,000 and 10 per cent. interest?—A. Yes, sir; that was correct.

Q. I do not know but you stated before, when the transaction was closed up and the money paid back?—A. I think it was some time during that same year; in the last of that year or the first of the year following; that is my recollection.

Q. The statement of Mr. Wilson upon that subject, you say, is substantially the truth?—A. Yes, sir.

Q. In relation to Mr. Patterson, of the Senate, I believe all your transactions with him were all gone over yesterday?—A. Yes, sir.

Q. The name of William B. Allison has been mentioned in connection with these transactions. Mr. Allison was then a member of the House, and is now a member elect to the Senate. Since your former testimony Mr. Allison has sent a telegram upon that subject stating what was his understanding in regard to it. Will you now state, in detail, the transaction between you and Mr. Allison in connection with that stock?—A. Mr. Allison, as I stated in my testimony, agreed to buy ten shares of Credit Mobilier stock. I received his dividends of 80 per cent. bonds on that stock, which sold at 97, and he paid me the difference in cash. In June he received a dividend of $600.

Q. You sold the bonds that you received on his stock as a dividend?—A. Yes, sir.

Q. What did they amount to?—A. They amounted to $800, less 3 per cent., $776.

Q. He paid you the balance?—A. He paid me the balance.

Q. Have you some memorandum of what that balance was?—A. The balance was $271.

Q. What is the date of that payment?—A. The date is April 24, 1868.

Q. That settled the balance of the stock?—A. Yes, sir.

Q. He had the stock at par, and interest from July previous?—A. Yes, sir.

Q. What was the amount of stock and interest?—A. One thousand and forty-seven dollars.

Q. The amount you received on the bonds was $776. He paid you the balance in money, $271. Where did you get this memorandum from which you are now testifying?—A. I got that from the entries on my books at home, and I find, in the office of the Sergeant-at-Arms here, the check indorsed by Mr. Allison.

Q. Did you say it was indorsed by him?—A. I am not sure about that. I found in his account, charged to him on that date, the balance covering the amount due on that stock, and the check for that amount.

Q. The balance which was due Mr. Allison for this stock I understand he gave you a check for on the Sergeant-at-Arms?—A. No. He drew the money himself, I suppose, and paid me the money.

Q. You got this entry at that date from your books at home?—A. Yes, sir; when I received that dividend from the Credit Mobilier I deposited $10,000 with the Sergeant-at-Arms here, and drew it out to pay these separate dividends.

Q. When was this money dividend paid to Mr. Allison?—A. About the middle or 30th of January, or somewhere thereabout.

Q. You paid that money dividend to him by check on the Sergeant-at-Arms, and you found the check of the Sergeant-at-Arms and the amount charged to you in your account in his office?—A. Yes, sir.

Q. Was this stock ever transferred to Mr. Allison?—A. No, sir.

Q. It still remains in your name?—A. Yes, sir.

Q. What has become of the stock received afterward as dividends upon it?—A. I have not given anybody any stock since July, except to Mr. Patterson, Mr. Bingham, and Mr. Painter. I held on to the rest, waiting for the result of this suit. It is due, and will be accounted for, but I have kept it in my possession until I know how this suit results.

Q. Has this contract between you and Mr. Allison ever been rescinded, or ever been given up and settled in any way?—A. He returned me the stock some time ago; his Union Pacific Railroad stock and Credit Mobilier stock.

Q. You gave him the certificates then?—A. I gave him the certificates, both the ten shares of Credit Mobilier stock and ten shares of Union Pacific Railroad stock. I thought it was returned this last fall, and I so stated in my testimony in answer to Mr. Merrick, I think. But I found that the letter of Mr. Allison, inclosing the stock, is mailed March 31.

Q. When did he receive the stock?—A. He received it at the time he paid me for it.

Q. He then took a certificate?—A. He then took a certificate.

Q. And kept it until last March?—A. I suppose so. That is the letter returning it; it has that date in the postmark.

Q. Is that letter here?—A. There was no letter; the envelope merely contained the certificates of stock. I do not know that it came from Mr. Allison; all I know is that it was mailed at Dubuque.

Q. You received it in that envelope, which you have retained?—A. Yes, sir.

Q. When did he receive his certificate of Union Pacific Railroad stock?—A. At the same time he received his Credit Mobilier stock. There was a dividend of 100 per cent. on Union Pacific Railroad stock at the same time of the first bond dividend. I received the dividend and handed it over to him.

Q. Does the envelope in which the stock was returned show the year?—A. No; that is all there is of it. It is postmarked Dubuque, March 31. The envelope I hand you is the one it came in.

Q. Are you confident it was last March?—A. I do not know.

Q. When do you think it was?—A. I thought it was later. Still I presume the postmark is correct.

Q. Are you confident that it was not earlier—further back than last March?—A. I simply give you my impression. I cannot remember certainly at all.

Q. Do you know that it was Mr. Allison who sent the certificate back to you?—A. No, sir; there was no letter inclosed, and nothing to show that it came from him. I did not know there was anybody else in Dubuque who owned Credit Mobilier stock, and took it for granted that it came from him, but I do not know that it did. It was not indorsed with any name.

Q. Do you know Mr. Allison's handwriting?—A. I do not know that I would.

Q. You would not be willing to swear that the address on this envelope is his handwriting?—A. No.

Q. The certificate of stock, I understand, you delivered to him in person?—A. That is my impression.

Q. That was in 1868?—A. Yes, sir.

Q. These certificates were returned to you, as you believe, last March, without any explanation accompanying them?—A. Yes, sir.

Q. Was there ever any conversation between you and Mr. Allison in reference to the contract being rescinded?—A. I do not know that there was.

Q. Have you any recollection of any such conversation?—A. No, sir. I suppose he might have considered the returning of the stock as explanation enough.

By Mr. McCrary:

Q. Did he return you any of the money that you had paid him in connection with that transaction?—A. I have no recollection that he did. I do not know of any.

Q. Have you examined to ascertain whether you received from him a check or a cash-draft on New York?—A. No, sir.

Q. You do not know whether that is the case or not?—A. No, sir.

Q. You are sure you gave him the stock in person. Might you not have sent it by mail to him?—A. I am not sure. I do not know that that would make any difference. He got it.

Q. Can you recollect any conversation you had with him when he told you he had concluded not to take the stock, and that you insisted on a repurchase on your part for a nominal sum?—A. There was something of that sort said after he found the suit was commenced.

Q. Did you offer him some little sum of money as payment for it, he to return his stock?—A. I do not know but I did.

Q. Do you know when that was?—A. No; I do not.

Q. What did Mr. Allison say at that time about it?—A. There was something said about a lawsuit, and my recollection is that it was after the suit was commenced.

Q. Was not the stock returned after the renomination of Mr. Allison, in the fall of 1868?—A. I do not recollect. It was some time ago.

Q. You understood from him at that time that he proposed to cancel the transaction, did you not?—A. Yes, sir; that was the idea.

Q. And you proposed to call it a repurchase by you of the stock?—A. I do not recollect how the thing was to be.

Q. Did he say he did not care what you called it, so that he got the thing entirely off his hands?—A. I think I recollect something of that sort. He did not want to have anything to do with the Credit Mobilier after the lawsuit was commenced.

Q. You do not know whether he has received any dividends that have not been returned to you?—A. He has had no dividends except what I have stated.

Q. That is $600, and he had previously paid you $1,000?—A. Yes, including the bonds I sold for him.

Q. What would be his profit if he had not returned you anything, provided it was canceled at the time?—A. He paid me $271 and received $600; that was all.

Q. You do not know whether he returned you that sum by draft to New York or not?—A. I do not think he did.

By the CHAIRMAN:

Q. Did you understand that this contract between you and this sale of stock to Mr. Allison was really rescinded and put an end to?—A. My idea was that he did not want to hold any Credit Mobilier stock after the suit was commenced, and proposed selling it back for a nominal sum; something like that.

Q. What we want to get at is, whether this was a real transaction, a real sale of it to you; did you so understand it?—A. I did not.

Q. How did you understand it?—A. I understood it to go just as he was a mind to have it.

Q. Did you pay him anything?—A. I think I did.

Q. How much?—A. I do not recollect. Some small sum; a mere nominal sum.

Q. Did you throw down a five-cent piece, or something like that?—A. Somewhere in that neighborhood; not a very big sum.

Q. Have you any idea when that was?—A. I think it must have been in the summer of 1868, after this suit was brought.

Q. Why did he not return you the certificates then?—A. I did not ask him. I think he had not them here. I supposed so; I do not know anything about it.

Q. Was anything said about his returning them to you?—A. I do not remember. I supposed if I bought it he ought to return it to me.

Q. Did you state that you bought it?—A. Yes, sir; if he was a mind to give it to me, and it seems he decided to, by inclosing it to me.

Q. What I want to know is whether this transaction between you and him had any real significance at all or whether it was a mere sham?—A. I think the amount of it was that if the lawsuit with McComb should amount to anything he would not own the Credit Mobilier stock; that he could call it mine or his, as he pleased.

Q. When these certificates were returned to you by mail, was it something that astonished you, or was it something you were expecting?—A. No; I was not expecting it.

Q. You say this transaction, when this nominal sum was repaid, was as far back as 1868?—A. I think so.

Q. And you did not receive the certificates until March, 1872?—A. That is my recollection.

Q. Had you not pretty much given up expecting them?—A. I did not look for them with a great deal of anxiety.

By Mr. MERRICK:

Q. Do I understand you to mean to convey the idea that this form of sale, for five cents, or whatever it was, was a mere nominal transaction, and that you considered yourself really as still holding the stock in his behalf?—A. I guess the receipt I gave him was that he was to hold the stock for me at the time the money was paid.

Q. Was it understood between you that in case the suit should prove disastrous you would be the holder of that for him?—A. That was my impression.

Q. It was therefore a device to avoid his being responsible for your lawsuit?—A. I think it was mixed up with these malicious charges of bribery which are made in the suit of McComb. That is the origin of this scandal.

Q. Do you mean that Mr. Allison demurred at the pecuniary responsibility which might be involved in it, or to some charge of impropriety?—A. Some charge of impropriety, I suppose. I do not know his ideas any further than that.

Q. Did this envelope in which you received the certificates by mail not also contain a check on New York?—A. No, sir.

Q. Do you believe that this money dividend that had been paid to Mr. Allison was ever repaid to you?—A. I do not think it was. I have no knowledge of it.

Q. I think his telegram says that he sent a check on New York with the certificate; was there any such check sent?—A. Not in that envelope.

Q. Did you ever receive a check from him?—A. Yes, sir; but that was in another matter.

Q. What was that?—A. An operation I went into with him in 1865, in Iowa, in the purchase of the stock and bonds of a failed road in Iowa.

Q. And the check you received was to close that transaction?—A. It was on account of that transaction

Q. Had it any reference to this money paid to him as a dividend?—A. No, sir.

Q. Have you any recollection or belief that that was ever repaid to you in any form?—A. No, sir.

The following memoranda from which witness testified in regard to Mr. Allison was here placed in evidence:

W. B. A.

Dr.			Cr.		
1868.			1868.		
April 24.	To ten shares Credit Mobilier of America stock..	$1,000	April 24.	By dividend of Union Pacific bonds, 80 per cent., $800, at 97 per cent....	$776
	Interest on same.........	47	April 24.	By cash of him.........	271
		1,047	June 17.	By dividend received for his account............	600
June 19.	To check...............	600			
		1,647			1,647

Q. I think you stated before in your testimony that neither Mr. Conkling, Mr. Fowler, nor Mr. Bayard, whose names have been mentioned in connection with this business, were ever holders of this stock?—A. Not to my knowledge. I had nothing to do with it.

Q. Neither of them ever paid you anything, or ever received anything from you?—A. No, sir.

Q. Neither of them were ever holders of the Credit Mobilier stock to your knowledge?—A. Not to my knowledge.

Q. You have no information that they were?—A. No, sir.

By the CHAIRMAN:

Q. In your letter of the 30th January, 1868, to Mr. McComb, you say, "I have placed some in New York, or have agreed to;" what was that you placed in New York?—A. I let Mr. Ham have some.

Q. The secretary of the Credit Mobilier?—A. Yes, sir.

Q. Is that all you refer to?—A. That is all I did.

Q. You stated somewhere, I think, that there was one going to New York; who was that one you refer to?—A. I did not let any go to New York, except to Mr. Ham.

Q. You testified before in relation to the matter between you and Speaker Blaine. You heard his statement, did you?—A. Yes, sir.

Q. Do you wish to make any further statement in reference to the transaction between you and him?—A. No, sir.

Q. Did he ever pay you anything?—A. No, sir.

Q. You never paid him anything?—A. I did not; his name is not on my books at all.

Q. There was a conversation between you, in reference to his becoming the purchaser of Credit Mobilier stock, but it never amounted to anything?—A. It did not. I looked the accounts over the other day, and I do not find his name on my books at all.

Q. Then whatever was the talk between you in reference to this transaction, he never made any investment?—A. No, sir.

Q. And never derived any advantage from the conversation, or in connection with Credit Mobilier stock in any way?—A. No, sir; only the advantage of being abused.

Q. Mr. Dawes, of Massachusetts, you stated, took some stock and settled for it; if I understand you right, he paid you $1,000?—A. Yes, sir.

Q. Have you some memoranda of the date of that?—A. It was about the time of the rest of them.

Q. Have you a memorandum of it?—A. No, sir; I have not. I had quite an account with Mr. Dawes; he bought some bonds of me. I recollect he paid me four or five thousand dollars at one time. I invested $1,500 in the Iowa Falls and Sioux City road for him.

Q. Did you ever receive any more than $1,000 from him to invest in Credit Mobilier stock?—A. Not in Credit Mobilier stock; he had ten shares of that.

Q. Did you pay him any dividends?—A. I think I did.

Q. Have you some memorandum account of that?—A. I paid him that $600 dividend in money. I paid him in part. He was owing me, and I paid him about $400, in settlement.

Q. The rest was applied to some other dealings between you and him?—A. Yes, sir.

Q. Can you tell us when it was that this matter was adjusted and ended between you and Mr. Dawes?—A. It was in December, 1868.

Q. He had already received his money from you by your accounting for the balance of the $600 dividend; did he receive anything more?—A. He received the bond dividend, I suppose, like the rest of them.

Q. Were the bonds delivered over to him?—A. I do not recollect. I probably sold them, or delivered them over; I do not know which.

Q. What became of the stock dividend of ten shares?—A. He did not take it; he got frightened about Mr. Larned and the Duff Green suit.

Q. That was to get the charter away?—A. Yes, sir; I settled with him on the 9th December, 1868.

Q. If I understand you, in this conversation, or settlement, so far as the Credit Mobilier stock was concerned he paid back his dividends, receiving ten per cent. interest on his money. Do you agree that that was the basis of the settlement?—A. That is my impression.

Q. I see, on this memorandum which you have here, $600 is charged to Mr. Dawes; that is a dividend?—A. That is a dividend.

Q. It says less $200.—A. That he owed me on some other transaction.

Q. Did Mr. Dawes receive any more on this investment except to get his money back and ten per cent. interest on it?—A. I think not. I had a memorandum, but I destroyed the memorandum. I kept this piece of paper, on which there is a note, which he gave me in the settlement, in 1868.

Q. That settlement embraced other things besides this?—A. Yes, sir.

Q. And there was a balance due you on the settlement for which he gave you his note?—A. Yes, sir.

Q. Please read the note.—A. It reads: "Washington, December 9, 1868. For value received, I promise to pay Oakes Ames, or order, $263.06, on demand, with interest. H. L. Dawes."

Q. Had you any detailed memoranda of the transaction between you and Mr. Dawes?—A. I had, but I gave it to him when I made the settlement.

Q. You believe that so far as your dealings are concerned with Mr. Dawes, you settled, giving him 10 per cent. interest upon his investment, and nothing more?—A. Yes, sir.

Q. Have you any memoranda by which you can give us the date when you received this $1,000 of Mr. Dawes?—A. I think in the memoranda which I gave him he paid me about $800 on the 11th January, 1868, and the balance on the 14th or 15th of the same month, some four or five days after.

Q. Was that the $1,000 you got, you think, in January, 1868, and not all in one sum?—A. No, sir; in two sums.

Q. In regard to Mr. Garfield, state to the committee the details of the transactions between you and him in reference to Credit Mobilier stock.—A. I got for Mr. Garfield ten shares of the Credit Mobilier stock, for which he paid par and interest.

Q. When did you agree with him for that?—A. That agreement was in December, 1867, or January, 1868; about that time; about the time I had these conversations with all of them. It was all about the same time.

Q. State what grew out of it.—A. Mr. Garfield did not pay me any money. I sold the bonds belonging to his $1,000 of stock at 97, making $776. In June I received a dividend in cash on his stock of $600, which left a balance due him of $329, which I paid him. That is all the transaction between us. I did not deliver him any stock before or since. That is the only transaction, and the only thing.

By Mr. MERRICK:

Q. The $329 which you paid him was the surplus of earnings on the stock above the amount to be paid for it, par value?—A. Yes, sir; he never had either his Credit Mobilier stock or Union Pacific Railroad stock. The only thing he realized on the transaction was the $329.

Q. I see in this statement of the account with General Garfield, there is a charge of $47; that is interest from the July previous, is it?—A. Yes, sir.

Q. And the $776 on the credit side of the account is the 80 per cent. bond dividend sold at 97?—A. Yes, sir.

Q. And the $600 on the credit side is the money dividend?—A. Yes, sir.

Q. And after you had received these two sums, they in the aggregate overpaid the price of stock and interest $329, which you paid him?—A. Yes, sir.

Q. How was that paid?—A. Paid in money, I believe.

Q. Did you make a statement of this to Mr. Garfield?—A. I presume so; I think I did with all of them; that is my impression.

Q. When you paid him this $329, did you understand it was the balance of his dividend after paying for his stock?—A. I supposed so; I do not know what else he could suppose.

Q. You did not deliver the certificate of stock to him?—A. No, sir; he said nothing about that.

Q. Why did he not receive his certificate?—A. I do not know.

Q. Do you remember any conversation between you and him in the adjustment of these accounts?—A. I do not.

Q. You understood that you were a holder of his ten shares?—A. Yes, sir.

Q. Did he so understand it?—A. I presume so. It seems to have gone from his mind, however.

Q. Was this the only dealing you had with him in reference to any stock?—A. I think so.

Q. Was it the only transaction of any kind?—A. The only transaction.

Q. Has that $329 ever been paid to you?—A. I have no recollection of it.

Q. Have you any belief that it ever has?—A. No, sir.

Q. Did you ever loan General Garfield $300?—A. Not to my knowledge; except that he calls this a loan.

Q. You do not call it a loan?—A. I did not at the time. I am willing it should go to suit him.

Q. What we want to get at is the exact truth.—A. I have told the truth in my statement.

Q. When you paid him $329, did he understand that he borrowed that money from you?—A. I do not suppose so.

Q. Have you any belief now that he supposed so?—A. No; only from what he said the other day. I do not dispute anybody.

Q. We want your judgment of the transaction.—A. My judgment of the transaction is just as I told you. There was but one thing about it.

Q. That amount has never been repaid to you? You did not suppose that you had any right to it, or any claim to it?—A. No, sir.

Q. You regarded that as money belonging to him after the stock was paid for?—A. Yes, sir.

Q. There were dividends of Union Pacific Railroad stock on these ten shares?—A. Yes, sir.

Q. Did General Garfield ever receive these?—A. No, sir; never has received but $329.

Q. And that he has received as his own money?—A. I suppose so; it did not belong to me. I should not have given it to him if it had not belonged to him.

Q. You did not understand it to belong to you as a loan; you never called for it, and have never received it back?—A. No, sir.

Q. Has there been any conversation between you and him in reference to the Pacific stock he was entitled to?—A. No, sir.

Q. Has he ever called for it?—A. No, sir.

Q. Have you ever offered it to him?—A. No, sir.

Q. Has there been any conversation in relation to it?—A. No, sir.

Q. Has there ever been anything said between you and him about rescinding the purchase of the ten shares of Credit Mobilier stock? Has there anything been said to you of its being thrown up, or abandoned, or surrendered?—A. No, sir; not until recently.

Q. How recently?—A. Since this matter came up.

Q. Since this investigation commenced?—A. Yes, sir.

By Mr. MERRICK:

Q. Did you consider at the commencement of this investigation that you held these other dividends, which you say you did not pay to him, in his behalf? Did you regard yourself as custodian of these dividends for him?—A. Yes, sir; he paid for his stock and is entitled to his dividends.

Q. Will the dividends come to him at any time on his demand?—A. Yes, sir, as soon as this suit is settled.

Q. You say that $329 was paid to him; how was it paid?—A. I presume by a check on the Sergeant-at-Arms. I find there are some checks filed without any letters or initials indicating who they were for.

Q. Have you had any correspondence, since this dividend was paid, with him in regard to this matter?—A. I do not know what matter you refer to.

Q. If you had any correspondence between you I would like to see it. —A. I have no copy of it.

Q. Have you the original?—A. No, sir. Mr. Garfield showed me a letter which he said he intended to inclose with some money sent me. I did not know who the money came from. He showed me a letter which he said he intended to have put in. I indorsed on the back of that letter my reply. I just turned over the letter and wrote what I wrote on the back of it, and let him have it.

Q. Your answer indorsed on the back of the letter was published in the newspapers?—A. Yes, sir. He published the letter, I believe.

Q. As published did they correspond with your recollection of the papers as written?—A. Yes, sir. I wrote it off hastily. He came to my room and said he had been accused of all kinds of crimes and misdemeanors. I told him I had made no such statement as he represented. He wanted me to say in writing that I had not. I took his letter, which he said he intended to have inclosed with the money, and wrote on the back of it that I had made no such statement.

Q. The published correspondence in the morning papers of the next day is your recollection of what occurred?—A. It agrees with my recollection, except that he says he left a letter for me at the Arlington. I never received that letter. I only saw the letter on which I indorsed my answer.

Q. Did he inclose the money?—A. Some money came to me inclosed in an envelope which he said he had sent. I gave it back to him.

Q. How much money was in that envelope?—A. Four hundred dollars.

The following memorandum refered to by witness as a statement of his account with Mr. Garfield was placed in evidence:

	J. A. G.,	Dr.
1868.	To 10 shares stock Credit Mobiler of A	$1,000 00
	Interest	47 00
June 19.	To cash	329 00
		1,376 00
		Cr.
1868.	By dividend bonds, Union Pacific Railroad, $1,000, at 80 per cent. less 3 per cent	$776 00
June 17.	By dividend collected for your account	600 00
		1,376 00

Q. Do you desire to make any additional statement in regard to Mr. Kelley?—A. No. Mr. Kelley's transaction was about the same as that of Mr. Garfield.

Q. Give the details of it and whether he agreed to take some stock.—A. Yes, sir.

Q. What amount?—A. One thousand dollars.

Q. Was that about the beginning of this same session of 1867 or 1868?—A. I think so.

Q. Did he pay you anything?—A. No, sir; it was the same as Mr. Garfield's—the same transaction precisely; he was to have ten shares.

Q. You received the bonds and sold them, and did you receive the money dividends also?—A. Yes, sir, and paid him over $329.

Q. The transaction in the amount and in its detail was the same as that of General Garfield?—A. Precisely.

Q. Can you give us the date of that?—A. I saw the check for that, with the initials "W. D. K." written, in the Sergeant-at-Arms' room. I put in the initials of his name in the check which is dated the 23d of June, and it was for the payment of that money dividend.

Q. He had the money for it?—A. I suppose so. I found it then taken up by the Sergeant-at-Arms and charged to me.

Q. You delivered the check to Mr. Kelley?—A. I presume so.

Q. When he received that check from you did he understand that that was the balance of his dividend after paying for his stock?—A. I suppose I gave him him a statement as I did the others.

Q. Did you think he understood that that was a loan from you to him, that he borrowed it of you?—A. I do not think so; still, I have loaned money to Mr. Kelley several times. He said the other day that I loaned him $1,000. I loaned him $750 the 27th September, and I think it probable he put that with this $329, to make the $1,000. I think he has it in his mind that he owes me $1,000.

The memorandum from which witness testified in regard to Mr. Kelley is as follows:

	W. D. K.,	Dr.
1868.	To 10 shares stock Credit Mobilier of A......	$1,000 00
	Interest..	47 00
January 19.	To cash..	329 00
		1,376 00

		Cr.
1868.	By dividend of bonds Union Pacific Railroad $1,000, at 80 per cent. less 3 per cent.........	$776 00
June 17.	By dividend collected for your account..........	600 00
		1,376 00
1868, September 29.	To cash loan..........................	700 00

Q. Do you think Mr. Kelley understood, when he received that check from you, that that was the money he was borrowing from you?—A. I did not think so; you can judge as well as I can of it.

Q. Was anything said about its being a loan?—A. Not that I know of.

Q. Did you have any conversation with Mr. Kelley after that in reference to this transaction in Credit Mobilier stock?—A. Yes, sir; he inquired about the dividends, whether there were any more. I told him there would not be any more until this suit was settled.

Q. Did you understand from that conversation that he considered himself entitled to further dividends if there were any more made?—A. I suppose so.

Q. You contiue to hold that stock for him?—A. I do, and that is all Mr. Kelley has received out of it, the $329.

By the CHAIRMAN:

Q. Do you remember the date of that cash dividend?—A. About the middle of June, I think. I deposited the money with the Sergeant-at-Arms the 17th June, on which I drew these checks.

Q. That was the June dividend of 60 per cent. in cash; where was it paid?—A. I received it in New York.

Q. Do you remember precisely when you received it?—A. The 17th or 18th June. I presume one day before I brought it here.

Q. Will you now state the entire transaction with Mr. Scofield?—A. Mr. Scofield got frightened in some way, as he states, in relation to his personal liability, and I settled the matter with him in the same way.

Q. You had a conversation with him about his taking some of this stock?—A. Yes, sir.

Q. Was this about the first of this same session do you think?—A. Yes, sir; he gave me money and I gave him a receipt for it, and was to get stock for him—$1,000.

Q. Can you give the date of that receipt?—A. I cannot; it was about the same as the rest, or a few days later; I think it was in January that he stated it, if I recollect right.

Q. Did you receive the bond dividend on that ten shares?—A. Yes, sir; I suppose so.

Q. How did you settle the matter with Mr. Scofield?—A. I do not recollect exactly how I did settle it; I settled it up and we squared the transactions.

Q. Mr. Scofield says you agreed to abandon this contract about the Credit Mobilier shares, and that he took other securities and invested his money in them?—A. Yes, he took some other bonds; he took some Cedar Rapids bonds.

Q. We want to know just what this transaction was.—A. I do not know that I can recollect accurately; I think he received his first dividends, and that he never took his Credit Mobilier stock; I gave him a receipt for the money but he never had his stock; I think I paid him his dividend of $600, and that after that we settled up the matter and I took it off his hands.

Q. How much did he make out of the $1,000 you received from him?—A. I don't recollect. I think he gave back the Credit Mobilier stock. I think he kept the ten shares of Union Pacific Railroad stock.

Q. That he had received as a dividend?—A. Yes, I think he kept that. I think he did not make much more than that out of it. He may have made a part of the June dividend; I do not recollect. He settled it up and we squared the account. He agreed to take the stock originally and gave me money to pay for it, but afterwards he declined to take it. I think he took his bond dividends. I do not recollect how it was closed up. There was no great deal of profit made by him beyond the ten shares of Union Pacific Railroad stock.

Q. Have you some memorandum of the dealings between you and

Mr. Scofield?—A. I do not find any. I find the check which I gave him for $600 was dated the 22d of June.

Q. That you supposed to be a money dividend?—A. A money dividend; yes, sir.

Q. You think you paid him the balance of the bond dividend?—A. I think so, but how we settled up I not remember.

Q. And that he also received the $600?—A. Yes, I think he received that; my memorandum says so.

Q. But he concluded that he did not want the Credit Mobilier stock, and the thing was closed up between you and him. Did he retain the ten shares of Pacific Railroad stock?—A. I think so.

Q. Did he take more Pacific Railroad stock and Pacific Railroad bonds?—A. No, sir; I do not think he did.

Q. Do you remember what amount of money he paid you, or you paid him, when the thing was finally adjusted?—A. I do not. We had other transactions. I sold him other bonds—sold him bonds several times.

Q. In your settlement, you accounted for the money you received from him, and he accounted for the dividends he had received from you?—A. Yes, sir.

Q. Can you state whether he had the same advantage or benefit of these dividends as though he had been the owner of the stock, and whether you accounted to him for them in the settlement you finally made?—A. I know it was settled satisfactorily to both of us. I am very sure he received Union Pacific Railroad stock, and that his returning me the receipt for Credit Mobilier stock was considered the same as paying me back the thousand dollars and interest. I do not recollect how we did settle it. I know he returned me the receipt.

Q. You say you have no memoranda of this transaction?—A. No, sir; I have not. I looked for it but I could not find it. All I could find in relation to this matter was the money he paid me to get the stock with, and the getting of this dividend of $600.

Q. Have you looked in the office of the Sergeant-at-Arms to see whether the matter was finally adjusted between you and him by check through that office?—A. No, sir.

Q. Do you think it would be done in that way?—A. I have no recollection what the balance was or how it was paid, whether I paid him or he me. I have no recollection. I know we settled it up.

Q. The settlement with Mr. Scofield was on a different basis, then, from your settlement with Mr. Kelley and Mr. Garfield which you produced here?—A. Yes, sir; Mr. Scofield paid me the money to get the stock with, and in the settlement he did not take the stock and returned the receipt.

Q. You considered that this ended all right and claim on his part to the stock—that it was your stock?—A. Yes, sir; it was my stock.

Q. And he took something else in lieu of his money?—A. Yes, sir.

Q. Can you tell when this final settlement occurred between you and Mr. Scofield?—A. I cannot. I think it was before the adjournment of that session of Congress, or else it was immediately after we came together the next session. I think we did not adjourn until late in July, 1868, and I think it was closed before that session ended.

Q. Mr. Bingham gave you the details of a transaction between you and him in regard to the Credit Mobilier stock; was his statement substantially accurate?—A. Yes, sir; his statement was substantially correct, and I have nothing to say in relation to it, except that he got me mixed up with his Nevada Mining Company, which I had nothing to do with.

Q. You received $2,000 from him to invest in Credit Mobilier stock?—A. Yes, sir.

Q. He received the entire dividends on that stock?—A. Yes, sir.

Q. The statement he gave of the account between you in his testimony is a statement of all that he received?—A. He has received all that he was entitled to, and his statement is correct, except in one particular, and that I do not suppose he claims he did not receive.

Q. What is that?—A. When I came back here he wanted the stock sold. I advised him not to sell it; that it would bring more. He said he wanted it closed up. We looked at the price-current in New York, (I refer now to the Union Pacific Railroad stock which he had received, or was to, as dividends on his Credit Mobilier stock.) I told him I would keep his stock until it brought a better price, and that whenever I did sell it I would pay him the difference. I think our settlement was made at 19 for the stock. When I sold it it had risen in price, so that I made for him about $800 more, which I paid to him as the difference. I did this at my own instance. I did not want him to sacrifice the stock, and kept it for him.

Q. When you sold his stock, you accounted to him for $800 more?—A. Yes, sir; that was something like a year later.

Q. Who do you consider the 20 shares you received back from Mr. Bingham in your settlement with him as now belonging to?—A. The stock belongs to me.

Q. It was understood, when you made the settlement, that he had no further claim on the stock?—A. Yes, sir; that was the end of it. I bought his stock back of him, and settled the whole thing.

Q. But he had the benefit of all the dividends between the time you received this money and the time the thing was settled?—A. Yes, sir.

Q. Were you present when J. F. Wilson made a statement before the committee the other day?—A. I was.

Q. Have you anything to say in reference to that statement of Mr. Wilson, in which you differ from it?—A. No, sir; that agrees with me exactly.

Q. You wish to make no qualification of it?—A. None whatever.

Q. The whole transaction was stated by him as it occurred?—A. Yes, sir; that is all square.

Q. There is one gentleman whose name appears on this list about whom as yet no inquiry has been made; that is Mr. Painter.—A. I suppose Mr. Painter had a right to buy it if I chose to sell it to him. He was not a member of Congress.

Q. Did he buy it?—A. Yes.

Q. And paid for it?—A. Yes.

Q. And got the dividends?—A. Yes.

Q. And owns it now?—A. I suppose so. I hope he has sold it at a good price.

Q. At the time of this transaction, when you were making these contracts for the sale of Credit Mobilier stock to various members of Congress, was there anything pending before Congress, on which legislation was desired or expected in reference to the interests of the Union Pacific Railroad Company?—A. No, sir. Nothing was expected, and nothing wanted, and nothing asked for.

Q. In one of your letters there is some allusion to "Washburn's move." That letter, I think, was late in January, 1868. What move of Washburn did you refer to?—A. I gave you a little slip yesterday; that I suppose was what I referred to. C. C. Washburn made a move somewhere about that time to regulate the rates of traffic over the road.

Q. Have you examined to see when that subject was started in Congress?—A. No, sir; I have not.

Q. Is that the thing you refer to in your letter as "Washburn's move?"—A. I presume so; I do not know of anything else.

Q. Was that resolution or bill of Mr. Washburn's, looking to the passage by Congress of some law regulating the rate of charges of the Union Pacific Railroad, introduced or pending in Congress at the time of this transaction?—A. It may have been; I don't know.

Q. Do you remember whether it was or not?—A. I do not know. I wish the resolution of Mr. Washburn had been passed; we could then get a great deal larger rates over the road than we do now.

Q. Did you want it passed then?—A. No, I thought it was improvident and impolitic.

Q. You did not vote for it?—A. I do not know whether I did or not. I have given some foolish votes since I have been here, and I may have voted for as foolish a thing as that.

Q. Have you examined to see how early in that session either of the Washburns introduced anything into Congress with reference to the Union Pacific Railroad?—A. No, sir; I have not.

Q. You think it was C. C. Washburn's resolution, or bill, about regulating the freights or fares referred to in your letter to Mr. McComb?—A. I think so.

Q. You infer from that that it had been introduced earlier than the date of that letter?—A. Probably, or else I should not have written about it.

Q. Was nothing said between you and any of these gentlemen, in any of these negotiations, about that matter of Mr. Washburn?—A. No, sir; with none of them.

Q. Had they any reference to it?—A. No, sir.

Q. Was that a matter about which you who were interested in the railroad felt an interest, to pass it?—A. Not much; no, sir. I did not care much about it. The road was being constructed then very rapidly. We were employing all our means for the transportation of iron, ties, supplies, and every kind of material, and it was very dangerous to take freight or passengers over the road, and we did not want them.

Q. Can you tell whether the men who were regarded as the friends of the Union Pacific Railroad voted for or against this resolution of Mr. Washburn?—A. I do not know anything about it. I don't think it ever came to a vote.

By Mr. MERRICK:

Q. In regard to these transactions with Mr. Painter, you say you let him have how much Credit Mobilier stock?—A. Thirty shares.

Q. Was that on his application or your proffer?—A. He said he had been promised by parties fifty shares, and he claimed fifty shares instead of thirty, but I hadn't it to give him.

Q. Did he say what parties had promised him?—A. I understood him that Mr. Durant, McComb, and Bushnell were some of these parties. He was not promised by me.

Q. Did he say anything of the reasons why it had been promised? Did he say what he was to do?—A. No, sir; I have no knowledge of that at all.

Q. Your knowledge is the simple fact that he had been promised fifty shares?—A. Yes; I think Mr. Painter stated that he had been promised fifty shares; but I could not give it to him. I had not enough to fill as much stock as had been promised. I gave him thirty shares.

Q. He had the promise originally from Mr. Bushnell?—A. I think from Mr. Bushnell and from Mr. Durant, and I don't know but McComb. I know I did not promise it.

Q. Did he assign any reasons to you why you should give it to him, beyond the naked fact that it had been promised?—A. No, sir.

Q. Was anything said in reference to his being concerned in or around Congress, so as to make it desirable that he should be the owner of this stock?—A. No, sir.

Q. Did he pay you for it in the same way as those other gentlemen did?—A. He did.

Q. Did he advance any money, or pay it out of the dividends?—A. I do not know but he advanced some money, perhaps before he got the $1,800 dividend. I presume he did. I should not have given him a check for $1,800 unless he had previously paid me the difference between the 80 per cent. of the dividend and the par of the stock and interest.

Q. Your transaction with him was identical, in point of time, with that of these other parties?—A. Yes, sir.

By the CHAIRMAN:

Q. Had you ever any reason to suppose Mr. Painter held this stock for the benefit of anybody else except himself?—A. No, sir.

Q. You think the transaction was on his own account and for his own benefit?—A. Yes; that is my supposition; I never heard anything else suggested.

Q. Have you any reason to suppose he held it for anybody else?—A. No, sir.

By Mr. NIBLACK:

Q. In your letter of January 25, 1868, to Mr. McComb, produced in his original testimony, to which reference has been made, you speak in detail of the manner in which you were to distribute this stock by States, and you say "One to Tennessee." Be good enough to state to whom you had reference.—A. To Senator Fowler.

Q. You have stated this morning that he did not take any stock.—A. No, sir; he did not.

By Mr. MERRICK:

Q. What is the aggregate of all the shares apportioned by you among these gentlemen?—A. I do not know. Mr. Wilson had twenty, Mr. Scofield ten, Mr. Patterson thirty, Mr. Painter thirty, Mr. Dawes ten, Mr. Bingham twenty, Mr. Colfax twenty, Mr. Kelley ten, Mr. Wilson of Iowa ten, Mr. Allison ten, Mr. Garfield ten.

Q. That foots up one hundred and eighty shares; what did you do with the residue of those shares which had been assigned to you and Mr. Durant by the company?—A. I let other people have them outside of Congress.

Q. Did anybody else from Tennessee take any of this stock before or since?—A. No, sir.

Q. You say that other parties outside of Congress have it?—A. Yes, sir.

Q. Are there any other Government officials who had any?—A. No, sir; and I don't think I would ever sell anything to any Government official or member of Congress again if I know it.

Q. You had not your experience at that time?—A. No, sir.

Q. Mr. Boutwell's name was mentioned at one time; did you ever have any negotiations with him?—A. I had some talk with him.

Q. Did you make any arrangement with him in regard to this stock?—A. No, sir.

Q. How was the negotiation broken off?—A. He declined to take it; that is how it was broken off.

Q. Did he at any time agree to take it?—A. No, sir; he talked about it, and I supposed at one time he would take it, but he declined taking it.

WASHINGTON, D. C., *January* 22, 1873.

WILLIAM B. ALLISON, United States Senator-elect from the State of Iowa, having been duly sworn, made the following statement:

I desire to state my recollection of my connection with the Credit Mobilier. Mr. Ames and myself had several conversations—perhaps three or more—concerning the stock, I think beginning early in 1867. He was very largely interested in Iowa railways at the time, and I had frequent conversations with him about general railway matters in Iowa. I said to him at one time, in some of these conversations, that I did not know but I would take an interest in the Credit Mobilier, if he was at liberty to sell me the same number of shares I had in what was originally an authorized branch of the Union Pacific Railroad, and afterward called the Sioux City and Pacific Railroad, in Iowa, being fifty shares, of $100 each. Mr. Ames said to me that, if I desired it, he thought there would be no trouble in getting the stock. The matter passed along, without anything more than casual conversations, until, I should say, the winter or spring of 1868, when he told me he thought he could let me have either ten or twenty shares. I said to him that I would see further about it.

After some time, Mr. Ames sent me ten shares of Credit Mobilier stock and ten shares of Union Pacific stock, with some memorandum containing a statement showing that the stock was nearly full-paid by the proceeds of sales of bonds which were accretions upon the stock. This statement disclosed, I think, a small balance due upon the stock. How this balance was paid, I do not now remember. I received a dividend of $600 in June, 1868, in the form of a check on the Sergeant-at-Arms of the House, which seems to have been placed to my credit with him on the 28th day of June, and dated June 20. About this time, I think, I stated to Mr. Ames that I was not certain whether I would hold the stock. He said, "Very well; if you do not wish to hold it, you can return it to me at any time."

Mr. Ames seems to have some statement here which, I think, is not correct in one particular; it may be in others. Very little more, if anything, was said until the winter of 1868, when I returned to Washington. I then said to Mr. Ames that I would not hold the stock, and gave my reasons therefor, which he may recollect, or may not. This was when I returned to Washington, in the fall session of 1868-'69; at least when I saw him on my return, perhaps not the first day or the first week of the session. He said, very well; that I could return it to him. The matter was not finally adjusted, however, until February, I think, 1869, when I included what was the difference between the dividend and the amount unpaid on the stock when sent to me in a check, which I drew to his order on New York, which also included another matter, and which was paid to him.

I have had a conversation with Mr. Ames in relation to this, and he says he does not recollect that the dividend was included. I recollect very distinctly that it was so intended by me, and, I think, so stated to him at the time. My recollection is very distinct, because in that check I made up to Mr. Ames all the money that he had at any time paid me. At this time the stock, with other papers, was in the city of New York. I offered to give him an order for it. He said that was not necessary, as the stock was already in his name, and he could draw dividends upon it without reference to whether he had the certificates in his possession, and that I could return him the certificates at my convenience. He has stated to me that I then gave him a receipt that I held the stock for him. That I have forgotten. He may be correct. From that time forward I have no recollection of paying any attention whatever to this stock, and I did not consider that I had any interest in it. After considerable time, I returned the original certificates to Mr. Ames. I know I must be right in reference to this date when it was finally understood that I should have nothing more to do with the shares, and I think Mr. Ames must have so understood it, because, although there were frequent dividends on the stock, Mr. Ames did not notify or say to me that there were such dividends, or make any further allusion to the transaction, and I never received but one dividend, which I have already referred to, of $600. Mr. Ames has some account about the stock, of which I know nothing.

I desire to say, in addition to this, that, having made this adjustment with Mr. Ames, I received no profits, and realized nothing whatever from the transaction in any manner.

By Mr. NIBLACK:

Question. Mr. Ames produced this morning the envelope in which the certificates were inclosed to him by you, and stated that his recollection was that he received the certificates at a later date, some time last fall, instead of March 31, when the envelope was post-marked.—Answer. I do not know what Mr. Ames's impression is about it. I should have said it was in 1871. If he has the envelope post-marked the 31st of March, I presume that is the date. It was after I went out of Congress. I had a number of papers relating to other matters in New York, and when I returned home I carried them on with me. Some time afterward, in looking them over, I found these certificates, and I immediately returned them to Mr. Ames. I have no recollection of sending any other letter to Mr. Ames since March, 1871, and I presume, therefore, that date is correct. The committee will understand my statement that, since 1869, I have had no interest in or interest to inquire about this Credit Mobilier in any manner, or in the Union Pacific Railroad stock arising therefrom.

By Mr. MERRICK:

Q. Your original arrangement with Mr. Ames was in January, 1868?—A. No; I should say now, having the dates, that it was at a later period. I had no particular arrangements with Mr. Ames. I should say that the ten shares of Credit Mobilier stock were sent to me in April or May, 1868.

Q. While you were here in Congress?—A. Yes; I was here in Congress; but in April and the first half of May engaged in the Treasury Department nearly all the time with a sub-Committe of Ways and Means, preparing tax-bill, and seldom in the House.

Q. You then received the two dividends spoken of?—A. No, sir; I never received but one dividend.

Q. Was that a money dividend?—A. That was a money dividend.

Q. That was in June, 1868?—A. It seems to be; Mr. Ames's check is dated June 20; I see his memorandum makes it the 19th; I must have received it between the 20th and 25th of June; I do not precisely understand the memorandum of Mr. Ames; there seems to have been an omission of a dividend; there was a dividend made between January, 1868, and the time when that memorandum was made, as I understand it.

Q. A dividend in money?—A. No, sir; in stock and bonds.

Q. Here is a statement of the first stock dividend on the credit side of your account with $776, the net proceeds of the bonds.—A. The committee may call that a dividend; I do not so call it, because I did not receive it; Mr. Ames sent me this Credit Mobilier stock, but he did not hand me any dividend, except the one I have spoken of.

Q. Did you pay him any money except the $271 on account of that stock?—A. I have no recollection of paying him the difference; that I should rather have said I did not pay him; but he says I did, and therefore I will not say that I did not, but do not know the amount.

Q. This account of his, corresponding with his accounts given in relation to others, was in substance that he contracted for $1,000 of Credit Mobilier stock, which he sold to you for par and interest from July, $1,047; that he credited you with the bond dividend of 80 per cent., which he sold at 97, netting $776; and that he received from you cash $271; that he then paid you in June afterward a dividend of $600, cash, and paid you the first dividend by way of crediting it on your purchase-money?—A. I understand that to be his statement. That statement of course I know nothing about. I only mention the fact that these two classes of stock were sent to me. It may be that I paid Mr. Ames $271. Until to-day I should have stated that my belief was that the balance due in the purchase of the stock was taken out of the $600 dividend, but he may be correct, and I think now he is, except as to amount.

Q. Did you apply to him originally for stock, or did he propose to you to take it?—A. I could not say in reference to that. Senator Grimes and myself were living together at the time. Senator Grimes had considerable interest in it, and Mr. Ames and I had frequent conversations about Iowa roads, and undoubtedly about this. I could not say whether he proposed to me to take it, or whether I asked him. At that time, I mean in 1867, I did not conceive there was anything improper in my holding it.

Q. Were you cognizant of any agitation in Congress, during that winter, in regard to the Union Pacific Railroad Company?—A. No, sir, I was not.

Q. Were you aware of any movement by Mr. Washburn?—A. There may have been movements made by Mr. Washburn, but I do not remember when they were made; certainly not at the time we were having these conversations.

Q. Was your mind ever directed to the fact that his movements bore upon the Credit Mobilier stock; that the interests of the stockholders were involved in any way in his movements or contemplated movements?—A. It may have been. I cannot say whether it was so or not at this distance of time.

Q. You do not know whether these matters were presented to your mind at that time?—A. No, sir.

Q. Did these agitations in Congress, and agitations in reference to this supposed lawsuit, have any influence, controlling or otherwise, in your abandonment of the purchase?—A. No, sir. I think they had no influence over my mind at the time. I do not think I knew that Mr. McComb had a lawsuit until I saw the publication in the newspapers during the campaign last fall.

Q. Why did you abandon the purchase?—A. The chief reason was that I owned a little stock in a branch road, the Sioux City and Pacific Railroad, in my own State, and was for a time a director. Friends and enemies criticised my owning stock in that company, and I thought it was not worth while to have this little matter of ten shares of stock in this company. I know very little about it, especially in reference to its profits. That was the motive that influenced me chiefly.

Q. It was public criticism upon your ownership in another company?—A. It was brought immediately to my attention in that way. My constituents seemed to think that it was better for me not to hold any of that sort of stock. I therefore desired to obey them in this regard, as they had just re-elected me to Congress.

Q. Your attention had not been called to any positive actual impropriety in holding this stock during the session of Congress, commencing December, 1867?—A. No, sir; I do not think it had. I do not think I regarded it as improper. I will say, as you have reached that point, that the only legislation I know of in reference to the Union Pacific Railroad during that period was in 1869, when I was a member of Congress, and that I understood to be in the nature of restrictive legislation. I know that those who had criticised the management of the Union Pacific Railroad voted for this legislation, as well as the friends of the road.

Q. You had parted with your interest in the Credit Mobilier at that time?—A. Entirely. I had no interest whatever. I remember that Mr. Washburn, who was not understood to be especially friendly to this road, voted for that proposition. The legislation which occurred in 1871, to which I have seen reference made, passed the House while I was out on a conference committee, in connection with Mr. Randall, of Pennsylvania, and Mr. Lawrence, of Ohio, so that I did not vote upon that proposition.

By Mr. McCrary:

Q. You told Mr. Ames that you would return him the stock. At the time you told him that, you had concluded not to take it?—A. Yes.

Q. Can you give us the conversation that occurred at the time? Can you state what Ames said about it, and whether he said anything about buying it back from you?—A. He did. He said, "I will buy the stock back again." I said to him that I did not wish to sell it; that I would return it.

Q. Please state all that occurred in that conversation.—A. I remember it very well. He threw down something of mere nominal value, and said, "I will buy it of you." I replied, "You may call it what you please, Mr. Ames."

Q. Did you suggest to him the propriety of the re-sale, or did he suggest it to you?—A. I am entirely sure that he suggested it to me. I had no idea of a re-sale, because I had never considered that I had the stock.

Q. Mr. Ames has left the impression, perhaps, that that was a mere ruse, so that the stock might be considered yours in case the litigation turned out favorably to the Credit Mobilier, but not otherwise. I want to ask you about that.—A. That could not be true, and Mr. Ames could not have so understood it, I think, from anything that was said.

Q. What was said about that litigation at the time?—A. I do not remember. Mr. Ames may have said to me that there was some litigation about the stock, or about the railroad, but it made no impression upon me as having anything to do with our transaction. It had nothing to do with my resolution to return the stock in any way.

Q. You had made up your mind after your re-nomination to return it?—A. Yes. I had a contest in my re-nomination, and a contest in my re-election, in which the whole matter of the Sioux City Railroad was the chief topic of discussion. I held debates during the canvass with my competitors, in which that was the chief topic; and, believing that it was a wise thing not to be interested in any matter that would be questioned before my constituents, this stock was never taken nor held by me, except as stated heretofore. This contest, I will say, began early in 1868, when the newspapers began to assail me as to the impropriety of my holding an interest in the Sioux City and Pacific Railroad. I thought, as I said, that it was a prudent thing to have no interest in these matters; and I want to say that I have no interest in any matter covertly that I am not willing the public, at any time, should know all about.

Q. Your recollection is distinct that that contest and the matters growing out of it, and not the litigation with Mr. McComb, instigated and induced you not to take the stock?—A. I am very clear in that statement.

Q. And I understand, also, that your recollection is very clear that you did not intend to hold on to this stock in any event, after the conversation you had with Mr. Ames?—A. Very clear, if you allude to the conversation in 1869.

Q. Was anything said by you, or by Mr. Ames, to that effect?—A. Nothing in any way to indicate any intention that I should hold the stock, either by him or by me. On the contrary, I must have given him distinctly to understand that I had no desire to be connected with it; and he must have so understood it, I think, at the time.

Q. I do not know whether you have stated the date of that conversation between you and Mr. Ames or not, in which you would not take the stock?—A. We had more than one conversation in reference to that subject. I could not give the exact date. The last one was about the time this check was given, in February, 1869.

Q. Why did you not return the certificates to him at that time?—A. The certificates had been transmitted to New York, and were in New York with a considerable number of other papers. As I stated, I offered to give Mr. Ames an order for these certificates, and he said that was not necessary, as the stock was already in his name on the books of the company, and he could draw the dividends; that I could hand him the stock at my convenience.

Q. The certificates remained there until you returned with your papers to Dubuque?—A. Yes; when I left Congress I took all the papers to my home, and afterward returned this stock to Mr. Ames.

Q. You seem not to have written him any letter at the time you returned the stock.—A. I am not certain about that. I do not recollect whether I wrote him anything or not. I should say there was some memorandum connected with it, but I would not be certain with reference to that. I should say that I wrote him a note suggesting the fact that I returned him the stock. What I have stated in relation to this whole affair is from memory, without memoranda before me, except as to the check, and not having charged my mind with the details, I may be in error as to some of them.

WASHINGTON, D. C., *January* 22, 1873.

N. G. ORDWAY sworn and examined.

By Mr. COLFAX:

Q. You are Sergeant-at-Arms of the House of Representatives?—A. Yes, sir.

Q. You have accounts with members from time to time?—A. I keep an account of their pay and mileage, which is a record of the Government. I also keep a set of books for deposits, in which I enter the accounts of money which members may have in my possession—a public and a private account.

Q. Have you examined my account during the year 1868?—A. I glanced over it this morning.

Q. In your public account did you find any entry besides salary and mileage?—A. The public account books are filed in the Treasury Department at the close of every Congress.

Q. In your public account there could not be anything except pay and mileage?—A. No, sir.

Q. In my private account do you find any deposit of $534?—A. I glanced over your account to see if there was anything except your salary and mileage, but I did not find anything else.

Q. That is an account of my private deposits?—A. Yes, sir.

Q. Mr. Ames deposited in 1868 a large sum of money with you, upon which he drew checks?—A. I have not looked at Mr. Ames's accounts carefully enough to know that. I understand there was some amount deposited.

Q. There have been some checks on that deposit signed by Mr. Ames?—A. Yes; he drew more than his salary and mileage considerably that session.

Q. Are these checks generally indorsed by the person who is to get the money?—A. Some of them are indorsed. Where one member gives a check to another, we do not require usually an indorsement, when it comes directly from the hall. When it comes through an outside party, we always require an indorsement.

Q. Mr. Ames testified to-day in regard to a check given by him to Mr. Allison; was that check indorsed?—A. My impression is that it was not. I looked them over twice with Mr. Ames and once with Mr. Allison.

Q. Did you see any of those checks drawn in June, 1868, that were indorsed?—A. I noticed one or more that were indorsed.

Q. By members?—A. By members; one was by a Senator.

Q. Did you see any check there to me?—A. I saw a check with the letters "S. C.," which Mr. Ames wrote down on a memorandum or piece of paper, opposite your name.

Q. "S. C. or bearer?"—A. Yes, sir.

Q. How much was that check for?—A. My recollection is that it was for $1,200.

Q. Is there any indorsement on it?—A. I think not.

Q. Do you remember ever having paid me any draft or check from Mr. Ames?—A. I have no such recollection, and I would not be likely to have, because I do not usually pay out the money or receive it myself.

Q. Who does pay it out generally?—A. The paying-teller. The arrangement in my office is, now, that he receives all the money and pays it out.

Q. What is the name of your paying-teller?—A. N. A. Fuller.

Q. Was he your paying-teller in 1868?—A. Not in 1868. I think Thomas P. Cheney was then acting in that capacity, with my son, George L. Ordway, as assistant.

Q. Were there any other checks drawn by Mr. Ames, payable by initials?—A. I think there were some.

Q. What were the initials?—A. I do not recall any of them now; I know there were initials on others.

Q. This amount was not placed to my credit as a private deposit, and, therefore, if paid, must have been deposited or gone elsewhere?—A. Yes, sir; I looked specially at your account this morning, for the purpose of ascertaining that fact. My attention was called to the subject only a few moments ago. I have not looked at the day-book; nothing of the sort appears upon the ledger.

Q. Who is your book-keeper?—A. Moses Dillon. He has occupied that position ever since I have occupied mine, except for a few months.

Q. Has he said anything to you on this subject?—A. He did say something when I came in this morning; I do not remember what it was. It was nothing to your injury, I can assure you.

By the CHAIRMAN:

Q. You have no personal recollection about these matters?—A. Not the least.

Q. This check would not have been likely to have been paid by you, whoever it was paid to?—A. No, sir; I refrain from handling money. I think it is better that one person should do it, and be responsible.

By Mr. COLFAX:

Q. Do you know where Mr. Cheney is now?—A. He has charge of the special railway mail-service of the New England States, with his headquarters at Boston.

Q. You never heard from him that he paid me any money?—A. No, sir; the subject was never called to my attention until recently.

By Mr. MCCRARY:

Q. A check of that kind would be paid to whoever presented it?—A. If it was an outside person who presented it, we should require an indorsement or an identification. All we want is to be sure that we are paying the money to the right person.

By the CHAIRMAN:

Q. This check which you looked at is payable to "S. C. or bearer?"—A. Yes, sir; it is one of our ordinary checks, signed by Oakes Ames. It was filed away after the close of the business of that session with all the other checks, and has so remained until within a few days.

Q. And is charged to Mr. Ames on his account?—A. Yes, sir.

By Mr. COLFAX:

Q. If he had drawn it himself, it would be charged to his account in the same way?—A. If he had drawn it, it would be charged in the same way. It is a common thing for parties drawing a check to pay for a draft to write in something to indicate the purpose for which it is drawn.

WASHINGTON, *January* 22, 1873.

JOHN B. ALLEY recalled and examined.

By Mr. COLFAX:

Question. You may remember that I said last September in a speech at South Bend that I had never received a dollar of dividends of any kind from the Credit Mobilier. Now, I would like you to state what Mr. Ames has said to you as to his recollection and mine in regard to this matter; whether they agree or disagree.—Answer. Mr. Ames stated to me before he went home—I think it was—that your statement was substantially in accordance with his. Upon reflection, I find that your statement was made on the 7th of January, after his return here. He, therefore, could not have alluded at that time to your statement before this committee. He must have alluded to your statement to him in conversation.

Q. But that the statement I made in conversation accorded substantially with his?—A. I understood there was no substantial disagreement. I am not quite certain now whether it was before or immediately after you made your statement here. I supposed he had conferred with you. I had never had any conference with you upon the matter.

Q. Mr. Ames testifies that he had some conversation with me early in the session, and that he made some statement before this committee based upon this conversation. He told you that the statement made to him accorded substantially with his recollection?—A. That is my impression. I do not know particularly about it.

By the CHAIRMAN:

Q. That was before the recess?—A. It must have been, because there certainly was a disagreement afterward. I did not regard it, and I did not suppose he regarded it, however, as any substantial disagreement even after the recess.

Q. There appears to be a substantial disagreement now?—A. Yes; quite different from what I supposed.

Q. Did Mr. Ames on that occasion go on to make his statement to you of the facts in relation to his dealings with Mr. Colfax? Did he undertake to narrate how the thing was?—A. No, sir.

Q. He merely said that he had had a conference with Mr. Colfax, and that they substantially agreed?—A. Yes, sir. It must have been previous to the recess, because I remember now that it was in the presence of his counsel, Mr. McMurtrie, who came here to look after his interests in connection with the Pennsylvania suit, and he has not been here since the holidays.

By Mr. MERRICK:

Q. Did Mr. Ames, when speaking of the substantial agreement between himself and Mr. Colfax, refer to any special statement in which there was this coincidence, so that you could identify the special correspondence he referred to?—A. I do not think he did. He was talking with the counsel and myself, speaking of the gentlemen who were implicated, and I remember his making that remark. Mr. Ames has told me since that when he went home and refreshed his recollection by his memoranda-books, &c., he found some things a little different from what he supposed when he gave his testimony. Whether that included Mr. Colfax or not, I do not think he stated.

Q. His first statement was given from general recollection, without reference to memoranda?—A. I understand so.

WASHINGTON, D. C., *January* 22, 1873.

MATTHEW G. EMERY sworn and examined.

By Mr. MERRICK:

Question. I will ask you if you had any communication with Senator Patterson in reference to any purchases or negotiations that he was making, or proposed to make, of stock of the Credit Mobilier?—Answer. Some two or three years since, perhaps two years, he called to see me to procure my indorsement of a note to enable him to raise money, as I understood, to purchase stock of Mr. Ames in the Union Pacific Railroad. I cannot recollect the exact time. By reference to our tickler, the note-book of the bank, I notice that I indorsed a note for $4,000 for him, which was discounted the 19th of February, 1870, and which he paid on maturity.

Q. Was that the only negotiation or loan?—A. I think I have indorsed notes for him two or three times before; I am not sure.

Q. Do you recollect the amounts of these notes or indorsements?—A. About the same amounts, perhaps from $2,000 to $4,000. I am not sure of the amounts.

Q. Did you make any indorsement for any such sum of money in the year 1868?—A. That was prior to the date I named, and I do not think that note was discounted in our bank. He may have used it in Mr. Kelly's bank. When it was I cannot tell you.

Q. Did he afterward speak with you in reference to the disposition he had made of that loan?—A. Some months afterward, perhaps a year, on his return to the next Congress, I asked him how his speculation in railroad stock had turned out. He said "Very well;" that "it was a very good thing."

Q. Did he speak of having received dividends?—A. It is my impression that he did not; I am not sure; I know he told me it resulted very well.

Q. Can you give us now, or hereafter by reference to any memoranda, the date of the earlier loan of which you speak?—A. If it was discounted in the Metropolitan Bank, I might; I do not know that I could by any record of my own.

Q. Was anything said between you and him with reference to Credit Mobilier stock at all?—A. Not at that time.

Q. At any time?—A. Since this investigation has been going on, I met him, and he asked me if I had any recollection of his ever saying anything in regard to his owning Credit Mobilier stock; I told him I had not; my impression at the time he borrowed the money was, that it was to purchase Union Pacific Railroad stock.

Q. As I understand you, both of these loans had reference, as you understood, to the purchase of railroad securities?—A. No, sir; I do not know in reference to that, and I cannot say whether the one I have named was for that purpose, or the previous one.

Q. Did you negotiate a loan in the National Bank of the Republic for $3,000?—A. No; I did for $4,000, the 19th of February, 1870.

Q. The other you suppose to have been negotiated at the National Metropolitan Bank?—A. I presume so.

Q. Did he or not inform you at the time he negotiated the first loan that he wanted to purchase of Oakes Ames stock in a company for building the Union Pacific Railroad?—A. My recollection is that he said Union Pacific Railroad stock. At that time I did not know that there was any other company for the purpose of building that road.

Q. Did he mention to you at any time the amount of dividends that he had received?—A. I do not know that he ever did.

Q. Do you recollect what Mr. Patterson said to you when he first approached you in reference to this loan of $3,000?—A. I do not know that he gave any intimation of what it was for.

Q. Did he mention Oakes Ames's name in connection with it?—A. He stated, in connection with one of the loans, that it was to purchase some railroad stock of Mr. Ames.

Q. Did he say anything about Mr. Ames having made a good investment for him?—A. I do not recollect as to that.

Q. Did he say anything to you about being able to get more than the cost of the stock within a short time?—A. No, sir. I have heard from him or somebody else—perhaps since this thing has been broached—within a year, that he received dividends upon the stock. I do not know that he did. I have no personal knowledge at all. I never saw him with any of the stock, or with anything pertaining to it.

Q. Of the two loans you aided him in, one was negotiated at the Bank of the Metropolis in 1871, and the other at the National Bank of the Republic in 1871?—A. I do not know the date of the one at the National Bank of the Metropolis.

Q. And you cannot, from your memory, state whether it was Credit Mobilier stock or stock to build a railroad that was mentioned?—A. No, sir; I recollect nothing of the kind at all as to the Credit Mobilier stock.

WASHINGTON, D. C., *January* 24, 1873.

OAKES AMES recalled and examined.

By Mr. KELLEY:

Question. I understand from your testimony day before yesterday that you hold as my property ten shares of Credit Mobilier stock?—Answer. Yes, sir.

Q. Will you be good enough to tell me when that became my property?—A. That became your property when you paid for it. When I paid you $329 in June, 1868. That is the way I considered it.

Q. About what date was that?—A. About the middle of June.

Q. Have there been any dividends declared upon these shares since June, 1868?—A. Yes.

Q. Will you be good enough to state in their chronological order what dividends have been declared?—A. I cannot. They were in certificates, in bonds, and in Union Pacific Railroad stock.

Q. Have you them to my credit?—A. I hold them for you.

Q. Then you cannot tell me what property of mine you have in your hands?—A. I can state that I have ten shares of Credit Mobilier and ten of Union Pacific Railroad stock.

Q. At what time did they come into your hands as my property?—A. The ten shares of Union Pacific Railroad stock came into my hands some time in February, 1868—in January or February of that year.

Q. If there are any assets, and if there have been dividends declared since then, in stocks or bonds, please give them to me in their chronological order.—A. I cannot tell you just what they are now. I have not the record here. There are two or three dividends, I think.

Q. Can you swear that you hold property for me, and yet cannot tell what it is?—A. I cannot tell you without looking at my memoranda showing when I received the stock.

Q. State as near as you can from memory, to be corrected from your memoranda.—A. I should say I hold forty or fifty shares Union Pacific Railroad stock for you and ten shares Credit Mobilier stock.

Q. Anything else?—A. I think I also have some certificates for first-mortgage bonds. The company were not able to get the bonds and exchanged them for income-bonds about a year afterward.

Q. About how much?—A. I cannot recollect the amount.

Q. Has there been any interest paid on any of this property of mine?—A. No, sir; it is drawing no interest.

Q. Is there interest due you?—A. No; you paid for your stock and there is no interest due me.

Q. Is there any interest due to me? I want to know, simply, what I am worth in this world.—A. I cannot state to you now what is due you. I will give you a statement.

Q. How soon can you furnish that list to the chairman of this committee—a list of property of mine now in your hands?—A. I think I can get the data to furnish it to-day or to-morrow.

Q. How did I pay for this Credit Mobilier stock?—A. In the first place, you were to pay me $1,000, and interest from 1st July, 1867, for the stock.

Q. Did I ever offer to pay you a dollar of money?—A. No, you never offered to pay me a dollar of money, but I did you. Do you deny it?

Q. Did I ever ask you for an investment in Credit Mobilier stock or anything else, or did you invite me to accept it?—A. I do not remember which way it was originally. I know you agreed to take it, and did take the dividends up to June.

Q. Do you remember meeting me in front of the Ebbitt House, on the south side of F street, near 14th, where I joined you casually that evening, as you seemed to be waiting for a car; when you rallied me about having become rich enough to throw away $1,000 for a subscription to the Credit Foncier?—A. No, sir; I do not remember that.

Q. Do you remember saying to me, after explaining that that would be a losing investment, and after being assured by me that I had no money to invest in any way, do you remember saying you could, as a friend, put me in the way of an investment that would probably be real, and have some profit in it?—A. I remember having some such conversation about it. I cannot tell where it was. I know there was a conversation.

Q. Were not you and I members of the national republican executive committee, meeting together as such frequently that year?—A. I believe so.

Q. Did I ever ask you for an investment, or about any investment?—A. I have no recollection of any investment except this thing.

Q. What I want to ask is, whether I was seeking for an investment and whether I suggested it?—A. I do not know whether you came to me or I to you.

Q. Then I want to ask you whether you ever loaned me any money?

The WITNESS. At what time?

Mr. KELLEY. At any time preceding this transaction?

A. I think I did.

Q. Did you not loan it to me because I told you of my extreme embarrassment?—A. I do not recollect. I loaned you $500 previous to this, and you repaid it.

Q. Did you loan me any other sum?—A. I have let you have some since.

Q. Did you not swear day before yesterday that you had also let me have $700?—A. I said I let you have $750.

Q. And $700?—A. No; $750.

Q. I was not here to hear your statement, but I understood that you stated both $700 and $750.—A. No; $750; nothing else. That was the 27th September.

Q. You state that you loaned me $500 previously. Did you subsequently let me have the amount of $1,000?—A. No.

Q. You were mistaken, then, on the 16th December last, in saying that you had loaned me $1,000?—A. I took it from you. You thought it was $1,000. You told me previous to this investigation that you had a thousand-dollar loan from me. I was willing to have it go in that way. I could not remember. I thought your memory must be better than mine.

Q. How soon can you deliver me the ten shares of Credit Mobilier stock which you say are mine?—A. I am ready to deliver it now, and you can have the dividends. (Witness here laid upon the table a certificate for ten shares of Credit Mobilier stock.)

Mr. KELLEY. You will please hand that to the chairman of the committee to be retained by him for my use, and please make me a statement of the dividends due me as soon as you can.—A. Very well. But if you do not own this stock, I do not see that you are entitled to any dividends.

Q. But you say I do own it, and am entitled to the dividends, and I wish to have a list of them as soon as you can furnish it.—A. Very well; that is what I agree to perfectly. (Certificate of stock referred to was then indorsed for transfer and handed to the chairman.)

Q. Then when I shall have received, or the chairman shall have received for me, all the dividends due me, will I, or will I not, be your debtor, in any sum or any account whatever?—A. Then $750 you owe me will be in part payment of what I am to deliver, I suppose.

Q. That is what I want you to state. I want to know whether, when I have received all the dividends due on my stock, I shall be your debtor, personally.—A. If you receive all the dividends you will owe me $750.

Q. Do I understand that the ten shares Credit Mobilier stock are paid for?—A. Yes.

Q. How paid?—A. Paid by the profits of the bond-dividend of February, 80 per cent., and by the cash dividend of June, leaving $329 due you, which I paid you.

Q. You appropriated these two dividends, then, for the payment of the stock?—A. Certainly; did you not so understand?

Q. That is what I want to understand; that is what I am trying to get at now in the presence of witnesses. You have sold the bonds which you say were mine, and have appropriated a certain amount of cash which you say was mine. Do I understand you that I still owe you for the stock?—A. No, you do not owe me for the stock. The stock has been paid for out of these dividends, as I stated. When all of the dividends shall have been turned over to you, you will then owe me the $750 loan.

(The chairman here explained to Mr. Kelley his understanding of the witness's statement.)

Q. I think I now understand it, then. If you turn over all the dividends except that which was applied to the purchase of that Credit

Mobilier stock, I will, according to your account, then owe you $750?—A. Yes, sir.

Q. Mr. Ames, did you ever hand me a check marked "W. D. K.?"—A. Yes, sir.

Q. You did?—A. Yes, sir; I did.

Q. Did you hand these other gentlemen whose names have been mentioned as receiving them such checks?—A. Yes, sir.

Q. Were there other checks in which the initials were written in other than those of W. D. K. and S. C., to which you have sworn?—A. Yes, sir; I think so.

Q. How many were marked with the initials?—A. I cannot tell you how many were marked; I think J. F. Wilson indorsed his check; I think Mr. Patterson indorsed his, and I do not know but some others.

Q. Did I indorse mine?—A. No, sir; I don't say you indorsed yours; you don't deny getting the $329?

Mr. KELLEY. I am not denying anything now; I am asking you questions.

The WITNESS. What, then, is the use of disputing about it, if you don't deny it?

Testimony of Mr. KELLEY:

Mr. KELLEY. I want to state to the committee that I do deny ever having received such a check, and I deny it under the responsibility of the oath I gave the other day, with a new affirmation, if you desire it. I say, in reference thereto, that I don't believe I received it; I cannot remember having received it; to the best of my knowledge and belief I did not receive it; and I add that I always thought it strange that, whatever I did receive from Mr. Ames, which I regarded in the shape of loans, was received in money, and not by check to my order or payable on demand.

By the CHAIRMAN:

Question. In your statement to the committee, if I remember right, Mr. Kelley, you stated you had borrowed a thousand dollars of Mr. Ames, and that you still owed him?—Answer. Yes, sir.

Q. Is it your recollection that you received the whole of the $1,000 at one time?—A. On the contrary, I have said, in the presence of other persons, that Mr. Ames gave me a round sum, which purported to be the money that he had about him, and that on the next day, or a few days thereafter, he handed me the remainder of the $1,000.

Q. Have you any memorandum of the transaction in any way?—A. I have not. I relied on Mr. Ames as a creditor keeping the account. Unhappily, I keep no books of my own.

Q. I think you stated the other day that you had no recollection about the time?—A. I cannot tell you about the time. I said the other day substantially this: The question was put to me whether the loan had any reference to the Credit Mobilier transaction. I replied that I would not undertake to state what was passing in my mind at a time so far distant; that if it was between the period at which Mr. Ames had proposed to carry ten shares of this stock for me, and the time he gave me notice that it was off—that it could not be done; it probably had reference to that transaction—that if it was after that, it could not have had any reference to it. I think that will be found to be substantially the answer I gave to that question, and so I say to-day. Of course, I do not undertake to judge what may have been passing in Mr. Ames's mind on the subject.

Q. You think the amount of money you received from Mr. Ames was, in all, a round thousand dollars?—A. It was a round thousand dollars; that is what I believe I had from him, and I have stated that I received it from him on two different occasions, and I now think I received these amounts on two successive days.

Q. Can you state, in reference to the division of the amount, as to how much you received at one time and how much on the other?—A. My recollection is that the amounts received were $700 and $300.

Q. Can you state which amount you received first?—A. Seven hundred dollars first.

The chairman inquired of Mr. Ames whether he desired to further examine Mr. Kelly.

Mr. Ames here handed to Mr. Kelley what seemed to be a written momorandum.

Mr. KELLEY. Mr. Ames asks me, on this paper, whether he shall put certain questions to me. It is not for me to say what he shall or shall not ask.

Mr. AMES. You have made it very important for me to ask you further questions. I have made my testimony heretofore as favorable to you as I could. I now ask you whether you have not come to me repeatedly, often, and wanted to know when you should get any more dividends on that stock?—A. No, sir.

Q. Did I not give you the $750 on account of dividends received on your stock?—A. I did not so understand it.

Q. Did you give me any receipt or voucher for that $750?—A. I do not think I did.

Q. Did you for the $329?—A. I think not; nor for the $500 I received previously.

Mr. AMES. Yes, you did; you gave me a note for it, which matured, and you paid it off before this transaction. You do not recollect any of these circumstances?—A. No, I do not recollect it. My recollection is very distinct, as I stated the other day, of going to Mr. Ames after his failure and expressing to him my regret that, as I was as much embarrassed as I had been when I borrowed it, I was unable to return him that $1,000, and of his saying that that $1,000 would not affect him much; that although they had squeezed him pretty tight, he thought he would not be seriously injured.

Q. You say now that you recollect no conversation in which you wanted to know when you were to get any more dividends on that stock?—A. In such conversations I recollect asking you in regard to your personal assets, as to how they were coming on.

Q. You have no recollection, then, of asking me when you were to get other dividends on that stock?—A. No, sir; not in reference to my interests.

Q. What was said when you asked me for $750?—A. Upon my word I cannot tell. I had asked you a little while before to loan me $1,000, and you gave me what you had about you, and, I think the next day, or within a few days afterward, you gave me the balance of it.

Q. I gave you $750?—A. $750, you say; $700, I say.

Mr. AMES. I do not know that this is at all important, but you asked me when there would be more dividends on that stock, and I told you that there had been dividends, but that they were tied up with the McComb suit.

Re-examination of Mr. AMES.

By the CHAIRMAN:

Q. Let me ask you a question in relation to your interrogatories to

Mr. Kelley. They seem to imply that he called on you from time to time to know if there were more dividends on his Credit Mobilier stock ?—A. Yes, sir; he did.

Q. At what time was that; was it after the $329 was paid ?—A. Yes, sir.

Q. Subsequently to that date you say Mr. Kelley came to you and made these inquiries ?—A. He did; yes, sir.

Q. And more than once, you say ?—A. Yes, sir. On one of these occasions, when he asked me, I told him there was a dividend declared, and I let him have $750, which I considered on account of the dividends; and I took from him no note, voucher, or receipt.

Q. You kept a memorandum of it ?—A. Yes, sir.

Q. The $329 you let him have was the balance due him after paying for the Credit Mobilier stock, and you say that was paid by a check on the Sergeant-at-Arms ?—A. Yes, sir; payable to W. D. K., or bearer.

Q. Was that the only check you gave him on the Sergeant-at-Arms ? —A. I think it was.

Q. The other payments were directly to him in money ?—A. I think so; it may be by check on some bank, I do not know what bank; and I do not know whether on some bank or on the Sergeant-at-Arms; I have no recollection.

Q. When he called on you to know if there were more dividends and stock, did you tell him there were dividends on the Union Pacific Railroad stock, &c. ?—A. Yes, sir; I presume so. The reason they were not turned over to him was in consequence of this suit.

Q. From your statement Mr. Kelley must have understood that he was the owner of the stock and entitled to dividends on it ?—A. He so considered it; at least I presume he did. I never heard anything to the contrary until the other day. I had always considered it as his stock.

Q. How recently do you think you had any conversation with Mr. Kelley on this subject before the present session ?—A. At every session since, and a number of times he has asked me when that thing was going to be settled, and when we could get our dividends.

Q. He knew, then, from your statement that you were holding some Union Pacific Railroad stock for him ?—A. I presume so; I have no reason to think he did not.

Q. Did you tell him so ?—A. I told him so when I made the first statement, and he knew that subsequent dividends were made.

Q. When he spoke to you about dividends did you tell him there had been stock dividends upon the Credit Mobilier stock ?—A. Yes, sir; the stock dividends were within a few months of that first transaction when I paid him the $329.

By Mr. MERRICK:

Q. The payment of the $329 was before the $750 ?—A. Yes, sir; the $750 was in September afterward.

WASHINGTON, D. C., *January* 24, 1873.

L. L. CROUNSE sworn and examined.

By Mr. COLFAX:

Question. You are acquainted with Mr. Ames ?—Answer. Yes, sir.

Q. Have you had any conversation with him in reference to the charges growing out of this investigation?—A. Yes, sir; quite a number of conversations.

Q. How many altogether?—A. I would not like to state the exact number, because it is my habit, in "pursuit of information under difficulties," to confer with him almost every day.

Q. Would you say five or six at least during the session?—A. Yes, sir; I would say at least that.

Q. Do you remember having any conversation with Mr. Ames about the time of the holiday recess, or when Congress re-assembled?—A. I remember having had a conversation with him; I think it was the 7th of January.

Q. In that conversation, did you allude to the statement sent by the Associated Press in regard to the testimony given by me on the 7th of January?—A. The circumstances of that conversation were about these: The House ordered the testimony taken by this committee to be made public. The order was made Monday, the 6th of January. I believe it was the next day that you made your statement. I think it was the afternoon of that day, after your statement had been made, that I had a casual conversation with Mr. Ames at his seat in the House.

Q. Did he say he had heard the statement made by me under oath?—A. I think he did; my recollection is not absolutely distinct as to whether he said he had heard your statement; but, as I alluded to it, I naturally inferred that he had.

Q. You are certain it was the afternoon of the next day, after the House re-assembled, on the 6th of January?—A. Yes, sir; I am quite certain as to that.

Q. What did Mr. Ames say about the matter in regard to my statement?—A. We had a general conversation about your statement, and there were other matters that entered into the conversation. I called his attention to the fact that your statement did not entirely agree with his testimony in the beginning. In response to that, he made a general remark that he had made no record of these matters; that he had always carried them in his head, as it were, and that Mr. Colfax was probably correct. These were about the words I understood him to use.

Q. He said he had no record in this matter at all?—A. He said this, as I recollect now: that he had never kept any record; that was the point, as I understood him—that he carried these things in his head.

Q. You are certain that he used the remark that he carried these things in his head?—A. He certainly did. He used these words, that he "carried these things in his head, largely."

Q. Did he say anything about having heard this testimony of mine?—A. No, sir; I do not think he did.

Q. What were the words he used?—A. I cannot say that with absolute positiveness; my recollection is that he stated Mr. Colfax was "probably correct." I think "probably correct" were the two words he did use.

Q. Did he say anything about the mistake in regard to the $1,200 dividend he had paid me?—A. No, sir; he did not say anything about it.

By Mr. AMES:

Q. Do you say I said that Mr. Colfax's statement was substantially correct; did I tell you anything of that sort?—A. I think you did, or that his statement was probably correct. That is what I understood.

Mr. AMES. I said nothing of the kind.

The WITNESS. Then I must say I shall have to withdraw my confidence in some statements made in regard to others. I so understood you, and the statement made such an impression upon my mind that I alluded to the fact that night in my dispatches.

Q. In the dispatches you sent to the Times the other night, did you state what had transpired in this committee?—A. I do not know which dispatch you refer to.

Q. I refer to the dispatch of the Washington correspondent in yesterday's paper. They are in direct contradiction to the testimony before this committee. If that is the character of your statements they ought not to have any authority with anybody.—A. There may possibly be an error there. I have only to say, if you impugn that dispatch, that only yesterday you were kind enough to say that my dispatches in the Times had been very fair.

Mr. AMES. Some of them, I think, have been, but that one yesterday is very unfair and very untruthful. And as to my saying that Mr. Colfax's testimony was correct, it is utterly untrue; I could not have said so.

By Mr. COLFAX:

Q. Was it in consequence of that dispatch sent the 7th of January that I asked you in a casual conversation what Mr. Ames had said; and did I not show you that dispatch in the Times a few days afterward?—A. I think, about a week after that, when I called with a friend at your room, after my friend had finished his call upon you, you directed my attention to this dispatch.

Q. Have you that dispatch with you?—A. I have a dispatch cut from the Times, sent the evening after my conversation with Mr. Ames.

Q. Will you present it to the committee?—A. I will read the paragraph to which you refer, and which alone has reference to Mr. Colfax, without reading the whole dispatch. It is as follows:

"Mr. Colfax appeared before the committee to-day, and made a very clear and explicit statement regarding his part in the matter, by which it appears that he pocketed a loss of $500 as the result of his negotiations, and that when he found the company was likely to be involved in a lawsuit he thought the matter one in which he ought to have no part. Mr. Ames's testimony, as published, does not accord in all respects with this statement of Mr. Colfax; but the former, in conversation to-day, says that his own memory is not clear in regard to this transaction, and he has no doubt Mr. Colfax is entirely right."

Q. That was sent the evening after your conversation with Mr. Ames?—A. Yes, sir; the conversation occurred in the afternoon.

By the CHAIRMAN:

Q. This conversation was at Mr. Ames's seat in the House. Did you understand Mr. Ames to say that he had no memorandum in regard to these matters, or that he did not have any when he testified?—A. He did not make any explicit statement in regard to that, except that he had carried these things in his head; that he did not have any record, by which I inferred that he did not make them a matter of absolute record as he would general business transactions.

Q. In what he said to you about vouchers did you understand Mr. Ames to mean that he had none, or that he had none when he gave his testimony before? He had already testified some time before.—A. I did not use the word "vouchers."

Q. Memorandum, then?—A. I am not sure about "memorandum." I think the word "record" was used.

Q. Did you understand it to refer to his not having kept any, or his not having any with him, when he made his statement?—A. I inferred from what he said that he had not kept any record of the transaction, that is, any general positive record, such as he would in dealing with somebody he had not entire confidence in.

Q. You understood that this transacton rested very largely in his memory?—A. Yes, sir; that is my impression.

Q. What is your best recollection of the precise words Mr. Ames used in speaking of Mr. Colfax's statement?—A. My best recollection of the precise words is, that he used the words "probably correct;" he conveyed the impression upon my mind that he yielded the uncertainties which were in his mind upon the subject to the positive statement of Mr. Colfax.

By Mr. BANKS:

Q. Did Mr. Ames say that he believed Mr. Colfax's statement was substantially correct as to the facts of the case, or as Mr. Colfax understood the facts?—A. I cannot say whether I drew the one inference or the other from what he said in regard to that.

By Mr. AMES:

Q. You knew I had testified before I went home, and that I then testified I thought Mr. Colfax had taken 20 shares of stock, paid for it, and received the dividends; that I stated that without reference to any memorandum, before I went home?—A. I had read your testimony; I so understood it.

Q. Did I say my testimony was wrong, and that Mr. Colfax was right, or anything of that sort? Did I give you to understand that I changed my testimony at all?—A. If I recollect rightly your testimony in regard to several of the members was much less clear than it appears to be now, and yet I will say that I was not aware at the time of this conversation that you thought you had any new evidence upon the subject, or that you had refreshed your memory in any way. It did not seem from anything you said to me that you had received any new light, but, on the contrary, you expressed a good deal of doubt upon the subject, as you did in several other conversations.

Q. Did you infer from anything I said that I wished to change in any respect my statement made in relation to Mr. Colfax before I went home?—A. No; I cannot say that your conversation conveyed that impression to me, but that, there being some discrepancy between you and Mr. Colfax, you were willing, apparently, to waive your recollection for his.

Re-examination of Mr. AMES:

Mr. AMES. I had not any conversation with Mr. Crounse such as he states. I did not say any such thing as he says I stated.

By the CHAIRMAN:

Q. Do you think there was anything said to you about Mr. Colfax's statement that day?—A. I do not recollect that there was. I do not think there was a word said about Mr. Colfax.

Q. Do you recollect where that conversation was, whatever it was?—A. He has spoken to me several times about the testimony here. I have refrained from saying much about it to anybody outside. As well as I can remember, I said nothing to him of the kind he has stated here at all.

Q. You knew that Mr. Crounse was a newspaper reporter?—A. Yes, sir.

By Mr. KELLEY:

Q. Do the ten shares of Credit Mobilier stock, which you have placed with the chairman of the committee, subject to my order, bear any proportion to the dividends on what has been spoken of here as the Oakes Ames contract?—A. Yes, sir; your stock draws the dividends of the Oakes Ames contract, and nothing else.

Q. These shares are entitled to whatever dividends were made on any stock?—A. Yes, sir.

Q. Then the statements you are to send to the chairman in my behalf will be the inventory of the dividends declared on the Oakes Ames contract, of my stock?—A. It will. I shall take great pleasure in sending it.

Mr. KELLEY. Mr. Chairman be kind enough to retain them subject to my order, as I do not wish them ever to come into my hands.

Re-examination of JOHN B. ALLEY.

By Mr. COLFAX:

Q. Day before yesterday you stated that in a conversation with Mr. Ames he said to you that his recollection and mine accorded substantially, but that you thought that was before the time I gave my testimony the 7th of January. Can you tell me about thetime it was you had this conversation? I do not mean the exact day, but as near as possible, within a week or ten days.—A. I could tell you, of course, within a week. It was near the time of the adjournment for the holidays. I think it was in the presence of the counsel of Mr. Ames.

Q. Will you repeat again, as near as you can, what he said at the time?—A. He said his impression was—of course he depended very much upon his memory at that time—but his impression was that there was no such irreconcilable difference; that was the idea conveyed to my mind—no such irreconcilable difference or conflict in the testimony that it could not be reconciled.

By the CHAIRMAN:

Q. Mr. Ames was speaking to you of a conversation with Mr. Colfax, not about his testimony?—A. Yes, sir; of a conversation.

Q. I will read your statement on the subject yesterday. You say "Mr. Ames stated to me before he went home, I think it was, that your statement was substantially in accordance with his. Upon reflection, I find that your statement was made on the 7th of January, after his return here; he therefore could not have alluded at that time to your statement before this committee. He must have alluded to your statement in conversation." You do not there use the words "irreconcilable difference," but you said that his statement was substantially in accordance with your recollection now?—A. Yes, sir; that is about what he said.

Re-examination of OAKES AMES.

By Mr. COLFAX:

Q. When I testified the 7th of January, and had closed all my statement, and asked Mr. Ames to cross-examine me, why did not you cross-examine me then in regard to my statement that I had received no dividend?—A. I did not want to contradict you. I was in hopes the thing would never be brought up again. I did not want to have it appear that there was any conflict between your testimony and mine if I could avoid it.

Q. You knew that I had received your $1,200 check?—A. I did know it.

Q. Why did you not at that time expose me?—A. You knew of the check.

Q. I stated in my examination the 7th of January that "a few weeks or months after this I heard a rumor that unpleasant controversies existed among the largest stockholders, which were certain to involve the organization in prolonged litigation. The very day I heard this rumor I told Mr. Ames that no profits present or prospective could induce me to buy into a lawsuit; that I had never been, during all my life, a plaintiff or a defendant in a court of justice."

What do you say in regard to that statement?—A. I do not know whether you said that or not. I cannot say. You might have said it. You certainly received the $1,200. Didn't you receive it?

Q. I did not. Did you not tell me that very session there were unpleasant differences existing among the larger stockholders?—A. I think it very likely. That suit of McComb's was probably what I referred to.

Q. At what time was that suit brought?—A. I think it was probably brought in July.

Q. Mr. McComb testifies that it was brought in November.—A. Then it was in November. I do not know whether Mr. McComb testified correctly about that or not. My impression is that it was in July. If it was in November, then the conversation must have been after November. I had no controversy with any one but McComb.

Q. Here is what Mr. Blaine testifies to on that subject: "I desire further to state that, some time in the spring of 1868—the precise date I will not affirm—Mr. Oakes Ames asked me, one day, if I would like to purchase some stock in the Credit Mobilier. He said it would prove a good investment, and he could sell me ten shares of the stock at a rate somewhat above par; I think some $1,060 for the ten shares. We had some conversation in regard to the matter, and Mr. Ames told me very frankly that, in regard to these shares, there was a lawsuit either pending or threatened, though he said his right to sell the shares was perfect and undoubted. I concluded that I did not desire to purchase the stock, and therefore declined Mr. Ames's offer." You stated here, to the chairman, that you agreed, substantially, to Mr. Blaine's statement?—A. Yes.

Q. Was it correct, as he states, that, in 1868, you told Mr. Blaine this lawsuit was pending?—A. I cannot say as to that.

Q. But you say you did not state that to me until the next session?—A. I did not say anything of the sort to you.

Q. Do you now say that the memorandum from which you testified day before yesterday, in regard to your transactions with me, is an exact copy of your private memorandum-book?—A. I think so.

Q. Do you know that you saw that memorandnm-book when you went home?—A. Yes.

Q. And you refreshed your memory from it?—A. I did.

Q. (Referring to the memorandum.) That is all the entry there is in regard to the amount for which you said you were trustee for me?—A. I do not know that I said I was trustee for you. It is the amount of stock I sold you, and the money I received from you, and the money I paid you; that is the whole of it.

Q. You told me, as I understood you to say, that I was to pay par and interest; what was the rate of interest?—A. Seven per cent.

Q. From what time?—A. From July 1, 1867.

Q. And I paid you that rate from July, 1867, till March 5?—A. Your check is dated March 5, I believe.

Q. Will you be kind enough to produce that private memorandum-book?—A. I cannot now; I have not it here.

Q. Is it at home?—A. It is at home.

Q. Does it contain an account with all the members with whom you had dealings?—A. No; some of them I settled with, and the memoranda were destroyed.

Q. You did not put them all down in your book?—A. No, sir.

Q. You put a part of them down?—A. Yes, sir.

Q. And you refreshed your memory by referring to them during the recess?—A. Yes.

Q. Why didn't you bring the private memorandum-book with you?—A. I brought all I thought was necessary. I brought enough to refresh my memory. I have here a list of the names that are on that private memorandum-book, taken from it.

Q. When you conversed with Mr. Alley, and stated to him that my recollection and yours were in accord, did you say anything to him about that $1,200 check?—A. My statement was not that my recollection accorded with your statement.

Q. You stated then that it accorded with a conversation we had at Wormley's early in the present session?—A. I do not know as I understand you.

Q. Mr. Alley stated day before yesterday that you told him your recollection substantially agreed with mine?—A. I do not recollect saying so anywhere. My recollection is very different.

Q. In that conversation I had with you at Wormley's, before which you called three times and did not find me, did I not tell you that I had received no dividends?—A. Not that I know of.

Q. Did I not tell you that I had never received a dividend from you?—A. I do not know, but you may have said so.

Q. Then when you told Mr. Alley, afterwards, before the recess, that your recollection of our conversation agreed with mine, why did you not add, except that you had paid me $1,200?—A. I do not think I said to Mr. Alley they agreed.

Q. In this private memorandum-book, which, I trust, the committee will have brought down here, have you down the names of all those to whom you sold stock and who received their dividends?—A. Yes, sir.

Q. All of them?—A. I do not know whether they are all there or not; a part of them are.

Q. Have you the names of the persons you have testified to here who are not owners of stock?—A. No, sir; their names would not be on it if they were not owners of stock?

Q. Now, sir, will you tell me why you made the check which you say you gave to me, that had the initials S. C. written in, while the check you gave to Mr. Allison had the full name of W. B. Allison written in?—A. I cannot give you an answer to that, only that I happened to write it so. In some cases I did not put in any initials at all; some I did, and others I put in the full name.

Q. Did I receipt to you for this check?—A. No; and there was no reason why you should; it did not belong to me; it belonged to you as a dividend.

Q. You state that you gave it to me?—A. Certainly I did. I did not deposit $10,000 to pay the dividends due here, and cheat some one out of $1,200; you do not suppose I would be guilty of fraud, do you?

Q. Have you ever told me, within the last four years, that I was the owner of this stock?—A. I do not know whether I have or not; I do not know that anybody has told me, within the last four years, that I owned my own hat.

Q. You testified a few moments ago that there was some remark made by me about my giving up these $500?—A. That you told me at your room before I testified.

Q. You testified, in answer to a question of Judge Poland about your recollections of that fact, that there was some such remark as giving up $500, and of my being sorry for your misfortune. Do you remember where this conversation occurred?—A. I think it was at Wormley's.

Q. I mean the conversation about giving up the $500, and that I was sorry for your misfortune?—A. You told me that you said so, and I presume you did, or I would not have so stated.

Q. You believe I said so? Did I not say it to you on the floor of the Senate after you had failed?—A. I do not know.

Q. Did you not tell me that the stock had gone down to 10 cents on the dollar, and that you had an extension by your creditors?—A. Everybody knew that.

Q. You remember that conversation?—A. It is very likely. I recollect seeing you over there in the Senate, but what was said I cannot remember. I do not dispute that you said so.

Q. Finally, after several questions, you remember that I spoke to you about the $500. Now, when I said to you that I was sorry for your misfortunes, and that I would not require you to return the $500 that I had paid you, why did you not state to me that you had paid me $1,200 against that, and that there was nothing to return?—A. I do not understand your version of the matter at all. When you spoke to me about that matter, you knew you had the $1,200, and so did I; there is proof of that on the books, and what is the use of trying to get round it? There is no getting round it or over it. The record shows for itself that I gave you the check.

Q. Where was I when you gave me the check?—A. I do not remember; in the House of Representatives, I suppose.

Q. Where was it—in the Speaker's chair or on the floor?—A. How can I remember six years ago where I was when I gave a man a check? That is ridiculous. I do not remember. I remember I gave it to you.

Q. Do you remember where it was that you gave it?—A. No, sir; I do not.

Re-examination of Mr. COLFAX:

Mr. COLFAX. I wish to repeat exactly what I stated day before yesterday: that I never received from Mr. Ames a dollar on any account whatsoever. I never saw this check. I never knew until I saw this check this morning, whether Mr. Ames signed his name O. Ames or Oakes Ames. Why, if the check was for me, he should have filled it out with S. C. or bearer, I cannot imagine. If I had seen a check so filled out, it would have struck me very forcibly. Now, I could not have had $1,200 added to my income without remembering it very positively. I could not have talked with Mr. Ames afterward about sympathizing with him in his misfortunes, and proposed to remit to him the $500 I had paid him, if I had received $1,200 from him.

During the whole four years, as he himself states, he has never proposed to pay me any of the dividends on the stock, although he recognized me as the owner of the stock; because when I said I told him I would not buy into a lawsuit, it must have occurred in the session of 1868, and which, as I have shown the committee, Mr. Blaine testifies to

Mr. Ames telling him the same in the summer of 1868, the committee will probably remember that I asked Mr. Ames a question before Mr. McCrary asked about Mr. Allison—whether I did not tell him I would not buy into a lawsuit, and that he then took a small piece of money out of his pocket, threw it down, and said I was to consider that it was bought back. I told him, "No, sir; I will have nothing to do with it, whatever."

By Mr. AMES:

Q. You told me that you paid the $534?—A. I stated originally to the committee that it was about $500, and that you then told me there were some dividends, but they were unadjusted. Mr. Ames has testified that there was a bond dividend which he sold for me without my authority, and he says there was a stock dividend which was unadjusted.

Q. You would not have given me a check for $534.72 unless it completed the purchase of the $2,000 stock?—A. I gave a check for the amount which Mr. Ames furnished to me.

By the CHAIRMAN:

Q. Mr. Ames says the amount he received from you was $534.72; do you concede that that was the amount?—A. I think it was. I supposed I had given him a check on a bank, and I had been to the bank for the purpose of ascertaining what the amount was. It did not occur to me that I had given a check on the Sergeant-at-Arms. I paid him the amount which he told me to pay.

Q. What was the precise conversation between you and Mr. Ames at that time, and how did you understand that this sum was made up in dollars and cents?—A. Mr. Ames told me the amount I was to pay was $534.72; he said there were some dividends that had accrued upon this stock; that they were not paid in cash, and that they were yet unadjusted; he did not offer any of them to me.

Q. Did you understand from Mr. Ames that this $534.72 was a balance from you to complete the payment for this stock?—A. I supposed it was a conjectural balance. He said I was to pay $534.72. I never saw his private memorandum-book. I never knew anything about his disposing of bonds, which he says belonged to me, at 3 per cent. off.

Q. You understood that it was at least an approximate balance?—A. I supposed that was to pay 25 per cent. of the purchase-money and interest.

Q. You say that you did not understand that it completed the payment of the stock?—A. I understood that there were dividends earned but unadjusted, which would probably make up the balance.

Q. You did not understand that this amount finished the payment of your stock, but you did understand that dividends had been earned which would probably amount to the price of it?—A. Yes, according to his statement, enough to pay and overrun the amount.

Q. You say that nothing was said to you by Mr. Ames of his having sold your bonds?—A. No, sir.

Q. Or of his having received the bonds?—A. Yes, I think he said the dividend was not in cash; that it was in bonds and stock.

Q. Do you remember his having said anything about having sold the bonds?—A. No, sir. I supposed he was holding them. My impression was that the bonds and stock would substantially cover this balance of 75 per cent. I supposed I was giving $500, and interest on the purchase, and, as I supposed, interest from the time I made the contract for the purchase.

Q. This sum, however, you did pay, and you did pay it by a draft on the Sergeant-at-Arms?—A. I suppose so. I have no doubt he is correct about that. I could not remember the exact amount. I stated in private conversation, as Mr. Niblack knows, that I thought it was about $530, as near as I could remember. (Mr. Niblack assented to the statement.)

Q. The $1,200 Mr. Ames said he paid you, you do not admit. You say you never received any such sum?—A. I am confident I never received a check from Mr. Ames, certainly never a check payable to "S. C. or bearer" for $1,200, or for any other sum. I have no recollection of it; not the slighest. It is utterly incredible. We could not have had that conversation in regard to returning the $500 if I received the $1,200. The only solution I can think of to reconcile the misunderstanding between us on that point is, that the initials were put in to distinguish, in his own mind, between dividends drawn for Oakes Ames, trustee, and for Oakes Ames personally, and that this "S. C." check was a memorandum for himself after I had informed him that the thing was off, and that I would not buy into a law-suit.

Q. When do you say that conversation occurred?—A. It was in the summer of 1868.

Q. You did not understand that you sold the stock back?—A. I understood that I gave it up. I had no certificate; I had no proceeds from it. I had made a payment on it, and I wanted to get out of it.

Q. Have you been in the habit of keeping a cash account yourself of your own disbursements?—A. Yes; I have endeavored, since I have been Speaker and Vice-President, to make my salary with my income pay my bills; and every month, or every two months, I have been in the habit of making a statement of my finances, to see how I was getting along.

Q. Have you preserved these memoranda so far back as 1868?—A. No, sir; I am sorry to say I have not preserved them even for the last session. I may say that I have fallen into the habit of always indorsing every check I drew. If you will examine the checks of the Sergeant-at-Arms or in the Frst National Bank, where I keep my account, you will find that, although they are payable to bearer, I always write my name on them. It has been a uniform habit with me.

Q. So that, if this check had been received by you, you would have made your indorsement upon it?—A. I call the attention of the committee to the fact that, except my own, there is but one of those checks payable to the initials or bearer.

By Mr. AMES:

Q. Did I not render you a statement of the price of the Credit Mobilier stock and interest, and give you a statement showing the dividends of 80 per cent. of bonds, which covered the price of your stock in it, $534.72, showing that balance, and did you not give me a check for that balance?—A. No, sir; I remember you told me I was to pay $534.72, and I will not be certain that you did not give me that amount on a slip of paper.

Q. You had more confidence in my statements then than you have now. I ask you if I did not make a statement to you at that time, giving you a balance of $534.72, showing you the amount of your $2,000 Credit Mobilier stock, with interest up to that date, giving you credit on the proceeds of 80 per cent. in bonds, and did you not give me a draft on the Sergeant-at-Arms for $534.72 to make up that balance; do you deny that?—A. I do deny that.

Mr. AMES. I am sorry for it.

The WITNESS. You gave me a slip of paper with the amount of the balance, $534.72, on it, and told me there were some dividends which had not been adjusted.

The CHAIRMAN, (to Mr. Ames:)

Do you wish to propound any more questions to Mr. Colfax?

Mr. AMES. If he denies that I made him this statement, I do not want to ask him any other question.

Re-examination of Mr. AMES.

By Mr. COLFAX:

Q. In the cross-examination of Mr. Ames on the 17th December, in response to the question, "Is he still the owner of that stock?" he replied, "It has never been transferred to him; I do not know whether he or I own that stock;" what did you mean by that?—A. There it is; you must draw your own inference. I understood that you owned it, but that you wanted me to own it.

Q. When did I tell you I wanted you to own it?—A. I cannot remember what you said about it. I have had several conversations with you. I called once or twice on you at Wormley's, and on one occasion I went down to your private room and talked the matter over. You told me you thought it very singular what I had said about the interest; that you did not understand it, and that you had often thought of what I had said about the interest.

Q. You say you called at my room and talked the matter over this winter?—A. Yes, sir.

Q. At Wormley's?—A. I called once or twice at Wormley's. I called on you the night before I testified last, and talked the matter over with you, to see if we could understand each other. I wanted to see whether we could understand each other. You said I must testify to the truth. I replied, "Certainly, I am going to do that." I left, and I suppose you thought, from your conversation with Mr. Crounse, that I was going to swear to what you testified the other day. You got the impression, from what you saw in the New York Times, that I was going to swear to that, and so you wanted me to tell the truth.

Q. I have not said anything of that kind.—A. It is an inference I draw, that you thought I was going to testify to that from what Mr. Crounse told you I had said about your testimony.

Q. In your testimony given on the 17th December, which was submitted to Mr. McMurtrie, and reduced to writing before you gave it, you state, "I am pretty confident he has paid me for it, though it was never transferred to him, nor can I remember having paid over to him any dividends;" how could you swear to that, if you knew you had paid me $1,200 dividends?—A. I can swear to it now, having refreshed my memory from my private memorandum-book, and your check on the Sergeant-at-Arms proves it. I do not think you can swear hard enough to get out of it. You stand in the same position with the rest of them. All the rest of them took their checks; that is the honest truth. You don't think I would be mean enough to cheat you out of $1,200?

Q. Yet you testified on the 17th December, "nor can I remember having paid over to him any dividends?"—A. I remember it now, and have got a voucher for it.

WASHINGTON, *January* 24, 1873.

N. G. ORDWAY, Sergeant-at-Arms, having been recalled, made the following statement:

I wish to say that in my statement the other day, I perhaps did not make myself sufficiently clear in respect to the manner in which the business is transacted in my office. I have seen in the newspapers some criticisms in regard to it, and I desire to state again that this book upon which these matters are kept is a private book, such as is kept by every bank, and is not the Government book in which the accounts of the members for pay and mileage are kept. That book is filed in the Department at the end of every Congress. This one, which is a private banker's book, has nothing to do with my official duties as Sergeant-at-Arms; it is a private account between myself and the members of Congress. I will ask the committee, inasmuch as this book is placed in their possession, that the examination of it may be confined to such matters simply as are before the committee. I make this request in justice to myself and these depositors.

By Mr. MCCRARY:

Question. You sometimes received the deposits of members in excess of their pay?—Answer. Yes, sir; members are constantly receiving drafts from home, and are remitting drafts for their families, which formerly required a messenger going backwards and forwards constantly to and from my office and the up-town banks. I arranged with General Spinner, United States Treasurer, to give drafts upon all parts of the country for large and small sums, and often as small as three or four dollars; and I also arranged with the banks to receive drafts from members and cash them. All the accounts for drafts and checks are entered in this book. Almost every member deposits his surplus money with me, which goes into his account, and is checked out by him as deposits are checked out of a bank.

Q. In other words, you kept just such an account as is kept in every bank?—A. I do. My books are balanced every night, so that any member may ascertain at any moment just how his account stands.

Q. Now turn to Oakes Ames's account on this book.—A. I have it here, commencing March, 1867, and going on to March 5, 1869. (Witness explained from the book the manner in which accounts are kept.)

By the CHAIRMAN:

Q. Mr. Ames stated in his testimony the other day, that, in June, 1868, he made a deposit with you of $10,000. Do you find an entry of that?—A. Yes; that is correct. I find here $10,000 deposited under date of June 20, 1868. I stated the other day, and repeat, that I do not know anything personally in regard to this deposit. This amount was not deposited with me; it was deposited with my book-keeper. I knew very little personally in regard to any of these matters. My book-keeper, however, knows all about the matter.

Q. The entry upon the books, however, satisfies you that it was made?—A. I have no doubt it was.

Q. Now, let me ask you whether the entries in this book are original entries, or whether they are taken from another book?—A. I am unable to state that; my book-keeper will give you all that information.

Q. Do you keep anything like a general cash-book?—A. The office of paying-teller was established two or three years ago. He keeps a daily blotter of all his transactions. Up to that time I had no paying-teller n my office; I had simply a book-keeper, messenger, and page.

Q. As far back as the summer of 1868, was there any entry of these transations except in this book?—A. I do not recollect whether there was or not. My book-keeper will have to answer that.

Q. Upon this book, under date of June 24, 1868, in Mr. Ames's account, there is charged W. D. K. $329; to what do the figures in the column I am now pointing to relate?—A. I am not familiar with the books, but presume that they relate to the pages of the day-book.

Q. In whose handwriting are these entries?—A. In the handwriting of Moses Dillon. Every entry in these books for more than ten years is in his handwriting.

Q. Can you produce this check of June 24, payable to W. D. K. or bearer?—A. I wish to say that about two weeks ago Mr. Ames came to my office, and asked me if I kept my old vouchers; I told him I thought I did, unless they were called for by the member to whom they belonged. We looked over the files, and I found this bundle of vouchers. He examined them, passed them to me, and they have been locked up in my safe since that time. I believe this is the check to which you refer. It reads as follows:

"WASHINGTON, *June* 23, 1868.

"SERGEANT-AT-ARMS, *U. S. House of Representatives*:

"Pay W. D. K. or bearer, $329."

Q. In whose handwriting is that check filled up?—A. I do not know. I never saw it until within a few days, to the best of my recollection.

Q. Do you know Mr. Ames's handwriting?—A. I judge that is his signature; I presume it was filled up by him; I am not considered an expert in handwriting.

Q. At that time (June, 1868) who was the man that actually paid out the money on checks in your office?—A. At that time my book-keeper did what he could. Thomas P. Cheney, the messenger, paid a large proportion of the money. My son was also a page in the office, and sometimes would make payments to members. I seldom ever pay these vouchers myself, except in an exceptional case.

By M. MCCRARY:

Q. Is it your practice that sometimes a member of Congress sends in a page with a check drawn by himself, and the money is returned by the page?—A. I presume so; still I have no knowledge upon that subject. I do not pay enough myself to know exactly what the practice is. During the session of Congress I attend to the wants of congressional committees and other duty, leaving other office-work to the book-keeper and paying-teller. Mr. Dillon and Mr. Cheney are both here, and will be glad to explain these transactions so far as they are disclosed by the books.

By Mr. KELLEY:

Q. Is that the only check drawn to "W. D. K?"—A. I think that is the only one.

By Mr. MCCRARY:

Q. I want you, in this connection, to state again whether it would be a common practice for a check to be made payable to "A. B.," "C. D.," or bearer, and for the member drawing it to send in a page for the money, receiving the money himself, and the letters indicating to him the purpose for which money was drawn?—A. I should consider that as legitimate. I have no recollection of such practice. I can conceive that the practice might very well be for such checks, given by one member to another, coming directly from the hall, and payable to bearer to be paid to the party who drew the check; the letters, or whatever is written in, being intended simply to indicate to the person drawing the check the purpose for which he intended to appropriate the money.

Q. (Mr. NIBLACK to Mr. Ames.) Was there any particular reason in your mind why you should put in the initials "W. D. K.," instead of writing Mr. Kelley's name in full?—A. (Mr. Ames.) No, sir; I have no recollection about it. I see that in some cases I put in the initials; in others I put in the names; and in some nothing is written in. I drew them in all ways. If I had considered it a bribe, of course I would not have put in either the name or the initials.

Q. (By Mr. McCRARY.) Did you draw up the checks the same day in paying out that dividend?—A. (Mr. Ames.) No, sir.

WASHINGTON, *January* 24, 1873.

THOMAS P. CHENEY sworn and examined.

By the CHAIRMAN:

Question. State your residence.—Answer. Ashland, New Hampshire.

Q. Were you employed in the office of the Sergeant-at-Arms, House of Representatives, in 1868?—A. I was, as messenger.

Q. Had you anything to do with paying out money in that office to members—A. That was a part of my duty.

Q. Was it your exclusive duty, or did others pay out money to members?—A. Perhaps I paid more than any others. Mr. Dillon, however, paid checks; and occasionally a son of the Sergeant-at-Arms, George Ordway, who was then in the office, would pay out money.

Q. Had you anything to do with keeping the books?—A. No, sir.

Q. Have you any idea how they were kept?—A. I have some general idea.

Q. Do you know whether there was a book from which the entries in this ledger were taken?—A. The first entries were made in the journal.

Q. Do you know what the column of figures I now point to in this ledger refer to?—A. I think that refers to the page in the journal.

Q. Here is an entry in this account of Oakes Ames, charging him, June 24, 1868, with a check payable to W. D. K., $329, and a check has been produced for $329, signed by Mr. Ames, payable to W. D. K. or bearer; have you any recollection in relation to the payment of that check?—A. None whatever. I could not have paid it; I was not in the office that day; I know I was away from about the 10th of June to about the 3d or 5th of July.

Q. You knew nothing about the payments made during that time?—A. No, sir; I had leave of absence, and was in New Hampshire during that time.

By Mr. COLFAX:

Q. Do you know anything of a check drawn by Mr. Ames payable to S. C. or bearer?—A. I never saw the check that I know of; that was paid, at any rate, while I was away in New Hampshire, and I know nothing about it.

WASHINGTON, *January* 24, 1873.

MOSES DILLON sworn and examined.

By the CHAIRMAN:

Question. In 1868 were you employed in the office of the Sergeant-at-Arms, House of Representatives, and in what capacity?—Answer. Yes, sir; as cashier and book-keeper.

Q. You remain there in the same capacity still?—A. Yes, sir.

Q. Was this book kept by you?—A. Yes, sir; every entry is in my handwriting.

Q. What is this book?—A. This is the deposit-ledger.

Q. I see a credit to Mr. Ames of $10,000, received June 17, 1868, by check on the Bank of Commerce, Boston.—A. Yes, sir; that is in my handwriting.

Q. Do you recollect anything about that transaction?—A. No, sir; there were a large number of transactions of that sort almost every day; I do not recollect that particular one.

Q. Can you state from what book this entry was taken?—A. It was posted from the journal.

Q. Is that journal in your office now?—A. I have it here.

Q. Mr. Cheney has stated that he ordinarily paid out money to members; that you also made such payments; but he says that from the 10th June until some day in July he was away. Were all the payments made during that time by you?—A. Not all of them; George Ordway sometimes would make payments.

Q. In this account of Mr. Ames, under date of June 24, there is a charge to W. D. K. of $329; have you any recollection in reference to the payment of that sum?—A. No, sir; not at all. I do not recollect to whom it was paid, and I do not recollect whether I paid it myself. I have no recollection at all of the transaction.

Q. Would you learn from the books to whom it was paid?—A. No, sir; not at all.

Q. You have no doubt it was paid, because the entry is in your book; but to whom it was paid you do not know?—A. I have no doubt it was paid, but I have no recollection about it, and nothing to show to whom it was paid.

Q. Turn now to the original entry in the journal.—A. Here it is, under date of June 24, $329 to W. D. K.

Q. What do you understand the letters W. D. K. to refer to?—A. I have no understanding at all about it. I suppose it was made in that way to identify the check. It indicates that that amount was paid on Oakes Ames's check to somebody; who that was, or what was the purpose of the letters, of course I know nothing about.

Q. Was there any other book in which you keep office-accounts?—A. No, sir; I keep a Government ledger—a pay and a mileage account; but this is the account of the private transactions of members; precisely such an account as is kept in every bank.

Q. There would not be another entry as a cash account?—A. No, sir; only this.

Q. So that if Mr. Ames gave a check on the Sergeant at-Arms it would only appear in these two books?—A. It would appear upon the journal, and then upon the ledger.

By Mr. KELLEY:

Q. If Mr. Ames appeared before the counter with his own check, marked "W. D. K. or bearer," would you have paid the check to him?—A. Certainly.

By Mr. McCrary:

Q. Is there anything to indicate whether the check was paid on that date?—A. The date of payment is here the 25th June; the date of the check is the 24th. I was in the habit, however, sometimes, when there were many checks, of charging the checks of two days under the same date. It may be, therefore, that this was paid on the 24th; I think very likely it was; it seems to be so posted.

By Mr. McCrary:

Q. State if it was a custom for members frequently to draw checks in their seats in the House, and send a page over to your office and get the money. Suppose his check was payable to order, would you pay it in that way?—A. Not without his indorsement, if it was payable to his order. If payable to bearer, we should.

Q. If a member brought you a check payable to bearer, or with simply the initials of his name, would you require him to indorse it?—A. Not at all.

Q. Under date of June 20th, in Mr. Ames's account, there is put down a charge to S. C., $1,200, and another to J. F. Wilson, $329. Do these entries read in the same way?—A. In the same way.

Q. These entries are both in your handwriting. Have you any recollection of the transactions?—A. I have not.

Q. And the entry gives no information as to whom the checks were paid?—A. No, sir.

By Mr. Ordway:

Q. I wish to ask the book-keeper whether, to his knowledge, there has ever been any money received and disbursed in any way in the office of the Sergeant-at-Arms, and entered upon these books, except in this open way?—A. There never has been to my knowledge.

By Mr. Colfax:

Q. At the time this payment was made on the S. C. check, there seems to have been another to J. F. Wilson, $329, entered in the same line. Would that indicate that the two checks came in together?—A. No; only that they came in the same day. They were both put upon one line as a matter of economy.

Q. Mr. Cheney says that he was away, and that you probably paid both these checks?—A. Probably I did.

Q. But you do not recollect anything in relation to paying them, or to whom they were paid?—A. No, sir.

Q. Do you not think it would have attracted your attention if I had come in with a check payable to S. C. instead of S. Colfax?—A. It might at the time; I don't know.

Q. Is it usual to give checks in this way with initials written in?—A. Some members come in and get the money themselves, and frequently put some marks upon them to identify the checks to refresh their memory as to what they used the money for.

Q. Here are several pages of checks; I don't see any others with the initials?—A. No, sir; that is the only one.

Q. Can you produce that check? (Check produced by Mr. Ordway.) Do you remember, in looking over this book, any other checks from Mr. Ames with initials entered upon them?—A. I did not notice any other.

Q. Now, if Mr. Ames had sent his check by a page, would you have paid it?—A. Yes, sir; or I would have paid it to Mr. Ames himself.

Q. Do you remember a check alluded to in the testimony day before yesterday, given by Mr. Ames to Mr. Allison; have you seen that check?—A. I presume so.

Q. Do you remember whether that is payable to W. B. A. or bearer?—A. I think it is W. B. Allison. I think the name is written in full. There is no general rule on the subject. There are some written with the full names, and some with the initials.

Q. These seem to be exceptional, however, in your entries?—A. Yes, sir.

By Mr. AMES:

Q. You will see that these checks are written, some payable to order, some without names, and some with initials. These books are correct?—A. I presume so.

Q. Do you make your entries the same day checks are paid?—A. Not always; sometimes the day afterwards. They are made at the same time substantially. Sometimes during the holidays they are not posted for four or five days.

Q. You received $10,000 on deposit from Mr. Ames the day of this entry for that amount?—A. I received the deposit of $10,000, and the checks show how it was drawn out.

By Mr. COLFAX:

Q. Have you ever figured to see whether that entire amount was drawn out by these mysterious checks?—A. No, sir; it was a running account.

Q. Please turn to the account of William B. Allison, and see if that check was passed to his credit.—A. Yes, I find here the check of Oakes Ames, $600, to his credit.

Q. Now turn to the account of Mr. Colfax, and see if the check of $534.72 is charged to me.—A. Yes, sir; it is charged to you and marked "draft." There is nothing credited to you, except your mileage and salary; no special item.

By the CHAIRMAN:

Q. You have no recollection whether this check of Mr. Colfax, March 5, 1868, which is marked "draft," was obtained for himself or Mr. Ames?—A. Of course I do not know anything about that.

Q. Have you anything in your office that will show?—A. No, sir; at that time we did not keep any memorandum of drafts from the Treasury; we do now.

By Mr. NIBLACK:

Q. Turn to Mr. Kelley's account and see if there is anything credited from him to Mr. Ames.—A. No, sir; there is nothing of his credited except his mileage and salary.

WASHINGTON, D. C., *January* 25, 1873.

OAKES AMES recalled and examined.

By the CHAIRMAN:

Question. Upon the books of the Sergeant-at-Arms produced yesterday, in the list of checks charged to you there was one of $329, to John A. Logan. The committee desire to ask you what that was for.—Answer. That seems to be a fashionable amount about these days, although, according to the testimony yesterday, a check does not prove anything.

Q. Will you state what the transaction was between you and Mr. Logan, out of which that check grew?—A. Yes. Mr. Logan agreed to take ten shares of Credit Mobilier stock. I made up a statement to him, showing a balance of $329 due him, and gave him a check for it. Awhile after that he paid me back the money and interest. I should prefer that you would call General Logan, as everything I say is disputed. Let us have the other side.

Q. We will hear you first.—A. That is my statement.

Q. At what time was the arrangement made between you and Mr Logan for this purchase?—A. I think in December, 1867.

Q. He paid you nothing?—A. No, sir; not originally. He paid me the money back with interest.

Q. You received the 80 per cent. dividend in bonds and sold them as you did for the others, at the same amount of 97?—A. Yes, sir.

Q. You afterward received 60 per cent., money dividend?—A. Yes, sir.

Q. Deducting from the dividend $1,000 and interest upon it from July, left a balance of $329?—A. Yes, sir.

Q. You paid that to Mr. Logan by check?—A. I suppose so, by his name appearing on the check.

Q. Do you not remember that?—A. I remember that the same as I did in regard to all the rest.

Q. Did Mr. Logan ever receive anything more from you?—A. No, sir; and he paid me back, as I have stated, with interest—$329 with interest.

Q. When was that repayment made to you?—A. I think the interest amounted to only two or three dollars on it.

Q. Then it was soon after he received the $329?—A. Yes. My memory is so defective as to dates that I should prefer that you would call General Logan.

Q. You think it was within a few months?—A. Yes, sir.

Q. What was the occasion of rescinding this contract?—A. I do not know what was in his mind about it at all.

Q. He just paid you back, and that was the end of it?—A. Yes, sir.

Q. When he paid back the $329, it was understood that the ten shares of stock remained yours?—A. Yes; I never paid him anything but the $329.

Q. So that Mr. Logan really made nothing out of the transaction?—A. Nothing at all. All he got from me he paid back as I stated. He was neither the better nor the worse for it except in the name of having $329.

Q. That has not affected him until now?—A. Not that I know of.

Q. That is all there is of this transaction with Mr. Logan?—A. That is all.

By Mr. MERRICK:

Q. What first brought you to Mr. Logan, or him to you, in connection with this transaction?—A. I think they came to me generally. As I stated originally, I received this stock to fulfill prior engagements. A great many people, after they thought there was going to be a profit in the enterprise, wanted to get stock. I promised a great many parties that if I could get the stock for them I would do so. In the latter part of October, 1867, there happened to be some stock in the hands of Dr. Durant, who had not paid for it, which was returned to the company. Of that stock I was assigned two hundred and fifty shares to enable me to fulfill engagments I had previously made. I found I had made so many that I could not begin to fulfill them. I gave some to parties with whom I had previously made no engagement. You heard the statement of Mr. Wilson, of Iowa, that he wanted $5,000, and I could not give him but $1,000. Mr. Painter had the promise of Dr. Durant that I should give him $5,000, and I only gave him $3,000. Mr. McComb wanted that I should give Senator Bayard $5,000, and I could not give him anything. Mr. Allison wanted more than he got; and so all through the list.

Q. Right there in regard to these engagements, I believe every one of the parties who have appeared here have stated the negotiations as occurring not earlier than December, 1867.—A. I guess Mr. Scofield said that he had talked about it a year before.

Q. That is just what I want to inquire about, whether any of these gentlemen, and, if so, which of them, made a prior engagement for any of this stock; whether you were under obligations to any of these members in consequence of conversations you had had with them prior to that session of Congress which commenced December, 1867.—A. I must say again that as to remembering dates I cannot do it; as I have before stated in my testimony, I had always been trying to get people interested in the Union Pacific Railroad and Credit Mobilier from the time I took an interest in it myself; I went so far as in a considerable number of instances to guarantee the parties against loss and 10 per cent. profit; I did this to Senator Grimes, to Mr. Gamaliel Bradford, of Boston, and Mr. Dana, of Boston, to Mr. Alley, and I offered to do it for Mr. Hooper, and for various other parties. My anxiety to get men into the enterprise was such as to induce me to make every effort, but I cannot remember all these conversations which occurred five or six years ago.

Q. This stock was put into your hands to enable you to fulfill engagements you had made before that time; now, what I want to get at is how many of these men in Congress, who received this stock, had made any engagements or had had any previous conversations with you on the subject?—A. My answer to that is simply this: I did not know before October that I could get any stock; I had talked with a great many parties, promising them that I would get them stock if I could.

Q. How early was it that it began to be understood that this was valuable stock and likely to pay a large profit?—A. I think not until about October; not until this contract was made which was assigned to trustees; we had not been able to sell our bonds previous to that.

Q. Can you state whether you had had any conversation with Mr. Colfax in reference to his taking any of that stock prior to the session which commenced in 1867?—A. I cannot positively.

Q. Can you in respect to Senator Wilson?—A. I think he did not have any money to invest until that money of his wife's alluded to.

Q. How in regard to Senator Patterson?—A. Senator Patterson says he talked with me on the subject long ago, when we were on an excursion or expedition to the northeastern frontier during the war, in 1864. I have no recollection of it.

Q. Not about the stock of this company?—A. So he says.

Q. There was then no connection between this company and the Pacific Railroad Company?—A. I do not know anything about it. I did not become interested in the Credit Mobilier until August, 1865.

Q. You remember no such thing?—A. No, sir.

Q. Do you remember whether you had any conversation prior to December, 1867, with Mr. Bingham, of Ohio?—A. I think I did. I think I talked with him about it the spring before.

Q. You think you had with Mr. Scofield; how was it with Mr. Garfield?—A. I cannot remember that I did.

Q. Did you with Mr. Kelley?—A. I cannot say; it is not fixed in my mind whether I did or not.

Q. I understood you to state that you had some other papers in reference to this transaction between you and Senator Patterson. Will you be good enough to produce them?—A. Senator Patterson testified that he never received any dividend from this stock, and that he had no money from me on account of it. Here is a receipt which I present to the committee.

(The paper referred to was placed in evidence, and is as follows:)

"WASHINGTON, *June* 22, 1868.

"Received of Oakes Ames $1,800, on account of dividend received by him as trustee on stock held for my account.

"J. W. PATTERSON."

Q. Did you see him sign this paper?—A. Yes. He gave it to me at the time. I wrote the receipt and he signed it. The receipt is in my writing, and the signature is his.

Q. And made at the time of the date?—A. Yes, sir. I also hand to the committee another paper.

(Paper placed in evidence as follows:)

"BOSTON, *May* 6, 1871.

"Received of Oakes Ames, two hundred shares Union Pacific Railroad stock, seven hundred and fifty-seven dollars and twenty-four cents in cash, on account of Credit Mobilier stock, and there are still due on the transaction thirty shares of stock in the Credit Mobilier of America, and two thousand in the income-bonds of the Union Pacific Railroad.

"J. W. PATTERSON."

Q. Was that signed by him in your presence and given to you?—A. Yes.

Q. And at the date it bears?—A. I presume so.

Q. The paper itself is in your own handwriting?—A. Yes, sir.

Q. This was the paper given at the time of the settlement made between you and him, of which you spoke in your testimony?—A. Yes, that $1,800 is the check I gave him on the Sergeant-at-Arms, for which he gave me the receipt. That is the final settlement.

Q. Have you still another paper?—A. I have a letter Mr. Patterson wrote me in relation to this matter. He wrote me several which I have destroyed. I found this last night in looking over my papers. It is a letter from Mr. Patterson.

Q. You received it through the mail?—A. I do not recollect how I received it. The letter is written here, and I received it here. I received several others, which, as I stated, I have torn up. This is all I have. This letter is written this winter since the present investigation commenced.

Q. Do you know whether it is in Mr. Patterson's own writing?—A. I do not know that I can swear it is.

Q. Have you had any conversation with him in reference to this letter?—A. I have had several interviews with him since the letter was written.

Q. In reference to the letter?—A. Not in reference to the letter, but in reference to matters the letter alludes to.

Q. In any of the conversations you have had with him, has the fact that he had written such a letter been mentioned?—A. I do not know that it has. I do not know whether it has or not. I think he asked me if I had got the letter he wrote me.

Q. Is this the only one you have received from him this winter?—A. No, sir; I have received several and torn them up. I did not know that I had this until last evening.

Q. Was there any envelope with it?—A. I destroyed the envelope which I received it in. I received it when I got back from home the 7th or 8th of January.

(The letter referred to was placed in evidence, and is as follows:)

"WASHINGTON, D. C., *January* 4, 1873.

"MY DEAR SIR: The facts in respect to the Credit Mobilier, so far as I had any connection with it, were as follows:

"You came to me one day, knowing that a want of means was a chronic evil with me, and said, 'Patterson, if you would like, I can let you have thirty shares of stock in the Credit Mobilier, which I think will be a profitable investment, and will be a good thing for you.'

"My reply, in substance, was that if you had anything which I could properly invest in, and out of which I could make some money, I should be glad to take it, but that I had not the money at that time, and must defer it until I could get it.

"Your reply was that you presumed I could have it later, when it might be convenient, and you regarded it a perfectly legitimate transaction. At that time you did not and could not anticipate you should ever ask for further legislation from Congress in respect to the road, and you never did except when it was forced upon you by the Secretary.

"After this conversation with me, you may have had the impression that I should take the stock some time, but for some reason or other, perhaps for a want of funds, I never took any of the stock. If I never had any stock in the company, I could not, as I did not have, its dividends.

"If pressed to know if I purchased at any time any bonds or stock of the road, you can say I did at the time they attempted to embarrass you when the value of the stock was depressed, and I paid you the full market value for it. I paid you $7,000 in money for stock and bonds.

"The stock I put into the hands of Mr. Morton immediately to sell as soon as it should go up reasonably in the market, which he did.

"I saw Mr. Morton on my way through, and he said he had never held any stock in the Credit Mobilier for any one, but did not wish to have his name brought into the examination if it could be avoided. I am going to Ohio. I will see you on my return. *Don't fail to correct your original statement before the committee. It must not be reported as it now stands.*

"Very truly,

"J. W. PATTERSON.

"Hon. OAKES AMES."

By the CHAIRMAN:

Q. Some days ago I gave you notice in writing to produce all the memorandum-books and papers that you had containing any entries relating to the dealings between you and these various gentlemen who have been named and have been examined here. You have produced what purports to be copies of some of these entries. Have you the original memorandum-books from which you made these copies?—A. No, sir; I have not.

Q. Where are they?—A. I suppose at Easton.

Q. The committee think these original memorandum-books must be produced.—A. Very well, sir; I will send for them.

Q. The committee desire that all the original papers and correspondence regarding this subject, in your possession, shall be produced.—A. I do not think I have any correspondence in relation to it.

By Mr. MERRICK:

Q. Have you refreshed your memory in relation to your dealings with any other members of Congress?—A. There is no other. The reason I did not name Mr. Logan before was that Mr. Blaine stated that this committee had nothing to do with Senators. You asked for any other member of the House. There was no other member of the House. I only allude to such names outside of the House as Mr. McComb and others had mentioned, such as were included in his litigation. General Logan is the only name in the Senate that has not been mentioned before, and there is now no other in either branch of Congress.

Q. Neither at that time nor any other time?—A. No other.

By Mr. MCCRARY:

Q. Did General Logan give you any reason for returning the money and canceling the contract?—A. I do not remember that he did.

Q. Is it not probable that he would have given you some reason for doing so?—A. I don't know that; it may be probable. I don't recollect any.

Q. Do you know whether he spoke of any lawsuit in connection with it?—A. I do not remember. I want to say further to the committee that I have been asked by them several times and by some of these parties why I held this stock and did not give it to them. The Credit Mobilier stock was not entitled to any dividends. The stockholders in that company who signed the stipulation making themselves personally liable under the Oakes Ames contract were the only parties who could draw dividends on account of having been stockholders in the Credit Mobilier; these parties holding stock here not having signed that stipulation could not draw dividends, and that was probably the reason why I retained the stock. It would not have been of any use to them, for they could not have drawn the dividends.

By Mr. MERRICK:

Q. You drew them in behalf of the parties, you having signed the stipulation of the Oakes Ames contract?—A. Yes; that was an after consideration, however.

By Mr. NIBLACK:

Q. Do I understand that, having signed the stipulation referred to under the Oakes Ames contract, you could draw the dividends belonging to these various members of Congress as their trustee, while they could not draw them without signing that paper and becoming personally responsible, and that, therefore, you retained their stock in your possession?—A. Yes, sir; I held on to it.

Q. You were trustee, then, for these persons?—A. My attorney in Boston said I was not trustee in any sense. I took this stock originally in my own name, and I put it in my name as trustee to distinguish it from my original stock. It was not the vote of the company at all that I should hold it as trustee. It was a whim of mine after I took it.

By Mr. BANKS:

Q. In answer to the question of the chairman as to whether you applied to General Logan or he to you, you said they generally applied first, and subsequently you stated that you made efforts to get people interested in the Union Pacific Railroad at an earlier period. What is your recollection of the reasons you gave to these different parties, some of whom you spoke to and others who spoke to you?—A. I cannot give you any particular reason for that. I thought it was going to be a very good thing, and that if I gave stock to any to whom I had not spoken before it was to give them the advantage of a good investment.

Q. You remember the fact clearly in regard to certain persons that you first spoke to them, and in regard to others that they had spoken to you?—A. Most of them had spoken to me. I do not remember speaking to any of them first on the subject; still it may have been the fact, as they say.

By Mr. MCCRARY:

Q. When the stock was below par you were trying to get people to take it, and you spoke to them generally, but after it got to be very valuable they spoke to you.—A. Yes, sir; there was a change of position in that regard.

By Mr. NIBLACK:

Q. This was a transaction which seemed not to be very generally public. How did these members ascertain that the stock was getting to be more valuable?—A. I do not know; I suppose they found it out. When stock becomes more valuable men are very likely to find it out.

Q. I suppose there will be no impropriety in saying here that I never had my attention called to the fact that there was that sort of thing going about at the time; I therefore wanted to know how others found it out.—A. I can let you have some now if you want; when anything becomes valuable you cannot keep the secret long.

Q. The idea that this stock was becoming valuable—a good thing to hold—was well understood, and you had no difficulty at that time in disposing of it?—A. None at all.

Q. There were plenty of people who would be willing to take it at par and interest?—A. Yes, sir.

Q. It would have been easy for you to have sold all of this stock at some advance above par at that time?—A. Very likely; my object in getting the stock, and the reason I gave for it, was to enable persons with whom I had previous contracts to get it; that is, I had told them I would try and get it for them if I could.

Q. It would appear by the testimony that most of the men in Congress who received some of this stock did not seem to understand that there was any previous engagement?—A. I think it very likely that there was not, with some of them.

Q. How did they come to have the stock at par and interest when no engagement had been made for it?—A. I always let everybody in on the ground floor. I used them all alike.

Q. Was there any special reason why men in Congress should have this favor more than people out of Congress?—A. No, sir.

Q. Did you receive a greater price for any of this stock that you disposed of to anybody than par and interest, from the preceding July?—A. No, sir; I served every man alike, in Congress and out.

Q. There was no distinction between men who were in Congress and those who were out, in the price they had to pay for it?—A. None at all.

Q. No part of this stock, which was assigned to you to enable you to fulfill contracts or engagements, received any greater price than par and interest?—A. No, sir; no part of it.

WASHINGTON, D. C., *January* 28, 1873.

HENRY C. SWAIN sworn and examined.

By the CHAIRMAN:

Question. Are you the cashier of the First National Bank of Washington?—Answer. I am.

Q. How long have you been cashier?—A. Since last April; since the death of Mr. Huntington.

Q. How long have you been connected with the bank in any capacity?—A. Since May, 1869.

Q. You were not in the bank in 1868?—A. I was not.

Q. Have you access to, and are you familiar with, the books of the bank?—A. I have control of them.

Q. Have you made any examination of the books of the bank to see whether Mr. Colfax kept his account there in 1868?—A. I think he did keep an account at the bank in 1868.

Q. Have you brought the books of the bank which show his account in 1868?—A. I have the books; yes, sir.

Q. Will you produce them, and turn to the account of Mr. Colfax for the month of June, 1868?—A. I would like to answer any question you may ask by referring to the books.

Q. Will you state from the ledger which is open before you, whether it appears that Mr. Colfax made a deposit on the 22d of June, 1868?—A. It does.

Q. What is the amount?—A. By reference to the books I find it was $1,968.63.

Q. From that entry you understand that that amount of money was deposited to his credit either by him or by somebody for him?—A. Yes, sir.

Q. State the various deposits made to his credit from that time during the month of July.—A. July 7, $400; July 8, $150; July 13, $1,543.87.

By Mr. AMES:

Q. Can you state whether that deposit on the 22d June was in money or checks?—A. It is entered as "cash items." It may have been money; it may have been checks.

By the CHAIRMAN:

Q. Your entries on that book do not show whether the amounts were received in money or checks?—A. No, sir.

Q. Nor on the journal either?—A. No, sir.

Q. Are these items entered upon an earlier book than either of these?—A. Yes, sir.

Q. Have you produced that book?—A. These items are the aggregate of items in the other book.

Q. Will you produce the blotter, or scratcher, or whatever you call it, the book of original entry?

The WITNESS. Referring to what dates?

The CHAIRMAN. We want you to produce all the entries and papers you have touching the deposits made by Mr. Colfax from the middle of June until the end of July, 1868.—A. I will have to send to the bank for a part of them. I can produce a part of them now.

Q. Can you produce the papers referring to that particular item of the 22d of June?—A. I can.

Q. Have you the deposit ticket with you? If so, you will please read it.—A. It reads: "Deposited in the First National Bank by Schuyler Colfax, June 22, 1868, United States and bank notes....... $1,200 00

Checks as follows	250 00
	18 63
	500 00
Total	1,968 63

Q. Will you look at your ledger and see when the last deposit of Mr. Colfax was made prior to the 22d June?—A. That was June 1st.

Q. There is no deposit made by him after that until June 22?—A. None.

Q. Do you know in whose handwriting this ticket is?—A. I should say it was in Mr. Colfax's handwriting. I am not much of an expert in handwriting.

Q. You are somewhat familiar with Mr. Colfax's handwriting?—A. Yes, sir.

By Mr. AMES:

Q. You cannot tell where that money came from, of course?—A. No; I know nothing about it.

WASHINGTON, *January* 28, 1873.

BENJAMIN F. HAM recalled and examined.

By the CHAIRMAN:

Question. When Mr. Dillon was on the stand he testified in relation to a loan by him to Mr. Neilson of $5,000 for fifty additional shares of Credit Mobilier stock; that he could not tell in reference to its repayment; that you kept his accounts at that time, and would probably be able to state the particulars; can you state whether that loan has been repaid?—Answer. I do not think he stated positively that I kept his accounts; he thought perhaps I did. I did not keep his accounts at that time. I have since kept track of some of his matters. At that time I was in the employ of the railroad company and of the Credit Mobilier. I was fully occupied, and had nothing to do with his private transactions.

Q. Have you had since?—A. Yes, sir, I have.

Q. Have you made any search among Mr. Dillon's books and papers for the purpose of ascertaining whether and how that $5,000 was repaid to Mr. Dillon?—A. Mr. Dillon does not, at the present time, keep any general books. He is engaged in three or four railroad contracts and has a book-keeper for each one, and a clerk who has charge of that particular matter, and I should not know where to look for any such thing.

Q. Has he not since you have known about his private affairs kept any books in reference to any private transactions of his?—A. No, sir.

Q. Are you familiar enough with his books to know whether he at that time, in February, 1868, kept any books of that description?—A. I do not think he did.

Q. Have you made any search among his books and papers to see whether anything can be found bearing upon that $5,000 transaction?—A. There is nothing to be found among the papers in my possession.

Q. Have you any knowledge in relation to that $5,000?—A. Nothing more than I stated in my former testimony.

Q. Any information about it?—A. No, sir.

By Mr. MERRICK:

Q. You were secretary of the Credit Mobilier at that time?—A. Yes, sir; assistant secretary.

Q. You cannot recall to mind anything that occurred in regard to this matter, independent of the books?—A. No, sir.

By the CHAIRMAN:

Q. Did you issue the certificate of these fifty shares to Neilson?—A. Yes, sir.

Q. Did you know in reference to the loan by Mr. Dillon, that Mr. Dillon loaned him the money to pay for it?—A. No, sir; I did not.

Q. Was the money paid to you?—A. Yes, sir.

Q. Who paid it to you?—A. That I do not know. These matters occurred in 1867, six years ago. My mind has been taken up with other business matters of my own since that time, and it has entirely escaped my memory.

Q. You have no recollection about the payment of this money, whether it was paid by Mr. Dillon, Mr. Neilson, or who paid it?—A. No, sir.

By Mr. MERRICK:

Q. Have you any recollection apart from the entries upon the books of the transfer of the stock?—A. No, sir; I was not in the habit of recollecting things. I was in the habit of keeping my accounts on the books in order to refer to them.

By the CHAIRMAN:

Q. It has been stated that a paper was drawn up and signed by several of the principal stockholders, authorizing the issue of these fifty shares to Neilson or Mr. Brooks. Do you know anything in reference to that paper?—A. Yes, sir; there was such a paper.

Q. Have you such a paper?—A. Yes, sir.

(Paper handed to the committee.)

Q. The name of Oakes Ames, here written in pencil, was not written by Oakes Ames?—A. No, sir.

Q. The paper had no date to it?—A. No, sir.

By Mr. BANKS:

Q. Was the name of Oakes Ames authorized to be appended?—A. I judge not; it looks as if Oliver Ames and Oakes Ames had been written in pencil to indicate that their signatures should be at the head.

By the CHAIRMAN:

Q. Do you know in whose handwriting the pencil signature of Mr. Ames is?—A. The signature in pencil, I do not know who wrote; the signature of Oliver Ames was first written in pencil, and afterward written by Oliver Ames himself in ink.

Q. The pencil-signature is not in the handwriting of Oliver Ames?—A. I think not. I do not think he would spell Oakes Ames without an *e* in the first name.

Q. Do you know anything about how this paper was gotten up, how it came to be made, and what was its object or purpose?—A. I do not

I presume the object was to sell Mr. Brooks fifty shares on account of his agreement with Mr. Durant.

Q. Have you any recollection about the getting up of that paper, as to who suggested it, or how it was to be made?—A. No, sir; none at all. I have no recollection of it.

Q. Did you hear any talk among persons connected with the company as to whether Mr. Brooks was entitled to two hundred and fifty additional shares?—A. I do not recollect of any discussion. It was none of my business to know anything about these things. I was simply a clerk; although I was styled assistant secretary, my business was simply to execute the wishes of parties in charge.

Q. Where did you find the paper?—A. This paper was in the hands of one of the attorneys of the company.

Q. You procured it from him recently?—A. Since I was here before.

Q. Do you know whether it was ever in your possession before?—A. I presume it was.

Q. How did it come to be in the attorney's hands; have you any knowledge?—A. I do not know. I presume it was handed to him for some purpose.

By Mr. MERRICK:

Q. Having that paper before you and referring to the erasure in the entry of the fifty shares to Mr. Neilson in your books, in regard to which you testified on a former occasion, are you enabled to recollect any of the circumstances connected with that erasure?—A. No, sir; nothing more than I stated before.

Q. Are you enabled to say whether or not, looking at that paper and recollecting the circumstances, that the name as originally entered for these fifty shares was the name of James Brooks and that it was changed to Neilson?—A. No, sir.

Q. Your mind is a blank upon that subject?—A. It has escaped my memory entirely. It is not improbable that Mr. Brooks's name was originally written there.

Q. Might that not have been naturally done in consequence of his name being used on this paper?—A. It might have been done for that reason.

By Mr. MCCRARY:

Q. Can you tell anything about the time that paper was written and signed?—A. It must have been written not long previous to the issue of the stock—which was the 29th of February, I think. Undoubtedly the paper was not all signed on one day, because some of these gentlemen resided in New York and some in Boston.

By the CHAIRMAN:

Q. You know the signatures of many of these men; that they are genuine?—A. I consider them genuine.

Q. Have you any doubt at all as to this being a genuine paper?—A. None at all except to the pencil-signature of Oakes Ames. I do not consider that genuine.

By Mr. MCCRARY:

Q. Can you recollect now, in seeing that paper, anything as to the reasons given for issuing that stock in the name of Mr. Neilson instead of Mr. Brooks?—A. No, sir; except that I was instructed to do so.

Q. I believe you stated before that you were instructed by Mr. Dillon to do so?—A. Yes, sir; I was simply acting in a clerical capacity and the reasons were not given to me.

Q. I understand you to repeat that you know nothing of the repayment of this money by Mr. Neilson or by Mr. Brooks?—A. No, sir.

Q. Do you know that it has ever been repaid?—A. No, sir; I do not.

Q. Have you examined the accounts of Mr. Dillon to see if you could find anything about the repayment of that loan by Mr. Neilson?—A. As I have stated before, he keeps no books, and has kept no books since I have had charge of his private matters. He keeps books of his different railroad companies.

Q. You know of no book account or memorandum of this transaction with Neilson?—A. No, sir.

Q. You think it might appear in some of the railroad-books?—A. It might; I do not know.

Q. Would Mr. Dillon be able to state where the account would appear?—A. I doubt if Mr. Dillon would know.

Q. Was he in the habit of making loans of $5,000 without any account of the matter in his books?—A. I do not know anything about that. I had nothing to do with him at that time, any more than I had with Mr. Alley or any other member of a railroad company.

By Mr. BANKS:

Q. Do you have charge of Mr. Dillon's private affairs now, and have you had since that time?—A. Yes, a portion of the time.

Q. If such an incident as this had occurred to you at any time since you have had charge would you remember it?—A. Yes, sir. If I had received it I could find it on my books. I have received no such sum of money on his account.

(The paper produced by witness in the above testimony is as follows:)

We, the undersigned, stockholders in the Credit Mobilier of America, consent to the sale of one hundred shares of its stock at par to General G. M. Dodge, chief engineer of the Union Pacific Railroad Company, and also to the sale to Hon. James Brooks of the balance he is entitled to under his agreement with T. C. Durant, the said Brooks to pay par value for the same.

OLIVER AMES.
[Pencil:] *OAKES AMES.*
(Not his, I believe.)
JOHN R. DUFF.
S. HOOPER & CO.
W. T. GLIDDEN.
E. H. BAKER.
F. NICKERSON.
JOS. NICKERSON.
R. E. ROBBINS.
THO. NICKERSON.
ISAAC THACKER.
HORATIO GILBERT.
HORATIO J. GILBERT.
T. W. ANDREWS.
S. H. FESSENDEN.
GAML. BRADFORD.
E. W. GILMORE.
O. S. CHAPMAN.
G. G. GRAY,
Per H. W. GRAY, *Attorney.*

WASHINGTON, D. C., *January* 28, 1873.

JOHN A. LOGAN, United States Senator from the State of Illinois, sworn and examined.

By the CHAIRMAN:

Question. Have you seen the testimony of Mr. Oakes Ames in which your name is mentioned in connection with the purchase of Credit Mobilier stock?—Answer. I have.

Q. Will you state to the committee your recollection in relation to the transaction between you and him in regard to the matter referred to?—A. I wish to say this at the commencement of my statement: I have nothing whatever to conceal in reference to this transaction as far as I am connected with it. Mr. Ames has stated that I agreed to purchase certain stock from him. I did so, as a mere business transaction, in the winter of 1867–'68, during the session of Congress. Mr. Ames, in a conversation with me, recommended this stock as valuable, and I agreed with him to purchase ten shares of it at par. I paid nothing to Mr. Ames at any time. He delivered to me no stock and no certificate of stock.

In June, 1868, following, on the 20th day, as my memorandum shows, and as, I suppose, the books will show, Mr. Ames came to me and said this stock was entitled to a dividend, or that there was a dividend on the stock. He made up a statement, and handed it to me, which showed that the dividends on the stock had paid for the purchase of $1,000, and that there was an amount coming to me, in excess, of $329. He handed me a check for the $329. I had paid Mr. Ames, as I say, no money, and he had delivered no certificate of stock to me, or to anybody else for me. I took the check, and said to Mr. Ames I would take it with the understanding that if I did not want to receive the stock I would let him know; that it was a matter I would consider about. Three or four days afterward, perhaps, I presented the check to the Sergeant-at-Arms, or some one who was in his office, and received the money on it, $329. I retained the money a few days. In the mean time I had received from a friend, with whom I was in communication, some letters which caused me to doubt whether it was good stock, or whether there would not be difficulty about it, and I said to Mr. Ames I believed I would not take the stock. Mr. Ames replied, "Very well," remarking that it was good stock, and that he thought it was a good investment, and that a man was very foolish, or something of that kind, not to retain it. I paid him back $329, and, I think, two dollars for interest. Mr. Ames hesitated about taking the small amount of interest, but I insisted on it, and paid him the amount, with interest, covering the whole transaction. That is all there is of it. I have examined my memorandum in regard to the transaction, and am able to give the date, which I could not do from memory. I received the check on the 20th June, and returned the money to Mr. Ames on the 10th July following.

I do not say this by way of excuse or covering up anything in this transaction, but simply to state the facts as they were. During the whole of this time I never received a share of this stock; I never had it in my possession; it was never delivered to me, or to anybody for me; nor did I ever receive anything from it, directly or indirectly, except as I have stated to the committee. And I wish to state further, inasmuch as the country is alarmed or excited about this matter, that I had no hesitation in making the agreement with Mr. Ames at the time, so far as any suggestion of corruption or wrong in the matter was concerned. I did not think of such a thing, and I had no suspicion that Mr. Ames thought of anything of the kind. There was no legislation before Congress at the time in connection with the Union Pacific Railroad, nor do I recollect any legislation occurring during the time this negotiation was going on between Mr. Ames and myself; if there was I do not remember it. I only say that so far as influence was concerned, in reference to the Union Pacific Railroad, it was entirely unnecessary for Mr. Ames or anybody else, if they had a desire, to have made any bargain with me out of which I could make profit to obtain my influence for that road. My constituency were immediately interested in its being constructed; I was entirely friendly to it, and have always aided and sustained it, because I thought it was right to do so in all proper things, and would just as willingly do so to-day, irrespective of this investigation, as I ever did. Whenever any matter for the benefit of the road has been before Congress which I considered proper I have always voted for it. I want now to ask Mr. Ames if any legislation, or proposed legislation, was pending during the period of which I have spoken?

Mr. AMES. I do not recollect anything.

By the CHAIRMAN:

Q. You were a member of the House at that time?—A. I was.

Q. Can you state about how early in the winter it was that you first had any negotiation upon the subject?—A. I do not remember the first conversation, because I kept no memorandum of it. I stated at the beginning the time I agreed to take this stock. I might have had frequent conversations with Mr. Ames prior to that agreement. I remember one conversation in reference to the stock in which he spoke of it as being good stock. This was some time along in the first part of that session of Congress. Afterward, on his recommendation, I agreed to purchase it. I cannot give you the date of these first conversations I had with him. The date at which I agreed to purchase was the 10th February, 1868. I then told him I would take ten shares of stock.

Q. Do you remember whether Mr. Ames had ever proposed to you to become a shareholder in the company prior to that session of Congress?—A. No, sir; I never had any conversation with him upon the subject prior to that session. We had some preliminary conversations, as I stated, prior to the 10th February, when I agreed to take ten shares.

Q. In the June following, as I understand you, he gave you a statement of the dividends and amount due you?—A. Yes, sir.

Q. There had been a bond dividend which he had sold and given you the benefit of, and also a cash dividend?—A. Yes, sir; he had received the dividends himself, and in his statement to me he accounted for the dividends, and stated that there was $329 due to me after paying for the stock.

Q. When you received the check from him you expressed some doubt as to whether you desired to make the contract complete, and stated that you would take the check and consider of it?—A. I did.

Q. And about the 10th July following you made up your mind, for some reason, that it was not desirable for you to go further in the transaction and returned him the money?—A. Yes, sir.

Q. I do not know whether it is very important for the committee to know the reasons that influenced you, but I would inquire whether it was some question in relation to the value of the stock that influenced you not to take it, or other considerations?—A. I had, as I said, my ideas in reference to the organization and matters in regard to the contract for building the road from the communications I had received from that friend who was entirely outside of this matter. It was from a contractor on the road. He had been writing to me, and had stated a good deal about the matter of these contracts, and the statements he made suggested to my mind that there might possibly be trouble ahead. If I had not received these letters perhaps I should have retained the money. If I had, I should certainly have come here and said so if the committee had sent for me.

Q. Did Mr. Ames, in the preliminary conversations you had with him prior to February, say anything as to the value of the stock, or how much you would realize on it?—A. He said it would be good stock; he did not make any extravagant statements to me about it.

Q. Do you remember whether he made any specific statement to you about its value?—A. I think he merely made general representations.

By Mr. NIBLACK:

Q. At that session of Congress I believe you were a member of the Pacific Railroad Committee?—A. I believe I was; I do not remember.

Q. Was it in consequence of your being a member of that committee that you had this correspondence with this friend of yours?—A. It may possibly have been; I do not remember the particular reasons that suggested it. I had several letters on the subject; I cannot say now what first gave me the suggestion that led me to reflect upon the subject, the result of which was that I concluded not to take the stock. I may say I had no reason to suppose there would be legislation, although I did not know but what there might be at some future time legislation in connection with the road. I saw nothing in the transaction on the part of Mr. Ames that showed anything more than a mere business matter.

By the CHAIRMAN:

Q. Do you remember whether in the conversations you had with Mr. Ames about it there was anything said as to there being any likelihood of the matter coming before Congress in any shape or form?—A. I do not remember that there was. I looked upon it simply as a transaction between him and myself as business men. He and I were good friends. He said to me that he was seeking prominent influential men in the country to invest in this stock. I mention that as a part of the conversation, because I desire to state everything.

By Mr. MERRICK:

Q. Were you or not advised of a resolution introduced by C. C. Washburn, 4th February, 1868, into the House, inquiring whether these roads had complied with the provisions of the twentieth section of the law incorporating them?—A. Probably I was advised at the time if it took place; I do not now remember it.

Q. You did not know that at the time you were making this contract with Mr. Ames?—A. It had no reference to it. I had had conversations with Mr. Ames long prior to that. This was the time I told him I would purchase.

Q. Suppose your attention had been called on the 10th of February, when you made your contract with him, to the fact that C. C. Washburn, on the 4th of February, had introduced a resolution inquiring as to whether these roads had complied with their obligations under the law?—A. I would have made the purchase just the same, because I did not look at it in any improper light.

Q. Would the fact of your being a member of the Pacific Railroad Committee, and this resolution being introduced the 4th of February, to inquire into the manner in which these roads had complied with their obligations, have been a sufficient inducement to have withheld you from the investment?—A. It might have been if I had thought anything about it. I had nothing in my mind at that time in reference to any such matter. In fact, I presume Mr. Ames proffered me the stock about which we had had prior conversations, and I said I was willing to make the purchase.

By the CHAIRMAN:

Q. You had learned from Mr. Ames that there was some connection between the Credit Mobilier and the Union Pacific Railroad?—A. I had learned this—and I dislike to confess my ignorance in the matter—I had learned that it was the stock of a company which was constructing the Union Pacific Railroad, but the details of the relations between them I did not know anything about, and really do not now thoroughly, for I have never investigated it.

[To Mr. Ames: Q. I wish to ask Mr. Ames whether the statement I have made accords with his recollection of the facts?—A. Substantially.]

The witness subsequently returned to the committee-room and said:

In my testimony this morning a statement was made which I desire to be corrected. In answer to the question of Mr. Niblack whether I was not a member of the Pacific Railroad Committee at the time, I replied that I did not know, perhaps I was. I went immediately and examined the Journal, and find that I was not a member of that committee at that time. I was not a member of the Pacific Railroad Committee during the 40th Congress. In 1869, in the 41st Congress, the Journal states the committee as follows: William A. Wheeler, chairman; John A. Logan; and so on. This was nearly a year after the transaction occurred. I was not appointed a member of that committee until March, 1869.

WASHINGTON, D. C., *January* 29, 1873.

SIDNEY DILLON recalled and examined.

By the CHAIRMAN:

Question. You stated the other day that you loaned $5,000 to Mr. Neilson to pay the fifty shares Credit Mobilier stock, and that you thought the money had been repaid to you, but was not clear by whom; your information then was that Mr. Ham was the man who had charge of the transaction, and could tell us. Mr. Ham has since been before the committee, and says he had nothing to do with matters of that sort for you. State whether you have yourself made any further examination since you were before the committee on a former occasion, for the purpose of ascertaining by whom that $5,000 was repaid to you, if it has been repaid.—Answer. I have made all the examination that is in my power to make, and I find no trace of it. When I referred the committee to Mr. Ham, I supposed he was my clerk at the period of this transaction, but I find he was not until some time afterward. The way my business has been done is this: I had some two or three different railroad contracts going on at the same time, one in New Hampshire and one in Massachusetts, and so on. I had an office in each place, where my business was done for that separate contract. I had no general office in New York until a comparatively recent date, when I employed Mr. Ham. Finding my different matters were getting mixed up in New York, and that I must keep an office there, I employed Mr. Ham to do my business. Before then, if a party came to me and wanted to borrow $5,000, or I wanted to borrow $5,000, or if I was in any trade in stock or bonds, it had been my custom to attend to the business myself, and keep the run of it in my head. All my railroad business I did with my clerks, as I have stated, but for these individual transactions I never kept any books and never kept any memorandum; I kept them all in my head. Such a matter as this with Neilson was a personal and private transaction, and there would be no record of it. I have no doubt it has been paid, but I have no knowledge on the subject. I cannot find the stock or bonds, and I think Mr. Neilson must have paid me. I may have sold the securities for his account, as they were about the same amount; if not, I must have returned them to him when I got my money back. I know of no other way to account for them unless they have been stolen from me, and I can tell you nothing further about it.

Q. You remember making the loan to Mr. Neilson—you remember that transaction as being with Mr. Neilson and not with Mr. Brooks?—A. It was with Mr. Neilson.

Q. Do you remember whether he gave you any note or obligation, or whether you made any memorandum of it?—A. I took no note and made no memorandum. I took collaterals from him.

Q. Would you be likely to loan the amount of $5,000 without having a note?—A. O, yes, I often do it; it is customary in New York. A man comes in, and wants five, ten, or twenty thousand dollars; "Here is my money; there are the collaterals; keep the collaterals until the money is paid." That was about the way of it when Mr. Neilson borrowed this money. He handed me his collaterals and I gave him the money. I think that is the fact; I am not sure. And he must have returned me the money and taken his collaterals without taking up the receipt.

Q. The receipt you gave for collaterals would state the amount of collaterals?—A. Yes, sir.

Q. You remember loaning the money; do you remember whether you did actually receive the collaterals?—A. I did receive collaterals at the time.

Q. Have you any recollection what they were?—A. They consisted of Union Pacific Railroad stock and bonds; none but Pacific Railroad securities.

Q. Do you remember the amount?—A. I cannot state the amount; it is not in my mind. I know it was satisfactory at the time to secure the return of the money.

Q. You have made search, and are not able to find any such securities belonging to Neilson in your possession now?—A. I have searched my entire papers, and had Mr. Ham search. I supposed at the time I was here, that Mr. Ham could trace the thing. I have employed him during the past year as a special clerk to look after things, such as I have been speaking of, for me.

Q. But the fact as to whether you have retained or surrendered these securities is entirely out of your memory?—A. I cannot remember; I do not remember the transaction.

Q. Then you have no personal recollection of this transaction between you and Neilson at all, except the fact that you loaned him the money?—A. That is the only recollection I have.

Q. So that you are utterly unable to say by whom the money was repaid, if it was repaid?—A. I am unable to say anything except that it would be natural that I should receive the money from the person who borrowed it. I cannot tell you as to the fact.

Q. Do you know anything in regard to the paper being gotten up and signed for the consent of the stockholders to Mr. Neilson's receiving the additional shares? You stated the other day that it referred only to this transaction of Neilson's.—A. I had forgotton that it referred to any other. I had not seen the paper for a long time.

Q. Can you state why the name of Mr. Brooks was put into that paper instead of Neilson's?—A. I can only state that as Mr Brooks's name had been identified with the transaction in the form in which it has been represented here, his name appeared by mistake in the paper instead of that of Neilson's. That is my impression now. I cannot state certainly.

Q. Can you state whether or not Mr. Brooks is the party who negotiated with you, or claimed that the thing should be done?—A. I think in my testimony I stated that Mr. Brooks talked with me about that.

Q. And that it was done upon his application and not upon the application of Neilson?—A. I think Mr. Brooks said the transaction was so and so, as has been represented here, and that, on consideration, of my own motion, I got up that paper to have Neilson get the fifty shares.

Q. Then I understand that it was upon the application of Mr. Brooks and not upon the application of Mr. Neilson that that transaction occurred?—A. I think it was brought to me in the first instance by Mr. Brooks.

WASHINGTON, D. C., *January* 29, 1873.

Robert S. Hale, esq., appeared before the committee in behalf of Mr. Colfax, and stated that it was the desire of Mr. Colfax to bring witnesses and adduce proof to rebut the testimony before the committee in regard to his connection with the Credit Mobilier. He wished now to recall a witness for the purpose of asking him a single question.

Permission having been granted by the committee, Henry C. Swain was recalled and examined by Mr. Hale.

Question. Will you state whether the books of the First National Bank show debits to Mr. Colfax on the day of the credits of which you spoke in your testimony yesterday—the 22d June, 1868?—Answer. They do.

Q. What are those debits?—A. I cannot state fully. Among them was a check of $1,000, paid on that day.

Q. Have you that check?—A. I have it here.

Q. Will you produce it?—A. This is the check referred to. It reads:

"WASHINGTON, D. C., *June* 22, 1868.

"First National Bank, pay to self or bearer $1,000.

"SCHUYLER COLFAX."

Q. State if you know how that was paid.—A. I think it was paid by a draft on New York, to the order of Mr. Colfax.

Q. Have you that draft?—A. I have.

Q. Produce it.—A. It is a draft of our bank on the Continental National Bank of New York, for $1,000, drawn to the order of Mr. Colfax, and signed by H. S. Flint, assistant cashier. It is indorsed:

"Pay to the order of A. H. Connor, Indianapolis.

"SCHUYLER COLFAX.

"A. H. CONNOR:

"Pay Winslow Lanier, or order.

"S. A. FLETCHER & CO."

Q. It was subsequently paid by the drawee, in New York?—A. Yes, sir.

Q. Are there any other debits to him on that day?—A. There may be. I cannot tell without referring to the books.

Q. Will you have the kindness, on returning to the bank, to examine the books, and advise the chairman if you find any other?—A. Yes, sir.

By Mr. AMES:

Q. Was this deposit of $1,200, and these checks referred to yesterday, the 22d June, 1868?—A. Yes, sir.

Q. He made the deposit, and then drew out $1,000, and sent it, in a draft, to New York?—A. We gave him a check on New York.

WASHINGTON, D. C., *January* 29, 1873.

Re-examination of OAKES AMES.

By the CHAIRMAN:

Q. Among the checks the Sergeant-at-Arms has laid before the committee dated in the month of June, 1868, drawn by you, is one payable to J. W. Patterson or bearer, $1,800, indorsed by Mr. Patterson; did you give that check to Mr. Patterson?—A. Yes, sir.

Q. For what was this $1,800 paid?—A. It was a dividend of 60 per cent. on $3,000 of Credit Mobilier stock.

Q. It was a cash dividend?—A. Yes, sir.

Q. Did you take a receipt from him?—A. I did.

Q. Have you that receipt?—A. I think you have it.

Q. Have you any other receipt from Mr. Patterson that you have not produced here?—A. Yes, sir.

Q. Will you produce it?—A. Here it is. It reads: "Washington, February 14, 1868. Received of Oakes Ames $2,328 for three bonds of Union Pacific Railroad Company sold for me, being a dividend of 80 per cent. in bonds on the stock of the Credit Mobilier of America, held by him as trustee on my account. J. W. Patterson."

Q. This was made at the time of the date?—A. I presume so; there would be no object in making it any other date.

Q. What are the figures at the bottom?—A. I think the figuring there is mine.

Q. The receipt, then, is written by you?—A. Yes, sir; and signed by Mr. Patterson.

Q. And the figures at the bottom show the transaction?—A. Yes, sir. I paid him $2,223, and deducted $105, which, I think, was the amount due for interest or on the purchase-money. Mr. Patterson would like to appear before you and make some explanation. He thinks there is some misunderstanding about the matter, and would like to have an opportunity to explain.

Q. The other day we examined the books of the Sergeant-at-Arms, and inquired of you in regard to all the names appearing upon the books except that of Mr. Logan, who was subsequently examined. In looking over the drafts, however, there are some which do not indicate in themselves by whom they were drawn, or for what purpose, and therefore we desire to inquire in reference to these. Here is a check drawn by you on the Sergeant-at-Arms, dated June 22, 1868: "Sergeant-at-Arms, House of Representatives, pay Oakes Ames." Then there is a letter S and some other filling, "[$600,] and charge to my account. Oakes Ames."—A. That was given to Mr. Scofield.

Q. The letters then are Sc.?—A. Yes, sir.

Q. These letters were put there to indicate that this, therefore, was for Mr. Scofield?—A. Yes, sir; I had forgotten all about it until I saw it the other day. I suppose I must have put it there for that purpose.

Q. Did you draw a check for Mr. Scofield for that dividend?—A. Yes, sir; my memorandum, which I showed the other day, says I did.

Q. Did Mr. Scofield receive this check from you, and get the money on it, as you supposed?—A. I suppose so.

Q. What was that dividend for?—A. Sixty per cent. dividend on the stock held.

Q. Did you receive a bond dividend on that stock prior to this?—A. Yes, sir.

Q. You sold the bonds?—A. Yes, sir.

Q. What was done with the money you received for the bonds?—A. I paid it out to these parties, as I have said.

Q. Did you pay the money to Mr. Scofield, or was it credited to him?—A. I do not recollect which it was; it was in the statement that I gave him.

Q. Had you paid over to Mr. Scofield the money you received for his bonds prior to June 22?—A. Yes, sir; I paid it over to him.

Q. You paid the proceeds of the bond dividend, and also this cash dividend?—A. Yes, sir.

Q. At what time do you think it was this transaction was rescinded between you and him?—A. I think it was the last part of that session of Congress or the first of the next.

Q. He concluded not to keep the stock?—A. He concluded not to keep the stock.

Q. Was that after the McComb suit was brought, do you think?—A. I think so.

Q. Is it your understanding that it was in consequence of that that he became alarmed about the transaction and did not choose to keep the stock?—A. I cannot tell you about that. He said something about personal liability. I cannot tell you what his ideas were.

Q. Please state what passed between you and him on that subject; do you remember it?—A. He wanted to sell and close up the matter, and we settled up in that way.

Q. These dividends were all he had received. Did he keep them or were they repaid to you?—A. I think they were repaid to me; all except ten shares of Union Pacific Railroad stock that he kept as profit.

Q. So that you got back the money and he made ten shares of Union Pacific Railroad stock?—A. I think so; I don't wish to state positively; his memory is probably better than mine upon that subject.

Q. But we want you to state your memory?—A. My memory is that he got ten shares of stock; I cannot say positively; but that is my remembrance of it.

Q. Here is another check upon the Sergeant-at-Arms of the same date, June 22, 1868: "Pay O. A. or bearer $329, and charge to my account. Oakes Ames." That seems to have been paid to somebody and taken up by the Sergeant-at-Arms. These initials are your own?—A. Yes, sir.

Q. Do you know who had the benefit of that check?—A. I cannot tell you.

Q. Do you think you received the money on it yourself?—A. I have no idea. I may have drawn the money and handed it to another person. It was paid on that transaction. It may have been paid to Mr. Garfield. There were several sums of that amount.

Q. Have you any memory in reference to this check?—A. No, sir; I have no memory as to that particular check. I found these checks in the package which the Sergeant-at-Arms gave me, and I find them on the Sergeant-at-Arms' books.

Q. You have some memory in regard to some of these men receiving payment of their dividends?—A. They all received payments of their dividends. There is no question of that in my mind. There may be in the minds of others.

Q. Is there any other gentleman here in Congress who received $329 dividend except those who have already been named by you?—A. I don't think of any other.

Q. In regard to Mr. Garfield, do you know whether you gave him a check or paid him the money?—A. I think I did not pay him the money. He got it from the Sergeant-at-Arms upon a check.

Q. You have testified to the check of $1,200, payable to S. C. or bearer; also to one $329 to Mr. Allison; also $329 to W. D. K.; the same amount to Mr. Wilson; and the same amount to John A. Logan, whose names appear here. These are all the names that appear on the books of the Sergeant-at-Arms of persons in Congress on that day. Are you satisfied that this check of $329, in which your own initials are written, was to pay some one a dividend on that stock?—A. Yes, sir. I don't know why I should draw a check for $329, except for that purpose.

Q. On the next day, June 23, there is a check given by you on the Sergeant-at-Arms for $272.79, without any name in it, payable to blank or bearer; have you any memory in reference to that check?—A. No, sir; I don't know that I can give you any information in regard to that.

Q. It does not correspond to any memorandum you have there?—A. No, sir.

Q. Would you infer from the sum and the manner in which the check is drawn that you drew the money?—A. I cannot say. I had no particular form of drawing my checks. There are quite a number drawn for other purposes having no reference to the Credit Mobilier.

Q. If you had wanted to draw out the money for yourself to use, would you be very likely to make a check for the fractional sum of $272.79?—A. That I cannot say; it might be for some remittance to pay some bill for board, or something like that.

Q. The fact, then, that there is no payee inserted in the check does not indicate to your mind that you received the money or did not receive it?—A. No, sir.

Q. If you drew out the money for yourself, would you not have been likely to draw a round sum, unless it was to pay some particular bill you had?—A. Unless it was to pay some bill or draft, or something of that sort. It may have been in settlement of some of these matters; I cannot say.

Q. Here is another check, July 3, 1867, for $1,200, which says, "Pay to draft."—A. That may be for a draft on Boston; I was in the habit of getting drafts on Boston and New York to send away.

Q. Have you any doubt, from the inspection of that check, that it was to get a draft to use for your own purposes?—A. No, sir; I don't suppose there is any doubt about that. I guess we adjourned about that time; but I may have wanted to remit it home for some purpose.

Q. Have you any memory in relation to this draft of $722, for what it was drawn?—A. None whatever. I may be able to find some memoranda; I have nothing here that will throw any light upon it.

Q. Did Mr. Dawes receive any money from you paid by check on the Sergeant-at-Arms?—A. I think he did.

Q. About what time?—A. I think about the same time with the rest of them.

Q. Have you examined all the checks that you gave the Sergeant-at-Arms?—A. I think I have.

Q. Did you find any check that you think was given to Mr. Dawes?—A. I do not know. Let me look over the checks again. My memorandum, that I have here, says I gave Mr. Dawes $600, less $200; there was a balance due me on some other matter.

Q. And you think you paid him $400, and that you paid it by check on the Sergeant-at-Arms?—A. I think I did, judging from this memoranda. The amount was $600, and $200 was deducted, and I must have given him $400. I had receipts from Mr. Dawes, but I settled with him as I stated, gave him the receipts and papers, and he gave me his note to balance the account.

Q. This $400 you think you paid Mr. Dawes as a portion of the money dividend on his ten shares?—A. Yes, sir.

Q. Who was W. W. Dungan?—A. He is a resident of this city.

Q. Has this check with his name anything to do with Credit Mobilier stock?—A. No, sir.

Q. Among these checks I do not find any for the sum of $400.—A. No, sir; I do not see any here. It might have been applied on account in our settlement.

Q. You think the check in which you wrote nothing to indicate the payee must have been for Mr. Garfield?—A. Yes, sir; that is my judgment.

Q. In relation to the dividends, you say you held the stock and certificates for bonds, and that you have drawn the dividends on these Credit Mobilier shares which have been transferred?—A. Yes, sir.

Q. If there had been any dividend paid upon any Union Pacific stock, that has not been divided?—A. No, sir.

Q. So that nothing has been received either by you, or could have been received by any of these gentlemen, on that account?—A. No, sir.

Q. You say you received certificates for bonds in payment of dividends; what kind of bonds were they?—A. They were dividend certificates for first-mortgage Union Pacific Railroad bonds, but the company did not have the bonds to make the dividend on, and they never were delivered.

Q. Would they have been delivered if they had been called for?—A. No, sir; the company had not the bonds to give.

Q. Did all the shareholders of the Credit Mobilier who were entitled to draw dividends receive an equal percentage of these certificates?—A. I presume so.

Q. If you had delivered the certificates for bonds to these gentlemen, would they have received the bonds?—A. No; and these gentlemen could not have drawn dividends at all. The dividends were not made, as I have before explained, upon the Credit Mobilier stock, but in consequence of the Oakes Ames contract, as it was called, and they were made to the shareholders of the Credit Mobilier who had signed the agreement making themselves personally responsible. These gentlemen had not signed that agreement, and therefore could not themselves receive the dividends.

Q. Suppose the parties declined to take the stock before this last dividend, and you had continued to be the owner of the stock itself, and had received certificates for the bonds, could you have got the bonds upon these certificates?—A. No, sir. About a year afterward we received what are called income bonds in payment of the certificates.

Q. Have these income bonds drawn any dividend?—A. Yes, sir. The receipts which I have from Mr. Patterson, Mr. Bingham, Mr. Painter, and others, show that I have given them dividends upon the bonds, and that I had accounted to them for all I had received.

Q. How was it in relation to Mr. Kelley and Mr. Garfield?—A. They have had nothing but the $329.

Q. Have you ever offered to deliver to them the other dividends?—A. No, sir.

Q. You say that Mr. Scofield, Mr. Dawes, Mr. Logan, and others with whom you made an adjustment, they having declined to take the shares of Credit Mobilier stock, did not receive these dividends?—A. No, sir; they went out after the 60 per cent. dividend; they had no more to do with it, and they were not entitled to anything more.

Q. But Mr. Kelley, you suppose, was entitled to receive the dividends, and will receive them when you settle with him?—A. Yes, sir; I expect to pay over to Mr. Kelley everything I have received on his stock.

Q. And in relation to Mr. Garfield?—A. The same in relation to him, if it is not borrowed money. I consider that I sold him the stock, and that he holds it.

Q. You have accounted to Mr. Patterson for his?—A. Yes, sir.

Q. You consider Mr. Colfax entitled to whatever you have on his stock?—A. I do.

Q. And the same with Mr. Allison?—A. Mr. Allison sent his stock back, and called the thing canceled.

Q. How did you call it?—A. If he sent his stock back and declined to have anything to do with it, I suppose the thing is off, as Mr. Colfax said.

Q. Is it off in consequence of the agreement you had with him; or, when he sent the certificate of stock back, did you treat that as an abandonment of the transaction?—A. I think Mr. Allison's idea was that he was in an excited political contest, and resolved to have nothing to do with it, so that it should not be brought up against him. I presume that is the fact. He knows his own motives; I cannot explain them.

Q. What we want to know is whether that was a real transaction or a nominal transaction which you described in regard to the resale of the stock to you?—A. I suppose he considered it a real transaction.

Q. Did you consider it so?—A. If you refer to the nickel, I did not consider that it amounted to anything; but when he returned it, I supposed the thing was canceled, and that that was an end of the transaction.

Q. Have you come to any other understanding or agreement with him at any other time except this small coin transaction?—A. No, sir; he returned the stock, and I suppose considered that as an end of it.

Q. Did you accept that as an end of the matter between you and him?—A. I so considered it, or he would not have returned it.

Q. He received the bond dividend and the cash dividend?—A. Yes, sir.

Q. Did he ever receive anything more upon his shares?—A. No, sir.

Q. The stock and the certificate for bonds you received afterward, and hold still?—A. Yes, sir.

Q. And you consider yourself entitled to these?—A. Yes, sir.

Q. Do you think that Mr. Allison ever returned to you in any way any part of the money you paid over to him?—A. He returned me the stock of the Credit Mobilier, and returned the $1,000 paid for it by returning the stock.

Q. He paid nothing for the stock?—A. He paid me something, or else he would not have received his $600 dividend.

Q. How much money did he pay you, and when?—A. I do not now remember how much. He must have paid it before the $600 dividend, of course.

Q. Do you remember how that was?—A. I remember he paid me for it, or I should not have given him the $600 dividend.

Q. Did he pay you for these ten shares of stock before the bond dividend?—A. No, sir; I received the bond dividend, and accounted for it toward the payment of the stock, and he paid me the balance in money. Afterward he received $600 cash dividend.

Q. Did he ever pay you back any part of the $600?—A. I did not so understand it.

Q. Do you so understand it?—A. He so understands it. When I gave my testimony before, I did not consider that he ever paid me back.

Q. Do you believe now that he ever paid you back?—A. No; I do not believe he did.

Q. Have you any doubt upon that subject?—A. Not much. Mr. Allison returned me his stock, but he has never paid me back any money, as I understand.

Q. You understand that Mr. Kelley and Mr. Garfield have each been bettered $329 by their transactions?—A. That is all there is of it. I have not seen Mr. Allison for a long time, until this winter. I cannot remember all these transactions, or everything that everybody says to me, very well.

Q. You heard Mr. Allison's statement upon that subject?—A. Yes, sir; he says he inclosed a draft on New York to me, to be applied on another transaction. I have no recollection of it.

Q. Do you recollect any transaction or any conversation by which it was agreed that he should pay you back this money?—A. I do not.

Q. And you do not believe he has paid it?—A. I do not recollect it.

Q. Have you had any correspondence with any of these gentlemen whose names have been brought in here, except Mr. Patterson, whose letter you have produced?—No, sir; I think not.

Q. You have had no communication with them?—A. No, sir; Mr. Patterson is the only one.

Q. How many of them have you had conversations with?—A. I have had conversations with almost all of them.

Q. What the committee want to learn is, whether, in conversations with any of these gentlemen, they have stated or admitted the matter to be different from what they have testified to before the committee.—A. I hardly know how to answer that question.

Q. Take any one that occurs to you; Mr. Merrick suggests Mr. Garfield.—A. Mr. Garfield has been to see me about the matter, and we have talked it over. A part of the time he thinks it was a loan; sometimes he thinks he has repaid me; and then again he is in doubt about it.

Q. You may state whether, in conversation with you, Mr. Garfield claims, as he claimed before us, that the only transaction between you was borrowing $300.—A. No, sir; he did not claim that with me.

Q. State how he does claim it with you; what was said? State all that occurred in conversation between you.—A. I cannot remember half of it. I have had two or three interviews with Mr. Garfield. He wants to put it on the basis of a loan. He states that when he came back from Europe, being in want of funds, he called on me to loan him a sum of money. He thought he had repaid it. I do not know. I cannot remember.

Q. What did you say to him in reference to that state of the case?—A. I stated to him that he never asked me to lend him any money; that I never knew he wanted to borrow any. I did not know he was short. I made a statement to him, showing the transaction, and what there was due on it; that, deducting the bond dividend and the cash dividend, there was $329 due him, for which I had given him a check; that he had never asked me to loan him any money, and I never loaned him any.

Q. After you had made that statement, what did he state in reply?—A. He wanted to have it go as a loan.

Q. Did he claim that it was in fact a loan?—A. No, sir; I do not think he did. No, he did not.

Q. Go on and state, then, what was said—all the discussion that took place.—A. I cannot tell you all; we had three or four talks. I cannot remember all that was said.

Q. How long after that transaction did he go to Europe?—A. I believe it was a year or two.

Q. Did you have any conversation in reference to the influence this transaction would have upon the election last fall?—A. Yes; he said it would be very injurious to him.

Q. What else in reference to that?—A. I am a very bad man to repeat conversation; I cannot remember.

Q. State all that you know in reference to it.—A. I told him he knew very well that that was a dividend. I made out a statement, and showed it to him at the time. In one conversation he admitted it, and said, as near as I can remember, that there was $2,400 due him in stock and bonds. He made a little memorandum of $1,000 and $1,400, and, as I recollect, said there was $1,000 of Union Pacific Railroad stock, $1,000 of Credit Mobilier stock, and $400 of stock or bonds, I do not recollect what.

Q. When was that memorandum made?—A. It was made in my room; I cannot remember the date. It was since this investigation commenced.

Q. Was it in that conversation that he referred to the influence this matter would have upon the election in his district?—A. I do not recollect whether it was in that one or some other. I have had two or three conversations with him.

Q. Tell us, as nearly as you can, precisely the remarks he made in that connection.—A. It was that it would injure his reputation; that it was a cruel thing. He felt very bad, was in great distress, and hardly knew what he did say.

Q. Did he make any request of you to make no statement in reference to it?—A. I am not positive about that.

Q. What is your best recollection in reference to it?—A. My impression is, that he wanted to say as little about it as he could, and to get off as easily as he could. That was about the conversation I had with him, about the long and short of it.

Q. Have you the memorandum that Mr. Garfield made?—A. I have the figures that he made.

Paper shown to the committee, containing figures as follows:

"$1,000
1,400
———
2,400"

Q. You say these figures were made by Mr. Garfield?—A. Yes, sir.

Q. What do these sums represent? How did he put them down?—A. $1,000 Union Pacific Railroad stock, $1,000 Credit Mobilier stock, and $400 which he could not remember whether it was to be in cash, stock, or bonds.

Q. Is that what he had received, or what he was entitled to?—A. What he was entitled to.

Q. That was his idea of what was coming to him?—A. Yes, sir.

Q. Was that about what he would have been entitled to?—A. He would have been entitled to the $1,000 in stock, and he would have been entitled to more than that. The $400 I think he is in error about. I gave him $329; I do not know whether the $400 referred to that.

Q. Did he put this down as his recollection of the statement you made to him?—A. I so understood it.

By Mr. MERRICK:

Q. It was in this conversation that these figures were made—that he deprecated the effect of the matter upon his election?—A. I do not know about his election; it was about his prospects, his reputation, &c.

Q. I understand that, in substance, he desired you to say as little as possible about it?—A. Yes, sir; and that is my desire.

Q. Will you repeat just about what he did say?—A. I cannot remember the conversation well enough to repeat it.

Q. You can repeat the substance of it?—A. I have given you the substance of it.

Q. How did you happen to retain that little stray memorandum?—A. I do not know. I found it on my table two or three days afterward. I did not pay any attention to it at the time, until I found there was to be a conflict of testimony, and I thought that might be something worth preserving.

Q. This conversation was in your room and the figures made there?—A. Yes, sir.

Q. Do I understand you that this loan which Mr. Garfield claims to have been made was in reference to a trip to Europe taken by him a year or two afterward?—A. I do not know when he took his trip. I know he did not go during that session of Congress. This payment was made to him during that session of 1867-'68.

Q. Do you know whether he went during that recess following?—A. I cannot say. I do not know.

Q. Do you not know that he did not go to Europe for nearly two years afterward?—A. No, I do not. It is my impression it was two years afterward, but I cannot remember dates. People ask me about things that occurred a year ago, and I cannot tell whether it was ten years ago or one.

By the CHAIRMAN:

Q. Did you understand in this conversation you had with General Garfield that you detailed to him the history of this matter as to how the statement you had let him have was made up; and did you understand him to concede your statement about it to be the truth?—A. Well, I cannot say. He would not have been very apt to recollect the amount there was due him if he had not acceded to my statement.

Q. From the whole conversation—from what he said and the figures that he made, did you understand him to concede the statement you had made to him as about the truth?—A. Yes; I so understood him.

Q. That statement you made to him was in substance the statement you have made to us in reference to him?—A. Yes, sir.

Q. Have you had any conversations with Judge Kelley upon this subject during this investigation?—A. I have had some conversations with him—yes, sir.

Q. Will you state what they were?

The WITNESS. When do you mean? before his testimony, or since, or both?

The CHAIRMAN. Both.

A. Mr. Kelley spoke to me about this matter, and said he called it a loan; he said he had stated it was a loan, and then wanted to pay me the amount. I told him that I did not so consider it—that I had let him have $750 on account of the dividends that I held. He wanted to call it a loan and wanted to repay me. He said he would give me a check on his bank, and wanted to know when he should date it. I told him that I did not know that it would make any difference, and he gave me a check for $1,000. That was before any testimony had been given, but after the investigation was ordered. I tore the check in two and handed it back to him and called it a payment.

Q. Did you understand that Mr. Kelley wanted to give you a check for $1,000 that he wished you to retain?—A. I did not consider that I had any business to retain it.

Q. Did you consider that the proposition made to you was that you should really get the money on that check?—A. I do not know but he may have so understood it. I did not consider that it belonged to me, and I tore it up and handed it back to him.

Q. What did he say when you did that?—A. We both appeared to be satisfied with the transaction.

Q. Do you say that he called the loan repaid after you did that?—A. I did not talk with him about it afterward.

Q. Was this thing done in a passion between you?—A. O, no, sir; it was done in no unfriendly spirit. If a man is in a passion with me I do not generally give him a check of $1,000.

Q. He gave you one?—A. That was in payment of a loan.

Q. We want to know precisely what that transaction was?—A. I have told you what it was. I suppose it was so that Mr. Kelley could say that he had paid that $1,000.

Q. Did you understand when he gave that check to you that he gave it with the expectation that you should return it to him?—A. I cannot say.

Q. Did you so understand it when that was done?—A. I have told you what was said.

By Mr. MERRICK:

Q. Did you receive it as a *bona-fide* check, which was to be paid in canceling the transaction between you?—A. I did not consider that he owed me anything. I had no business with Mr. Kelley's check of $1,000.

Q. You told him so?—A. Yes, sir.

Q. Did he deny the transaction being as you claimed it?—A. No, sir.

By the CHAIRMAN:

Q. He wanted to call it something else?—A. That is my idea. I may be mistaken.

Q. Is that the way you understood him?—A. He wanted to be clear from this transaction. That was the idea; so that he could say he had not any interest in it.

Q. You did, however, state to him what the transaction was, and give a history of it as you gave it to us?—A. No, sir; I did not state that to him. He knew the history of it as well as I did.

Q. You stated to him that it was not a loan?—A. Yes, sir. He might call the $750 a loan. I gave him the money without taking any note or receipt for it. When a man loans money he usually takes a note or receipt.

Q. When you paid him that $750, did you understand that it was to be considered on account of his dividends?—A. Yes, sir.

Q. Did you state to him in this conversation that you had not loaned him any money, but that you had paid it over to him on his stock?—A. I do not know whether I did or not.

Q. Did he not understand that that was what you claimed?—A. I suppose he did.

Q. You told him he did not owe you anything, and he understood that was the claim you made?—A. I suppose so, and he never disputed it.

Q. You can say whether when he drew this check and handed it to you, you think he did it with any serious expectation that you were going to keep the check and get the money?—A. I do not think he did, and still I did not ask him. I expect he did it for the purpose of being able to say that he did not own any of this stock when called on to testify before this committee.

Q. He did not express any surprise when you tore up the check, but was apparantly satisfied?—A. He did not say he was not; he evinced no astonishment.

Q. And you think the transaction, taking place as it did, was one he expected to call a payment of the loan?—A. I supposed so; that was my supposition.

By Mr. MERRICK:

Q. In this conversation with Mr. Garfield, was anything said by him to you about your being an old man near the end of your career, and of his being comparatively a young man?—A. No, sir; nothing of that sort.

By Mr. McCRARY:

Q. You had an envelope the other day in which, you stated, Mr. Allison returned his stock, and the postmark on which shows it was mailed in Dubuque in March; the year was not given?—A. No, sir.

Q. You were in error then, in your first statement, in saying that he returned his stock last fall?—A. Yes, sir; according to the postmark. As I told you, I cannot remember dates. It may have been three years ago, and still I might have thought it was last fall.

Q. You have no reason to doubt the correctness of the postmark on the envelope?—A. No, sir; I do not expect, of course, that that was a forgery.

WASHINGTON, D. C., *January* 29, 1873.

JAMES BROOKS, recalled at his own instance, read the following statement:

Mr. Brooks desires to make record of the fact—

That in the *printed* exhibit of the supreme court of Pennsylvania,

January term, 1868, (No. 19, equity,) in the suit McComb *vs.* the Credit Mobilier of America, was filed a sworn list of the Credit Mobilier stockholders, dated December 12, 1867, and that in the list is Charles H. Neilson, one hundred shares, and Charles H. Neilson, fifty shares; and that therefore nearly three months before Mr. Brooks became Government director it was a matter of notoriety in the highest court of Pennsylvania that Mr. Neilson owned one hundred and fifty shares in his own name and right.

Mr. Brooks also desires to make matter of record the names of all the Government directors, when he was one of them, such names as Hon. George Ashman, of Massachusetts; Hon. James S. Rollins, of Missouri; Hon. Jesse L. Williams, of Indiana; Hon. Ben. Wade, of Ohio, and others; and to the facts on the record of the Union Pacific Railroad books, that these directors generally, if not always, were in accord with him (Mr. Brooks) as to the duties they owed to the Government and to the road; and that during that time Hon. John A. Dix, governor of New York, was president of the road, and the late United States Senator, Hon. E. D. Morgan, of New York, one of the trustees of the bonds of said company.

Mr. Brooks also calls attention to his resolution in the October meeting, 1872, of the Union Pacific Railroad directors, in which he demands the revocation of the Wyoming Coal Company contract, and that his resolution prevailed, with but one dissenting voice.

By. Mr. MERRICK:

Question. What was the duration of your commission, which you received as Government director?—Answer. I was appointed 1st October, 1867, but I was not sworn in until March 23, 1868, and my commission expired October 1, 1868.

Q. You stated at your former examination that your commission was in October, 1867; that you were not sworn in till March 23, 1868; did you not receive another commission the 11th March, 1868, under which you were sworn in?

The WITNESS. Commission from whom?

Mr. MERRICK. Under the Government, from the same authority under which you were first commissioned.—A. I am quite sure there could not have been such a commission. I was searching the books of the Interior Department, the other day, to find out everything in connection with that subject, and I recollect seeing no such thing.

Q. I understand, then, that you were not commissioned twice, but that your first commission was anterior to the date of your being sworn in?—A. I recollect no commission except that of October, 1867; I do not see why there should have been another. I may have had notice that I must either accept or not accept; that I must either be sworn in or not be sworn in, or something of that sort.

Q. I have been advised that there was a commission on the 11th March, as well as on the 1st October, 1867, and I therefore asked the question.—A. The records of the Department at which I have looked show that I was sworn in 23d March, and I have a letter from Mr. Cowan, Acting Secretary of the Interior, to that effect, after a thorough search of all the papers.

By Mr. NIBLACK:

Q. Why were you not duly qualified, under your commission of October 1, before March?—A. I stated in my first examination that there was discord in the board, and that I did not want to get into a row.

Q. Were you not recommissioned in October, 1868?—A. No; I was never recommissioned. The Government directors held on until their successors were appointed. I held on until soon after General Grant came in, when my successor was appointed. I have already stated that I was very much disinclined to go into the board as a Government director, but that I went in because I had promised to go. I made great sacrifices, personally, in going in.

By the CHAIRMAN:

Q. If I remember your testimony you stated that you had no knowledge in reference to this paper that was gotten up and signed by the shareholders of the Credit Mobilier authorizing the issuing of these fifty shares?—A. I never heard of it until since this investigation commenced.

Q. You never saw the paper?—A. I never saw it and never heard of it, and never knew of the existence of such a paper.

Q. Have you ever seen that paper?—A. Not until yesterday, when the reporter showed me a copy of it.

Q. How your name came to be used in it you have no knowledge?—A. Not the least, except as a matter of guess-work, and you can guess as well as I from the testimony that has been elicited here. I have not the least idea, unless from the general conversation in the office, and the constant talk, in which it may have been stated that Durant's shares were Brooks's shares; in the haste of preparation the clerks drawing up such a paper may have inserted my name instead of that of Neilson. But there is nothing in that, I repeat again. It is demonstrated by this record of the court of Pennsylvania that Neilson at that time had one hundred shares standing in his name, and fifty additional shares standing in his name.

Q. I did not understand that the books show Neilson as becoming the owner of the fifty shares until some time late in February.—A. February 29, 1868; and he got his other shares, the one hundred shares, December 26, 1867.

Q. This printed paper purports to give a list of the shareholders the 12th December. That was prior to the transfer to Neilson of the one hundred shares?—A. I can account for that by supposing, which would not be at all unusual, that the records of the Credit Mobilier would show the transaction when it was agreed upon, although the stock might not have been actually transferred until a later period. Sometimes a man does not actually get his stock for months after he is the owner of it.

Q. At the time of the negotiation which ended in the adjustment of your claim, by which you or Neilson was to have the hundred shares, was there nothing said in relation to fifty additional shares?—A. No; he was to have all the rights the one hundred shares were entitled to. There was nothing said specifically upon that subject that I remember. I know I was very much dissatisfied with the settlement; I thought that I ought to have, or that Neilson ought to have, two hundred shares instead of the one hundred.

Q. Did you not receive as compensation for the additional shares $25,000 of the Union Pacific Railroad securities?

The WITNESS. What $25,000?

The CHAIRMAN. Two hundred shares Union Pacific Railroad stock and $5,000 bonds?—A. No, sir; Mr. Neilson did—not I.

Q. That was by special agreement?—A. That was by special agreement.

Q. It was not because these securities went with the stoek as belonging to it?—A. Doctor Durant settled the matter in his own way; I remember very little of the transaction.

Q. In the transaction between you and Mr. Durant, which resulted in this adjustment or settlement, was it understood that you were entitled to fifty shares additional upon the one hundred shares?—A. I do not recollect any conversation between us on that subject. In point of fact, I was extremely ignorant of the affairs of the Credit Mobilier.

Q. Mr. Durant says there was nothing of that kind understood; that the one hundred shares were not entitled to the accretion of fifty additional shares.—A. It seems, by the testimony that has been given, that there was no question on the part of the company as to Mr. Neilson's right to the fifty shares. The only question was whether it should come from Mr. Durant or from the company, and that was a point in dispute of which I knew nothing, but it seems to have led to the signing of this paper.

Q. Have you made any examination of your papers, so as to give any further information in relation to the money you advanced Mr. Neilson, or as to whether you did advance it for him?—A. I loaned him money; there is no doubt of that. I showed my check-book the other day, in which it appeared that there must be some mistake in the statement of Mr. Crane about my check of $7,000. I am quite sure I advanced the money, but it may have been in the form of some other person's check. It is very unimportant whether it was or not. I loaned Neilson the $10,000.

Q. Can you state anything more in relation to the $5,000 which Mr. Neilson says he borrowed from Mr. Dillon to pay for the fifty shares?—A. I never knew anything of the transaction.

Q. Have you examined your papers so as to be able to state whether you paid that money to Mr. Dillon?—A. I have looked over everything I had, and have seen no symptom of it; nothing in my check-book, and nothing in my memorandum-book. As I testified the other day, I am very sure I never paid it to Mr. Dillon.

Q. Do you keep no account between yourself and Neilson?—A. It is a very rough, slovenly account. We have a general understanding in regard to our dealings, but it is a rough, slovenly account. I have a great many transactions with him and he with me. I have transactions of this sort, if you will allow me to state them: On the night of October 4, after I had gone home, very late at night, (I had been addressing some of my constituents,) a man, who is the money-writer of my paper, stated to me that he had news from Washington which would enable me to make any amount of money the next day, if I acted early in the day, before the information became known in Wall street. The information was that on the Monday following an order would be issued from the Treasury Department inflating the currency, I think, four or five millions, increasing the sales of gold four or five millions, and increasing the purchase of bonds four or five millions, making about thirteen millions in all of inflation, which would go into the Bank of Commerce and the Fourth National Bank of New York. Everybody knew that if the currency of New York was to be inflated the Monday following thirteen millions of dollars, to be deposited in two banks, that stocks must go up any amount. In point of fact, the stocks on Wall street did go up in the aggregate $40,000,000 within a few days. I said to the money-writer of my paper that I could not go down town in the morning, but that he might take to my son-in-law, Mr. Neilson, blank checks of mine for a limited amount, and that with that he could make any amount of money he pleased. Until the other day when he was here, I supposed he had made four or five thousand dollars out of it, which any man who had the information I had could very easily have done. Any man using a large amount of capital could have made tens of thousands and hundreds of thousands. I was very sorry he did not act upon that information, as he certainly would have done if I had gone down town the next morning.

Q. With these large dealings between you and Mr. Neilson, do you keep no account of them?—A. I keep little books like this memorandum-book I showed you the other day.

Q. Nothing that you have found on your books or papers gives you any information of having paid $5,000 to Mr. Dillon to cancel this loan?—A. Nothing whatever.

Q. And you have no recollection or belief that you did?—A. I know I did not. There is no reason why I should.

WASHINGTON, *January* 30, 1873.

THOMAS C. DURANT, having been recalled at his own instance, made the following statement:

Mr. John B. Alley prefaced his testimony on the 7th day of January instant, in his examination before your committee, with what he calls a "few observations." His statements are so at variance with the actual facts as to the two corporations, and so untrue and unjust to individuals, both living and deceased, that I avail myself of the privilege you have granted me of replying to the same, which I do, supported by the records, to which I shall constantly make my appeal, in the belief that these rash statements should not be suffered to go out to the world without the refutation which the record of the history of the Union Pacific Railroad abundantly furnishes.

This company was organized by the election of a board of thirty directors, on the 29th day of October, 1863, upon a subscription to its stock of $2,180,000, on which an installment of 10 per cent. was paid. In the following spring its charter was amended by Congress. In the fall of the year 1863, the company commenced operations by breaking ground at Omaha, and prosecuted the work until its resources were exhausted, and contracted large obligations. Finding it impossible to proceed in the work on their own part, a committee was appointed on the 12th day of May, 1864, to negotiate a contract for the construction of one hundred miles of their railway. On the 8th day of August, 1864, H. M. Hoxie proposed to build the same for $50,000 per mile, subscribing for a portion of the stock. This proposition was accepted. A copy of this contract I submit, marked A.

Unable to secure the assistance of gentlemen of sufficient capital to enable him to execute the contract, he was about to abandon it, when I proposed to guarantee him against loss, and find those who were able and willing to take up the work and carry it forward. A subscription was circulated to obtain names of parties willing to take an interest in the contract, fixing the aggregate amount to be furnished at $1,600,000.

I submit a copy to you, marked B.

The subscribers paid 25 per cent. of their subscriptions, and this amount was expended on the work. The second installment being called for, many failed to respond, being doubtful of the success of the enterprise, and of a return of their investment, and fearful lest, acting as copartners, they would individually incur large liability. It therefore became necessary to devise some measure for limiting the liability of these parties to the amount they were willing to risk in the enterprise. For this purpose the Credit Mobilier of America, a Pennsylvania corporation of ample powers, was made use of. On the 15th day of March, 1865, that corporation, by an agreement in that behalf, assumed to carry out and guarantee the performance of Hoxie's contract. That contract was by him assigned to a trustee, who afterward assigned it to said corporation.

Copies are submitted, marked C.

The parties who had taken interest in the Hoxie contract transferred their subscriptions, and others were procured, amounting to upward of $2,000,000, to that corporation, and it proceeded with the work. At the time of making this contract the country was involved in civil war; iron was high, labor difficult to obtain, the Indians troublesome, transportation expensive, the only means of communication being by the tedious and uncertain navigation of the Missouri River, and no railroad communication through the State of Iowa, the price of gold being 145.

Government bonds to be issued to the company, being payable in currency, were of doubtful market-value, and the company's securities were unsalable. The company was not in a position to hold the contractors to their agreement, having failed on its part to comply with the requirements of the same, and the parties interested in the Hoxie contract were largely in advance. Thus it was by force of unforeseen circumstances that the Credit Mobilier became connected with the construction of the road, and built two hundred and forty-seven miles. Without the aid of this company, or some other formed for similar purposes, the railroad could not have been built at that time. Such construction companies have since been used in all important railway operations.

Mr. Ames, Mr. Alley, and their friends were not original subscribers in the Union Pacific, their only interest in the said company being acquired by them as contractors or as stockholders in the Credit Mobilier. At the October election of directors, in 1866, of the Union Pacific Railroad Company, and after the completion of the Hoxie contract, several of these gentlemen were elected into its direction. On the 5th day of January, 1867, at a meeting of the directors of the railroad company, the following resolution was passed:

"*Resolved*, That the Union Pacific Railroad Company will, and do hereby, consider the Hoxie contract extended to the point already completed, viz, 305 miles west from Omaha, and that the officers of this company are hereby authorized to settle with the Credit Mobilier at fifty thousand dollars per mile for the additional fifty-eight miles."

Against this I entered the following protest:

"*To the board of directors of the Union Pacific Railroad Company:*

"GENTLEMEN: I protest against the passage of the resolution, appearing on your minutes as passed January 5, 1867, purporting to treat and consider the Hoxie contract as extended to the point already completed, namely, three hundred and five (305) miles west of Omaha, and authorizing the officers of the company to settle with the Credit Mobilier at fifty thousand dollars per mile for the additional fifty-eight miles. Said resolution was moved and adopted while I was absent from the meeting of the board on necessary business of the company. I make this protest on the ground that said fifty-eight miles has been constructed at much less cost than fifty thousand dollars per mile, and has been accepted by the

United States Government as complete, and that it was not constructed under the Hoxie contract, and that a considerable portion of the cost thereof had been paid by the company before the adoption of said resolution, and that said resolution does not provide any compensation or advantage to the company by requiring stock subscriptions or stipulations for the construction of additional portions of the company's railroad, or by any other means or stipulations whatsoever, but leaves the company to sustain a very great and unrequited loss.

"Respectfully, yours,

"THOMAS C. DURANT."

I also obtained an injunction from the New York supreme court, restraining the board of directors from carrying out the said resolution; whereupon they rescinded it. On the 1st of March, 1867, Mr. J. M. S. Williams presented a proposition to build a portion of the road, commencing at the 100th meridian, covering the said fifty-eight miles; also, an additional number of miles already built. The board accepted the same by resolution, and on the 27th of March I again protested against their action, as appears by the following:

"UNION PACIFIC RAILROAD COMPANY,
"PRESIDENT'S OFFICE, NO. 20 NASSAU STREET,
"*New York, March* 27, 1867.

"*To the directors of the Union Pacific Railroad Company:*

"GENTLEMEN: I protest against the resolution of the board of directors passed at your last meeting, which proposes to give the contract of the road of this company, commencing at the 100th meridian of longitude, for the reason that a section of the road already accepted is included in the contract, and it does not appear that this company derives any benefit adequate to the price paid over the cost of construction, by the purchase of securities or otherwise, and does not in the future require, as an essential point in the contract, the completion of the road within the shortest possible time; and for other reasons named in a previous protest relative to the extension of the 'Hoxie contract,' at the rate of fifty thousand dollars per mile for that portion of the road completed and accepted by the Government commissioners.

"I beg to call your attention again to the fact that a part of this road has been done for months, and contracts made and materials delivered for nearly 150 miles of road which the company have paid for, as will be shown by the books.

"Respectfully,

"T. C. DURANT."

On motion of Mr. McComb, my protest was ordered to be received and filed, but not entered on the minutes.

Mr. Williams had agreed to assign his contract, when made, to the Credit Mobilier. Again I sued out an injunction from the New York supreme court, restraining the board from making said contract. That injunction still stands undissolved. I filed an amended complaint in the action, stating "that I was willing to consent to such a contract as is proposed only upon the consideration that the same is approved by all the stockolders of the Union Pacific Railroad Company," some of whom were not members of the Credit Mobilier. As I have already stated, at the October election persons holding a large amount of stock in the Credit Mobilier became directors in the Union Pacific, so that contracts between the two corporations were, in fact, contracts of one person with himself.

I deemed it my duty, as an officer of the Union Pacific, to do all in my power to protect the interests of those of the stockholders who were not stockholders in the Credit Mobilier. I knew my course was not approved by Mr. Alley and his friends. They seemed to consider all sums saved to the Union Pacific as robbed from them, as stockholders in the Credit Mobilier; and here was the issue joined between us. Of course I was not a popular candidate at their next election in May, and I do not object to Mr. Alley's term, "ousted," in that connection. Since that day the Credit Mobilier has had nothing to do with the construction of the Pacific Railway.

Mr. Alley, in his statement, says: "That Durant, McComb, and their supporters believed that everything that could be made must be made in the construction of the road," &c.

In this statement he has, with unparalleled impudence, attributed to Mr. Ames and his party the views and policy of their opponents. My protests and complaints before the courts, made to protect the interests of the stockholders, are the best evidence of what my views and actions were at the time. I strenuously resisted their efforts to make an enormous sum of money on the construction of the work, rather than to secure an investment profitable in the legitimate earnings of the road. These gentlemen, soon after they had acquired a voice in the direction, developed several plans which increased the cost of construction to the railroad company.

One of these plans was the payment of large commissions to themselves for loans to the company, or procuring for it such loans, Locomotives which had been purchased at Government sale of condemned property, and being repaired, were forced upon the company by Oakes Ames.

They well knew that the one hundred and fifty miles of the road next west of the one hundredth meridian was being built for about $20,000 per mile, exclusive of equipment and station-houses. This appears from the Boomer contract, Gesner, agent, under which the work was done, of which contract I furnish a copy, marked D. This contract, made by me, but never formally recognized by the board, except by payments under it, shows my anxiety to secure the construction of the road at a low figure, in which I was sustained by the advice of General Dix, the president, and John J. Cisco, the treasurer, and other conservative members of the board.

Mr. Alley testifies to what he calls great irregularities in management by me of the affairs of the Credit Mobilier.

The facts are simply these: In order, as I suppose, to influence the next election of the board of directors of the Union Pacific Railroad Company, an account was stated by them, improperly charging me with many items, and neglecting to credit me with others to which I was entitled, so that they placed me in a false position.

Mr. Hazard, one of their number, instituted a suit in the courts of Rhode Island, based upon said accounts. In refutation of these charges, and to show how outrageous was the account, as stated by them, I introduce affidavits filed in said suit of Sidney Dillon, their president, Mr. Ham, their assistant treasurer, and Henry C. Crane, of which the following are copies:

"In the supreme court of the State of Rhode Island—in equity.

"*Isaac P. Hazard* vs. *Thomas C. Durant et al. Suits Nos.* 1 *and* 2.

"AFFIDAVIT OF SIDNEY DILLON.

"*City and County of New York, ss:*

"Sidney Dillon, being duly sworn, says: That he was president of the Credit Mobilier of America, from May, 1867, to the present time, and a member of the railway bureau of said corporation from July 27, 1865; that deponent has examined Schedule E, in above suit No. 2, annexed to the bill of complaint therein.

"That, according to his knowledge and belief, all the items in said Schedule E were payments by, for, or on account of, the Union Pacific Railroad Company, and none of them for or on account of the Credit Mobilier of America, and that all said items were charged by the Credit Mobilier of America to the Union Pacific Railroad Company, and were acknowledged by said railroad company, and allowed in a general settlement and adjustment of accounts between said two corporations, and said Credit Mobilier of America has no charge or claim against any other person therefor.

"That the Gesner drafts in said bill of complaint mentioned were never in the accounts of the Credit Mobilier of America, and never belonged there, and that said drafts were paid by the Union Pacific Railroad Company, and, when paid, were charged by the last-named company to said Gesner, agent.

"SIDNEY DILLON.

"In the supreme court of Rhode Island—in equity.

"*Isaac P. Hazard et al.* vs. *Thomas C. Durant et al. Nos.* 1 *and* 2.

"AFFIDAVIT OF HENRY C. CRANE.

"*City and County of New York, ss:*

"Henry C. Crane, being duly sworn, says: That he was assistant treasurer of the Credit Mobilier of America, from the time of its establishment in New York until May, 1867, and was well acquainted with the affairs of the Union Pacific Railroad Company until 1869; that deponent has seen a copy of Exhibit E, attached to the bill in suit No. 2; that all the items in said Exhibit E, under date of 1864, were payments made by the Union Pacific Railroad Company on demands against it, and not by or for the Credit Mobilier of America, and that the last-named corporation had not, at any of said dates, money or means to any such amounts; that the books of the Credit Mobilier of America do not contain any entry showing that said Thomas C. Durant received of said corporation any of the sums mentioned in said Exhibit E, and that, in fact, said Thomas C. Durant did not receive the same, nor any part thereof; that said T. C. Durant had no interest in the $46,000 mentioned in the bill of complaint in suit No. 2; that deponent received that sum as trustee, and disposed thereof according to the direction of the board of directors of said corporation, in discharge of claims upon it for preliminary expenses, and it was paid out by deponent under said authority, and said Durant had nothing to do with such disbursement thereof; and that the said sum came to deponent's hands by virtue of a resolution of the board of directors of said company, at a meeting thereof in Philadelphia, October 20, 1864, at which meeting the said Durant was not present, of which resolution the following is a copy:

"'On motion, the treasurer of the company, or assistant treasurer, be, and he is hereby, authorized to pay forty-six thousand dollars to H. C. Crane, trustee, New York, for preliminary expenses of the company.'

"That a large amount was earned by Mr. Hoxie, on his contract, for labor and materials, prior to December 31, 1864, and the same appears by the estimate of the Union Pacific Railroad Company's engineer in charge, of which a copy is hereto annexed; that all which was so earned and remained unpaid to that date was allowed by the Credit Mobilier of America to said Hoxie, and paid pursuant to the agreement between said corporation and said Hoxie, and was collected by said corporation from the Union Pacific Railroad Company.

"That Thomas C. Durant at various times advanced money to said Union Pacific Railroad Company, and also to said Credit Mobilier of America, from time to time, as each required it, and said several corporations, from time to time, made payments on said loans.

"That the $35,000 of bonds mentioned in the bill came to Thomas C. Durant from the Credit Mobilier of America as collateral security upon a loan of $25,000 made thereto by said Durant, and he received the same as such pledge in good faith, and rightfully controls the same as security for said loan, which remains unpaid.

"That the item $25,000, in Exhibit E of bill in suit No. 2, was money paid to Cornelius S. Bushnell by the Credit Mobilier of America, and for which said Bushnell's receipt was taken at the time, and still is held therefor; and the same was so paid to said Bushnell on account of interest and commissions on a loan of $1,000,000.

"H. C. CRANE.

"Sworn to before me this 8th day of August, A. D. 1870.

[SEAL.] "EDWIN F. COREY,

"*Commissioner for the State of Rhode Island in New York.*

[Copy.]

"UNION PACIFIC RAILROAD COMPANY.

"THIRD MONTHLY ESTIMATE.

"*To the contractors for building the first hundred miles.*

"DECEMBER 31, 1864.

"Ten miles grading and bridging completed east of the Elkhorn River, at $50,000	$500,000	
"19,500 ties, at 50 cents	9,750	
		$509,750 00
"Deduct for unfinished work, as follows:		
"Station-buildings, equipments, &c., per mile	5,000	
"Iron ties, spikes, chains, and track-laying	15,700	
"Ten miles deducted, at $20,700 per mile	207,000	
"Two miles' bridging deducted, at $7,000 per mile	14,000	
"Disbursements made by company	47,176	
		268,176 00
		241,574 00

"WEST OF ELKHORN RIVER.

"6 miles completed, at $50,000		$300,000	
"Deduct for station-buildings, equipments, iron, ties, spikes, chains, and track-laying, as above	$20,700		
"Bridging	1,800		
"Difference in grading west of Elkhorn	5,500		
	28,000		
"6 miles deducted, at $28,000 per mile		168,000	
			$132,000 00
"10 miles nearly completed, at $50,000		500,000	
"Deduct for station-buildings, equipments, iron, ties, spikes, chains, track-laying, bridging, and extra costs for grading	28,000		
"Amount required to finish	1,000		
	29,000		
"10 miles at amount required to finish, at $29,000 per mile		290,000	
			210,000 00
			583,574 00
"Add for extra work, as directed by the special committee of the board			168,874 45
			752,448 45
"Deduct November estimate			544,954 45
			207,494 00

"OMAHA, *December* 31, 1864.

"I hereby certify that the above estimate to the contractors for building the first hundred miles of the Union Pacific Railroad, amounting to two hundred and seven thousand four hundred and ninety-four dollars, is correct.

"J. E. HOUSE,
"*Division Engineer.*

"H. C. CRANE.

"In the supreme court of the State of Rhode Island.

"*Isaac P. Hazard* vs. *Thomas C. Durant* et al. *In Equity. Suits Nos.* 1 *and* 2.

"CITY AND COUNTY OF NEW YORK, *ss:*

"Benjamin F. Ham, being duly sworn, says: That he was assistant secretary and assistant treasurer of the Credit Mobilier of America, and auditor of the Union Pacific Railroad Company, from May, 1867, to May, 1869; that during that period deponent had charge of the books of account of both said corporations; that deponent has examined Schedule E in above suit No. 2, annexed to the bill of complaint therein.

"That all the items in said Schedule E were payments by, for, or on account of, the Union Pacific Railroad Company, and none of them for or on account of the Credit Mobilier of America, and that all said items were charged by the Credit Mobilier of America to the Union Pacific Railroad Company, and were acknowledged by said railroad company and allowed in a general settlement and adjustment of accounts between said two corporations; and said Credit Mobilier of America has no charge or claim against any other person therefor.

"That the Gesner drafts in said bill of complaint mentioned were never in the accounts of the Credit Mobilier of America, and never belonged there, and that said drafts were paid by the Union Pacific Railroad Company, and, when paid, were charged by the last-named company to said Gesner, agent.

"BENJAMIN F. HAM.

"Subscribed and sworn to this 24th day of August, 1870.

"In witness whereof I have hereto signed my name and affixed my official seal, the day and year first above written.

[SEAL.] "GEORGE W. COLLES,

"*Commissioner for Rhode Island, in New York.*"

Mr. Alley states that McComb and friends, finding themselves ousted from the Credit Mobilier, associated themselves with Jim Fisk in a scheme to wrest the road from the rightful owners, and that, to thwart such scheme, they had to raise the enormous sum of fifteen millions of dollars in a single day.

The facts are these:

Mr. Ames, then acting president of the company, gave directions to the treasurer to receive no subscription for stock except when accompanied with payment of the full par value thereof. Thereafter Mr. Alley and his friends proceeded to subscribe for stock. On the first subscription being made, a parcel of greenbacks was produced by the party making subscription, stating to the treasurer that it was a tender of fifty-five per cent. of the amount of the par value of his subscription, which was, of course, refused by the treasurer, as the party well knew it would be. The amount thus pretended to be tendered was not, as I understand, ever counted by the treasurer, but was retained by the party so offering to subscribe, to be used the next minute on another subscription. Among the subscriptions made in such a way at this time are three in the name of John B. Alley, and John B. Alley trustee, amounting in the aggregate to $28,500,000. This farcical subscription and tender thereon was continued for the period of about ten minutes in time, and reached in amount the sum of about sixty millions of dollars. Not a dollar of this money passed into the hands of the company, nor was it intended it should so pass. All this took place about five days before the election of directors. The by-laws of the company provided that no stock could be voted on which had not stood on the books of the company, in the name of the person offering to vote thereon, for ten days previous to the election.

On the day of the election Mr. Alley and his friends, with General B. F. Butler present as their counsel in the stockholders' meeting, passed a resolution amending these by-laws to suit their desire, appointed new inspectors, and opened the polls, the duly-appointed inspectors having previously opened the polls and commenced receiving votes. All parties were enjoined from voting upon subscriptions for stock on which no money had been paid at this election, but I understand General Butler succeeded in some way in getting one of the injunctions modified; the election being carried on in two polls, with two sets of inspectors, in the same room; one ticket representing the old board, and the other that of Mr. Alley and his friends. Each board of inspectors declared their ticket elected. An injunction restraining Mr. Alley's bogus board from acting was at once procured and served on them, to which they gracefully submitted and never moved to dissolve the same.

At the first meeting thereafter of the regular board of directors of the Union Pacific Railroad Company,

Mr. McComb offered the following resolution, which was adopted unanimously:

"Whereas the Hon. John A. Dix, heretofore elected a director and president of this company, has accepted the office of minister plenipotentiary at the court of the Emperor of the French, and is now, and has been for several months past, absent at the post of his duty as such minister, and we are thereby deprived of his valuable aid and services in the management of the company; and

"Whereas, also, C. H. McCormick, of Illinois, and Charles A. Lambard, of Massachusetts, heretofore directors of this company, have also left the country on their necessary and proper business unconnected with the affairs of this company: Therefore

"*Resolved*, That while we deeply regret the loss which we have sustained, and must continue to sustain, from the absence of the gentlemen named, and particularly from the want of the able and wise counsels which General Dix would give, if he were here with us, in the present condition of our affairs, the necessity of having a full board of directors compels us to fill the places made vacant by the absence of the persons mentioned."

On motion of Mr. McComb, Mr. John B. Alley was elected a director of this company, to fill one of the vacancies existing.

On motion of Mr. McComb, Mr. Franklin Gordon Dexter was elected a director of this company, to fill one of the vacancies.

On motion, Benjamin E. Bates was elected a director of the company, to fill one of the vacancies.

Mr. Tuttle here tendered his resignation as a member of the board of directors.

Mr. McComb offered the following resolution, which was adopted:

"*Resolved*, That the resignation of Mr. Tuttle be accepted, and this board tender to Mr. Tuttle their parting regrets, and express their appreciation of his services and his uniformly kind and gentlemanly deportment."

On motion, it was voted that William T. Glidden be elected a director of this company, to fill the vacancy occasioned by the resignation of Mr. Tuttle, and the board thus constituted transacted the business of the company until the next election.

So much for the statement that Durant, McComb, and friends were turned out of the direction and some of them finally re-instated upon a compromise.

Another statement which Mr. Alley makes, the reverse of the facts, is that he was opposed to a distribution of the profits arising under the Ames contract. In contradiction to that, I herewith submit a transcript of the resolution of the board of trustees relative to the said dividend, and showing the vote thereon:

"NEW YORK, *December* 12, 1867.

"Present: Messrs. Ames, Durant, Dillon, McComb, Bushnell, Alley, and Bates.

"Mr. Bushnell offered the following resolution: That the treasurer, Benjamin E. Bates, be authorized and instructed to procure from the Union Pacific Railroad Company at least $2,000,000 of their first-mortgage bonds, and purchase an equal amount of full-paid stock of said company: *Provided*, Said amount shall be found due on account of the contract, and whenever the owners of full-paid stock in the Union Pacific Railroad company shall have signed a written approval of the contract between said company and Oakes Ames, then a division shall be made to the holder of the stock of the Credit Mobilier of America, say 60 per cent. in said bonds and 60 per cent. in said Union Pacific Railroad stock.

"Aye and nay vote being called, carried, six voting aye; Mr. McComb, *no*."

Subsequently it was deemed advisable by the conservative element in the trusteeship that the Union Pacific Railroad Company should have the advantage of keeping all their first-mortgage bonds on hand for the time being, in order to meet their requirements and enable them to raise money, and that the trustees should receive from them in lieu thereof, for division under their trust, certificates entitling the holder to receive first-mortgage bonds from the Union Pacific Railroad Company at some future time, when it might be more convenient for the company to deliver them.

Upon a resolution to adopt this proposition being brought before the trustees, Mr. Alley was the only one who voted *nay*.

Subsequently, at a meeting held on the 3d of January, at which were present Messrs. Ames, Durant, Dillon, McComb, Bushnell, Bates, and Alley, a resolution was offered that a supplemental dividend be made of twenty per cent., in bonds of the Union Pacific Railroad Company; which resolution was adopted, Mr. Bushnell being the only one voting against it.

Upon the occasion of declaring the first dividend, Mr. Alley, in a general conversation, before any resolution was offered, suggested a delay of a few days in making a dividend. I was informed that he was at that time short of stock, having sold, as I have since learned, at about 200, that standing in his own name, in which Mr. Oakes Ames had half interest.

Upon being advised of this circumstance, I gave him a refusal for ten days of 250 shares, at 160. His receipt therefor is already put in before your committee as testimony. Thereupon, a resolution being offered declaring a dividend, Mr. Alley voted in favor of the same, as the record will show. I think the change of views which he experienced shows that his claims for his patriotic and unselfish course, in connection with this enterprise, are as baseless as many of his other statements have been by the record shown to be. This and other transactions of his before the eyes of the other trustees so disgusted the majority of them that his resignation was insisted upon; and it was under such circumstances that he was permitted to put upon the record his letter of resignation, enabling the trustees, in filling the vacancy, to avail themselves of the counsel and advice of Mr. John Duff, a gentleman of great railway experience.

So far from desiring to exclude me from the direction of the road in consequence of any extravagance or mismanagement on my part, the letter which I here present from Oakes Ames to Mr. McComb, dated 17th September, 1867, (at which time I was insisting that every stockholder should assent to any contract for construction which might be made with themselves,) shows the real object of these gentlemen in seeking to exclude me from the direction:

"N. EASTON, *September* 17, 1867.

"H. S. McCOMB, Esq.:

"DEAR SIR: I have called on Governor John A. Andrew, and got his consent to act as one of the Government directors, if he should be appointed; and it is our wish to have him.

"I wish you to put the matter in the hands of Judge Black, if that is the best channel to do it.

"I don't suppose the change will be made until October.

"Hope you will get everything ready to run smooth on the contract.

"I don't feel that we should do right to put Durant in as director, unless he withdraws his injunction suits, and submits to the will of the majority. He cannot hurt us half so badly out of the direction as he can in;

and there is no pleasure, peace, safety, or comfort with him, unless he agrees to abide the decision of the majority, as the rest of us do.

"Yours, truly,

"OAKES AMES."

On the 16th of August, 1867, Mr. Oakes Ames made to the company a written proposition, of which the following is a copy:

"NEW YORK, *August* 16, 1867.

"*To the president and board of directors of the Union Pacific Railroad Company:*

"GENTLEMEN: I propose to construct for your company 667 miles of your road, commencing at the 100th meridian westward, for the following prices, viz: First 100 miles, at $42,000 per mile; second 167 miles, at $45,000 per mile; third 100 miles, at $96,000 per mile; fourth 100 miles, at $80,000 per mile; fifth 100 miles, at $90,000 per mile; sixth 100 miles, at $96,000 per mile; provided the details of a contract can be arranged by a committee of your board and myself satisfactory.

"Respectfully,

"OAKES AMES."

On the same day this proposition was accepted, and referred to the executive committee by the following resolution:

"*Resolved*, That the contracts adopted this day be referred to the executive committee, with authority to settle the details; and when the same is approved by said executive committee, that the president *pro tem.* and secretary are hereby authorized to execute the same in the name of the company."

At the time that this proposition was accepted, it was generally understood that in some way the contract would be placed in other hands for execution, for the benefit of all interested, Mr. Ames's name being used merely as that of John Doe, or Richard Roe, or that of any irresponsible person might have been inserted. And of these facts Mr. Alley must have been aware, for a similar proposition had been made for a contract in which the names of Mr. Alley and Mr. Crane were used; but some objection being made to Mr. Alley, by persons better acquainted with him than I was at that time, his proposition was withdrawn at the same time that Mr. Ames's proposition was made, as the records of the company will show. It was further understood that the assent of all the stockholders in the company should be secured to the execution of the contract; and this alone placed it in their power to dictate how it should be used, although Mr. Ames was not called upon to make any promise as to what he should do with it. The form of a contract was carefully drawn up, and submitted to several of the members of the executive committee for approval as to the details, in order that the several copies of the same might be prepared for execution, ready to be submitted to the whole committee at their first meeting. Among the signers of that approval were Springer Harbaugh and myself. Mr. Harbaugh appended on the same paper, below his signature, to be used in case he was not present at the first meeting, a note addressed to the executive committee, of which the following is a copy:

"*To the Executive Committee:*

"As one of the executive committee, I herewith accompany its acceptance on my part with a letter reserving an option, as expressed in said letter.

"SPRINGER HARBAUGH,

"*Government Director, and one of the Executive Committee.*"

I also append a note, of which the following is a copy:

"AUGUST 18, 1867.

"I recommend the above with the understanding that the assent of all the stockholders is to be obtained.

"T. C. DURANT."

At the first meeting of the executive committee, October 1, 1867, I found upon the books of the company the contract, already executed, between Mr. Oliver Ames, as president of the corporation, and Mr. Oakes Ames, his brother, with our names appended to the same, as being approved *without reservation or condition.* A resolution was immediately offered to approve the contract as above; which resolution was lost. The following resolution was then offered and adopted:

"*Resolved*, That the foregoing contract between the Union Pacific Railroad Company and Oakes Ames, referred to the executive committee by a resolution of the board, August 16, 1867, to settle the details, be approved, and that the proper officers of the company be instructed to execute the same, subject, however, to the written approval of the stockholders of the company, as understood by the board of directors when the same was voted upon."

These records of the executive committee were on the same day submitted to the board, and by the board, by resolution, approved.

Subsequently, and on the 15th of October, Mr. Ames assigned the said contract to seven trustees—the terms of which assignment, and other papers relative thereto, I submit herewith, marked F.

Previous to such assignment of said contract, the board, by resolution, agreed to recognize said assignment, and accepted the guarantee of the Credit Mobilier Company, and to release the said Oakes Ames from all liabilities under the same, referring the details of such assignment to the executive committee. A full release from all liabilities under the contract was duly executed by the proper officers of the company.

The enormous responsibility which Mr. Ames had assumed—amounting, as Mr. Alley says, to $47,000,000—was thus completely wiped out. The risk would have been somewhat modified by the fact that between two and three hundred miles of this road, embraced in this contract, had been actually completed; the difference in price between the actual cost of which and the contract price amounted to upwards of $3,000,000.

In reference to Mr. Alley's testimony relative to the resolution of July, 1868, conferring upon me, as vice-president, full authority to act upon the line of the road, amenable only to the executive committee, and practically ignoring the president and chief engineer, and also his letter purporting to have been written July 25, expressing dissatisfaction with such resolution, and his reference therein to General Dodge, the chief engineer, and the pretended pledges which he and that officer and Mr. Ames have made, I have this to say:

That upon examining the condition of the work, I found that the president had never been on that portion of the line then being constructed; that the chief engineer, under a salary of $10,000 per annum, was also a member of Congress, at that time in Washington, instead of being on the road; and upon my remonstrating against this, I was informed that he could do more good in Washington, where he had great influence. I further found that his wife was the owner of one hundred shares of Credit Mobilier stock, and was, therefore, a large participant in the profits to be made by the contractors. I also found that with the large force of men and teams then employed on the line, (some 20,000 men and 6,000 or 8,000 teams,) the company were liable to be called upon for damages for not having the road located in time for the construction. I issued to the engineers an order, designated as *General Order No.* 1, in which I instructed the consulting engineer of the company, Colonel Silas Seymour, (a man of large experience in locating railroads,) to go over the line in connection with the division engineer, to determine some points as to location, giving him power of chief engineer while that official was absent from duty.

I do not mean to insinuate that I thought that the chief engineer would be unduly influenced in his duties or estimates by any interest which his wife might have in the construction contract. Subsequently, and in the early part of 1869, on my return from the line of the road, I found that $11,000,000 had been paid to the Oakes Ames contractors on account of construction; and I called, by resolution, in the executive committee, upon the treasurer of the company to know by what authority such payment was made.

The following is a transcript of said resolution:

"NEW YORK, *February* 25, 1869.

"On motion of Mr. Durant,

"*Resolved*, That the treasurer report to this committee the authority on which a check for $50,000, dated July 27, 1868, was paid; also, whether there is any deficiency in the cash or bond account of the company; the authority on which the payment of $11,000,000, or thereabouts, was made contractors in January; and also an explanation of the check for $3,000, said to be given for a commission on a loan which was not received."

On the next day, February 26, 1869, the committee received the following report from the treasurer:

"UNION PACIFIC RAILROAD OFFICE,
"*New York, February* 26, 1869.

"In reply to the questions propounded by the executive committee of the company, February 25, 1869, I have to report:

"1. The check for $50,000 referred to, was given on the order of Mr. Ames, president, and Messrs. Bushnell and Alley; said to be for legal expenses.

"2. A deficiency is reported by the accountant, in the cash, said to be the result of an overpayment on a loan. The auditor is now engaged in trying to correct the same. There is also a deficiency of $110,000 in Government bonds; but whether lost, stolen, or in the hands of some party from whom loans have been made, the accountant or assistant treasurer are as yet unable to determine.

"3. The payment of $11,000,000 to the contractors was done by order of the president, on the following certificate of the chief engineer of the amount due the contractors.

"4. The check for $3,000 was given by the assistant treasurer, as he says, by the direction of Mr. Ames, president.

"As to the resolution relating to the bonds, I have given instructions to have the statement made up in full, which I hope to be able to lay before you in a short time.

"Respectfully submitted.

"JOHN J. CISCO, *Treasurer*."

A copy of the engineer's certificate, referred to in said report, I submit herewith, marked E.

It will be seen by this estimate that the chief engineer had included in the amount due, under the Oakes Ames contract, a large amount of work done beyond 667 miles, and for which the board had approved no contract, or submitted the same to the stockholders. At their first meeting, being March 9, 1869, I submitted the following communication:

"NEW YORK, *March* 4, 1869

"*To the executive committee, or the board of directors, of the Union Pacific Railroad Company:*

"GENTLEMEN: I learn that while I was absent on business of the company, payments were made to the assignees of the Oakes Ames contract out of funds of the company for the construction or equipment, or both, on the lines of the road west of the 667 miles mentioned in that contract. As no assent of the stockholders has been given to any contract, or the extension of any contract for construction west of said 667 miles, and no authority exists for such payments, I protest against the same, and demand that all such payments, if made, be recalled, and the sums so paid be restored to the company.

"Respectfully, yours,

"THOMAS C. DURANT."

I also, on the 8th of March, sent the following telegram to the chief engineer:

"MARCH 8, 1869.

"General G. M. DODGE,

"*Chief Engineer, Washington, D. C.:*

"You have so largely overestimated the amount due contractors that it becomes my duty to suspend your acting as chief engineer until you give a satisfactory explanation of the same. A mistake of a trifling amount might occur; but when it gives contractors hundreds of thousands of dollars it creates the suspicion that all is not right. Your immediate attention is requested, in order that if you have an explanation to give, it may be done before the report becomes public.

"T. C. DURANT, *Vice-President.*"

In reply to which I received the following:

WASHINGTON, D. C., *March* 8, 1869.

"To T. C. DURANT, 20 *Nassau Street:*

"The last estimate was made up by data furnished by Mr. Reed and Mr. Crane. If there is any mistake in it I could not detect it, as all of my estimates are made from data furnished by them. I will be in New York to-morrow.

"G. M. DODGE."

It is only necessary here to state that Mr. Reed and Mr. Crane were not in the employ of the railway company, but were both in the employ of the contractors, to show how closely Mr. Ames, Mr. Alley, and the chief engineer were looking after the interests of the road. This estimate was not made by the chief engineer with the intent (as I believe) to defraud the company, but is introduced to show how little he knew of the affairs of the company, when he went beyond the Oakes Ames contract, before any extension thereof or additional contract was approved.

I am aware that I expended more money in building the road than some thought advisable. This I did in order to secure good work. The railroad company was not the loser, for it was to pay a fixed sum per mile, and by my action the contractors only were deprived of a portion of their profits by the increased expenditure.

And in order that there might be no cause of complaint on the part of the public or the Government, I did, upon one occasion, when I heard of the appointment of a new commissioner, send the following telegram to the President of the United States:

"U. P. R. R. Co.,
"*End of track, October* 29, 1868.

"*To the President of the United States, Washington, D. C.:*

"One of the commissioners appointed to re-examine the Union Pacific Railroad, now completed, and also to examine the location of the line west thereof, has been for some time in the employ of this company as civil engineer, and located that portion of the line above referred to. I would, therefore, most respectfully suggest, that the commission be composed entirely of disinterested persons, believing their decision will be more satisfactory to the Government, the stockholders, and the public, and relieve all parties from unfriendly criticism.

"Respectfully, yours,

"THOS. C. DURANT,
"*Vice-President U. P. R. R. Co.*"

Although at some time previous, Mr. Ames, the president, by virtue of a resolution of the board, had appointed an auditor for the accounts in New York, and the details of payment were not in my department, I still considered it my duty, as vice-president, acting under resolution, to inquire occasionally as to their doings.

At a meeting of the executive committee, on the same day on which the treasurer made his report referred to, I offered the following resolution:

"*Resolved*, That the treasurer be called upon to report whether there are any certificates outstanding for Government bonds, on completed sections of the road, for which the company has received the Government bonds, and also if the bonds so received are in the possession of the company, or in any manner disposed of.

"Whether there is not a large amount of our securities remaining in the hands of brokers or other parties on which the loans have been paid.

"That he also be called upon for a statement of the certificates for Government bonds, to whom sold, and the difference between price obtained and the price of Government certificates on the date of sale.

"That he also report whether it has been the habit of the company to give refusals at a price, for any length of time, for the sale of Government bonds, to whom, and by what authority.

"And further, what rates of interest and commissions have been paid on loans, the securities given for the same, and whether such rates or commissions are paid by the contractors or the company, including the amount of loans now outstanding, and the securities now hypothecated for the same."

Mr. McComb offered the following amendment, which was adoped:

"That the treasurer also report the amount of loans carried for individual or individuals, on the bonds of the company, or otherwise, for what length of time the same have been carried, and what amount is now due on such loans."

My resolution was then adopted with the amendment.

At a meeting of the board, March 11, 1869, the road being completed within a few miles, I addressed to it the following communication:

"NEW YORK, *March* 11, 1869.

"*To the board of directors of the Union Pacific Railroad Company:*

"GENTLEMEN: The object of the resolution of the executive committee adopted July 3, 1868, having been fully accomplished, I therefore resign all authority conferred by said resolution or by any resolution of the board.

"Yours, &c.,

"T. C. DURANT."

My resignation was accepted, and the following resolutions were passed virtually annulling the powers of the executive committee:

"On motion of Mr. Alley,

"*Resolved*, That the executive committee shall have no power to make any of its actions final and binding upon the company until reported to and ratified by the board, and any vote or resolution heretofore passed inconsistent herewith is hereby rescinded."

In order still to get at the report, I offered the following resolution:

"On motion of Mr. Durant,

"*Resolved*, That the treasurer be required to furnish the information to this board called for by the executive committee by its resolutions of February 25 and 26, 1869, and that a committee of two be appointed to investigate the matters therein mentioned."

The president appointed Mr. Alley and Mr. Harris said committee.

I have never been able to learn that this committee made a report, although in the settlement of the Oakes Ames contract and the contract known as the Davis contract in extension, the matters of difference on the payments for construction were adjusted, and the company suffered no loss thereby. I submit a copy of the Davis contract, marked "G."

In reference to the accounts mentioned by John B. Alley, as between the Union Pacific Railroad Company and myself, and the suits of I. P. Hazard, I will simply refer to the affidavits filed in said suit of Sidney Dillon, Benjamin F. Ham, and Henry C. Crane, which I have before read in another connection, as well as the affidavits of John J. Cisco, treasurer, John A. Dix, Oliver Ames, the president, Josiah Bardwell, and Cornelius S. Bushnell, which I now submit:

"In the supreme court of the State of Rhode Island.

"ISAAC P. HAZARD ET AL. *vs.* THOMAS C. DURANT ET AL.—IN EQUITY, NOS. 1 AND 2.

"*Affidavit of Oliver Ames.*

"I, Oliver Ames, of North Easton, in the county of Bristol, and Commonwealth of Massachusetts, on oath depose and say that I am the president of the Union Pacific Railroad Company; that in January, 1867, I, together with John J. Cisco, the treasurer of said corporation, was appointed a committee under a resolution of the board of directors of said corporation, a copy of which is hereto annexed, marked A; that prior to the 11th day of September, of that year, I, together with the said Cisco, made all the investigations required by said board of directors, in a manner and to an extent which enabled us satisfactorily to make a report of our doings to said board of directors, a copy of which is hereto annexed, marked B, and that I believe the facts set forth in said report to be true; that upon an examination of

Schedule B, annexed to the bill in equity of Isaac P. Hazard against Thomas C. Durant and others, now pending in the supreme court of the State of Rhode Island, and of Schedule E, annexed to the bill in equity of said Hazard against the said Durant and myself and others, and Credit Mobilier of America and the Union Pacific Railroad Company and Rowland G. Hazard as defendants, I find each of the sums in said schedules to be the same, or in part the same, which formed the suspense-account set forth in our report as such committee, saving and excepting that the item in said suspense-account under date of 1865, December 29th, T. C. Durant $112,000, is in said Exhibit B, attached to said bill of said Hazard, carried out $120,000; further saving and excepting two items in said Exhibit E, annexed to the bill of said Hazard, the one under date of January 25th, 1867, of $30,081, the other under date of March 9, 1867, of $25,000.

"The report thus made by me and Mr. Cisco was accepted by the board of directors.

"OLIVER AMES.

"Subscribed and sworn to before me, a notary public, this 12th day of July, 1870.

[L. S.]

"JOHN R. DUFF,
"*Notary Public.*"

Mr. Lambard offered the following resolution, which was adopted:

"*Resolved,* That Oliver Ames, president *pro tem.*, and John J. Cisco, treasurer, be a committee to inform themselves in regard to the details of the so-called suspense-account of this company; also to audit any further claims on this account, and *that their statement to this board that the facts in the premises are satisfactory to them shall end all further discussion,* and that the accounts shall be closed and charged to construction.

"Meeting of board of directors, January 4, 1867."

[Copy.]

Messrs. Ames & Cisco, a committee appointed by virtue of a resolution passed at a meeting of the board of directors of January 4, 1867, report as follows:

"*Statement of suspense-account.*

1864.			
August	1.	T. C. Durant	$44,549 45
"	25.	T. C. Durant	4,000 00
Sept.	1.	T. C. Durant	66,325 00
"	14.	T. C. Durant	13,128 13
"	14.	T. C. Durant	6,500 00
"	21.	C. S. Bushnell	5,751 63
"	26.	G. T. M. Davis	3,000 00
"	29.	James C. Kennedy	2,000 00
"	29.	Alexander Hay	4,000 00
"	30.	T. C. Durant	50,000 00
"	30.	T. C. Durant	8,000 00
March	21.	T. C. Durant	30,000 00
"	21.	T. C. Durant	5,500 00
"	21.	H. S. McComb	1,000 00

1865.			
Dec.	29.	T. C. Durant	$112,000 00
1866.			
March	30.	Special committee	50,000 00
May	10.	Special committee	20,000 00
			435,754 21

"*To the board of directors of the Union Pacific Railroad Company:*

"The undersigned special committee, appointed by the resolution of this board passed January 4, 1867, respectfully report: That we have informed ourselves as to the details of the accounts of which the foregoing is a settlement, and have found that the several amounts were paid, as above contained, upon proper authority, and that the facts in the premises are satisfactory to us.

(Signed) "OLIVER AMES.
"JOHN J. CISCO.

"NEW YORK, *September* 11, 1867.

"On motion of Mr. McCOMB,

"*Resolved*, That the report of the special committee in respect to certain suspense-accounts be approved and adopted, and that said accounts be closed and charged to construction."

"In the supreme court of Rhode Island, county of Newport.

"ISAAC P. HAZARD ET AL. *vs.* THOMAS C. DURANT ET AL.—IN EQUITY.

"*Affidavit of John A. Dix.*

"John A. Dix, of the city, county, and State of New York, on oath deposes and says, that he was president of the Union Pacific Railroad Company from its first organization under its act of incorporation on the 30th day of October, 1863, until November, 1866, and exercised a general supervision over the affairs of said company and the conduct of its business during the whole of said period; that John J. Cisco was treasurer of said company during said period and subsequently; that this affiant never knew of any sums of money paid by said treasurer out of the funds of said company except upon proper vouchers and under proper authority, according to the rules and regulations of the board of directors, and in the legitimate and proper business of the company; that Thomas C. Durant was vice-president of said company during the whole of said period, and was actively engaged in the construction of said railroad; that this affiant never knew of any sums of money intrusted to said Durant for disbursement which were not fully and satisfactorily accounted for, and that the treasurer had no authority to pay to the vice-president, or to any other person, any sums of money unless upon satisfactory vouchers, approved as required by the regulations of the board of directors; that this affiant was never informed of any claim on behalf of said company against said Thomas C. Durant for moneys not accounted for, and does not believe any such claim ever existed; that no request was ever made to him as president, and none to the board of directors, to his knowledge, to prosecute any such claim by Isaac P. Hazard, or by any other person; and this affiant believes the said Durant to be a man of large means, and amply able to respond to all claims against him.

"JOHN A. DIX.

"COMMONWEALTH OF MASSACHUSETTS, BARNSTABLE, *ss*,
"*Chatham Town, August* 24, 1870:

"There personally appeared John A. Dix and made oath to this, the within written instrument, before me.

[SEAL.] "WARREN ROGERS,
"*Notary Public.*"

"In the supreme court of the State of Rhode Island, for the county of Newport.

"ISAAC P. HAZARD ET AL. *vs.* THOMAS C. DURANT ET AL.—IN EQUITY, NOS. 1 AND 2.

"*Affidavit of John J. Cisco.*

"John J. Cisco, of the city, county, and State of New York, on oath deposes and says that he was treasurer of the Union Pacific Railroad Company from its organization until the removal of the office of the corporation from New York to Boston, in the year 1869; that during that period all sums of money disbursed by said corporation were paid by this affiant, and that no sums were paid without proper vouchers and under proper authority, produced and verified to me as treasurer at the time of such payment; that I have examined the items in the statement, "Exhibit B," annexed to the bill of complaint in the case known as No. 1, and know that the sums therein set forth as having been delivered to Thomas C. Durant were paid at the dates annexed, upon proper vouchers then produced to me, audited by the proper committee, and were entered as having been paid in the proper and legitimate business of said corporation; that subsequently the said items were carried into what was known as a suspense-account, created for the purpose of having the items contained in it apportioned to the divisions of the road to which they were properly chargeable in construction-account; that in January, 1867, Oliver Ames, president of said corporation, and this affiant were appointed a committee to audit and settle said items, a copy of which resolution is hereto annexed; that said committee examined said items, and the vouchers therefor, and found the same satisfactory, and directed the same to be charged to the proper construction-account, and made their report to that effect, bearing date September 11, 1867, a copy of which is hereto annexed; that there was no such item as that of $120,000 in such statement, but under the same date there was an item of $112,000, which is probably the item referred to; that no one of said sums was at any time a proper charge against said Durant, and after said final adjustment they did not appear on the books of said company as claims against any person.

"And he further states that, according to his knowledge, information, and belief, said Thomas C. Durant was never liable to pay any one of said sums to said corporation. And he further states that, in the early history of the corporation, the said Thomas C. Durant, from time to time, loaned large sums of money to the corporation, which were repaid to him by me, as treasurer, in the same manner and upon the same authority that other loans for borrowed money were repaid.

"JOHN J. CISCO.

"STATE OF NEW YORK,
"*City and County of New York:*

"Sworn to before me this 27th August, 1870.

[L. S.] "EDWIN F. COREY,
"*Commissioner for Rhode Island in New York.*"

"EXHIBIT B.

"*Statement of moneys received by Thomas C. Durant, or by others, on his orders, from the Union Pacific Railroad Company.*

"August 25, 1864	$4,000 00
"September 14, 1864	13,128 13
"September 14, 1864	6,500 00
"December 29, 1865	120,000 00
"March 30, 1866	50,000 00
"May 10, 1866	20,000 00
"G. T. M. Davis	3,000 00
"James C. Kennedy	2,000 00
"Alexander Hay	4,000 00

"(Indorsed:) Exhibit B. I. P. Hazard *et al. vs.* T. C. Durant *et al.*

"STATE OF RHODE ISLAND AND PROVIDENCE PLANTATIONS.

"*Office clerk supreme court, county of Newport, ss:*

"I, Thomas W. Wood, clerk of the court aforesaid, for and within the State and county aforesaid, do hereby certify that the foregoing one page contains a true and correct copy of the Exhibit B, filed in cause I. P. Hazard *et al. vs.* T. C. Durant *et al.*, No. 1, as compared by me this day with the original filed in this office on the 22d day of August, A. D. 1869.

"In testimony whereof I have hereunto set my hand, and affixed the seal of said court, this 22d day of August, A. D. 1869.

[SEAL.] "THOMAS W. WOOD, *Clerk.*"
[Stamp.]

"In equity.

"ISAAC P. HAZARD ET AL. *vs.* T. C. DURANT ET AL.

"*Affidavit of Josiah Bardwell.*

"Josiah Bardwell, of the city of Boston, Commonwealth of Massachusetts, being duly sworn, says that he was a director of the Union Pacific Railroad Company during the time covered by the complainants' bills in equity, and also a stockholder in the Credit Mobilier of America, and thoroughly conversant with all the transactions of said Thomas C. Durant set forth in said bills; that he does not, according to the best of his knowledge and belief, consider any of the allegations in each and either of said bills that the said Durant fraudulently or otherwise appropriated the moneys of either or each of said companies to his own use or benefit, or that said Durant is or was at the filing of said bills indebted to either of said companies; but he says that all of said moneys set forth in said bills and schedules were paid by the properly authorized officers of said companies, and were duly audited and settled by the properly constituted officers and committees of the said respective companies. He further says that he believes that there is no foundation either in law or fact for said bills in equity, and that the same are instigated and are prosecuted by said Rowland G. Hazard from malice and ill-feeling towards said Durant. He further says that he believes the said Durant to be of ample and sufficient means to pay at any time any and all charges and damages claimed and recovered against him.

"JOSIAH BARDWELL.

"STATE OF MASSACHUSETTS,
"*County of Suffolk, City of Boston, ss:*
"Subscribed and sworn to this 12th day of July, A. D. 1870, before me.
[SEAL.] "CHARLES B. F. ADAMS,
"*Commissioner of State of Rhode Island.*

"ISAAC P. HAZARD ET AL.
vs.
THOMAS C. DURANT ET AL. } In equity.

"*Affidavit of Cornelius S. Bushnell.*

"CORNELIUS S. BUSHNELL, of the city of New Haven, State of Connecticut, being duly sworn, says that he was, during all the period of time during which the complainants' bill alleges certain transactions to have taken place on the part of Thomas C. Durant, a director of the Credit Mobilier of America, of the railway bureau of said company, also a director in the Union Pacific Railroad Company, and a member of the executive committee, and is thoroughly conversant with all the transactions covered by both of said bills of complaint; that to the best of his knowledge, information, and belief, the said Thomas C. Durant is not indebted to either of said corporations, nor has he ever, fraudulently or otherwise, appointed or expended any of the funds or moneys of each or either of said corporators to his own use or benefit.

"The sum charged against said defendant in each of said bills, and the schedules annexed thereto, was expended for the benefit of each and either of said corporations by their properly and duly appointed officers, or were subsequently audited and allowed by duly appointed committees of each and both of said corporations, and allowed, charged off, and settled formally and duly.

"Your affiant further says that he believes that both of said suits are instigated and maintained by said Rowland G. Hazard from malice and ill-feeling towards said Durant, and that the said Durant is possessed of large and ample substantial means to pay any and all charges and damages properly claimed and recovered from him.

"C. S. BUSHNELL.

"Subscribed and sworn to before me, a notary public, this 12th day of July, 1870.

"JOHN R. DUFF,
"*Notary Public.*"

As to Mr. Alley's statement that a committee was appointed, on behalf of the Credit Mobilier, to examine my accounts, I will state that at my instance a committee was appointed, when I ceased to have any connection with the company, consisting of Mr. McComb and Mr. Williams. That committee not acting promptly, I invited several gentlemen, who were large stockholders, to examine my accounts with the Credit Mobilier; and on the day following Mr. Alley and Mr. Oakes Ames, a self-constituted committee, called on me. How far these gentlemen went into the investigation I do not recollect. I was willing to show them all my accounts connected with the Credit Mobilier; but when they came as a self-constituted committee on the part of that corporation to inquire into my accounts as an officer of the Union Pacific Railroad Company, with such railroad company, as to those matters, I have no doubt that I treated them cavalierly, and gave them very little information; but I deny ever having stated to Mr. Alley that I paid Mr. Thaddeus Stevens any money whatever. I deny ever having quarreled with that gentleman, never having seen him, except on one occasion, from the time the bill passed to the time of his death. I now state that I never paid or promised to pay Mr. Stevens any sum of money whatever, or any stock, bonds, or other property. I may have stated that a section introduced by Mr. Stevens, and insisted upon by him in his committee, in the amendment of 1864, had cost this company even a larger sum of money than that named. In regard to that section, not understanding why it was in, I once called upon Mr. Stevens, in company with Mr. Alexander Hay, and was informed that the affairs of the Leavenworth, Pawnee, and Western Road, (since called the Union Pacific, Eastern Division,) were in such shape that, if the amendment passed, as was proposed, without the said section, the lien prior to the Government lien would amount to a larger sum than the issue of Government bonds, per mile, to the road, to which the said prior lien was to be restricted; that the company, having already issued bonds, and also in its various negotiations incurred other liens and complications, so that there was even a doubt as to what parties controlled its franchise.

Mr. Stevens distinctly asserted that unless these matters were so arranged as to convince him that the Government lien would be what it purported to be, in theproposed amendment, he should insist upon a clause that would protect the Government, and recommended that those matters be adjusted among ourselves. It was in consequence of this interview that matters in dispute were, to a certain extent, arranged between the parties interested before the bill passed, in accomplishing which a large amount of money was used. At that time the Pacific Railroad was a popular measure, and there was no difficulty in passing any reasonable amendment in Congress which would insure the completion of the road. The difficulties we encountered were from the parties interested in the several companies named in said bill of 1862, growing, in a great measure, out of their own complications and local rivalries as to location of the termini and control of the franchises. In addition to the money expended in this effort, the company did part with a valuable portion of its franchise, on the representations of Mr. Oakes Ames that Iowa, and perhaps Massachusetts Representatives, would oppose this amendment of 1864, unless the Sioux City branch was given up to other corporations. This also I supposed was done to conciliate local interests.

As to the 650 shares referred to in Mr. Alley's statement, the facts are these: That amount made up my full subscription to the Credit Mobilier stock. At that time, if my just credits had been entered in the books of the company, the stock would have been more than paid for. When the said certificate was issued, instead of taking it from the office of the company, it was transferred, by power of attorney on the back of the same, and left in the hands of the assistant treasurer of the company, and the certificate had never been taken from the office of the company. The assistant treasurer, as I was absent from New York most of the time, was instructed to deliver said stock to the parties to whom I had promised stock, and who might call in my absence to receive and pay for the same. At the time I ceased to be an officer of the company, and the general administration of the Credit Mobilier was changed, and while I was absent on the road, that certificate was in the possession of the assistant treasurer; and, upon being asked for it by the new administration, it was surrendered, with a letter stating the fact that he held it in trust for the parties to whom it had been promised.

In reference to Mr. Alley's statement as to the connection of Mr. McComb and myself with the Fisk suit, in justice to Mr. McComb, I will state that, after the date of Mr. Ames's letter, which has been given in evidence on this examination, it was proposed that several parties become subscribers to the stock of the Union Pacific Railroad Company.

Among them, Mr. McComb and myself proposed to subscribe. When we met at the office to make our subscriptions, and tender the amount which we supposed the company were entitled to, (55 per cent. then being the amount that had been called by the board of directors,) we found that the treasurer had been instructed to receive nothing less than par. We were provided with certified checks to pay for subscriptions amounting to $500,000. While offering these subscriptions, Mr. Fisk came into the office to inquire relative to certain parties from Boston, who expected to be in town that day, and who, he said, proposed to subscribe to stock in the Union Pacific Railroad Company, and during that time made subscriptions himself. On Mr. McComb stating that he intended making a subscription for the account of a Mr. Turner, Mr. Fisk remarked, "I will make it for you," and made the subscription referred to; and that was all the subscription that Mr. McComb had any connection with.

After Mr. Fisk commenced his suit against the company, Mr. Turner, through his attorneys, notified the company that Mr. Fisk was not his agent, and forbid their settling with him for said subscription. This is all the connection that I know of Mr. McComb having with the matter.

I have made this statement as brief as I could. A full and detailed statement of all the facts connected with the matter upon which Mr. Alley testifies would exhaust your patience. Those who know the history of the Union Pacific Railroad Company do not need to be informed that the claim which Mr. Alley puts forward for Mr. Ames and his other friends, that this great national enterprise owes its success entirely to them, is utterly unfounded. But many are uninformed upon the facts. At the risk of seeming to magnify my services, I beg to take this opportunity to say one word on that subject.

As I have stated, Mr. Ames, Mr. Alley, and their friends were not original stockholders in the company. They came into it by virtue of their character as contractors and their interest in the Credit Mobilier, and did not come into the direction until after several hundred miles of road had been completed, and nearly five hundred miles had been completed at the time of the execution and assignment of the Oakes Ames contract. The claim of patriotism and of a far-seeing, intelligent, and honest policy, put forward in their behalf, is ridiculous. In fact, so uninformed were they of the mode of conducting the entire business, that they did not distinguish and at times seemed incapable of distinguishing between the railroad company and the Credit Mobilier. And I may here state that it does not seem to me strange that gentlemen, members of Congress, to whom Mr. Ames sold interests, mistook the company in which they held stock, for I do not think Mr. Ames himself could hardly have given them a clear idea on the subject.

Early in 1856, while in connection with C. W. Durant and Henry Farnham, engaged in constructing a railroad in Iowa, we employed engineers to make examinations for a favorable point for crossing the Missouri River, and to make observations as to a general route for a railway to the Rocky Mountains. In the fall of 1863, and prior to the organization of the company, at my private expense, I sent engineering parties into the field to explore the whole country to be traversed by the road. Lines were run through Cheyenne, Bridge, and all the other principal passes in the mountains, while five different lines from the Missouri were run to a common point in the Platte Valley. I did this before the company had obtained subscriptions enough to enable them to organize, so that when it should be ready to commence work, valuable time which would be required to make surveys and run lines might be saved; and I also sent a geologist to make examinations as to coal and iron lands on the line and in the vicinity. I submitted a report of my action to the company at the first meeting of the board of directors.

So, too, in respect of taking the stock. The matter long languished in the hands of men of the highest character, until the time limited for organization had nearly expired. Believing the enterprise would ultimately succeed, I made my own subscription, and, finding it impossible to induce capitalists to engage in the enterprise, I succeeded in obtaining subscriptions for the requisite amount only by inducing my friends to subscribe, I advancing the money to pay their first installment of ten per cent. thereon, giving them the option to retain the stock by returning me my advances, or I would find parties to take the stock off their hands. All of this stock, amounting to three-fourths of the whole stock ($2,000,000) required to be subscribed, was subsequently transferred to me, the parties not choosing, even after the amendment in 1864, to take any risk in the enterprise.

While conducting personally the actual construction of the road, I often found it imperatively necessary fearlessly to assume responsibility in correcting errors in any department, and still more fearlessly to oppose those who were ready to sacrifice ultimate success for immediate profit.

So placed and acting, it is not strange that I met the malignant opposition of a few persons whose calumnies I should never have noticed, had not the statement of Mr. Alley being placed on record seemed to demand a refutation on my part.

I would also add, with reference to the general belief that extraordinary profits were realized from the construction of this road, that, taking the cost of the road from its eastern terminus to that point to which the estimates were made, and upon which the last dividends were paid, as shown by the schedule given your committee, comprising a distance of more than 900 miles, on an expenditure of about $74,000,000, the entire profits, estimating the average market value of the securities divided, would amount only to between sixteen and eighteen per cent. on the sum paid—a profit less than is generally anticipated in all railroad contracts. The estimates for the cost of the remaining 140 miles, or thereabouts, embraced in the Davis contract, are not included in this estimate of cost, my connection with the company having ceased upon the laying of the last rail, and prior to the accounts being finally closed.

The rapidity with which the work was completed, being in less than one-fourth of the time ordinarily required for such work, makes this profit appear larger than if the construction had extended for the period usually required.

The company, while they complied on their part with the requirements of the law, felt they had cause to complain of want of good faith on the part of the Government, by which their securities were depreciated and the cost otherwise increased.

First. By its passing an act allowing the Union Pacific, Eastern Division, which was, by the acts of 1862 and 1864, to have been a branch connecting with the main line at or near the 100th meridian, to construct their road up the Smoky Hill Fork, thereby not only making it a rival line for a long distance, but depriving the Union Pacific Company of the benefits of a connection with the Central Branch from Atchison.

Second. By allowing the Central Pacific Railroad Company to extend its road eastward to a point beyond that designated in the acts of 1862 and 1864.

Third. By fixing arbitrarily the junction of the two roads at or near Ogden.

Fourth. By delaying the work of construction, in neglecting promptly to establish the point at the base of the Rocky Mountains where the increased issue of bonds should commence.

Fifth. By neglecting and refusing in some instances to accept the location of the road made by the company until in one case after the track was actually laid on the same for a distance of upward of two hundred miles, though the maps had been filed in the proper department of the Government. This deprived the company of the use of the bonds to be issued on said portion, compelling them to raise large sums of money at ruinous rates.

Sixth. By their neglect to certify to the company large portions of land to which they were entitled.

Seventh. To the action of Government in retaining the money due in accordance with the act for the transportation of Government freights, mails, and troops, at a time when the company was greatly in debt, and depending on the sale of their securities, thereby causing, on the part of capitalists, a general distrust in the good faith of the Government toward the company; and compelling the company to make sacrifices, thus increasing the apparent cost of the road.

A.

NEW YORK, *August* 8, 1864.

To the president and committee on contracts of the Union Pacific Railroad Company:

GENTLEMEN: I propose to enter into a contract to build and equip one hundred miles of your railroad and telegraph, commencing at Omaha City, complying as far as practicable to the general specifications hereunto annexed, upon the following terms and conditions, viz:

To proceed at once with the grading and bridging, and complete the same within the time required by the acts of Congress specified, and in such manner as will comply with the same; to assume all your contracts for ties, iron, and equipment, the company reserving the right, if they elect, to dispose of what iron they have, with the exception of, say, five hundred tons, which may be required to facilitate the grading, and also to dispose of the equipment not needed this season, except three locomotives and ten platform-cars; but, in case they elect to do so, shall give me written notice of their intention prior to the first day of October next.

To build all necessary side-track not exceeding six per cent. in length of the main line, the contractor to have the right to change grades, provided the maximum grade shall not exceed that of the New York Central Railroad. Also to have the right to enter upon all lands belonging to said company, for the purpose of obtaining material used in the construction of the road.

Should the company decide to Burnetize the cottonwood used for ties, they shall pay in addition sixteen cents for each tie, and for all other timber in like proportion.

The contractor shall not be required to expend, in the construction of any one bridge, over eighty-five thousand dollars, nor shall he be required to expend for the erection of station-buildings, machinery, machine-shops, tanks, equipments, &c., more than five thousand dollars per mile, or five hundred thousand dollars in the aggregate, but the same shall be expended as directed by the engineer. The contractor to have the use of the road until the contract is completed. The work on the sections near Omaha, which have been let by the company, or which have been commenced, to be continued by them or transferred to me as may be agreed upon hereafter, and the cost of the same to be charged to me in final settlement. Any excess in the cost of iron above one hundred and thirty dollars per ton at Omaha to be allowed by the company. Right of way to be furnished by the company. The expense of engineers engaged in the construction to be paid by the contractor. The company to pay for the same at the rate of fifty thousand dollars for each and every mile so completed. Payments to be made as the work progresses, upon the estimate of the engineers, in making which the engineer shall deduct from each section its proportion of the cost of equipment not then furnished, station-buildings, superstructure, and cost of telegraph; but all material delivered or in transit for the account of the company may be estimated for. The contractor to furnish money upon the securities of the company, as hereinafter provided for in the construction of each section of the length required by the acts of Congress hereinbefore referred to, viz:

The company shall proceed to mortgage the land acquired from the Government at not more than sixteen thousand dollars per mile, bearing seven per cent. interest, payable semi-annually in the city of New York, which bonds shall be receivable as the bonds of the company at such prices as may be fixed upon from time to time as the cash price of the lands. The company to proceed to the preparing of the first-mortgage bonds, as provided for under the act, made and put on record, the mortgage securing the same, so that the bonds may be ready for use as soon as the provisions of the law are complied with; and shall do everything necessary and requisite to obtain the Government bonds at an early day. In the mean time, if required, the company to execute certificates of an amount to correspond to the first-mortgage and Government bonds, chargeable for the same upon the company's obtaining the United States bonds. Said certificates to bear interest, payable semi-annually, at the rate of six per cent. On these certificates I will advance, or procure to be advanced, the necessary funds to the company at the rate of eighty per cent. of their par value, and on the land-grant bonds seventy per cent., reserving the right to dispose of them whenever the amount so advanced, including what may be due on construction, shall exceed five hundred thousand dollars, or whenever said advance shall have been made over four months, but not to do so for less than the prices above named. The company in their option to decide whether I take the bonds, or any portion of them, at the prices above named, in payment for advances and interest, if called upon to do so within thirty days thereafter. I will also subscribe, or cause to be subscribed, to the capital stock of your company five hundred thousand dollars. I will assume and pay such obligations or accounts as may have been certified to by the committee appointed by your board or executive committee for services and expenses, the company paying me the amount of the obligation so certified to and assumed. In making this proposition it may be well to state that I am connected with and agent for parties who have machines, oxen, and necessary outfit for prosecuting the work, and are prepared to commence at once, having sent cattle and tools to Nebraska.

H. M. HOXIE,
By H. C. CRANE,
Attorney

H. M. HOXIE, Esq.:

DEAR SIR: You will please go on with the work under the above proposition, and if the company do not accept it before the first day of October next, they will pay you upon the same terms and conditions for what work may be done, as shown by the estimates of the engineers, made as provided in this proposition, first giving you thirty days' notice that they do not accept.

GEORGE T. M. DAVIS,
Special Committee.

Above contract is approved and ratified.

[SEAL.]

JOHN A. DIX.
C. S. BUSHNELL.
GEORGE T. M. DAVIS.

SEPTEMBER 23, 1864.

NEW YORK, *October* 4, 1864.

To the president and executive committee of the Union Pacific Railroad Company:

On condition that your railroad company will extend my contract from its present length for one hundred miles, so as to embrace all that portion of the road between Omaha and the one hundredth meridian of longitude, I will subscribe, or cause to be subscribed, for five hundred thousand dollars of the stock of your company.

Respectfully, yours,

H. M. HOXIE,
By H. C. CRANE,
Attorney.

The above proposition is hereby accepted for and on behalf of the Union Pacific Railroad Company.

JOHN A. DIX,
C. S. BUSHNELL,
GEO. T. M. DAVIS,
Special Committee.

OCTOBER 3, 1864.

B.

NEW YORK, *October* 7, 1864.

Whereas H. M. Hoxie, esq., of the State of Iowa, has a certain contract, bearing date the 8th day of August, 1864, for the construction of a portion of the road of the Union Pacific Railroad Company, which contract the said Hoxie has agreed to assign to Thos. C. Durant, esq., of the city of New York, or to such party or parties as he may designate, by agreement bearing date the 30th day of September, 1864, the terms of which assignment form a part of this agreement:

Now, therefore, we, the undersigned, hereby agree to take an interest in the said contract to the extent set opposite our respective names, depositing at the same time, in the hands of said Thos. C. Durant, 25 per centum in cash on the interest so subscribed. And the parties hereto agree, one with the other, that should default be made in payment of the balance of the interest so subscribed as required, the party so defaulting shall not be entitled to any further interest in said contract than the amount paid bears to the amount subscribed. It is understood that the amount subscribed for the carrying out of this contract shall be $1,600,000.

Thos. C. Durant, $600,000; C. S. Bushnell, $400,000; Chas. A. Lambard, $100,000; H. S. McComb, $100,000; H. W. Gray, $200,000, &c.

C.

Know all men by these presents, that I, Herbert M. Hoxie, for and in consideration of one dollar to me in hand paid, the receipt whereof is hereby acknowledged, and for divers other good and valuable considerations me thereunto moving, do hereby sell, assign, transfer, and make over unto John Duff, trustee, all and singular the agreements, between the Union Pacific Railroad Company and myself, made by and contained in a certain proposition in writing, signed by me, and dated August 8, 1864, and an acceptance thereof by said company, under its seal, dated September 23, 1864, both which proposition and acceptance are hereto annexed; and also all my rights under said agreement, and all moneys, property, privileges, payments, benefits, and advantages to me or to my heirs, representatives, or assigns by said agreement provided for or secured, with full power to use my name whenever necessary or proper for obtaining, receiving, or enforcing the said rights, moneys, property, privileges, payments, benefits, and advantages, as fully as I myself could do the same; subject, nevertheless, to my agreement with the Credit Mobilier of America, dated the 15th of March, 1865, and all my rights thereunder.

In witness whereof, I have hereunto set my hand and seal this 15th day of March, 1865.

[SEAL.] HERBERT M. HOXIE.

[United States internal-revenue stamp, $1, canceled.]

N. B.—l. 24, "March," written on erasure before execution.

Witness: BENJAMIN F. BUNKER.

Whereas Herbert M. Hoxie and the Union Pacific Railroad Company have entered into an agreement by means of the foregoing writings, (namely, a proposition from said Hoxie, dated August 8, 1864, and an acceptance thereof, dated September 23, 1864:)

Now these presents witness, that the Credit Mobilier of America, in consideration of one dollar to them in hand paid, the receipt whereof is hereby acknowledged, and for divers other good and valuable considerations them thereunto moving, do hereby covenant and agree to guarantee, and hereby do guarantee, to and with the said Union Pacific Railroad Company, that the said Herbert M. Hoxie, or his representatives or assigns, shall, and will, well, truly, and perfectly perform and fulfill the said agreement in all things on his part to be done or performed according to the terms and true intent of said agreement, as in said foregoing writings contained.

In witness whereof, the said Credit Mobilier of America have caused these presents to be sealed with their corporate seal and signed by their president, this 15th day of March, 1865, at their agency in the city of New York.

[SEAL.] THOMAS C. DURANT,
President.

Attest: B. F. BUNKER,
Assistant Secretary.

Memorandum of an agreement made the 15th day of March, 1865, between the Credit Mobilier of America, a corporation organized under the laws of the State of Pennsylvania, of one part, and Herbert M. Hoxie, of the other part:

Whereas, by certain writings hereto annexed, and forming part of these presents, a contract has been made by and between the Union Pacific Railroad Company and said Hoxie; and whereas said Hoxie has partly performed the same:

Now, in consideration of the premises, and of the mutual grants and agreements herein contained, the parties to these presents grant and agree as follows:

Said Credit Mobilier agrees to execute to said company a guarantee of the performance of said contract by said Hoxie, and also to make to said Hoxie all advances of money which may be necessary to provide and pay for labor, materials, services, and all other expenses and charges in the construction of the railroad, and other performance of said contract on said Hoxie's part; and also to provide for, secure, and obtain all subscriptions to capital stock required by said contract from said Hoxie. Said Hoxie agrees to, and hereby does, assign to said Credit Mobilier all his right to have and receive from said company securities, stocks, moneys, profits, and payments due or to become due for constructing the railroad, or other performance of said contract, upon said Hoxie's being paid for all work done and materials furnished, as by adjustment certificates of the engineer or settlement made in December last; and he hereby appoints said Credit Mobilier his lawful attorney, irrevocable, to take, collect, and receive for their use all the matters and things so assigned.

And for the better securing said Credit Mobilier against being made chargeable on said guarantee by any default of said Hoxie, and against any loss of the matter and things above assigned, said Hoxie hereby appoints said Credit Mobilier his lawful attorney, irrevocable, to name, constitute, employ, and at their pleasure remove, all agents and subagents which said Credit Mobilier may deem necessary or proper to conduct, manage, and do the business of constructing the railroad, otherwise performing said contract, and to pay out and apply the moneys so to be advanced to the uses for which the same are to be advanced, and does hereby pledge and transfer to said Credit Mobilier the said contract and all his rights under the same, as collateral security for the performance of said contract on his part, with full power to enforce such pledge on default without notice.

The said Credit Mobilier agrees to save said Hoxie harmless and indemnified against all claims under said contract, and to pay the said Hoxie five thousand dollars in cash and ten thousand dollars in the stock of the Union Pacific Railroad Company, and to carry out the conditions relating to a construction bureau, as shown by specifications hereto annexed.

In witness whereof said Credit Mobilier has executed this memorandum, under its seal and signature of its president, and said Hoxie has signed and sealed the same the day and year first above written, at their agency in the city of New York.

T. C. DURANT,
President.
H. M. HOXIE.

Witness:
B. F. BUNKER.

D.

NEW YORK, *November* 10, 1866.

SIR: Referring to our informal agreement for the construction of a portion of the Union Pacific Railroad, I hand you the following memorandum of contract, which, if in accordance with your understanding as to details, you will please indorse as accepted, and return me one copy, retaining the other for yourself.

1st. You to assume such existing contracts for material, grading, bridging, &c., as may properly belong or appertain to the construction of one hundred and fifty miles of the road westward from the 100th meridian of longitude, including an agreement for the grading and superstruction of that portion of the road between the 100th meridian of longitude and the west bank of the North Platte River, at the rate of nineteen thousand five hundred dollars per mile, exclusive of the bridge over the said river, which bridge is to be paid for at the actual cost of construction.

2d. All the present employés on construction are to be retained and employed under this contract, unless discharged for inefficiency or other good reasons. That the work shall be under my supervision, or that of the engineer or person designated by the company, and through the superintendents, engineers, agents, and contractors now on the work, in order that the present effective organization may not be impaired or changed until the railroad company decide whether they let the contract for building and equipping the balance of the road to parties who may wish to have the advantage of the present organization or do the work themselves as a corporation; but nothing in this shall be construed to prevent the employment of other agents, if thereby the work can be more expeditiously and economically prosecuted.

3d. The grading, bridging, and superstructure to be completed to the satisfaction of the company's engineer and the acceptance of the Government commissioners, and of the same character as to workmanship, material, and kind of iron, &c., as in the construction of the one hundred miles east of the 100th meridian of longitude.

4th. Work on station-buildings, depot-grounds, tank-houses, or anything appertaining thereto, or equipment and rolling-stock, to be an additional charge, but all such work is to be done with the sanction and under the direction of the engineer in charge. The side-track and turnouts necessary for the immediate requirements of the company, at the several stations established on the line, as indicated by the engineers at the present time, to be constructed at the expense of the contractor. If more should be required, the same is to be constructed at the expense of the company.

5th. The cost of iron, delivered at Omaha, is guaranteed not to exceed one hundred and thirty dollars per ton; and if ties or bridge-material are burned or destroyed, the company to pay the actual cost of the same. The transportation of men and material, &c., used for the construction, to be free of charge to the contractor over the completed portion of the road.

6th. The work to be pushed with the same rapidity as heretofore, and, if required, to be completed at the rate of two miles for each pleasant working-day, provided the company deliver and transport the necessary material therefor over the completed portion of the road without causing detention.

In case the engineer in charge is of the opinion the grading, &c., is not progressing as fast as required to comply with the contract, he shall be at liberty to place more men on the work, at the cost of the contractor; but the company shall not require grading to be done while the ground is frozen, unless at their own cost and expense; neither shall the contractor be liable for delays from high water or causes entirely beyond his control.

7th. In consideration of the faithful performance on your part of the above work, you shall be paid twenty thousand dollars per mile for each and every mile so completed west of the North Platte River bridge to the termination of the fourth hundred miles westward from Omaha, and nineteen thousand five hundred dollars per mile, and the cost of the North Platte River bridge, for each and every mile between the one hundredth meridian and the west bank of the North Platte River, as hereinbefore referred to. Payments to be made as the work progresses, on the monthly estimates of the engineer in charge of the work, and that material delivered or in transit may be estimated when the same has been shipped for account of the company.

THOS. C. DURANT,
Agent.

L. B. BOOMER, Esq.,
Chicago, Illinois.

I hereby accept the above.

L. B. BOOMER.

I hereby become personally responsible for the payment to you of the above.

THOS. C. DURANT.

The within contract may be terminated by giving me ten days' notice, in writing, and the payment, according to the terms thereof, of all sums that may be due for work performed and material furnished.

L. B. BOOMER.

E.

CERTIFICATE OF ENGINEER, REFERRED TO IN ABOVE REPORT OF THE TREASURER OF THE UNION PACIFIC RAILROAD COMPANY.

Estimate to contractors for building road west of 100*th meridian, December* 31, 1868.

100	miles, at $42,000 per mile	$4,200,000
167	miles, at $45,000 per mile	7,515,000
100	miles, at $96,000 per mile	9,600,000
100	miles, at $80,000 per mile	8,000,000
100	miles, at $90,000 per mile	9,000,000
100	miles, at $96,000 per mile	9,600,000
46	miles, at $90,000 per mile	4,140,000
400,000	ties, at $1 each	400,000
10,875	tons iron, at $110 per ton	1,196,250
30	tons splice-bars, at $185 per ton	5,550
100	frogs and switches, at $100 each	10,000
1,000	telegraph poles, at $2 each	2,000
100	miles wire, at $50 per mile	5,000
500,000	F. M. B. bridge-timber, at $50 per M	25,000
100,000	F. M. V. lumber, at $45 per M	4,500
100	miles grading, at $20,000 per mile	2,000,000
	Equipment:	
103	locomotives, at $14,000 each	1,442,000
16	first-class passenger cars, at $4,000 each	96,000
8	second-class passenger cars, at $3,500 each	28,000
14	baggage and express cars, at $2,800 each	39,200
81	caboose-cars, at $2,000 each	162,000
949	box freight-cars, at $900 each	444,600
1,589	platform-cars, at $767 each	1,218,763
54	station-houses, at $2,500 each	135,000
60	tank-houses, at $1,500 each	90,000
70	wind-mills, at $1,500 each	105,000
10	coal-houses, at $1,800 each	18,000
12	turn-tables, at $1,500 each	18,000
	North Platte round-house	80,000
	North Platte shops	150,000
	North Platte eating-house	15,000
	Sidney round-house	20,000
	Cheyenne round-house	80,000
	Cheyenne shops	100,000
	Cheyenne eating-house	22,000
	Sherman round-house	20,000
	Laramie round-house	80,000
	Laramie shops	200,000
	Laramie eating-house	45,000
	Medicine Bow round-house	20,000
	Rawlings Springs round-house	40,000
	Rawlings Springs shops	150,000
	Rawlings Springs eating-house	27,000
	Bitter Creek round-house	40,000
	Machinery for Bryan shops	150,000
		60,738,863

Deduct unfinished work, as follows:	
713 miles equipment, per contract, at $7,500 per mile..	$5,347,500
	55,391,363
Amount received from company....................	43,725,000
	11,666,363

G. M. DODGE,
Chief Engineer.

F.

THE "OAKES AMES CONTRACT," AND THE TRANSFERS OF THE SAME.

Copy of contract U. P. R. R. C. with Oakes Ames, and transfer to T. C. Durant and others.

Agreement made this sixteenth day of August, one thousand eight hundred and sixty-seven, between the Union Pacific Railroad Company, party of the first part, and Oakes Ames, party of the second part, witnesseth:

That the party of the first part agrees to let and contract, and the party of the second part agrees to contract, as follows, to wit:

First. The party of the second part agrees and binds himself, his heirs, executors, administrators, and assigns, to build and equip the following-named portions of the railroad and telegraph line of the party of the first part, commencing at the 100th meridian of longitude, upon the following terms and conditions, to wit:

1st. 100 miles at and for the rate of $42,000 per mile.
2d. 167 miles at and for the rate of $45,000 per mile.
3d. 100 miles at and for the rate of $96,000 per mile.
4th. 100 miles at and for the rate of $80,000 per mile.
5th. 100 miles at and for the rate of $90,000 per mile.
6th. 100 miles at and for the rate of $96,000 per mile.

Second. At least three hundred and fifty miles shall be, if possible, completed and ready for acceptance before the first day of January, 1868, provided the Union Pacific Railroad Company transport the material. The whole to be constructed in a good and workmanlike manner, upon the same general plan and specifications as adopted east of the 100th meridian of longitude. The party of the second part shall erect all such necessary depots, machine-shops, machinery, tanks, turn-tables, and provide all necessary machinery and rolling-stock, at a cost of not less than $7,500 per mile, in cash, and shall construct all such necessary side-track as may be required by the party of the first part, not exceeding six per cent. of the length of the road constructed, and to be constructed, under this contract. The kind of timber used for ties, and in the bridges, and in its preparation, shall be such as from time to time may be ordered or prescribed by the general agent, or the company, under the rules and regulation, and standard, as recommended by the Secretary of the Interior, of the date of February —, 1866.

Third. Whenever one of the above-named sections of the road shall be finished to the satisfaction and acceptance of the Government commissioners, the same shall be delivered into the possession of the party of the first part, and upon such portions of the road, as well as on that part east of the 100th meridian now completed, the party of the first part shall transport, without delay, all men and material to be used in construction, at a price to be agreed upon by the party of the second part, his heirs, executors, administrators, or assigns, and the general agent, but not less than cost to the party of the first part.

Fourth. The party of the second part, his heirs, executors, administrators, or assigns, shall have the right to enter upon all lands belonging to the company, or upon which the company may have any rights, and take therefrom any material used in the construction of the road, and may have the right to change the grade and curvature within the limits of the provisions of the act of Congress, for the temporary purpose of hastening the completion of the road, but the estimated cost of reducing the same to the grade and curvatures, as established by the chief engineer, or as approved from time to time by the company, shall be deducted and retained by the party of the first part, until such grade and curvature is so reduced.

Fifth. The party of the second part, his heirs, executors, administrators, or assigns, is to receive from the company and enjoy the benefit of all existing contracts, and shall assume all such contracts and all liabilities of the company accrued or arising therefrom for work done or to be done, and material furnished or to be furnished, for or on account of the road west of the 100th meridian, crediting, however, the party of the first part on this contract all moneys heretofore paid or expended on account thereof.

Sixth. The party of the second part, for himself, his heirs, executors, administrators, and assigns, stipulates and agrees that the work shall be prosecuted and completed with energy and all possible speed, so as to complete the same at the earliest practicable day, it being understood that the speed of construction and time of completion is the essence of this contract, and at the same time the road to be a first-class road, with equipments; and if the same, in the opinion of the chief engineer, is not so prosecuted, both as regards quality and dispatch, that then the said party of the first part shall and may, through its general agent or other officer detailed for that purpose, take charge of said work, and carry the same on at proper cost and expense of the party of the second part.

Seventh. The grading, bridging, and superstructure, to be completed under the supervision of the general agent of the company, to the satisfaction of the chief engineer, and to be of the same character as to the workmanship and materials as in the construction of the road east of the one hundredth meridian.

It is, however, understood that all iron hereafter purchased, or contracted for, shall be of the weight of not less than fifty-six pounds to the yard, and to be fish-bar joints.

Eighth. All the expenses of the engineering are to be charged and paid by the party of the second part, except the pay and salary of the chief engineer and consulting engineer, and their immediate assistants, and the expenses of the general survey of the route.

Ninth. The depot buildings, machine-shops, water-tanks, and also bridges, shall be of the most approved pattern, and they, as well as the kind of masonry and other material used, shall be previously approved by the general agent and chief engineer of the company, and all tunnels shall be of the proper width for a double track, and shall be arched with brick or stone, when necessary for the protection of the same.

Tenth. Payments to be made as the work progresses, upon the estimates of the chief engineer—in making which the engineer shall deduct from each section its proportion of the cost of equipment not then furnished, station-buildings, superstructure, and cost of telegraph, but all materials delivered or in transit for the account of the company may be estimated for.

Eleventh. Payments hereon shall be made to the party of the second part, his heirs, executors, administrators, or assigns, in cash; but if the Government bonds received by the company cannot be converted into money at their par value net, and the first-mortgage bonds of the company at ninety cents on the dollar net, then the said party of the second part, his heirs, executors, administrators, and assigns shall be charged hereon the difference between the amount realized and the above-named rates; provided the first-mortgage bonds are not sold for less than eighty cents on the dollar; and if there shall not be realized from the sale of such bonds an amount sufficient to pay the party of the second part, his heirs, executors, administrators, or assigns, for work as stipulated in this contract, according to the terms thereof, then such deficiency shall, from time to time, be subscribed by said party of the second part, his heirs, executors, administrators, or assigns, to the capital stock of said company, and proceeds of such subscription shall be paid to said party of the second part, his heirs, executors, administrators, or assigns, on this contract.

Twelfth. On the first 100 miles on this contract there shall be added to the equipment now provided for, and intended to apply on this section, as follows, viz: six locomotives, fifty box-cars, four passenger-cars, two baggage-cars, and a proportionate amount of equipment of like character be supplied on the second section of 100 miles after the same is completed.

Thirteenth. The amount provided to be expended for equipment, station-buildings, &c., shall be expended under the direction of the party of the first part, and in such proportion for cars, locomotives, machine-shops, station-buildings, &c., and at such points as they may determine. The party of the first part to have the full benefit of such expenditures without profit to the contractor, or they may, in their option, purchase the equipment, and expend any portion of said amount provided at any point on the road where they may deem the same most advantageous to the company, whether on the section on which said reservation occurs or not.

Fourteenth. The telegraph line is included herein under the term "railroad," and is to be constructed in the same manner and with similar materials as in the line east of the one hundredth meridian.

The said parties hereto, in consideration of the premises and of their covenants herein, do mutually agree, severally, to perform and fulfill their several and respective agreements above written.

This contract having been submitted to the executive committee by resolution of the board of directors, August 16, 1867, and we having examined the details of the same, recommend its execution by the proper officers of the company with Hon. Oakes Ames, the party named as the second part.

(Signed) OLIVER AMES,
C. S. BUSHNELL,
SPRINGER HARBAUGH,
THOMAS C. DURANT,
Executive Committee Union Pacific Railroad Company.

At a meeting of the executive committee, held on the 1st day of October, 1867, a resolution was offered to approve the foregoing contract, which was lost. Thereupon the following resolutions were offered and adopted:

Resolved, That the foregoing contract between the Union Pacific Railroad Company and Oakes Ames, referred to the executive committee by a resolution of the board, August 16, 1867, to settle the details, be approved, and that the proper officers of the company be instructed to execute the same, subject, however, to the written approval of the stockholders of the company, as understood by the board of directors when the same was voted upon.

Resolved, That the option to extend this contract to Salt Lake be referred to the board, with recommendation that said option be accepted.

Assignment of contract to T. C. Durant and others.

Memorandum of agreement, in triplicate, made this fifteenth day of October, one thousand eight hundred and sixty-seven, between Oakes Ames, of North Easton, Massachusetts, party of the first part; Thomas C. Durant, of the city of New York; Oliver Ames, of North Easton, Massachusetts; John B. Alley, of Lynn, Massachusetts; Sidney Dillon, of the city of New York; Cornelius S. Bushnell, of New Haven, Connecticut; Henry S. McComb, of Wilmington, Delaware, and Benjamin E. Bates, of Boston, Massachusetts, parties of the second part, and the Credit Mobilier of America, party of the third part:

That whereas the party of the first part has undertaken a certain large contract for the construction of a certain portion therein named of the railroad and telegraph line of the Union Pacific Railroad Company over the plains and through and over the Rocky Mountains, which will require a very large and hazardous outlay of capital, which capital he is desirous to be assured of raising, at such times and in such sums as will enable him to complete and perform the said contract according to its terms and condiditions;

And whereas the Credit Mobilier of America, the party of the third part, a corporation duly established by law, is empowered by its charter to advance and loan money in aid of such enterprises, and can control large amounts of capital for such purposes, and is willing to loan to said party of the first part such sums as may be found necessary to complete said contract, provided sufficient assurance may be made to said party of the third part therein that said sums shall be duly expended in the work of completing said railroad and telegraph line, and that the payments for the faithful performance of said contract by said railroad company shall be held and applied to re-imburse said party of the third part for their loans and advances, together with a reasonable interest for the use of the money so loaned and advanced;

And whereas said party of the third part fully believes that said contract, if honestly and faithfully executed, will be both profitable and advantageous to the parties performing the same, are therefore willing to guarantee the performance and execution of the same for a reasonable commission to be paid therefor;

Ahd whereas both parties of the first and third part have confidence and reliance in the integrity, business capacity, and ability of the several persons named as parties of the second part hereto, and confidently believe that said persons have large interests as well in the Union Pacific Railroad Company as in the Credit Mobilier of America, they will execute and perform the said contract, and faithfully hold the proceeds thereof to the just use and benefit of the parties entitled thereto;

Therefore it is agreed by and between the said parties of the first, second, and third part hereto, as follows, that is to say:

That said Oakes Ames, party of the first part hereto, hereby, for and in consideration of one dollar lawful money of the United States, to him duly paid by the party of the second part, and for divers other good and valuable considerations herein thereunto moving, doth hereby assign, set over, and transfer unto the said Thomas C. Durant, Oliver Ames, John B. Alley, Sidney Dillon, Cornelius S. Bushnell, Henry S. McComb, and Benjamin E. Bates, parties of the second part, all the right, title, and interest of, in, and to the said certain contract heretofore made and executed by and between the Union Pacific Railroad Company and the said Oakes Ames, bearing date the 16th day of August, 1867, for the construction of portions of the railroad and telegraph line of said railroad company, to which contract reference is herein made, for them, the said parties of the second part, to have and to hold the same to them and their survivors and successors forever in trust.

Nevertheless, upon the following trusts and conditions and limitations, to wit:

First. That they, the said parties of the second part, shall perform all the terms and conditions of the said contract so assigned, in all respects, which in and by the terms and conditions thereof is undertaken and assumed and agreed to be done and performed by the said party of the first part herein named.

Second. That they, the said parties of the second part, shall hold all the avails and proceeds of the said contract, and therefrom shall reimburse themselves and the party of the third part hereto all moneys advanced and expended by them, or either of them, in executing or performing the said contract, with interest and commission thereon as hereinafter provided.

Third. Out of the said avails and proceeds, to pay unto the parties of the second part a reasonable sum as compensation for their services as such trustees for executing and performing the terms and conditions of this agreement, which compensation shall not exceed the sum of three thousand dollars per annum to each and every one of the parties of the second part.

Fourth. To hold all the rest and residue of the said proceeds and avails for the use and benefit of such of the several persons holding and owning shares in the capital stock of the said Credit Mobilier of America, on the day of the date hereof, in proportion to the number of shares which said stockholders now severally hold and own, and for the use and benefit of such of the several assignees and holders of such shares of stock at the times herein set forth, for the distribution of said residue and remainder of said avails and proceeds, who shall comply with the provisions, conditions, and limitations herein contained, which are on their part to be complied with.

Fifth. To pay over, on or before the first Wednesday of June and December in each year, or within thirty days thereafter, his just share and proportion of the residue and remainder of the said proceeds and avails as shall be justly estimated by the said trustees to have been made and earned as net profit on said contract, during the preceding six months, to each shareholder only in said Credit Mobilier of America, who being a stockholder in the Union Pacific Railroad, shall have made and executed his power of attorney or proxy, irrevocable, to said several parties of the second part, their survivors and successors, empowering them, the said parties of the second part, to vote upon at least six-tenths of all the shares of stock owned by said shareholders of the Credit Mobilier of

America in the capital stock of the Union Pacific Railroad Company, on the day of the date hereof, and six-tenths of any stock in said Union Pacific Railroad Company he may have received as dividend, or otherwise, because or by virtue of having been a stockholder in said Credit Mobilier of America, or which may appertain to any shares in said Union Pacific Railroad Company which had been so assigned to him at the time or times of the distribution of the said profits as herein provided; and this trust is made and declared upon the express condition and limitation that it shall not inure in any manner or degree to the use or benefit of any stockholder of the Credit Mobilier of America who shall neglect or refuse to execute and deliver unto the said parties of the second part his proxy or power of attorney, in the manner and for the purpose hereinbefore provided, or who shall in any way, or by any proceeding, knowingly hinder, delay, or interfere with the execution or performance of the trust and conditions herein declared and set forth.

And the above transfer and conveyance of said contract is made upon these further trusts and conditions, to wit:

First. The said parties of the second part, their survivors and successors, trustees as aforesaid, in all their acts and doings in the execution and performance of said contract, and in the execution of their several trusts and conditions herein set forth, shall act by the concurrent assent of four of their number, expressed in writing, or by yea and nay vote, at a meeting of said trustees, either or both of which shall be recorded in a book of proceedings of said trustees, kept for the purpose by their secretary, and not otherwise.

Second. Said parties of the second part shall keep an office in the city of New York for the transaction of the business incidental to said trust. Meetings of said trustees may be held on call of the secretary, on request of any two of their number; such call may be made personally or by mail.

Third. The said trustees shall appoint a competent person as secretary, who shall keep a faithful record of all their acts, proceedings and contracts, in books to be provided for that purpose, and shall cause to be kept suitable books of accounts and vouchers of all their business transactions, which books shall at all times be open to the inspection of any of said trustees.

Fourth. The said trustees shall cause a monthly statement to be made, showing the amount due from the Union Pacific Railroad Company on account of work done, or equipment or material furnished under the contract according to the estimates of the engineer of the Union Pacific Railroad Company, as provided in said contract, a copy of which statement shall be furnished to the Credit Mobilier of America.

And the above transfer and conveyance of said contract is made upon the further trust and condition:

First. That in case of death, declination, disability, by reason of sickness or absence from the country for the space of six months, or neglect to fulfill the duties and obligations of said trust for the same time, by either of said trustees, the remaining or surviving trustees may declare the place of such trustee to be vacant, and fill such vacancy by vote in manner aforesaid.

Second. That in case any one of said trustees shall willfully neglect or evade the performance of his duties as such trustee, or shall willfully attempt to hinder, delay, obstruct, or interfere with the execution or performance of said contract, or the due execution and performance of said trust and conditions, according to the true intent thereof, or shall appropriate to his own use or benefit any money or other valuable thing belonging to or appertaining to said trust, fund, or property, he shall not be entitled further to act as such trustee, or to receive any of the benefits of said trusts, either as shareholder in said Credit Mobilier of America, or otherwise.

The parties of the second part do hereby accept the said trust, and agree faithfully to execute and perform the same according to the terms, conditions, and limitations herein set forth.

The party of the third part, in consideration of the premises, hereby agree to advance, as upon a loan, to the said parties of the second part, their survivors and successors, all such sums of money, and at such times as may be necessary, to enable said trustees economically and promptly to execute and perform the conditions of said contract, upon the call of said parties of the second part, their survivors and successors, such sums, never to exceed in the whole the amount provided for in said contract, to be paid by the Union Pacific Railroad Company for the execution and performance thereof, and to receive therefor interest at the rate of seven per centum per annum, payable semi-annually, on each sum so advanced, until the same are repaid.

And said party of the third part do further agree, for the consideration aforesaid, and for an amount equal to two and one-half per cent. on the amount to be by them advanced, to be paid to them as commission, to, and do hereby, guarantee unto the parties of the first and second part the due performance and execution of the said contract, according to its terms and conditions, and to indemnify and hold harmless the said parties of the first and second part, of and from all costs, liability, loss, or damage to them, or either of them, arising from or on account of said contract, and to the faithful performance of the agreements, contracts, and conditions hereinabove specified to be done and performed by each.

And this conveyance and transfer is made upon the further trust and condition that the trustees shall adjust and pay over to the Credit Mobilier of America such portion of the net profits of the work done and material furnished on the first 100 miles west of the one hundredth meridian as was done and performed prior to January 1, 1867.

In witness whereof, the party of the first part, the several parties of the second part, in their own proper persons, have hereunto set their hands and seals, and the party of the third part has caused these presents to be executed by its president, attested by its secretary with the seal of the said company, on the day and year above written.

(Signed) OAKES AMES.
THOS. C. DURANT.
OLIVER AMES.
JOHN B. ALLEY.
SIDNEY DILLON.
CORNELIUS S. BUSHNELL.
H. S. McCOMB.
BENJAMIN E. BATES.

Signed, sealed, and delivered in presence of—
CLARK BELL.

(Signed) THE CREDIT MOBILIER OF AMERICA,
By its president, SIDNEY DILLON.

Attest: BENJAMIN F. HAM,
Assistant Secretary.

G.

NEW YORK, *February* 26, 1869.

The executive committee of the board of directors of the Union Pacific Rrilroad Company, pursuant to adjournment, met this day at the office of the company.

Present: Messrs. Ames, Durant, McComb, Duff, and Bushnell.

The following communication was then received from the vice-president, Mr. Durant:

NEW YORK, *November* 27, 1868.

To the board of directors of the Union Pacific Railroad Company:

GENTLEMEN: I hand you herewith copy of contract and an assignment of the same in trust to the same parties who are trustees for the assignees of the Ames contract, the whole subject to the approval of the stockholders of the Union Pacific Railroad Company. I found it absolutely necessary, in order to carry out the wishes of the board, to commence work of this portion of the road at once. The present organization, with its large outfit of teams, tools, and men, presented the most available means of doing the same. To have created an entirely new organization would cause so much delay that the programme of the company for the year would have been endangered. Should your stockholders not sanction the contract, you will have to make some fair arrangement with the trustees of the Ames contract for the use of their outfit. On the other hand, if approved, the work can go on under the same organization as heretofore.

Referring the whole subject of your action,

I remain, very respectfully, yours, &c.,

THOMAS C. DURANT,
Vice-President and General Agent.

There having been no meeting of your board since the date hereof, I hand the report to your executive committee. You will perceive I have taken the terms of the Oakes Ames contract as a base, believing that to be the wishes of the stockholders who approved said contract.

WEBER, *November* 1, 1868.

SIR: I will build and equip, according to the specifications of the contract made by your company with Oakes Ames, esq., all that portion of your road not embraced in the said contract and west of the same, upon the conditions and terms embraced in said contract, for the *pro rata* price per mile according to the amount of work to be done, which rate shall be established by competent engineers, or in such manner as your board shall determine.

Yours, &c.,

(Signed) JAMES W. DAVIS.

THOMAS C. DURANT,
Vice-President and General Agent, Union Pacific Railroad Company.

Accepted, subject to approval of all the stockholders of November 1.

(Signed) THOMAS C. DURANT,
Vice-President and General Agent.

WEBER, *November* 6, 1868.

Know all men by these presents, that I, J. W. Davis, do hereby, in consideration of one dollar lawful money of the United States to me in hand paid, and for other considerations to me satisfactory, do hereby assign, transfer, and set over to Oliver Ames, Thomas C. Durant, John Duff, Sidney Dillon, H. S. McComb, B. E. Bates, and C. S. Bushnell, trustees for the stockholders of the Union Pacific Railroad Company, the contract made with me for building a portion of their road, dated November 1, to have and to hold the same, as trustees aforesaid, and all benefits and profits accruing from the same, they assuming and paying all losses and liabilities of every kind; said profits, if any, to be divided *pro rata* according to the amount of stock held by each stockholder, or to which he was entitled on the 1st day of November. This assignment and the contract referred to being subject to the approval of the aforesaid stockholders.

(Signed) JAMES W. DAVIS.

Witness:

(Signed) C. L. FROST.

By resolution, my action as to this contract was approved, and a committee appointed to obtain the assent of the stockholders.

WASHINGTON, D. C., *January* 30, 1873.

JOHN B. ALLEY, having been recalled at his own request, made the following statement:

I wish to make a statement and have it go upon your record in relation to this matter of the Credit Mobilier. There has been some misapprehension in regard to the exact position of the case, I judge from the statements that I see in some of the Massachusetts papers, which represent that there is a great discrepancy between Mr. Ames's statements and mine before this committee and those made by us before the court of Pennsylvania. I wish to say that there is not the slightest discrepancy. The statements made by Mr. Ames and myself before this committee may not have been as full or explanatory as they were before that court, and for very obvious reasons to the committee. The committee sitting in another room in this Capitol will probably go more fully into that subject than this committee.

Now, the statement which was in some of the Massachusetts papers—the Springfield Republican and one or two others—represents that we both stated before the courts of Pennsylvania that there had been but one dividend, or two small dividends, made by the Credit Mobilier corporation; that Mr. Ames was asked by this committee how many and what was the character of the dividends that were made by the Credit Mobilier, and without explanation it appears from the testimony, as published in this paper, that he went on to treat all the dividends made under the Oakes Ames contract as having been made by the Credit Mobilier. It is my recollection, however, that Mr. Ames stated to the committee distinctly, as I certainly did, that these dividends referred entirely to the Oakes Ames contract, and were not dividends of the Credit Mobilier, but were to be treated as dividends under the Oakes Ames contract alone. Now, the facts are just these: In this suit in Pennsylvania we both stated, as did all the officers of the company, I believe, and several of the large stockholders, and I believe it is the concurrent opinion of all the officers and stockholders of both companies, with a single exception, perhaps, of Mr. McComb, that these dividends were made by the trustees under the Oakes Ames contract, and had nothing whatever to do with the Credit Mobilier as a corporation.

The Chairman stated that this whole subject had been very fully gone into; that the facts were before the committee, who could form their own judgment in regard to them.

WITNESS. I desired only briefly to allude to it, taking it for granted that the committee have the records before them, and understand the case just as well as I do; and I think it was under that impression that Mr. Ames referred to the dividends without making this explanation on each occasion. I merely wished to call attention at this point to the parties who have misapprehended or misrepresented the facts. I ought to be charitable enough, I presume, to believe they misapprehended the point. Certainly there is no variation in the slightest degree in the testimony we have given before this committee from that which was given to the court.

By the CHAIRMAN:

Q. There is one subject I wish to make an inquiry of you about. When this stock was assigned to Mr. Ames—these 650 shares—Mr. Ames claimed that he wanted it for the purpose of fulfilling engagements that he had made with various persons to let them have stock. Now, will you state what you know in reference to any negotiations or conversations between Mr. Ames and any of these gentlemen in Congress, who afterward received stock, about letting them have it prior to December, 1867. From the testimony of nearly all these gentlemen it would seem that their negotiations began about December, 1867, a considerabe time after the stock had been assigned to Mr. Ames.—A. I never knew anything about any negotiation, except with the three gentlemen I have named. At a meeting of the executive committee at New York, or at least a meeting of quite a large number of the stockholders and officers, of both companies, the statement was made by him that he wanted this stock to fulfill engagements he had made; in some instances partial promises, in others full promises. He said he did not think he ought to take it out of his own stock; that he had promised to get stock for various parties. If he told who the parties were I do not remember; I do not think he did; and the only ones in Congress that I happen to know about were Senator Wilson, Mr. Boutwell, and Mr. Dawes; and I am not certain about Mr. Dawes. Senator Wilson spoke to me some time before that in regard to stock for his wife; I think it must have been as early as the July previous, and may have been even earlier than that; but we did not ascertain until June, 1867, that these 650 shares of stock was held in the manner we found it was. When the new direction came in, in May, 1867, we found soon afterwards that 650 shares stood in Mr. Durant's name, unpaid for, and was soon after transferred to Mr. Dillon, the new president, from Mr. Durant, who stated that he held it in trust, and that he had engaged it, or most of it, to other parties. Then it was that Mr. Ames, as I understood it, tried to dispose of it to insiders and to outsiders without much success. I know that about the first of July, while I was in Washington, though not then a member of Congress, Mr. Winthrop Gray, of New York, said to me that he had 50 shares which he would like to sell, and offered it at 95. Mr. Ames turned to me and said, "I have no money; I wish you would buy this." I replied, "I do not want it; I am not largely interested, but still I have as much as I want." He then said to me, "If you will buy it I will agree to guarantee you against loss, and ten per cent. for your money, and we will share the profits on it." I said, "Very well, if you will do that I will take it;" and I did take it upon those terms. He was very anxious that other stock should be sold, and he exerted himself to place it, as he called it. I refer to these 650 shares. I am very sure that Mr. Wilson spoke to me in July on this subject. Mr. Ames thinks it was in December, but I think he is mistaken, for I called his attention to the fact that it was while I was here, and that I was not here in December; he acknowledged that he must be mistaken. His attention was not then called to the fact that there had been two extra sessions of Congress in 1867. There was one from the 1st of July until the 20th, and another from the 20th of November; and the conversation I had with Mr. Dawes may have been in that November session. Mr. Dawes thinks it was not earlier than the 1st of December.

Q. What I want to get at is your knowledge of any negotiations had with any of these gentlemen prior to the time stated by them.—A. I have no knowledge except as I have said. I do not know anyting about any members of Congress except these three gentlemen I have named.

Q. You are confident now that he had conversations with Mr. Wilson and Mr. Boutwell, prior to the commencement of the session of 1867–'68?—A. O, yes, sir.

Q. And what is your belief as to Mr. Dawes?—A. My belief would have been that my conversation with him was in the July session. But Mr. Dawes is very confident that it was not until the commencement of the session in November.

Q. Laying aside his recollection, what is your recollection?—A. I have no recollection about it, more than this: I think it could not have been in December, for I was not here in December, and I am certain that the conversation between us took place here.

Q. Were you here in November?—A. I was here at the commencement of the session in November, and I was here again in January.

Q. The point of this, if there is any point about it, is, how many of these men had negotiations with Mr. Ames prior to the time of getting the stock?—A. He stated there in New York that he had made negotiations for even more than the amount of stock which was then assigned to him. There was considerable opposition to letting him have it, because the stock at that time was worth more than it had been before. He may have designated the parties with whom he had made engagements, but I do not remember it; he regarded them as obligations. I do not think he said he had positively promised but very few, and I do not know that he stated the name of anybody. I happened to know of the parties I have mentioned, because of my conversations with them.

Q. You do not know, then, that Mr. Ames at any time previously mentioned the names of any of these men in Congress to you?—A. No, sir; I do not. I remember that he said afterward to me that he was very much embarrassed by his promises; that he made more promises than he could fulfill.

Q. Did he think that some of them claimed promises where he had not made them?—A. I do not know about that; they claimed more than he had stock to give. I do not think he referred to members of Congress particularly, more than to others. He had some outside purchasers.

Q. If I recollect aright, at the time this transfer was made to Mr. Ames, Mr. McComb was there and objected to it?—A. Mr. McComb said there was no reason why Mr. Ames should have his promises carried out any more than Mr. McComb should his; that he (McComb) had made promises.

Q. Whom did Mr. McComb say he had made obligations with for stock?—A. He said, I think, that he had promised stock to Mr. Bayard, Mr. Fowler, and some other gentlemen. I think he said he had promised Mr. Wilson, of Iowa, thirty or fifty shares; I had forgotten it until Mr. Wilson named it the other day.

Q. Did he say anything about Mr. Allison?—A. My impression is that he did. Mr. Allison was one of the parties that he had promised stock to. He denied Mr. Ames's right to promise stock, and finally Mr. Ames said he would do the best he could to help Mr. McComb with any promises he had made. That was about his reply.

WASHINGTON, D. C., *January* 30, 1873.

BENJAMIN F. HAM recalled and examined.

By Mr. ALLEY:

Question. In your cross-examination the other day, by Judge Black, I notice by the record that he asked you if you knew anything about the arrangements of the assignment of the Oakes Ames contract to trustees. You said you did know something about it, but not much. He asked you further, if that was not done for the purpose of evading the taxes in Pennsylvania. Your reply, as it stands upon the record, was that you did not know, but you supposed so. Am I correct in that?—Answer. I have tried to get access to the record, so that I might see in regard to that, but have not been able to see the printed record. If I was so reported, I should like to have it corrected. My information upon that subject was from other sources, and so far as I knew anything about it, it was for other purposes that the assignment was made to trustees rather than to the Credit Mobilier direct.

Q. I wish to ask you if you ever heard an intimation from the officers of either company, or from any party in interest in that Oakes Ames contract, that there was any such design or purpose or thought upon the part of anybody?—A. I did not.

WASHINGTON, *January* 31, 1873.

CHARLES H. NEILSON recalled and examined.

By the CHAIRMAN:

Question. Do you keep an account of the transactions between you and Mr. Brooks in the dealings you have with each other?—Answer. I have not kept any formal account—any book-account.

Q. Do you keep any account at all in any way in writing or any memorandum of the dealings between you and him?—A. I have no memorandum made out in my own handwriting of it.

Q. Has it been your habit, whenever you have paid him any money, or received money from him, to keep no record of it?—A. When I have paid him any money, it has been by check.

Q. Have you not kept any memorandum or account of your dealings between yourself and him?—A. No, sir; not formal memoranda.

Q. I don't know what you mean by formal. Have you kept anything by which you could show the transactions between you?—A. I have given Mr. Brooks a check for $9,000 on account of a loan that was given in a check.

Q. He advanced $10,000 to pay for one hundred shares; was it just $10,000?—A. Just $10,000.

Q. Did you have any account of that, or any memoranda of it; anything in writing?—A. I have nothing in writing to show.

Q. Did you at any time make any memorandum of it?—A. No.

Q. Do you know whether Mr. Brooks made any?—A. Not to my knowledge.

Q. Did you give him any note or any obligation?—A. I gave him no note.

Q. There was nothing in writing on his part, or your part, as far as you know?—A. No, sir.

Q. I have forgotten whether you stated that you gave him any security for the $10,000?—A. I gave him collateral security for it in Union Pacific first-mortgage bonds.

Q. The same bonds you received with the stock?—A. They were bonds I received from the company.

Q. At the time you received these 100 shares of stock, there went with it $5,000 in bonds, and $20,000 in stock of the Union Pacific Railroad Company, if I remember right. Did you have that?—A. That was given to me.

Q. Was that the security you gave to Mr. Brooks?—A. I gave the bonds as a part of the security to Mr. Brooks; I hypothecated them with him; I did not give them to him; they were mine; I merely hypothecated them.

Q. Did he receive from you the same securities, bonds and stock, that you received at the time you got the 100 shares?—A. When I got the 100 shares I received at the same time 200 shares Union Pacific Railroad stock and five first-mortgage bonds; I gave him the five first-mortgage bonds.

Q. Did you give him the stock?—A. I do not think I did; the shares were made out in my name and I did not transfer them.

Q. He did not receive the 200 shares and never had that stock?—A. I always retained the stock.

Q. But the $5,000 in bonds were given over to him as collateral security?—A. Yes, sir; as a part of the collateral security I gave him.

Q. Did you give him other bonds than these?—A. Not at the time I received the Credit Mobilier stock.

Q. Did you at any time to secure that loan?—A. Afterward, as I received bonds from the company as an allotment, I gave him some bonds, enough to cover the loan.

Q. But these were bonds you subsequently received as dividends upon the stock?—A. Bonds that I received from the company, ten first-mortgage bonds.

Q. Did you receive them from the company as dividends upon the stock?—A. I received them as dividends, or allotments, whatever you may call it.

Q. So that all the collateral security you gave him were bonds which you received as dividends or allotments on the 100 shares of Credit Mobilier stock?—A. Not quite; I think the $5,000 I first received were dividends upon that stock; those I gave him subsequently I received from the company by virtue of holding the 100 shares.

Q. Soon after receiving the 100 shares there was a bond dividend?—A. Yes, sir.

Q. And you then delivered these bonds to Mr. Brooks as security?—

A. Yes, sir; I delivered them to him as I would do to any New York man from whom I borrowed money.

Q. Soon after you received the 100 shares there was a cash dividend?—A. There was a cash dividend that I received on the 100 shares, how soon I cannot say now.

Q. Do you know when you received that cash dividend?—A. Yes; the 18th of June, 1868, I received $9,000 in cash.

Q. That is 60 per cent. on the 150 shares?—A. Yes, sir.

Q. That you paid over to Mr. Brooks?—A. That I gave to Mr. Brooks as part payment of the money I owed him.

Q. Did you pay him anything before that?—A. Not any money; I had merely hypothecated the bonds I had received previously.

Q. Had you other loans from Mr. Brooks?—A. I have borrowed money from time to time as I required it.

Q. Do you know whether you were then indebted to him for any loans of money at that time?—A. I do not think I was; I may have been for some small sum of one hundred dollars or something of that sort which he had loaned me. This $10,000 was the only sum of any amount that I owed him.

Q. Had you repaid any part of this loan prior to the check of $9,000?—A. I had not repaid him anything.

Q. You paid it over to him at the time or about the time you received it?—A. The same day. I gave it in at his office to his cashier; he was not then in town. I left with his cashier a check to his order and took a receipt from Mr. Kingsland, his cashier, for it.

Q. Have you that receipt here?—A. I have.

The following receipt was handed to the committee:

"NEW YORK, *January* 18, 1868.

"Received from Mr. Charles H. Neilson his check for $9,000, to order of Mr. James Brooks, and on said James Brooks's accounts.

"JAMES B. KINGSLAND."

Mr. Brooks also handed to the chairman his check-book, showing a deposit in his bank to his credit of that amount at the date referred to.

Q. Have you paid Mr. Brooks the balance of the $10,000?—A. No; I have not paid him any money; I have given him this collateral security for it.

Q. The same collateral you have spoken of?—A. Yes, sir.

Q. Does he hold all these collaterals yet?—A. I owe Mr. James Brooks in the aggregate now about $15,000; he has let me have other moneys since that time.

Q. Does he still hold all the securities that you put into his hands, or has any part of them been returned to you?—A. They have not been returned to me, for I have not settled my account with him.

Q. What was the entire amount of security you put into the hands of James Brooks?—A. Sixteen first-mortgage bonds.

Q. He has them yet?—A. Yes, sir; he holds them yet.

Q. Since the advancement of this first amount you have received other loans from him to what amount?—A. To the amount of $14,000, about the value of the security he holds as collateral.

Q. The only cash payment you have made him is the $9,000, which you received as a dividend on the stock?—A. Yes, sir.

Q. The fifty shares you afterward received Mr. Dillon advanced the money to pay for?—A. He advanced me the money.

Q. Has that been repaid to Mr. Dillon?—A. Mr. Dillon says it has been paid. I find no memorandum on my check-book, nor any evidence of it. I have examined Mr. Brooks's check-book and find that he has not yet paid it. Mr. Dillon must have sold the securities and repaid himself, as he was justified in doing under the circumstances.

Q. You have never paid him in any other way?—A. In no way.

Q. What was the security you gave to Mr. Dillon?—A. Four first-mortgage bonds, and fifty shares Union Pacific Railroad stock.

Q. Were these bonds and stock the same you received by way of dividends upon these shares?—A. I received them as dividends upon the one hundred shares of Credit Mobilier stock. I got no dividends upon the fifty shares until I had paid for them.

Q. The securities you gave Mr. Dillon were the same you received by way of dividends upon the one hundred shares?—A. Upon the one hundred shares; yes, sir.

Q. If Mr. Dillon has been paid at all, it must have been by a sale of these securities?—A. I think he must have sold them. The loan has been running a long time. It was a small loan to him. I think he just sold the securities on account of the loan and paid himself in that way. I do not know that to be a fact; it is my theory, from all I can gather.

Q. Have you ever had any conversation with Mr. Dillon about it?—A. Not until this question came up; he assures me that the loan has been paid or has been settled—probably in that way.

Q. Have you ever received back from him any of the securities?—A. I never received any of the securities back.

Q. Has he ever paid you anything?—A. He never has paid me anything beyond the $5,000, and the small amount in addition for interest.

Q. Has he ever paid you anything of the proceeds of the securities you put into his hands?—A. No, sir.

Q. You let him have $4,000 of bonds and 500 shares of stock; the bonds were worth par, were they not?—A. No. They never have been sold at par in the market that I am aware of.

Q. What was the market price of these bonds at the time?—A. I could not tell you; they have no fixed price; they were fluctuating.

Q. Were they not nearly at par? Mr. Ames has reported sales at about that time at 97.—A. I do not know of their being sold in the market for any such price; they may have been; I do not know whether they were or not.

Q. What was the stock worth at that time?—A. I do not know whether the stock was on the market generally at that time; I do not recollect any sales.

Q. You have never had any settlement or adjustment in any way with Mr. Dillon?—A. No, sir.

Q. It would be a little remarkable, would it not, if a sale of these securities should exactly balance your loan?—A. I have a right to go to Mr. Dillon now and give him my check for the amount of the loan and interest to the present date and demand back my securities.

Q. Had he any authority for selling them?—A. No authority, except that he could easily replace them at any time if demanded.

Q. Was there any conversation in regard to replacing the securities?—A. No conversation.

Q. Has there been anything said between you and Mr. Dillon upon that subject from the time you got that money and put these securities into his hands until this winter?—A. Nothing at all. I saw Mr. Dillon about a week ago; he told me he thought the loan had been paid; that he had not the securities; in other words, that he must have sold the securities in order to pay the loan.

Q. That is a mere conjecture of his, because he has no such securities in his possession?—A. A mere conjecture.

Q. Did you ask him how much he sold them for?—A. No, sir.

Q. You never made any inquiry about it?—A. He was very busy at the time, and I did not talk long with him about it.

Q. This loan was made five years ago?—A. Yes. It has always been my custom when I have made a loan on favorable terms to wait until I am notified to take it up.

Q. Did you not suppose that the securities you put into his hands were of greater value than the amount of the loan?—A. No, sir; I suppose they are of less value now than the loan and interest.

Q. At that time did you not suppose the securities put into his hands were worth more than the amount of the loan?—A. I supposed they were worth just about the amount. I considered the bonds worth about 80.

Q. We have no evidence as to the value of the bonds, except that Mr. Ames sold his at that time for 97.—A. I never sold any of my bonds at that price, and never had any such offer.

Q. Did you make any effort to sell your bonds at that time?—A. No, sir; a man may make a private sale at a certain price which he could not get in open market at all.

Q. You have never called on Mr. Dillon for any adjustment of the loan?—A. No, sir.

Q. And have never inquired of him?—A. No, sir.

Q. Did you not regard it as somewhat out of the ordinary course of business that a matter of this sort should go on four or five years without some effort at adjustment?—A. No, sir; I do not think it is. I have known loans to lie as long as that where a security was satisfactory to the person who had loaned the money.

Q. The securities that you put into Mr. Brooks's hands you suppose he still retains, or has he sold them?—A. I presume he retains them. He has assured me of that fact—that he has them yet—and holds them as collateral security for the money I still owe him.

Q. Do you still hold the stock you received by way of dividends on your Credit Mobilier stock?—A. I hold some of it.

Q. Some you have sold?—A. I have sold some.

Q. How high a price has that stock ever brought in the market, to your knowledge?—A. Somewhere in the neighborhood of 42 or 43. I have not heard of any higher than that.

Q. Do you know what its value is in the market?—A. I do not know what it is to-day. Somewhere in the neighborhood of 35. It may be a little higher or a little lower.

Q. In any of the conversations you have had with Mr. Dillon, has he given any account of what he got for the securities you put into his hands?—A. No, sir; he cannot give any account of them.

Q. He does not claim there is anything due from you to him?—A. He does not claim there is anything due.

Q. Is this the only transaction between you and him?—A. It is the only transaction.

Q. Whether there is any balance between you and him you do not know?—A. I do not know. I do not see how it can be.

Q. That depends upon how much he sold his securities for.—A. If he owes me the money he will pay it, I have no doubt. If I owe him I will pay him.

Q. Does he admit that he owes you money?—A. He says the loan has been settled, but he does not know how.

Q. He infers that from the fact that he does not find any securities in his hands; he does not profess to have any knowledge about it?—A. No, sir.

Q. Did you receive more bonds by way of dividends upon this stock than those you placed in the hands of Mr. Brooks and in the hands of Mr. Dillon?—A. No more.

Q. All the bonds were received by way of dividends, which went into Mr. Brooks's hands and into Mr. Dillon's hands, and all went either as security or payment for the stock received?—A. Yes, sir; I hypothecated the bonds and paid Mr. Brooks $9,000 on the loan.

Q. I think you have stated when you were here before all you knew in reference to obtaining the fifty shares; that when you received the one hundred shares you did not know that you were entitled to fifty shares more?—A. No, sir.

Q. But subsequently you were informed by Mr. Brooks that you were entitled to fifty shares more?—A. I heard I was entitled to fifty shares more.

Q. You made no effort yourself about the fifty shares, except to go and call for them?—A. I went and called for them.

Q. You had no knowledge in relation to the paper that was gotten up and signed by the stockholders?—A. No, sir; I knew nothing about that.

Q. Did you ever hear of such a paper?—A. I never heard of it.

Q You had no such paper at the time?—A. No, sir; I had no such paper.

Q. You presented no such paper?—A. No, sir; I simply went and demanded my rights.

Q. If there was anything done—any effort made in any way to get these shares more than going and calling for them—it was not done by you?—A. I was not a party to anything that was done.

Q. Mr. Brooks told you that you were entitled to them, and could get them by going after them?—A. He told me I was entitled to fifty more shares.

Q. Can you tell how long after you got the one hundred shares before you received your fifty others?—A. It was in the latter part of February, 1868.

Q. You went and got the fifty shares after you received this information from Mr. Brooks?—A. Very shortly afterward.

Q. At that time you did not know you were entitled to fifty shares?—A. I did not know that I was entitled to any more.

By Mr. NIBLACK:

Q. You say it was your habit when you had a favorable loan not to repay it until you were called upon. When the loan was secured by collaterals why did you not apply this principle in regard to your loan of Mr. Brooks? Why were you so particular to take this cash dividend to him as soon as you received it?—A. Because I wished to obtain some other money from him afterward.

Q. Could you not just as well have retained this and allowed the loan to run on with the collaterals as security?—A. I do not know but I might.

Q. Why did you not retain this money instead of applying it on the loan from Mr. Brooks while he had your collaterals as security?—A. Because I had the money there, and I thought it was better to repay him that loan.

Q. Do you think he was any more entitled to that particular money than any other money you might receive?—A. I was not in the habit of receiving checks for $9,000 every day.

Q. Did you turn over the identical check you received?—A. No, sir; I deposited the check I received in my own bank, and deposited with his cashier my check for the amount.

Q. You gave him a large part of the bonds you received as collateral for the $10,000?—A. He held these bonds as collateral before I gave him the $9,000.

Q. After you gave him the $9,000 you allowed him to still continue to hold the collaterals?—A. I did; but I subsequently borrowed of him $14,000 more.

Q. And he still holds the bonds as collateral?—A. He stills holds them.

Q. Do these bonds draw interest?—A. They do.

Q. Who receives the interest upon them?—A. Mr. Brooks has given me, from time to time, a portion of the interest coupons.

Q. Does he charge you interest upon the loan?—A. I expect to pay him interest upon it when the account between us is settled.

Q, You have not closed your account with him during the last five years?—A. No, sir; it was natural, I presume, that I should obtain money from Mr. Brooks when I needed money.

Q. Yet you did not keep any formal books with him?—A. I do not keep any formal books with him.

By the CHAIRMAN:

Q. What evidence has Mr. Brooks of this loan? Does he hold any note or other obligation from you?—A. No; I presume Mr. Brooks keeps a memorandum of the money he has let me have.

Q. Do you know whether he does or not?—A. I do not know that he does. All the money I have received of him lately I have a memorandum of.

Q. He has no obligations signed by you?—A. No obligations. Being my father-in-law, I did not suppose it was necessary to be as formal in regard to these things as would otherwise be required.

Q, Do you keep in any form a memorandum of the money you receive from Mr. Brooks?—A. I deposited in my bank the money I received from him—$14,000. There is an entry in my check-book that I deposited at one time $13,750, and subsequently $350 additional. This transaction had nothing to do with the $10,000 for the Credit Mobilier stock.

Q. How does this entry come to be in your check-book?—A. I received his individual check, deposited it in the bank, and made a memorandum of it upon my check-book as a deposit.

Q. Have you that memorandum here?—A. I have not my check-book here.

Q. Is there any reason why such a memorandum as that should be in your check-book?—A. Certainly; because I received his check for it and deposited it in my own bank—the Leather Manufacturers' Bank.

Q. Your check-book is a book of checks that you draw yourself, is it not?—A. It is a book in which I keep on one side the money deposited in the bank, and on the other side a memorandum of the checks I draw. It is the ordinary form of check-book.

Q. That is the only written evidence you have that shows anything of these transactions between you and Mr. Brooks?—A. That is the only evidence I have.

By Mr. McCRARY:

Q. You have received from Mr. Brooks $14,000 since you paid him $9,000; was that all received at one time, or at different times?—A. I have stated that $13,750 was received at one time, and $350 at another time.

Q. Can you tell when you received the $13,750?—A. I think it was this last summer. I cannot tell you the exact date—probably about August.

Q. When was the $350 received?—A. About that time.

Q. The $14,000 was received during the last summer, more than four years after you paid him the $9,000?—A. Yes, sir.

Q. And during all that time he held your collaterals?—A. He held them.

Q. Why did you leave so large amount of collaterals in his possession when you had but $1,000 of the loan remaining?—A. I was living in the same house with Mr. Brooks at that time. I kept sundry articles in Mr. Brooks's safe in which these bonds were deposited, and they were lying right alongside. If I had received them back from Mr. Brooks, I should have deposited them in the same place.

Q. There were, then, about as much yours as his?—A. They were lying right alongside of some silver I had in the same safe.

Q. The loan you obtained from Mr. Dillon was simply by the deposit of collaterals without giving any note or obligation; is it customary for transactions of that sort to keep a note-book account of it?—A. There is no fixed custom about it. This thing was done hastily with Mr. Dillon.

Q. Would it not be a very unusual transaction if you had received these collaterals and just sold them without making any account of the amount for which they were sold?—A. Mr. Dillon does not acknowledge that he has sold them. He does not recollect anything more than that he had the securities, and does not now find them in his possession. From that he infers that the loan was canceled in some way, and I think it was not unnatural, as the securities held as collateral would have sold for just about the amount of the loan and interest.

Q. Would not almost any business man have an account of the proceeds of the sale somewhere, according to your custom, in New York?—A. If these securities were sold by Mr. Dillon, I can call upon him to give a bill of sale of them; but he does not yet acknowledge that they have been sold.

Q. If they have been sold there is no account of the transaction. Is not that something unusual as a business matter?—A. I do not know whether it is unusual with Mr. Dillon. He gave me a receipt for the bonds, which is sufficient proof to me that he had my bonds.

By Mr. MERRICK:

Q. Did you not keep a book in which you made entries of these various transactions?—A. My regular business is not that of a stockholder. My regular business is of a different nature, in connection with insurance. I keep regular books in my regular business; but for my private transactions the record is kept by my broker. I receive nothing more than notices that he has bought or sold for me such securities at such prices, and occasionally he renders an account showing my balance. That is the custom of doing that kind of business, I think. I am not a banker or broker.

Q. If I understand you, you dealt very frequently in stock operations?—A. Yes, sir.

Q. Yet you never kept any regular account of them?—A. Nothing beyond the bills of sale and purchases and the orders I gave. The accounts are kept by the broker. You will find that is customary for persons doing business as I do. I am not a member of the brokers' board myself, and I do not operate for other people.

By the CHAIRMAN:

Q. The interest upon the bonds Mr. Brooks holds is in part drawn by you?—A. He has given me some coupons. He has given me the coupons from five of the bonds, as per agreement. The coupons on the other ten bonds he draws himself.

Q. Then he has had the interest on the ten thousand dollar bonds?—A. Yes, sir.

Q. And the other six thousand you have had the interest on?—A. No; I have only had interest on five thousand.

Q. Then he has had interest on eleven thousand?—A. Yes; Mr. Brooks from time to time has made me some presents of five hundred dollars about Christmas or New Year's.

Q. That had no reference to the transactions of the bonds?—A. It has. He receives the money, and I suppose thinks it prudent to pay it over to me occasionally.

Q. Do you understand the interest he receives on these bonds to be a matter of account between you?—A. A matter of account between us.

Q. Then, the payments he has made were not presents at all?—A. Not all. I wish to correct that. He has given me the money to go into our general account.

Q. Would he be any more likely to give it at Christmas or New Year's than at any other portion of the year?—A. No; he did not always give it at New Year's.

Q. Was the interest on the bonds payable at either of these dates?—A. The interest on the bonds is payable the first of January, and that is the way I got the coupons the first of January.

Q. You got it, then, not because it was New Year's, but because the interest was due?—A. Because the interest was then due.

Q. Have you kept any account of what you have received from Mr. Brooks in that way?—A. No, sir. I have not kept any book-account.

Q. Do you know whether he does?—A. I presume he has some evidence of it. I do not know whether he has or not.

Q. Can you tell us what amount you have received by checks in that way?—A. I cannot.

Q. Can you give some approximate impression of the amount you have received from these coupons?—A. Yes, sir; I have obtained in the aggregate from Mr. Brooks about $24,000, and I have given him securities that would not sell for that in the market in the aggregate.

Q. In ascertaining the sum you owe Mr. Brooks do you add in it the checks you have received from him in this way?—A. Yes, sir; I shall consider them as added into our general account.

Q. Have you done it?—A. I shall reckon it into the general account.

Q. Was that reckoned into the two loans of $13,750 and $350?—A. No, sir; I received checks from him for these specific amounts, $350 or $375, I think perhaps the latter was.

Q. Do these two sums make up the entire amount you are indebted to Mr. Brooks?—A. I owe him a thousand dollars still on the Credit Mobilier matter.

Q. What becomes of these checks you have received from time to time; have you reckoned them in to make up the aggregate sum?—A.

Not to make up the aggregate sum I owe him. These checks were for coupons on the bonds.

Q. You say now you do not suppose they were presents, but that they were received by you on account from Mr. Brooks?—A. Yes; to be accounted for in our general settlement.

Q. You have kept no account of them?—A. I may have a memorandum deposited in my check-book; I probably have not, however, in full, because I have probably taken them sometimes to the bank, drawn the money myself on them, and put them in my pocket, so that they would not go on to my check-book.

Q. Have you any idea of the whole amount you have received in that way from him?—A. I should think it must be in the aggregate $3,500 in all that I have received from him on account of these coupons, in the checks he has given me.

Q. What is the rate of interest on these bonds?—A. Six per cent. in gold.

Q. You have received coupons of $5,000 for this whole period of time; do you regard the money you got in that way as yours, or as belonging to Mr. Brooks?—A. Simply as mine; it is money he paid me as interest.

Q. Were you to account to Mr. Brooks for it?—A. I consider that as so much to go against the collaterals, when we come to settle up the account.

By Mr. BROOKS:

Q. Have you any memorandum of the transactions you had with Mr. Ham, in regard to the dividends in your Credit Mobilier stock?—A. I have some notices which I received. I have a couple of notices of dividends which are all I happen to have with me when I left New York; I was hurried off toward the end. The first is dated March 3, 1868, notifying me there are some dividends due me on one hundred shares of Credit Mobilier stock standing in my name. It is signed by Benjamin F. Ham, assistant secretary. The other is dated the next day, March 4, 1868, stating there are still some dividends due, and asking me to call that afternoon and receive them.

Q. What does the notice of March 3 refer to?—A. It refers to dividends due me on one hundred shares Credit Mobilier stock which I owned at that time.

Mr. Brooks stated that he introduced this evidence for the purpose of showing that the stock was recorded at the office as belonging to Mr. Neilson. The notice was directed to Mr. Neilson's place of business, 42 Pine street, showing that the transaction was Mr. Neilson's and not his.

Q. What were the dividends which you received in pursuance of the notice of March 3?—A. I think one hundred shares of railroad stock.

Q. Why did you receive another notice the next day?—A. Because March 3 I purchased from the company fifty shares, and paid for them; and on the 4th I received a notice that there were some dividends due me on the fifty shares.

By the CHAIRMAN:

Q. You got just the same dividends *pro rata* on the fifty shares that you did on the one hundred shares?—A. The same *pro rata*, I presume.

Q. The same per cent. in bonds, money, and stock?—A. The books will show what I received; that was my understanding.

Q. I understand you to say that the coupons on some of these bonds you received and collected yourself?—A. I collected them myself.

Q. Why did you allow this loan from Mr. Dillon to run so long?—A. Because it was a favorable loan to me; and I should probably have to raise the money somewhere else, if I had paid it off. Mr. Dillon never notified me to take it up. It was satisfactory to both parties apparently to allow it to run.

By Mr. BROOKS:

Q. You were speaking of an unsettled account between you and Mr. Brooks; will your check-books, or any memoranda you have, show how that account stands?—A. My check-books will probably show on my side, and his check-books will show on his, when we come to a final settlement.

Q. Any check you have received from me will be entered in your check-book; and anything received by me will be entered in my check-book?—A. Yes, sir.

Q. So that there is a basis of settlement whenever we come to a final settlement?—A. Yes, sir; there is no doubt about that.

Q. Have you ever dealt in any other Pacific Railroad securities besides those that have been spoken of here?—A. Yes, sir.

Q. In what form?—A. I have bought them for a rise of one or two per cent., and sold them through my broker.

Q. This, then, is not the only transaction you ever had in Union Pacific securities?—A. No, sir; I have dealt in almost every stock on the list, at different times.

Q. You have not kept any more private memoranda in your dealings in stock for yourself with others than you have with me?—A. No; I have not kept them. My broker has kept them for me. I have, as I stated, never dealt as a broker.

Q. Tell me what is the practice on Wall street, especially in exciting times, in the matter of call loans, like this with Mr. Dillon. Suppose there was a great movement in stocks, and there should be a decided fall or rise, what would a man holding collaterals for a loan be likely to do in such a time of excitement?—A. He would be likely, if he could not find the man to whom the money was loaned, to sell the securities and take care of himself; I think I should do it.

Q. Is that at all an uncommon thing in Wall street?—A. No, sir; it is very often done, when a man's margin has run down.

Q. Would it have been natural for Mr. Dillon to have paid himself in that way in 1871; for instance, when the suspension of Oakes Ames took place, and all the securities of the Union Pacific Railroad Company went down as they did?—A. I don't think it would have been unnatural for him to have paid himself at all.

Q. Is it unnatural that you, holding a favorable loan, should let it run five, six, or seven years, if the person loaning the money to you did not demand it?—A. No; that would not be unnatural.

By the CHAIRMAN:

Q. What was the rate of interest you were to pay Mr. Dillon?—A. Seven per cent,

Q. Was there any special agreement about the interest?—A. That is the ordinary rate that I should expect to pay; that is the rate I have always paid to my brokers. I think probably there was no rate fixed between us. That was the current rate of interest at that time.

Q. Was there anything said at the time about the rate of interest you were to pay?—A. There was nothing said that I recollect.

Q. Was there anything said about the length of time you would be likely to want the money?—A. No, sir.

Q. Nothing said when he would want it of you?—A. No, sir; this was a call loan; it was not a loan on time. He had the right to call on me the next day to pay the money back. He had the right to call for it at any time he wanted it, and I had the right to pay whenever I got ready.

Q. Do you mean to say that it is customary or usual for loans made in that way to run five years?—A. I have known them to run longer than that. I think it is a usual thing; at least it is not an unusual or extraordinary thing.

Q. Do you think a large proportion of the loans made in this way, which you call call loans in New York, run five years?—A. A large proportion do not, I presume; but there are instances where they do.

Q. There are some instances where they are never paid, are there not?—A. Yes, sir; there are some instances where the security turns out to be valueless.

Q. You do not think it strange or odd that Mr. Dillon should not call on you for all that long period of time?—A. It is a matter that seems to have been neglected by Mr. Dillon. He never called on me to pay it; and I did not go to him. I did not think anything more about it. I had my stock. I recollected it was there, and that I held Mr. Dillon's receipt for the securities. I knew I could get them at any time.

Q. These securities are fluctuating, more or less, are they not?—A. Yes; if they had gone up very much, I should have called for them, and paid the loan; if they had gone down, he would have sold them and paid himself.

Q. Did you keep that in mind, and watch the market in reference to these securities?—A. In reference to my general speculations, I did.

Q. There was no time when the state of the market made it for your interest to go and take them?—A. No. If I had taken the securities from Mr. Dillon, I should have had to borrow the money somewhere else, and I could not have obtained as favorable a loan.

Q. I think you stated the other day that if this money had been paid to Mr. Dillon, it must have been paid by Mr. Brooks?—A. That was merely an assumption. I am sure now, since I have looked over Mr. Brooks's check-book, that he never paid it.

Q. Had you then any idea that Mr. Brooks had paid it?—A. I had no proof in my possession that he had paid it.

Q. Had you any idea in your mind that he had paid it?—A. I had no ground for thinking that he had paid it; my remark was that I had not paid it. Mr. Dillon claimed that it had been paid, and I said that if anybody had paid it it must have been Mr. Brooks.

Q. Did you know, prior to the time you testified before, that Mr. Dillon said it had been paid?—A. I had not seen Mr. Dillon previous to that. Since then I have seen him, and he says he has not got the securities.

Q. So that what you testified on that subject when you were before the committee at a former period was mere supposition on your part?—A. My supposition was that the loan was still due to Mr. Dillon; the impression on my mind was that it had never been settled.

Q. You supposed that you held the money for Mr. Dillon, and that he held the securities; but you have since learned, in some way, that the securities have gone out of his hands, so that he has got his pay, and you infer that simply from the fact that he has not the securities?—A. That is all.

Q. You have never received them?—A. I have never received them.

By Mr. MERRICK:

Q. You say you had a conversation with Mr. Dillon the other day, in which Mr. Dillon stated that the loan had been paid; did you state to him that you held the receipt for the collaterals?—A. I told him. He said he wanted to investigate it further; that he could not find the securities, but was going to make further examination. Since then I have not talked to him about it.

Q. Did you notify him that you were in possession of the receipt?—A. I did.

Q. Did you offer to return it to him?—A. I did not have it at the time. If he is satisfied the loan has been paid, and wants the receipt, I will give it to him at any time. I am perfectly willing to acquiesce in the settlement of the loan in that way; it is to my advantage to consider that it has been settled.

Q. Then why not return the receipt?—A. If he wants it I will give it to him. He has not stated that the loan has been canceled yet; he merely infers it from the fact that he cannot find the securities.

Q. Then you consider it an open question between you and himself whether the loan has been paid or not?—A. Yes, sir; until we arrive at some positive conclusion.

By Mr. BROOKS:

Q. Were not these Union Pacific Railroad stocks and mortgage-bonds, while you were living in my house and using my safe, as much in your possession as mine?—A. I could have got them at any time by paying you $1,000. I did not take them because I owed you still $1,000, and expected I would be obliged to borrow more money on them.

Q. Were they permitted to lie there as a place of better security than any other you could put them in?—A. Yes, sir; under my own observation.

WASHINGTON, D. C., *January* 31, 1873.

JOHN B. ALLEY, recalled at his own request, made the following statement:

I only wish to say a word in reference to what was said the other day, and not reply at length to the paper which Dr. Durant has just read. I supposed, when I made some remarks the other day, that this committee, as the other had not been appointed, would go into a more thorough investigation than now appears to be its purpose. I therefore took occasion then to say that if a thorough and complete investigation of all the transactions connected with the Union Pacific Railroad Company and the Credit Mobilier could be had, the American people would discover that the cry of "stop thief" was raised by the thieves themselves. I do not expect now that this committee will go into that investigation; but I hope the other committee, known as the "Wilson committee," will make a thorough investigation of this whole matter.

It seems necessary that I should say a word or two upon some of the points presented by Dr. Durant to-day. He says, with regard to the statement I made the other day, that we found great irregularities when I came into the direction of that company; that large sums of money had been expended and unaccounted for, that it is false. He has sworn before this committee and before the other committee that $435,000 has thus been spent by him. There has been no satisfactory account given, certainly to me, and the testimony of Oliver Ames, the president of the company, before the other committee, fully corroborates. With regard to that matter I will further remark, that the individual who is charged with having received $250,000 of that money is now confined in jail by order of the House of Representatives for contempt in refusing to state where this money went to. That is the answer I have to make to his remarks upon that point, and no reports or affidavits of others can make it right.

With regard to Mr. Thaddeus Stevens, I stated distinctly that when Mr. Durant told me that story I did not believe a word of it. I never believed a word of it. I stated then that Mr. Stevens's character and position forbid its belief. Mr. Oliver Ames has testified before the other committee the same thing precisely; so that upon that point I am corroborated. Mr. Oakes Ames told me, and I suppose he will testify before that committee also, that Mr. Durant told him the same. So far as that is concerned, it is unnecessary for me to say another word. Dr. Durant has spoken of a large subscription by myself and others in that connection upon that day. He does not state directly, but the inference would be from his statement, that that subscription preceded, instead of followed the Fisk-Durant-McComb subscription. As a matter of fact, it was subsequent to that subscription, grew out of it, and was necessitated by it. As I stated the other day, it occasioned our raising immense sums of money in order to effect that subscription; and having stated that fact, it is unnecessary for me to go any further into the matter, as the whole transaction will come out, probably, before the other committee.

Now, in regard to Mr. McComb's and Mr. Durant's connection with Fisk. The doctor speaks of it as accidental, when it is notorious to those who were connected with the company, and knew about it, that these three gentlemen undertook by that movement to get possession of the road. The only excuse Fisk had for appearing in the matter, as he himself admitted to me, was an interest of $240; and the only excuse he could give for making the demand he did of the company, which was, that unless the company paid him $100,000 he would injure them a million; to which I replied that, so far as I was concerned, the company should never pay him a single dollar, no matter what might be the consequences. I denounced it before him as a black-mailing operation. He replied that Dr. Durant and McComb, finding they did not succeed, had gone back upon him, as he expressed it; and that was the reason, and the only reason, he gave for making this outrageous demand upon the company. And subsequently Durant made these affidavits against him. With regard to the statement which has been made here to-day about General Dodge, all I have to say is that General Dodge is well known to the country, and I need not say a word about him. He is certanly well known to one of the gentlemen who sits at this table as a member of this committee, as a very able and true man, and an honest man. I do not think there is a man of good character and reputation in that company who has not always had the utmost faith and confidence in General Dodge. The insinuations the gentleman has made against him here I deem very unjust. In regard to my position in all these controversies, and my view of these men and their purposes, my letter to Oliver Ames, the president of the company, of July 25, 1868, in which I stated what I thought was due to the Government, to the stockholders, and to all parties in interest, fully explained. The views therein expressed furnish my own vindication. You will remember that in that letter I cautioned Oliver Ames against these very things. The chairman suggests that this is a matter entirely collateral to this investigation, and I will not say another word upon that point.

I wish to make this additional statement in respect to the payment of the dividends upon the Oakes Ames contract. As I stated before the other committee, it was not because I was opposed to it upon the ground that any wrong was done to anybody, because all the stockholders of the Union Pacific Railroad Company were to receive substantially their proportionate share of the profits; but it was on account of the personal peril to Oakes Ames and those associated with him, who were my friends, that I opposed the contract, as he will state to you. Dr. Durant has said that I did not oppose the payment of the dividend, and he has copied from the record to show that. His statement is true so far as the record goes; but it will be in proof, and it was perfectly notorious to those gentlemen, that it was something which I thought should not be done, as I deemed it improper in a business point of view. Still, I said to both the Ameses, from first to last, that my interest was so small, so trifling as compared to theirs, and indeed to almost anybody's, that while my judgment was against it, and my feelings adverse to it, if they finally decided that it was best, and I could not convince them by fair argument, I should not be factious and an obstacle in the way; that I should not vote against the contract or the dividends. And they will testify that from first to last I constantly expressed that opinion both in regard to the contract and the dividends.

Dr. Durant has alluded to giving me a call for two hundred and fifty shares of stock as an inducement for me to vote as he desired—in other words, that he purchased my vote for that price; that is what it means. Now, what are the facts? It is true, as he says, that he gave me a call for two hundred and fifty shares at 160; he first offered to sell because he wanted to increase my interest, and he gave, of course, other reasons; I did not then suppose that he had any improper motive in it; I declined to buy at his offer, as I thought I could purchase of another party at the same or a less price; I did not, therefore, choose to take it; he then said he would give me a call for ten days; at the expiration of the ten days it was worth considerably more than 160, and I took it, of course. So far as his attempt to purchase me in that way, all that he says may be true; I do not doubt it; it was his habit to buy votes when needed by inducing them to make some operation by which it would be for their interest to go for him; that was the constant complaint I think of all parties in interest, that he would always do these things; fortunately for me I shall be able to show, and so show it before the other committee, if a thorough investigation is had, that from first to last I stated to Oliver Ames and to Oakes Ames that I should go for these dividends, and that I should vote for the contract if, after full consideration, they really desired it. Dr. Durant's statement that he said there would be no difficulty in getting my vote because he had done what he had, I have heard of before to-day Oakes Ames could have told him, in reply, that he had made a great mistake if he had given me the right to purchase any stock for less than its real value, because I had given him my word that, if he and his brother desired it, I should vote for what they deemed to be their interest, inasmuch as my interest was so trifling in comparison with theirs. Mr. Oakes Ames will testify to that fact; so that if there was any wrong in this matter it seems to be with Dr. Durant entirely, who does not pretend, of course, that I knew anything about his purpose in giving me this call.

I do not suppose it is necessary for me to claim the attention of the committee further upon this subject, except for a single word in regard to the report of the committee on which Oliver Ames and Mr. Cisco were appointed in regard to this expenditure of four or five hundred thousand dollars. All this occurred long before we had anything to do with the company. Oliver Ames has testified that, upon a further knowledge of the facts, he did not believe the money was spent, although Durant told him that he gave, indirectly, some sixty or eighty thousand dollars to Thaddeus Stevens by way of purchasing a foundery; that he did not believe the story, and that will be corroborated so far as my testimony goes.

In regard to the $50,000 which was paid or charged as counsel-fees in the Fisk suit, I have already gone fully into the subject in the other committee; and I only desire now to say that the matter is there fully explained; that it is shown conclusively that I had nothing whatever to do with it; that when a knowledge of it came to me I denounced it; and that I had no connection whatever with it in any shape.

WASHINGTON, *February* 1, 1873.

H. S. McCOMB re-called and examined.

By the CHAIRMAN:

Question. At the time of your former examination you proposed to produce some further letters from Mr. Ames.—Answer. I have made search for them and have found some, but some I have not found.

Q. Will you produce such as you have found?—A. I have some unimportant ones here, some that I have not before referred to. I have not examined all of them, and I do not know very well what is in them.

Q. Are they all the letters from Mr. Ames you have?—A. These are all I can find. I find here in Mr. McMurtrie's letter to Mr. Gowen, he refers to one that I put in as an exhibit in the Pennsylvania case, dated April 13. I cannot find anything but that letter. I have one of March, one of September, and one of November, 1868, and also one of February, 1868; but I cannot find the one referred to in Mr. McMurtrie's letter to Mr. Gowen. I took all these letters back from the examiner and left copies. I do not know what this letter contained; I do not recollect it at all.

Q. Were the letters you had mentioned that you did not find filed as exhibits in the Pennsylvania case?—A. That one of April 13 was the only one.

Q. And the letters you produce here now are all the letters you have from Mr. Ames?—A. They are all the letters I can find. My house has been a perfect pell-mell for the past six months. I put a new mansard roof on it, and had from ten to thirty men at work on it. These papers were carried to my house, and my things have been moved and shifted about and knocked about so that they are in great confusion. I have made very diligent search for these letters. (The letters referred to were examined by the committee and not placed in evidence, as having no reference to this transaction.)

Q. You did not produce this letter of April 13, 1867?—A. I think I did, but I cannot find it.

Q. You think that letter was not left with the master?—A. No, sir; that was produced before the examiner. All my papers that were produced have been marked as exhibits. I took the originals all back, because I was afraid to leave them there.

Q. You have looked among your papers enough to satisfy you that you have not that letter?—A. I have looked over my papers enough to satisfy myself that I cannot lay my hand upon that letter.

Q. Can you state the contents of the letter?—A. I can state something of its contents, but I would rather not speak of the substance of it, because I have not the letter to produce. I have already testified in substance what was in it, and the substance of my personal conversation on the same subject, as well as what was in the letter. I might say that there is a letter here from General Dodge, in which reference is made to a resolution before Congress. He was a member of Congress at that time. This letter was written to me as chairman of the bridge committee, and the postscript refers to defeating the rate bill. I would like to have Mr. McMurtrie's letter to which I have referred placed in evidence, because it shows, as I have said, that Mr. McMurtrie refused to go on with my cross-examination unless these original letters of Mr. Ames were put in.

Q. Did you say you could state the substance of this letter of Mr. Ames to you of April 13, 1867?—A. It was not that letter I said I could state the substance of, but another one. I have not the remotest idea of the contents of that letter any more than if I had never seen it. My only recollection of having seen it is by reference to the McMurtrie letter to Gowen.

Q. What letter do you refer to that you can state the substance of?—A. The letter of Mr. Ames of some time in February, I think 1868; that is the letter that I have searched for and been particularly desirous to find.

Q. State what was said in that letter.—A. I have already repeated about the substance of it.

Q. Have you repeated the substance of it as being in that letter?—A. I stated it as having been said to me, and as having been written by Mr. Ames.

Q. State, as nearly as you can remember, what the letter said.—A. The letter said in substance, (I do not give you the phraseology,) "Did not the stock transferred to Colfax pay?" referring to some ruling he had made in regard to some legislation; that is the substance of the letter; they are not the words; it was a letter written, I should say, the latter part of February, 1868.

Q. Do you remember whether it was about the time you received this letter from General Dodge?—A. I think so; that is what induced me to look up General Dodge's letter; I thought I had something from somebody else on the same subject.

Q. The conversation you speak of with Mr. Ames in reference to Mr. Colfax was before or after you received the letter?—A. I think it was very nearly the same time; there was not many days' difference.

Q. You received the letter from Mr. Ames here at Washington?—A. O, yes; it was written from Washington to me, at Wilmington.

Q. Do you think Mr. Colfax was named in the letter; that he was referred to by name by Mr. Ames?—A. I think he was either referred to by name, or as Speaker; I think the letter referred to him by name; that is my recollection about it.

Q. You are satisfied, from your examination, that you have no further letters or documents?—A. Not that I can find; I have no idea that anything is destroyed; I cannot put my hand upon them; I have looked very diligently for them; I should have brought them, most unquestionably, if I could have found them.

By Mr. McCrary:

Q. You have referred to some ruling of the Speaker.—A. Yes, sir;

that is my recollection. The substance of it was, did not I think the stock which had been placed in that direction had paid in that instance.

Q. Do you know what ruling the Speaker had made?—A. No, sir; I do not; I have no knowledge of the congressional proceedings referred to, and have not read anything in reference to it.

By Mr. NIBLACK:

Q. I understood you, when you were before the committee on another occasion, that he had made some ruling in reference to some move of Mr. Washburne's?—A. I think that relates to Mr. Ames's letter of the 30th of January; that letter relates to Washburne's move and Durant's action in New York. He said nothing could be done here, and he did not care, or did not know, what Durant might do in New York. That was the reference made to Washburne's move. The other was a personal conversation, and the letter which I stated the substance of.

By Mr. MCCRARY:

Q. You have not examined the Globe to see what that ruling was?—A. I have not; nor any other congressional record.

Q. Perhaps I misunderstood you. I understood that you were on the floor of the House when some ruling was made?—A. You must have mistaken me; I don't know that I was ever on the floor of the House when the House was in session.

Q. The letter you cannot find you think is dated February 28th?—A. I did not give that date; I said it was dated in February.

Q. Does not the letter of Mr. McMurtrie refer to that date?—A. No, sir; it does not.

Q. Does Mr. McMurtrie's letter refer to the letter you speak of?—A. No, sir; it gives no date of any letter except that of April 13th, 1867.

Q. Did you receive any letter touching the matter referred to, about the distribution of gifts or shares to members of Congress, except the letters you have filed?—A. No, sir; only the two filed.

Q. That expression, then, must have referred to one or the other of these?—A. It must have referred to one of the two; I subsequently produced another letter of February 22, which Mr. McMurtrie did not refer to; I had furnished Mr. McMurtrie before with copies of these letters over my own signature; I had originally not intended to have these letters made any part of the record; I did not desire that they should be made public; but furnishing him with the copies seemed to whet his appetite and induced him to bring out the originals, and when the originals were produced they got into the newspapers.

Q. I understand the letter you refer to was dated some time in February, 1868, but that you do not know the date?—A. No, sir; I do not know the date, and I would rather not speak of a letter when I cannot give the date. My recollection of the conversation between us is more fresh in my mind.

Q. What had the Speaker done that, in the estimation of Mr. Ames, made the transaction with him "pay?"—A. I could not tell you. It was something relating to the proceedings of Congress.

Q. What did Mr. Ames tell you?—A. No specific thing; nothing more than something that had been up.

Q. Did you infer that it was some ruling he had made as Speaker; did Mr. Ames say something of that kind?—A. I inferred from his expressions that it was some parliamentary maneuver which a presiding officer could perhaps judiciously use, and which resulted in benefiting the company in some way. That is the inference I drew.

Q. The reason I desire to be particular is that if there was any such ruling it will appear in the Globe?—A. Yes, that is the reason that I am very careful in speaking about it. I am not certain that Mr. Colfax's name was used, or whether he was referred to as Speaker.

By Mr. BANKS:

Q. Is it not possible that another member might have been referred to?—A. Such things are possible.

By Mr. MCCRARY:

Q. The transaction must have occurred in January or February?—A. Yes, that is my idea. Mr. Ames's letter evidently had reference to no particular day, but to quite a space of time.

By the CHAIRMAN:

Q. The idea you had from Mr. Ames about it was that this ruling had been in some way influenced by his distribution of stock?—A. Yes, most emphatically. That I am very decided about. One fact I wanted to bring out this morning especially was a conversation with a gentleman with whom I sat at table this morning, and who recollects a conversation between himself and myself in reference to what I said of a conversation between Mr. Brooks and Mr. Alley, during Mr. Durant's absence. If he were present I would like to call upon him this morning to state it.

Q. Is it merely what you said that you want him to testify to?—A. Yes, during Mr. Durant's absence in Europe.

Q. And before the subject was agitated in public?—A. Yes, sir; that gentleman is Mr. Crane; he said he would be here, and if he is I would like to ask him one or two questions. There is one other matter that I want to state, if the committee will allow me. I have examined a copy of the minutes of the executive committee of the Union Pacific Railroad Company, owned by Mr. Durant. I saw in that book, on the 2d January, 1868, that James Brooks acted as member of the executive committee of that company. This was two days before that large dividend was declared, and six days after he had received his first hundred shares Credit Mobilier stock. I want to state further that on the 9th of March, 1868, two days before his appointment, as is stated, as Government director, he acted as inspector of the board of directors; at least he was so appointed by the board as one of the committee of inspectors. If you will ask for the production of these record-books you will see that that is the fact.

Q. These were the proceedings in the election of directors of the Union Pacific Railroad?—A. Yes. I have this morning asked, in the other committee-room, to see a copy of the original minute-book of the Union Pacific Railroad Company of that date. They tell me that book is missing; that the original minutes are missing from October, 1867, to March, 1868; that they cannot get them. Mr. Durant has a copy of that book, and I saw what I have stated on his copy of the minutes of the executive committee. I had myself a personal recollection of the fact, and I looked over these minutes to refresh my recollection.

Q. Do you think Mr. Brooks's right to act in the capacity of a Government director would be affected by his being the holder of Credit Mobilier stock?—A. Yes, sir; the point I make is that Mr. Brooks produced a letter from the Interior Department, stating that he did not qualify as Government director until March 23, 1868; and I want to show that, notwithstanding, he acted as a director before then—at least that he acted as a member of the executive committee, which he could only do by virtue of his appointment as a Government director.

Q. Do you say that prior to the time of his taking the oath he acted as Government director?—A. Yes. He was on the executive committee as Government director of the Union Pacific Railroad Company.

By Mr. NIBLACK:

Q. From what books do you derive that information?—A. From Mr. Durant's copy of the executive committee's minute-books.

Q. The copy Mr. Durant has purports to be taken from the original book?—A. Yes, sir.

By Mr. BANKS:

Q. By whom was that copy made?—A. I do not recollect. It has a notarial seal on it; it is a notarial copy.

By Mr. NIBLACK:

Q. I have learned, more from testimony taken in the other committee than this, that there was some money missing, or not accounted for, which it is claimed was expended here in Washington for the procurement of certain legislation. Have you any knowledge in regard to that matter?

WITNESS. What do you refer to?

Mr. NIBLACK. I cannot very well define it. I think the allegation was that at the time the legislation in Congress in the interest of the Union Pacific Railroad Company was obtained in 1864, some expenditures were made or credits claimed for such expenditures, about which there was some difficulty in producing vouchers for the items. There has also appeared some statement about a large amount of money having been paid at Willard's Hotel at one time.—A. I only paid my own bills at Willard's Hotel. I can answer for that.

Q. Have you any knowledge of this transaction by men connected with the Union Pacific Railroad?—A. I have no knowledge myself, personally, of the expenditure of a dollar in Washington for any such purpose. I was on a committee in conjunction with Josiah Bardwell, of Boston, and John B. Alley, to examine Mr. Durant's accounts for four or five hundred thousand dollars. Mr. Bardwell and myself were ready to proceed with the examination. Mr. Alley wanted to have Oakes Ames present before we should join in making the examination, and telegraphed for him to come on. Mr. Durant produced his vouchers. Mr. Bardwell and myself took a minute of them, and checked off every voucher produced. They were either certified to by J. F. M. Davies and Mr. Bushnell jointly, or by one of them. They were authorized by the resolution of the board to make these certificates. We examined the vouchers in conformity with the resolutions of the board authorizing them to be certified. We took a minute of them and checked them off, as I said. I prepared a report upon the subject and presented it to Mr. Alley to sign, telling him that they were all right. His reply was that if it was all right they must not let the people know it; that Mr. Durant must not be relieved from the odium placed upon him by the statement that these vouchers were for the expenditures of money that he could not account for. That remark struck me with very great force. I remember saying that if Mr. Alley was that stripe of a man he and I must be two people from that time on.

Q. Did you pass on all the items of Mr. Durant's account in that way?—A. Yes; and Mr. Bardwell made a memorandum of them.

Q. You have heard of two $5,000 checks which Dr. Durant says he gave to influence the election in Iowa in 1867; do you recollect about those checks or vouchers?—A. I recollect seeing the checks.

Q. Do you recollect whether he claimed them as vouchers for money expended for the Union Pacific Railroad?—A. I think not; I think that was his individual expenditure. They were not included among the vouchers presented to us to audit. My recollection is that they were not vouchers submitted to us to be audited.

By Mr. ALLEY:

Q. Do you say that Oakes Ames was on this committee?—A. No, sir; I did not say any such thing.

Q. Do you say that he was present?—A. I did not say any such thing.

Q. I know you did not; I ask you the question now.—A. I say he was not present at our interview when we had this talk.

Q. Was there any one present with us when I made the declaration you have alluded to?—A. Nobody who could hear you, because their ears would be closed for anything you said that was not according to your view.

Q. I thought there would be nobody present to hear that conversation.—A. That was a conversation between you and myself.

Q. Did you not swear in Philadelphia that I was the only person who refused to sign that report, and the reason I gave was that Mr. Durant was a dishonest man; that these vouchers were not satisfactory, and I utterly refused to sign that report?—A. I did testify to that, and I repeat that testimony now. You were one of the three men appointed on that committee, you were a tacitly-appointed member. I do not know whether you were regularly appointed or not. You and Mr. Ames came in subsequently and examined the vouchers for yourselves. What conclusions you came to for your own edification I do not know.

The following are the letters placed in evidence by witness in the above testimony, May 21, 1872.

MCCOMB *vs.* THE CREDIT MOBILIER.

DEAR SIR: On Thursday, December 23d, you have appointed to close the cross-examination of Mr. McComb, and to proceed with your evidence.

Allow me to remind you of promises made by your client at the prior meetings, many months since, to furnish or produce the papers or documents, from copies of which he spoke or referred to, or to memoranda taken from them. Some, at least, were to be sent me *next day.* None have been sent. He stated the other day they had been withheld for a purpose. I must ask that you will require him to produce, at the meeting on Thursday, if you desire me to cross-examine, the following letter from Oakes Ames in reference to the disposing 375 shares as gifts to members of Congress. His books showing the original entries of dividends or sums stated to have been received as dividends:

April	1866
July	1866
September	1866
December	1866
January	1868

I would also like to have a copy of Mr. Ames's letter of April 13, 1867. Exhibit No. 2, Awn.

Very truly,

R. C. McMURTRIE.

JAS. E. GOWEN, Esq.

[Private.]

FORTIETH CONGRESS UNITED STATES,
HOUSE OF REPRESENTATIVES,
Washington, D. C., February 17, 1868.

H. S. McCOMB, *Washington:*

I write Tracy to-day. When you go to New York, get my report to you and let him read it. It is important that he should take a decided stand for the Childs' Mill crossing; also for the C. B. transfer grounds. If we swing away south we will be virtually in the wilderness with our transfer—no train or accommodation near—and will strike a fatal blow to the interests of Western Iowa. The C. R. I. & P. R. R. certainly do not want to add five to eight miles to the distance to Chicago for benefit of B. & Mo. R. R., when most of the southern trade will leave us at Kearney and go by the Atchison Branch, which will finish their road to Kearney this year.

Truly,

G. M. DODGE.

P. S.—We beat the rate resolution to-day, 61 to 73; close vote.

John B. ALLEY, having been recalled at his own instance, made the following statement:

I will merely state that, so far as having made any declaration of the kind sated by Mr. McComb, in regard to the reasons which I gave for not signing that report, providing for the expenditure, by Dr. Durant, of $435,000, it is utterly false in every particular. It is a sheer fabrication, without any foundation whatever. I wish to say that my interest in the Union Pacific Railroad at the time of the Oakes Ames contract was in the neighborhood of one thousand one hundred shares. The capital, at that time, was about six millions. My interest in the Credit Mobilier corporation at the time this contract went into operation was two hundred and ninety shares, the capital being $3,750,000; showing that if any one was wronged by that contract it was myself, as my interest in the Union Pacific Railroad Company was relatively and proportionately nearly three times as much as in the Credit Mobilier.

I will say, further, in relation to my position on the subject of declaring dividends, that I stated it fully yesterday. I might mention this fact, that Oakes Ames in his letter, as you will all remember, complained of me as being the only person opposed to their making these dividends. That was some time subsequent to the sale of the two hundred and fifty shares to me by Durant, and the conversation I narrated yesterday. My judgment and my feeling were in perfect consistency from first to last in regard to that matter.

HENRY C. CRANE recalled and examined.

By the CHAIRMAN:

Question. Do you know anything in reference to the conversation between Mr. Brooks and Mr. Alley in regard to Mr. Brooks having fifty shares of Credit Mobilier stock?—Answer. I know nothing about it.

Q. Did you have any information on the subject at the time?—A. No, sir.

Q. Did you hear anybody say anything about it?—A. I do not think I did.

Q. Did you hear Mr. McComb say anything about it?—A. I do not think I did.

Q. Mr. McComb informed us that he had some conversation in regard to it about the time. You had no information from Mr. McComb on the subject?—A. No, sir.

Q. Did Mr. McComb, about the time of the issuing of these fifty shares to Neilson, say anything to you in relation to Mr. Brooks's action or in regard to what Mr. Brooks did?—A. Mr. Durant was in Europe then. I was in correspondence with him. Mr. Brooks was always supposed to be a friend of Mr. Durant. Mr. McComb came to me and wanted me to keep my own counsel, saying that Mr. Brooks had showed himself out to the other parties.

Q. That is all he said?—A. He gave me to understand that I had better keep my own counsel; keep my matters to myself; that in case I wanted to consult him on anything I was to meet him at the Fifth Avenue Hotel,

Q. Was anything said in relation to this Credit Mobilier stock?—A. I think not. I have no recollection of it.

By Mr. McCrary:

Q. Did Mr. McComb tell you he had heard a conversation between Mr. Alley and Mr. Brooks about the matter?—A. I have no recollection of any such thing. I know there were meetings being held there all the while between the parties. Mr. McComb was keeping me posted in what I could not pick up for myself. He knew, I supposed, that Mr. Brooks's relations were friendly to Mr. Durant, and so he gave me this warning, which it was very satisfactory for me to have.

Q. You do not remember that he told you he heard any conversation between Mr. Alley and Mr. Brooks?—A. No, sir; I do not.

Q. Did you ever make any report of this conversation you had with Mr. McComb in writing to Mr. Durant?—A. I did, either by letter or telegram. I do not know what it was. I was writing to him very often. I was looking after his business.

Q. You either wrote to Dr. Durant or telegraphed him to that effect?—A. I think so. I kept posted on these matters and kept him posted. I do not know what I did say to him.

Washington, D. C., *February* 6, 1873.

Horace F. Clark sworn and examined.

By Mr. Brooks:

Question. Please state whether you had any interest in the Credit Mobilier?—Answer. I have not, and never had at any time. I had no connection of any sort or description with the Union Pacific Railroad Company until March 7, 1872.

Q. And you have had no interest in the Credit Mobilier since that time, direct or indirect?—A. Never, at any time. I never purchased a share of Union Pacific Railroad stock until after January, 1872. I not only have no interest in the Credit Mobilier, but in fact my interest is adverse to that corporation.

Q. Will you define in plain English the meaning of the French words Credit Mobilier, when applied to the building of a railroad in this country under the circumstances attending the building of the Union Pacific Railroad?—A. Premising that all I know of the Credit Mobilier is derived from the public history of the times and from such examination as it has been my duty to make, as president of the Union Pacific Railroad Company since my election in 1872, I will say that the Credit Mobilier, in this case, was a construction company to build this road and make money by the construction.

Q. Were you invited in 1866 or 1867 to take an interest in this construction company?—A. I was; some time about 1866 the matter was called to my attention. I declined because I deemed the venture too hazardous—beyond the limits of ordinary prudence.

Q. Why did you deem it too hazardous?—A. Without, perhaps, judging correctly as to the future, I thought the road if built would be worthless as property, and I saw no temptation to invest money in an enterprise where the whole capital, in my judgment, would be lost.

Q. Did you or not hear at the time that the surveyors who were making reconnaissances of this road were obliged to be accompanied by troops of cavalry; that they could not venture among the Indians without armed escorts?—A. Being considerably connected with railroads I gave some general attention to the subject which I suppose every intelligent man is more or less familiar with, and I came to the conclusion that the whole enterprise except as a Government measure was beyond the range of ordinary prudence.

Q. Did you found that opinion upon the extreme danger the builders of the road would incur?—A. I thought that no reliable estimate could be made of the cost of construction under the circumstances, and that when constructed the property itself would probably be worthless; that is, that the road could not be so managed, when built, that it could pay its running expenses. The reasons which impelled me to that conclusion were the character of the country, and the whole circumstances surrounding the case. I, therefore, let it go by, notwithstanding all the promises of successful speculation; and, as I said, never became interested in it until after the act of March, 1871, was passed by Congress, and then became interested in it by reason of the very large interest I then had and now have in its eastern connections.

Q. Were you aware, from general information, or from reading the reports of the engineers, that the construction trains for that road had to be armed with light artillery, Sharp's rifles, and outlying guards, against the savages infesting that country?—A. It was well understood by railroad men that a part of the force were armed to guard the remainder at work. To invest money in a railroad to be built under such circumstances appeared to me preposterous; perhaps I was mistaken.

Q. Did you ever know any railroad in the United States to be built under such trying or difficult circumstances?—A. Nothing compared with it in the history of this country.

Q. Have you or not been largely engaged in the construction of railroads in different parts of the United States?—A. I have been interested in the construction of a very considerable number of railroads, and am now interested in the construction of several railroads, but not of that character. The railroads, the construction of which I have been and am connected with, are branches extending from main trunk lines, in which I am largely interested. I am president of the Lake Shore and Michigan Southern Railroad Company, a railroad extending from Buffalo to Chicago. I am interested in the construction of several feeders or lateral branches leading to the main line. The purpose of their construction and of my interest in them is to add to the business of the main line, but in all these cases, when constructed, a fair amount of traffic is insured. In case of the Union Pacific Railroad Company, unless finished to the Pacific, there would probably have been no traffic, and I had no anticipation of any settlement of the country which would insure it.

Q. Is it not also true that when the construction of the Union Pacific Railroad was commenced there were no termini east or west, and no connections with it?—A. There was no line of railroad from Chicago to the Missouri River; it impressed me as a wild adventure.

Q. In the construction of such a road as that through a savage wilderness, over an unexplored country, what should be the difference of profit on its construction from that in constructing railroads in Ohio, Michigan, Illinois, New York, or any of the older States?—A. The ordinary tests cannot be applied. The amount of reasonable profits depends upon the character of the risk. As I said before, I saw no inducement, because of any probable amount of profit, to invest money in an enterprise where the capital might possibly, and, in my judgment, would probably, be utterly lost.

Q. You would not, therefore, go into it at all?—A. I declined to go into it at all.

Q. There have been two modes of building railroads since you have been upon the stage. The first was by subscription of the stock, and the next by construction companies. Will you give us a little history, as an expert, of the difference in the two modes of building?—A. In the early history of railroads in this country, subscriptions were made to the capital stock and the roads were constructed for account of the stockholders. It resulted, in almost every instance, that the money invested by the stockholders was a total loss. For many years past, I should say ten or more, few roads have been built except by means of construction companies; and by construction companies I mean by parties associating themselves together, with or without the protection of a charter, who take all the securities and all the stock for better or for worse, and provide the means for the construction.

Q. What is the difference, then, between such a company and the Credit Mobilier?—A. The only difference is, that in this case the directors of the Union Pacific Railroad Company—some of them—were also the directors and managers of the Credit Mobilier. They, therefore, dealt with themselves, and became subject to the rules of equity urisprudence affecting the relations of trustees and *cestui que trusts*. I have never been connected with any construction company which sustained the technical relation of directors of the company whose railroads were being constructed. In this particular case, it may be said, perhaps justly, that these men bargained with themselves, and perhaps are liable to have the question raised upon them under the general rules of equity jurisprudence to which I have referred, the result of which is that if a profit is realized they must surrender it, and if a loss is incurred they must sustain it.

Q. Were or were not the contracts for building the Union Pacific Railroad entered into with the assent of all the stockholders of that company?—A. It is so alleged. It is alleged that there are upon the records of the Union Pacific Railroad Company evidence showing that that corporation, Government directors and all, assented to these dealings with the Credit Mobilier. There is also upon the records evidence going to show that the stockholders of the Union Pacific Railroad Company, who were the parties ultimately interested in this matter, assented to this scheme of construction. The question remains whether, when the stock was subsequently sold and passed, as it has passed into the hands of *bona-fide* purchasers, it was received shorn of its claims to the large and, as some allege, inordinate profits made by the construction company, or whether they can enforce the rights which the prior owners of the stock could enforce in case there has been a violation of the proper relations between trustees and *cestui que trusts.* I am one of the new class of *bona-fide* purchasers of stock who came in in 1872, and ascertained that these large dividends have been received by other parties in the course of construction; and whether we have or have not claims against such of the directors of the Credit Mobilier as sustained the technical relations of directors of the Union Pacific Railroad Company, is a legal question which may or may not arise; and it is a question that has not perhaps been adjudicated, as to what right stockholders purchasing stock in the open market acquire in respect to past transactions which may be subject to criticism.

Q. About how large a percentage of profit have you known to be made by railroad credit mobiliers or large construction companies for building railroads in the old and settled States?—A. It is the practice nowadays, as I have stated, for the construction companies to take all the securities, bonds, stocks, and everything, for better or for worse, and the profit which ought to be made of course depends upon the character of the risk. No profit, as I said before, would tempt me to the possible hazard of the principal. I have never been engaged in any enterprise where there was not a reasonable expectation that the property would not be worth something.

Q. What is the largest profit you have known to be made on the construction of a railroad in one of the old States?—A. I was connected with a railroad from the State of New York into the interior of the State of Vermont, in which I believe we took the bonds at par and an equivalent amount of the stock, and we expected to make 100 per cent. out of the transaction; but I am under the impression that the entire amount of the investment is a total loss. I am now speaking of the Harlem extension. In the construction of lateral roads connecting with the great trunk lines east and west, the laterals extending, for instance, into coal-fields, over which roads, when finished, there must be a greater or less amount of traffic, 100 per cent. has not been regarded as an excessive or inordinate profit. Nobody is wronged in any event, because the enterprise itself and the results of it belong to the parties who hazard their money, and who take the results for better or for worse.

Q. Have you heard of a larger profit than 100 per cent.?—A. It so happens that the development of business may bring about a larger profit. Any profit commensurate with the risk incurred would not be regarded by railroad men as unreasonable.

Q. Can capitalists in New York be tempted to go into northwestern railroads or southwestern railroads without the promise of very large profits?—A. Of course not. In a new country the future of a railroad enterprise is always more or less uncertain, because there is no local traffic to sustain it insured in advance.

Q. As a Government director, associated with such men as ex-Vice-President Wade, George Ashmum, now dead, Mr. Williams, of Indiana, and others with whom I was associated, I want to ask you two questions. First, what time this Credit Mobilier was organized?—A. From my examination of its history I believe the Credit Mobilier was a charter granted by the State of Pennsylvania in the year 1859, under the name of the Pennsylvania Fiscal Agency. Its name was changed by authority of the legislature of Pennsylvania to the Credit Mobilier of America about 1863. The charter is one of a class of charters which had been granted by several of the legislatures of the Northern States, and which are supposed to confer powers and franchises sufficient to enable the companies organized under them to do business in any part of the world, and to protect the stockholders against personal responsibilities. The State of Connecticut has a general law under which enterprises are being conducted in various parts of the world. Mining companies are organized under the general laws of New York, which carry on their operations in Colorado, Utah, and even in Australia. It has been supposed that these State charters give the protection against personal responsibility which the Credit Mobilier charter assumed to give. This Credit Mobilier charter was no better than half a dozen thers for oil production, pipe-lines, and many mining operations conducted in various parts of the country under State charters. The Panama Railroad was built under a charter from the State of New York. In the case of the Union Pacific Railroad there was an absolute necessity for the intervention of a corporation to protect against personal responsibility the men engaged in an enterprise of so much magnitude and hazard. If the gentlemen sitting around this table combine to build a railroad, they are liable, *in solido*, for its contracts. Where the enterprise is especially hazardous, or the amounts larger than the ordinary means of capitalists, no man of prudence would embark in it, except where his liability was limited by the extent of his subscription under a charter limiting personal responsibility. In case of a small enterprise, not extra hazardous and promising well, parties of responsibility may be willing to invest without the intervention of such a corporation. It the other case it would be hardly considered as within the limits of ordinary prudence.

Q. Under that presentation of facts, on the 2d of January, 1868, some two or three years after the creation of this company, would you deem it the duty of a Government director to break up its contract and dissolve its connection with the railroad company?—A. It is my understanding from the history of this matter that the Government directors had previous to that time assented to a contract of this corporation with the Union Pacific Railroad Company. There was no opposition at any time manifested against these proceedings on the part of the Government directors, so far as I am aware.

Q. What, in your judgment, was my duty as a Government director, on the 2d of January, 1868, in regard to this Credit Mobilier proceeding; was it to break up its relation to the Union Pacific Railroad, and risk the road not being built, or not?—A. If it was for the interest of the Government to kill the enterprise, perhaps that was your duty; if it was the object of the Government to secure the construction of the road, means must be resorted to to accomplish the result. I do not know whether you were a Government director under the scheme of 1862 or that of 1864.

Mr. Brooks. I was a Government director under the law of 1864.

Witness. Under the law of 1862, the scheme of organization was this: There were thirteen directors elected by the stockholders, and two additional directors were appointed by the President. That law of 1862 contained a provision directory upon the President of the United States to appoint two Government directors, persons who were not stockholders of the company. The law of 1864 changed that scheme, and provided for twenty directors, fifteen to be elected by the stockholders, and five to be appointed by the President; but it does not contain a provision directing that the President shall appoint the five Government directors from persons who were others than stockholders; the act of 1864 is silent upon that point. The act of 1862 does not contain any provision that the acquisition of stock in the Union Pacific Railroad shall void their seats; but directs the President to appoint as I have said. You seem to have assumed that there is a disability upon the part of Government directors, under the scheme of 1864, to hold stock; I have not been able to construe the law in that light. I have supposed it to be a general rule of statutory construction that when the subject-matter of an old law is covered by the new, and new regulations are made in relation to the same subject, there is a repeal, by implication, of the old; and I do not find in the law of 1864 any inhibition against a Government director owning stock in the Union Pacific Railroad Company. If you are to presume that Congress, in the law of 1864, meant to retain the provisions as to Government directors which are not repealed by the law of 1862, then I am mistaken; but I have supposed otherwise.

Q. The number of directors was increased under the act of 1864?—A. The number of Government directors was increased from two to five.

Q. And the new law was made applicable to the five?—A. The act is entirely silent as to the qualifications of the five. It ought, perhaps, to be stated that the same reason existed in 1864 as in 1862 why this class of Government directors should be parties adverse, if you please, to the interests of the stockholders of the Union Pacific Railroad; but there is entire silence in the law upon that question. I do not know what the views were, or what the policy of Congress. It is certain that there appears upon the records no objection on the part of the Government directors, at any time, to that Credit Mobilier scheme of construction.

Q. I am asking these questions because it is alleged that the use of my son-in-law's name was a mere cover for me to own the stock myself. What I want to ask you is, whether there was anything in the contract of the Credit Mobilier which made it necessary that a man owning stock in that corporation should also own stock in the Union Pacific Railroad Company?—A. By the scheme adopted, as I understand it, a stockholder in the Credit Mobilier might or might not become a stockholder in the Union Pacific Railroad Company. As a matter of fact the stock of the Union Pacific Railroad Company was divided among the stockholders of the Credit Mobilier, and the division of such stock was anticipated in the event of the Government securities and the first-mortgage bonds not realizing from their sale a sufficient amount to cover the sum embraced in the contract.

Q. Let me ask you whether the profit realized by the Credit Mobilier on the construction of the Union Pacific Railroad was larger than in the construction of the Panama Railroad, or of the Nicaragua route, judging by sales of stock?—A. I think that stock has been as high as 240, and down as low as 50; the depreciation resulting from the change in the course of trade, by reason of the construction of the Pacific Railroad. The earnings of the Panama Railroad were very large during the early emigration to California, and during the gold excitement. I do not feel able to say what would be regarded as an inordinate or extravagant profit, considering the hazards of this enterprise. There can be no rule applied to it. Practically the directors of this road had to build the road east through the State of Iowa. After that road was built they had to bridge the chasm of the Missouri River. They were compelled to construct their road over a country furnishing no timber, no traffic, no fuel, and no water. That was too much for me. I do not know what profits those engaged in the construction of this road realized; I never heard of any profit sufficient to tempt me to incur the hazard of investing in it.

Q. Would you, or would the public, have justified me and my associate directors if we had prevented the construction of this road by breaking up or denouncing the contracts of the company with the Credit Mobilier?—A. If it could have been possible to have built it for less money I think you would have discharged your duty better, and that the present stockholders would have been in a better condition if it had cost half as much.

Q. Was it possible?—A. I think not. I think you could not have obtained subscriptions to build that road. If there was no road now I do not think you could, although the promises for the next year are that the traffic will reach ten million dollars; I do not think you could raise the capital to build it to-day.

Q. State what peculiar difficulties and dangers the road encountered in consequence of snow-storms during the last winter.—A. I came in as president in March, 1872; the road was blockaded with snow for about two months. We were deprived of a revenue of one million dollars, and we have expended between five and six hundred thousand dollars the present year in order to prevent the recurrence of similar snow-blockades this winter.

By Mr. BANKS:

Q. You have been president of the Union Pacific Railroad Company since March 6, 1872, and you know, naturally, what the interests of the company are now?—A. I am the executive officer of the Union Pacific Railroad Company, which is a corporation entirely distinct from the Credit Mobilier.

Q. If there has been any irregularity in connection with the Credit Mobilier organization; if they have deprived anybody of their rights, upon whom has that injury fallen, in your judgment?—A. Upon the stockholders of the Union Pacific Railroad Company.

Q. Upon them rather than the Government of the United States?—A. The position of the Government in regard to this road is that of a second-mortgage bondholder; the Government is the creditor of the road to the extent of twenty-seven millions of dollars, which originally was the first mortgage on the road. In 1864 the Government subordinated that lien to a mortgage on the road for an equal amount. The Government is, therefore, a creditor with that lien upon the property for $27,000,000. The wrong, if wrong there was—and upon that subject I do not wish to be understood as having expressed any opinion, because my interest is adverse to the parties in interest in the Credit Mobilier—I say the wrong, if wrong there was, has fallen upon the stockholders of the Union Pacific Railroad Company. The Government is interested in the maintenance of the road, in its being kept in a condition to do the services for which the corporation was created. It holds the position, simply, of a creditor with a debt not yet due, and not that of a creditor at large.

Q. You have stated that as it was your duty as president, you have looked into the history of the company; was that before or since you took charge of the company as president?—A. Since.

Q. Then you have learned its history from the records?—A. I have.

Q. As the representative of the company, how have you regarded the transactions of the Credit Mobilier?—A. It has seemed to me that there has been a technical violation of the rule of equity jurisprudence to which I have referred. I have doubted whether there might not be a remedy, provided inordinate profits had been derived in the course of that construction.

Q. How have you regarded it yourself as a practical business man having a practical interest in the matter?—A. It is only recently that developments have been made as to the whole history of the construction of the road. We have waited for such a development of the facts as might disclose to us our remedy on the one hand, or which on the other might show circumstances to exonerate the parties constructing the road from responsibility.

Q. What I desire is a statement of your own opinion.—A. My own opinion is that some time or other, as between gentlemen sustaining the technical relations to which I have referred, there might be such a state of facts as to justify a court of equity in looking at the question as to whether the profits were or were not unreasonable under all the circumstances.

Q. You have not, then, yourself pronounced any opinion upon the matter as president of the company?—A. No; I should not be justified in saying what would be the action of the company. So far as I am concerned I should endeavor to be just. I would not insist that men should take such hazard as this for six, seven, or eight per cent. I do not even know how much they got. I have stated my opinion of the law as applicable to such enterprises.

Q. Since your official relation with the company have you known Mr. Oakes Ames in connection with its affairs and as a business man?—A. I know Oakes Ames very well; I first met him in 1872. I have had business relations with him since that time; he has always attended the meetings of the board, and has always exhibited a very deep interest in the affairs of the company.

Q. Are you permitted to state your views of his action or connection with the company in regard to its interests?—A. Certainly; I have no secrets in that respect.

Q. What is your idea of his character as a business man in connection with the affairs of the company?—A. Mr. Ames is a peculiar man; he has impressed me as a thoroughly honest man, without that accuracy, and without, perhaps, that peculiar culture which some men have acquired.

Q. I ask for his general character as a business man?—A. I think very well of Mr. Ames; I should not regard him as the most accurate man; I should not regard him as a full man in his explanations. He is not a man of many words; I believe him to be a thoroughly honest man.

By the CHAIRMAN:

Q. I supposed the stockholders of the Union Pacific Railroad Company and of the Credit Mobilier were to a large extent the same persons?—A. That being true might relieve the case of difficulty, except as to the non-assenting stockholders.

Q. If the stockholders had been identically the same there could be no question as to the propriety of this proceeding?—A. No, sir; but that was not the case.

Q. I understand it to have been not absolutely the case, but that the great mass of the stockholders of the Union Pacific Railroad Company were also stockholders of the Credit Mobilier?—A. I think they either were or had the opportunity to become so. I ought to have stated that it is asserted, in behalf of these gentlemen, that the stockholders of the Union Pacific Railroad Company who did not become stockholders of the Credit Mobilier sold out their stock.

Q. As you understand it, the stockholders of the Union Pacific Railroad were all allowed to come in and become stockholders of the Credit Mobilier?—A. It is so alleged, and I believe it was as a matter of fact.

Q. And the great mass of them did so?—A. They did.

Q. So that if there was any exorbitant price paid for the construction of the road, the profit on it was divided substantially among the stockholders of the Union Pacific Railroad Company itself?—A. I am satisfied that was done. The question I have been discussing was whether the present stockholders received their stock shorn of that right, and that is a view of the case which has not, I think, been presented.

Q. Have you examined so as to be able to give us any opinion as to the quantity of Union Pacific stock that was not represented in the Credit Mobilier?—A. From the best inquiries I have made, I suppose about 20,000 shares were not. I think 360,000 shares were issued. But it is claimed by these gentlemen, and that ought not to be suppressed, that the holders of this stock either sold it or else acquired the right to participate in the contracts with the Credit Mobilier.

Q. It was one of the conditions that the stockholders should sign the Oakes Ames contract in order to participate in its benefits?—A. The condition was that the dividends should only be paid to such stockholders of the Credit Mobilier as, being owners of the stock of the Union Pacific Railroad Company, should give a perpetual proxy.

Q. Your first connection with the road was less than a year ago; had you any knowledge at all in reference to the distribution of the stock of the Credit Mobilier prior to that time?—A. I had not. I ought to say that when I purchased a large amount of stock in 1872, I knew there had been a construction company, and that their profits had been large; precisely how large I did not then and do not now know.

Q. Did you know to whom that stock went?—A. I did not. My first information was derived during the late political canvass, when it was published in the newspapers. I found it out as the public generally did as one of the scandals of the day.

By Mr. BROOKS:

Q. If this railroad is allowed to be conducted as other railroads are what is your opinion as to its power to pay the debt it will owe the Government at the time when the second mortgage becomes due?—A. With friendly relations on the part of the Government to the company, and not otherwise, because it is in the power of the Government to destroy it, as it is in the power of a State government to destroy a franchise of its own creation—I say, assuming friendly relations with the Government, with the present expectations as to lands, and as to coal-lands particularly; assuming that the transportation of supplies for the Government does not fall off to any great extent, I should think that without some special calamity befalling the enterprise the Government is secure enough. We are all astonished at the growth of settlements along the road. We are carrying every year an army which guards the line, the effect of which is to diminish the transportation for the Government, except as to the mail-service, which is increasing. Under the circumstances, I think there is a reasonable hope that the second mortgage of the Government is good, with friendly relations, but not otherwise.

By Mr. McCRARY:

Q. Suppose the statute to be construed as you construe it, not to prohibit the holder of Union Pacific Railroad stock from acting as Government director, do you think the same construction would prohibit the owner of Credit Mobilier stock from acting in that capacity?—A. I did not mean to assert positively the opinion that a Government director was not inhibited from holding Union Pacific Railroad stock. I think the policy and purpose of the provision of the law of 1862 might be held to apply to the law of 1864. That would be a question of construction.

Q. Suppose the law of 1864 had expressly stated that a Government director should not be the holder of Union Pacific Railroad stock, then the question is whether the spirit of that would not apply equally to the Credit Mobilier?—A. In other words, as a holder of Credit Mobilier stock might acquire stock of the Union Pacific Railroad as a dividend in the event provided for, which event did happen, the position of the Government director holding Credit Mobilier stock would be attended with some embarrassment. The same general rule which applies to directors dealing with themselves would, of course, apply.

Q. The holder of stock in the Credit Mobilier would be equally interested against the Government?—A. Not until he acquired Union Pacific Railroad stock. Of course, as the holder of Credit Mobilier stock, he was engaged in a speculation to make money out of the construction of the road.

By Mr. MERRICK:

Q. Do you think a Government director could be engaged in a speculation to make money out of the construction of an enterprise in which he was Government director, with propriety?—A. Perhaps not; but referring, if I may do so, to his position as a member of Congress, the holder of an interest either in the Credit Mobilier or the Union Pacific Railroad Company might practically be disqualified from voting in any case where a direct interest ought to disqualify him. So that Mr. Ames, in the distribution of this stock, practically incapacitated his friends from sustaining the road in case of a Government raid upon it.

Q. That is, provided they took that view?—A. Let me say that there is no better rule of law than that there is a presumption of the correct performance of official duty. Whenever a question arises in which a member of Congress has an interest different from that of the world at large, and peculiar to himself, he will be compelled to withhold his vote.

WASHINGTON, D. C., *February* 6, 1873.

JAMES BROOKS, recalled at his own instance, made the following statement:

I desire to make a correction in my former testimony in regard to my appointment and commission as a Government director of the Union Pacific Railroad Company. I stated that my appointment was dated October 1, 1867, and that I took the oath as such on the 23d of March following. Not having formally accepted the appointment, I supposed it had not been renewed before I qualified for the position by taking the oath. I depended upon the records of the Interior Department for these dates. I find now that the appointment was renewed March 21, 1868. Since testifying before the committee I have seen what I presume is an accurate copy of the books of the Union Pacific Railroad Company, from which I find that I acted at Government director, the 2d of January, 1868, prior to my qualification as such, and prior to taking the oath. I am willing to accept the statement that I did so act January 2, 1868, as correct. I repeat that the only guide I have had in regard to these dates has been the records of the Department. This seems to be an official record, and I accept it as such.

By the CHAIRMAN:

Question. It appears, by this extract from the minutes of the Union Pacific Railroad Company, that you acted as a director at a meeting held 2d of January, and at another meeting held 6th of February.—Answer. I presume that is correct, and I desire so to correct and shape my testimony in the conflicting dates of the Interior Department and the Union Pacific Railroad Company.

Q. These minutes also show that on the 11th of March you acted as one of the inspectors of election?—A. Yes. I might have done that, I presume, without having been even a director. I do not know how it is, but I presume they have the right to call anybody as an inspector of election.

I want, also, to make record of the fact here, so as to make the consistency of my statement appear, that it was December 26, 1867, when Mr. Neilson received his shares from Dr. Durant. This was prior to January 2, 1868, and therefore I was perfectly accurate in stating that I had no interest, direct or indirect, in the Credit Mobilier when I became a Government director. That was the only issue in the case. I want to bring these dates into consistence as much as possible, and I want to impress upon the committee that I was led into the inaccuracy I have referred to by the records of the Interior Department, to which alone I had access when that statement was made by me.

The following papers, referred to in the above testimony, were placed in evidence:

"DEPARTMENT OF THE INTERIOR,
"*Washington, D. C., March* 21, 1868.

"SIR: I have the honor to transmit herewith a commission from the President of the United States, appointing you to be a Government director of the Union Pacific Railroad Company.

"If you accept the appointment, please signify the same, and take, subscribe, and return the inclosed oath to this Department.

"I am, sir, very respectfully, your obedient servant,

"O. H. BROWNING,
"*Secretary.*

"Hon. JAMES BROOKS,
"*New York.*"

NEW YORK, *January* 2, 1868.

Pursuant to the call of Mr. Oliver Ames, president *pro tem.*, the board of directors of the Union Pacific Railroad Company met this day at the office of the company. Present: Messrs. Ames, Alley, Bushnell, Duff, Durant, Dexter, Cook, Cisco, Glidden, McComb, Macy, Ashman, McKee, Brooks, and Bardwell.

Pursuant to adjournment the board of directors of the Union Pacific Railroad Company met this third day of January, 1868. Present: Messrs. Ames, Alley, Bushnell, Bates, Dillon, Dexter, Durant, Cisco, Cook, Glidden, McComb, Ashman, McKee, and Brooks.

NEW YORK, *February* 6, 1868.

Board met pursuant to call of president. Present: Messrs. Ames,

Alley, Bushnell, Bardwell, Bates, Duff, Dillon, Dexter, Cisco, Glidden, McComb, Ashman, McKee, Williams, and Brooks.

Mr. Ashman offered resolution that a committee of three be appointed to negotiate in relation to franchise, &c., of telegraph line, and that Messrs. Dillon, Bushnell, and Brooks be such committee, and that they report to this board. Passed.

Extract from the minutes of the board of directors of the Union Pacific Railroad Company at a meeting held March 11, 1868.

Mr. John J. Cisco reported to the meeting that the board of directors of the company had designated the following persons as inspectors of election to preside at the election of directors at this meeting of stockholders, viz: John J. Cisco, John B. Alley, and James Brooks.

Mr. James Brooks, from the inspectors, reported as the result of the election, that the following-named gentlemen were duly elected directors of the company for the ensuing year, having a majority of all the votes cast, viz: Thomas C. Durant, Oliver Ames, H. S. McComb, Charles A. Lambard, John Duff, John J. Cisco, C. S. Bushnell, Josiah Bardwell, John F. Tracy, Sidney Dillon, W. H. Macy, F. G. Dexter, Benjamin E. Bates, John B. Alley, and Henry C. Crane.

STATE OF NEW YORK,
City and County of New York, ss:

This may certify that I, Merritt A. Potter, a notary public in and for said county and State, duly commissioned and sworn, and residing in said city, have compared the foregoing extracts from the book of minutes of the board of directors of the Union Pacific Railroad Company with the original thereof, and that the same are true copies of said original.

In witness whereof I have hereunto set my hand and official seal the fourth day of February, 1873.

M. A. POTTER,
Notary Public, N. Y. Co.

WASHINGTON, D. C., *February* 6, 1873.

AUGUSTUS SCHELL sworn, and examined by Mr. Brooks:

Question. I want to ask you if in 1866, or the early part of 1867, I came to you and desired to interest you and your associates in railroad matters in the stock of the Credit Mobilier?—Answer. Some time in 1867 or 1868, you called upon me and called my attention to my becoming interested in the Union Pacific Railroad.

Q. What makes you think it was in 1868?—A. I am not sure about the time; I said in 1867 or 1868; I was over a part of the road in 1866; I think this was in the summer of 1867.

Q. Do you remember the substance of the conversation that occurred between us?—A. You called my attention to it as being a very important enterprise, or one that gentlemen associated in railroads would find it advantageous to themselves to become connected with. You asked me to examine into it, and if I thought well of it to take an interest in it, and to interest those who were associated with me in other enterprises to take an interest in it. I replied that I would examine into the matter, and at your suggestion I went to the office of the Union Pacific Railroad Company in New York, and had an interview with Dr. Durant, who was at the head of the enterprise. He explained to me the condition of the affairs of the company and the arrangements for the construction of the road. I reflected upon the matter and declined to interest myself in it.

Q. Have you any objection to stating the general reasons why you declined to enter into it?—A. It was a great enterprise, involving very large amounts of money, and although the profits and advantages seemed to be desirable, yet I was unwilling to embark my own money in it and take the risk incident upon so large an enterprise.

Q. With some few exceptions, did any of the capitalists of New York come into it at that time?—A. Very few with whom I was associated.

Q. Did it or not seem to be too hazardous an exterprise to put money in it?—A. It seemed to me the risk would be very great for the profits and advantages which were to be derived from it.

Q. Do you recollect anything about the value of the stock at that time; would you have gone into the Credit Mobilier at par or not at that time?—A. I do not know that it was dealt in to any considerable extent in the market.

By the CHAIRMAN:

Q. Did you understand from Mr. Brooks whether he was a stockholder or not?—A. I did not.

Q. Did you understand that Mr. Brooks was acting in behalf of this Credit Mobilier corporation?—A. I understood that he was a friend of the enterprise.

Q. Did you know at that time that the stock of the company was regarded as very valuable, and was selling at very much above par?—A. No, sir; I never had any interest in it, and did not watch it at all.

Q. You knew nothing in relation to the price of the stock at any time?—A. No, sir.

WASHINGTON, D. C., *February* 6, 1873.

JAMES B. BECK, a member of the United States House of Representatives from the State of Kentucky, sworn, and examined by Mr. Brooks:

Question. Having been charged by Mr. McComb with receiving fifty shares of Credit Mobilier stock for the purpose of bribing or influencing members of Congress, my first inclination was to call the entire one hundred democratic members on that subject; I thought that would incumber the record too much, and therefore I have called two who have been in official relations with this Union Pacific Railroad question, Mr. Voorhees, a member of the Pacific Railroad Committee, and Mr. Beck, a member of the committee of conference in which this matter of interest was decided. I wish to ask whether I have had any conversation with you at any time in regard to the Union Pacific Railroad when any matter affecting its interest was before Congress for adjudication?—Answer. When I was summoned a few moments ago to appear before this committee, I could not imagine what the purpose was. I have been on terms of intimacy with Mr. Brooks for several years. We served together during one Congress upon the Committee on Reconstruction, and were very intimate, especially because in the Fortieth Congress I, with the other Kentucky men, had put our cases in his charge when we ourselves were kept out six months because of some doubt as to our loyalty; and during all the time I have been in Congress our relations have been more than usually intimate. I have no recollection that Mr. Brooks ever spoke to me on the subject of the interests of the Union Pacific Railroad in Congress at any time, in any shape or form, directly or indirectly. The question in regard to the payment of interest was brought before the Committee on Appropriations, by, I think, Mr. Lawrence, of Ohio. A very full discussion of the legal questions involved in relation to it took place in that committee, and my recollection is that, after a full investigation, I, with a majority of the committee, came to the conclusion that the law was in favor of the railroads. I knew nothing about the Credit Mobilier, and had no idea there was any question of this sort involved in it. The question was simply discussed as to the rights of parties under the law of 1862 as modified by the law of 1864, to wit, whether it gave the Secretary of the Treasury the right to collect more than one-half the transportation over the Pacific Railroads. I know I was very anxious that the United States should sue the companies, and so test the legal question. I had not much faith in Mr. Akerman's opinion; I did not think it was sound law; and upon a full investigation of the subject, the committee came to that conclusion. I did not want this question to come up on an appropriation bill, and I preferred that it should be discussed on its own merits and in connection with no other question. The question was reported on and decided, in spite of my protest, when the conference report was adopted, as you know, and so far as Mr. Brooks was concerned, I have not the slightest recollection that he ever mentioned the matter to me in any shape or form.

WASHINGTON, D. C., *February* 6, 1873.

DANIEL W. VOORHEES, a member of the United States House of Representatives from Indiana, sworn, and examined by Mr. Brooks:

Question. Were you a member of the Pacific Railroad Committee during the Forty-first Congress?—Answer. Yes, sir.

Q. Did you have questions before you often affecting the interests of the Union Pacific Railroad and the Central Pacific Railroad Companies, and their various branches?—A. We had; at least I so understood. I remember more distinctly than anything else the question which arose in regard to the junction between the Union Pacific and the Central Pacific at or near Ogden, in which there was quite a spirited controversy before us between the two roads.

Q. Did I ever appear before that committee to advocate, as member of Congress, in any way or manner, the interests of the Union Pacific Railroad?—A. I will state to the committee that during that Congress my relations with Mr. Brooks were quite intimate; we were democrats together on the same side of the House; he never spoke to me on the subject of the Union Pacific Railroad; he never came before that committee, so far as I have any recollection; and he never approached me or spoke to me in any way on the subject.

WASHINGTON, D. C., *February* 11, 1873.

The CHAIRMAN stated that Mr. Oakes Ames had been notified to be present this morning for further examination; as he had not yet reached the committee-room, and Mr. Colfax was present, if he had any further statement to make or testimony to adduce the committee were ready to hear it.

Mr. ROBERT S. HALE stated in behalf of Mr. Colfax that he deemed it due to him that the testimony of Mr. Ames in relation to him, which was now incomplete, should be completed, and the original memoranda referred to by him be produced, before Mr. Colfax should adduce any testimony.

The CHAIRMAN said the committee would delay further proceedings until Mr. Ames's arrival.

Re-examination of OAKES AMES.

Mr. Ames subsequently appeared and was examined as follows:

By the CHAIRMAN:

Question. Have you the original of the memoranda that you produced before the committee in your former examination?—Answer. I have it; but I understand there is evidence to be put in to impeach my testimony in relation to Mr. Colfax, and my friends say I should have that in and know what to reply to before I produce my book.

The CHAIRMAN. The committee think your evidence cannot be considered as complete with only copies of your memoranda before them. These copies cannot be considered strictly as legal evidence at all. The originals ought to be produced, not only in relation to Mr. Colfax but all the others concerning whom you have testified from memoranda, and the committee think they should be produced now.

WITNESS. I have left my book with a friend, who has legal knowledge in the matter, to examine.

The CHAIRMAN. You will please send for it. The committee must be guided by their own judgment as to the course they should legally pursue.

WITNESS. My advisers say I should have the testimony of Mr. Colfax before I should be called on to produce the book.

The CHAIRMAN. The committee are so unfortunate as to differ with that gentleman, whoever he may be, and they direct that you send for the book, or the committee will send for it if you will tell them whom to send to.

WITNESS. Horace F. Clark has the book, at the Arlington Hotel.

(A messenger was therefore dispatched to the Arlington with an order from Mr. Ames to bring the book referred to.)

Q. Have you the originals of any of the others of these memoranda now with you?—A. Yes, sir.

Q. The committee want the originals of all the copies you have given them, and they will go on with such as you have.—A. I have not much in the books I have here. Mr. Clark has the book for 1868, which contains most of the entries I have referred to.

Q. Do those you have here contain the original of any of the entries of which you have given the committee copies?—A. I do not recollect whether I gave you copies or not. I have tried to get the printed testimony in this case. I sent to the Printing-Office twice for it, but was unable to get it. I would like to have an opportunity of looking over the printed testimony, and of seeing what has been testified to before going on with my testimony. I think it is important that I should have it. The book I have here contains three entries relating to this matter. One is that on May 10, 1867, I sold Gamaliel Bradford one hundred shares Credit Mobilier stock, giving him a discount of 5 per cent., making it 95. There is another entry, which is different from what I supposed when I gave my testimony; I find that Mr. Patterson paid me $3,000 for Credit Mobilier stock on the 31st of August, 1867. My memory when I testified was, that it was in the December following. That is what there is on this book relating to this matter. It is a private memorandum-book, and relates to a great many of my private transactions. I desire, therefore, that the committee will retain it in their own possession and not allow others access to it.

The book referred to was handed to the chairman, who, after examination, read the following entries:

SATURDAY, *August* 31, 1867.

J. W. Patterson, credit by check for C. M. of A.	$3,000 00

MAY 4, 1867.

Sold G. Bradford 100 C. M. at par	$10,000 00
Interest to May 4	61 67
Less 5 per cent. commission	500 00
	9,561 67

Q. Did you make these entries at the time?—A. Yes, sir; these are the only two entries in this book that relate to this matter in any way.

Q. Have you looked it all through to ascertain that fact?—A. Yes, sir.

Q. These items you have given us are all that relate to this matter in any way?—A. Yes, sir; the book of 1868 contains most of the memoranda I have testified to.

The memorandum-book referred to was subsequently brought to the committee-room by Horace F. Clark, who, with the permission of the committee, acted as counsel for Mr. Ames, on his examination as to the entries in the memorandum-book of 1868.

Mr. CLARK. I wish, if the committee will allow me, to ask at whose instance this memorandum-book was called out in evidence.

The CHAIRMAN. At the instance of the committee. I gave Mr. Ames notice, verbally, to produce the book before he went home for the Christmas holidays, but he seemed to think that copies would answer as well, and I subsequently gave him written notice to produce the original memoranda.

Mr. CLARK. If the chairman will permit me to say a few words, I will state the circumstances under which I appear as counsel for Mr. Ames on this examination to-day. I may say that friendly relations have existed between Mr. Ames and myself, but there have been no professional relations between us, and with respect to the matter of the Credit Mobilier we are in adverse relations and interests. Mr. Ames said to me that he would regard it as a favor if I would advise him as to his legal rights and duties touching the production of the memorandum-book, which I now have in my hand, and which I produce and now deliver to him in the presence of the committee. I have given some consideration to the subject, and if the committee will grant me a few moments' indulgence I will give to Mr. Ames, in the presence of the committee, the advice which I think I ought to give him upon the request he has made. This memorandum-book was, as I am informed, referred to by Mr. Ames, or rather extracts from it produced before the committee, were referred to by Mr. Ames for the purpose of refreshing his recollection as to the circumstances in respect of which the committee saw fit to make inquiries. I have to say to him that in my opinion this memorandum-book is not evidence *per se*. It cannot speak irrespective of him. Produced, examined, and read, it would not afford even *prima-facie* or presumptive evidence of the truth of its entries. But he has produced alleged extracts from it, or certain statements which he alleges embody the substance of extracts from it, for the purpose of refreshing his recollection. Inasmuch, therefore, as this memorandum-book and its entries are evidence standing alone, I think it is his private property. You will find, if you examine it, that it has reference to transactions having no relation whatever to the subject-matter of your inquiry. It embraces transactions with other parties not members of Congress, but private citizens, residing in various States, and is, for the most part, a memorandum in respect of transactions with which you have no concern, and which are not in anywise material or pertinent to the subject-matter of your inquiry; and I may add the expression of my opinion that you would not be at liberty to institute inquiries in relation to these transactions under the order of the House, by virtue of which you are empowered.

This being but a memorandum made by the witness, (and you may assume it to have been made contemporaneously,) by which he has refreshed his recollection, it seems to me that, under the well-settled laws of evidence, it cannot be used except for the purpose of impeachment of the witness. It cannot be used, I think, in corroboration of any statement he has made or may make. As I understand the rule of evidence, the adverse party to the witness who has made the memorandum which refreshes his recollection can use it for the purpose of impeaching the witness in respect of his statement. If, referring to his memorandum, he alleges a particular transaction, and states that his recollection of it is refreshed by it, I suppose the adverse party, if he can get hold of that memorandum, can use it for the purpose of impeachment, but not for the purpose of corroboration.

The book is Mr. Ames's private property, and in respect of its custody, and in respect of any developments not material to your inquiry, which might result from its exhibition, he is protected by law against any unreasonable search. I think no court would require a witness to produce his private papers for the purpose of showing whether a statement he has made is true or untrue; but the adverse party to him, if he produces it, may refer to it for the purpose of showing that the statement he has made is not sustained by the memorandum by which he has refreshed his recollection.

Now, this book was not before the committee when Mr. Ames gave his testimony, and that testimony stands or falls irrespective of the memorandum. I think, therefore, the committee cannot require him to produce these memoranda for the purposes of corroboration without disregarding those rules of evidence which human experience has shown are best calculated to elicit the truth. I think it is only by the voluntary action of Mr. Ames that you can enforce the production of this book.

But there are considerations connected with this case—and, Mr. Ames, I wish you to understand that this is my advice to you—which take it out of the ordinary course of judicial proceeding, and which incline me to advise you to withhold no fact which the committee may deem material to the investigation they are authorized to make.

I have to advise you, Mr. Ames, that if the Vice-President, or any other gentleman whose name has been connected with these transactions, or whose name may rightfully be connected with these investigations, desires that this memorandum-book may be produced for the purpose of impeachment of any statement you may make, or for the purpose of corroboration of any statement he has made or may make, I would advise you to produce all that part of it which relates to any such individual, or to any transaction with which his name may be associated.

I understand that collateral issues have arisen in the course of the investigation, and that this memorandum-book bears upon such collateral issues rather than upon the main issue. The main question submitted to you for inquiry by the House was, if I mistake not, as to the ownership of stock in the Credit Mobilier by members of Congress. I think that is the point of the investigation, and that the particular examinations in respect of which reference is sought to be had to this book bears upon the question whether there has or has not been prevarication upon the part of gentlemen whose names have been associated with these transactions.

Now, I have examined this memorandum-book and am able to say that the great bulk of it relates to matters utterly foreign to this inquiry; but I would advise Mr. Ames that he should produce it for the private inspection of the committee, feeling satisfied that they have no desire to indulge any prurient taste on the part of the public; that they are not inclined to enlarge the area of scandal and calumny which has already attended the investigation of this case; and I would suggest to him that at the request of any of the gentlemen whose names have been associated with the Credit Mobilier transaction he should furnish a sworn copy of any entry relating to them which may tend to the ascertainment of the real truth. Mr. Ames is here as a witness, and has certainly not lost all his rights because of his being a member of the honorable body to which you, gentlemen of the committee, belong. He is protected by that bill of rights which was intended to protect as well the right of private papers as the right of home, and he ought not to be forced to spread in detail all his private transactions for the past few years before the public, which seems to me are looking rather for calumny than for truth.

I now return to Mr. Ames the book, advising him that he ought to withhold from the committee no evidence which bears upon the case of any one of the gentlemen whose names are connected with these transactions, but that when he goes beyond and exposes through the press, or otherwise, his transactions with other parties, who have never had any relations with Congress, he surrenders rights as a private citizen, which, it seems to me, he ought not to surrender except to superior force.

The CHAIRMAN. The committee do not entertain precisely the same view of the law of evidence that has been expressed. I understand that when a question arises between two men, one of whom claims to have paid a sum of money to the other, that the man claiming to have made the payment, if he has made an entry in some book contemporaneous with the transaction itself, may produce that entry, and it will be received as the strongest kind of corroborative testimony. The committee think that such a memorandum is admissible, not only for the purpose of impeachment, but for the purpose of corroborating the statement of the witness himself, and that it is very strong competent evidence to that end.

Mr. CLARK. Does the committee take the ground that Mr. Ames could produce this book for the purpose of corroborating his own evidence?

The CHAIRMAN. Certainly; that is well settled in the law of evidence, as I understand it. In a suit for the recovery of money, if the party produce his memorandum-book, and it appears upon its face that the entries were fairly made in due course of business, these entries would be strongly corroborative of his testimony.

Mr. CLARK. The entries made in books kept in the ordinary course of business would be received as evidence *per se*, but I think there is no such rule in regard to a private memorandum.

The CHAIRMAN stated that the rule was extended in the case of a congressional investigation, and that the committee had decided the memorandum-book in question must be produced.

Mr. CLARK stated that Mr. Ames had exhibited no reluctance to producing the book, but that he had advised him that he owed it to the public interest not to extend the range of scandal beyond what had already grown out of this investigation, by exhibiting, unless for the private inspection of the committee, the entire book, with all its entries of private matters having no relation to this inquiry, unless compelled to do so by the superior power of the House.

Mr. AMES thereupon produced the memorandum-book in question, and was directed to read the first entry he found relating to any of the persons named.

WITNESS. The first entry I find is the following:

1868.

TUESDAY, *January* 14*th*.

Henry Wilson, cr. for cash on act. of C. M. of A.............. 70 00

I will say that I had several other matters with Mr. Wilson, which are referred to in this book, and which do not relate to the Credit Mobilier at all.

The next entry I find referring to Mr. Wilson is the following:

1868.

MONDAY, *February* 10*th*.

For $1,600 bonds.

Paid H. Wilson		548 00
In Scofield check	195 33	
U. P. R. R. check	308 72	
Sergt.-of-Arms	44 00	
	548 05	

Mr. CLARK stated that he was informed by the witness that these memoranda were not in every instance made at the time, but that they referred back to the true dates of the transactions.

By the CHAIRMAN:

Q. Do you remember anything in relation to this entry, except what appears upon the face of the entry itself?—A. No, sir; I do not.

Q. These various items go to make up the sum of $548?—A. Yes; these items are correct.

Q. The amount seems to be made up of three items: Scofield check, Union Pacific Railroad check, and check on the Sergeant-at-Arms?—A. Yes, sir.

Q. Do these items refresh your recollection so that you are able to state whether this sum which you paid him was a dividend on the Credit Mobilier stock?—A. No, sir, I cannot remember; I might ascertain by looking further at the book. (After examination.) I think that must have been on this transaction. It is for $1,600 of bonds.

Q. You suppose that $1,600 to be a dividend on 20 shares?—A. I think so. Schofield's check was a check which he gave me for $195.33 in settlement of this bond dividend. He took the bond and gave me a check for that amount.

Q. Is that Mr. Scofield of the House?—A. Yes, sir; and this amount is transferred to his account.

Q. You suppose that transaction to have been at the time?—A. Yes, sir.

Q. And you suppose this entry to have been made at the time?—A. Yes, sir; under date of March 5, I find an entry of a transaction with Mr. Henry Wilson, which refers to a Cedar Rapids bond, and has nothing to do with the Credit Mobilier.

The CHAIRMAN. You need not read that.

WITNESS. Under date of June 22 I find the following entry:

1868.

MONDAY, *June* 22.

Hon. Henry Wilson.

By div. from U. P. R. R.		1,200
Cash	223 00	
IC. R. & M. R. bd	950	
Intst. from Feb. 1	27	——1,200
Bond to be ded.		
Check on Bk. of Commerce		223

Q. Have you any further memoranda in reference to Mr. Wilson?—A. I think there is no other.

Q. Have you anything to state in reference to the final settlement of this transaction with Mr. Wilson different from your former testimony?—A. No, sir.

Q. Now turn to the earliest memoranda you have in reference to any one of the other persons named?—A. I find, under the date of January 11, 1868, the following:

1868.

SATURDAY, *January* 11.

Recd. of Hon. H. L. Dawes.
Cash on acct. of stock in C. M. of A.
$800, Jany. 11th.
235 " 14th. $1.035.

Q. That was the par value of 10 shares of stock with interest upon it up to that time, and these sums paid by him to you were for the 10 shares of stock?—A. Yes, sir.

Q. Have you any further entries in relation to Mr. Dawes?—A. I presume so.

Mr. CLARK. Do I understand the committee to claim the right to examine every memorandum relating to this matter on this book, whether it has been referred to in testimony or not, and whether it is asked for or not, either for the purpose of the impeachment of Mr. Ames, or for the purpose of corroboration?

The CHAIRMAN. Certainly. We are not trying a case between anybody. This is a proceeding in rem., if I may so express it. It is more in the nature of an inquisition than a trial.

Mr. NIBLACK suggested that the circumstances under which the transaction took place were the most important part of the transaction.

WITNESS. There is the check on the Sergeant-at-Arms given to Mr. Dawes; there is also in the cash account the entry, "Henry L. Dawes, by cash $1,035."

Q. That is the $1,035 you have before referred to?—A. That is the

$1,035 before referred to. The entire entry to which I refer is a statement of the whole transaction as it then stood, as follows:

Henry L. Dawes.

	by Cash	1,035
	by am't due on bond	195 23
to bond	1,000	
C. M	1,000	
U. P	1,000	

Q. Can you state when this entry was made?—A. That was made, I suppose, previous to the June dividend, as the June dividend does not appear there. This was a statement of accounts as they stood after deducting the bond dividends.

Q. The entry "by cash $1,035," as I understand, is the amount he paid for ten shares of stock?—A. Yes, sir; instead of my selling the bond for him he took the bond itself for the 80 per cent., and paid me the difference.

Q. That was equivalent to taking his 80 per cent. dividend in bonds?—A. Yes sir.

Q. Then this entry says, "to bond 1,000."—A. That is the bond he paid for.

Q. That is intended to signify the same transaction?—A. Yes, sir.

Q. The next entry is "C. M. 1,000."—A. That is the stock he paid for.

Q. The next is "U. P. 1,000."—A. That was the dividend he was entitled to in the Union Pacific Railroad stock.

Q. I see it printed at the top of this page "cash account, March."—A. That does not signify anything. This was a vacant page that did not come into my records, and I made my memorandum there for the purpose of convenience.

Q. The fact that the heading is printed March is no indication that it was in March?—A. No, sir.

Q. On the contrary you think this entry was made before June?—A. Yes, sir; because it does not embrace the cash dividend for June; it only shows what he was entitled to then.

Q. Is there any further entry in reference to Mr. Dawes?—A. Nothing further except that I gave him a check on the Sergeant-at-Arms for $600, in payment of his dividend in June, 1868. That you will find with the Sergeant-at-Arms.

Q. Your book shows no entry of that?—A. I have no entry of that.

Q. At the top of the page containing these cash entries of dividends, the date is printed Saturday, January 2, 1869.—A. This book runs a day or two over into the next year. The date has nothing to do with the entry. This is simply an account of the transactions between myself and the different individuals who were entitled to receive their dividends. This was the list of names. The following is the entry referred to:

1868.

SATURDAY, *January* 2, 1869.

H. L. Dawes	×	600
Scofield	×	600
Patterson	×	1,800
Painter	×	1,800
Wilson	×	1,200

Colfax.. × 1,200
Bingham.. × 1,200
Allison.. × 600
Kelley.. × 329
Wilson... × 329
Garfield... × 329

Q. You put down in this list what was to be paid to these men; it is not an entry of the payment you had actually made?—A. It is a list of payments to be made and which were made in different ways, some in one way and some in another.

Q. Is there anything further in that book in regard to your dealings with Mr. Dawes, in reference to these 10 shares of stock?—A. No, sir, I do not think there is.

Q. Having examined the sevarious entries in your memorandum-book, have you any alteration to make in your statement before made as to the ultimate terms of settlement, or as to the time when you settled with Mr. Dawes and took the stock back?—A. No, sir, none whatever.

Q. Now state the next entry you have in regard to any one of the others whose names have been mentioned.—A. I find the following in regard to Mr. Colfax:

1868.

THURSDAY, *March* 5.

Rec'd of Schuyler Colfax check balance........................ 534 72

Q. You made this entry?—A. Yes, sir.

Q. You think it was made at this date?—A. Yes, sir.

Q. You have already stated in your testimony that, after applying the proceeds of the sale of the 80 per cent. bond dividend to the purchase of the stock, it left a balance due you of $534.72, which Mr. Colfax paid you?—A. Yes, sir.

Q. And this is the entry of it?—A. This is the entry. My next entry in regard to Mr. Colfax is the check of the Sergeant-at-Arms for $1,200.

Q. In this list, before referred to under the printed date of January 2, 1869, Mr. Colfax's name appears with $1,200 opposite. This list, I understand you, shows the amount these parties were entitled to from the cash dividend you received in June?—A. Yes, sir.

Q. You put down this list, as you say, to show what you were to pay to each one whose name appears on it?—A. Yes, sir; it shows the parties to whom I was responsible for the 60 per cent. dividend of June and which I was to pay.

Q. This entry is, "S. Colfax, $1,200."—A. Yes, sir. The next entry in regard to Mr. Colfax is the following, which is a general statement, such as I made out in each case:

Colfax:

20 shares Credit M. cost....................................	2,000 00
7 mos. 10 days' int'st..	86 72
	2,086 72
Less 80 pr. ct. bds. at 97....................................	1,552 00
Paid, March 5..	534 72

2,000 U. P. stock.
2,000 C. M. stock.

Q. When was this entry made?—A. It was made previous to June. It was made after I had received the bond dividend, and shows the condition of the account after receiving that dividend.

Q. You made up a statement with each of these individuals and put it down in your book?—A. Yes, sir. Here is the original statement which I found among my papers, and which was shown to each man. (Paper handed to chairman.)

Q. This is a calculation you made out, showing how you stood with any man having 30 shares, or 20 shares, or 10 shares?—A. Yes, sir.

The paper referred to is as follows:

30 shares of Credit Mobilier, at 100		3,000
7 mos. 10 days' int'st, at 7 pr. ct		130 08
		3,130 08
Less div. in bonds, 80 pr. ct	2,400	
Less 3 pr. ct	72	2,328 00
		802 08

$3,000 or 30 shares U. P. R. Rd.
3,000 or 30 shares Credit Mobilier.

20 shares Credit Mobilier		2,000
7 mos. 10 days' int'st		86 72
		2,086 72
Div. in bonds, 80 pr. ct	1,600	
Less dis. 3 pr. ct	48 00	
		1,552 00
	1,552 00	
		534 72

10 shares of Credit Mobilier of America		1,000
7 mos. 10 days' int'st		43 36
		1,043 36
80 pr. ct. div. in bonds	800	
Less discount of 3 pr. ct	24 00	776
		267 36

10 shares 1,000 U. P. R. stock, 1,000.
10 Credit Mobilier stock, 1,000.

Q. This is a calculation you made up before you made any of the entries in this book?—A. Yes, sir.

Q. And by reference to it, if a man had thirty shares you could state his account without making a separate calculation. If he had twenty shares you could state his account, and if he had ten shares you could state his account?—A. Yes, sir.

Q. This was not made out with reference to the account of any particular individual?—A. No, sir, but it shows the account of any one having ten, twenty, or thirty shares. It was a formula made for that purpose.

Q. Do you know whether you showed that paper to any one of these gentlemen?—A. I showed it or a copy of it. I think I made up a little statement for each man, or at least that I did it generally.

Q. Have you any other entry on that book referring to Mr. Colfax?—A. Nothing except the $1,200 check on the Sergeant-at-Arms.

Q. I notice that opposite each of the names on this list with the printed heading of January 2, 1869, you have put a little cross or check; what does that signify?—A. That the amount was paid.

Q. You put that cross or check opposite Mr. Colfax's name when you made a settlement with him?—A. Yes, sir, I did.

Mr. CLARK suggested that on the next page of the memorandum-book would be found the same names, with statement of accounts, some of which are and others are not crossed off, the explanation of which is that in some cases there had been no final settlement with the parties.

Q. Where you made out a statement of the account of each man I notice that some of them are marked across the entire account; that indicates, as I understand, that the transaction is closed, and where the account is not so crossed out the indication is that it has not been finally closed?—A. Yes, sir; that is the explanation of it.

Q. This account with Mr. Colfax which I have read is not crossed off?—A. No, sir.

Q. Have you any further entry on this book of dealings with Mr. Colfax?—A. I have this. (Handing to chairman.) The entry referred to is as follows:

1868.

SUNDAY, *June* 31.

Checks on commerce, deposited with Sergeant-at-Arms	10,000	
P'd S. Colfax	1,200	00
" James F. Wilson	329	00
" H. L. Dawes	600	
" William B. Allison	600	
" G. W. Scofield	600	
" J. W. Patterson	1,800	
" John A. Logan	329	
" James A. Garfield	329	
" William D. Kelley	329	
" Henry Wilson	1,200	
" John A. Bingham	1,200	

Q. This entry, "Paid S. Colfax $1,200," is the amount which you paid by this check on the Sergeant-at-Arms?—A. Yes, sir.

Q. Was this entry upon this page of these various names intended to show the amount you were to pay or that you had paid; was that made at this date?—A. I do not know; it was made about that time. I would not have written it on Sunday; it is not very likely. It was made on a blank page. It is simply a list of names.

Q. Were these names put down after you had made the payments or before, do you think?—A. Before, I think.

Q. You think you made this list before the parties referred to had actually received their checks, or received the money?—A. Yes, sir; that was to show whom I had to pay, and who were entitled to receive the 60 per cent. dividend. It shows whom I had to pay here in Washington——

Q. It says "paid."—A. Yes, sir; well, I did pay it.

Q. What I want to know is, whether the list was made out before or after payment?—A. About the same time, I suppose; probably before.

Q. Have you any entry in this book or any other book in reference to Mr. Colfax?—A. I have one of a later date in another book which I will show you when you have got through this.

The CHAIRMAN. You will please produce it now.

Mr. CLARK said that Mr. Ames was of opinion he should not be compelled to bring forward, one by one, his corroborations in respect to each individual. He desired, before producing this other book, to know what Mr. Colfax himself says, so that he might be able to apply the corroborating circumstances from entries in the book as they should be required.

The CHAIRMAN said the committee required the book referred to to be produced at this time.

(Book produced by witness.)

Q. This is the memorandum-book you kept for 1869?—A. Yes, sir.

Q. The entry to which you direct attention is—

"FRIDAY, *January* 22, 1869.

"Paid S. Colfax $60.75 for interest on $1,500, certificate of U. P. R. R." You made this entry?—A. Yes, sir.

Q. Do you think it was made on that day?—A. I think the entry was made on that day, and I presume the payment was.

Q. What were these certificates of the Union Pacific Railroad?—A. The trustees of the Oakes Ames contract made a dividend of 75 per cent. first-mortgage bonds. They did not have the bonds, and never had them. This was, I think, in July, 1868. On the January following they paid the interest on the certificates the same as they would have done on the bonds. Mr. Colfax was entitled to the interest on $1,500, the same as if the bonds themselves had actually been divided. I collected the interest and paid it to Mr. Colfax.

Q. The certificate itself was a dividend on the Credit Mobilier stock?—A. Yes, sir; or rather a dividend on the Oakes Ames contract. The two seemed to get mixed up.

Q. The interest on that certificate was $60.75, which was due Mr. Colfax, and you paid it to him?—A. Yes, sir.

Q. And you think the payment was made on this day?—A. I think so.

Q. Do you remember that it was so paid?—A. It was paid here in Washington.

Q. In what way?—A. In money.

Q. Have you any recollection as to whether it was by check or cash?—A. It was cash. They were small items. I made a list of these gentlemen's names, and the amounts they were entitled to, the amount of interest each one was entitled to on these certificates. I did that on a slip of paper; and I paid them all off in that way. It was a small slip of paper. The amount twenty shares was entitled to was $60 and odd cents. The amount thirty shares was entitled to was $90, and so on.

Q. That amount you paid to Mr. Colfax?—A. I did.

Q. And you entered it upon this book at the time of payment?—A. Yes, sir.

Q. Have you any further entry in any book in regard to Mr. Colfax?—A. I have not looked over them very carefully. I do not think there is any other for Mr. Colfax.

Q. Have you been able to find any receipt signed by Mr. Colfax for money you paid him?—A. I have not looked very particularly.

Q. Have you been able to find any receipt signed by Mr. Colfax?—A. I am having my papers looked over to see if I can find anything.

Q. You have not found anything yet?—A. No, sir.

Q. You think the memoranda you have given us are all you have seen on your books?—A. They are all I can find on the books.

Mr. CLARK inquired whether the committee desired the entries in this book in reference to parties when there was no discrepancy of statement between them and Mr. Ames.

The CHAIRMAN replied that the committee did not feel absolutely certain even when Mr. Ames and the parties themselves agreed. They wanted all the memoranda Mr. Ames had in regard to these transactions.

Witness next produced the following entry from his memorandum-book:

1868.

WEDNESDAY, *January* 29.

Rec'd of Glenni W. Scofield, check on Serg't-of-Arms......		708 50
10 coupons, 350 East..............................	350	
Less 5 p'r c't....................................	17 50	332 50
		1,041 00

to be invested in 10 shares of the Credit Mobilier of America, as trustee by me, No. 346.

Q. This transaction was the payment by Mr. Scofield for 10 shares of stock?—A. Yes, sir. I was to get him his stock, and I gave him my receipt.

Q. What were the 10 coupons referred to?—A. I think, on Cedar Rapids bonds which I had sold him before. I am not positive about that.

Q. You took them as money?—A. Yes, sir.

Q. I find on your memorandum-book, right below the entry just given, the following:

"Feb'y 1st, 1868.—Del'd to Hon. Glenni W. Scofield certificate No. 346, for 10 shares of stock on Credit Mobilier, bot. for his account."

That certificate of 10 shares was delivered to Mr. Scofield?—A. I guess it was afterwards; I cannot remember.

Q. Do you think you gave him the certificate at that time?—A. I think not. I think I did not have the certificate at that time. I think I gave him a receipt for the money.

Q. That was the 29th of January, as your first entry shows. This entry, dated the 1st of February, is written immediately underneath, and states that you delivered him the certificate. Do you remember whether you did or not?—A. No, sir; but I presume I should not have made the entry if I had not.

Q. You presume you did give him the certificate?—A. I do not know that; but I should not have made the entry if I had not.

Q. When the matter was adjusted between you and him you returned the certificate?—A. Yes, sir; I think I did.

Q. Is there any other entry in relation to Mr. Scofield?—A. I think there is. I find the following:

1868.

SUNDAY, *February* 9.

Reached Washington from N. Y.

D'l'd Glenni W. Scofield one bond............................	1,000
10 shares stock..	1,000

Rec'd of G. W. Scofield, for balance due on his bond over his div., $195.33, & endorsed the same on my receipt.

Q. He took $1,000 bond and the difference between the bond and the eighty per cent. he paid you?—A. Yes, sir.

Q. So that it was equivalent to his taking his eighty per cent. dividend?—A. Yes, sir.

Q. Have you any further entry in relation to Mr. Scofield?—A. There was a check for $600 on the Sergeant-at-Arms. His name is on the list which you already have of the dividends paid in June, 1868. There is also the same detailed statement in the back of the book, as follows:

G. W. Scofield.

By cash	1,041
On bond	195 33
	1,236 33
Dl'd him one Bond	1,000
	236 33

1,000 Credit.
1,000 U. P. R. R'd.

Q. That entry is crossed out, which indicates, I presume, that the transaction was settled, and closed up between you?—A. Yes, sir.

Q. Mr. Scofield thought he had only received his money back in his final settlement of the matter. Your statement differed with his in that respect; you thought he made out of it his ten shares of Union Pacific Railroad stock?—A. That was my impression.

Q. Is that your impression now?—A. Only from memory; and I, perhaps, ought not to put my memory against his.

Q. You now think that he made ten shares of Union Pacific Railroad stock out of the transaction?—A. That is my memory. I am not certain.

Q. Now give us your next entry.

WITNESS. Is there any necessity of going through with all these names? They amount, substantially, to the same thing.

The CHAIRMAN. The committee prefer to have all the entries. Which is the next name you have?—A. The next is that of Mr. Painter.

The CHAIRMAN. We do not care anything about the entries relative to Mr. Painter. We have heard Mr. Painter's case as much as is necessary.

WITNESS. I do not see why Mr. Painter should be neglected. The next is in relation to Mr. Allison, and the following is the first entry:

1868.

FRIDAY, *April* 24.

Rec'd of Wm. B. Allison 271 00
for balance due on stock sold him, 1,000 in Credit Mobilier, and 1,000 in Union Pacific R. road.

Q. You received the bond dividend of 80 per cent., and sold the bonds?—A. Yes, sir; and he gave me his check for the balance.

Q. The $271 was the balance in payment of the stock, after deducting the bond dividend?—A. Yes, sir.

Q. The ten shares Union Pacific Railroad stock was what belonged to him as a dividend on his Credit Mobilier stock?—A. Yes, sir.

Q. Is that what your memorandum signifies?—A. Yes, sir; that is stock which he returned to me afterward.

Q. Have you any other entry in regard to Mr. Allison?—A. Yes, sir; there is the $600 check for the June dividend, and the same general enumeration at the back of the book.

Q. That $600 was paid by check on the Sergeant-at-Arms?—A. Yes, sir; and a corresponding entry made in the list of June dividends, which you have. The general statement is as follows.

Wm. B. Allison.

10 shares Credit M	1,000
Int'st to May	46
	1,046
Div. in Bonds 80 pr. ct. sold at 97	776
Cash to balance	270
1,000 C. M.	
1,000 U. P.	

It is crossed off, which shows that the matter has been finally settled. The next is James F. Wilson, and I find the following general statement of his account, corresponding with that made out for the others:

James F. Wilson.

10 shares C. M	1,000
7 mos. 10 days	43 36
	1,043 36
80 pr. cent. Div. at 97	776
	267 36
Int'st to June 20	3 64
	271 00
1,000 U. P.	
1,000 C. M.	

Q. That is crossed off, showing that it was settled?—A. Yes, sir. This statement left a balance due him of $379, for which I gave him a check on the Sergeant-at-Arms.

Q. Afterward he sold his stock, and there the matter ended so far as you were concerned?—A. Yes, sir. The next on the list is J. W. Patterson. I gave you this morning the first entry I had in his case, from my memorandum-book of 1867. The first I find in this is the following:

1868.

Friday, February 14.

Paid J. W. Patterson, for 2,400$ bonds of Union Pacific R. R. Co., as dividend, less 3 pr. ct.	$2,328
Less interest paid	105
P'd cash	$2,223
Per receipt.	

Q. That you paid him and took his receipt, which has already been before us?—A. I think that receipt has been shown. There is there the same general enumeration at the end of the book, as follows:

Rec'd of J. W. Patterson:

Cash and Interest	3,105 00
Rec'd for 3 Bonds	2,328
	5,433 00
Feb'y 14, to Cash	2,328
	3,105 00

3,000 U. P. stock.
3,000 C. M. A. "

Q. That is crossed off to indicate that it has been settled?—A. Yes, sir. I gave him afterward a check on the Sergeant-at-Arms, for which I produced his receipt.

Q. Have you any further receipts from Mr. Patterson than those which you have already shown to the committee?—A. I have not. I think I have produced three.

Q. This account, as I said, seems to have been crossed off. Have you anything more to say in reference to the dealings between you and Mr. Patterson than you stated before?—A. No, sir.

Q. He had thirty shares of the stock and the dividends accruing from it?—A. Yes, sir. The next on the list is Mr. Bingham. I do not believe I have any special entry in reference to Mr. Bingham, except the general statement at the end of the book. We kept receipts and memorandums. We boarded together, and occasionally we would change off receipts and burn them up. The general statement is as follows:

John A. Bingham.

by Cash		2,086 72
" Note		399 32
to bonds	2,000	
Stock	2,000	
C. M	2,000	

He took two bonds and paid me the difference at par.

The CHAIRMAN. There does not seem to be any necessity of taking any time with Mr. Bingham. He admits having the stock, and admits that he had the benefit of it. This account is crossed off?—A. Yes, sir; it is crossed off.

Q. Now show us the first entry you have in reference to Mr. Kelley.—A. I do not think there is anything except the general statement and this check for $329. His general statement is as follows:

Wm. D. Kelley.

10 shares C. M. A	1,000
7 mos. 10 days' int'st	43 36
	1,043 36
80 p'r c't bond div., at 97	776
	267 36
Int'st to June 20	3 64
	271 00

1,000 U. P. stock.
1,000 C. M.

Q. You received his money dividend in June?—A. Yes, sir.

Q. And paid him his balance of $329?—A. Yes, sir; that I gave him by a check on the Sergeant-at-Arms, which has been shown to the committee.

Q. His name is on this list and when it was paid it was checked off?—A. Yes, sir.

Q. This general statement of his is not marked across?—A. No, sir; I delivered his Credit Mobilier stock to you the other day. His Union Pacific Railroad stock I have not yet delivered.

Q. This cross opposite the $329 indicates that he received his check?—A. Yes, sir.

Q. Have you an entry on your books of the $750 which Mr. Kelley received of you subsequently?—A. Yes, sir; I find the following:

1868.

Tuesday, September 29.

William D. Kelley, on com	$750

Q. Have you anything more to say in reference to the purpose of that payment than you said before?—A. No, sir.

Q. Now turn to any entries you may have in reference to Mr. Garfield.—A. Mr. Garfield's payments were just the same as Mr. Kelley's.

Q. I find Mr. Kelley's name on the list of June dividend payments for $329. That I understand you to be the amount of the June dividend after paying the balance due on his stock?—A. Yes, sir; the general statement made up for Mr. Garfield is as follows:

Garfield.

10 shares Credit M	1,000
7 mos. 10 days	43 36
	1,043 36
80 per ct. bd. div., at 97	776
	267 36
Int'st to June 20	3 64
	271 00

1,000 C. M.
1,000 U. P.

Q. You received $600 cash dividend on his ten shares?—A. Yes, sir.

Q. And, as you say, paid him $329, as the balance of the dividend due him?—A. I think I did.

Q. This general statement is not crossed off?—A. No, sir.

Q. In this list of names for the June dividend, Mr. Garfield's name is down for $329.—A. That would be the balance due.

Q. The cross opposite his name indicates that the money was paid to him?—A. Yes, sir.

Mr. CLARK remarked that Mr. Ames was not certain whether this amount was paid Mr. Garfield by check or in currency.

The WITNESS. If I drew the check I may have paid him off in currency, as I find no check with initials corresponding to his.

Q. We find three checks for the amount of $329 each; one is in blank; there are no initials written in. There are, however, the same number of checks for that amount as are called for by the names on this list for that amount.—A. I am not sure how I paid Mr. Garfield; I paid him in some form.

Q. This statement of Mr. Garfield's account is not crossed off, which indicates, does it, that the matter has never been settled or adjusted?—A. No, sir; it never has.

Mr. CLARK remarked that he supposed it was understood that no one of these gentlemen had ever seen the entries in this book.

Q. Can you state whether you have any other entry in your book relating to Mr. Garfield?—A. No, sir. I want to explain one item. You questioned me very closely when I was before you the other day in reference to a check for $272.79 on the Sergeant-at-Arms. I find in the memorandum I have here of the payments I made to Mr. Painter, a check on the Sergeant-at-Arms for just that amount in payment of a balance due him on the $1,800 cash dividend, which accounts for this check which I could not then explain.

Q. Have you found on your memorandum-book any entry in reference to Speaker Blaine?—A. No, sir; I have had nothing of Mr. Blaine, and his name does not appear on my book at all.

Q. There is one other gentleman whose name appears here—that of General Logan; what entry have you in regard to him?—A. I have his general statement, as follows:

Logan.

10 shares C. M. A.	1,000	
7 mos. 10 days	43	36
	1.043	36
80 pr. ct. Div. at 97	776	
	267	36
Int'st to June 20	3	64
	271	00
1,000 U. P.		
1,000 C. M.		

Q. You gave him a check for $329?—A. I gave him a check for $329.

Q. This account of General Logan has been crossed off, showing that it has been adjusted?—A. Yes, sir.

Q. Have you found in looking over your memorandums or papers any entries showing any dealings between you and any other member of Congress in regard to the Credit Mobilier, in addition to those you have named?—A. No, sir.

Q. These are all?—A. These are all.

Q. You believe you have now shown us all the entries you have in regard to all the gentlemen named?—A. These are all, I believe. I may have failed to give the general statement, for Mr. Henry Wilson. It is as follows:

Henry Wilson.

Rec'd of him	1,000
two bonds 1,000	
Less 3 pr. cent	1,552
Cash	70
	2,622
p'd Cash & Int'st	1,548
	1,074

2,000 Credit.
2,000 U. P. stock.

Q. That includes all who were then in Congress with whom you had dealings in reference to this stock?—A. Yes, and all who were ever in Congress, so far as I now remember, except Mr. Grimes, who was in the company originally, and therefore, I suppose, had the right to have stock in the Credit Mobilier.

Q. If there is anything you wish to say relative to any of the matters in reference to which you have been inquired of, you may now have the opportunity of doing so.—A. Mr. Garfield understands this matter as a loan; he says I did not explain it to him.

Q. You need not say what Mr. Garfield says; tell us what you think. —A. Mr. Garfield might have misunderstood me.

Q. Mr. Garfield has told us how he understood it; what the committee desire to know of you is your understanding of the matter.—A. I supposed it was like all the rest; but when Mr. Garfield says he mistook it for a loan; that he always understood it to be a loan; that I did not make any explanation to him and did not make any statement to him, I may be mistaken. I am a man of few words, and I may not have made myself understood to him.

Q. We do not want you to mix up your recollection with that of Mr. Garfield.—A. I have stated it as I remember it; but I may be mistaken.

Q. Do you remember it so now?—A. I think I do.

By Mr. NIBLACK:

Q. You told me privately the other morning, while coming up in the cars, before you went home, that you had taken receipts from nearly all these gentlemen, and that when you went home you would be able to find receipts from nearly all of them. State whether you have searched for these receipts, and whether you have found any that you have not produced.—A. I have found none that amount to anything; I found a receipt from Mr. Allison that he had bought ten shares of stock from me. There is no date to it.

Q. Have you searched for receipts among your papers?—A. I have somewhat. I told my clerk to search for papers relating to this matter, and he is doing it.

Q. Your examination is not exhausted, then?—A. No, sir.

Q. How soon will you be able to know whether you have any such receipts or not?—A. I think I ought to be able to know this week. If he finds any, he will advise me. If he does not, he will not. The receipt from Mr. Allison is as follows:

Received of Oakes Ames ten shares of the stock of the Credit Mobilier of America, which I hold subject to his order.

WM. B. ALLISON.

That is the receipt Mr. Allison alluded to.

Q. When was that given?—A. I do not know; it has no date.

Q. Upon what occasion was it given? Was it at the time of the talk you had about the nickel?—A. Yes; it was part of that transaction.

Q. Did you say you thought you had made a similar arrangement with Mr. Colfax, in reference to the repurchase of his stock?—A. Yes, sir. I thought I had such a paper from him, but I could not find it. Mr. Colfax alluded to the transaction in his testimony, and I do not know but such a receipt may have been given, but I did not find it.

By Mr. HALE:

Q. You first testified before this committee the 17th of December last or in December, did you not?—A. I do not remember the date.

Q. Do you remember whether it was in December?—A. I think it was in December.

Q. After that you went home?—A. I did.

Q. When did you go home?—A. I do not remember the precise date.

Q. Did you go home before Christmas?—A. I think I did.

Q. How long were you at home?—A. I went home about the time Congress adjourned, and returned about the time Congress reconvened.

Q. When did you return home again?—A. I went home the 29th or 30th of January.

Q. And remained at home about how long then?—A. I think I got back yesterday morning.

Q. During your visit home, in the holidays, did you examine your memorandum-books which have now been produced here?—A. Yes, sir.

Q. Did you make up from them certain statements which you presented to the committee after your return?—A. My book-keeper prepared them, and I presented them.

Q. Then, you did not prepare them?—A. No, sir.

Q. Your book-keeper prepared them?—A. Yes, sir.

Q. Were they prepared under your eye, you reading and knowing they were correct?—A. Yes, sir.

Q. In all cases?—A. I think so.

Q. Are you sure you looked over and compared the copy made by your book-keeper with your original entries?—A. I did.

Q. In every instance?—A. I think I did.

Q. So that when you testified on your return, from the copies you presented, you testified of what you knew of your own knowledge?—A. I think so.

Q. What did you do with these memorandum-books at the time you returned to Washington?—A. I left them in my office.

Q. Where?—A. At Easton.

Q. You left all three you have presented here?—A. Yes, sir.

Q. Did none of those books come back to Washington when you returned, after the holidays?—A. No, sir.

Q. Was neither of these books in Washington between the time you returned, after the holidays, and your coming back on the 29th January?—A. Yes, sir; one of them was.

Q. Which one?—A. That of 1868.

Q. When did that come back to Washington?—A. I do not know as I can tell you the exact date.

Q. As nearly as you can tell?—A. I cannot tell you exactly.

Q. How did it come to Washington?—A. I think my son brought it on his way to New Orleans.

Q. And delivered it to you?—A. Yes, sir.

Q. And was it in your possession from that time to the present?—A. No, sir.

Q. Was it in your possession from that time until you returned to Washington?—A. No, sir.

Q. Where was it?—A. It went back to Easton with Mr. Kennedy, after being copied.

Q. With George W. Kennedy?—A. Yes, sir.

Q. Did he carry it back to Easton?—A. I think he did.

Q. By your request?—A. I do not know about that; I had got through with it; I did not suppose anybody wanted it further.

Q. That was your presumption?—A. Yes, sir.

Q. Mr. Kennedy is your book-keeper?—A. He is the book-keeper of Oliver Ames & Sons; he is not my book-keeper.

Q. The book-keeper of the firm of which you are a member?—A. Yes, sir.

Q. Can you tell what day your son arrived in Washington, on his way to New Orleans?—A. No, sir.

Q. Have you any means of telling?—A. I do not know whether I have or not.

Q. Will you ascertain from any memoranda which you have, and inform the committee, what day he arrived here?—A. I do not know that I can tell you. He went through here. If you can tell the day Mr. Kennedy came down to be examined, I can tell you when my son came. They came together. I cannot tell you now what day they arrived.

Q. Then the memorandum which you presented to this committee as made from these books was not made at your home in Easton during the holidays?—A. No, sir; they were made by Mr. Kennedy, and presented here.

Q. You understand me to refer to the copies or statements which you presented to the committee as copied from these memorandum-books; do you mean to say that they were made here, and not at Easton?—A. Yes, sir; they were in Mr. Kennedy's handwriting; they were made by him while he was here.

Q. Have you not said that during your visit home for the holidays these copies were there made from these books by your book-keeper, under your own eye, and that you left the books at Easton when you came back?—A. I do not think I said any such thing; if I did, I misunderstood your question. They were made here from the book here.

Q. When did this committee first call upon you to produce these memorandum-books?—A. I do not know.

Q. Can you not tell?—A. No, sir; I cannot tell.

The CHAIRMAN stated that written notice to Mr. Ames was given after Mr. Kennedy testified before the committee.

Mr. HALE. That was after verbal notice.

The CHAIRMAN said that when Mr. Ames went home for the holidays he notified him verbally that the committee would want all his books and papers showing this transaction; and that written notice was served after Mr. Kennedy had testified.

WITNESS. When that call was made for all my memorandum-books, large books, and everything else, I asked you whether, if I brought you a statement in relation to these cases, that would not be satisfactory, and you replied it would. Then Mr. Colfax afterward called for the books, and you re-ordered them.

The CHAIRMAN said the witness must have misunderstood him in that regard.

By Mr. HALE:

Q. Have you now on this cross-examination for the first time disclosed to the committee that either of these memorandum-books had been in Washington during this investigation until since you last returned?—A. I do not know whether I have or not. I do not know that they asked me.

Q. Do you say upon your oath that you do not know whether you have or not disclosed that fact?—A. I do not remember whether I said anything about it or not.

Q. Do you mean that you have or have not disclosed the fact that you had that book when Mr. Kennedy's testimony was taken?—A. I do not know whether I did or not.

Q. I am asking for your recollection, whether you made that statement or not?—A. I do not know that I did.

Q. Do you know whether you did or not?—A. I do not know that I have stated anything about it.

Mr. CLARK suggested that if there was any material issue upon which the counsel was endeavoring to show the witness had made contradictory statements in his former evidence, such evidence should be first read to him.

The CHAIRMAN said the counsel was entitled to an answer to his question whether Mr. Ames recollected the fact inquired about.

WITNESS. I do not remember it.

Q. I am asking the witness whether he has any remembrance of having developed that fact?—A. I do not know that I have; I do not think I have.

Mr. HALE. I do not think that is quite an answer to my question.

WITNESS. Well, see if you can get it any different.

Mr. HALE. I wish to ask the chairman whether I am entitled to a square answer to that question.

The CHAIRMAN said he understood the witness to have answered substantially that he could not remember whether he had stated anything about it.

Q. I want to ask the witness again to answer me the question, if he does or does not know whether he has or has not so stated?

WITNESS. I have answered it to the best of my ability; if you can get anything more out of it you may try to.

Mr. HALE. That answer I will take. There is no more of a cat than her skin. In your testimony, before your last visit home, on the 22d of January, you were asked where these original memorandums were from which your statement was taken, and you answered that it was in a small pocket memorandum-book, and some of it on slips of paper. Have you produced here all the slips of paper which you referred to as a part of the foundation of your statement?—A. No, sir; I have not been able to find them.

Q. Where are they?—A. I suppose they were destroyed when the transactions were ended. I had a slip of paper containing a list of the names of persons who were entitled to interest on the certificates, but when I came to search for them, I found they had been destroyed.

Q. You think they were destroyed in 1868?—A. Yes, sir; or 1869.

Q. What did you mean, then, when you said these memorandums were made up in part from slips of paper?—A. I did not say from slips of paper; I said they were made up from this memorandum-book; and they all show that they were made from this book. These slips of paper were in 1868.

Q. Then these slips of paper were not before you and Mr. Kennedy when you made up the statements that you produced here in January?—A. No; the statements were made from the book.

Q. And from the book alone?—A. I think so.

Q. Please refer to page 288 of the printed testimony, on which appears what purports to be a memorandum, or printed copy of a memorandum, which you produced to the committee. Now, will you show me on your memorandum-book the original entry of which this is a copy?—A. (Handing memorandum-book to Mr. Hale.) That is the first item.

Q. I want the original entry from which this statement is a copy.—A. Well, that is the first item.

Q. What I want is the original statement on your book handed in here, from which this copy, as it purports to be, on page 288 of the printed testimony, was taken.

WITNESS. I expect the reporter has that copy.

Q. I asked you to point me on this memorandum the original statement, of which the paper you handed in here was a copy, and which paper is in print on page 288?—A. I made that statement up from items in the book as memoranda, and I have shown you the first item, which gives the payment of the $534.72.

Q. Where does that appear?—A. Under date of March 5. The memorandum says, "Received of Schuyler Colfax check for balance, $534.72."

Q. Have you read everything that appears there in relation to Mr. Colfax?—A. That is the entire entry under that date.

Q. There are no other words, figures, or letters?—A. Not there.

Q. I now ask you for the next entry.—A. I do not find here the entry of the bonds. But I made a statement to Mr. Colfax, and if you have that statement there you can see it.

Q. I am not asking you about any statement. I am asking you about what is in this book.—A. I made up an account which shows that $534.72 was the balance due me for $2,000 of Credit Mobilier stock.

Q. That is not an answer to my question.—A. This sum makes up the amount from the *data* and figures I have shown. Mr. Colfax does not dispute that he gave me the balance on his account, does he?

The CHAIRMAN. The Chair understands that this is an account which Mr. Ames made up for Mr. Colfax.

Mr. HALE. If the chairman will turn to page 323 of the printed testimony, he will see that the witness used this language:

"Q. Do you now say that the memorandum from which you testified day before yesterday, in regard to your transactions with me, is an exact copy of your private memorandum-book?—A. I think so.

"Q. Do you know that you saw that memorandum-book when you went home?—A. Yes.

"Q. And you refreshed your memory from it?—A. I did."

My question is, do you now say that you can find on your memorandum-book, or on any memorandum-book that you have produced, the original entry from which this statement on page 288 is a copy?—A. That is a copy of the transaction, sir. I made up that statement from these items in this book. I am not a book-keeper, but I understand that to be a correct statement.

By the CHAIRMAN:

Q. Do you mean to say that in your books the statement which is here printed is set down in the form in which it is here, and that you copied it from any of the books in that form?—A. No, sir; I did not have on any of my memorandum-books an account drawn off in that way. This statement was prepared in that way to show what I have paid to and received from Mr. Colfax.

By Mr. HALE:

Q. Then, instead of being a copy of an original entry, it is a statement of account made up by yourself derived from various entries and various sources?—A. The original entries are in the memorandum-book. Mr. Colfax would not have given me the $534.72 unless——

Mr. HALE. I do not want that to go in as a part of my cross-examination. The witness is a man of few words I know, but they come in sometimes at improper places.

WITNESS. That is very probable.

Q. In regard to the statements which you produced of your transactions with some of these other gentlemen, as, for instance, in Mr. Garfield's case, printed on page 297, and Mr. Kelley's, on page 298, were they of the same character? Were they copies of original entries, or statements made up from various entries?—A. They were statements made up from entries of different transactions, occurring on different dates; some were from books, and some from other memoranda.

Q. Pray tell me what other memoranda they were from?—A. I made memoranda of all these transactions, and handed them to these parties at different times. I made one for Mr. Colfax when he paid me the balance of $534.72.

Q. Do you mean that these statements were made up from memoranda which you had delivered to the parties to be used before?—A. No; they were made up from memoranda that I had.

Q. Where are all these memoranda?—A. I do not know where they are now.

Q. Do you mean the memoranda from which Mr. Kennedy made the statement?—A. Yes, sir; from the books and from the facts where I had delivered to parties bonds, and the parties admitted it.

Q. Did Mr. Kennedy make that statement from any other written documents than from the books?—A. We had written documents showing that the papers were received and that the bonds were received.

Q. I am now inquiring of you of the statements Mr. Kennedy made up and which you presented here; what did he make them from?—A. I think mostly from this book.

Q. What else?—A. We had these statements here to make them from.

Q. Did you have any papers besides the book to make them from?—A. I think not.

Q. Does the book contain all the items embraced in these statements, or were they made in part from memory?—A. I think this includes all the items.

Q. Were these statements made up in part from memory, as to the transactions of these parties?—A. No, sir; these statements were made up from this book of 1868.

Q. Turn now to page 298, and give me in your book the entry that is copied in your statement on that page of the printed testimony.—A. Here is the entry [handing book to Mr. Hale] of the various items making up Mr. Kelley's account.

Q. Is that the whole of the entry?—A. That is the whole of it.

Q. And do you say that the statement made by Mr. Kennedy, which is printed here, is a correct transcript of that entry?—A. It is correct, is it not?

Q. Take this item of $47 for interest.—A. There are two items on the memorandum-book which make up that amount.

Q. Now tell me what there is on the debit side in your memorandum-book.—A. There is nothing on the debit side of this entry.

Q. This statement contains two items on the debit side and one on the credit side, showing a balance of $271. Where are the other entries that make up the statement printed on page 298?—A. The other entries are the 80 per cent. bond dividend collected for his account, amounting to $776.

Q. I ask you whether that is in your memorandum-book?—A. The memorandum-book does not come up so far as this cash dividend of June, from which he received $600.

Q. Is there any entry in your memorandum-book, under date of June 19, "To cash, $329?"—A. No, sir.

Q. That is not in the memorandum-book?—A. No.

Q. Is there any entry on your memorandum-book of "Dividend collected for your account, $600, June 17?"—A. Yes, sir; here it is.

Q. That is on the list you describe?—A. It is on the list of parties who were entitled to dividends.

Q. Is that the only place where it appears in your book?—A. No, sir.

Q. Where else?—A. Upon this other list, under date of June 21.

Q. In both these cases the memorandum was made by you of amounts due the parties, and not amounts you had paid them?—A. They were paid.

Q. I did not ask you that. I ask you what the entry was intended to indicate?—A. The entry showed that the parties were entitled to receive dividends, and I paid them the dividends.

Q. I did not ask you that.

WITNESS. What do you ask?

Q. I will now ask your another question. Turn to the entry in this printed book, of the payment of $329 to Mr. Kelley, and show me where you find that entry?—A. Not on this book; the Sergeant-at-Arms will show it to you.

Q. It is not, then, on your book?—A. Yes; and there is an entry of $329.

Q. But that is the amount to be paid?—A. It was to be paid before it was paid, and it has been paid since.

Q. But you say that is not an entry of actual payment?—A. I say it is, if it is crossed off. It was an entry to be paid, and when it was paid it was crossed off.

Q. Now I want to ask Mr. Ames, who comes here and says he presents to the committee a statement which is a transcript of his book, to point me the place on his book where that entry is made.

WITNESS. I have shown you where.

The CHAIRMAN stated that the committee had gone over all these matters until they understood them very thoroughly; and unless it was necessary for the counsel for his own enlightenment to go over them again, the committee would not be receiving any additional information from it. If there was any inconsistency in Mr. Ames's statements the committee had already all the means of ascertaining it.

Mr. HALE said the witness had sworn to certain statements as having been copied from his memorandum-book, and he was asking him to point out the entries from which the copies were made.

The CHAIRMAN said he understood the witness to state that he had produced all the memoranda he had. If the object of the counsel was to find further memoranda, he might proceed with his examination.

But if the object was simply to prove inconsistency of statements, the committee had all the means which any further examination would be likely to elicit.

Mr. HALE said that if the committee were satisfied Mr. Ames was telling two widely different stories, he had no desire to proceed further.

The CHAIRMAN said the counsel was not authorized to draw any conclusions on that subject. His object in interrupting him was to save time.

Q. Please show me where the entry is on your memorandum-book of "By dividends for your account, six hundred dollars?"—A. I collected the dividend.

Q. Where is the entry on your memorandum-book showing it?—A. I do not know much about book-keeping, but I am not so stupid that I cannot make such a calculation as will show that 271 from 600 will leave 329. I can explain that, as big a fool as I am, and if you will allow me I will do so. Mr. Kelley owed $271. Then he was entitled to a dividend of $600. Taking 271 from 600 left a balance of 329 due, which I paid. That, I think, is a plain statement of book-keeping.

Q. Very likely that is so; but what I ask you for is to state where you find such an entry on that book?—A. Yes; I find that he was entitled to $329, the balance due him on the $600 dividend after deducting $271 which he owed.

The CHAIRMAN said the committee had traveled all over this ground until they were entirely familiar with it, and that the counsel was apparently not so familiar with it, or he would not desire to go over it again.

Mr. HALE said he would not dispute that statement, although inclined to think that appearances did not fully warrant it. He would, however, proceed no further in this line of examination.

Q. Did you take any receipt, voucher, or acknowledgment from Mr. Colfax in payment of the $1,200 which you stated you gave him in June?—A. I do not think I did. I gave him a check and he drew the money.

Q. The last part of your answer is not responsive to my question.—A. It is true, nevertheless.

Q. Have you stated within the last month repeatedly to different persons in the city of Washington that you had such a receipt from Mr. Colfax?—A. No, sir; I have not.

Q. Have you not stated to different persons that you were very sure you had such a receipt?—A. I do not think I have. I know I have not. I did not suppose I was entitled to a receipt for the $1,200 belonging to Mr. Colfax, as a dividend on his stock. He paid me for the stock, and why should I take a receipt from him for his own money?

Q. Did you not state to John B. Alley that you had such a receipt?—A. No, sir.

Q. Did you not state to different persons in this city that you had such a receipt from Mr. Colfax?—A. How many times do you want me to answer that question? I say I did not to anybody.

Q. You have not said that to Judge Niblack, Judge Poland, or any member of this committee.—A. I do not think I have. I must have been asleep when I did it.

Q. That is very possible.—A. I was in hopes I should find one when I went home, but I did not. I did not suppose anybody would dispute the payment after the evidence that has been presented.

Q. The payment you have now testified to of $60.75, made on the 22d of January, 1869—did you take any voucher or receipt for that?—A.

No, sir; it was his money. It was a dividend on a certificate for bonds which I held for him, and which belonged to him.

Q. You do not think you were entitled to a receipt?—A. No, sir.

Q. You took a receipt from some gentlemen to whom you paid money?—A. I did from two or three. I do not know why I did.

Q. Can you give any reason why you took a receipt from Mr. Patterson and none from Mr. Colfax?—A. No; I did not know that I had Mr. Patterson's receipts when this investigation commenced. He paid me $3,000 in August, and I got the stock from him afterward. Of course I should give him a receipt for the money.

Q. You have said several times that you paid $1,200 to Mr. Colfax?—A. I said I gave him a check for that amount.

Q. Do you make that statement from any recollection you have? Do you remember giving Mr. Colfax a check for $1,200?—A. I do.

Q. Where did you give it to him?—A. I do not know.

Q. When did you give it to him?—A. Probably at the time; the date of the check will show.

Q. Can you state when from memory?—A. I do not know.

Q. Who was present and under what circumstances did you give it to him?—A. I gave it to him because I owed it to him. That is the circumstance.

Q. Can you state all the circumstances?—A. No.

Q. Do you mean to say you can remember a fact as occurring and not remember any circumstance or incident connected with that fact?—A. Sometimes I could. This was simply the fact of giving him a check. He was entitled to receive $1,200. I held the money and gave him a check for the amount.

Q. Do you remember giving the check?—A. I remember that.

Q. Did you hand it to him in person?—A. I did.

Q. That you know?—A. There has never been any person between us. What we have done we have done ourselves in person. There were no go-betweens.

Q. How long has your memory been so positive on that subject?—A. There are some things I can remember positively.

Q. How long has your memory been positive in regard to this?—A. Ever since I gave him the check.

Q. You have had no lapse of memory in regard to that?—A. No, sir; and I gave a check to all the rest of them, too.

Q. On the 17th day of December, when you testified before this committee, you produced a written statement and read it to the committee, in which, on page 20, appear these words: "Mr. Colfax is one mentioned. I cannot remember which of us first mentioned the subject, but I know he wanted to get some stock. I am pretty confident he has paid me for it, though I have never transferred to him, nor can I remember having paid to him any dividends." Was that a written statement carefully prepared and brought in by you before this committee, as your evidence?—A. Yes, sir. He cannot say he has received no dividends.

Q. I want you to answer the question.—A. I will answer the question in my own way. This statement was made up in December without any memoranda, or anything to refresh my memory with. It relates to transactions which occurred four or five years ago, of very little consequence, as I then considered it, and, with the immense amount of business I have had on hand, it would not be strange that all these details would not at the moment be very clear in my mind. I made up the statement to the best of my recollection then.

Q. On page 23 the chairman put to you this question: "Is the committee to understand that you put this in as your testimony, and swear to the truth of it?" To which the answer given is, "Yes, sir." That is true?—A. Yes, sir.

Q. Now, then, did you, when that paper was prepared, and when it was read by you before this committee, and when you swore to the truth of it in answer to this last question, remember to have paid $1,200 to Mr. Colfax?—A. I supposed I had paid him dividends. I could not remember without data things that took place four or five years ago. My impression was, as I stated in that testimony, that I had paid him dividends.

Q. Did you remember that you had paid him dividends?—A. That was my impression.

Q. Is that your only answer?—A. That was my impression, and that is my only answer.

Q. When you said in this testimony "nor can I remember of having paid over to him any dividends," did you intend to speak the truth or speak a lie?

Mr. CLARKE submitted to the committee, in justice to the witness, that the question propounded by counsel was not a respectful one.

Mr. HALE said, although the question might be a little more polite, he thought the question was a proper one.

Mr. MERRICK remarked that, to do justice to the witness, his whole statement should be presented to him. In the same examination, on page 26, in answer to the question, "Do you know whether he has received any dividends on it?" the witness answers, "It is my impression that he has; but I am not certain."

Mr. HALE. The committee will remember I do not charge falsehood; I am quite willing to change the phraseology of the question, and to put it in this form: Did you intend to speak the truth or not?—A. I will not answer that question; it is an impudent question. I have rights here as well as you. I am not to be bullied here by any man.

Mr. HALE. I accept that as an answer, that you will not answer my question.—A. No; not in that form.

Q. Do you now say, in answer to my question a few minutes ago, that you have always remembered, ever since you gave that check for $1,200, that you gave it?—A. I should have remembered it at any time, upon looking at my memoranda.

Q. My question is this: Do you now say that you did remember when you testified before?—A. I said it was my impression when I testified. The answer I gave in my first examination was right enough. I intended to make it as favorable as I could to Mr. Colfax, but when I heard it was said they intended to break me down I could not do otherwise than state everything.

Q. Do you now say that when you testified before, from this prepared statement, that you knew that you had given him dividends?—A. I stated in that examination that I presumed I had given him dividends, did I not?

Q. You will please answer my question.

WITNESS. I said so, did I not?

The CHAIRMAN remarked that it was admitted in presence of the committee that the statement referred to was prepared by counsel of Mr. Ames, and portions of it were objected to by counsel.

Mr. HALE. Is that true, that the statement given as your testimony was prepared by your counsel, or by yourself?—A. Mr. MacMurtrie prepared it.

Q. Was it prepared from your dictation?—A. Partly.

The CHAIRMAN said that course of inquiry need not be pursued. The witness was cautioned that no part of the statement would be accepted as testimony unless its truth was sworn to by him.

Q. Is there any reason why you remember giving this check to Mr. Colfax, and do not remember giving other checks to other parties?—A. I do remember, and my memorandum shows that I gave checks to others, and when I see these entries in my book I know they are true, and I know that I paid these amounts.

Q. I want to call your attention to page 26, to this testimony given by you:

"Q. Did you pay him the dividends yourself?—A. I cannot recollect.

"Q. If this stock stood in your name on the books, the dividends would have been paid to you, I suppose?—A. That would be a natural consequence.

"Q. And can you recollect, do you recollect, whether you paid dividends to Mr. Colfax?—A. No, sir; I do not recollect; it is my impression that I did."

Q. Is that statement true?—A. That was my impression.

Q. Do you now modify the answers you then gave, to any extent?—A. I make them stronger now. I did pay the dividends.

Q. That is what I supposed. You do now modify these answers?—A. Yes.

Q. In testifying in Mr. Garfield's case you say you may have drawn the money on the check and paid him; is not that answer equally applicable to the case of Mr. Colfax?—A. No, sir.

Q. Why not?—A. I put Mr. Colfax's initials in the check, while I put no initials into Mr. Garfield's check, and I may have drawn the money myself.

Q. Do you say that if you put any initials before the words "or bearer" into a check, that is evidence that you gave him the check, and that he drew the money on it?—A. I am satisfied that I gave him the check any way, because it belonged to him.

Q. Did not Mr. Garfield's check belong to him?—A. Mr. Garfield had not paid for his stock. He was entitled to $329 balance; but Mr. Colfax had paid for his stock, and I had no business with his $1,200.

Q. Is your recollection in regard to this payment to Mr. Colfax any more clear than your recollection as to the payment to Mr. Garfield?—A. Yes, sir, I think it is. Do you doubt that I gave him, Colfax, the check?

Q. That is not a proper question for me to answer; if it were I should answer it very frankly. Do you say that you have never presented to the Sergeant-at-Arms, and drew money on, checks payable to initials or bearer, or to a fictitious name or bearer, or to somebody's name or bearer?—A. I do not think I have.

Q. Can you so testify from your knowledge?—A. I cannot say that I have or have not. I have drawn a great many checks on the Sergeant-at-Arms within the last ten years, and I cannot remember how I have drawn every check.

Q. On the 29th day of December, in this room, as reported on page 353 of the printed testimony, is the following:

"Q. Here is another check upon the Sergeant-at-Arms of the same date, June 22, 1868: 'Pay O. A. or bearer, $329, and charge to my account. Oakes Ames.' That seems to have been paid to somebody and taken up by the Sergeant-at-Arms. These initials are your own?—A. Yes, sir.

"Q. Do you know who had the benefit of that check?—A. I cannot tell you.

"Q. Do you think you received the money on it yourself?—A. I have no idea. I may have drawn the money and handed it to another person. It was paid on that transaction. It may have been paid to Mr. Garfield. There were several sums of that amount."

Do you think that was possibly the case as to the $329 and not possibly the case as to the $1,200?—A. I have no recollection of drawing any of them myself.

Q. That is your answer?—A. Yes, it is. I have no recollection of drawing any one of them. But I could not have drawn the money on one of those containing the initials without remembering it. I do not think I drew any of them myself.

Q. Is there any reason why your memory should be any clearer in regard to the $1,200 check than in regard to the $329 check?—A. I should not have put Mr. Colfax's initials into the $1,200 check if I had been going to draw the money myself.

Q. Do you remember positively that you gave Mr. Colfax a statement showing the condition of his account?—A. I gave him one, or showed him one. I exhibited one to him; I am sure of that.

Q. That you are positive of?—A. I am.

Q. On page 282, in your examination of the 22d January, I find this report:

"Q. Did I offer to pay you, or did you give to me, or ask me to pay you that?—A. That I cannot tell you. I suppose I handed you a statement showing the balance due, and that you gave me the check.

"Q. Do you swear that you did hand me a statement?—A. No; I will not swear to it."

A. Well, I exhibited one to him, if I did not give him one; and he gave me a check for the balance. It is not very likely he would have given me a check for $534.72 without knowing what it was for. I do not think he was as green as that.

Q. Again, on page 285: "You do not think you told me that, do you?—A. I do not know whether I did; I suppose I gave him a statement."—A. Well, I suppose I did.

Q. Do you now modify that answer?—A. No; I think I did give him a statement.

Q. Do you mean to say that all you can say is that you suppose you gave him one?—A. I do suppose I gave him one; I do not think there is any doubt of it.

Q. Do you mean to say you remember positively that you gave him one, or showed him one?—A. I gave him one, or showed him one; there is no doubt about that; does anybody question that fact?

Q. Now, then, on page 327, while Mr. Colfax was under examination, you asked him this question:

"You had more confidence in my statements then than you have now. I ask you if I did not make a statement to you at that time, giving you a balance of $534.72, showing you the amount of your $2,000 Credit Mobilier stock, with interest up to that date, giving you credit on the proceeds of 80 per cent. in bonds, and did you not give me a draft on the Sergeant-at-Arms for $534.72 to make up that balance; do you deny that?—A. I deny that.

"Mr. AMES. I am sorry for it.

"The WITNESS. You gave me a slip of paper with the amount of the balance, $534.72, on it, and told me there were some dividends which had not been adjusted.

"The CHAIRMAN, (to Mr. Ames:)

"Do you wish to propound any more questions to Mr. Colfax?

"Mr. AMES. If he denies that I made him this statement, I do not want to ask him any other question."

These remarks made to you by Mr. Colfax were based on your former testimony that you supposed you had given him the statement?—A. Yes, sir; I supposed I had given him one; I know I gave him one or exhibited one to him; I am sure of that.

Q. Now go back to page 4 of this testimony, on which appears your letter to Mr. McComb, in which you say, "I have assigned as far as I have gone to 4 from Mass., 1 from N. H., 1 Delaware, 1 Tenn., 1 Ohio, 2 Penn., 1 Ind., 1 Maine, & I have 3 to place, which I shall put where they will do most good to us." Will you state to me what transactions you intended by those from each State there enumerated?

The CHAIRMAN stated that all this matter had been gone over thoroughly, and the committee understood what Mr. Ames's explanation of that letter was.

Mr. HALE desired an answer to this question, for the purpose of showing that it was a falsification on the part of the witness; that when he stated he had placed stock with certain persons designated, his own testimony before this committee proved that he had never transferred stock to them or to several of them.

The CHAIRMAN said the committee had determined they had all the light they were likely to get upon that subject, and declined to allow the counsel to make further inquiries in regard to it.

Q. On page 40 appears a list of dividends declared by the Credit Mobilier, numbering twelve in all, which you say you think are correct, except as to the first three, which were not dividends. To what dividends do you claim Mr. Colfax to be entitled?—A. He was entitled to 80 per cent. first-mortgage bonds that I gave to him. He was entitled to 100 per cent. Union Pacific Railroad stock. He was entitled to 60 per cent. in cash, that I paid him; and to 40 per cent. in Union Pacific Railroad stock. Then he was entitled to 75 per cent. first-mortgage bonds, which were never received, but for which a certificate was given, and I paid the interest on that certificate to Mr. Colfax. He was entitled to his interest on that $1,500 of bonds, and I paid it to him. Then he was entitled to 100 per cent. Union Pacific Railroad stock. I think there is a mistake in this list. I think this dividend of 75 per cent. first-mortgage bonds is repeated in July and September, where it should only be stated once. He also was entitled to 200 per cent. Union Pacific Railroad Company stock, in his dividend declared December 19, 1868.

Q. Was Mr. Colfax entitled to all these dividends?—A. Yes, he was, and is, as far as he has not received them. That is my impression.

Q. Are you sure the 75 per cent. bond dividend, to which you refer, is an error as printed in this testimony?—A. I think so. I cannot tell now; my books will show.

Q. Have you drawn all these dividends?—A. I think I have.

Q. Have you paid over any of them to Mr. Colfax?—A. None, except those I have mentioned. I gave him the stock when he made his first payment; I mean the 100 per cent. Union Pacific Railroad stock. At least that is my impression. His recollection is probably better than mine as to that.

Q. You have no recollection of paying him any dividends except the three you have mentioned?—A. No, sir; I have paid no others, excepting the 80 per cent. bond dividend, the 100 per cent. Union Pacific Railroad stock, and the 60 per cent. in cash.

Q. On the 75 per cent. first-mortgage-bond dividend you paid him the interest in January?—A. I collected the interest in New York, and paid it over to him. That is my recollection.

Q. Where did you pay him that $60 and odd cents?—A. Here in Washington.

Q. By check?—A. No; in money.

Q. Can you not tell the place?—A. No.

Q. Nor any circumstances connected with it?—A. Only this entry on my book. I should not have charged Mr. Colfax with the money if I had not let him have it.

Q. Do you mean to say that you remember it as you have it on your book?—A. I do not mean to say anything of the sort.

Q. Then you have no recollection of it?—A. I did not have until I saw it on the books.

Q. Have you now any recollection of it?—A. Not except that I know I paid it, as I entered it on the books as paid. Do you suppose I would cheat Mr. Colfax out of $60?

Q. You say you do remember paying these $60 to Mr. Colfax?—A. I cannot state the circumstance. I found the entry on my book.

Q. Now, will you show me the entry on your book of $60.75?—A. Yes; you shall have all the entries. Here it is: "Paid Schuyler Colfax $60.75 for interest on 1,590 certificates of U. P. R. R."

Q. That is all your knowledge in relation to it?—A. Yes, sir.

Q. You testified on your former examination that you had no recollection of paying him any money on account of these dividends except $1,200?—A. Excepting the $1,200; I did not remember this interest then.

Q. And do not remember it now?—A. No; except that I have it entered on my book.

Q. You are confident of the correctness of your book-keeping?—A. Yes, sir. I do not think I should charge Mr. Colfax with $60, if I had not paid it.

Q. On page 279 you say, "I never delivered to Mr. Colfax anything else, and never received anything from him except that time. He paid me for the balance of the stock, and I paid him a cash dividend." That is your testimony, is it?—A. Yes, sir.

Q. Have you ever given him any information that he was entitled to these dividends?—A. I do not know. I think I must have. This suit of McComb was brought against the company, and I have been holding these dividends until the result of that suit.

Q. You have no knowledge of giving him information as to his being entitled to this large amount of dividends?—A. I have no recollection except of having given him a statement when he paid me the $534.

Q. I now call your attention again to page 35:

"Q. Did you pay them a dividend declared June 17, 1868, of 60 per cent., cash currency, and the same day one of 40 per cent. Union Pacific Railroad stock?—A. I cannot tell you. I presume I did to those who had paid for their stock. Some of them never paid for their stock, and were therefore not entitled to the dividends."

A. That was my recollection at the time.

Q. Do you modify that answer in any respect now?—A. I say I did pay them the cash dividend.

Q. Again on the same page I read as follows:

"Q. The same question is asked you in reference to a dividend declared September 3, 1868, of 100 per cent. Union Pacific Railroad stock, and the same day 75 per cent. first-mortgage bonds Union Pacific Railroad Company?—A. It is my impression that I did. I do not recollect. It depended on the conditions on which they took the stock. Some gave up their stock, and some did not pay, and, therefore, did not get their dividends, of course."

Q. Do you modify that answer now?—A. I think I hardly understood the question asked. I am a little hard of hearing, and some of these questions were put to me which I did not hear distinctly. I know I did pay them to Mr. Patterson and to James F. Wilson, and several others. Some of them I have not settled with, and some I had settled with before, and taken back the stock.

Q. Do you modify that part of the answer in which you say that some gave up their stock, and some did not pay, and therefore did not get their dividends, of course?—A. Those who did not pay for their stock did not get their dividends, of course.

Q. Did not Mr. Colfax give up his stock?—A. Not that I know of.

Q. Did not Mr. Colfax notify you that he would not take his stock, and did not you testify to that on a former occasion?—A. I think not.

Q. You never understood that he gave up his stock?—A. Not until this investigation. I never before heard anything about its being given up; at least I do not think I did. I have no recollection of it.

Q. On page 20 of your former testimony did not you say in regard to Mr. Colfax that at the next session he said to you something about that thing being off, when he came on here?—A. There were a good many people, when this matter became public, in connection with McComb's suit and the canvass of last fall, who came to me and wanted to know how I understood the matter, and among others Mr. Colfax. I had none of my books here with me, and nothing to refresh my recollection with, and I was inclined to let it go as they wanted it, as far as I could. I did not know but their recollection might be better than mine. I stated it as well as I could for their side generally, and if my recollection differed from theirs I would rather lean to their opinions, supposing they might be right instead of myself. I had no recollection of Mr. Colfax saying anything about it being off until after I came back this winter.

Q. You state that you have no recollection of Mr. Colfax saying anything about being off until this investigation commenced?—A. No, sir.

Q. Did you in your former testimony state that Mr. Colfax said something to you about $500 you owed him in 1870 or 1871?—A. No, sir; I did not say anything about any $500 I owed him in 1870 or 1871, or ever, to my recollection.

Q. On page 286 of this testimony, in answer to Mr. Colfax's question, "After this conversation in which I told you to never mind the $500, did you not regard it as off?" you said, "No, sir; I supposed I had to pay the $500. I did not know who had the certificate, you or I." Do you modify that answer now?—A. Well, sir, I do not know. I do not recollect hearing Mr. Colfax ask the question. Mr. Colfax speaks very rapidly and rather low. I am a little hard of hearing. I did not catch a great many of his questions, and it is very likely that I did not understand that question.

Q. Do you say now that you did not mean to say you had to pay him the $500 back?—A. I do not see how I could ever make such an answer as that. I did not pay any $500 back, and I do not remember the question he asked at all.

Q. Again, on page 280 there is this question by the chairman of the committee: "What do you say in reference to that statement about his making a present to you of $500, saying that you might keep the $500 he paid you?—A. He made some remark of that sort to me.

"Q. Will you state what was the whole conversation?—A. I cannot remember that all; he made some such statement that he was sorry for my misfortune, or something like that.

"Q. How late was that?—A. That was about two years ago—about 1871."

Q. Did you fully understand these questions when they were put to you?—A. I said he made some such statement to me as that he was sorry for my misfortunes, or something like that; that was my answer to one of the questions, and when he asked me the date of it I said it was about two years ago; that was all right.

Q. Do you modify your answer in any respect?—A. I do not, except that I do not know that he ever offered to pay me $500.

Q. Do you modify your answer, then?—A. I do not know that I do; I should want to examine precisely what I am reported as saying; my answer was that he made some such statement, that he was sorry for my misfortune; I think that is right; and then the question is put about the time when he was sympathizing with me about my misfortunes, which I said was about two years ago; that answer is correct; I do not know that he ever offered to pay me $500.

Q. Did you understand the question of the chairman when he asked, "What do you say in reference to that statement about his making a present to you of $500, saying you might keep the $500 he paid you?" Is your answer correctly reported?—A. The answer given is, "He made some remark of that sort to me." He did make some statement of that sort to me this winter.

Q. Your answer is that he made some statement to you of that sort this winter, but never before to your knowledge?—A. Yes, sir.

Q. Did you understand the question put to you by the chairman, "How late was that," to which you answered "That was about two years ago—about 1871?"—A. My understanding was that it was about the time of my misfortune—about two years ago. That is the way I understood the question, and it is the way I understand it now. The question refers to my misfortune, and my answer that it was about two years ago is correct.

Q. Now turn back to Mr. Colfax's statement when he testified that this conversation did take place in 1870 or '71, which statement you heard. Take that with the question first put to you by the chairman—"Did you hear Mr. Colfax's statement when he was before the committee the other day," to which you replied, "I did," and the question immediately following, "What do you say in reference to that statement about his making a present to you of $500, saying you might keep the present until he paid you?" to which your answer is, "He made some remark of that sort to me?"—A. That is the statement he made here the other day in his testimony before the committee.

Q. And that statement you understood?—A. I heard him make that statement.

Q. And your answer, in reference to that particular statement, that "He made some remark of that sort to me," is correct?—A. Yes; that was this winter.

Q. Then, in answer to that question, you now say that you understood it to refer to a conversation with Mr. Colfax this winter?—A. No; I did not say any such thing. I say that I do not recollect hearing him say anything about the $500 I owed him until this winter; but I said that my misfortunes, about which he inquired, went back to 1870 or 1871.

Mr. HALE. I will simply ask the attention of the committee to the statement of Mr. Colfax on this subject, on page 82. He says, "The next year, or the year after, Mr. Ames suspended payment, in consequence, as was said, of financial involvements connected with the Pacific Railroad, and his creditors gave him an extension on his liabilities. But regretting his failure and its cause, I voluntarily told him to dismiss from his mind the small amount of money between us."

Q. Will you please turn now to the entry in your private memorandum-book of the payment of $1,200 to Mr. Colfax?—A. Yes, sir. Here are the three entries I have already placed in evidence.

Mr. HALE then inquired of Mr. Dillon, book-keeper for the Sergeant-at-Arms, who at his request had brought the books of his office for 1868, what was the meaning of the letter "C" placed in the ledger account of two checks, one dated May 15, and the other May 23.

Mr. DILLON replied that the entry meant cash, and that where the letter was inserted in the ledger account the check was usually payable to self.

FEBRUARY 13, 1873.

Mr. Ames appeared before the committee and asked leave to make the following explanation, which was allowed to be made:

Wherever in my testimony I have used the words "dividends of or to the Credit Mobilier," I mean the dividends made to the parties interested in the Oakes Ames contract, viz, the trustees to whom it was assigned, and the persons who in writing made themselves liable upon the Oakes Ames contract.

WASHINGTON, D. C., *February* 11, 1873.

MOSES DILLON recalled and examined by Mr. Hale.

Question. Have you any recollection, distinct or indistinct, as to how you paid this $1,200 check, having the initials S. C. written in it?—Answer. When I was before the committee the other day, I said I had no recollection, although I had an impression. I supposed an impression would not be evidence. I had a very positive impression as to how that and several of the other checks out of this ten-thousand-dollar deposit were paid—that they were paid to Mr. Ames.

Q. Is that your impression now as to this $1,200 check?—A. It is my impression now. Still I was not certain or clear in my own mind about it.

Q. Have you any recollection as to the amount of the bills you gave for this $1,200 check?—A. Yes, sir; I think I paid him two $500 bills and two $100 bills. That was my impression when I was before the committee the other day; and I will state that, within the last thirty hours, I asked Mr. Ames if he did not think I paid the check to him; and he replied he thought it very likely.

By the CHAIRMAN:

Q. Do you think that you recollect that you paid that particular $1,200 check to Mr. Ames?—A. Not with sufficient distinctness to say that I recollect it. It is my impression. A man has a right to have an impression without being able to recollect distinctly. My recollection does not go that far.

Q. Do you think you remember that you paid that to Mr. Ames?—A. I cannot say as an act of memory that I do. My impression was the other day, and has been ever since, that I paid the money to Mr. Ames himself.

Q. You mean to say that is your recollection?—A. You may call it so; I would not make oath to it, because it is too far off to testify to distinctly.

Q. You mean the committee to understand that it is your recollection that you paid it to him?—A. That is my impression.

Q. Do you mean to say that is your recollection, either positive or less than positive?—A. I do not know how to put my answer into better language; it is my impression.

Q. I do not know how a man can know anything of a past transaction except by recollection; and what I want to get at is whether it is your recollection, whether you remember that it was so?—A. I cannot say that I remember it. That is an impression I have.

Q. How do you get any impression about it except from memory?—A. Of course you must attribute it to memory, and nothing else.

Q. Then you wish the committee to understand that you remember you paid that $1,200 to Mr. Ames?—A. Not with sufficient distinctness to swear to. I say again, that that is my impression, and I have no doubt in my own mind about it.

Q. Is your recollection sufficiently distinct to enable you to say that you remember having paid it to Mr. Ames himself?—A. I think I paid it to him.

Q. You say you think you paid other checks to Mr. Ames?—A. There were several of these checks I think I paid.

Q. Be good enough to name any one in particular that you think you paid.—A. I do not know that I could name any except this larger one.

Q. Is there any circumstance in your memory by which you can fasten upon the fact that this $1,200 check was paid to Mr. Ames?—A. No, sir; only as I have stated it as my impression.

Q. Do you now remember it? Does your memory go back to the payment of that $1,200 to anybody?—A. Only to the extent I have stated. I think I paid it to Mr. Ames; and my impression that I did is very strong.

Q. Was the circumstance recalled to your memory on seeing the check payable to the order of S. C. or bearer?—A. That was in my memory when the check was first produced; when Mr. Ames first asked to see it; and I so stated to Mr. Ordway; but when I was brought before the committee under the sanctity of an oath I could not say positively that I had done it.

Q. These checks were paid four or five years ago, and have remained on file in the office of the Sergeant-at-Arms ever since. You have had no occasion to look them up since, have you, until the other day?—A. Not until called for by Mr. Ames.

Q. Mr. Ames was the man who came to get you to look them up?—A. Yes, sir.

Q. Did you look them over with him?—A. Mr. Ordway did.

Q. Did you look them over yourself?—A. Yes, sir.

Q. Did you see this one, payable to S. C. or bearer?—A. Yes, sir.

Q. Did it occur to your memory then that you had paid it to anybody?—A. It occurred to me that I had paid it to Mr. Ames himself.

Q. Do you remember now that you ever saw that check before?—A. Not to give legal evidence, perhaps, that I recollect it; that is my impression.

Q. Do you remember the circumstance of a check being presented by anybody payable to S. C.?—A. No, sir; I could not recollect the circumstance that it was payable to S. C. After inquiries were made about it my mind was led to the idea that I had paid that check for $1,200 to Mr. Ames himself, without remembering that S. C. or any other initials were in it. I had no doubt about it in my own mind.

Q. Is there any circumstance which connects it with any other transaction in your mind—which fastens the fact upon your mind?—A. No, sir; I had a strong impression upon my mind of the $10,000 having been deposited by Mr. Ames as chairman of a committee, and that he was paying it out for the expenses of the committee. That was on my mind at the time. I could not account for it in any other way than that. I supposed Mr. Ames had deposited this money to pay it out to persons entitled to it. Several checks were payable to individuals who indorsed them; the others I think he got himself—most of them.

Q. There were several checks given by Mr. Ames payable to some person by name; do you think all these persons drew the sums themselves?—A. Yes, sir.

Q. Have you any memory whether they did or not?—A. No, sir; I presume they did.

Q. You judge of that from what they would be likely to do in the ordinary course of business?—A. Yes, sir; I judge of it from the ordinary course of business.

Q. There is a check payable to O. A. or bearer; have you any recollection of that?—A. That was paid to himself.

Q. Have you any memory that it was, or do you judge of that by the form in which the check is drawn?—A. No; I have no distinct memory about it. I have no doubt myself that I paid that to Mr. Ames.

Q. Have you any other reason for your belief that you did, except that it is payable to O. A. or bearer?—A. No, sir.

Q. Have you any other reason whatever for supposing you paid it to him than that?—A. No, sir.

Q. There is another, payable to W. D. K. or bearer; have you any memory about the payment of that?—A. No, sir; only I presume I paid that to Mr. Ames himself. I think I paid all these checks payable to initials to Mr. Ames.

Q. Have you any memory about that?—A. No, sir; no distinct memory.

Q. Have you any memory at all?—A. Yes; I think I have a very good one, generally.

Q. Whatever a man knows about a transaction, he knows from memory. I want to ascertain just precisely how well and how strongly you remember these facts.—A. I do not remember them well, and that was the reason I stated that I had merely an impression; but it is a very strong impression.

Q. If you supposed a man could not testify to his recollection, unless it was a positive and absolute recollection, you did not understand the law on that subject. What we want to know is, how firm your memory is in this regard.—A. Well, sir, I would not swear that I paid it to Mr. Ames, or to Mr. anybody else. I can only repeat again, that it is my impression I did. I cannot state that I recollect it positively.

Q. Do you mean to say that you have no recollection about it?—A. Yes, sir; I have.

By Mr. HALE:

Q. Do you mean to say that you have a recollection, but that it is not a positive recollection upon the subject?—A. That is it precisely; that is what I do mean to say.

Q. You use the word "impression" to denote an imperfect recollection? —A. That is it; not to be too positive about it.

By the CHAIRMAN:

Q. In this account of Mr. Ames, on the 29th June, there is an item of $1,800?—A. That was payable to Mr. Patterson, was it not?

The CHAIRMAN. Your ledger does not say.

WITNESS. It says J. W. P., does it not?

The CHAIRMAN. No; it does not say anything.

WITNESS, [after examining the journal of the Sergeant-at-Arms' office.] Yes, sir; that $1,800 was paid to Mr. Patterson.

Q. That was a draft payable to him?—A. No, sir; that was a check on the Sergeant-at-Arms payable to him, as I see by the original entry.

Q. Do you remember what kind of money you paid him in?—A. No, sir.

Q. Have you no impression on that subject?—A. No, sir; I do not think I have.

Q. You seem to have some idea of the denomination of the bills which you paid for the $1,200?—A. An indistinct recollection. Mr. Ames, when he drew large checks, always got large money.

Q. Was there anything peculiar to Mr. Ames about that?—A. I do not know. He always drew notes of large denominations.

By Mr. AMES:

Q. Did I not get drafts when I wanted large amounts?—A. You generally did.

Q. Did you ever know me to take a large amount in bills?—A. Yes, sir, I have; particularly when you were purchasing iron down about Alexandria.

By the CHAIRMAN:

Q. Under date of June 29 there is an entry of $1,000 to Mr. Ames's account; what is that?—A. That was cash, I presume.

Q. Have you any recollection what sort of money he got that in?—A. No, sir; I have no doubt he got a thousand-dollar note if he got it himself.

Q. What I want to ascertain is, how you have the impression that Mr. Ames drew the $1,200 in two $500 notes and two $100 notes; now do you remember any such thing?—A. I have an indistinct memory of such a thing.

Q. Is there any circumstance which recalls it to your mind?—A. Only that he was in the habit of getting bills of large denominations.

Q. Can you give any other reason except that he usually got large bills?—A. No, sir.

By Mr. BANKS:

Q. At what time was this purchase of iron?—A. After the war he was purchasing iron, I believe; I do not know anything about his business; I only heard so.

By Mr. AMES:

Q. This check of June 29, of $1,000, was given on the Sergeant-at-Arms to Eldridge & Co., of Alexandria; I did not draw the bills at all?—A. I guess you did; otherwise I should have paid the check to Eldridge & Co., and should have so put it down in the book.

By Mr. BANKS:

Q. When you saw this check the other day, did you recognize it as one you had seen before?—A. I said I had an indistinct recollection of having seen it; I could not state when, or anything about it.

Q. What was there about it that led you to think you had seen it before?—A. Nothing further than the size of the check, and the initials in it, without knowing for whom they were intended. I did not know it was intended for Mr. Colfax until it was brought out recently.

Q. Did you observe the initials at first?—A. Yes, sir.

Q. You remember the initials?—A. No, sir; I do not remember them distinctly.

By Mr. HALE:

Q. You say that Mr. Ames, within the last twenty-four hours, told you he thought it very likely he drew the money. State the whole conversation that occurred between you and Mr. Ames.—A. Mr. Ames was at the office looking over the different checks this morning or yesterday afternoon. I said to Mr. Ames, "Did I not pay you that check?" And he replied, "I think it very likely."

By Mr. AMES:

Q. Did you not tell me you could not tell?—A. I did not tell you anything about it.

Q. Have you not been before this committee and testified that you could not recollect who you paid the checks to?—A. I said so under the sanctity of an oath. My mind was not sufficiently clear to state under oath that I recollected to whom I had paid it, but my impression was as strong then as it is now.

Q. Can you remember who you paid checks to four or five years ago?—A. No, sir; not often.

Q. Why do you remember this so distinctly; has anything refreshed your memory?—A. My memory has not been refreshed; I supposed I would not be allowed to state a general impression in evidence, and therefore I stated in my testimony that I could not recollect.

Q. You have not examined your memorandum-book since, have you?—A. No, sir; I have not.

By Mr. MCCRARY:

Q. Did you pay all the checks drawn on the Sergeant-at-Arms?—A. Not all of them.

Q. Did you pay most of them about that time?—A. I did most of them about that time.

Q. Was this an unusually large check?—A. Yes, sir; we very seldom had a check for $1,200. The salary of a member was $416 a month, and they mostly drew it out every month; sometimes they would allow it to run up to $1,000, but it was something unusual.

WASHINGTON, *February* 11, 1873.

SCHUYLER COLFAX recalled at his own instance and examined.

By Mr. HALE:

Question. You will please make in your own language such statement to the committee as you desire.—Answer. The chairman of the committee will remember that after Mr. McComb had testified, and his testimony had been printed to the effect that Mr. Ames had written and said to him that I had made some ruling or parliamentary maneuver by which Mr. Washburn's move against the Union Pacific Railroad had been thwarted, and the stock proffered to me made to pay, I addressed a letter to the chairman of this committee asking that Mr. McComb should either produce the letter or else designate the particular ruling to which he referred, so that it could be examined by a parliamentary expert and its correctness tested. Upon further examination Mr. McComb did not point out the ruling nor give any date, except that it must have been in the winter of 1867–'68.

The CHAIRMAN stated that he had received the letter referred to, and had made the inquiries, as requested, of Mr. McComb.

The WITNESS. Yes, sir; but in the same testimony Mr. McComb reiterates his statement of a conversation with Mr. Ames, and a letter which he could not find in which Mr. Ames stated that by some parliamentary maneuver I had thwarted some move of Mr. Washburn against the Pacific Railroad. Not being able, therefore, to obtain any satisfactory or precise statement of what ruling was alluded to, I took the liberty of asking a gentleman, who I suppose the members of the committee will recognize as one of the ablest parliamentarians in the country, the journal-clerk for twenty-five years of the House of Representatives, to examine every ruling made by me on the subject of the Union Pacific Railroad during the winter of 1867–'68. Mr. Barclay was in ill-health, and made the examination from the Globe at his own house and sent me the following reply, which is dated from the Clerk's office in the Capitol:

"CLERK'S OFFICE,
"HOUSE OF REPRESENTATIVES UNITED STATES,
February 10, 1873.

"DEAR SIR: At your request I have examined the proceedings of the House of Representatives for the session of Congress commencing December, 1867, and ending July, 1868, as reported in the Congressional Globe.

"I have examined all your rulings as Speaker on every proposition made during the entire session by Hon. E. B. Washburne and Hon. C. C. Washburn in relation to the Union Pacific Railroad, and find no ruling made by you that was not (in my judgment) commanded and justified by parliamentary law.

"Very respectfully, your obedient servant,
"JOHN M. BARCLAY,
"*Journal-Clerk, House of Representatives.*

"Hon. SCHUYLER COLFAX."

Last fall I was one of a number of persons in public life charged with having been bribed with gifts of stock in the Credit Mobilier, from which enormous dividends had been secured, and for which certain legislation had been exacted. I replied to these charges in a speech at South Bend, Indiana, September 25, 1872, in which, after showing that the most important of this legislation had been enacted four years before the alleged bribery, I responded to the personal attack as follows, which I now read from the Chicago Inter-Ocean of the next day:

"Never having had in my life a dollar of stock of any kind I did not pay for, I claim the right to purchase stock in the Credit Mobilier or credit immobilier, if there is one; nor do I know of any law prohibiting it. * * * * *

"Do I need to add that neither Oakes Ames nor any other person ever gave me, or offered to give me, one share or twenty shares or two hundred shares in the Credit Mobilier, or any other railroad stock, and that, unfortunately, I have never seen nor received the value of a farthing out of the 270 per cent. dividends, nor the 800 per cent. dividends in cash, stock, or bonds, you have read about for the past month, nor 100 per cent., nor the tenth part of one per cent. I have said that if twenty shares of it could be purchased at par without buying into a prospective lawsuit, it would be a good investment, if as valuable a stock as represented. * * * But never having been plaintiff nor defendant in a court of justice, I want no stock at any price, with a lawsuit on the top of it."

It will be seen from these extracts that I publicly claimed last fall the right to purchase the stock, and avowed frankly that I would have been willing to pay par for twenty shares if I did not buy into a prospective lawsuit, but that no possible profits could induce me to involve myself in litigation. Having over four years before this speech voluntarily abandoned a contract to purchase at the rate I had stated and on the very ground that I had stated, and having no certificate nor ownership of stock in it, my answer to the charges then made are the exact truth. And then I frankly accepted also whatever odium there might attach to willingness to purchase and to hold its stock, as I then understood it. I will add that what I thus said last September, "that Oakes Ames, nor any other person, ever gave or offered to give me any of this stock," has been repeatedly printed during this session with the essential word "give" entirely omitted, entirely changing its sense.

Mr. Ames having sworn, December 17, in his original statement before the committee, which he declared (see page 21 of the evidence) embodied the exact facts, that he could not remember having paid me any dividends, now declares that in June, 1868, a check payable to the initials "S. C. or bearer," for $1,200, but not indorsed by me nor any one else, was paid by him to me as a cash dividend of the Credit Mobilier.

In answer to this charge I repeat again that I have not the slightest knowledge, recollection, or belief that I ever saw this check or any other check of Mr. Ames till he presented it before this committee, nor that I have ever been paid or proffered by him, directly or indirectly, in check, stock, or bonds, $1,200, or $100, or $1, or any amount whatever. I further state that I have not the slightest knowledge, recollection, or belief that I ever heard there was or could be any cash dividend on the Credit Mobilier till the discussion of last fall; and I am as positive as as I can be of any fact in the past, that Mr. Ames never spoke to me of this last dividend, and never paid or proffered to me, in person or through any other channel, any check, or money, or bonds on that or any other account.

It seems to me impossible and incredible that I should have received the check without remembering that addition to my income, and especially in a check drawn so singularly to initials, and not containing my name at all. Nor could I have talked to him when he failed, as I did, about letting the $500 go, which I had paid him on the dividend stock, if he had paid me an overplus of $700.

I must add that till to-day I have never heard of the certificate for fifteen hundred dollars of Union Pacific bonds, sixty dollars interest on which Mr. Ames says he paid me in January, 1869, and I would not have been more astounded to have been charged by him with the assassination of one of his own family than I have been by his charges that he paid me either twelve hundred dollars, or sixty dollars, on any other account whatever on the stock that I had abandoned.

I will add that for over four years I have spoken in my family of this transaction exactly as I described it in my testimony of January 7, namely: that I had contracted to purchase, had paid about $500, had heard of threatened and acrimonious litigation among its principal stockholders, and had therefore abandoned it without receiving any dividend or certificate, but at a loss of the money I had paid upon it, and of the fact of these conversations I will produce evidence.

I come now to the bank deposit of $1,200 in bills from June 22, 1868, and the committee will remember that I really invited the examination of my bank-accounts, by stating to them unasked that I kept my accounts at the First National Bank, where all my checks would be found indorsed by me, whether payable to order or bearer.

Difficult as it is to recall all the transactions of five years of a public man's life, I will state to the committee where all the money came from deposited from June 22, 1868, and will add that it was the month immediately succeeding my nomination for the office I now hold.

The total deposit was $1,968.63, and there being no previous deposit later than the 1st of June, it shows that this amount was the accumulation of money paid to me during most of the intervening time. This is also proven by the dates of the checks deposited. One check was for $18.63, dated June 13, signed by J. N. Seymour, since deceased; one for $250, dated June 12, signed by E. C. Cowdin, and one for $500, dated June 17, signed by T. Denny & Co., none of them having the slightest connection with the subject of investigation before this committee.

Of the deposit of bills, two hundred dollars, I am positive, were paid me by my step-father, Mr. Matthews, on account of a debt which he owed me. In December, 1867, I paid $455 for a piano bought of Steinway & Co., through W. G. Metzerott, for his daughter, the check for which is in the bank, and agreed to wait for the most of it till the summer, when he expected to be better able to pay me. After my nomination, in May, 1868, I had numberless appeals for contributions for political expenses in various localities, processions, bands, charity, religious aid, &c., and I had promised to contribute as promptly and largely as possible to the legitimate expenses of the canvass in my own sharply contested State of Indiana, and I often paid out $50, and sometimes as high as $100, per day, as friends were unexpectedly liberal in their contributions to me. I therefore asked Mr. Matthews to pay me his indebtedness as soon as he could raise it, to assist me in meeting these demands incident to my new position. During the month of June, 1868, and, as nearly as I can fix the time, about the middle of the month, he paid me $200 in bills on account, and early the next month he paid me another installment, completing the whole payment before Congress adjourned, late in July. I am very confident that this $200 formed part of this $1,200 deposit, being part of my cash receipts previous to the deposit of June 22.

About the time of this payment, and, as near as I can fix the date, about the middle of the month of June, and very soon after the payment by Mr. Matthews, I was opening my letter-mail at the breakfast-table, in accordance with my usual custom, and found an envelope within another envelope postmarked New York. On opening the inner envelope I found it contained a letter written by George F. Nesbitt congratulating me most cordially and warmly on my nomination for the Vice-Presidency, and saying that the writer desired to send me confidentially the remittance inclosed to aid me in the heavy expenses of the canvass, but wished it kept a secret, as neither his family nor any one else would ever know of it unless I told them. Inclosed in this letter was a greenback or national bank bill of $1,000. It was as gratifying as it was liberal, and holding up the letter and the bill I asked the attention of all my family to it, and then read them the letter. The fact of sending so large a bill by mail was commented on, and the magnitude of the gift was discussed, when Mr. Matthews remarked that it came in good time, either he or I then referring specially to the appeal of Mr. Conner, chairman of the Indiana republican committee, for money to aid in arranging for the canvass already in active progress there. The bill was then passed around from hand to hand, and examined. I am sure I deposited it with the $200 I had received from Mr. Matthews, and purchasing on the very same day, as the bank-books show, a draft for the exact amount of this remittance, and in exact accordance with the donor's wish, and exactly as discussed at my table at the time, sent it at once to the chairman of the republican committee at Indianapolis.

Fortunately, this does not rest on my own testimony alone. Living witnesses will tell the committee that they remember the receipt of this bill, and the contents of the letter in which it was inclosed, and that it was at once discussed how it could be used to carry out Mr. Nesbitt's desire; and the draft presented and sworn to by the cashier of the bank proves that the very day I deposited $1,200 in bills I bought and remitted out of my deposit a draft for $1,000 to the chairman of the Indiana State committee. The draft, indorsed by Mr. Conner, was found in the bank here and laid before your committee the next day after the bank deposit was testified to, my counsel at the time promising to connect it with my evidence.

My family at the time consisted of my mother, since deceased, my step-father, Mr. Matthews, and my half-sister, Mrs. Hollister, whose residence is in a distant Territory beyond the Rocky Mountains.

I said it was fortunate there were living witnesses to this besides myself, for, on a thorough examination of the accounts and papers of Mr. Nesbitt, made by his executor at my request, (Mr. Nesbitt having died the next year,) no trace of it is there found. He had carried out what he wrote, that it was intended to be confidential, unknown even to his family, and if it was revealed it would have to be by me; and he evidently sent it in a bill the more surely to accomplish the object.

During the last eight or ten years the accumulation of my letters has been so extraordinary that it has been my regular habit to destroy fully nine-tenths of them. Those that are not destroyed are not filed, but kept in their envelopes until they crowd my drawers and tables, and are then tied up, but not chronologically, to be stowed away wherever room for them can be found. Indeed, Mr. Chauncey, one of the House employés, after I had left that wing of the Capitol for the Senate wing in 1869, happened to find a box full of old letters thus tied up, the loss of which I had entirely overlooked. I have gone three times over all the letters I have preserved, and have not found this letter, or any political letters for June, 1868. The acknowledgment of this draft of $1,000, sent to Indiana, cannot be found, though, fortunately, the bank was able to find the draft itself. The letters accompanying the three checks deposited on the 22d of June have also been destroyed, so that I am unable to produce either of the five letters relating to the transactions of that day.

I remember distinctly that after my nomination my mail increased enormously, amounting to fifty if not sometimes one hundred letters per day, and their preservation seemed so impossible that I remember, as others do, more than once almost filling a waste-basket with the fragments of destroyed letters. But, as I have said, besides the draft, which testifies for itself, there are living witnesses here to prove that I received at that time the $1,000 bill, one of them having made a three thousand mile midwinter journey alone to tell this committee her recollection of it. When my bank account was examined here the cashier was asked what the forty-five thousand footings meant, and he replied to the inquiry that it was the amount of the debits and credits when the accounts were finally balanced. It was telegraphed to the New York Tribune that night that the books showed I deposited $45,000 in one year, and the inference was that I could therefore easily have forgotten the $1,200 in question. As my general accounts have thus been made a subject of public discussion, and as I have no secrets in regard to them, I feel it my right now to correct this misstatement.

This total was for three years, not one year, namely, from December, 1865, to October, 1868, inclusive, and embraced, besides other cash accounts, the changes made in my investments, the avails of a laborious life, and which changes were mainly on the advice of valued friends in New York, Baltimore, and the West. On the debtor side are purchases of $5,000 seven-thirties of the bank, between December, 1865, and April, 1866, mainly from the receipts for lecturing; one share of New York Tribune stock, at $6,000, in January, 1867; a present of $1,000 in the early part of the same year to my mother, then the head of my family; an investment of $5,000 in an iron company of Lake Superior; an investment of $5,000 in bonds of the Pennsylvania Steel Company; a house and lot in South Bend, near the post-office, which I am glad to state is worth now nearly double the $2,200 I paid for it; a loan of $455 to Mr. Matthews, as stated; an investment of $5,000 in a western rolling-mill; and a payment of $1,750 to Ricketson Burroughs, for money borrowed of him. This amounts to $30,000 out of the $45,000 transactions of those three years.

The deposits on the credit side that enabled me to pay these amounts were as follows: During these years I was lecturing on my stage-coach ride of 1865 across the continent—during November, the holiday recess, Saturdays, in the early part of the session, and during the spring when Congress adjourned in March—receiving $100 to $200 per lecture. I received in all over $12,000 from this source, of which I estimate about $10,000 was deposited here. I sold the $5,000 seven-thirties, and also sold the Tribune share at $6,100, and Mr. Matthews returned me the $455 he owed me. Besides these items, I sold sixty-two shares of Adams Express at 72¼, and $6,000 in second-mortgage bonds of the Alton and Terre Haute Railroad for $4,920, making about $31,000 in all, which offsets the $30,000 of investments charged against them.

Of course, the committee understand that in bank-accounts where changes of investments are made the same money often figures three or four times over. Thus, I deposited my lecturing-money, bought seven-thirties, sold them at an advance, and used the proceeds for another investment. I bought a Tribune share mainly out of similar receipts, sold it at an advance, and again invested the proceeds. A large part of the money I drew from the Sergeant-at-Arms for my salary was deposited in the bank, as I paid my housekeeping expenses there. It has taken all my dividends, besides my salary, to pay my expenses for the past half dozen years, and hence my willingness to follow the counsel of better financiers than myself to investments and changes of investments.

Q. State whether in your own mind, as well as in conversation with-others with whom you spoke upon the subject, from the time of your leaving or abandoning this investment, you considered yourself, spoke of yourself, and believed yourself a loser to the extent of $500 by the operation, instead of being a gainer to the extent of $700.—A. I will state that all the transactions of which I have spoken were understood by and made a matter of conversation in my family as early as the summer of 1868; I say as early as the summer of '68, because my recollection is that it was in the spring of 1868 that Mr. Ames states he told Mr. Blaine frankly a lawsuit was pending, or threatened. I told my family that I had abandoned this contract of purchase, and therefore when I spoke to Mr. Ames, after his failure, failing as he did on account of his Pacific Railroad investment, resulting in an extension from his creditors, the supposition being at the time, as it has not turned out since, that the failure was an unfortunate one pecuniarily, it would have been impossible that I could have offered to relieve him from the payment of the $500 he owed me if he had paid me the $1,200 to which he testifies. He would of course have replied, "You have already got your money back and $700 more." From that time in the spring or summer of 1868, with all the persons in and out of my family to whom I have spoken on the subject, I have spoken of the contract as abandoned by me. I made no claim upon him for dividends, I received no certificates from him, and he proffered me no certificates.

Q. Has it been a matter of conversation in your family that you were a loser by that amount in the investment?—A. Yes, sir.

Q. Have you ever had any knowledge, information, or suspicion that there were bonds, stocks, or dividends to any amount whatever, to which you were entitled, in the hands of Mr. Ames, as coming from that source?—A. I have not; I mean since the time I abandoned the contract, which was when I heard of the threatened litigation, or of the prospective lawsuit to which I referred in my speech at South Bend.

Q. About what time was that?—A. I cannot fix the time to a day.

Q. Are you sure it was before the adjournment of Congress?—A. Certainly I am. It was the subject of discussion in my family during the trip made to Colorado, immediately after the adjournment, and it was because of that prospective lawsuit, I said in my speech that "if twenty shares of it could be purchased at par, without buying into a *prospective* lawsuit, it would be a good investment, if it was as valuable a stock as represented," but that I wanted "no stock of any kind, at any price, with a lawsuit on top of it."

Q. State right there where you went immediately after the adjournment of Congress in 1868.—A. Congress adjourned Monday, the 27th of July, and my family and myself left either on Monday or Tuesday, I cannot now recall to mind which. We arrived at South Bend, and left there the ensuing Monday, or within a day or two thereafter. I think about the 4th of August I went with my mother, my half-sister, the lady who is now my wife, then unmarried, and who went with my mother at her request, and other persons outside of my family, to Colorado. We were in the mountains and on the plains during the month of August, arriving home about the middle of September. I think the trip occupied altogether about six weeks. On that trip this matter was talked about in my family. The abandonment of the contract was spoken of, the matter was talked of a great deal by the person who was then the head of my family, and who is now deceased, who spoke of it to others.

By the CHAIRMAN:

Q. Can you state whether this conversation between you and Mr.

Ames, with reference to the rescinding of this purchase of stock, was earlier than the 20th of June?—A. I think so decidedly. As I said, my impression is that it was late in the spring. The payment of the $534.72 was made the 5th of March. I looked for that check in the bank, because I intended to present it to the committee, and had forgotten it was drawn on the Sergeant-at-Arms. I then stated to Mr. Niblack my recollection that the sum was about $530. I could not call to mind the exact amount, and that I thought it was in March. It was soon after that I heard there was great difficulty between the principal stockholders of the company.

Q. Do you know now from whom you had that information?—A. I cannot now recollect. It seems to me I heard it as a rumor, and that I then asked Mr. Ames as to its truth. I cannot now distinctly state from whom I heard it. Mr. Ames admits the truth of Mr. Blaine's statement, that in the spring of 1868 they had some conversation about the matter, and that Mr. Ames told him there was a lawsuit either pending or threatened. That confirms me in my recollection that this information came to me in the spring of that year. Still, I have no means by which I can fix the exact date, except that it was in that session of Congress.

Q. Did you hear anything in relation to Mr. McComb?—A. No, sir; I do not think I heard his name mentioned. I heard that the principal stockholders had quarreled. I understood that it was a difficulty that would involve the company itself in prolonged litigation. The impression upon my mind is that I heard there was a possibility it would all be tied up in expensive litigation.

Q. Who was the Mr. Nesbitt to whom you referred?—A. He was a gentleman in New York in the stationery business, originally a printer.

Q. You are not able to find this letter?—A. I am not. I cannot find any political letter of June, 1868, at all. I have made a thorough search three times over, including this box full of letters found by Mr. Chauncey, and brought to me, as I stated, in 1869.

Q. You have made such a search among your papers as to be satisfied that you have not possession of the letter now?—A. Yes, sir.

Q. Do you remember whether you received this $1,000 before or after you received the $200 from Mr. Matthews?—A. My impression is that it was after—I should say a day or so after—and this impression I have is deepened from the fact that when I showed the letter and bill, Mr. Matthews, whom I had asked to pay me, at once said that it came in very excellent time for me, as he had heard of the need I had for money, and the promise I had made that I would send a large contribution to Indiana. My impression is that he had heard of the specific promise I had made that I would send $1,000.

Q. Had you ever any conversation with Mr. Ames from the time you had this talk with him in the spring of 1868, when you understood this matter was ended between you and him, upon the subject of that stock up to the time of this conversation after his embarrassment?—A. None that I remember; I have no recollection of his addressing me a word upon the subject, or of my addressing him upon the subject. I regarded it as a rather poor financial investment upon my part, but thought I had saved the money I would have had to pay a lawyer if I had continued my interest and the company had been involved in litigation. This conversation with Mr. Ames was in 1870.

Q. That was two years after your last preceding conversation?—A. I think it was about two years afterward.

Q. And you have no memory of any conversation between yourself and Mr. Ames during this period?—A. Not on this subject. We were in the Capitol together, and probably had conversations in regard to other matters. I may add, that when I said to Mr. Ames that I must be off or out of it, he put his hand in his pocket, took out a small coin, and said, "Consider that I have bought it back." I said to him, "No, sir; I want it to be understood that I am out of it entirely," because I did not want to be in any lawsuit.

Q. What did he say to that?—A. He assented to that; I cannot call to mind his words; he did not dissent; I understood that he assented, but that he had his way of paying me something so as to regard it as bought back; my idea was that I had no certificate and no dividends, and I wanted to get out of the concern altogether.

Q. That conversation was not very long after you paid the $534?—A. It was not longer than that season; this payment was at the opening of spring, and the conversation to which I have referred could not have been later than the latter part of spring; it must have been before June; that is my very best recollection.

Q. Between that time and June you think this conversation took place about the trade being at an end?—A. Yes, sir; and that I heard the same thing he told Mr. Blaine of, that there was to be a lawsuit.

Q. You understood him to assent to bringing the trade to a close?—A. I did.

Q. Was anything said to him on that occasion about the $534 you had paid?—A. There was not.

Q. Nothing by you nor by him?—A. By me nor by him; I said to him that I must be off; that "I must be out of this thing."

Q. Do you remember whether in your own mind you had any idea about this sum of $534? You had received nothing?—A. I had received nothing.

Q. Do you remember whether you were to receive it from Mr. Ames?—A. I had this impression about that; I thought Mr. Ames had come to me as a friend to give me an opportunity to make an investment which would be a valuable investment, and that he had done it out of friendship to me. He had said nothing to me about any legislation. I had nothing in my own mind about any legislation; on the contrary, I supposed there could not be any. When I heard of this lawsuit, I had always had an instinctive dread of having anything to do with a lawsuit. I had carried on the printing business for twenty years, with a great many men failing to pay me what they owed, and I had never sued a man in my life. I had paid this amount of money to Mr. Ames in a matter which I understood as a friendly act on his part to me, and when I made up my mind to get out of it I also made up my mind to say nothing to him on the subject of the payment I had made. If I withdrew from a bargain that proved distasteful, I did not feel I had any right to make any conditions. I had made up my mind to get out of it, and I think the events of the last year have showed that I was wise in trying to get out of it.

Q. Did he make any mention of the money you had paid?—A. He did not, except by the single expression that he wanted me to consider he had bought it back.

Q. The amount he offered would not have made it much more, even if you had taken it?—A. No, sir; it would not.

Q. Do you remember whether you had heard at that time anything in relation to the value of this stock, by rumor or in any way?—A. No, sir; except so far as Mr. Ames had told me of the possible profits.

Q. Are you able to say that you had any just idea that this stock, if you had held on to it, and there had been no liability of getting into litigation, was to earn for you the large profits which have been stated?—A. Nothing like so large as have been stated since that time. I had traveled across the country in a stage-coach, having previously made numberless speeches in favor of a Pacific railroad, for the purpose of endeavoring, with the gentlemen who accompanied me, to make a public opinion in favor of the road being promptly built for the proffer of the Government. We had decided in our own minds, from the observations we made, that the road could be built for this proffer of the Government, and a profit realized upon it. I understood from Mr. Ames, when he spoke to me about the purchase of the stock, that the gentlemen of capital who had gone into the Pacific road, instead of letting the work out to contractors who would receive large profits for their risk, were to build it themselves, and thereby would realize themselves the profits which would otherwise go to contractors, and that that would amount to a considerable sum. I have the impression that I thought it would probably amount to 100 per cent. I think there was something said about 100 per cent. on some three millions of stock.

Q. What I want to get at is whether from what you had then heard of the probable earnings of the stock, you supposed Mr. Ames would in any way be the loser, even if he paid back the money he had received from you?—A. No, sir; I should suppose not. I really did not know anything about what dividends might be made upon it, or how the threatened legislation would affect the concern. The road was at that time being pushed forward as rapidly as possible.

Q. What I want to get at is, whether from what you then understood in reference to this stock, you did not suppose Mr. Ames could very well afford to take back the stock without any reference to this $534 you had paid?—A. I should suppose so; but did not ask any such condition.

Q. Did you then suppose so?—A. I do not remember whether I did or not. My only object then was to get out of the scrape.

Q. From what you learned about it you were willing to get out of it with the loss of $534?—A. I would have been. If I had paid twice as much I would have rather lost it than to be compelled to go into court or into a lawsuit.

Q. The interest upon the $500, a memorandum of which Mr. Ames has now produced as being entered upon his book, you have no memory of having received?—A. Not the slightest of any money received from him, or anything else, whether as interest, dividends, certificates, stock, or bonds.

Q. The date Mr. Ames gives of the payment of interest is in January, 1869. That would have been between the time when you say the contract was rescinded or thrown up, and the time when you had this conversation with him, after his failure or embarrassment; you have no recollection of any transaction between you in reference to this stock during that period of time?—A. I have none. My recollection coincides exactly with his testimony of January 22, except so far as the $1,200 is concerned on the 22d of June. He swore then "he has no recollection of having delivered to me anything else." He did not deliver any check or money to me, to the best of my knowledge, recollection, and belief, and why it was drawn payable to "S. C., or bearer," I cannot imagine, except upon the supposition that it was some memorandum for his own use. I do not impute to him or to anybody else an intention to state falsely.

Q. The $60 which Mr. Ames states was paid to you, not in a check, but in money, would not be likely to be deposited by you, or any so small amount if you had received it?—A. I do not know. I cannot tell whether if I received a small amount of money like that I would deposit it or not. Sometimes I did not go to the bank for weeks at all. I frequently passed there in the morning on my way to the Capitol before the bank was opened for regular business.

By Mr. HALE:

Q. You have not examined your bank account for 1869?—A. I have not.

Q. You heard for the first time to-day in regard to that $60, and therefore have had no opportunity of examining it?—A. I never heard of it until to-day.

By Mr. McCRARY:

Q. Have you any means of fixing the date of the receipt of that $1,000 from New York?—A. Only that it was about or a little after the middle of the month. It was the month succeeding my nomination. Reference was made directly in the letter to the nomination, and his congratulation upon it seemed the impelling cause of sending the money. It was to be used by me for political purposes. I think it was about the middle of the month, or it may possibly have been a very few days later.

Q. The nomination was the 21st of May?—A. The 21st or 22d; I think it was the 21st.

Q. It was your custom to deposit always amounts as large as that you received from New York?—A. O, yes, sir.

Q. If you had received $1,000 from New York and $1,200 from Mr. Ames, you would have deposited both?—A. I would have deposited both.

By Mr. HALE:

Q. Do you remember whether the $1,000 from New York was received before or after the payment of the $200 by Mr. Matthews?—A. I am very clear it was afterward, because the impelling cause of Mr. Matthews's remark about it seemed to be based on the money he had paid me at my request.

By Mr. McCRARY:

Q. I believe you have stated, as nearly as you can remember, the date of your conversation with Mr. Ames when he proposed a nominal resale of this Credit Mobilier stock?—A. Yes, sir; I should say it was late in the spring, but I will state frankly that I have not the data by which I can fix the exact date.

By Mr. MERRICK:

Q. Do you remember any other occasion when you kept so large a sum as $1,200 for so long a period before depositing it?—A. I do not know how long this was kept; probably less than a week; perhaps but two or three days.

Q. You have stated that it was about the middle of the month you received it?—A. I said about or soon after the middle. I cannot fix it perhaps so accurately as other witnesses here can. My recollection is that it was about the middle that Mr. Matthews paid me, and that it was within a day or so after that I received this money. I made no deposit from the 1st until the 22d of June, and out of this $1,200 I sent the check for the $1,000 in accordance with the talk we had at its receipt, and in accordance with the donor's wish.

By Mr. HALE :

Q. At that time where did you live?—A. I lived in a two-story white house on the left side of Lafayette Square.

Q. Your duties called you to the Capitol, and you were in the Capitol daily?—A. I was, with the exception of when I was sick. I always left as soon as breakfast was over. My correspondence was immense, and my duties somewhat laborious, and I therefore passed the bank on my way to the Capitol early in the morning, and did not go into the bank frequently for a considerable time.

Q. You usually came to the Capitol before the bank opened in the morning and returned after it closed?—A. I used sometimes to go in, and they would take my deposits, because they knew my habits and my necessities as to time, although the bank was not regularly opened.

Q. State whether at that time you were particularly occupied with the duties of your office and with your correspondence?—A. Yes, sir; my time is very much engrossed; and the calls I had were numberless, commencing before I got up in the morning, and not ceasing till after I went to bed; and with the calls, correspondence, and duties of my position, my time was entirely occupied and engrossed.

By the CHAIRMAN :

Q. Do you know at what time the bank ordinarily opens?—A. It opens for business purposes at 10 o'clock; but a little after 9 I would go in, and they always received my deposits. Sometimes the cashier would not be there to sign a draft if I wanted one, and then they would send them up by messenger to me at the Capitol.

Q. You do not mean, then, that you made fewer deposits because you could not get into the bank on your way up to the Capitol?—A. No, sir. I could generally get into the bank if I had the time to spare; but I very often would get into the carriage and drive directly to the Capitol.

WASHINGTON, *February* 11, 1873.

GEORGE W. MATTHEWS sworn and examined by Mr. Hale.

Question. You are the step-father of Vice-President Colfax?—Answer. I married his mother.

Q. She is now deceased?—A. Yes, sir.

Q. You are a clerk in the office of the House of Representatives, and have been for some years?—A. Yes, sir.

Q. In 1868, during the session of Congress, where did you reside in Washington, and who made up your household?—A. I lived on the west side of Lafayette Square, No. 7. The household consisted of my wife, her son, (Mr. Colfax,) my daughter, and myself. My daughter, now Mrs. Hollister, was then unmarried.

Q. Have you any recollection in regard to your payments of money to Mr. Colfax in the summer of 1868?—A. Yes, sir.

Q. State as definitely and particularly as you can what they were.—A. Mr. Colfax has stated the contract made by him at my desire about the piano. I think it was about the 12th or 13th day of June that Mr. Colfax said to me, one day, "Mr. Conner is here and wants to raise money for the campaign in Indiana. I would be glad if you would raise all the money you can in the next few days, because I desire to send him some money." I told him I would do so. I had about $125 in my pocket, and on the 15th, when my month had half expired, I went in and asked the privilege to draw on my salary for the month, which I did; and on the 16th June I paid him $200. That was all I was able to pay him at that time. At the time of the purchase of the piano I paid him $50, which, with five dollars he had borrowed of his mother, made the payment of fifty-five dollars. About the 3d or 4th day of July, I do not remember which—I am pretty certain it was not the 1st or 2d—I realized for some coupons or bonds I had, and paid him another $100; and when Congress adjourned, which I think was the 25th or 26th of July, if I remember correctly, I drew my pay for that month, and paid him the other $100. I went home pretty well strapped, but out of debt.

Q. Have you any knowledge in regard to the receipt of moneys through the mail, by Mr. Colfax, in June, 1868?—A. Yes, sir; I remember it very well.

Q. State fully and distinctly all your recollection of that transaction.—A. According to my memory, from the way I see it now before me, I think it must have been three or four days after I paid Mr. Colfax this $200. At the breakfast-table one morning, as usual, Mr. Colfax had spread out his letters and papers at the table, and was opening them while the meats were being brought on. I remember that by the time the servant had finished bringing on the meats he had broken open several letters and read them. I noticed that he seemed to be particularly engaged with one letter—that he seemed to be very much interested in it. He nodded to the servant to step aside, which he did. After the servant went out he opened the letter, which was written on ordinary letter-paper, and held it up, with his thumb pressed upon a bank-bill, as I now hold this sheet of paper, (illustrating.) He held it up for a moment or two so that we could look at it, and said, "A thousand-dollar bill from a gentleman who is almost a stranger; this is the second letter I have received from him." I remarked, "That comes in good time." "Yes," says he, "this will help me fix out Ham Conner, for he is clamorous for money." This was the very remark he made at the time. His mother said, "Read the letter, Schuyler." He laid down the bill and read the letter. It was a short letter, written on one page of letter-paper. I remember some of the contents of it. It was a pleasant, congratulatory letter. Mr. Nesbitt said he had great regard for Mr. Colfax as a public man; seemed to be greatly delighted that the convention selected him, one of the craft, as one of its standard-bearers. He supposed that Mr. Colfax had not a great amount of money, and he begged him to accept the inclosed. He did not mention any amount except the inclosed. He said Mr. Colfax might feel delicate about receiving it, but that he had no political favors to ask, and as no member of his family knew or would know of his sending the money, they could not claim anything on account of it. That was about all there was in the letter. It was a very friendly letter. My wife and I spoke of it a great many times, for it was an uncommon thing for a letter containing a thousand-dollar bill to come into the family. It gratified her very much. We talked about it frequently.

Q. That is the substance of your knowledge of the transaction?—A. That is all I know about it. I think it was about three days after I paid him the $200 I have mentioned.

Q. Do you remember the subject of hearing an interest Mr. Colfax had in Credit Mobilier being talked over in the family?—A. We talked it over several times in the family. I have heard much said upon the subject. It was spoken of several times, to my recollection. Of course you will understand there has been a good deal said about it this winter.

Q. I am now speaking of what was said as far back as 1868?—A. We had some conversation on the subject.

Q. Will you state what was said as to his being a loser or gainer in that transaction?—A. Early in the spring of 1868, Mr. Colfax remarked to his mother, and to the family, that he thought he should take a trip on the Union Pacific Railroad to the end of the track, as he had a pass, or could get a pass, to go over the road. I jokingly told him that I would take the trip too, as I had an interest in the road, and they ought to give me a pass also. He asked me what interest I had; I told him I had purchased a bond when they had first offered their bonds in the market; our bank advertised them, and I purchased a bond at 90, which I thought was a pretty good investment. I told Mr. Colfax I had purchased this bond. He remarked to me, "I expect to have something better than that." I asked him what he expected to get. He said he was about to contract for some stock in the Credit Mobilier. I asked him what they proposed to do. He said they proposed to pay good dividends. I made some little further inquiries about the institution, and the conclusion, I think, was, that there was a little rivalry between us as to our investment. I told him it looked to me like the place where the big fish eat up the little ones, and I did not think much of it. I thought I had the best investment. This was in the winter or early in the spring of 1868. In the course of perhaps a couple of months after that, I asked him how about the Credit Mobilier; I wanted to know whether he had as good an opinion of it as I had of my bond, and whether I had not made the best investment. He said, "That thing has gone up." I asked him how it had gone up. He said there was a prospect of a lawsuit, and, as he had never been in one, he backed out; that he did not have any interest in it. That was about all he said at the time. Some time after that, perhaps a year or two, I do not know how long, my wife read in the newspapers something which she was very much distressed about; that it was probable Mr. Ames had met with reverses and would have to suspend payment. My wife and Mrs. Ames were very intimate. She sympathized very much with Mrs. Ames. Mrs. Matthews always expressed great love and affection for Mrs. Ames; so much so that she used to say, "My Mrs. Ames, she is so good and so kind;" she spoke of her always in a very affectionate way. Her son remarked, "Never mind; Mr. Ames owes me a little, and I will never ask him for it until he gets able to pay it." He mentioned the amount of $500. This is all I ever heard at the time of the Credit Mobilier or of his stock in it.

By the CHAIRMAN:

Q. This is all the conversation you had with Mr. Colfax or heard in his family in reference to his owning stock; did he say anything then in relation to how much he had paid?—A. No, sir; I understood him that he was about to make a contract for some shares; he did not say how much.

Q. Did you ever hear anything from him in relation to the $500, until this conversation you had about Mr. Ames's failure?—A. I do not think I ever heard him mention it; I think he never mentioned, to my knowledge, how much stock he owned, or anything about the terms of it. It was just a little pleasant rivalry between us, about our investment. That was the conversation we had upon the subject.

Q. In this dealing between you and Mr. Colfax, did any note or obligation pass between you for the money you owed him?—A. No, sir.

Q. There was nothing in writing about it?—A. No, sir; nothing.

Q. There was no memorandum kept by you?—A. I kept a little memorandum of my payments. I had very little cash balance except simply the receipt of my salary, which I generally gave to my wife and daughter to use for their purposes, and, being in society, they could easily dispose of it.

Q. Do you know whether you made any memorandum of the $200 payment by you?—A. I think I put it down in a little memorandum-book I had.

Q. Do you think you now have that?—A. I could not say, indeed, whether I have or not.

Q. Were you in the habit of carrying such a memorandum-book?—A. I always do carry a little memorandum-book, in which I have occasion sometimes to put down any such little transaction.

Q. Do you think that memorandum which you kept in 1868 is in existence now?—A. I have not the least idea whether it is or not.

Q. You have made no search for it?—A. No, sir; I have not.

Q. If you have that memorandum-book now, it probably shows this entry of $200?—A. I think probably it does.

Q. If you have preserved it at all, it is probably here in Washington?—A. No, sir; I have no memorandum-book in Washington of any date longer ago than last fall.

Q. You do not spend your time here except during the session?—A. That is all. All the transactions that I had in money beyond the ordinary receipt of my salary was the payment of this $400 which I owed to Mr. Colfax.

Q. In this conversation in which Mr. Colfax spoke of Mr. Ames having become embarrassed, and of his owing him $500, did he say what it was for?—A. He did not that I remember.

Q. He did not make any explanation?—A. No, sir; his conversation was with his mother; he did not speak to me about it.

Q. Did he speak of owing it to Mr. Ames, or of Mr. Ames owing it to him?—A. He said, "Mother, Mr. Ames owes me $500, and I shall never ask him for it until he is able to pay it." It was in reply to her expression of sympathy.

Q. She was a friend of Mr. Ames's wife?—A. Yes, sir. The ladies were very intimate. I know my wife regarded Mrs. Ames very well, as a lady; she was always asking about Mrs. Ames; and in speaking or her, as I have said, spoke of her as "My Mrs. Ames;" she did it in that way to designate her as Mrs. Oakes Ames.

WASHINGTON, D. C., *February* 11, 1873.

MRS. CAROLINE HOLLISTER sworn and examined.

By Mr. HALE:

Question. Where do you now reside?—Answer. In Utah.

Q. What is your husband's name?—A. Ovando.

Q. You are the half-sister of Mr. Colfax?—A. Yes, sir.

Q. In the summer of 1868 were you unmarried?—A. Yes, sir.

Q. Mr. Colfax was also unmarried?—A. Yes, sir.

Q. Where did you reside?—A. With him in Washington.

Q. You have come from Utah here for the purpose of giving your testimony in this case, on the request of your brother?—A. Yes.

Q. State if you have any recollection or knowledge of the receipt of a letter by him, inclosing a thousand-dollar bill, in June, 1868; if so, state fully all your knowledge in relation to it.—A. I remember he received a thousand-dollar bill in June, and that he said it came from Mr. Nesbitt, of New York. It was inclosed in a letter which he read to us. It was a letter congratulating him upon his success at Chicago. He seemed to be delighted, and wanted to do something for Mr. Colfax, and begged him to accept the thousand-dollar bill, which he sent in a bill, as I remember it, so that there could be no record of it. He did not wish his family even to know about it. Mr. Colfax was rather doubtful of the propriety at first of receiving it, lest the gentleman might want his influence in some way. My mother thought he was too sensitive about such things; that is just as I remember it.

Q. Can you fix the time any more definitely than you have? You say you think it was in June; do you know that it was after the nomination?—A. Yes, sir; it was during the first excitement after the nomination, when he was receiving congratulations from every one.

Q. How long did that excitement last?—A. He was receiving congratulations three or four weeks.

Q. After you left Washington, at the close of the session, you took a journey to Colorado with your brother, your father, and your mother, and several others, and among them Miss Wade, who is now Mrs. Colfax?—A. Yes, sir.

Q. Do you remember at that time, on that journey, that this $1,000 was spoken of, and of conversing with any person in relation to it?—A. I do not remember distinctly; I have the impression that I talked about it with my friends.

Q. Can you say with whom?—A. Not positively. I should think, likely, I talked with Miss Wade, and, perhaps, with my cousin; it was natural that I should.

Q. Of that you are not positive?—A. No, sir.

Q. You have stated all your knowledge of the matter as fully as you remember it?—A. Yes, sir; just as I recollect it.

By the CHAIRMAN:

Q. Did you state the name of the gentleman from whom this letter came?—A. It was from Mr. Nesbitt, of New York.

Q. Was he a person you had ever heard of before?—A. Yes, sir; I had heard of him.

Q. You did not know him?—A. No, sir; I did not know him then.

Q. Did you happen to know in relation to your father paying Mr. Colfax $200 about that time?—A. No, sir; I did not. I knew he had loaned my father money, and I presumed he did pay him about that time. I have thought of it, but I do not know certainly.

Q. You knew of this arrangement about the purchase of a piano between them?—A. Yes, sir.

Q. Do you now remember of hearing or knowing anything in relation to your father's paying Mr. Colfax $200 anywhere about the time of the receipt of the letter containing the $1,000?—A. No, sir; I do not remember.

Q. You saw the money that came in the letter?—A. I cannot positively say that I saw it. I knew of it, and I think I must have seen it. I know that I heard the letter read.

Q. Do you remember whether Mr. Colfax exhibited the money that was in it so that you could see it?—A. I could not say as to that.

Q. You remember more distinctly as to the contents of the letter?—A. I remember the letter distinctly, and the bill, and that it was in June.

Q. Is there any circumstance by which you can fix the date any nearer than that as to what part of June it was?—A. No, sir; nothing.

Mr. HALE stated that Mrs. Colfax was present, and if the committee desired to inquire of her she would be able to testify in regard to conversations about the thousand dollars during the trip referred to to Colorado. As the counsel of Mr. Colfax, he did not wish to offer her as a witness, but would leave it for the committee to call her if they so desired.

The CHAIRMAN stated that the committee would not call Mrs. Colfax of their own motion as a witness.

The following letter was directed by the committee to be incorporated with the testimony:

"WASHINGTON, D. C., *February* 8, 1873.

"In my statement of facts heretofore made, I submitted a letter from the Interior Department, showing that I was appointed a Government director October 3, 1867, but did not qualify until March 3, 1868. Relying upon this record, the only one then before me to refresh my memory, and having then no access to the Union Pacific Railroad records, copies of which I have just seen, it is now due to your committee, and to myself, to add, that January 2, 1868, I began to *act* as director, prior to the qualification March 23d, as I should have stated at the start if I had known it.

"It will be seen, however, in Mr. Durant's, Mr. Crane's, and Mr. Ham's testimony, and from the Credit Mobilier certificates of Mr. Neilson, that December 26, 1867, *before* I acted as Government director, I dispossessed myself of every possible interest in the Credit Mobilier, and hence, when I acted, I had no interest, direct or indirect, in that property.

"Yours, respectfully,

"JAMES BROOKS.

"Hon. L. P. POLAND, *Chairman, &c., &c., &c.*"

The following is the certificate and indorsement handed by Oakes Ames to the chairman, by request of Mr. Kelley, as set forth in the testimony:

Incorporated under a special act of the State of Pennsylvania.

THE CREDIT MOBILIER OF AMERICA.

Par value of shares, [Stamp,] One Hundred Dollars.

No. 373. 10 Shares.

This certifies that Oakes Ames, Trustee, is entitled to Ten Shares in the Capital Stock of the Credit Mobilier of America, transferable on the books of the company in person or by Attorney at the office of the Treasurer, in the city of Philadelphia, or at any Transfer Agency established by the Company, only upon surrender of this certificate.

Witness the signatures of the President and Secretary of the company, Dated at the Transfer Agency in the City of New York, this thirteenth day of March, 1868.

SIDNEY DILLON,
President.

BENJAMIN F. HAM,
Ass't Secretary.

Capital $2,500,000, in 25,000 Shares of $100 each, with power to increase to $10,000,000.

[Stamped as follows:] Credit Mobilier of America, Philadelphia, 1859.

[Indorsed on the back as follows:]

For value received the undersigned hereby asssign and transfer unto Shares of the capital stock of the Credit Mobilier, and do hereby constitute and appoint Oakes Ames Trustee, true and lawful Attorney, irrevocably, for and in name and behalf, to make and execute all necessary acts of assignment and transfer required by the regulations and by-laws of said company.

In witness whereof ha hereunto set hand and seal this day of , 186

OAKES AMES, *Trustee.*

Sealed and delivered in the presence of—

Re-examination of OAKES AMES.

By Mr. MERRICK:

Question. Have you any knowledge in reference to any money being used or advanced to aid in the election of Senator Carpenter to the Senate of the United States?—Answer. No, sir; I have not.

Q. Have you any knowledge whether he was employed ostensibly as counsel for the Union Pacific Railroad Company, prior to his election?—A. I think he never was; not to my knowledge.

Q. Were any overtures made to you by any person, or suggestion made to you, to pay him any sum of money, or to retain him as counsel for the Union Pacific Railroad Company, and pay him any sum of money in that capacity?—A. Yes, sir; there was.

Q. By whom?—A. General Butler recommended that we should employ Mr. Carpenter as counsel for the road.

Q. Did you employ him in consequence of General Butler's recommendation?—A. No, sir; I did not know that we wanted any counsel. I wrote to my brother, who was then president of the road, about it. It was about the time Mr. Carpenter was a candidate for the Senate. My brother declined to employ him; said he thought, under the circumstances, it seemed highly improper that we should employ him as counsel, or spend any money for any such purpose; we were not a political corporation, and had no right to meddle with political affairs.

Q. Was there any suggestion made to employ him especially as counsel and pay him a compensation as an electioneering fund, to aid him in his election?—A. I cannot say that that was the intention; it might look like that.

Q. Was that suggestion or any suggestion of that sort made?—A. I am not clear enough about it to state that.

Q. You say he was not employed?—A. He was not employed to my knowledge; I do not think he was; I have no reason to suppose he was.

Q. Have you any recollection as to whether the sum of $10,000 was paid to him nominally as counsel by the Union Pacific Railroad Company?—A. No, sir; not to my knowledge. I never knew of anything of the sort, or heard of it. It was suggested and nothing more.

Q. Did you not refuse in the first instance, and afterward, being pressed, consent to have him so employed?—A. No, sir; I did not. I told General Butler I would refer it; that I had no authority in the matter. I was not a director at the time. I told him I would write to my brother about it, as I did, but he declined to do it.

Q. Did you not make a statement in the hearing of Mr. Buffinton, to the effect that when the application was first made it was rejected, but that afterward it was acquiesced in?—A. No, sir; it never was acquiesced in to my knowledge. The suggestion was made, as I said, about his being employed as counsel, and it was at the time when he was a candidate for the Senate.

Q. Did you not make a statement to Mr. Buffinton of what transpired in that connection?—A. I could not have made any statement to him that Mr. Carpenter was so employed, for it was not a fact to my knowledge.

Q. As far as you know there was no money given to him as counsel, which was charged up against the Union Pacific Railroad Company?—A. I do think there was.

Q. You made no payment?—A. No, sir; the suggestion was made that we should employ him as counsel, and pay him $10,000.

Q. That suggestion was made by General Butler? Was there any reason given, such as that it would be important to have his influence in the Senate as a friend of the Union Pacific Railroad?—A. I am inclined to think there was; I do not think he stated distinctly that that was what it was for; that was my inference.

Q. You have no recollection of making any statement in the presence or hearing of Mr. Buffinton of its having been done?—A. No, sir; I could not have done it; I may have said that Mr. Butler made such an application; that is very likely.

Q. But you stated that you refused to acquiesce in it, and that it was not done?—A. My brother refused to acquiesce in it. I told General Butler I would refer it; that I had no authority in the matter.

Q. Have you any other knowledge in reference to that subject?—A. No, sir; I have not.

Q. Have you had any communication with Mr. Alley in connection with that subject?—A. I do not know. I may have mentioned it to Mr. Alley at the time. He was a director then, I think.

Q. Have you or Mr. Alley, or any others, acted upon that direction and caused the thing to be done?—A. No, sir; I do not think it was done. I am very sure it was not; if it was, it was without my knowledge.

By the CHAIRMAN:

Q. At the time of this conversation between you and General Butler, was General Butler the counsel for the company?—A. No, sir; I did not so consider him.

Q. Was this conversation between you and General Butler prior to Mr. Carpenter's election to the Senate?—A. Yes, sir; it was prior to that.

Q. Was this advice of General Butler given in view of the expectation that Mr. Carpenter was coming to the Senate?—A. I supposed he wanted to have him elected from that conversation.

Q. You understood that this advice was given upon the basis that Mr. Carpenter was coming to the Senate?—A. I drew that inference; I do not know whether I had any right to draw it or not, but I did draw that inference.

By Mr. MERRICK:

Q. Did General Butler make any such remark, or assign any such reason as that it was important that there should be some man there who could talk in behalf of the road, or who had a mouth?—A. No, sir; I think the expression was that Mr. Carpenter had a tongue in his head; I think that was the reason assigned; I am not positive, but that is my impression. I am a very bad hand to repeat conversation, but that is my recollection of it.

By Mr. McCRARY:

Q. Do you know whether an application was made to the Central Pacific Railroad to retain Mr. Carpenter?—A. No, sir; I have no knowledge of it. I never heard of it until within a few days. I have heard it mentioned here in this committee-room or the other; I never heard of it until quite recently.

WASHINGTON, D. C., *February* 11, 1873.

JAMES BUFFINTON, a member of the United States House of Representatives from the State of Massachusetts, sworn and examined.

By Mr. MERRICK:

Q. Did you have any conversation with Oakes Ames, or hear any conversation with Oakes Ames, relating to the employment of Mr. Carpenter as counsel for the Union Pacific Railroad Company?—A. No, sir; I never heard him speak of it.

Q. Did you have any conversation or hear any conversation, with General Butler, with reference to any application or suggestion he had made to Mr. Ames in regard to his employment as counsel?—A. It was some time ago, I think as long ago as the winter of 1868–'69, that I heard General Butler state that an offer had been made for the Union Pacific Railroad Company to retain Mr. Carpenter as counsel; this was before he was Senator.

Q. State all the facts and all that was said in reference to it.—A. Well, it would be impossible for me to state particularly all that was said. General Butler stated that Mr. Carpenter's friends, as near as I can recollect, had sent down here to have Mr. Carpenter retained for a certain sum of money, and he named the sum.

Q. What was the sum?—A. I think it was $10,000.

Q. What else was said?—A. He said that Mr. Alley, of my State, objected to its being paid. I do not mean to be understood as quoting his exact words; I cannot remember them; that was the substance.

Q. Did he state whether or not it had been paid?—A. It had not up to that time; that was the inference I drew.

Q. Did he make a statement that he had suggested or urged it upon Oakes Ames?—A. I could not say as to that; I do not remember that he did; he remarked that Mr. Alley objected to the payment of the $10,000.

By Mr. NIBLACK:

Q. What reason was assigned, if any, why Mr. Carpenter should be employed?—A. I could not say there was any reason given.

By Mr. MERRICK:

Q. You stated that he said the suggestion had come down from the friends of Mr. Carpenter that a fund should be provided to promote his election?—A. I so understood it.

Q. Was anything said in regard to the importance of having Mr. Carpenter in the Senate as a friend of the Union Pacific Railroad?—A. Nothing, to my knowledge.

Q. Then, why should the Union Pacific Railroad furnish a fund for his election?—A. I do not know that they did.

Q. Why should it have been suggested that they should?—A. That is impossible for me to say.

Q. Of course it is, so far as it may have been spoken of by others; I ask the question to see whether it recalls your memory of the conversation.—A. I do not think that General Butler, in any conversation I had with him or he with me, stated any reason why it should be given.

Q. Did he or not say that he made an overture to Mr. Ames?—A. I do not recollect his saying anything of that kind; the overture was made, as I understood, not by Mr. Butler but by Mr. Carpenter's friends to the railroad company, for funds to assist in his election.

Q. Do you or not recollect whether it was stated that the overture was at first refused, but afterward acquiesced in?—A. No, sir; I do not think it was at the time of the conversation I had with him; I inferred that nothing had been given at all; he remarked that the thing was objected to by Mr. Alley.

By the CHAIRMAN:

Q. When was this conversation with General Butler?—A. I cannot fix the precise date; my impression is that it was four years ago; probably in the month of February, before the meeting of the Forty-first Congress.

By Mr. MCCRARY:

Q. It was before Mr. Carpenter's election to the Senate?—A. It was before Mr. Carpenter's election to the Senate.

By Mr. MERRICK:

Q. The only person with whom you conversed upon the subject was General Butler?—A. Only with General Butler at that time. I never exchanged a word with Oakes Ames upon the subject, that I remember; and I do not wish to be understood that General Butler presented this proposition to retain Mr. Carpenter as counsel at all, or that he advocated its acceptance by the Union Pacific Railroad Company. His statement to me was simply that such a proposition had been made by Mr. Carpenter's friends, but was objected to by Mr. Alley.

WASHINGTON, D. C., *February* 19, 1873.

The committee met. Present: the chairman, and Messrs. McCrary, Niblack, and Merrick.

Mr. SCHUYLER COLFAX again appeared before the committee, attended by his counsel, Robert S. Hale.

The CHAIRMAN remarked that the committee had learned from Mr. Colfax that he desired to make some further statement.

Mr. HALE. I wish to state to the committee that when Mr. Colfax was on the stand, (on the 11th, I think,) the immediate question before the committee on which he was called upon for an explanation related to the deposit of $1,200 on the 22d of June, in the First National Bank. I examined him only in relation to the source from which that money came, understanding that to be the question as to which testimony was desired. At that time I had full knowledge of the letters and remittances at other times made by Mr. Nesbitt to him, which Mr. Colfax will explain this morning; (producing the letters before the committee;) but

I advised him, as his counsel, that I did not see how he could properly go into that subject, (his relations with Mr. Nesbitt, and his remittances to him at other times,) unless it should be called out by inquiries from the committee or from other parties. I advised him that his testimony should be confined to the point at issue, and that it seemed to me that that was entirely outside. Of course, if any question had been raised as to his acquaintance with Mr. Nesbitt, and receiving remittances from him at any other time, that would have been fully stated. In that opinion I was influenced mainly by my desire to confine the testimony to the point in issue, but I also saw, from the nature of the letters themselves and from the injunctions contained in them, that they were of a confidential character, and certainly ought not to be, voluntarily and without any sufficient reason, brought before the public. Since Mr. Colfax testified I have learned that the committee had been instituting inquiries concerning his bank-account, deposits, and transactions at other times, outside the immediate connection with the deposit of June 22, 1868; and, on that fact, I advised Mr. Colfax to lay the whole matter before the committee; and he accordingly communicated to the committee the letter of last Monday. He desires now to lay before the committee those letters from Mr. Nesbitt, not as having any connection with the transaction, but as explaining fully all his connection with Mr. Nesbitt and everything connected with his receipts from him during that whole session of Congress, and as far beyond that as the committee may desire. The letters will speak for themselves, and the transaction throughout will speak for itself. Now I will ask Mr. Colfax to proceed and give to the committee the narrative of his entire connection, correspondence, acquaintance, and transactions with Mr. Nesbitt during the whole year.

Mr. COLFAX. On the 18th of April, 1868, over a month before I was nominated for the vice-presidency, I received the following letter, inclosing a check for $1,000:

"NEW YORK, *April* 17, 1868.

"DEAR SIR: I beg your acceptance of the inclosed to assist in defraying your *personal* expenses during the present political campaign.

"I beg to say that I am ever ready to forward the interest of a deserving member of the craft, and as I am pleased with you, (though personally unacquainted,) and knowing that to occupy a desirable position in politics is expensive, I have taken the liberty of offering my trifle, with the assurance that if the matter is known beyond ourselves it will be through you, and against my wish.

"Very respectfully, your obedient servant,

"GEORGE F. NESBITT.

"Hon. SCHUYLER COLFAX,
"*Speaker House of Representatives, Washington, D. C.*"

At the foot of the letter is the following paragraph, written in pencil, as part of the letter:

"I inclose a check for safety; if you had rather receive it in another way, please name your wish."

This letter I received on the morning of the 18th of April. It came from a gentleman whom I knew by reputation, but who was personally an entire stranger to me. I thought over it a good deal as to what I should do in relation to it. It struck me as surprising and needing explanation. I was struck with the pencil memorandum at the end of the letter, as if it had been the original intention of the writer to send the money in some other way—by bill or otherwise—but had finally decided on sending it in a check for safety. In the afternoon of that day I replied to this letter. I have no copy of my letter, for it was not my habit to preserve copies. This was a personal gift. It was not to be put into a general fund for political purposes. The letter said that it was "to assist in defraying your personal expenses during the present political campaign."

I replied to the gentleman, as nearly as I can recollect, as follows: That I was surprised at the receipt of this large gift from him, but that I could not accept it if it involved any obligation on my part for any favor, express or implied, personal or official. That was the substance of my answer. In the mean time I held the check. It did not pass through the bank till the 2d of May. To that letter I received the following reply:

"NEW YORK, *April* 20, 1868.

"DEAR SIR: Your favor of the 18th was duly received.

"I beg to assure you that in presenting the affair referred to, I had no idea of placing myself in a position where I could ask or expect a favor. When I ask in my note of the 17th that the matter may be confined to ourselves, I mean it. If it should be known that we correspond, I should probably be annoyed beyond anything I desire.

"I have my party predilections and personal preferences for men, and I am ever ready to contribute to the success of either or both, and in doing so I usually adopt the course I have in this instance, with the only condition that it may be known only by the parties interested. I think it better to contribute in this way than through a committee, where much is lost by friction.

"Very respectfully, yours,

"GEORGE F. NESBITT.

"Hon. SCHUYLER COLFAX,
"*Washington, D. C.*"

The reason why I desire to submit these letters first privately to the committee, and then—if considered necessary for the ends of justice—to be made public, was for the reason that they all exhibit the same desire that the matter should be strictly between ourselves. His generosity to me was lavish; his regard for me was very great; and I desired, in behalf of a deceased friend, not to say anything in reference to this transaction except so far as was necessary for my own vindication. But, after I found that my bank-account was examined in relation to other dates than the 22d of June, and that an unfavorable impression was sought to be created out of it, I felt that if this friend could come back, he would say that for my vindication he would have no objection to publicity.

Mr. HALE, (to Mr. Colfax.) You heard my statement as to the advice given you as counsel?

Mr. COLFAX. Yes, sir.

Mr. HALE. Was that correct?

Mr. COLFAX. That was correct. I showed Mr. Hale these letters, and I told him that perhaps the best course was to allude to them or to state them. He advised me very decidedly against it, on the ground that it was not relevant; and when the $45,000 of deposits was pointed out in my bank-account as for one year, (but which afterward turned out to be for three years,) I felt, contrary to his advice, that it was better to state to the committee the changes in investments which I had made, and that these changes in investments during three years accounted for $30,000 of that $45,000. Mr. Hale advised me against doing that;

but I felt disposed that the committee should know everything. I had had no disguises about it, nor about any transaction in my life.

The next letter that I received was the one inclosing the $1,000 bill, which was deposited on 22d June. That was the letter which was read at the breakfast table, and the circumstances in relation to which have been described by myself and by others. It was received very soon after the middle of the month, (I cannot fix the exact day,) and was deposited on Monday morning the 22d. I suppose it was received during the preceding week, and toward the latter part of the week. The conversation at the table has been spoken of by other witnesses as well as by myself—about its coming at an opportune time to send to Mr. Conner, chairman of the Indiana republican committee, who was anxious for money, and to whom I had promised to send money to assist in organizing the campaign, which was already in progress, (for the Indiana campaign opens in the spring always.) The check which I drew for the $1,000 draft to Mr. Conner has been exhibited here. It is payable to self or bearer. Attached to it is the draft purchased by it. The draft is dated June 22, 1868. It is issued by the First National Bank of Washington, and is payable to my order. It is indorsed by me, "Pay to the order of Hon. A. H. Conner, of Indianapolis;" is indorsed by him, and has passed through the banking-house of Winslow, Lanier & Co. At this time I sometimes received from fifty to one hundred letters a day. That was during the month after my nomination. In the letter from Mr. Nesbitt inclosing the $1,000 bill he said that it was to be confidential between ourselves; that it was not known to any of his family. I cannot recollect certainly whether or not he said that the letter was to be destroyed. I have stated that I could not find that letter, and could not find, on an examination of Mr. Nesbitt's accounts, any trace of it. I do remember, however, very distinctly, that the matter was frequently talked of between myself and my mother, now deceased. Since the committee closed its public testimony I received a telegram from my sister in Iowa, who might be here, but that, unfortunately, she has a child who is in a very dangerous condition of health. I have received from her a letter which I will read to the committee simply as corroborative of what others have testified to:

"KELLOGG, *February* 12, 1873.

"MY DARLING BROTHER: I received your telegram on Tuesday and answered immediately, because of remembering circumstances that it brought up in my mind, and fully believing I could find the letter, but on searching find I have *not a* letter in the house back of 1872. I generally destroy all old letters and papers once a year, as I have no way of keeping them without lying around. I am very, very sorry about it. I remember mother writing about the nomination. In the next letter, she wrote about a friend sending Schuyler *a* $1,000 *bill*, and says at the same time, 'Who can say they don't appreciate my boy?' In the same letter she told about your all going to Denver, and I distinctly remember how I felt, for I thought, well, I am glad my friends can run around and have a good time if we do have bad luck on the farm, and told Elijah that $1,000 was more than we could make from our farm in four years."

Carrying out the conversation at the breakfast table between Mr. Mathews and myself, carrying out the wish of the gentleman who sent me the money, and carrying out my pledge to Mr. Conner, I sent him this money to assist in the campaign. On the very same day that I made the deposit, I turned the bill into this draft which is here. On the 11th of July, just after the New York papers had announced that the Mississippi election, the first election of the canvass, had been carried by the republicans, and when Congress was expected to adjourn in a few days, I received a letter from Mr. Nesbitt, inclosing a check for $1,000. I speak of the New York papers having announced the result of the Mississippi election because, in the first place I remember the incident, and in the second place I think it important to state it in this connection. The letter which I received is as follows:

"NEW YORK, *July* 11, 1868.

"DEAR SIR: Allow me to congratulate you upon the result of the first battle of the political campaign, and to predict a satisfactory result at its close. As you are about to leave your present occupation for the more active and expensive one of a canvass for the approaching election, I beg to offer the inclosed to assist in paying the cost. You need have no fear that I shall trouble you for office, as I am better calculated for business than political position. Nor do I desire that it shall be known that we correspond. If it should be, I would probably be importuned for letters of introduction to an extent that would be anything but pleasant to you or myself. I, like yourself, am a New Yorker born, and am ever ready to contribute to the honor of New York or her sons. I, like yourself, was at an early age sent forth to earn a living and establish a character. In the first I have succeeded to my utmost deserving; for the latter I refer to those who know me best. Your career has been different from mine. You aimed to be a statesman, a position more full of honor than profit. Thus far your friends must be satisfied with your position and reputation. In a pecuniary point of view I doubt if it can be very satisfactory. Observation has taught me to know that it is almost impossible for a poor boy to become prominent as a statesman unless he has friends who will assist him in his financial necessities. If not assisted he must remain in the back-ground, and the places of statesmen be filled in many instances by persons having more money than ability. Where would have been our Webster, Clay, and many others if it had not been for friends who came forward to help them during financial embarassment? I hope and believe you may have many friends who will assist you to attain to the high position your character and ability so fully entitle you, and you will not accuse me of flattery, I hope, when I say there is no position under our Government for which I think you unqualified. The present campaign will be an expensive one, and if you find you are in want of funds, you are at liberty to call upon me, with the assurance that if I have money to spare you shall have it. If I have not I will so inform you, and in either case the matter will there terminate.

"I have the honor to be your obedient servant,

"GEORGE F. NESBITT.

"HON. SCHUYLER COLFAX, *Washington*."

This letter, as the committee will see, not only inclosed the check for $1,000, but gave me a *carte blanche* to draw on him for any amount of money I wanted. I need scarcely say to the committee that I did not draw upon him for anything. Whatever he sent was sent voluntarily. I beg also to state how it was that these letters were found. I remember that when Congress adjourned my table was filled with letters. I had barely time at the close of the session to read all the letters that I received, much less to answer all of them. When Congress adjourned I took all the letters that were on my table, tied them up, threw them into a trunk, and did not see them again from that day till the time that this committee commenced its investigation.

I wish to say furthermore that Mr. Nesbitt never asked a favor of me of any kind, personal or official, political or relating to any contract or business whatever. He never asked me for a favor. We met that fall at his house, and he with his family at my house; and when I said to him, with a heart full of gratitude, "What can I do to show you my appreciation of your generosity toward me?" he said to me, in my own house, "If you will get tickets for myself and family so that we can see you inaugurated, I shall be amply repaid."

Mr. HALE. Is that the only favor he asked of you?

Mr. COLFAX. That is the only favor he ever asked of me. In conversation he told me that he believed in administering on his own estate. He told me that he had assisted six other persons, and that what he did for me had given him more gratification than what he did for the rest. He made a great many other kind remarks; but I do not think that even the scrutiny into private matters, which this committee permitted, renders it necessary for me to repeat them. I acknowledged the receipt of this third thousand dollars with a great deal of gratitude on my part toward him, scarcely knowing how to express myself, because I never had found such a large-hearted friend in all my life; and to that letter he replied as follows:

"NEW YORK, *July* 18, 1868.

"MY DEAR SIR: Your favor of the 12th was duly received. I fear it is too late for you to think of engaging in business unless you are defeated in the coming election, which is not probable. The opposition will resort to all and any means to elect their ticket, and they have an untold amount of money to back them. But with all these we will beat them—not by remaining idle, however, for we have much and hard work to do, and *the party* will require money, but the furnishing of this must be left to the political organizations. Persons who are in office will pay in the hope that they will be retained, and others who are out will pay in the hope that they may get in. Between the two I think *the party* will be supplied. Not so with you. Your friends must supply you, and the money must come without any promises on your part, either expressed or implied. I have but little experience in political matters and may not be a safe adviser, but I might be allowed to suggest that your reputation is sufficient for present purposes, and would not probably be improved by letter-writing or speaking in public. I think if you were put away somewhere it would be about as well. If you should be coming North, and wish to spend a few days quietly and out of the way, I would like you to get in one of the cars of the New Haven Railroad and take a trip to the quiet little town of Stamford; there land, and ask the first hackman you see to take you to my summer home. I am about one and one-half miles from the depot, in a very quiet neighborhood, and live very plainly. My family make no fuss when friends call. They are therefore allowed to and do feel at home. I am at home at all times, except Wednesdays and Saturdays, when I am in New York, and would have my carriage at the depot to meet you, if I knew when to expect you. You shall not be annoyed by company, unless there should be some friend of yours in the town whom you would like to see. The Sabbath is a delightful day with us. I regret that we are not personally acquainted, I never having seen you except from the gallery of the House, and you never having seen me at all. I feel that I am taking liberties with you, but I do assure you I am anxious only for your success. In the first place because you are a son of New York, but more particularly because you have shown conspicuously that, though born of humble parentage, you have been tendered almost the highest honor in the power of your fellow-citizens to bestow, without resorting to the low devices of the politician, but rather exhibiting all those Christian virtues so well becoming a true gentleman of honor. About the 1st of November next I shall have another one thousand dollars for your use, and will require your address at that time. You do not probably fully understand me, but in order that you may I will explain.

"I have made it a rule to inform my children as soon as they were old enough to understand me, that it was my intention, if I had the means at the time of my death, to leave them sufficient to provide them with the necessaries of life. As for the luxuries, they must work for them as I had done, if they required them. This rule I am preparing to carry out. It enables me to do some good while living, and probably will save some of my children from the disadvantages too often attending the acquisition of money not earned. My children are being educated to earn their living at such occupation as seems best adapted to the disposition of each. I have written more than I meant to, and more probably than will be interesting to you. I will close as I began. It is too late for you to think of being anything but a statesman. If that does not pay, your friends must make up the difference. While I can, I will contribute. When I can do it no longer some other friend will appear to take my place. Please believe me, when I say I desire most particularly that our correspondence should be private, and when a discontinuance would appear desirable by you, you are only to notify me and your wish shall be respected.

"Very respectfully, your obedient servant,

"GEORGE F. NESBITT.

"Hon. SCHUYLER COLFAX, *Washington, D. C.*"

This letter alludes to a remittance which the writer intended to make about the 1st of November, and which I have no doubt he did make. The letter, however, cannot be found, although I have made search for it among all my letters at home. I have no doubt that I received it. In fact, I have a distinct recollection of it.

The CHAIRMAN. You mean the letter inclosing the $1,000 check in the fall afterward?

Mr. COLFAX. Yes, sir; I am certain that I received that $1,000, but the letter itself cannot be found; so that, for two of these remittances only can I produce the letters. As to the other two I can only produce the circumstantial facts bearing on them. And now before handing these letters to the reporter of the committee, I desire to make one remark. Those letters of July 11 and July 18 are from a gentleman who had surely shown a very great interest in me. Although written after my nomination to the vice-presidency, neither of them contains the slightest allusion to that nomination. But as I have testified to the committee, and as my family has testified, the letter which I am unable to produce, and which contained the one thousand dollar bill, was a congratulatory letter, warmly so, one which I might expect from a man who would lavish four thousand dollars upon me in a single year. This gentleman died very soon after I was inaugurated.

Mr. HALE. These letters are all inclosed in the original envelopes, and some of them are postmarked?

Mr. COLFAX. Yes, sir; and the committee will recollect that I said that the letter inclosing the thousand dollar bill, came in an envelope inclosed in another envelope. One of these letters came in the same way.

It will be seen, therefore, by the committee, that in April, 1868, I received $1,000 from Mr. Nesbitt as a personal gift. It will be also seen, from my testimony, that I received $2,000 afterward, before the session of Congress closed, and $1,000 at the close of the campaign, in November; but that has no bearing on this matter. These three amounts of $1,000 each, received during the session, were all deposited in the bank. The 11th of April check was not deposited until the 2d of May. I am reminded by a gentleman here that I promised at a meeting of Indianians, to contribute $2,000 to the political canvass in Indiana, if I could.

This matter about Mr. Nesbitt I kept as confidential as I could. I did speak of it to a few friends; but Mr. Nesbitt had desired it to be kept so secret that I avoided reference to it as much as I could. It appears, however, that there were a few persons with whom I did converse on the subject. I have here an affidavit which was received by me, first through the telegraph, and afterward through the mail, and which I will read to the committee. It was sworn to by a gentleman who is on intimate terms with me. He came into the town of South Bend and heard a good deal said about Colfax's statement before this committee. He did not read my statement, as he swears, but he immediately made an affidavit containing 393 words and sent it to me by telegraph. The original affidavit has since come by mail. The gentleman who made this has lived for thirty years or more at South Bend. He is a gentleman of prominence, whose character is unquestionable, whose veracity nobody would dispute; who has occupied positions of trust there, and would occupy more if he was willing to accept them, and about whose credibility the committee may consult General Packard, who, I believe, knows him personally.

The affidavit is as follows:

STATE OF INDIANA, *Saint Joseph County, ss:*

Ricketson Burroughs, a citizen of South Bend, in said county and State, being duly sworn, deposes as follows: "During the summer of 1868, after the return of Mr. Colfax from Washington, in consultation about the approaching political campaign, he (Colfax) related to me the circumstance of his having made the acquaintance of an old gentleman in New York City by the name of Nesbitt; that he (Nesbitt) stated to Mr. Colfax that neither he nor his friends wanted any office; in common parlance, 'He had no axes to grind,' and he had abundance of means for himself and family, and wished, if Mr. Colfax would accept, to bestow a part of his wealth in such manner as would assist Mr. Colfax in defraying his increasing expenses incident to said campaign, and then offered him (Colfax) the sum of $1,000 or $2,000, I am not certain now which sum, but it was either $1,000 or $2,000, for such purpose, and that all the favor he (Nesbitt) would ask in return was that he (Colfax) would call on him (Nesbitt) and take tea with him. I have frequently spoken of said conversation to many of my neighbors and friends in South Bend during the last few weeks, and having just been informed this evening that Mr. Colfax had recently made a statement in relation to said matter before an investigation committee in Washington, (although I have not seen said statement yet,) I take pleasure in making this affidavit in proof of that transaction about receiving said money from said Nesbitt, in hope that it may in some measure serve the cause of truth, and help to vindicate the character of a just and truthful man whom I have intimately known for more than thirty years, against the malicious aspersions with which his good name is assailed, and I will add further that Mr. Colfax informed me, during the conversation above referred to, that said Nesbitt did give him $1,000 or $2,000, (I am not certain which sum,) and that he (Colfax) soon after sent the amount so received to the chairman of the central committee at Indianapolis.

RICKETSON BURROUGHS.

Subscribed and sworn to before me this 13th day of February, A.D. 1873.
[SEAL.] GEORGE H. ALWARD,
Notary Public.

The committee will notice that although my testimony was confined, the last day I appeared before it, to the thousand dollars received on the 22d of June, and the draft which was sent to the Indiana central committee, and although that was all that was talked about at South Bend and all over the country, yet Mr. Burroughs, three or four times in the affidavit, speaks of my having told him of one or two thousand dollars, evidently recollecting two thousand, without any prompting from my statement, or in any way whatever. The committee will also remember that I stated that I received one thousand dollars in April as a personal gift, and two thousand dollars in June and July to be used for political purposes. This check was in the letter of the 11th of July, and was received here on the 12th of July. I was then engaged in paying up the expenses of the session of Congress, and in closing up my affairs before leaving for home. I had given twenty or thirty dinner-parties during the session; my expenses had been very large, and I was paying the bills. I took the thousand-dollar check of Mr. Nesbitt's, and deposited it on the 13th of July to my account in the bank. I remembered his desire that that should be used for political purposes, and I was faithful to the trust, as I have been faithful to every trust. Five days after that time, on the 18th of July, I went to the office of the Sergeant-at-Arms and drew the amount in cash which the chairman will find there, (handing a memorandum to the chairman,) $1,044.49.

Mr. HALE. That was drawn on account of salary?

Mr. COLFAX. On account of salary. What the $44.49 is for I am unable to tell the commitee. I have endeavored to find out everything in relation to my financial matters; but this $44.49 I will frankly say I cannot explain. The second thousand dollars from Mr. Nesbitt was sent, on the same day that I drew the money from the Sergeant-at-Arms, to Mr. Conner, in this draft, (handing it to the chairman.)

The CHAIRMAN stated that the draft was dated July 18, 1868, for one thousand dollars, was payable to the order of Mr. Colfax, was indorsed by Mr. Colfax, "Pay to the order of Hon. A. H. Conner, of Indianapolis," was indorsed by Mr. Conner, and passed through the banking-house of Winslow, Lanier & Co.

Mr. HALE, (to Mr. Colfax.) State when the present existence of this draft first came to your knowledge.

Mr. COLFAX. I have examined everywhere to find this draft, but, as it was purchased with cash, received from the Sergeant-at-Arms, and not with a check, I could not find it. Since the committee met this morning it has been found by the merest accident at the bank. It is now here and speaks for itself.

Mr. HALE. It has been brought here this morning by your secretary, Mr. Todd.

Mr. COLFAX. Yes, sir. Not being connected with a check, it was difficult to trace it. I presented the account of the Sergeant-at-Arms to show that I drew that very day $1,044.49 in cash. There are a good many other items in my cash account of that year that I am not able to account for. If the committee would like to know how much money I spent that year, I can show all my political experiences, my personal expenses, and my gifts; and I will say frankly to the committee that I desire this to be done. These experiences are, of course, unpleasant, but if there is a further examination desired into my accounts, I will state all of them, and show what I expended politically, personally, and for household expenses.

The CHAIRMAN. I do not see that the committee has any desire to inquire into that. The reason that we inquire at all was to try and settle this difference between yourself and Mr. Ames, which Mr. Ames claimed that you had. That is the point of the inquiry, and it would not be likely to be elucidated by what you propose.

Mr. COLFAX. I would like to state it, however.

Mr. HALE. O, I would not touch it.

Mr. COLFAX. All the money that I sent to Indiana, and I expended still more in that State than this, was for legitimate expenses of the campaign, and was all furnished by friends. I have been blessed with good friends. I remember that once in a congressional campaign a gentleman, who was not worth over twenty thousand dollars, gave me a thousand dollars, which was five per cent. of his whole fortune. What friends offered for political purposes, I felt no hesitation in receiving. My hesitation about the first thousand dollars from Mr. Nesbitt was because it was a personal gift. I accepted other sums for political use in that campaign, and used them for legitimate and honorable political purposes.

The CHAIRMAN. The point of all our inquiry is to ascertain whether any of these sums were paid by the money received from Mr, Ames; and as some allusion has been made to the action of the committee, I think I can say for myself and all my associates, that our only desire has been to ascertain the precise and exact truth in regard to everything which we were undertaking to inquire about. After the statement of Mr. Colfax on the last occasion, which was finished pretty late in the evening, and after a long and severe day's work, I remembered that there appeared on Mr. Colfax's bank-book, on the 1st day of June, a deposit of $1,200, and it occurred to me that any one might say, in looking over our proceedings, that we were remiss in not having inquired about that $1,200, because the time of its being paid was not precisely indefinitely stated, and because it was possible that the thousand dollars received from Mr. Nesbitt might have gone in those $1,200. In conversation and consultation with the committee, we thought that, in order to justify ourselves, it might be well to ascertain about that $1,200 which was deposited on the 1st of June, and so, by the direction of the committee, I obtained a copy of the deposit certificate of that day. We had some conversation with Mr. Ames on the subject, and Mr. Ames said that some of the subsequent deposits he thought were of a larger amount than $1,200, and that the thousand dollars which Mr. Colfax received from New York might have gone into the subsequent deposits. We could see that it might be important to determine and to know precisely what each of these deposits was made up of, and accordingly I have procured from the bank the copies of all the deposit checks. Our purpose was to satisfy ourselves whether or not that thousand dollars had gone into some other deposits; and if we found anything which made for one side or the other in the controversy about this twelve hundred dollars, we intended at the proper time to have put it on the record.

Mr. HALE. It was in view of that action of the committee that I said to Mr. Colfax that it was evidently his duty now to present those letters in reference to the other transactions.

Mr. COLFAX. I desire to state, in reference to the twelve hundred dollars of the 1st of June, that I was informed at the bank that a gentleman had called there, and stated that he represented the Poland committee, and that he desired to examine Mr. Colfax's account of the 1st of June for twelve hundred dollars. The cashier told him that he would like to have some authority from the committee before he would let him examine the books, (although it appears that my bank-account is very accessible, and has been the subject of a good deal of scrutiny.) I said to the cashier, "Why did you not show it?" He said, "Because it is not our way." The deposit of the 1st of June was composed of a seven-hundred-dollar draft or check from Mr. Sinclair, one of the payments on the New York Tribune stock, of a one-hundred-dollar check which I received from the First National Bank of South Bend, and of a four-hundred-dollar check which I think was perhaps on account of my salary. The check which I received from Mr. Nesbitt on the 11th of July, I deposited on the 13th of July. Five days afterward I got $1,044 in cash from the Sergeant-at-Arms, and, on that very same day, I sent this second draft for a thousand dollars, in compliance with my promise, to Mr. Conner. I must evidently have stated to Mr. Burroughs that I received two thousand dollars from Mr. Nesbitt, and sent it to the chairman of the republican committee in Indiana.

Mr. NIBLACK. What was Mr. Nesbitt's business?

Mr. COLFAX. He was a large stationer—one of the old-time stationers of New York. Years before his relations with me, he obtained a contract for Government envelopes, and held it until the time of his death. He never spoke to me about his contract; never asked me to do anything about it; but, on the contrary, told me that he had instructed his family never to ask a favor of me.

Mr. NIBLACK. Had you any connection with him before that as a Government contractor?

Mr. COLFAX. Never.

Mr. NIBLACK. It has been suggested to me that he had contracts under the Government while you were chairman of the Post-Office Committee of the House?

Mr. COLFAX. That is entirely beyond my knowledge.

Mr. NIBLACK. It has also been intimated that he had received favors from you in that way?

Mr. COLFAX. The first acquaintance that I ever had with him was in 1868, five years after I became Speaker, and of course five years after I was chairman of the Post-Office Committee. I did not make his personal acquaintance till the fall of 1868. Let me say furthermore (as it has been stated that I had forgotten this draft of the 13th of July) that I can never forget the generosity of this man toward me. I can never forget the manner in which he spoke of me to myself and my family. And as I have been so misrepresented, I desire to say to these gentlemen reporters that, as I have been speaking freely of a deceased mother, I trust there will be no misrepresentation in regard to that.

The CHAIRMAN. I would like to say in reference to our communications with the bank that I never sent anybody to the bank, and that I do not know what Mr. Colfax refers to or what the bank cashier refers to.

Mr. COLFAX. I have no doubt that that was a canard. Mr. Swain, cashier, said to me that he thought that this was an enterprising reporter.

The CHAIRMAN. So far as I know, no person knew anything of our purpose except the members of the committee and the cashier of the bank; and, in order to satisfy the cashier, I assured him that whatever communication should be made to us would be made no use of unless it was thought fit to go on the record of the committee; and that, if so, we should call him publicly before us to state it.

Mr. COLFAX. I have no complaint to make on any point.

The CHAIRMAN. I desire that the action of the committee should not be misunderstood. We desire to do no disfavor to anybody.

Mr. HALE. There is no disposition on our part to criticise in the least the action of the committee.

Mr. COLFAX. If the committee has any questions to ask I am ready to answer them.

The CHAIRMAN. I have here a deposit-check, of 22d of June, and I have copies of all the deposit-checks from June 1. I think it would be just all around if those deposit-checks were put on the record.

Mr. COLFAX. Certainly, sir.

Mr. HALE. I wish to inquire the extent of time covered by these deposit-checks?

The CHAIRMAN. June and July.

Mr. HALE. I would be glad also to include May.

The CHAIRMAN. We were satisfied that those sums which Mr. Colfax received were received after his nomination, so that we did not inquire for any earlier date.

Mr. COLFAX. If it would not be lumbering up the records too much, I should like to have the deposit-checks of the entire session put in.

The CHAIRMAN. There is no need of that. I learned that there was no deposits between the 21st of May and the first of June, so that these deposit-checks already copied give the details of all the deposits made after the nomination of Mr. Colfax to the end of that session, and until he left Washington. (To Mr. Colfax.) Do you recollect whether, in Mr. Nesbitt's letter inclosing the thousand-dollar bill, there was any reference to the fact of his sending money instead of a check?

Mr. COLFAX. I do not think there was. My impression is that there was not, because I did not discover the bill until I read the letter through. It was inclosed in the inside of the sheet, and the whole letter was on the first page. The letter was inclosed in two envelopes. It was a letter of congratulation on my nomination, a very cordial and earnest letter of congratulation and of good wishes for my success.

The CHAIRMAN. That was the first letter you received from him after you were nominated?

Mr. COLFAX. Yes, sir; and the only one received until the letter of July, which contained no reference to my nomination at all, showing that there must have been some intervening letter.

The CHAIRMAN. Had you ever had any correspondence with Mr. Nesbitt before the first letter of April?

Mr. COLFAX. No, sir.

The CHAIRMAN. So far as you know, it was the first letter that you received from him?

Mr. COLFAX. I am quite positive it is the first letter I received from him, because I was so surprised at receiving it.

Mr. MCCRARY. I take it from your statement that Mr. Nesbitt's generosity made a very distinct impression upon your mind?

Mr. COLFAX. It did; very distinct, indeed. He told me afterward about his habit of giving money—that his wife and himself gave money often without consultation with each other.

Mr. McCRARY. Have you now any distinct recollection as to the total sum which you received from him?

Mr. COLFAX. I received $4,000 in 1868. I have a distinct recollection of it, for I have often spoken of it.

Mr. McCRARY. You have no question that it was $4,000—not $3,000?

Mr. COLFAX. Yes; it was $1,000 before my nomination, as a personal gift, (as he stated,) $2,000 after my nomination and before I left here, and $1,000 in the fall. There were three remittances during the session.

Mr. McCRARY. You do not think there was any possibility of your being mistaken, and that the total was not $3,000, but $4,000?

Mr. COLFAX. No, sir; I am positive about it being $4,000 during 1868. The affidavit which I have presented corroborates that I received the $2,000 from him after my nomination, and during the session of Congress, because when I went home I told this confidential friend, Mr. Burroughs, about it, and about my having received from him (as Burroughs says) $1,000 or $2,000, and he evidently thinks it was $2,000, showing the impression that was made on his mind, and about my having sent the money to the chairman of the central committee; and I have presented the two drafts corresponding in time.

By Mr. OAKES AMES:

Question. You say that you received a check from Mr. Nesbitt on the 18th of April?—Answer. Yes; the check is dated the 17th, and it arrived on the 18th.

Q. A check for $1,000?—A. Yes.

Q. And you say that on the bottom of the letter is a paragraph in pencil asking whether you wished the money sent in any other way?—A. Yes, sir.

Q. Did you instruct him to send the next money in a bill?—A. I made no reference to the matter in my reply, because I made no claim for any money whatever. Whatever he sent, he sent voluntarily.

Q. Can you account for his sending the next remittance in a bill, while he sent all the other remittances in checks?—A. I do not know whether the one sent in November was a check or a bill. This postscript in pencil seems to show that he thought first of sending a bill in April.

Q. You say that the remittance of the 22d June was in a bill?—A. Yes.

Q. And you say that it was often talked about in the family, and that it excited a good deal of comment and surprise that so liberal a donation should be made by a man who was comparatively a stranger?—A. Yes.

Q. Can you account for so much being said about that thousand dollars when the other three thousand dollars excited no attention at all?—A. When I opened my mail at the breakfast-table and saw this one thousand dollar bill I was very much surprised. It was a bill which had evidently been somewhat worn, because I remember it had none of the crispness of a new bill; the rattle was all out of it. I held it up, and we talked of it.

Mr. AMES. It made a rattling sensation at the breakfast-table which the checks did not make.

Mr. COLFAX. It lacked the rattling sensation.

Q. That $1,000 bill which you received—did you deposit it on the 22d or 23d of June?—A. On the 22d of June.

Q. Why was it so important to make that deposit of just $1,200, the same amount as Mr. Ordway's check? Why did you have to get $200 from somebody else to make it up?—A. I never saw Mr. Ordway's check or $1,200 till I saw it here in the committee-room.

Mr. AMES. All right; there is no use in discussing that any further.

Mr. COLFAX. I have not alluded to it.

Q. And you received another thousand-dollar check on July 11?—A. Yes.

Q. And another one in November?—A. I have not got the letter inclosing it, but I have no doubt I received the thousand he promised to send then.

Mr. AMES. And these three checks excited no comment and made no impression on your mind, while the thousand-dollar bill was a subject of conversation at the breakfast-table, and all the way to Colorado and back?

Mr. COLFAX. Indeed they did; they made a very decided impression.

Q. Was not this Mr. Nesbitt a contractor with the Post-Office Department for furnishing envelopes?—A. So I understand.

Q. For four or five years, while you were chairman of the Post-Office Committee?—A. I have no recollection of it; I had no connection with it. It was a contract given to the lowest bidder. He never spoke to me in 1868, or in any year preceding 1868, or up to the day of his death, in 1868, in reference to a post-office contract. He never asked me to do anything directly or indirectly in regard to it at any time.

Mr. AMES. It seems that this man always got the contract every year, whether he was the highest or the lowest bidder.

Mr. COLFAX. That I know nothing about.

Mr. AMES. So I am informed, and I did not know but that these donations may have been something as bad as Credit Mobilier stock.

Mr. COLFAX. As I have said, they were accepted with a distinct understanding that they would not involve any obligation, expressed or implied, personal or official; and it was so acquiesced in, and Mr. Nesbitt so instructed his family. The only favor he ever asked me was to get tickets for his family to see the inauguration.

Mr. AMES. He must have been a singular man.

Mr. COLFAX. He was a very large-hearted man.

Mr. AMES. No doubt of it.

Mr. COLFAX. His letters show that very conclusively.

By Mr. MCCRARY:

Q. Do you know how the contracts were let for supplying those envelopes?—A. I believe by receiving bids, which are decided by the Postmaster-General on the recommendation of a board of some of his officials, which he creates. He has two or three officials who examine the specimens. I know nothing of it personally. I never saw any letting of any envelope contracts, and I have no personal knowledge how envelope contracts are let.

Q. They were let to the lowest bidder?—A. There has been a question, as I understand it, sometimes as to who was the lowest bidder, because there was some difference as to the quality of the specimens. But I repeat again that Mr. Nesbitt never asked me anything about it. On the contrary, it was a distinct understanding that no favor should ever be asked of me by him.

The CHAIRMAN. This contract was a contract with the Post-Office Department?

Mr. COLFAX. Yes, sir. Mr. Nesbitt had it for a number of years.

Mr. AMES. You were chairman of the Post-Office Committee during this contract?

Mr. COLFAX. I do not know whether I was or not, for I do not know when the contract began. The Postmaster-General never asked me anything about such contracts while I was chairman of that committee.

The CHAIRMAN. Was Mr. Nesbitt a contractor to supply the House with stationery?

Mr. COLFAX. Not that I know of. The contract he had was for furnishing stamped envelopes.

Mr. HALE. I am very confident that the stamped envelopes were not introduced until a later date than Mr. Ames mentions, and until Mr. Colfax became Speaker of the House.

Mr. COLFAX. Let me repeat. I never had a word with Mr. Nesbitt, by letter, by paper, by personal interview, before April 11, 1868.

The CHAIRMAN. Mr. Nesbitt never, as far as you know, had any contract to supply the House with stationery?

Mr. COLFAX. No, sir; never, so far as I know.

The following are the deposit-checks, and summary thereof, that were put in evidence:

Deposited with First National Bank, by ———, June 1, 1868:

Notes	
Checks, as follows	$400 00
	700 00
	100 00
	1,200 00

SCHUYLER COLFAX.

Deposited with the First National Bank, by ———, July 7, 1868:

United States and bank notes	
Checks, as follows	$100 00
	200 00
	100 00
	400 00

(Signed) SCHUYLER COLFAX.

Deposited with the First National Bank, by Schuyler Colfax, July 8:

United States and bank notes	
Checks, as follows	$150 00

Deposited with the First National Bank, by Schuyler Colfax, July 13, 1868:

United States and bank notes	
Checks, as follows	$1,000 00
	500 00
	43 88
	1,543 88

Deposited with the First National Bank, by Schuyler Colfax, July 27, 1868:

United States and bank notes	
Checks, as follows	$74 22
	100 00
	174 22

June 1, 1868.	C. W. Guthrie, Cas. on Merchants' Nat., N. Y.	$100 00	
	S. Sinclair, Park	700 00	
	(Check noted, and dep. ticket don't find)	400 00	
June 22, 1868.	E. C. Cowdin, Metro., N. Y.	250 00	
	T. Denny & Co., Am. Ex., N. Y.	500 00	
	I. N. Seymour, tr.	18 63	
July 7, 1868.	J. L. Everett, Cas., note, Broadway	100 00	
	C. W. Guthrie, Cas., Merchants', N. Y.,	200 00	
	S. M. Pettingill & Co., Nassau	100 00	
July 8, 1868.	(Don't find)		$150 00
July 13, 1868.	I. N. Seymour, leather man	43 88	
	G. F. Nesbitt, man. co	1,000 00	
	Thomas Cornell, First N. Y.	500 00	
July 27, 1868.	W. Orton, Comm	74 22	
	Devlin & Co., Broadway	100 00	

WASHINGTON, D. C., *February* 19, 1873.

J. S. FOWLER, formerly Senator from Tennessee, appeared before the committee and made the following statement under oath:

Some time in 1867, toward the close of the year, I met Mr. McComb, a friend of mine, and after the usual compliments had passed, he remarked to me that Oakes Ames had some stock of the Credit Mobilier to dispose of, and he said, "I want my friends to have some of that stock, and not his have all. I want you to have some, and I want Mr. Bayard, of Delaware, to have some." He made a few remarks about the stock, as that it would be very valuable, &c., and he said, "I am going to let both of you have some." That is about all that occurred between us, of any importance, pertaining to that subject. Some time afterward, I do not know how long, I met Mr. Ames. I met him very frequently; we were members of the same committee; I mean the national union republican committee. I think I remarked to him, "Mr. Ames, what about that Credit Mobilier stock, that Mr. McComb has been speaking to me about?" (Mr. McComb had also spoken to Mr. Ames about letting me have it.) Mr. Ames remarked, that he had had some of that stock to dispose of, but that he did not think that he had any then. That was all that took place of any importance at that time. A day or two afterward I met Mr. Ames, and we conversed over that matter, and over Pacific Railroad matters generally. Mr. Ames never offered me any of the stock. I do not know that I ever owned a dollar's worth of stock in any institution, until last December, when I purchased a little stock in an insurance company. I certainly never received a cent in dividends from any stock; if I did, it is to be discovered yet by me. Mr. Ames never proposed anything to me in this matter. It was altogether through Mr. McComb that my name was connected with it, and the first that I knew of it was by the publication in the New York Sun last summer. I had no chance then to give an explanation of it.

By the CHAIRMAN:

Q. Was this conversation between you and McComb, when the matter was first spoken of, after the commencement of the session of Congress in December, 1867?—A. I think it was during that session. I am satisfied that it was here at Washington, and it must have been during that session of Congress, because I met him in the Capitol. The reason why I did not charge my memory with the date was, that I did not attribute any particular importance to what he said on the occasion. He, however, seemed to be very earnest in the matter.

Q. And he told you that Mr. Ames had some of that stock to distribute?—A. Not to distribute, but to dispose of.

Q. And he wanted some of his friends to have some of it?—A. Yes, sir; he said, I want you, and Mr. Bayard, of Delaware, to have some.

Q. Mr. Bayard was then in the Senate, and you were also in the Senate?—A. Yes, sir.

Q. Can you tell about what time it was that you had the first conversation with Mr. Ames about it?—A. It may have been ten days or two weeks after our conversation with McComb.

Q. Was it in the early part of that winter?—A. I think so; it was immediately following the conversation I had with Mr. McComb.

Q. What do you say was Mr. Ames's answer to you?—A. He spoke about the stock, and said that he had had some of it, but he did not think he had any then. I remember his saying that he had let Mr. Patterson have $3,000 worth of the stock.

Q. Do you recollect whether he named anybody else in connection with it?—A. No, sir; I remember that very distinctly.

Q. Did Mr. McComb name any other person to you except yourself and Senator Bayard?—A. Not to the best of my recollection. He said that he wanted his friends to have some of that stock, and I recollect that he mentioned Mr. Bayard by name. I did not understand Mr. McComb as meaning that stock was to be distributed, but that it was to be purchased.

The CHAIRMAN. When I used the word "distributed" I did not mean that the stock was to be given away.

The WITNESS. I understood the same idea to be conveyed by Mr. Ames in relation to Mr. Patterson's stock. Mr. Ames spoke of it as having sold the stock to Mr. Patterson.

Q. You did not understand from Mr. McComb that Ames had stock to give away?—A. No, sir.

By Mr. MERRICK:

Q. Did you understand that stock was to be transferred at anything less than its full market-value?—A. No, sir; there was no understanding about it. I did not know what its value was.

Q. There was nothing said with reference to its value?—A. No, sir, not then; because I did not press the inquiry in the matter at all. Mr. McComb said it would be valuable.

Q. Did they describe to you the exact relations between the Credit Mobilier and the Union Pacific Railroad Company, as they are now understood and developed?—A. No, sir; Mr. McComb did not. Mr. Ames and I had a full conversation about those relations.

Q. Tell what description he gave you about these relations—what impression was left on your mind?—A. He stated that the Credit Mobilier was a company which had been formed for the purpose of building the Union Pacific Railroad, and I understood from him that they were to receive their pay from the subsidies given the Union Pacific Railroad Company; that the dividends were all to come from the profits on the contract. Mr. Ames did not seem anxious to dispose of any of the stock.

Q. Did you understand that those dividends were to consist in whole or in part of the stock of the Union Pacific Railroad Company itself?—A. I did not.

Q. Was there anything in the account and description which he gave to you of the Credit Mobilier, and its operations in connection with the Union Pacific Railroad Company, that would suggest to your mind or to the mind of any other intelligent gentleman any antagonism that might arise between the relations of the holder of that stock and his duties as a disinterested law-maker of the country?—A. There was such a possibility.

Q. And they were incompatible, as you understood?—A. Of course, they might be. Mr. Ames did not state that any legislation would be required by the company, but I, myself, could see such a contingency.

Mr. MERRICK. Yes; I speak of what you derived from his statement.

The WITNESS. My conclusion was that this question might come before Congress, and that if I held the stock I might be required to vote on measures affecting it; no more from his statement than from my own knowledge of the matter.

Q. Influencing your private interests?—A. Possibly; I would consider it about the same as a vote on the question of national banks, in which I might hold stock, or something of that kind. I should regard the interests of the national bank in which I held stock, if I held any, as placing me in precisely the same attitude as I would have been placed in if I held this stock. I did not understand that either Mr. McComb or Mr. Ames kept back any explanation.

Q. Do I understand from you that you declined to take the stock?—A. No, sir; I did not. Mr. Ames did not offer me any.

Q. If stock had been offered to you, would you have taken it with the knowledge which you had of the possible complications which might arise between your private interests and your public duty?—A. That is a question, of course, which goes to my motive, and if I were to answer, it might be only a vindication of myself and self-laudation. I would prefer that the country should judge what I would have done from my character. It would be easy for me to say now that I would not have taken the stock.

Q. It is easy for you to say whether you would or not?—A. Throughout my whole life I never had received any consideration for duty performed by me, except legitimate fees for professional service.

Mr. NIBLACK. As a matter of fact you ought to state what was your impression and the motives that operated on you.

The WITNESS. I would state that it has been a rule of my life never to place myself in an attitude in which my private interests would conflict with my public duties.

Mr. MERRICK. And the conversation was sufficient to indicate to your mind that that complication might arise in certain contingencies.

The WITNESS. Unquestionably there was such a possibility.

By Mr. MCCRARY:

Q. Was any of your conversations with Mr. Ames during the summer of 1868 and during the presidential campaign?—A. I think not; and for this reason, that in 1868 I became isolated from the members of the republican party, and I do not think we conversed on the subject after that.

Q. Your latest conversation, then, with Mr. Ames was probably in the latter part of the winter of 1867-'68?—A. Perhaps so. I do not know that my relations with Mr. Ames were materially affected, but the impeachment trial came on and isolated me from the republican party.

Mr. McCRARY. I want to fix the date of your last negotiations with Mr. Ames.

The WITNESS. I did not have any negotiations with him about it.

Mr. McCRARY. Well, your conversation.

The WITNESS. I presume that if I say in 1868, it will cover the ground; possibly I may in 1869.

Q. And he gave you to understand that he had none of this stock to dispose of?—A. Yes, sir.

Q. I suppose that was prior to June, 1868?—A. There may have been some conversation in 1868; if there was it was very early in the year, because the impeachment trial came on and then I had no conversation with Mr. Ames on the subject—certainly not until after June.

Q. What time did you leave the Senate?—A. In 1871.

Mr. AMES. Did I say anything to you about wanting any legislation, or did I try to influence you or to affect your vote in any way?

The WITNESS. Not in the slightest degree. I considered Mr. Ames's statement sufficiently full and explicit to satisfy me in regard to this whole matter. If it was as full to others there would be no trouble in coming to a knowledge of the whole matter.

Mr. AMES. You spoke to me about the matter in consequence of Mr. McComb's recommending you to come to me about it?

The WITNESS. Yes, sir; and only on that account.

LETTER FROM MR. BROOKS.

The following letter from Mr. Brooks was handed to Mr. Poland, the chairman of the committee, on the morning of the 17th, complaining of the exclusion of testimony in his favor:

WASHINGTON, *February* 17,
Before the Committee-Room,
Monday, a. m., 10 *o'clock and* 5 *minntes.*

Hon. LUKE P. POLAND, *Chairman, &c.:*

Finding your door closed, I demand, before you reach any conclusion on my case, what the greatest criminal has a right to demand—a sight of the indictment against me. The only public charge made against me, and upon which I had reason to think the whole case turned, was the charge of McComb that Mr. Alley gave me fifty shares of Credit Mobilier stock to bribe or influence democratic members of Congress. This has been proven by no one, but on the contrary disproved by Alley, Dillon, Ham, Neilson, and Brooks. If there be any other charge, I demand the right of defense upon it and to see the charge, and when it is presented I will undertake to prove negatives to the entire satisfaction of the court. I will show by all or nearly all the clerks in the Union Pacific Railroad office, and in the Credit Mobilier office, and by others, that all my transactions were open and above-board, and in nothing under cover. It is cruel, in secret committee, then, without notice, to damn a man's unstained record of twenty years of public life, without a full and fair trial. I have asked you to summon the Government directors, to show my uprightness and co-ordinate action with them. It has not been done. I have asked you to call for Government records within a mile of your court-room, to show that McComb was not a good witness. It has not been done. I have been permitted to have but Messrs. Voorhees and Beck as my witnesses, against the dozen or more called by you during the ten days you were arraigning me.

I most respectfully submit that this is unjust, illegal, and partial, and before any conclusion is reached, I respectfully demand such an opportunity for defense as would be given a criminal in a common police court.

Yours respectfully, but in haste,

JAMES BROOKS.

INDEX.

34 x

○

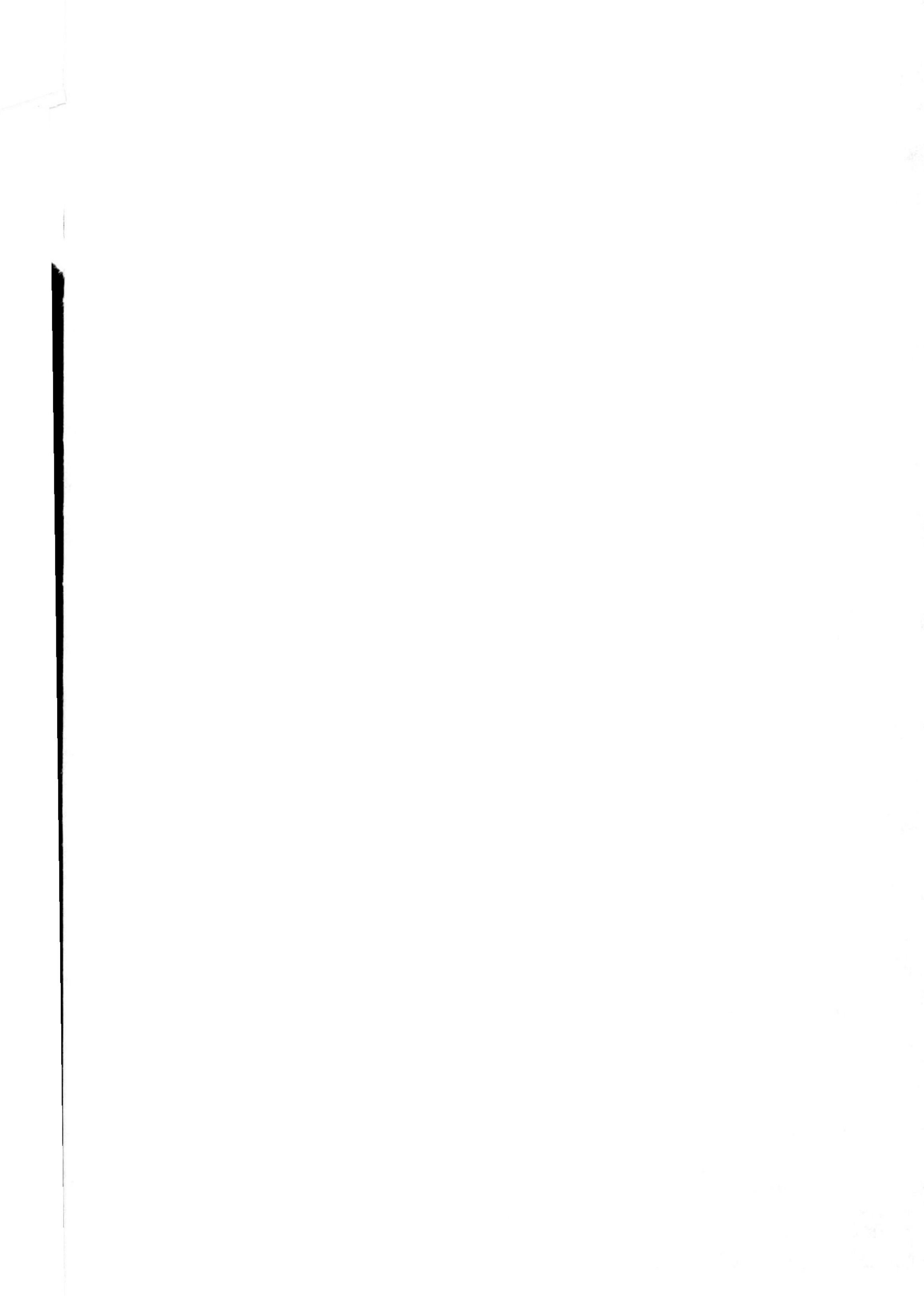

www.ingramcontent.com/pod-product-compliance
Lightning Source LLC
LaVergne TN
LVHW021258110826
845150LV00003B/426

* 9 7 8 1 4 2 5 5 6 0 6 7 6 *